Purchasing
and the Manageme
of Materials

Purchasing and the Management of Materials

SEVENTH EDITION

Gary J. Zenz
Florida State University

With the assistance of George H. Thompson
Trinity University
San Antonio, Texas

JOHN WILEY & SONS, INC.
New York • Chichester • Brisbane • Toronto • Singapore

ACQUISITIONS EDITOR Timothy J. Kent
MARKETING MANAGER Debra Riegert
SENIOR PRODUCTION EDITOR Marjorie Shustak
DESIGN SUPERVISOR Ann Marie Renzi
MANUFACTURING MANAGER Andrea Price
ILLUSTRATION COORDINATOR Jaime Perea
TEXT DESIGN Lee Goldstein
COVER DESIGN David Levy

This book was set in Times Roman by General Graphic Services and printed and bound by Malloy Lithographing, Inc. The cover was printed by Phoenix Color Corp.

Recognizing the importance of preserving what has been written, it is a policy of John Wiley & Sons, Inc. to have books of enduring value published in the United States printed on acid-free paper, and we exert our best efforts to that end.

Library of Congress Cataloging in Publication Data:
Zenz, Gary Joseph.
    Purchasing and the management of materials / Gary J. Zenz; edited by George H. Thompson. — 7th ed.
        p.   cm.
    Includes indexes.
    ISBN 0-471-54983-5
    1. Industrial procurement—Management.   2. Materials management.
I. Thompson, George (George H.)   II. Title.
HD39.5.W47   1994
658.7′2—dc20   93-5911
                                                                                                                CIP

Printed in the United States of America

10 9 8 7 6 5 4 3 2 1

Printed and bound by Malloy Lithographing, Inc.

To Mary Thompson for the support which she so generously provided, and to the new generation, particularly Michael Sanders, Erin Evans, and Jennifer and Eric Landis.
May they meet their future challenges with courage, integrity and compassion.

About the Author

Dr. Gary J. Zenz is an internationally recognized leader in the fields of purchasing and materials management. His background combines an intimate knowledge of practical business conditions, gained through executive positions, with comprehensive academic credentials. He was director of purchasing and director of market research for three major corporations before entering academia. He has also consulted with leading organizations, including members of the Fortune 500 as well as the Chicago Board of Trade, OAS, and Merrill Lynch. Dr. Zenz lectures at leading universities and is a frequent speaker at national and international conferences throughout the United States and Canada.

Dr. Zenz received a Ph.D. in Business and Economics from the University of Wisconsin and has taught at several universities. He is currently Full Professor in the College of Business at The Florida State University. He has been named an "Outstanding Educator of America," is the author or co-author of numerous articles and several books, and holds memberships and offices in professional organizations.

Dr. George H. Thompson combines chemical engineering and MBA degrees from Tulane University with five years of Navy Supply Corps duty and over 17 years with Union Carbide Corporation, where he was responsible for purchasing organic chemicals worldwide and worked in plant operations and construction. He earned the Ph.D. degree in management and economics at the University of North Texas under a National Association of Purchasing Management doctoral fellowship. He has taught at the University of North Texas and at Trinity University, where he was named an "Outstanding Educator of America" and served as department chairman, now Professor Emeritus.

He is an original lifetime Certified Purchasing Manager (C.P.M.) and has served on NAPM's Academic Planning Committee. He and his students have consulted for over 400 small businesses. He has conducted numerous academic and industrial conferences and regularly reviews books in the purchasing and materials management field.

Preface

As a new dawn breaks in purchasing and materials management, strong evidence persists that the struggle for global position changes people, products, processes, procedures, partnerships, precincts, and even provinces. This book directs the reader toward changes in strategic purchasing and the purchasing manager's expanding role in many organizations, in buyer–supplier partner relationships, and in trading throughout the global marketplace. The buyer moves toward greater productivity as telephone, fax, and computer speed up transmitting a reply to the query, ''Which way?'' in the supply chain.

I find a greater complexity in the economy, as a direct result of scarcer resource input. It requires greater knowledge to resolve conflicting aims. The paradox looms: fewer raw materials increase the demand for labor. Cheap labor may come at the expense of quality. Total quality management requires everyone's commitment within the firm that strives to compete successfully in a global marketplace. Most businesses label these as exciting times.

ORGANIZATION OF THE BOOK

This new edition introduces each chapter with a vignette of what the chapter describes. Each chapter begins with Chapter Contents and ends with Discussion Questions, identifying the core substance. I have added Chapter Summaries to recap what each chapter covers. Several chapters provide exercises for drill. Three appendices contain details for the most interested reader. A Glossary points to what I mean when using new or key terms.

TOPICAL COVERAGE

The book specifies vast changes that have occurred in the global market-place. However, the emphasis fixes on management, chiefly within firms in the private sector. Just-in-time purchasing has changed the manner common among businesspeople. Specifically, many firms operate with fewer suppliers and carriers, more certified suppliers, fewer purchase orders, longer commitments and annual contracts, relationships longer than spot contracts, and more reliance on quality goods delivered in precise time slots. Desktop computing in purchasing makes possible electronic data interchanges with vendors and carriers.

CHANGES IN THE SEVENTH EDITION

I have arranged the chapters in new sequence: the first 11 chapters instruct the unsophisticated reader in the work performance of the purchasing and materials management functions. The remainder of the chapters address specific topics that offer most to experienced as well as novice buyers.

Two new chapters, one on purchasing strategy and forecasting and the other on health care purchasing, appear because of rising importance. I have expanded reclamation and salvage procedures to embrace the purchasing manager's responsibility to the environmental protection issue—many times the ultimate economy, a profitable pursuit as well as meeting mandates. Also, the international chapter features heightened attention due to changes during the past 10 years. Past users will recognize that three former chapters now fit as follows: computers, into almost every chapter in the book; audit and control, into the purchasing performance measurement chapter; and purchasing research, into organizational considerations.

With all the many changes in this edition and in the global market, I have maintained the fundamental coverage of purchasing and related materials management—concerns that provided the framework for the prior six editions.

FEATURES OF THE BOOK

The back-to-basics theme centers on managing the functions that commit the largest recurring expenditures for most industrial firms today. I balance theory and practice by grounding theory in reality. Throughout the book I explain the theoretical frameworks that guide managerial activities, and then provide illustrations and examples of how and when those theories work and don't work. I use examples and discuss management in both large and small businesses as well as in nonprofit organizations.

ACKNOWLEDGMENTS

ABI/INFORM Ondisc served as the delivery mechanism for a vast database of current international literature. Credit for the intellectual property goes to UMI/Data Courier.

Dr. George H. Thompson is especially acknowledged for his major revision efforts in this seventh edition. His extensive academic and professional experience provided the background for writings throughout the book. He provided the foundation of this revision, and for this I am very grateful.

Gary J. Zenz

Contents

9

Negotiation and Cost–Price Analysis, 245

10

Purchasing in a Global Marketplace, 269

11

Purchasing Performance Measurement with Internal Audit and Feedback, 295

12

Purchasing and Materials Management in the Public and Nonprofit Sectors, 343

13

Human Resources Management in Purchasing and Materials Management, 373

14

Legal Considerations, 399

15

Health-Care Purchasing, 429

16

Acquisition and Disposal of Capital Equipment, 443

17

Value Analysis, 467

Purchasing
and the Management
of Materials

=1

The Functions and Contributions of Purchasing and Materials Management

A new materials manager has just joined the firm. Six department managers report to her: Purchasing, Traffic, Inventory Control, Storage, Cafeteria, and Security. How will she accomplish change, considering that the people presently involved may not want to give up their privileges, for one reason or another? How should she decide what needs changing? As her boss, what advice would you offer?

CHAPTER CONTENTS

U.S. purchasing managers spend trillions of dollars. Business establishments, individuals, or organizations that purchase products or services to use in producing other products or services represented $6.7 trillion in manufacturing and trade sales in 1992. To this figure add the institutional market—educational institutions, hospitals, prisons, and nonprofit organizations including museums, foundations, and libraries. Finally, add the government market: federal, state, and local governments.[1]

The twentieth century's final decade brings America's purchasing managers and materials managers face-to-face with a world turned upside down. The 1990s challenge, as never before, the people who will be buying goods and services for America's business firms.

Since the 1970s economic power has shifted rapidly to the Pacific Rim and to Europe, and away from the United States. How should American managers of purchasing and materials respond? Communism's decline in Eastern Europe and the resulting new markets for U.S. goods and services and stiff global competition compel America's purchasing managers to take on world-class operations in a global marketplace.

In 1984, for the first time since 1910, the United States became a debtor nation, as its cumulative current account slid from a break-even point at the end of 1983 to more than a $4 trillion deficit. Three percent of the gross national product came from abroad in 1960; by 1988, the figure had reached 12 percent. By 1990, 70 percent of U.S. products competed with foreign competitors outside or within the United States.

The nation's productivity growth suddenly fell during the 1980s from nearly 3 percent a year to 1 percent. The student achievement test score decline that began in 1967 made its major impact on productivity growth in the 1980s. As the better educated workers retire, replaced by less and less well educated workers, the U.S. skilled labor shortage staggers strategic planners. How can America's firms buy and sell competitively in domestic and foreign markets with too few skilled workers? As technology expands throughout the United States and world economies, the supply of skilled and highly educated workers shrinks even further.

Skilled labor shortage in the 1990s focuses on business information, telecommunications, and specialty retailers that use computers to raise labor productivity. Paine Webber, the investment firm, foresees computer power and semiconductors becoming a commodity. Telecommunications and business information promise the path to growth.

In such a high-tech climate, buyers find it necessary to become world-class customers. They need to know their business so that they can effec-

---

[1] *Survey of Current Business* (February 1993), p. S-2.

tively and efficiently satisfy the increasingly complex needs of their internal customers.

In the past, many procurement operations focused on transaction processing. Today, they concentrate on analysis of the best strategic sources, shifting focus from current suppliers to full supply markets.

Buyers find that they have to examine the ethical behavior of foreign suppliers. Buyers' own firms may shrink in size as a result of cost-containment measures. Corporate downsizing has changed the logistics roles that shippers and carriers play. Public and contract warehouses rise to increasing opportunities as providers of a broad range of third-party services.

Until recently, purchasing managers and buyers followed a reactive approach designed to reduce production costs in an effort to neutralize the threat of foreign competition. Today, they develop a proactive strategy that pursues a sustainable competitive advantage through international sourcing.

Personal savings increased at a much faster rate as the 1990s began. It may reach $500 billion annually by 1993. Baby-boomers—those 76 million people born between 1946 and 1964—have generally satisfied their larger financial burdens and now represent the ''high savers.'' This new source of venture capital has the potential to underwrite the U.S. drive to profit from the Eastern Europe shift towards free enterprise and the Pacific Rim's bright future.

Recycling, reducing solid waste 40 percent by 1995, removing hazards in the work place, choosing products that minimize downtime by employees: These items all confront the decade's purchasing managers.

The U.S. dollar weakens against the yen and other currencies. This event attracts foreign investors to buy U.S. property. Do the Japanese really own 40 percent of downtown Los Angeles?

The savings and loan crisis exploded in the 1980s, brought on by greed, fraud, and mismanagement. Special liquidity banking bailed out insolvent thrifts at taxpayer expense. Stock markets tensed, signaling investors to place their money elsewhere. Who finances Third-World debts? Who feeds the starving, who relieves world poverty?

Global market purchasing and materials managers face the question: How could America, the land of the free, best operate in a world turned upside down?

This chapter considers procurement activities in terms of these shifts in actions and previews the comprehensive chapters that follow. The book as a whole is designed to present the principles and procedures that represent the most professional approach to purchasing and materials management in the private, public, and nonprofit sectors of our economy. This approach focuses mainly on industrial purchasing or commercial purchasing in contrast to purchasing by household consumers.

The study of purchasing and materials management attracts many students on college campuses today. The practice of purchasing and materials management rewards the professional career person with increasing respect, position, and salary.

HISTORICAL PERSPECTIVE

There are few historical records of the origin of purchasing. This is to be expected, since the first industrial purchase was made in the dim past when someone bought materials or supplies to be used in making an article to be sold instead of used. Before 1900 there were few instances of purchasing departments separate and distinct from production or other operating departments; such purchasing departments as did exist were found mostly in the railroad field. The first book dealing specifically with the purchasing function was published in 1887. The fact that the earliest writings on this function were railroad publications—on railroad purchasing and written by railroad personnel—can be explained by the predominance at that time of railroad organizations in the economy of the country.

At about the same time, occasional articles began to appear in some of the technical trade publications dealing with some of the aspects of purchasing. One such article, by James M. Cremer, entitled "The Engineer as a Purchasing Agent," appeared in the August 1908 issue of *Cassier's Magazine*, an engineering publication. In an article appearing in *Iron Age* in January 1913, John C. Jay, Jr., general manager of sales of the Pennsylvania Steel Corporation, suggested the organization of a group to promote the interests of purchasing agents through more publicity regarding their activities. Although this article did not result in the immediate organization of the National Association of Purchasing Agents, it definitely indicated emerging interest in the purchasing function.

The National Association of Purchasing Agents was founded in 1915. Purchasing came of age during the early part of World War I, under the impact of the expanded production brought about by the war. At its fifty-second annual convention in Washington, D.C. (May 1967), the association voted to change its name to The National Association of Purchasing Management, in recognition of the managerial status that purchasing had attained.

OVERVIEW OF PRESENT PROCUREMENT OPERATIONS

Organizations view procurement as a professional activity that includes all the activities involved in obtaining materials at minimum cost, transporting them, storing them, and moving them toward the production process. Included in this modern approach is the economic analysis of supply, demand, and price and the assessment of international events as they affect materials.

The diversity of the purchasing function is reflected in many organizations that utilize purchasing economists to provide economic assistance for buyers. Purchasing personnel often perform as practicing economists as they project prices and demand–supply relationships, strive to achieve delicate inventory balance support to operations with minimum cost and capital, and uphold supplier relationships.

Considerable variation exists among organizations in the proportion of income dollars that they spend on purchasing goods and services. In highly mechanized mass-production industries, labor costs are low and the proportion of income dollars spent for goods and services is relatively high. For instance, the petroleum industry spends 90 percent of its sales dollar on goods and services. Craft organizations, in which skilled labor predominates, like printing and publishing, have a lower-than-average purchase percentage, namely 35 percent.[2] In addition, the proportion spent by the government is usually smaller than in private industry; federal government expends approximately 38.7 percent of its revenues on purchased goods and services,[3] as Table 12-3 in Chapter 12 shows. The distribution of expenditures among federal, state, and local governments continually shifts with the political philosophy of the times.

PURCHASING AND THE ECONOMY

In analyzing business operations, the phrase *value-added concept* expresses the difference between the cost of the component materials and the selling price of a finished product. The amount of the differential represents the unique contribution of each organization to the production process. In our interrelated economy, firms tend to specialize and produce segments of total products. Many companies produce component parts and materials for other firms, utilizing economies resulting from a combined demand for their specialized products. As a result, the average U.S. firm now buys more than half of the dollar value of its sales; the value added is typically less than 50 percent of its sales. Conversely, the average company purchases materials valued at more than half of what it sells. An organization's profit is thus, to a large extent, determined by how effectively it procures and manages these materials.

The efficiency of any organization is correspondingly contingent on the

---

[2] U.S. Bureau of the Census, *Annual Survey of Manufactures: 1990.*
[3] *Survey of Current Business,* January 1993, Table 3.2.

availability of component parts and materials in the proper quantity, quality, and price range. Failure in any of these areas increases costs and decreases profit and can precipitate an economic crisis.

A MANAGERIAL PROCESS: MULTIPLE OBJECTIVES

Purchasing is a managerial process that goes far beyond simply buying materials. It includes planning and policy procedures that cover a wide range of related activities, including research and development as required for the proper selection of materials and sources; ascertainment of delivery; inspection of documents on incoming shipments to ensure quantity and quality compliance; development of procedures to implement buying policies; coordination of purchasing activities with other internal divisions of the concern such as engineering, production, and accounting; and development of effective communications with top management in order to ensure a complete appraisal of the performance of the purchasing function.

In achieving these multiple objectives, purchasing contributes to the value of the firm in extraordinary ways. It provides stability in the marketplace. It embraces a body of ethics that commands consideration. It plans toward a long-term horizon of strategy and tactics for integrating the materials management process. Purchasing attracts college-trained men and women who aspire to add value to their organization by integrating the process.

The nonprofit sector has its opportunities for adding value. For example, key top-level initiatives within the United States Postal Service facilitated the integration of a materiel management operation employing almost 800,000 people, managing some 40,000 different activities or organizations, and processing annually almost 155 billion pieces of mail.[4]

As part of its managerial process, Texas Instruments moves people out of the transaction mode and into the strategic mode. TI's vice president of corporate procurement and material management looks for people who can plan supply strategies for long-term corporate advantage.[5]

The latest trends in the purchasing function call for important changes in many organizations—greater computerization, fewer suppliers, longer contracts, more reliable quality, and leaner inventories. Business as usual doesn't rule any longer. The career purchasing manager finds importance in these changes, serving, in a manner of speaking, as the manager of operations outside the firm. In the chaotic times of the 1990s, managers and

---

[4] "Integrated Materiel Management in a Large Semi-Public Organization," *Journal of Purchasing and Materials Management* (Summer 1990), p. 12.
[5] "Technocrat No Longer Stands for Professional," *Purchasing* (April 16, 1992), p. 17.

owners with long-standing relationships with their customers, vendors, and bank find customers cruising the world for deals, vendors negotiating goal-oriented contracting,[6] and strangers running the bank. In fact, the bank's name may have changed twice in five years.

PURCHASING AS A SOCIOECONOMIC FORCE

As a major factor behind the allocation of trillions of business dollars, purchasing is increasingly recognized, and in some cases formalized, as a significant socioeconomic force. By challenging price increases and promoting competition between firms and materials, purchasing's efforts have a direct impact on costs and prices, hence inflationary pressures within the economy. Efficient use of scrap and by-products, a major purchasing role, has important repercussions on the nation's resource supply. In the process of vendor selection, purchasing influences environmental policies by considering the pollution-control policies of prospective suppliers. Similarly, the concerns expressed by purchasing personnel to prospective vendors about their hiring of minorities influences the employment policies of these firms, collectively influencing the nation in these areas. Finally, decisions on the use of foreign sources of supply directly influence the nation's balance of trade payments and the international status of the currencies involved.

The significance of purchasing's role in societal developments is sometimes formalized in an organization's policy statements on social issues. In the area of environmental responsibility, purchasing managers may stress that industry has an obligation to resolve water, air, and noise pollution problems as well as to conserve natural resources rather than depending on government to initiate such programs.

PURCHASING AND PROFIT: THE PROFIT MULTIPLIER

The purchasing function plays an important role in an organization's profit-making ability. The impact of procurement on profits can be illustrated by the *purchasing profit multiplier*. This multiplier indicates the amount of sales increase necessary to equal a dollar saved in purchasing.

The relationship between profit and purchasing depends on a firm's gross profit margin. Assuming a gross profit margin of 10 percent, a firm requires $10 of sales for every $1 in profits. Because a dollar saved in purchasing is equal to a dollar increase in profits, one can substitute pur-

---

[6] "Long-term Relationships Call for Clever Contracts," *Purchasing* (December 12, 1991).

TABLE 1-1. Sales Increase to Contribute the Same Profit as a $1 Savings in Purchasing

Gross Margin (percent)	Purchasing Profit Multiplier[a]
2.5	$40.00
5.0	20.00
7.5	13.33
10.0	10.00
15.0	6.67

[a]Sales increase necessary.

chasing for savings so that a dollar increase in profits results from a dollar savings in purchasing. For example, say the gross margin is 5 percent, and the question is posed, "What amount of sales increase would be necessary to equal a $1 savings in purchasing?" The algebraic equation becomes

$0.05x = \$1$ increase in profits
Solution: $\$1/0.05 = \$20$

The solution states that a $1 savings in purchasing is equivalent to a $20 increase in sales for a firm with a gross margin of 5 percent.

The purchasing profit multiplier for alternative gross margins is shown in Table 1-1 as the equivalent amount of sales increase needed to equal a $1 savings in purchasing.

PURCHASING AND MATERIALS MANAGEMENT

A widely used organizational approach to purchasing management involves a concept known as materials management. This concept recognizes purchasing as one of several activities dealing with the planning for, acquisition of, and utilization of materials. In this approach, organization is structured so that all activities bringing materials into and through the plant are combined under one person known as the materials manager. The basic rationale for this type of organization is that, taken alone, the functions of purchasing have conflicting objectives. For example, purchasing's concern that supply be continuous may conflict with inventory control's emphasis on minimizing inventory levels, or with traffic's objective of shipping in full loads. The expanded use of computers has made it possible for the materials manager to coordinate this increased level of operations.

The concept of materials management as a function to obtain the lowest overall cost of materials will be utilized throughout this text by presenting the materials management principles in each materials function as they relate to and interact with one another and with purchasing operations.

Physical distribution takes over after the materials management function completes its actions. Physical distribution takes the output—finished goods—from the end of the firm's production process to the customer. This transaction may involve packaging, finished goods warehousing, outbound transportation, delivery to customers, customer complaints, and accounting for all product costs since the product left the production line.

Logistics contributes to both the materials management and the physical distribution functions. The American Production and Inventory Control Society considers Logistics to manage the shipment of all incoming goods from suppliers and all outgoing goods to customers. The firm's traffic manager typically carries out these activities.

PURCHASING OBJECTIVES

In general, purchasing's responsibility is to buy materials of the right quality, in the right quantity, at the right time, at the right price, from the right source, with delivery at the right place.

In most concerns continuity of operations is of critical importance. The purchasing function must not allow production to be disrupted by a lack of needed materials. Furthermore, this objective must be achieved with a minimum investment in inventories. Achieving this objective of security with a minimum investment demands a fine balancing of various factors: risk of shutdown, the cost inherent in forward buying, and the economies of quantity purchases. Weighing these factors calls for experience and a high order of professional judgment.

Another objective is the maintenance of adequate quality. Quality refers primarily to the suitability of an item for its intended purpose. The objective is to procure the goods that are best suited rather than those of highest absolute quality. In addition to product quality, the services offered by the suppliers must be evaluated in the light of the organization's own needs. An initial low cost quoted by one supplier may legitimately be rejected in favor of a supplier with a higher initial cost balanced by valuable service factors.

A further objective of purchasing is to avoid duplication, waste, and obsolescence of the various items purchased. The purchasing department can do much to eliminate these risks by considering each purchase in relation to long-range operating plans as well as the short-range considerations of the immediate purchase.

The purchasing manager also has the objective of sustaining the company's competitive position. This requires constant examination of specifications to ensure that quality standards are not higher than those of competitors, while considering the demands of the ultimate consumers.

As representatives of a company dealing with many suppliers, purchasing personnel also have an external objective. They must be concerned with the supplier's image of the company. A favorable image enhances purchasing's ability to obtain valuable technical assistance, including innovative techniques that may reduce costs while improving performance. Good personal relations and a favorable image also help purchasing obtain materials during periods of shortages and affect the outcome of delicate price negotiations.

A final objective of sound purchasing is the development of internal relationships that lead to understanding and harmony among the various organizational units within the company. Probably no other function involves more contact with and reliance upon other departments than purchasing. Purchasing decisions and actions influence production (component procurement), finance (dollar expenditures), inspection (quality of purchases), engineering (design, material, and tolerance specifications), sales (brand names and quality of components), and accounting (control of receipts and payments). To be effective, purchasing must have the respect and cooperation of all these associates and be capable of interaction in all management decisions about material costs and controls. This decision-making participation in turn requires that purchasing, as one of its major objectives, educate top management about its ultimate profit-contributing potential.

THE PURCHASING PROCESS

Two approaches may be used to analyze the work performed by the purchasing department. One approach emphasizes the time spent as related to the various tasks performed by purchasing personnel. An alternative approach emphasizes the qualitative aspect of the activities of a purchasing department. The qualitative approach to purchasing activities is presented in the following paragraphs.

Recognition of Need

All purchase transactions begin with recognition of the need for an item by someone in the organization. Generally, the need is recognized by the person in charge of a using department, the head of one of the manufacturing operations, the office manager, or the maintenance engineer. The need may often be satisfied by a transfer of materials from available (on-hand) inventory. However, internal supplies must eventually be replenished. Thus, either directly or indirectly, purchases originate with the recognition of the need for an item by a using department.

Ideally, purchasing anticipates the needs of the departments involved. Projecting advance needs is a major consideration in determining the appropriate quantity of an item to buy. In turn, determining the most economical quantity to buy requires recognition that increasing the quantity normally decreases cost, while simultaneously increasing the cost of carrying the item until it is needed. This is the classic economic order quantity dilemma, which necessitates balancing the economics of acquisition against the costs of possession; this problem will be discussed in a later chapter.

Description of the Need

Once a need has been recognized, it must be accurately described. To secure an adequate and complete description of needs, purchasing personnel must have comprehensive knowledge of the items and their function within the organization.

Selection of Sources

The next step in the purchase transaction is the selection of the source or sources for the requisitioned item. For most purchases there are many comparable alternative suppliers. Considerations such as price, service, delivery, and quality predominate in inventory selection, but goodwill and even personalities have an impact on this decision. Sources of information about potential vendors include salespeople, catalogs, trade associations and publications, and other buying organizations. Personal interviews, plant visits, financial analyses, and reference checks all help purchasing personnel to select the appropriate vendor.

Price Determination

During the process of source selection, price is a major consideration. For items that have been bought repeatedly, catalogs, price lists, and discount schedules may be useful. However, catalog prices are not binding on the seller and are not considered legal offers.

Another method of determining price is direct negotiation. This method is especially suited to goods made to the specifications of the buyer. The negotiation process offers a flexible method of buying, permitting adjustments in requirements and specifications that are difficult to effect when standard items are bought either from price lists or on a bid basis.

A third method of securing price information is the competitive bid. This method is widely used in government procurement because governments have statutory requirements. It is also occasionally employed by industrial purchasing departments, especially for buying fabricated parts to be incorporated into a finished product. Ideally, the bid process stimulates competition among suppliers on an equitable and open basis, although a considerable amount of time may be consumed in the process, and considerable negotiation flexibility is lost.

Placing the Order

Among the first considerations relevant to purchasing is the placement of an order with a supplier. As we have seen, a considerable amount of work must be done before arriving at this step. It amounts to a routine culmination of previous purchasing activities and is usually accomplished by a clerk, under close supervision and control. All orders should be in writing on formal purchase forms. A restricted number of persons are usually authorized to sign and place purchase orders that commit the company to the expenditure of funds.

Follow-up of the Order

Once the order has been placed, purchasing's responsibilities do not end; most purchasing departments have responsibility for confirming orders. Follow-up is necessary to ensure that the seller has received the order, that the price and terms are mutually understood, and, most importantly, that delivery will occur as requested.

Responsibility for follow-up is generally assigned to the buyer who placed the order. The clerical work may be performed by an expediter or follow-up clerk who keeps the necessary records and forms and takes routine actions. Orders requiring special action are referred to the buyer, who has responsibility for such action.

Follow-up consists essentially of actualizing a supplier's promise of delivery. Although many purchasing agents use the terms follow-up and expediting interchangeably, there is a distinction between the two. Follow-up is defined as strengthening an effect by further action, whereas expediting is defined as accelerating a process or progress. The follow-up of a purchase order involves regular communication with a supplier until an explicit acceptance of the order is received and a commitment made as to delivery date. At this point, if it is deemed necessary, the purchasing department may attempt to expedite the order—that is, attempt to pinpoint and remove barriers to on-time delivery.

Maintenance of Records

A purchasing department typically maintains computer records and files pertaining to purchase transactions. Since a large proportion of all purchases consists of repeat orders, these sources are consulted frequently. Buyers typically refer to the records of previous transactions for guidance in current relations with suppliers. Purchase orders are legal contracts and must be preserved as long as they have legal significance. Requisitions and similar documents should be preserved by the purchasing department, since they constitute the authority on which the department took its actions in buying a given item.

Professional Vendor Relations

A crucial aspect of the purchasing function is the maintenance of good professional relations with the vendors with whom the company deals. Relationship management skills are based on mutual trust and confidence and grow out of dealings over a period of time. Much emphasis is placed on the importance of this phase of purchasing. Professional respect and vendor goodwill help the purchasing department achieve its objective of buying the right goods in terms of quality, quantity, price, time, and place.

MANAGEMENT EXPECTATIONS OF PURCHASING PERSONNEL

Productivity depends on cooperation and motivation. To achieve optimal interaction, management must meet the vocational and personal needs of the purchasing employee, and the materials and purchasing managers must regard and respond to general management expectations. These expectations of management include the professional and personal qualifications that the employee brings to the job. Naturally, management, for its part, expects proficiency in the basic purchasing expertise and skills necessary to sustain the efficient operation of the firm's manufacturing or service enterprises. The following are some of the most important skills needed.

Negotiation

First of all, purchasing must be able both to negotiate effectively with suppliers at all levels of management and, at the same time, to encourage their respect and confidence. This art requires the purchasing agent to know when to stop during an interchange in which both parties' objectives conflict. The supplier will attempt to obtain the highest possible price, whereas the buyer must reduce the price as much as possible. Therefore, the art of negotiation is to push price into an area both parties find reasonable while retaining respect and cooperation. Negotiation also naturally extends to other purchasing–sales variables, such as delivery times, terms, and adjustments for rejected goods.

Electronic Data Processing

Among the technical skills needed by purchasing is the ability to utilize electronic data processing equipment, including knowledge of how and when a computer can assume clerical burdens and maximize information retrieval. This technical expertise is one of those most sought after in purchasing personnel.

Materials Management

Management is concerned with the cost and control of materials as a separate and distinct profit center. Accordingly, the materials management concept, which incorporates all functions involved in obtaining and bringing materials into the plant, is now being viewed as the answer to many coordination and control problems. Therefore, management expects to find purchasing personnel who have the expertise necessary to organize and administer all the activities involved in each of these materials functions. Purchasing personnel normally have close contact with all these activities, but some may lack the in-depth knowledge of specific techniques, particularly in areas of inventory and production control. Purchasing personnel need to be aware of this need for expertise and take the necessary steps to educate themselves in these areas, either through occupational interaction or by taking courses on these subjects.

Commodity Futures and Hedging

As we face the future, the realities of erratic and often violent price changes will become increasingly pronounced, mainly as a result of an international scarcity of many basic raw materials. Therefore, purchasing personnel must be knowledgeable about all the ways in which to hedge price changes, including commodities futures trading. By the use of hedging techniques, costs can be predetermined and sale prices protected long before physical stock is received. Similarly, declining inventory values can be cushioned without liquidating physical stock, and in many cases favorable prices can be obtained without need for contracts with specific suppliers. In addition, international purchases can be safeguarded against currency fluctuations by means of international currency hedges. Tomorrow's purchasing manager should expend the effort necessary to become well versed in the functioning of commodity and currency markets and to master the techniques of hedging.

Professionalism and Administrative Abilities

Management looks for evidence of the professionalism of the candidate for a job in purchasing. Membership in local and national purchasing organizations and activities directed toward improving personal abilities such as communication and comprehension are evidence of professionalism.

In addition to specific expertise, management expects administrative abilities in its purchasing personnel, including the ability to recruit, direct, and motivate peers and subordinates. Empathy, a keen sense of individual motivations, and patience are needed to obtain maximum performance from others. The ability to express oneself effectively in written communications is also necessary for this task. In addition, care for personal appearance evidences concern for one's own physical well-being. Other personal considerations include the self-motivation of the individual, since purchasing involves many opportunities to take actions that are entirely at the discretion of the buyer. For example, new vendors and new materials and processes can be explored or left as is. Finally, a very great concern of management is that purchasing personnel have high personal ethics. Management increasingly realizes how important it is that responsibility for safeguarding the purchasing dollar be placed in the hands of persons who have the highest ethical and moral standards.

OCCUPATIONAL OUTLOOK

The decade of the 1990s and those following hold broadening opportunities for the purchasing professional, for three threats face American industry: increased involvement in a shortage-prone world marketplace, periodic high inflation levels, and heightened foreign competition. Because of these threats, top management in all organizations needs purchasing professionals' particular expertise and experience and will continue to need them throughout the twenty-first century. In short, purchasing is reaching for a new high in professionalism and influence. A 3732-response survey conducted by *Purchasing* magazine[7] indicates a 1992 average annual salary of $48,800 for men and $33,900 for women. The average two-year increase in pay was 9.0 percent, while the cost of living rose 7.6 percent. The survey also shows that purchasing salaries increase with company size. The field looks especially bright for college graduates, particularly those possessing graduate business

[7] December 10, 1992, p. 76.

degrees and some degree of technical training. Certification as a C.P.M. (Certified Purchasing Manager) by the National Association of Purchasing Management (Tempe, AZ 85285) pays off. The salary average for non-C.P.M.s was $42,800; for C.P.M.s, it was $54,200, or 7 percent more than the previous year, plus a better chance for a bonus. The highest salary listed by a non-C.P.M. was $200,000; for C.P.M.s, the highest was $240,000. Professional certification becomes increasingly important to today's organizations.

CHAPTER SUMMARY

U.S. purchasing and materials managers spend trillions of dollars yearly to supply industrial, commercial, institutional, and governmental establishments. They buy materials and services from very simple nuts and bolts to very complex objects like stealth aircraft. They impact every department of the typical organization, helping users specify what they need, finding sources, negotiating purchases, and scheduling deliveries.

The materials management concept brings into one group, reporting to one executive, two or more of the functions relating to materials. Closer coordination of effort results in reducing inventories, eliminating duplication, simplifying procedures, pinpointing accountability, and containing costs.

Worldwide trends bring new value to the profession's career opportunities. The U.S. economic power no longer dominates the world's markets. Political friendships change, closing once open supply sources. Competing nations contend for scarce materials. Advancing technologies bring new processes and products into demand. The environment requires alert stewardship of dwindling forests and overcrowded dumping grounds for toxic waste. Adjusting to the trends, the purchasing profession serves its constituents' needs.

The study of purchasing and materials management challenges many students on college campuses today. The practice of purchasing and materials management rewards the professional career person with increasing respect, position, and salary.

Discussion Questions

1. Describe the relationship between the organizational concept of materials management and the field of purchasing.

2. Outline the important factors the purchasing manager must consider in order to provide continuity of production.

3. State the rationale for having follow-up handled by purchasing rather than another department.

4. Delineate positive arguments for assigning the invoice-checking function to the purchasing department.

5. In what ways does purchasing aid production?
6. What does the purchasing multiplier indicate?
7. Define purchasing in the socioeconomic sense described in the text.
8. What are the objectives of purchasing activities?
9. What does management expect of its purchasing department?
10. What social issues can be influenced by purchasing?
11. Describe the influence of purchasing on the economy.
12. What rationale can be given for purchasing's assumption of an active role in socioeconomic issues?
13. What is the difference between follow-up and expediting?
14. Describe the effective purchasing manager of the future.

===2

Purchase Strategy and Forecasting

Leo Baekeland sold the rights to his invention, Velox photographic printing paper, to Eastman Kodak in 1899. It was the first commercially successful photographic paper and he sold it to Eastman Kodak for $1 million. Baekeland had planned to ask $50,000 and to go down to $25,000 if necessary, but fortunately for him, Eastman spoke first.*

CHAPTER CONTENTS

Planning Strategic Goals and Tactical Goals

Interrelated Strategies

Strategic Supplier Involvement/Supplier Partnering

Strategic Sourcing

Outsourcing

Outsourcing Disadvantages

Mathematical Models

International Forecasting

Inventory Simulation Models

Exponential Smoothing

Regression Analysis

Trend Line Projection

Economic Projections

*Source: Asimov, *Biographical Encyclopedia of Science and Technology,* second revised edition (New York: Doubleday, 1982).

The strategic planning concept spread rapidly through organizations in the 1960s and 1970s as a major management phenomenon. Corporate planners positioned themselves near the top executives and brought in staffs with special techniques and visions of the future. The entire environment of a business came under scrutiny. As a general rule, managers committed funds for planning only if they could anticipate, in the foreseeable future, a return on planning expenses as a result of the long-range planning analysis.[1] Purchasing and materials management became closely involved, as a major contributor to bottom-line results.

A total of 297 of the *Fortune 1000* asserted in a 1987 study that a substantially higher percentage of the purchasing departments had assumed an increased role/responsibility since 1980. Strategic planning topped the list of newly assigned activities, at 43 percent, followed by "providing economic forecasts/indicators" at 41 percent.[2]

PLANNING STRATEGIC GOALS AND TACTICAL GOALS

Purchase planning typically involves a production or operations master plan that stretches out 15 to 30 months into the future. Some organizations tie in their marketing master forecast to the specific items to be brought in via the purchase plan.

Purchase planning starts by defining the objectives and goals for the company's purchasing efforts. These goals mean more than mere objectives, because they specifically spell out how much and when. Specifying these objectives as goals encourages employees to focus on day-to-day performance and helps managers measure progress toward attaining these goals.

Strategic goals, on the other hand, concentrate on broad, general issues. The organization's top management sets these goals, for the organization and for themselves. These goals typically involve large sums of money and cover long periods into the future.

Tactical goals focus on how to achieve the strategic goals. Middle managers—including purchasing, materials, and transportation managers—set tactical goals. For example, Certified Grocers of Florida operates a fleet of 75 tractors and 160 trailers to service 200 supermarkets. The transportation manager for Certified Grocers made the tactical decision to use a life-cycle cost approach when adding 11 standard Kenworth T800s. His analysis

---

[1] Samuel C. Certo, *Modern Management,* 5th ed. (Boston: Allyn & Bacon, 1992), p. 189.
[2] *Purchasing Organizational Relationships* (Center for Advanced Purchasing Studies, Tempe, AZ, 1988).

TABLE 2-1. Definitions of Strategic Planning Terms

Term	Meaning	Example
Objective	Desired outcome	Lower-cost purchasing
Goal	Quantified objective	2 percent lower purchasing department operating costs by end of year
Forecast	Expected event	3 percent inflation in current year
Strategy	Action plan to reach objective	Increase buyers' skills of negotiating
Tactics	Specific steps to secure the objective designated by a strategy	Conduct negotiations seminar—half on buyers time, half on company time
Policy	A guide to action	Only buyers with over 4 years on the job will negotiate with vendors

indicated that, despite higher initial cost, the life-cycle cost included resale value for a lower long-term cost.[3]

In summary, organizations' purchasing operation works within the framework of top management's *strategic goals,* with specifics as developed by the corresponding *tactical goals.* The result is a *purchasing plan* that is translated into action by the specific set of *purchasing strategies* which take account of the market, competition, and resources that exist at the present time. Table 2-1 provides definitions of terms.

INTERRELATED STRATEGIES

Strategic purchasing often involves a set of interrelated strategies in the planning process. For example, materials managers and purchasing managers constantly juggle cost trade-offs in their daily operations.

> The concept of balancing conflicting cost patterns is at the heart of logistics management and is essential to strategic planning. Understanding that major cost-service elements such as transportation versus inventory, production versus distribution, and customer service versus all logistics costs are in trade-off, or conflict, with each other helps to set the scope of the logistics plan.[4]

[3] "Cost Study Cuts Expenses," *Fleet Equipment* (November 1991) pp. 20–23.
[4] Ronald H. Ballou, *Basic Business Logistics,* 2nd ed. (Englewood Cliffs, NJ: Prentice Hall, 1987), p. 347.

A manager for a large distributor summarizes his company's purchasing strategy in the following categories:

Asset Management: Relating to total inventory investment measured in "days in inventory" versus actual cost of sales in a given month. Also, the control and review of closeouts (slow movers) and management of specials.

Marketing Objectives: Relating to a market-driven focus on specific product categories. Includes two-way communication with marketing on new items, deleted items, promotion items, and on continuing feedback. A strategy of matching purchasing techniques with overall marketing objectives to optimize profits is the ultimate goal.

Vendor Support: Utilization of vendors in a "partnering concept" to effect a stronger supplier base, specific vendor evaluations and a sharing of information and risks for overall mutual rewards. A trend toward fewer, qualified vendors is the goal for a long-term relationship.*

Strategic management incorporates the broad concept of supply management. The department's responsibilities include anything that involves inbound material or services. Purchasing functions as an entrepreneurial team member responsible for product development and bottom-line results. The department's completely proactive stance provides strong input to the creation of corporate values and plans.

In some firms, the people in the purchasing function perform little or no actual purchasing. Rather, they act as the focal points of supply relationships between various engineering and manufacturing people in the two firms.

To earn regard as an equal contributor to the strategy and success of the organization, an alert purchasing department strives to develop its activities, its management approaches, its budgetary structures, and its personnel skills as it evolves toward strategic management.[5]

Purchasing strategy must consider the strong forces that deregulate commodities like natural gas and that move the market in the direction of competition and customers. Customer service levels take on greater importance when competition arises to claim part of the field. Firms that desire a high degree of transactional control will have to develop a staff to implement and monitor these strategies.[6]

---

* Specified in conversation with the author, June 4, 1992.
[5] "Fitting Purchasing to the Strategic Firm: Frameworks, Processes, and Values," *Journal of Purchasing and Materials Management* (Winter 1990), pp. 6–10.
[6] "Purchasing Strategies for Natural Gas in a Deregulating Market," ibid. p. 27.

Strategic purchasing planning necessitates a professional purchasing manager who can identify specific trends in the market, and at the same time grasp the big picture of environmental impact and economic advantage.

As purchasing takes a greater role in strategic decision planning for the firm, it develops a deeper understanding of the company goals for the long term. Then it asks how purchasing may contribute significantly to these goals, in what areas, and where does purchasing need to increase its participation to match purchasing's goals with the company's goals?[7]

Purchasing managers realize the importance of supply strategies: the outgrowths of corporate thinking about competitiveness in the 1990s. Much of that thinking leads to the conclusion that corporate success ties in to supplier performance. Along those lines, the heads of top buying operations speculated on the most important factors in their companies' competitive success and offered the following list, in order of importance:

Cost control
Customer satisfaction
Product quality
Prices paid
Development of new products/technologies
Competitive prices of our products
Ability to attract top suppliers[8]

STRATEGIC SUPPLIER INVOLVEMENT/SUPPLIER PARTNERING

Over the period from the late 1980s into the 1990s American firms have developed the concept of close cooperation with their suppliers, which some identify as strategic involvement, supplier partnering, or related terms. Essentially, the concept means using the resources of a supplier to the maximum benefit possible. It looks at a supplier as an extension of the buying organization—specifically an extension of the purchaser's research capabilities, storage potentials, financial backing, and manufacturing and quality-control needs.

U.S. managers borrowed the Japanese concept of extremely close supplier interaction and cooperation. The practice consists of selecting the "best" suppliers, working closely with them, and entering into long-term relationships based on mutual need and trust. The specific benefits that

---

[7] "Are You Valuable to Your Company—or Just a Clerk?" *Purchasing* (May 7, 1992), p. 21.
[8] "A Glimmer of the Radical Changes that Lie Ahead," ibid. (March 5, 1992), p. 17.

hopefully would derive include improved delivery and quality performance, reduced administrative cost, technology sharing, inventory reduction, and lower prices.

Reported success indicators usually include JIT (just-in-time) inventory stocking procedures, inventory reductions, and a smaller supplier base. New United Motors Manufacturing Company defined their philosophy on the premise that quality dominates. They used a strong JIT program, which involved more than the traditional materials handling, to include plant layout, scheduling, and service managing inventory.[9]

A survey of purchasing managers found general agreement in the fact that supplier partnering reduced the number of suppliers. All who responded stated that they had cut or were in the process of reducing the number of suppliers. They cited the following main reasons for these reductions: (1) supplier development is expensive and cannot become cost effective unless limited to the suppliers with which they do sizable business; (2) close working relationships require restricting the number of suppliers; and (3) a small supplier base ensures that the supplier who commits to partnering and quality improvements receives rewards of substantial business.[10] Chapter 5, "Sourcing," presents additional information concerning partnering.

STRATEGIC SOURCING

A growing number of businesses look at strategic sourcing as a means of economic advantage.[11] The intense competitive pressures of the global marketplace put renewed emphasis on finding the right sources of materials and services. While purchasing traditionally has conducted sourcing, management's growing interest in sourcing will not lead automatically to a more significant role for purchasing. How this movement will translate into corporate policy remains unclear.

Strategic sourcing, according to one statement,[12] will require purchasing departments to increase their suppliers' capabilities, answer to more accountability for results, explain what goes on in greater detail, and work much more effectively with other functions. This latter point may mean sharing its power as the ultimate decision maker regarding supplier selection.

---

[9] "Japanese Philosophy Puts Power in Purchasing Partnership," *Purchasing World* (October 1987).
[10] "Building World-Class Supplier Relationships," *Purchasing World* (August 16, 1990).
[11] "Strategic Sourcing: How Relevant Is Purchasing?" *Purchasing* (April 2, 1992), p. 15.
[12] "Strategic Sourcing Rises to the Top," ibid., p. 54.

Still another statement asserts comprehensiveness as the key to establishing effective strategic sourcing management.[13] That strategy involves:

1. A total supply chain vision focusing on the ultimate customer.
2. The technology to improve or design the firm's finished products.
3. A process for reviewing components and materials in order to maximize standardization.
4. A competent systematic cross-functional make/buy competitive analysis process for determining how much of the design and manufacturing phases to do in-house or outside.
5. Value-oriented management techniques applied where appropriate.
6. Processes for developing systematic supplier evaluation and supply-base strategy.

As a driving force for implementing the sourcing strategy, purchasing looks beyond a tradition of transaction processing. Instead, it focuses on using strategic sourcing with the highest levels of management as part of competitiveness planning.[14]

A recently designed strategic sourcing model augments the traditional cost analysis for a purchase. It considers strategic and technological factors by examining process technology's role and maturity in providing competitive advantage. It examines competitors' process technology positions. After following the model's guidelines, the tentative sourcing decision reduces to one of the following: Make, develop internal capability, buy or develop suppliers.[15]

During the 1980s, many firms developed supply chains—although some have existed for a long time, like Kraft and Pillsbury for refrigerated product distribution and DuPont and Burlington Industries for fibers. Supply chains function as cooperative links in the buying and selling interface, all the way from daily transactions to long-term research and product offerings. For example, Merck joined with Johnson & Johnson to combine the research and manufacturing advantages of one firm with the distribution and marketing strengths of the other.[16] And Wal-Mart leverages procurement power to obtain manufacturers' merchandise at lower prices and passes them to its customers, thus optimizing the total supply chain.[17]

---

[13] "Strategic Sourcing Management," ibid., p. 52.

[14] "How Strategic Sourcing Can Affect Your Career," ibid. (June 18, 1992), p. 17.

[15] "Strategic Sourcing: A Progressive Approach to the Make-or-Buy Decision," *Academy of Management Executive* (February 1992), pp. 23–31.

[16] "Identifying Interfirm Total Cost Advantages for Supply Chain Competitiveness," *International Journal of Purchasing and Materials Management* (Fall 1991), pp. 10–15.

[17] "The End of a Trade Promotion Paradigm?" *Discount Merchandiser* (April 1991), pp. 62–64.

OUTSOURCING

Outsourcing is a collective term applied to the result of supplier partnering, with its attendant reduction in number of suppliers and the increased reliance on the resources of these suppliers.

When considering outsourcing, managers need to: (1) establish a strategy for the proper balancing of management, contracting, and consulting; (2) establish a strategy to deal with possible reduced staff; (3) intimately integrate potential outsource vendors; and (4) provide close communication channels. Employees may need time to adjust to the new workstyle.

Cost savings may accrue for outsourcing vendors in reduced salaries, superior management techniques and systems, the timely application of new technology, and the ability to supply critical, high-priced help on an as-needed basis.[18]

OUTSOURCING DISADVANTAGES

The improper use of outsourcing may contribute to a competitive decline. For example, the decline in the U.S. consumer electronics industry has been attributed by some as partially a result of outsourcing. The problem with outsourcing is that while a series of incremental outsourcing decisions, taken individually, make economic sense, collectively they represent the surrender of the business's competitive advantages. Outsourcing often involves the following four questionable assumptions:[19]

1. Strategy primarily involves competitive position in the marketplace.
2. Brand share is defensible without manufacturing share.
3. Design and manufacturing are separable.
4. Market knowledge is separable from manufacturing.

These assumptions may or may not be appropriate to a given situation. If not, a loss of the buying organizations' competitive advantage may result from the outsourcing practice. Analysts can forecast the outcome of limiting the number of supplies too tightly.

The chapter now addresses forecasting.

---

[18] "The Real Costs of Outsourcing," *Information Systems Management* (Winter 1992), pp. 78–81.
[19] "Outsourcing and Industrial Decline," *Academy of Management Executive* (February 1992), pp. 7–22.

MATHEMATICAL MODELS

Econometrics is a computerized combination of economics, statistics, and mathematics applied to specific decision-making situations. It has been developed because our economy has become more complex and unstable. Using relationships based on past data, econometrics enables an analyst to describe the economy or a distinct part of the economy in terms of an equation or set of equations. The equations form a model of the economy or of an individual market.

Data Resources, Inc., Chase Econometrics Associates, and Wharton Econometrics offer a wide variety of services. These include models of the U.S. and international economies, inflation monitoring services, regional and state forecasting, demographic predictions, and models of specific industries, such as petrochemical, agriculture, plastics and rubber, and steel.

Monsanto decided against "an ivory tower, from-the-top-down" forecasting approach which assumes that their managers are the most knowledgable about market conditions. However, they use a general econometric model of demands to check on bottom-up forecasts and to pick up on economic turnarounds. The final valuations come from comparing the forecast model against what managers hear from other information sources. When management and forecasters differ on predictions, the company reexamines its base assumptions.

Some non-measurable factors cannot be reduced to a mathematical format, such as the psychology of an industry or a new technology. However, econometric models at least force users to ask the right questions and allow managers to develop alternate strategies.

The information that purchasers get from these tools, when tempered with their experience in the market, can give them an informational and analytical advantage.[20]

INTERNATIONAL FORECASTING

When forecasting for an international purchase, many elements appear the same as in domestic purchasing. Other elements, such as JIT methods and hand-to-mouth buying, require serious reevaluation in light of the extended lead times and transportation requirements. The large volume buyer also will have to study exchange rate fluctuations in order to forecast currencies and know how to pay for a product internationally.

[20] "Econometrics: Forecasting Tool for Buyers," *Chemical Marketing Reporter* (January 10, 1977), pp. 11, 12, 14.

button. Extending the trend line makes it possible to determine three items: (1) When will Demand reach a certain level? (2) What Demand level will occur at a particular time? (3) What happens in between?

ECONOMIC PROJECTIONS

Probable price changes and the availability of purchased commodities are forecast in economic projections; they constitute an extension of vendor and commodity research. Price forecasting is of considerable significance to purchasing professionals, helping them to determine how and when the price of materials will move in a rapidly changing economy. Price predictions are based on past rises in prices; standardized published price indexes such as the Wholesale Price Index, which predicts overall industrial averages for a certain index; vendor and business surveys; economic models; information from a forecasting service; or a combination, such as commodity price histories and forecasts. Economic and political developments, such as inflationary trends in nations that are large suppliers for specific commodities and changes in relations between super powers are watched and analyzed to determine their effect on prices and availability.

The NAPM Survey

An important and much-utilized predictor of macroeconomic conditions is the NAPM's *Report on Business*. Of great value to purchasing personnel, it projects commodity prices and availability as they follow the ups and downs of the overall economy. When the economy is coming out of a recession, the survey respondents should collectively report higher output moving upward; when the economy is on the way down into a recession, the reverse is true. Appendix B contains details on the features of this important monthly report.

Purchasing personnel can use all survey components to predict changes in prices and demand–supply commodity variables. Since economic forecasting is an art rather than a science, obvious adjustments must be made as these measures are used in specific situations. The adjustments consist of the following steps.

1. Maintain charts of the individual organization's activity and relate them to those of the survey to determine the relation (or lack of one) between it and the individual survey components.
2. Relate survey results to key commodities and key vendors to determine overall relationships and the degree of lead, lag, or coincidental relationships.

3. Study the findings from the first two steps, considering both the absolute changes as well as rates of change.

4. Consider extenuating circumstances of the individual organization in respect to commodities and vendors, before making a predictive analysis.

This survey has been in operation for over 50 years and has been receiving increased attention from economics experts in government and industry as one of the most useful measures in economic forecasting. Properly adapted, it can be helpful for forecasting prices and availability. As such, the survey can be of great assistance in developing buying policies relative to inventory levels, degrees of forward commitments, and types of purchase contracts. Forecasting services are another important means for buyers to acquire dependable analyses of commodity and economy movements.

Forecasting Requirements

In the process of forecasting, two statistical measures are useful: correlation analysis and cyclical analysis.

Correlation analysis is a statistical expression of the relation between two sets of data. One set, which is to be forecast, is called dependent data; the other, the independent data, is the set used as the basis for the forecast. Using a purchasing example, one could possibly project the number of houses in a society (the dependent variable) by establishing the correlation existing with births seven years earlier (the independent variable). A bit of a lead–lag relationship would probably appear in this example.

In buying practice, if the independent variable can be estimated fairly accurately, and a high degree of correlation between the two sets of data is found to exist, the dependent variable can be similarly forecast with a high level of accuracy. Generally, the more "macro" the independent variable is, the easier it is to forecast. A buyer of lumber might conceivably find that the level of overall construction is projected quite accurately for a three-month period on the basis of building permits issued. Correspondingly, a correlation should be found between construction activity and the projected level of lumber prices (i.e., as construction increases, a correlative increase in lumber prices can be predicted).

Long-term (10 to 15 years) market data are assumed to consist of four types of variations: long-term underlying (secular) movements; so-called cyclical movements (typically, movements within three- to five-year cycles); seasonal fluctuations (occurring within a 12-month period); and irregular, unpredictable fluctuations. *Cyclical analysis,* as a forecasting technique, attempts to isolate and predict the cyclical directions of the economy. This approach assumes that buyers are primarily concerned with the short-run (three to five years) influences on the demand, supply, and price variables. In practice, using specific yearly data, cyclical analysis isolates and removes the seasonal variations, the long-term secular trend, and irregular influences, leaving the cyclical variation, which is then analyzed and projected.

CHAPTER SUMMARY

Global competition brings pressure to bear on managers to enlarge the scope of strategic long-range, large dollar planning for the firm. Due to the importance that suppliers make in creating and sustaining competitiveness, strategic planning brings the purchasing function into new relationships with top management. Purchasing no longer holds the sole responsibility for selecting suppliers. More and more companies report the involvement of top management in finding stable suppliers who will ship uniform quality goods to meet exacting customer specifications. The assignment of responsibility and accountability, however, needs clarifying.

Purchasing managers in many companies for years have provided economic forecasts for upper-level management, including the President of the United States. The expanding emphasis on strategic planning obliges firms to gather data from many marketplaces. The professional purchasing officer contributes his or her experiences, observations, and speculations to the information-gathering efforts of upper management. The desktop and portable laptop computer facilitates gathering and analyzing the growing volume of data available that is indeed vital to the business decision maker.

Discussion Questions

1. What is the objective of strategic planning?
2. Describe purchasing strategy.
3. Explain how interrelated strategies benefit the buyer's firm.
4. Discuss the application and importance of the NAPM business survey for purchase forecasting, specifically.

5. How does the NAPM survey reflect the upward and downward trends of the overall economy?
6. How might the purchasing department utilize statistical forecasting?

Suggested Cases

Ajax Sewing Machine Company
Factory Enterprises, Inc.
Gamma Corporation

Megalopolis City
Powers Company

Exercise

Using exponential smoothing, compute four periods of forecasts where demand remains constant at 95 units and the initial forecast equals 100. Select Alpha the smoothing constant as 0.3.

3

Basic Procedures and Purchasing Techniques

The Great Atlantic & Pacific Tea Company switched to central buying at a time when most retailers and wholesalers decided to continue buying locally. A&P points to several reasons for establishing a central buying department: more efficient buying and planning of sales events, better asset management, and greater inventory control. Some observers have stated that A&P buys centrally in order to cut down on division overhead costs by eliminating positions. Few suppliers think that central buying can result in better prices, but it may achieve efficiencies through more centralized invoicing and accounts payable.*

*Source: ''The Best Buy: Controlled or Decentralized?'' *Progressive Grocer* (February 1991), pp. 79–84.

Systems Contracting

Purchasing Services

Small-Order Procedures

Strategic Partnering

Most organizations require coordinated efforts by interdependent individuals and departments. Standard procedures make routine coordination possible. Moreover, such procedures, if well known, provide for unusual events and exceptions. Procedures guide participants in handling the exceptions in accord with the organization's policies.

Purchasing departments vary because their companies vary in organization, size, and operating policies. Therefore, most of this book is devoted to a consideration of purchasing policies and the means of implementing them. The emphasis on policies rather than procedures is meant to delineate the importance of purchasing in most business organizations. In any purchasing department there is always the hazard of so emphasizing forms and procedures that the vital functions of the department are overlooked.

However, to provide a realistic background against which to picture the purchasing policies and procedures discussed later, this chapter is devoted to a description of the procedures, forms, and automated storage retrieval methods most generally used in a purchasing department.

Applications of automation in purchasing range from sophisticated computer models to electronic typewriters. Electronic data processing equipment is used by an increasing number of companies with a heavy load of paperwork. A number of systems of automating the procedural processes have been developed, and such systems must be tailored to the requirements within a company. This chapter will concentrate on the basic storage, retrieval, and analysis tasks involved in purchasing.

A purchasing manual delineates the written policies and procedures for the internal operations of a purchasing department and its significant relationships with other departments within the organization. The typical manual will set forth the policy adopted by the company on a specific aspect of the purchasing function and then detail the procedures to be followed in adhering to that policy.

The major benefit of a manual is that it provides support for the authority of the purchasing department. It informs other departments within the company of purchasing policies and procedures and, by keeping purchasing personnel advised of policies and procedures, it aids in their training.

Each company has its own individually designed set of policies consistent with its company objectives, and procedures are similarly individualized.

PURCHASING PROCEDURE

Procedure, in the present context, refers to the mechanism by which a purchase transaction is carried through from its inception to its conclusion. Company and purchasing department policies outline the broad objectives to be accomplished and the guidelines within which the procedures must accomplish the desired results. Procedures outline in detail the functions to be performed by the people who carry out the operations of purchasing. Forms and records are used to implement both procedures and policies. The first part of this chapter outlines procedures—that is, the way the purchasing function is conducted in a typical purchasing department—and the second part focuses on the forms and records necessary for efficiency in performing procedures.

Since there are wide variations in industries, companies, products, and personnel, it would not be feasible to establish a single set of procedures that would apply to all cases. The following steps, however, must be taken, in one way or another, to complete a purchasing transaction. These may be called the basic steps of the operation.

1. Recognition of need
2. Description of requirement
3. Selection of possible sources of supply
4. Determination of price and availability
5. Placement of the order
6. Follow-up and expediting of the order
7. Verification of charges
8. Processing of discrepancies and rejections
9. Closing of completed or canceled orders
10. Maintenance of records and files

Related activities such as receiving, storekeeping, and inspection are often a part of the purchasing procedure; however, we will concentrate here on the functions specifically performed by the purchasing department.

Recognition of Need

The term *recognition of need* refers to the means by which a needed item is officially brought to the attention of the purchasing department. Two procedures are followed. In one the department concerned or the stores department issues a requisition. In the other a bill of materials is issued.

A purchase requisition describes the needed item and becomes the basis for action by the purchasing department. It is issued by the inventory control department or in cases of urgently needed items, a using department. This form is usually prepared in duplicate, and the carbon copy is retained by the issuing department as a record of its action. Requisitions must be signed by authorized individuals in order to avoid irresponsible purchase requests. In some companies requisitions for inventory items, as opposed to those for items for immediate use, are initiated in the department responsible for maintaining inventory. Requisitions are issued when stocks diminish to the reorder point and are sent to the purchasing department for action.

Requisitions from using departments are routed through the stores department. If the item is in inventory, it is supplied from stock instead of being purchased. Requisitions for items not in inventory are sent on to the purchasing department for action. In government agencies and institutions that operate on a budget, the requisition is generally routed to the purchasing department through the financial officer in order to ensure that funds are available.

A bill of materials is a list of all items to be incorporated into the finished product. Such bills are generally prepared when engineering blueprints for the item are made. Under this method of establishing need, the production planning department notifies the purchasing department of the manufacturing schedule. The buyer then multiplies the items listed in the bill of materials by the total units planned for production to determine total requirements. After the total needs have been adjusted to make use of existing inventories, the quantity to be purchased is determined. Bills of materials are used primarily to purchase standard parts and small expendable tools. Supplies and similar needs are usually handled by requisitions.

Description of Requirement

The requisition describes the required item. To assure complete and accurate information for ordering, the requisition includes all necessary information in a standardized form that is readily checked and verified. Since a bill of materials is usually prepared by the engineering department as a part of the original plan for the product, it can be used for the descriptions.

The buyer checks requisitions carefully, utilizing personal knowledge of the item and records of past purchases. Buyers do not change inadequate requisitions but refer them to their source.

The buyer acts as a help desk, an advocate, often with experience and expert knowledge of available alternatives. This knowledge assists the requisitioner in preparing his or her description of need. Artificial intelligence technology makes expert systems such as this one closer to reality. And companies have begun to make computer networking available to their engineering and operating personnel, for displaying alternative specifications.[1]

Selection of Possible Sources of Supply

The buyer must next select the sources from which to secure prices. This process involves narrowing down a large list of potential suppliers to a relative few from whom quotations will be requested.

For items purchased frequently, prequalified preferred suppliers are usually contacted. For nonroutine purchases, the process requires a careful survey of potential sources of supply. The extent and thoroughness of the survey is determined by the cost of the item and its importance to production.

From many potential suppliers the list is reduced to the few with whom negotiations are to be conducted. Many sources of information are used during this stage of the purchase transaction, including internal records of potential suppliers, visits to prospective suppliers' plants, and recommendations of salespeople and other purchasers. Government purchasers are required by law or regulation to grant all qualified suppliers an opportunity to bid for the business. Private sector buyers choose from many suppliers only those with whom they wish to negotiate.

Determination of Price and Availability

The next step in the purchasing transaction is to secure the price for the items to be purchased. This may be accomplished in several ways. For low-volume standard items, suppliers' catalogs and price lists are available for pricing data.

Negotiation is a second method of establishing price; this implies bargaining between buyer and seller. The buyer should approach the process of negotiation with an open mind and with as much information as possible about the commodity under consideration—the buying firm's rate of use, the production facilities of the supplier, market conditions, and any other factors that may bear on the outcome of the negotiations. (See Chapter 9 for negotiation techniques.)

The third method of securing price is through a request for quotes. It is standard practice to solicit quotes from prospective suppliers by means of a quote request form that specifies the requirements. At the end of a specified period of time stated on the quote requests, the bidding is closed and quotes

---

[1] "Capture That Information on an Expert System," *Journal of Business Strategy* (January/February 1990), pp. 11–15.

are analyzed and compared. The purchase order is then issued to the chosen firm.

Government purchasing policies frequently require that bids be opened publicly, with the award made to the lowest qualified bidder. In private sector purchasing there is no such requirement. Nonetheless, if buyers have carefully selected the suppliers from whom bids are requested, and the bids are responsive to the specifications, there is no economic reason why they should not accept the lowest bid. Practice varies whether unsuccessful bidders are notified and what notification procedure is used. Early notification benefits unsuccessful bidders so that they may release for sale the items they reserved for the buyer's order.

Placing the Order

The legal order is placed with the supplier on a form known as a purchase order. Most companies insist that every purchase be placed in this manner. When an order is placed by telephone or telegraph, it is the practice to confirm it by sending the supplier a regular purchase order. Such an order should be clearly marked "confirming" to avoid possible confusion with a second order.

The buyer records on the original requisition the name of the company receiving the order, the price, the quantity, and other pertinent data. The purchase order is then prepared for the signature of the authorized individual in the purchasing department.

Companies vary in the number of copies of the purchase order required and in the disposition of the copies. The original is sent to the supplier and is usually accompanied by one carbon, known as the acknowledgement copy. On this copy the supplier confirms acceptance of the order and indicates the date on which delivery is to be made. Other purchase order copies are often sent to the receiving, accounting, using, inspection, and inventory control departments, and the follow-up section of the purchasing department. One copy is always retained for the purchasing department's files.

Follow-Up

The method employed in following up an order varies among organizations. Typically, orders are listed in the computer by scheduled shipping dates; critical and past-due orders are followed up by further communication with the supplier.

Follow-up routines include securing an acceptance and a promise of delivery. Outstanding orders are reviewed at regular intervals and communication with suppliers is conducted as required.

Verifying Charges

Invoice checking consists of verifying the data on the seller's invoice against the buyer's records. The seller's invoice is compared with the original order and the receiving record.

The invoice quantity is checked against the quantity specified on the purchase order and the quantity received. Terms and prices are checked against the purchase order. The description of the goods is verified on both forms. If an invoice is correct in all respects, it is approved and forwarded to accounting for payment.

Processing Discrepancies and Rejections

If discrepancies are found, the buyer is notified. If the invoice is in error, the buyer returns it to the vendor for correction. When material is rejected it is customary to obtain the vendor's authorization for return and replacement. If the material is urgently needed, the buyer may subject it to 100 percent inspection. When every piece must be checked to verify that it meets specifications, the buyer will seek to recover the increased costs from the supplier. Total inspection costs more than partial inspection.

Closing Completed Orders

Since most purchasing departments maintain a file copy of unfilled orders, the department needs a procedure for closing orders when they are completed. Before closing an order, the purchase order must be checked against both the receiving reports and the vendor's invoice. A previous section of this chapter describes the checking of invoices. There may be only one receiving report to check. However, when partial shipments occur, several receiving reports will be used. All except the last one should be marked "partial," and the last one, which completes the shipments of the order, should be marked "final."

After the invoices and receiving reports match the file copy of the order, a notation of this fact should be made on it. It should then be removed and stored in the file of closed orders. In most departments closed orders are filed according to the purchase order number sequence so that they may be readily located if reference is required.

Maintenance of Records and Files

The final step in the purchasing process is maintaining records of the transaction. This process, normally computerized, is routine in nature. Many companies maintain computerized records of purchases arranged by both product and vendor. Decisions on the extent of detailed records to be maintained, the length of time they are maintained, and the form in which they are kept are policy matters determined by legal as well as management principles.

CANCELLATIONS

Once an order has been placed by the buyer and accepted by the seller, it constitutes a legal and binding contract between both parties. However, there are occasions when it will be necessary for a buyer to seek to cancel although the seller stands ready to fulfill the contract. An excessive accumulation of inventory, an engineering or design change in the buyer's finished product, a basic change in the products being made, or a sudden change in demand for the product may make such cancellations necessary.

Cancellations for the convenience of the buyer often involve potential financial losses. The seller may have begun production, or refused other orders because of this commitment, or expended funds or materials specifically designed for the order.

Cancellation charges are usually arrived at in negotiations between the buyer and the seller after the cancellation has been made. Occasionally, formulas governing cancellation charges are a part of the contract. The governing factor is the amount of actual loss or cost incurred by the seller. If the cancellation relates to standard material or a product regularly sold by the seller, there is naturally less presumption of loss than if specialized products are canceled. If the amount of the loss cannot be established through negotiations, formal arbitration or ultimately a court trial may be necessary.

There are also instances when a seller may cancel a buyer's order. Cancellations are especially likely during periods of price increases and in times of growth and economic acceleration. During such periods suppliers may not be able to fill all their orders, and those they do fill may be of substandard quality because quality control procedures have been relaxed owing to heavy demand. Under the Uniform Commercial Code, the seller can be held liable for such defective goods. During periods of very short supply or heavy demand, an ''impossible'' situation may develop whereby a vendor is not bound to deliver as contracted. The potential for situations developing in which orders cannot be delivered reinforces the need for good vendor relations and a working knowledge of the legal rights and responsibilities of both parties.

AUTOMATION OF PROCEDURES

The large volume of orders processed through a purchasing department, many of which are repeated frequently throughout the year, has led purchasing departments to automate much of the paperwork. Automation, in this context, does not necessarily mean computerization. Rather, it refers to procedures that reduce the paperwork necessary to place purchase orders by reducing the number and volume of forms. Computerization often provides file and retrieval assistance and may be an ultimate part of these procedures.

The regular release of shipping orders under a purchase contract is an illustration of the automation of a purchasing procedure. The calendar triggers the releases, which go out without further action.

Again, suppose that a company has a frequent demand for an item. A *traveling requisition* can be used instead of making a new requisition each time the item is needed. The traveling requisition form lists all descriptive information about the item requested, the approved vendors and their addresses, and past pricing information, all in permanent blocks. The form also has a series of spaces in which the requisitioning department lists the current stock of the item, the desired quantity, and the date. The form is then sent to the purchasing department, which fills the order by issuing a purchase order for the desired item and indicates the action. The form then goes back to the requisitioning department to be held for future use. The use of the traveling requisition saves the time and trouble of filling out repetitive requisitions and also cuts down on the amount of paperwork the purchasing department must handle.

Automation has also greatly facilitated the maintenance of stock records. Machines and techniques have been developed to simplify and quicken the entering of inventory receipts and disbursements and to provide reports of inventory levels. The use of such equipment saves considerable time and clerical effort and provides current information on inventories of materials.

Automation of records is often expensive; purchasing executives must constantly weigh the benefits against the costs. The final determination depends on such factors as the size of the firm, the purchasing system employed, and the accounting and internal control methods in effect.

Computerized Purchasing

Integrated materials management systems and effective computerized purchasing applications assist the buyer in selecting vendors more wisely through using an automated database. The buying process begins with the buyer receiving a requisition for specific goods or services, something previously purchased, or a new item. The buyer may assist in writing the specs.

"Buying screens" on the desktop computer aid in making the initial buy and subsequent repeat buys. The "delivery screen" assists the buyer in reviewing the anticipated stock level or a possible stock-out situation. The "vendor performance screen" provides the buyer with recent history concerning the company's vendors. The "open purchase order screen" serves as a sales representative's performance review, showing delays or promises kept.[2]

Information flows into and out of the typical purchasing system as Figure 3-1 depicts. When the purchasing system uses a computer, computerized purchasing manages those information flows among various functions (e.g., transportation), databases (e.g., price histories), records (e.g., vendor information), and reports (e.g., buyer workload). Figure 3-2 represents computerized purchasing as a flowchart. The computer operates the electronic data interchange with suppliers, as this chapter discusses later.

Desktop or personal computers (PCs) with hard disk drives help businesses access large amounts of information in such applications as desktop publishing, database management, and networking. An estimated 85 percent of PCs sold in the United States in 1990 had hard disk drives. A hard disk drive contains nonremovable disks that allow repeated recording, editing, and erasing of data. Data on a hard drive transfers easily to a floppy disk for portability or regular back-up.[3]

Compact Disk-Read Only Memory (CD-ROM) add enormous capacity to the purchasing department's PCs, making large databases accessible. Thomas Publishing Company, for example, has placed the entire Thomas Register of American Manufacturers on compact disk (CD-ROM). To load and read the Thomas Register CD-ROM, the buyer connects an optical disk drive to the desktop PC.[4] For the materials manager, literature searches of on-line databases can provide access to research and other data to assist in making objective, informed, defensible purchasing decisions.[5]

Major responsibility for buying computers, workstations, and peripherals comes under purchasing's control, according to a recent survey.[6] The purchasing department's role encompasses identifying needs, evaluating brands, obtaining purchase authority, and upgrading existing systems.

Americans often complain about the problems of selecting a personal computer, but the Japanese buyer faces far worse dilemmas. Multiple incompatible standards fill the PC market. The keyboard does not suit the

---

[2] "What Buyers Can Expect from Computer Assisted Purchasing," *Purchasing World* (April 1990), pp. 48–52.

[3] "The Hard Facts about Hard Disks," *Today's Office* (January 1990), pp. 52–53.

[4] "Put a Thomas Register in Your PC," *Purchasing World* (June 1989), pp. 63/M7–64/M8.

[5] "Searching the Literature: More Resources to Make the Purchase Decision," *Hospital Material Management Quarterly* (May 1992), pp. 42–54.

[6] "Purchasing Takes Reins of PC Buy," *Purchasing* (August 13, 1992), pp. 83–84.

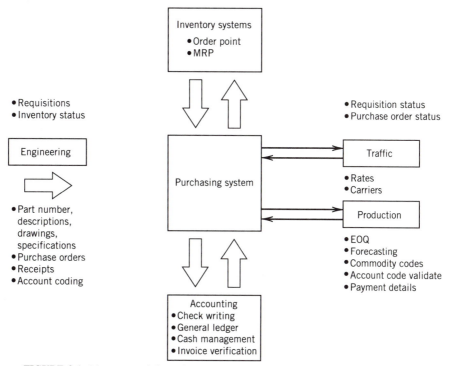

FIGURE 3-1. Management information system (MIS) showing purchasing at the core.

Japanese language, and cramped office space leaves little room for a bulky computer footprint. Only 2 percent of Japan's population use PCs, compared with 10 percent of the U.S. population.[7]

The Defense Department has launched a pilot project to give suppliers a standard way to bid electronically on government purchases under $25,000. Of the $151 billion in Defense Department purchases made each year, about 98 percent falls into the under $25,000 category. The Electronic Commerce Procurement Pilot promises to widen supplier access to procurement and to eliminate paper in the procurement process.[8]

To provide for such interaction, an organization may job-out some or all of its information processing services, a step known as facilities management or outsourcing. The Civil Aviation Authority, for example, subcontracts computer operations to outside suppliers, embracing what some analysts call the biggest trend in computing since the PC's development.[9]

---

[7] "Desktop Deprivation," *Computerworld Supplement* (August 13, 1990), pp. 18–20.
[8] "EDI Suppliers to Test Fed Purchasing Net," *Network World* (June 22, 1992), pp. 43–44.
[9] "IT Goes Out," *Management Today* (April 1992), pp. 80–83.

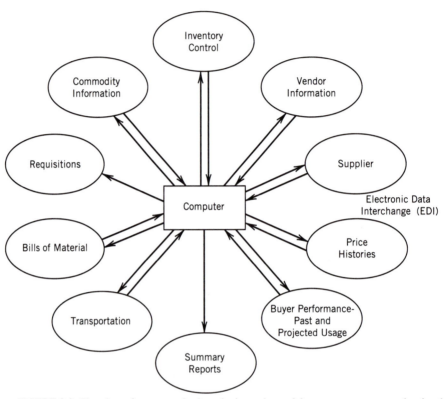

FIGURE 3-2. Flowchart of a computerized purchasing and materials management system, showing the inputs and outputs of information about materials, and electronic data interchange with a supplier.

Practitioners believe that independent specialists can provide computing service more cheaply and efficiently, decreasing overhead by removing expensive computer equipment and staff. Blue Cross and Blue Shield of Massachusetts contracts with Electronic Data Systems Corporation to provide all of its information technology services into the next century, committing some $800 million to the contract.

Even though outsourcing data processing (DP) to a third party can expose the organization to the risk of losing control over DP,[10] systems integration by specialists becomes part of the collective computational experience of most major global corporations. Estimates for the general

---

[10] "Outsmart Your Outsourcer: The Three P's of Negotiation," *Credit Union Executive* (May–June 1992), pp. 23–29.

systems integration market reach the $35 billion range by 1995, up from $6 billion in 1989.[11]

PURCHASE REQUISITIONS, FORMS, AND RECORDS

Requisitions

In many organizations, two basic types of purchase requisition are used. One of these, frequently called a traveling requisition, is used for inventory items that are ordered repeatedly and, as was mentioned previously, is the simplest step toward automation. The second, used for all other requirements, may be called a descriptive requisition.

As stated earlier, the traveling requisition includes a complete description of the item to be ordered, a listing of the preselected vendors, and a space to record the purchase order number, the date ordered, and the vendor selected. The quantity to be ordered may be specified by the stores department or be determined by the purchasing department in accordance with economic order quantity (EOQ) procedure.* The buyer selects the vendor to be used and the price to be paid. The requisition is then forwarded to the typist, who prepares the order. After the purchase order has been prepared, the traveling requisition is returned to the person who originated it.

A simple form of descriptive requisition includes space for the purchase order number, the date, the description of the required item, the date the item is needed, the signature of the individual originating the requisition, and the action taken by the purchasing department.

The form is usually prepared in duplicate, with the original copy going to the purchasing department and a copy retained by the requisitioner. Some companies use a more elaborate form of requisition in which the original copy can be forwarded directly to the vendor as a purchase copy for items of small value. In other cases the original may be used as a master for the reproduction of purchase orders and related forms. The requisition usually bears the prominent heading or title ''purchase requisition'' to differentiate it from other similar forms or the actual purchase order.

Other Forms

The request-for-quotation form is shown in Figure 3-3. This form is used when a potential supplier is asked to furnish prices and terms on a proposed

---

[11] "What the Brochures Won't Tell You about Systems Integrators," *Information Strategy: The Executive's Journal* (Fall 1992), pp. 18–25.
* See Chapter 6 for a more detailed discussion of EOQ procedure.

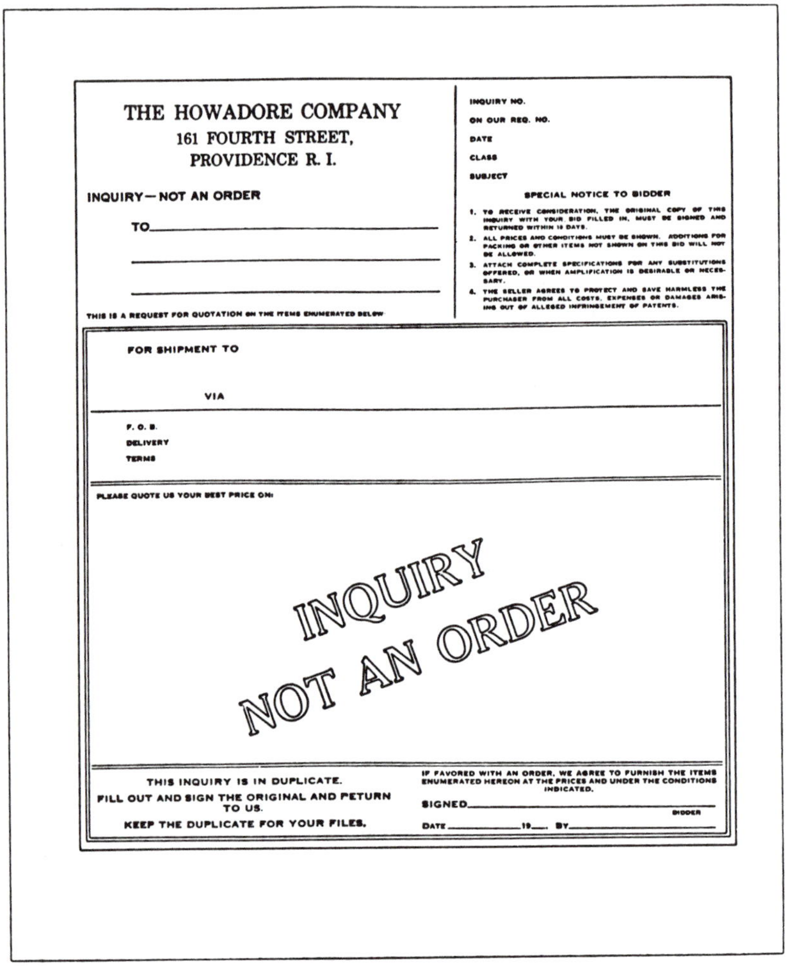
THE HOWADORE COMPANY
161 FOURTH STREET,
PROVIDENCE R. I.

INQUIRY—NOT AN ORDER

TO____________________

THIS IS A REQUEST FOR QUOTATION ON THE ITEMS ENUMERATED BELOW

INQUIRY NO.
ON OUR REQ. NO.
DATE
CLASS
SUBJECT

SPECIAL NOTICE TO BIDDER

1. TO RECEIVE CONSIDERATION, THE ORIGINAL COPY OF THIS INQUIRY WITH YOUR BID FILLED IN, MUST BE SIGNED AND RETURNED WITHIN 10 DAYS.
2. ALL PRICES AND CONDITIONS MUST BE SHOWN. ADDITIONS FOR PACKING OR OTHER ITEMS NOT SHOWN ON THIS BID WILL NOT BE ALLOWED.
3. ATTACH COMPLETE SPECIFICATIONS FOR ANY SUBSTITUTIONS OFFERED, OR WHEN AMPLIFICATION IS DESIRABLE OR NECESSARY.
4. THE SELLER AGREES TO PROTECT AND SAVE HARMLESS THE PURCHASER FROM ALL COSTS, EXPENSES OR DAMAGES ARISING OUT OF ALLEGED INFRINGEMENT OF PATENTS.

FOR SHIPMENT TO

VIA

F. O. B.
DELIVERY
TERMS

PLEASE QUOTE US YOUR BEST PRICE ON:

INQUIRY
NOT AN ORDER

THIS INQUIRY IS IN DUPLICATE.
FILL OUT AND SIGN THE ORIGINAL AND PETURN TO US.
KEEP THE DUPLICATE FOR YOUR FILES.

IF FAVORED WITH AN ORDER, WE AGREE TO FURNISH THE ITEMS ENUMERATED HEREON AT THE PRICES AND UNDER THE CONDITIONS INDICATED.

SIGNED____________________
BIDDER

DATE__________ 19___. BY________________

FIGURE 3-3. An example of a form requesting a price quotation from a supplier.

purchase. To avoid being mistaken for an order, it bears very clear identification across its face.

The request-for-quotation form describes the proposed purchase in detail, including a description of the item, the quantity required, the time and the place of delivery, and the terms. Like other forms, it bears an identifying serial number and may also include a number identifying the purchase requisition that initiated the inquiry.

This form ordinarily specifies a date by which the response must be received. Many companies permit a prospective supplier to quote on the basis of alterations or substitutions in the original specifications, provided that such changes are clearly noted and accompanied by complete specifications. This practice makes it possible for suppliers with good alternatives to make the suggestion without prejudicing their chances to secure the order.

A comparable form, usually called an invitation for bid, is extensively used in purchasing for government units. Legislative requirements generally specify that public bidding is open to all qualified suppliers. Unlike private sector purchasing, government requests for quotations do not permit variations from the specifications on the form.

Government purchasing solicits proposals that, when accepted, create a legal contract. This is accomplished through the use of an invitation-for-proposal form sent to competent suppliers. When a completed invitation-to-bid form is submitted in response by a supplier, it has the legal status of an offer. The purchasing agent can complete the contract by promptly notifying the vendor of acceptance of the offer. This notification may be done by letter, followed with a copy of the agent's own purchase order.

Purchase Orders

A purchase order is a legal contract when it is issued in acceptance of a formal quotation or offer. Purchase orders vary from the simple form illustrated in Figure 3-4 to highly complex and detailed documents. Efforts to standardize purchase order forms have failed because they are legal documents and businesses differ in the degree of legal precaution they require in their purchasing activity.

However, all purchase orders contain the date of issue, a purchase order number for identification purposes, the name and address of the vendor, the quantity, the description, the price of the goods, the signature of the buyer, and the conditions or terms that govern the purchase. On the form in Figure 3-4 the conditions and terms are on the back.

More complex purchase order forms typically have many more conditions or clauses governing the purchase.* Most include space for indicating desired routings and shipping instructions. Most forms assign space to indicate the date by which the shipment should be made. Others, such as the form in Figure 3-4, require that the buyer type in such information on purchases for which a specific delivery date must be met.

FORM DESIGN

Forms simplify the data collection process and enable ultimate retrieval of information vital to efficient purchasing. Observance of the following prin-

---

* See Chapter 14 for a more detailed discussion of the types of clauses.

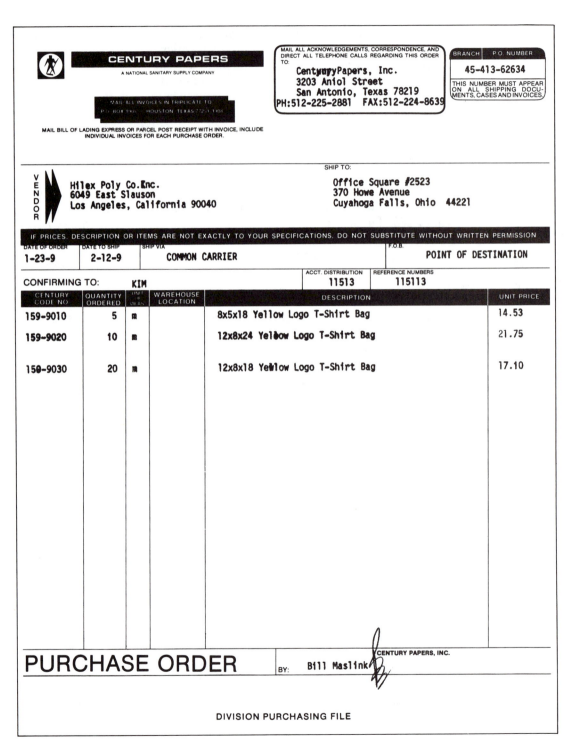

FIGURE 3-4. An example of a purchase order form.

ciples of good form design assures efficiency and maximum use. An effective form does the following:

1. Facilitates the entering of data.
2. Makes significant information both understandable and obvious.
3. Makes it easy for those who use it to obtain the pertinent data.
4. Minimizes the possibility of errors in entry or use of data.
5. Is economical to reproduce.

Since a form is designed to centralize data about which decisions are to be made, it is important that it be designed to make the entry of the data as simple as possible. Sufficient space must be allowed, and the form arranged so that the data can be entered in a logical and proper sequence. It should also be designed with adequate and properly placed instructions.

Forms influence the mental attitudes of the persons using them. Consequently, physical appearance is important. Good appearance can be achieved by a proper original design and good reproduction. A form that looks crowded or is poorly reproduced tends to create an indifferent attitude in the person who uses it.

After forms are completed they become the basis for action. Clerical errors must be minimized. A form will tend to reduce errors if it includes only essential data, clearly segregates columns in which statistical data are required, simplifies reading lines across the page, and generates an attitude of respect on the part of the clerk who enters the data by suggesting that management has planned the form carefully and reproduced it with quality.

Finally, one of the most important criteria in form design is to keep down paper and printing costs. Elimination of unnecessary duplication in gathering data, use of standard-sized dimensions of paper stock, elimination of unnecessary duplicates, and use of durable paper stock consistent with the use to which the form will be put all help eliminate unnecessary expense.

Although only two examples are illustrated in this chapter, most firms have a much greater number. These examples show the simplest types available, to illustrate the principles without presenting the complicating details many organizations include for purposes of internal administration.

Follow-up Forms

Frequently it is necessary to follow-up a purchase order to secure acceptance and compliance. For routine follow-up, specially designed form postcards are frequently used. Such cards include the purchase order number, the date the material is required, space for the promised shipping date, and the signature of the individual making the promise.

For urgent orders, or for those with special problems, the follow-up is often done by telegram or telephone. The follow-up may be by an expediter or by the buyer personally if its importance justifies such action.

Receiving Forms

On all incoming shipments the receiving department itemizes receipts on a receiving slip form. This form provides space for the date of receipt, the name of the vendor, and the common carrier who made the delivery. Space is also provided for noting the amount paid to the carrier if the shipment was not prepaid.

The body of the form reports the quantity and type of materials received. Usually, no special space is provided for reporting damaged goods, but a notation of the damage is written across the face of the form when it is discovered during the receiving operation. The form has a space for the signature of the checker.

Rejection Forms

Most companies require that all material received be forwarded to the receiving inspection department. This department makes a detailed inspection of the material, checking it against the specifications on the order. If it does not meet the specifications, the material is rejected or must be modified. The purchasing department is notified of this situation by some type of rejection form, frequently called an inspection report. This report may suggest the return and replacement of the material or state that the material is usable but request that the vendor be notified of the discrepancies found so they will not occur on future orders.

Other Purchasing Forms

The forms described are used by most business concerns. Others that are used by some purchasing departments include change-of-order notices, exception reports, sample test forms, and stock record forms.

RECORDS AND DATA RETRIEVAL

Well-organized records promote efficient operations and also provide the basis whereby past experience can be used to repeat successes and avoid mistakes. A complete record system adds to the cost of operating a department but is more than compensated for by the savings it produces in facilitating the purchasing process.

The records of a purchasing department include copies of the forms, which are usually put into a computer. The following are additional sources of information.

Purchase Record

A record is maintained to indicate each purchase of all commodities. The purchase record is often combined in a single file with the perpetual inventory records to indicate all receipts and disbursements of the commodities purchased.

The purchase record has a separate entry for each item in use, including a description of the item and a list of suppliers. The body of the record contains data on orders placed, including purchase order number, quantity, date, vendor, and price.

Vendor Record

The vendor record is a file maintained primarily as an aid to order writing. It is a list of all vendors and their complete mailing addresses. This file is intended to simplify the work of the buyer, and the order-processing clerk, who fills in supplementary information for the file.

Blueprint and Specification Record

In business many items are purchased by blueprint specification. Such specifications are often very detailed and cannot be reproduced on the purchase order. Brief descriptions of the parts needed are written on the purchase order with a reference to the blueprints and specifications, which are enclosed and made a legal part of the order.

To streamline the forwarding of such specifications, the purchasing department maintains blueprints and specifications covering all parts in current use. For repeat orders to established suppliers, corrected copies are sent only when a change in a blueprint or specification is made.

Contract Files

When goods are bought under term contracts, purchasing maintains a record of such contracts. These records are especially important for open contracts, against which orders may be placed within the contract period.

Record of Printed Forms

Every concern uses printed forms and usually keeps records of those in use, including samples and descriptions of each.

Tool and Die Record

The tool and die record, sometimes known as a pattern record, is used by companies that purchase fabricated parts, castings, and the like that are made with a tool, die, or pattern furnished by the buyer. Such patterns are the property of the buyer, who should maintain a record of their location at all times. Frequently the record is also a guide to determining replacement requirements.

Purchase Order Sequences

Most purchasing departments maintain accounts of all purchase orders placed. The vendor and dollar value of the order are entered in this record for two purposes. It is useful in preparing reports on the activity of the department involved, and it gives the company an indication of the expenses to which the company is being committed. This record is also useful in relating actual purchases to volume.

Commodity Coding

Commodity coding is a common application of computer technology. Essentially, it collects data for analyzing specific commodities bought in large amounts by blanket and multilocation blanket contracts. Commodity coding also allows purchasing to compare the capabilities of vendors with the organization's requirements.

Commodity coding has other uses. (1) For newly designed products it permits quick reference to already-used components, and it assists in product simplications for existing products. (2) It can be used to identify components made by similar manufacturing processes. Their manufacture may then be simplified and their costs reduced. (3) It provides the essential information for many aspects of inventory control.

Information management advances, and artificial intelligence amplifies, managers' perceptions of the 1990s. Information Resource Management (IRM) makes certain that information-processing employees effectively use their equipment and databases.[12] With more and more information to pro-

---

[12] "The IRMing of America," *CIO* (March 1989), pp. 61–62.

cess, purchasing managers rely on numerous purchasing techniques for cost-cutting, profit-generating opportunities.

Major Costs in Ordering Low-Value Items

An analysis of a typical buyer's purchased items usually indicates that 80 percent of them constitute only 20 percent of the purchased value. This 80 percent of low-value components includes, but is not limited to, such items as maintenance, repair, and operating (MRO) supplies. The cost of purchasing such items, in terms of labor and paperwork, is disproportionately high in relation to their value. The buying techniques discussed in this chapter are designed to reduce such costs without impairing the quality of the product or service.

Inventory Carrying Charges

Inventory ownership is another cost of concern to all purchasing managers. Ownership and storage may constitute as much as 40 percent of the costs of inventory. These costs include interest on the investment, the charges for storage space and for physical handling and protection, and the money lost through deterioration or obsolescence of the inventories. Some of the procedures described herein completely eliminate inventory carrying by the purchasing company and thus eliminate this cost for the purchaser. To the extent that the carrying cost is also reduced for the seller, the total cost of the products is lowered.

The objective of all the specialized techniques discussed in this chapter is to decrease material costs as well as operating costs and to order from fewer suppliers. Often the types of items purchased, quotations by suppliers, and suppliers for a given item are all reduced in number; and because of the time savings previously discussed, purchasing overall becomes more effective.

BLANKET ORDERS

The blanket order is the most popular alternative to the single-item, fixed-price order. A blanket order may be an agreement to provide a designated quantity of items over a period of time at an agreed price. If the price is not specified, a method of determining it is included in the contract. Deliveries are then made under a specified release system. A second type of blanket order is an agreement to furnish all the buyer's needs for particular items over a designated period of time. Under this type of ''evergreen blanket'' agreement the total quantity is not fixed but is calculated at the end of the period covered by the contract. Estimates of demand are usually provided during the bidding stage.

The unique purpose of a blanket order is to purchase a variety of items for which there are frequent deliveries from one source. The blanket order is best for items with low unit value but high annual usage, because their rate of use cannot be precisely anticipated.

Typically, a blanket order covers a 12-month period, although other time periods are also used. For example, in the automobile industry two-, three-, and five-year agreements have been used to provide suppliers with justifications for substantial tooling expenditures. The basic interests of the purchasing department employing the blanket order procedure are usually best served by staggering the expiration dates of its blanket orders in order to avoid concentrating the work of negotiating new orders.

Blanket purchase orders provide central control for managing the billions of dollars spent yearly on office supplies. The typical one-year transferable orders find best use for generic items such as cardboard, tape, packing peanuts, and computer paper, saving 15 to 20 percent on office supplies costs. Controlling supplies requires monitoring supplies on hand, selecting an optimum inventory, and replenishing stock on an as-needed basis, using blanket purchase orders.[13]

The description of products may be handled in one of three ways. The blanket order may completely itemize and describe each product; the order may be written to cover broadly described categories of goods (e.g., fasteners); or the order may specify that it covers all items the supplier is able to furnish.

Price is also handled in a number of ways. Firm prices may be negotiated for each item covered. The blanket order may specify a market price and include a method of determining such a price. Sometimes a ceiling price is established, and the actual sale price is designated each time the supplier releases an item under the order. If the price exceeds the ceiling figure, the transaction is treated as a new and separate purchase which the buyer and seller must negotiate as a single-purchase transaction.

A consideration in establishing blanket orders is the procedure to be employed in releasing goods. The buyer must retain basic responsibility for providing materials to the firm when needed and controlling the amount spent. Releases must be arranged so that the buyer does not lose control even when authority to issue releases is delegated to another department.

---

[13] "From Pencils to Peanuts: Strategies for Supply Management," *Catalog Age* (August 1989), pp. 77–80.

Blanket Leveraging

Some organizations have used blanket orders to gain price reductions from suppliers through a practice called leveraging. Leveraging refers to the process of obtaining a percentage discount directly related to the volume of materials ordered (e.g., an additional 10 percent discount on an order of 100 million-plus parts). Chapter 12 describes cooperative purchasing at the state and local levels. Cooperative purchasing flourishes in the private sector, as well. In small firms, a buying group, like Gold Leaf Office Products Ltd.,[14] may support an independent office for bulk buying, publish catalogs for all its members, print the advertising flyers, and run a group-wide private brand of supplies. It may also provide accounting systems and product quality testing. Large organizations may use a different type of pooling wherein many divisions of the same firm join efforts to use buying leverage, as United Technology Corporation does. Consolidating buyers forms a different purchasing technique from the vendor consolidation that just-in-time purchasing creates.

United Technology Corporation (UTC) makes heavy use of leverage in conjunction with its blanket orders. It purchases more than $30 million every business day, or more than $7 billion a year. Office supplies cost $3 million yearly. In 1985, UTC employed a special purchasing technique: pooling the combined leverage of UTC divisions.[15] It established the Consolidated Purchasing Program, initially targeting commodities in general use, such as office supplies. The program now devotes itself to purchasing supplies and services, computers, office systems, energy, and transportation. The program involves 200 employees in 19 cross-division councils within UTC. A senior buyer sits on the Senior Purchasing Advisory Board, representing each of the corporation's business groups—Pratt & Whitney Aircraft (engines), Sikorsky (helicopters), Hamilton Standard (aerospace systems), Norden (defense) Systems, Carrier (heating and air conditioning systems), Otis (elevators and escalators), and Essex Wire & Cable. The program worked out many agreements, one of which directs all operating units across the United States to purchase office supplies from one firm. The first year's savings amounted to $650,000.

Advantages of a Blanket Order Procedure

Among the benefits available to the buyer who uses the blanket order system are the following.

---

[14] "Strategies: Pulling Together," *Canadian Business* (November 1988), pp. 27–28.
[15] "Mission Impossible," *Purchasing* (May 18, 1989), pp. 60–61.

1. Simplification of paperwork involved in orders and invoices.
2. Assurance of regular supply—that is, a quantity agreed made in advance may be held in the distributor's stock and shipped immediately upon request.
3. Reduction of inventory investment through reliable, immediately available stock.
4. More time for purchasing to deal with more crucial concerns.
5. More effective use of sales calls and elimination of unproductive ones.

Disadvantages to Suppliers

Suppliers are sometimes leery of large-volume blanket orders, for the following reasons.

1. Figures of estimated annual usage are often unrealistic and inflated.
2. When actual usage is below the estimate, the supplier is burdened with needless special inventory at the end of the contract.
3. Biased terms negotiated by the buyer's attorney sometimes result in inequitable benefits to the contract parties involved.
4. Demands for cost-plus pricing require the supplier to show its bookkeeping to the purchaser.
5. A discontinued contract for a large number of items may leave the supplier with a large void in sales if a subsequent contract is given to a competitor.
6. The buyer often operates an electronic data processing system and requires, as part of the contract, that the supplier adapt paper flow to accommodate the system, which may increase accounting costs.
7. There is an overemphasis on price.

Suppliers have reported various problems with blanket orders. In some of the instances just listed, the buyer presents the supplier with unrealistic or inflated figures for the quantities used annually. This may cause losses to the supplier, who based the price quotation on anticipated high usage. It may also mean that an inventory item is overstocked.

Nonetheless, blanket orders are important to suppliers because of the potential savings brought about by such arrangements. Once a supplier has been selected and the negotiations leading to a blanket order contract are concluded, selling costs are almost eliminated. The assurance of a specified or estimated volume of sales enables the supplier to plan production and inventory more accurately. Since most blanket order contracts specify monthly invoicing, it follows that the supplier's paperwork can also be significantly reduced.

Effects of Blanket Ordering

Some authorities predict an eventual merging of the pertinent purchasing and inventory system of buying and selling firms using blanket contracts. Electronic data processing communication between buyer and seller, in which stipulated stock levels at the buyer's plant trigger order releases at the seller's plant, operates effectively in many firms through electronic data interchange (EDI), as Margaret Emmelhainz explains.[16] Telephone release systems and those triggered by computers rely on standard blanket ordering procedures.

Another effect of blanket ordering on purchasing policy is greater reliance on a single source, rather than on multiple sources of supply. In fact, many of the blanket orders being written require such single sourcing as part of the arrangement.

Other effects of blanket order purchasing include the stimulation of supplier service to embrace assembly, acquisition of related items, and technical service; significantly greater standardization of requirements by the buying firm; a tendency to remain with the same supplier for a much longer period of time; and motivation to develop much more comprehensive systems by which to evaluate suppliers. (Since blanket orders cover a wide range of products rather than a limited number, the economic order quantity concept described in Chapter 6 is not applicable; the cost of purchasing input to the formula will no longer be valid). Finally, management, as opposed to the line buyer and seller, may be involved as part of the team negotiating the blanket order.

ELECTRONIC DATA INTERCHANGE (EDI)

Electronic data interchange (EDI) is the computer-to-computer exchange of business documents between companies. It enables placing an order and receiving acknowledgement without a telephone call or mailed document.[17] A buyer needs trading partners with compatible computers, willing to interact in software that translates documents into a standard format.

In the computer-integrated manufacturing (CIM) environment, a fully

---

[16] Margaret A. Emmelhainz, *Electronic Data Interchange: A Total Management Guide* (New York: Van Nostrand Reinhold, 1990).

[17] "EDI: A New Method of Sending Your Orders," *Production and Inventory Management Review and APICS News* (April 1990), pp. 50, 52.

integrated electronic data interchange plan can reduce substantially the overhead and burden. EDI can serve as the catalyst for cleaning out old systems, manual as well as computerized. Companies wanting to fully integrate EDI should probably begin with their external customers and then force their suppliers to do EDI with them, according to one source.[18]

EDI systems are classified under two categories: (1) one-to-many systems, through which one company establishes links with other companies, and (2) clearinghouse systems, in which participants use third-party vendors who serve as a mailbox or who translate documents from industry format to the buyer's format.[19]

Purchasing department personnel using EDI transmit purchase orders, invoices, shipping notices, receiving advices, financial information, and payment (called Electronic Funds Transfer). Traditional paper-based purchasing information flow involves entering the purchase order numbers 22 times, along with other data. Seventy percent of one company's data output eventually becomes another company's data input. This traditional process creates problems: increased time, low accuracy, high labor usage, and increased uncertainty due to several mailings and many processing delays.[20]

When Gemini Industries (Clifton, New Jersey) first adopted its 24-hour shipping policy, it processed less than 100 orders a day. However, when Gemini, which manufactures television and cable equipment, expanded its product lines, it needed a more advanced computer system to handle the increasing orders that had grown from 2000 a month to 18,000. Under the new system, about half of Gemini's current customers submit their orders via computer, which saves time and the need to maintain a large clerical staff.[21]

A library departed from the normal pattern of sending orders electronically to a vendor. Instead, the vendor dialed into the library's mainframe to receive and send messages using a low-cost packet-switching network, at transmission costs of less than a postage stamp.[22] For the government or the commercial firm, the prospects of vendors dialing into the computer raises information security issues. The Foreign Corrupt Practices Act of 1977 mandates that businesses take measures to ensure the security and integrity of assets, including accounting and ledger information stored and processed on electronic data processing systems.[23]

The Automotive Industry Action Group (AIAG) has published industry-

---

[18] "EDI's Role in CIM," ibid. (May 1990), pp. 46–47.

[19] "Paperless Business: Where Are We Now?" *Business* (January–March 1990), pp. 55–59.

[20] Emmelhainz, op. cit.

[21] "A Promise Is a Promise," *Manufacturing Systems* (March 1990), pp. 37–38.

[22] "Exploring Costs of Electronically Transmitting Information between a Library and a Vendor," *Information Technology and Libraries* (March 1990), pp. 53–65.

[23] "Security Is Big Business," *UNIX Review* (November 1989), pp. 60–67.

wide guidelines that will make it easier for automakers and their suppliers to purchase, ship, receive, and pay for goods electronically.[24]

NATIONAL CONTRACTS

The multiplant company will do some of its purchasing through a master or nationwide contract. Such a contract, generally referred to as a national contract, is normally negotiated by the corporate purchasing staff. The purpose of such contracts is to take advantage of the overall company purchasing strength by consolidating requirements in the negotiation process.

Once the national agreement has been signed, the individual plant purchasing managers are notified of its existence and of how they may proceed to place orders (releases) against the master agreement. Some firms use preprinted release forms, which are provided to the plant manager with details of the agreement. The purpose of the national contract is to gain a volume-bargaining advantage; it does not constitute an attempt to centralize completely the purchasing function at the corporate level.

Prudential Insurance Company of America (Newark, New Jersey) spends more money each year on furniture than any other commodity except paper. A 20-person purchasing staff at Prudential's headquarters negotiates national agreements with 14 furniture suppliers to maximize Prudential's immense buying power. These national contracts fill the furniture needs for their insurance field offices and securities traders.[25]

Phillips Petroleum Company negotiated a national contract with Businessland for purchasing personal computers. In a separate transaction, Phillips decided to lease Xerox copiers rather than buy, since copier technology changes so rapidly. The blanket agreement includes maintenance. These deals fit into Phillips' overall procurement goals: (1) to reduce the number of vendors by moving into single-sourcing partnerships, (2) to employ fewer and better-trained personnel, and (3) to add electronic data interchange.[26]

From the sellers' side of the table, the National Account Marketing Association fosters leading-edge changes in national account marketing as a strategic focus for corporate growth. The European Community's opening

---

[24] "EDI Rules Simplified," *Purchasing* (November 7, 1991), p. 32A3.

[25] "Pru Exercises the Power of Agreements," *Facilities Design & Management* (January 1989), pp. 60–63.

[26] "Office Products & Business Systems: Deals, Deals, Deals," *Purchasing* (October 26, 1989), pp. 66–67.

in 1992 and a trend toward "strategic partnering" enlarged the national account concept's international dynamics.[27]

STOCKLESS PURCHASING

Under a stockless purchasing system the buying company has no financial responsibility for the inventory of goods being purchased. The supplier owns the inventory. The goods may be stored at either the supplier's or the buyer's plant. The term *consignment buying* is often used to designate the second arrangement.

In order for a stockless purchasing system to succeed, the buyer and the supplier must work together very closely, with service a vital consideration. If inventories are to be maintained at the supplier's plant, nearby suppliers are obviously preferable.

Under a stockless purchasing system prices may be slightly higher, since the supplier assumes most of the warehousing and inventory costs. However, the cost at the point of use may well be lower; sellers may be able to perform these functions more economically than buyers because sellers are specialists in the products and handle their own inventory.

In general, stockless agreements cover standard off-the-shelf items that are used by several industries. Such items are typically purchased at frequent but irregular intervals, with the prices of suppliers remaining relatively constant. Some contracts contain a clause requiring the supplier to maintain a stipulated amount of backup inventory for the buyer's protection. When this is done, a clause is usually included in the contract whereby at its termination the buyer will purchase the backup stock of items that are special or have become obsolete.

Advantages of Stockless Purchasing

Stockless buying has advantages for both buyer and seller. The buyer profits by a reduction in the amount of capital tied up in inventory, in the amount of inventory becoming obsolete, and in lead time. Paperwork is also significantly reduced so that departmental personnel are freed to devote time to other elements of their job. Finally, the buyer is likely to enjoy a lower price, not only because of inherent economics but also because the seller may be inclined to make price concessions, knowing that all a customer's business is to be gained.

[27] "The National Account Marketing Association: Turning Silver into Gold," *Journal of Personal Selling & Sales Management* (Fall 1989), pp. 65–66.

The advantages to the seller are equally significant. Since the successful bidder on a stockless contract has the assurance of the customer's business during the contract period, selling efforts can be devoted to other customers. The seller, like the buyer, has a significant reduction in time-consuming paperwork. If consignment buying is employed, the seller's requirements for warehouse space may be reduced. If the product is equipment, customers are more likely to acquire the equipment as it becomes available because they do not have stocks of spare parts. The supplier can also eliminate obsolete spare parts from inventory more rapidly. The seller, particularly a middleman, has the opportunity to buy in the most advantageous quantities and at the most advantageous periods within the constraints of the contract.

JUST-IN-TIME PURCHASING

A variation of stockless purchasing is just-in-time (JIT) purchasing, a practice extensively used by the Japanese. JIT, as used in Japan, emphasizes small quantities, better supplier evaluation and selection, and flexible design specifications.

JIT purchasing is an integral part of the entire JIT manufacturing concept. The JIT manufacturing system is based on the idea that "inventory is evil" because it covers up quality problems and costs a great deal of money to maintain. Therefore, the JIT system is set up to eliminate reliance on inventories of finished goods, raw materials, and parts.

The elimination or reduction of these inventories forces the manufacturing system to be able to provide raw materials "just-in-time" to be assembled into finished goods, which are then shipped "just-in-time" for sale. Obviously, this means that all these materials must be of high quality, since there are no extras to substitute for rejects. This is where JIT purchasing becomes vital to the smooth functioning of the system.

JIT purchasing depends on the supplier to furnish parts on time and in amounts required for daily use. In the United States, the auto industry has adopted the JIT system for the purchase of many automobile components needed on a daily basis, thereby reducing in-stock inventories and associated costs.

Under JIT, purchasers are often encouraged to deal with only one vendor for a specified part. It is assumed that one vendor producing in small quantities will produce a better-quality product, thereby permitting less time to be spent on inspection at the receiving point. Specific benefits associated with JIT are depicted in Table 3-1.

There are some drawbacks associated with the JIT system. It necessi-

TABLE 3-1. The Effect of JIT Purchasing Practice on Quality

Purchasing Activities	JIT Practice	Effect on Quality
Lot size	Purchase in small lot sizes with frequent deliveries	Fast detection and correction of defects
Supplier evaluation	Supplier evaluated on ability to provide high-quality products	Suppliers put more emphasis on their product quality
Supplier selection	Single source in close geographical area	Frequent on-site visits by technical people; rapid and better understanding of quality requirements
Product specification	Fully specify only essential product characteristics	Suppliers have more discretion in product design and manufacturing methods, which means specs that are more likely to be attainable
Bidding	Stay with same suppliers; do informal value analysis to reduce bid price; no annual rebidding	Suppliers can afford cost of long-term commitment to meet quality requirements, and they become more aware of buyer's true requirements
Receiving inspection	Vendor certifies quality; receiving inspections are reduced and eventually eliminated	Quality at the source (the supplier) is more effective and less costly
Paperwork	Less formal system; reduced volume of paperwork	More time available for purchasing people to devote to quality matters

Source: Richard J. Schonberger and Ansari Abdolhossein, ''Just-In-Time Purchasing Can Improve Quality,'' *Journal of Purchasing and Materials Management* (Spring 1984), pp. 2–7.

tates a great deal of emphasis on quality, which may reduce purchasing's ability to negotiate lowest possible prices. A balance between the two methodologies is necessary. JIT also reduces the number of competitors; ultimately it may be possible to raise prices because there is so little competition.

NCR Corporation's printer manufacturing plant in Ithaca, New York launched its JIT program in 1986, after several unprofitable years with drastic workforce reductions.[28] NCR-Ithaca points to some notable outcomes: On-hand inventory shrank from 110 days' worth to just 21 days, output quality improved, parts shortages decreased dramatically, work-in-process was reduced by 80 percent, and the manufacturing cycle time was reduced by 90 percent.

However, many small supplier companies, having annual revenues of less than $10 million, turn down potential business because it would require frequent shipments in small lots. For example, a Cleveland, Ohio custom fabrication and machining shop lost a $500,000-a-year contract because it put an extra burden on paperwork and packaging to ship in much smaller lot sizes. Increased costs for inspection, higher inventory, shipping, and paperwork forced up their prices to recover the costs, and they ended up losing the contract.[29]

Some JIT features prove highly useful, as strategic partnering firms attest later in this chapter.

Several leading manufacturers have tried just-in-time (JIT) sourcing simultaneously with global sourcing, or outsourcing. However, the incompatibility of the two approaches calls for rigid managing of the longer inventory supply line while reducing lead times and enhancing flexibility.[30]

A study reports the financial, operational, and buyer–supplier relationship results obtained by 40 firms in a variety of industries. Most of the buyers reported successful implementation of just-in-time purchasing. One quarter of the respondents reported paying lower prices for inputs they purchased using JIT. Sales of products with JIT-purchased inputs rose. The quality of product inputs and manufactured output using JIT inputs improved. However, the most important outcome of the JIT implementation may be the augmented strategic role for purchasing and a change in its traditional objectives.[31]

SYSTEMS CONTRACTING

Systems contracting is a technique designed to permit ordering and stocking of repeated-use materials with a minimum of administrative expense.

Systems contracts avoid inventory duplication, cost of acquiring, cost of

---

[28] See also Grieco, Gozzo, and Claunch, *Just-In-Time Purchasing: In Pursuit of Excellence* (Plantsville, CT: PT Publications, Inc., 1988), and "JIT in Purchasing: A Progress Report," *Purchasing* (September 14, 1989).

[29] Ibid.

[30] "Exploring the Logistics Interface between Global and JIT Sourcing," *International Journal of Physical Distribution & Logistics Management* (1992), pp. 3–14.

[31] "Buyer Experiences with JIT: Some New Roles for Buyers," *Mid-Atlantic Journal of Business* (June 1992), pp. 113–123.

possessing, and repetitive buying. They do not require requisitions or purchase orders; instead, systems contracts involve a master contract negotiated with suppliers to cover large groups of materials or supplies that the contract details, with terms of supplier delivery. Systems contracts for MRO items typically reduce inventories, provide better information on usage and product interchangeability, reduce and simplify buying workloads, and provide higher turnover rates (i.e., the number of times a particular stock of goods is issued and restocked during a given period of time). Systems contracts reduce errors, turnaround time (i.e., in purchase terms, the time elapsed between determining the need for a particular good and its delivery into the user's hands), order processing, and administrative time. They establish an exclusive supply arrangement for specified products for a period of time with set prices.

There may be some confusion in differentiating a systems contract from blanket order buying, national purchase agreements, automatic purchasing arrangements, and other similar procedures. The essential difference is that the systems contract is long-term and involves stocking, warehousing and related services by the vendor, with relatively infrequent changes in suppliers.

Systems contracts merge the firm's ordering and inventory functions, more than do blanket contracts. Compared to blanket contracts or orders, systems contracts are much more likely to: (1) be informal in nature, (2) rely on periodic billing procedures, (3) allow nonpurchasing personnel to issue order releases, (4) use special catalogs, (5) require vendors to maintain minimum inventory levels, and (6) not specify the volume of contract items a buyer must purchase.[32]

Inland Steel, the nation's fourth largest steel producer, relies heavily on systems contracts for its fax machines that link all aspects of the steel-making process. The purchasing department at the Indiana Harbor Works negotiated a long-term lease agreement on a systems contract with Ricoh Corporation for the six different fax models it uses, a free 30-day trial, free installation, and competitive monthly rates.[33]

Many company buyers require fax capabilities as part of systems contracts. Fax capability helps to move the purchasing activity closer to the requisitioner. Unlike computer ordering, fax allows instant transmission of product specifications and drawings along with the purchase order.

As a result of negotiating through systems contracts, Inland Steel saves $1.5 million yearly in janitorial supplies.

---

[32] "A Comparison of Blanket and Systems Contracts," *Journal of Purchasing and Materials Management* (Summer 1989), pp. 35–40.
[33] "All Systems Go," *Purchasing* (March 23, 1989), pp. 106–107.

The McDonnell Douglas Corporation's $1.5 billion systems contract provides the U.S. Air Force with aircraft, training, and flight simulators for the service's Tanker/Transport Training System.[34]

Industrial buyers become increasingly receptive to partnering agreements that extend and formalize the relationships. Firms find such relationships central to systems contracts. The distributor can provide the buyer with: (1) customer service, (2) assorted conveniences, (3) credit and financial assistance, and (4) advice and technical support. The partnership develops closer relationships between vendor and buyer through better communication and higher service levels.[35]

How Systems Contracts Differ

A systems contract differs from other special techniques in a few specific ways.

Choice of Vendor.   Under the systems concept, not only will the agreement be of longer duration, but there will be a high degree of trust and interdependence. The service requirements imposed on the vendor by the contract are likely to be extensive. A specified price is commonly an integral part of the arrangement, but total costs for all items and services covered in a systems contract are the determining factor.

Analysis of Requirements.   A selected vendor will generally assist the buyer in analyzing requirements in order to have the contract reflect the product variations and appropriate prices. The prior rate of use will be determined, as well as the frequency of reordering over some past period.

Since such analyses require a study of closed purchase orders, a policy question arises about the wisdom of providing access to such records to the vendor.

Standardization.   Under a systems contract the buyer receives only the brands produced or sold by the contractor, which generally means that a standardization program must be adopted, a practice usually desirable for its own sake.

Catalogs.   The catalog is vital to a systems contract because all the items must be identified. This catalog is usually prepared by the vendor and

---

[34] "McDonnell Douglas Team Wins USAF Training System Contract," *Aviation Week & Space Technology* (February 26, 1990), pp. 18–19.

[35] "Selling to Purchasing," *Industrial Distribution* (April 1988), pp. 60–65.

utilizes its numbering system. Unit packaging is typically specified to facilitate requisitioning in economic order quantities (EOQ). Because the negotiated price is listed in the catalog, the accounting department will not need copies of all purchase orders as a basis for checking the prices at which items are invoiced.

Catalogs listing confidential information such as price are given to the purchasing, accounting, and auditing departments. Catalogs that do not list prices are distributed to the requisition points within the organization.

Requisitioning. In a systems contract, the burden of inventory acquisition and availability is placed on the stocking distributor instead of on the buyer's storeroom. Shifting the inventory back to the distributor eliminates duplication and reduces the carrying cost, simultaneously improving both stock turnover and return on invested capital. The systems contract vendor guarantees availability. A requisition, properly countersigned by the purchase approval agent, is forwarded directly to the contractor.

Order Filling by Vendor. The systems contracts vendor assigns a number to the requisition when it is received. The numbers are consecutive under each contract, and this numbering system permits better control than the usual numbering sequence in which all vendors' requisitions are intermingled.

The vendor prices the initially unpriced requisition and then selects the method of shipment. Because timely delivery is a crucial element in the systems contract, most vendors agree to deliver on 24-hour notice, about the same time lapse as when requisitioning from a company storeroom.

Payment. A periodic payment is customary even though each requisition technically constitutes an invoice. The periodic payment is made on the basis of a simple tally sheet of all transactions with a vendor for a stipulated period of time. The consecutive numbers on the requisitions ensure both parties that the periodic payment is complete.

Advantages of Systems Contracting

The foregoing comparison of systems contracting with regular purchasing procedures illustrates its significant advantages. The majority of repeatedly purchased items are delivered within a 24-hour work period, which is often faster than delivery from a company-controlled inventory. The systems contract substantially reduces inventory records, requests for quotations, bids, purchase orders, follow-ups, shipping notices, and invoices. The reduction in storeroom requirements constitutes a savings in personnel and space.

The chance of errors in ordering is reduced since the original requisition is used as the notification to the supplier to ship. The potential for errors in copying or typing orders, packing slips, invoices, and so on is eliminated.

Most companies that have adopted systems contracting report a reduction in inventory levels. Savings are accomplished by eliminating nonessential items and carrying a bare minimum of items that can be stocked and requisitioned from the supplier's investment and floor space. Obsolescence risks are also reduced: lower inventories permit design changes that would otherwise be impossible because heavy inventory would be lost.

Other benefits realized with this approach are fewer calls made by distributor suppliers; back orders reduced or eliminated; a predetermined price structure; time freed for the purchasing department to perform value analysis and negotiating functions for higher-value items; better planning between maintenance and operations; reduction of pilferage; standardization; and improved profitability through reduced costs of acquisition and possession.

Evidence appears to be rather conclusive that the advantages of this approach far outweigh the disadvantages. However, the problems that do exist seem to be concentrated in the area of implementation and its associated training and education difficulties. Many companies have discovered that true systems contracting is difficult to achieve and that vendors need to acquire more knowledge about systems contracting. Many companies would prefer that distributors take a more aggressive role in selling, expanding, and maintaining the systems approach.

Vendors share the responsibility for improving systems contracts; price itself is not the most critical factor; and the use of such contracts has meant a greater degree of responsibility and control on the part of an organization's purchasing department. However, it should be noted that the measurable dollar savings from systems contracts are likely to be minimal unless personnel are actually removed.

A systems contract has significant advantages to the vendor as well. Salespersons' time and efforts can be directed in more effective areas than taking sales orders. The supplier can concentrate attention on new items and materials not covered under the contract.

There are also significant savings in paperwork for the vendor. All pricing is done from the catalog. Individual invoices, packing lists, and so on do not have to be prepared. The quantities sold to a customer are greater because the vendor furnishes all the buyer's requirements for the items under contract.

PURCHASING SERVICES

In the early 1970s, for the first time in U.S. history, the nation spent more dollars for services than for buying goods. In 1989, the U.S. Department of Commerce classified 79 percent of all jobs as service sector jobs, up from 27 percent in 1973. The industry is still growing, but at a slower rate.[36]

Business services span a broad spectrum, including these considerations:

Accounting	Grounds maintenance
Advertising	Insurance (liability)
Architecture	Laundry
Banking	Legal
Cleaning	Moving
Computer	Personnel
Construction	Security
Data processing	Surveying
Engineering	Testing
Equipment repairs	Travel
Food services	Waste disposal

Systems contracts may purchase these services, as this chapter here and elsewhere discusses. For example, SaskPower Corporation (Saskatchewan, Canada) decided to contract out its electric meter testing and repair work to Schlumberger Industries. The utility thus avoided extremely heavy capital expenditure for state-of-the-art meter laboratory equipment. The utility reduced its direct employed staff by 27 percent, by contracting out power line maintenance and construction and power plant maintenance, under systems contracts.[37]

SMALL-ORDER PROCEDURES

All companies have a significant volume of purchase transactions of a nonrecurring as well as recurring nature that involve insignificant sums of money and individual transactions. The specialized techniques described in

---

[36] "Business Services & Supplies," *Forbes* (January 8, 1990), pp. 124–125.
[37] "SaskPower Contracts-Out Meter Maintenance," *Transmission and Distribution* (March 1989), pp. 126–128.

this chapter cannot usually be adapted to meet this problem. To save costs in this area one cannot increase the value of the transactions, and so the alternative, reducing the handling costs per purchase transaction must provide the answer.

The specialized small-order techniques described in the following pages are designed to reduce the costs of buying while protecting the quality of the services received.

It is difficult to anticipate the need for small, nonrecurring purchases because the situations that generate such needs are usually not related to one another. The item involved can frequently be bought only from a single supplier, precluding the possibility of combining orders to increase total value. Furthermore, because such items are usually needed promptly, one cannot hold and accumulate orders to increase the total value of the transaction.

When the nonrecurring purchase is a particular item for a single department in the company, it may be possible to develop specialized procedures to bypass the usual receiving, inspection, storage, and similar functions. This shortcutting not only reduces the amount of paperwork but also speeds up the purchasing cycle.

Petty Cash System

Petty cash is a system that virtually eliminates paperwork by setting aside a sum of money for cash payments of minor expenses. This procedure is the most effective for purchasing small orders from local sources and often employs runners to handle the transaction physically.

A requisition is given to the roving buyer, with the source indicated. The buyer makes the pickup and pays for the item immediately. The sales slip becomes both the receiving document and the petty cash voucher. Invoicing and accounts payable, as well as purchase order procedures, are eliminated.

When this technique is employed, the general petty cash fund or a special fund for small purchases must be under the control of the purchasing department to preserve the advantages of centralized purchasing.

Cash-on-Delivery Ordering System

Although some companies have argued against the use of the cash-on-delivery (COD) system because its use may be interpreted as a reflection on a company's credit standing, such a system has advantages. A COD system can reduce administrative costs significantly. The savings are primarily connected with invoice and accounts payable procedures, although some companies have also used telephone ordering of COD items to eliminate purchase order writing. A major consideration in the adoption of such a system is the difference between the COD fees and the costs of the paperwork eliminated.

Telephone Orders

The use of the telephone to order small-value nonrecurring purchases is logical. A buyer receives a requisition from a using department and must, in any situation, telephone a supplier to determine the availability and price of the item. When telephone orders are authorized, the buyer merely goes one step further and places the order over the telephone, providing the supplier with an order number that is also used to identify the requisition. The written purchase order is thus eliminated.

Copies of requisitions are given to both the receiving and accounting departments. The accounting department is normally authorized to use this requisition, which contains the price data obtained over the telephone, as the invoice for payment purposes.

Some companies realize further savings in paperwork by making an agreement with suppliers on a charge account system for telephone orders. Instead of paying for each order, they accumulate orders and pay for them periodically, in most instances bimonthly, without the seller rendering an invoice.

The state of California adopted a streamlined telephone system to be used for ordering more than 25,000 items, each with a value of less than $1000. The items made up 80 percent of all transactions of the state's purchasing departments and only 15 to 20 percent of the total dollar cost. Competitive quotations were secured, a supplier chosen, and the order was placed, all by phone. The time lapse between the writing of the requisition and the issuance of the written purchase order was cut to fewer than 10 days. Appendix A's and Chapter 6's ABC analysis delve further into this concept.

Electronic Ordering

Electronic ordering systems, like EDI discussed earlier, representing the combined efforts of the telephone companies and electronic firms, are commercially available. In essence, such systems connect a prepunched card system in the buyer's office to a receiving system in the supplier's facility. The buyer simply places a purchase requisition in the form of a punched card into a card reader and dials the vendor's number. The purchase data are then automatically transmitted over the telephone lines. The process is fast, accurate, and particularly useful for repeatedly ordered small-value items. Fax machines transmit purchase orders and other documents with ease.

Check Payment Ordering System

Paperless purchasing is another common term for a check payment ordering system. This purchase order draft system combines a purchase order and blank check for payment purposes. Besides the product description, the purchase order section will contain shipping instructions, account number, unit price, quantity, applicable sales tax, discounts, and the terms of payment.

The supplier completes the presigned blank check, which bears a notation that it is limited to a fairly low dollar maximum, such as $500. A duplicate copy of the blank check is sent and returned to the buyer. Partial shipments are not permitted under the system. It frequently is possible to negotiate an additional cash discount because of the immediate payment feature on such orders and the associated reduction of paperwork for accounts payable.

Small-Order Problems

The small-order problem is not one that can be solved by the elimination of all small orders. The need for small orders is inevitable in the business enterprise. The effort of the analyst who seeks to minimize the problem of ordering items in small numbers must be to reduce costs connected with the procedure for handling such orders. The order itself cannot be eliminated, but several steps in the purchasing process can be combined or bypassed, and savings can be effected. As noted earlier, the greatest opportunities for effecting economies are within the steps involved in the payment for such purchases.

Small orders for recurring or nonrecurring types of purchases can be handled in a number of ways that would minimize the cost and reduce the size of this problem. Better planning and scheduling can reduce such small orders by combining several into a single-purchase transaction. Special arrangements for combining invoices on the part of the supplier can reduce the paperwork usually connected with handling a large volume of invoices.

It must be emphasized that whatever procedures a firm adopts to meet its small-order problems, they must be designed to meet the specific needs of that firm. No standard answer can apply to all firms and all situations.

It should be noted that many small orders occur because of carelessness, errors, and ignorance on the part of purchasing personnel or related departments. This chapter has not discussed steps that might be taken to reduce small orders. Improvements in internal efficiency and management of the purchasing function automatically lessen this problem at the same time.

The proper approach to solving the problems created by small orders has at least three steps.

1. Analyze and categorize the small orders that have been processed in the department for a specific period of time to determine whether the orders had to be small.
2. Determine whether any procedure could be adopted to reduce the costs of handling such orders, the clerical function within any other departments of the company, or the related functions in the supplier's plant.
3. Exercise ingenuity in proposing and testing alternative procedures for handling small orders, especially consolidating orders.

STRATEGIC PARTNERING

Partnering in purchasing replaces the adversarial relationship between buyer and seller. It involves a long-term agreement that places high value on quality, efficiency, and performance. Partnering develops trust and thrives on it. Long-term business partners do not tolerate nonperformance.

The traditional American purchasing system not only tolerates nonperformance and waste but has even created jobs dedicated to dealing with it. The whole field of expediting exists because of supplier nonperformance. We have created a whole job description and a career path based on waste. Incoming inspection (another nonperformance example) adds three to six cents to each purchase dollar.[38]

Northern Telecom, Inc. of Nashville, Tennessee, the second largest telecommunications manufacturer in the United States, spends more than $150 million on office products in the United States, and another $150 million globally. Its dynamic office procurement system features such strategies as writing national contracts, partnering with suppliers, and implementing an extensive electronic data interchange system.[39]

Partnering agreements on maintenance, repair, and operating (MRO) supplies require buyers to make commitments for all of such products from a single distributor who promises to sell at determined prices, and have the goods when called for. This form of stockless purchasing provides Hyster Company with lower overall pricing, reduced inventory, and better quality

---

[38] "Partnering in Purchasing," *NAPM/Insights* (February 1990), pp. 21–22.
[39] "Office Products and Business Systems: Training of the Shrewd," *Purchasing* (February 23, 1989), pp. 54–57.

control. SMS Supply Company reports that long-term commitments providing exceptionally good communications also provide a strong understanding of the business.[40]

Industrial buyers become increasingly receptive to partnering agreements that extend and formalize the relationship central to systems contracts. To establish a long-term relationship, the distributor examines the customer's operations to determine where it can make an impact on the customer's business. The distributor can provide the buyer several features:[41]

1. Customer service
2. Assortment convenience
3. Credit and financial assistance
4. Advice and technical support

Apple Computer manages worldwide procurement with such leading-edge purchasing procedures as just-in-time implementation and vendor consolidation (through partnering).[42]

American business has benefited from partnering for decades. Donald Wills Douglas built his first plane in 1922 for the U.S. Navy. It successfully lifted its own weight in payload, a feat never before accomplished. By this fact, Douglas' first plane established the economic basis for all future air transportation.[43] He relied on partnership relationships with a few suppliers—aluminum framers, engine builders, fuel distributors—to work closely with his engineers and his tempermental self. He counted on his supplier-partners to change designs, to try new specifications, and to accept delayed payments.

The purchasing strategy of partnering encounters barriers to wide usage. Any local, state, or federal procurement officer who spends appropriated funds must operate under rigid and long-standing rules: three bids, low bidder, minority supplier whenever appropriate. Thus, he or she cannot develop a long-term partnership with a single-source supplier except when no one else makes the specialty good or service.

Private firms find that tradition, past practice, and precedent form strong tides to buck. Conventional wisdom says:

---

[40] "Partnering Is a Strategy—Not a Gizmo for Selling MRO," *Purchasing* (April 28, 1988), pp. 60–71.
[41] "Selling to Purchasing," *Industrial Distribution* (April 1988), pp. 60–65.
[42] "Front Line Buyers Have Worldwide Buying Clout," *Purchasing* (June 22, 1989), pp. 42–47.
[43] "Tomorrow's Airplane," *Fortune* (July 1938), p. 88 and Clinton Woods, "The Douglas Aircraft Story," *Ideas that Became Big Business* (Baltimore, MD: Founders, Inc., 1959), p. 79.

Like the county, we've always bought on a three-bid, bottom-dollar basis. That's the free market competitive way, isn't it? Without competition, vendors would never lower their prices.

A barrier emerges when complacency sets in among partners. A price hike here, a price hike there—the buyer finds it uneconomical to continue the partnering relationship.

In the Information Age of the 1990s, with the free flow of vast information deluging buyers on a global stage, it still takes close surveillance to maintain honest relationships and lowest cost.

CHAPTER SUMMARY

Procedures outline in detail the functions that purchasing and materials management personnel carry out to obtain materials and services for the company. Basic procedures vary so little from firm to firm that experienced persons may fit easily into different companies. There they learn to handle variations according to industry practice or company tradition.

Many purchasing departments automate their procedures with computers and fax machines. Both machines generate forms such as purchase orders and transmit them speedily to vendors. Automated procedures release personnel from routines and repetitive tasks, thus freeing them for developing new sources of supply.

Specialized purchasing procedures reduce the cost of handling small purchase orders. Better planning and scheduling can reduce small orders by combining several into a single-purchase transaction. Special arrangements for combining invoices on the supplier's part may reduce the paperwork usually connected with handling a large volume of invoices. Many small order problems result from carelessness, errors, and ignorance on the part of purchasing personnel or related departments. Improvements in internal efficiency and management of the purchasing function would improve automatically the small order problem, at the same time correcting other purchasing problems, like delays, poor quality, or inferior substitutes.

Strategic partnering brings a buyer closer to a selected supplier who favors the buyer with better service and lower prices, at least for a while.

Discussion Questions

1. What are the basic steps required to complete a purchasing transaction?
2. What is the difference between a purchase order and a requisition?
3. Define *bill of materials* and indicate its use.
4. What methods are available to buyers to ascertain price?
5. What procedure is involved in closing an order?

6. Describe the benefits and the drawbacks of automated purchasing procedures.

7. What are the basic concepts involved in designing a good business form?

8. What is the difference between a purchase record and a vendor record?

9. Describe what you consider to be the three most important forms used in a purchasing department.

10. Describe electronic data interchange (EDI).

11. Why is it necessary to develop specialized purchasing procedures?

12. What is the purpose of a blanket order and how does the buying firm benefit from its use?

13. Define blanket leveraging.

14. What are some of the problems that have developed with blanket order systems? Suggest solutions to those problems.

15. What are national contracts?

16. What is meant by stockless purchasing? What are its benefits?

17. What is a systems contract and what are its advantages?

18. Describe the petty cash system of purchasing. For what types of purchases should it be used?

19. Describe the check payment order system. For what types of purchases should it be used?

20. Describe just-in-time purchasing. What are its advantages and disadvantages?

21. Describe how to set up a systems contract. How does systems contracting differ from other similar procedures?

22. In what ways does purchasing services differ from purchasing goods?

23. Why should or should not purchasing services appear as a specialized purchasing technique?

24. Strategic partnering has what advantages? Disadvantages?

Suggested Cases

Ajax Sewing Machine Company

Evans Corporation

Expediting Problems

Howell Chuck Company (A)

John Roberts Manufacturing Company

King County

Roberts Fibre Products Company

The Wagner Corporation (A)

4

Organizational Considerations and Alternatives

Intel Corporation's office products purchasing has made significant improvements in cost savings, delivery, and product quality since it changed its management style. After a year of reorganizing, the microprocessor manufacturer has a semicentralized purchasing department with commodity teams and solid purchasing expenditure plans. The new corporate structure has allowed the company to establish a number of national contracts, control costs, standardize equipment, and increase negotiating power because of higher volume. The key to Intel's success is that the purchasing departments have simplified structure and organization but retained flexibility. The commodity team was invaluable when the Office Products-Forms group reconsidered its forms manufacturer. It set guidelines for stocked items and reduced the number of items stocked by 20 percent and the number of active items by 15 percent.*

CHAPTER CONTENTS

*Source: "Reorganizing with Commodity Teams," *Purchasing* (February 21, 1991), pp. 54–58.

Organization for Research

The Purchasing Library

Areas of Research

PERT and CPM

Purchasing and PERT

Research—an Expanding Field

Many organizations attempt to structure functions to attain maximum total effectiveness, along with encouraging the greatest possible output of the individuals involved. Essentially this process has two dimensions. One dimension is the motivation of the individuals and subgroups to achieve optimal contributions. The second consists of the pattern of formal interactions that tie the members of the groups together. These dimensions are usually expressed in organizational charts.

The elementary issues to be weighed in organizing a purchasing department include the need for and advisability of a staff-and-line approach and centralization versus decentralization of purchasing operations. Significant interdepartmental relationships involving purchasing and other functions should then be examined. All these considerations are combined in the materials management concept. The extent of its recent growth, and the factors in the business and materials environment that have contributed to the acceptance of this concept, are examined in this chapter.

HISTORICAL PERSPECTIVE

Organizational changes have occurred throughout American history as organizations have responded to the specific needs of particular times.

In the early 1900s, during the phase of so-called classical scientific management, organizational concern focused on the physical working conditions and the individual performing the work. In this phase the use of time and motion study as a tool to determine optimal approaches to tasks was introduced, and orientation to work and tasks was emphasized.

The 1930s were a period of so-called classical administrative management, in which the organization as a whole rather than its individual components was the prime focus. Managerial duties were segregated into those involving planning, organization, and control; the firm was compartmentalized into functional areas such as manufacturing, sales, finance, and purchasing. In addition, a distinction was made between activities classified as line (operating) and staff (planning). The substance of this system was the concept that tasks are relatively independent and that functional specialization improves efficiency and productivity.

In the 1940s, operations research techniques that evolved from World War II contributed to the decision-making process in organizations. Mathematical models and economic decision making grew in use as corporate America sought to shift from a war economy to one that recovered at home and reconstructed abroad. The emphasis of organizational thinking shifted from the organization as a whole to the individuals making up the organization. During this era of so-called human relations management, concern focused on the effect of the group on the output of the individual; the fact that performance is affected by a worker's social situation at work was recognized. The emphasis on group interaction resulted in the growth of organizational activities such as company athletic events, company cafeterias, and even company towns.

An interdisciplinary approach to management evolved during the 1950s. Uniting the behavioral and classical points of view, this concept promoted organizational structures that embodied both functional specialization and the recognition of group influences. The so-called marketing concept[1] and the materials management approach to organizations are identified as part of this movement. The interdisciplinary approach essentially provides a systems orientation to organizations. It recognizes both the interdependence of individual subfunctions, such as purchasing and inventory control, and the synergistic effect of having these functions under one organizational head.

During the 1960s, religion contemplated situation ethics: judging right or wrong depends upon the situation. Business contemplated contingency theory: a course of action in any given situation depends upon many factors, including financial strength, the economic outlook, top-management values and attitudes, and organizational strategy. Organizational behavior theory drew from a broad, interdisciplinary base of psychology, sociology, anthropology, economics, and medicine. This approach took a holistic view to consider individual, group, *and* organizational processes. Managers must consider as many relevant elements (contingencies) as possible in every new situation.[2]

In the 1960s and 1970s, systems theory caught on. American business adopted biological research's way of looking at a unit's impact on its surrounding environment, as well as the environment's impact on the unit. Interdependency of units within the organization came under closer scrutiny and clearer understanding.

---

[1] The marketing concept usually means emphasizing the customer orientation of the firm and grouping all marketing activities under the organizational component called the marketing manager.

[2] Based on Griffin, *Management*, 3rd ed. (Boston: Houghton Mifflin), 1990.

Theory Z emerged in 1981. It attempted to integrate common business practices in the United States and Japan into one middle-ground framework for organizations. It borrowed concepts from each culture to cope with lagging worker productivity, robotics displacing wage earners, multilayered organizations stifling initiative, and poor performance quality. The Type Z organization values long-term employment, collective decision making, individual responsibility, and holistic concern for each employee including family. The U.S. Congress has recognized the pull toward this latter organizational concern by supporting day-care centers and illness leave legislation for all but the smallest businesses.

Thinning the middle manager ranks of American organizations and holding decision makers accountable have become the ongoing challenges for the 1990s. Purchasing managers hold pivotal positions in America's quest for world-class operations on one hand and economic survival on the other.

This chapter presents the organizational concerns that apply to the purchasing function individually and then examines the relevant principles of materials management, which combines purchasing with the other organizational activities of moving materials into and through the organization. The chapter also discusses research in purchasing.

ORGANIZATIONAL PRINCIPLES

Organization is essential. It promotes greater productivity of working systems because it provides clear assignment of responsibilities to personnel and clear definition of authority, improves use of executive time, establishes a chain of promotion, and improves personnel relations and morale. When the assignment of responsibilities is unclear, work may not get done and efforts may be duplicated. Clear definition of authority provides better communication because personnel know their reporting responsibilities. When responsibility and authority are properly delegated, subordinates make more decisions, thus freeing executive time for broader procedural and policy matters. The establishment of a chain of promotion, by the development of clear job specifications, makes it easier to train personnel for their particular positions and for those immediately above them. The existence of such a promotion chain and systematic training strengthens and improves performance and morale within an organization.

It should be recognized that there are distinct limitations to what can be achieved through organization, and there are certain organizational weaknesses to be avoided in setting up a business organization. An inherent limitation to any organization is the personnel who staff it. The best principles of organization are of little value if the personnel employed to carry out various responsibilities are incapable of doing so. Frequently, organizational principles must be compromised in order to assign responsibilities to personnel who are capable of handling them. Many organizational charts do not accurately reflect the lines of authority and responsibility, which flow through persons as well as through their positions.

Another factor to consider is the possibility of over-organization. There are many organizations in which all duties and responsibilities are so minutely defined that excessive "red tape" prevails rather than order. Over-organization slows down decision making because the channel to the decision-making executive is too long or too devious. A highly refined organization can be made to run smoothly by retaining policy control at the upper levels and delegating authority and responsibility to lower levels, subject only to reporting and review. On the whole, though, there is greater risk of poor performance due to under-organizing than to over-organizing.

In purchasing there are two major organizational problems: (1) the role of the purchasing department in the overall company structure and (2) the internal organization of the department. The first problem consists of two basic issues: the desired degree of centralization of the purchasing function within the company, and to what executive (or division) the purchasing officer should be responsible.

Centralization versus Decentralization in Multiplant Operations

With a multiplant firm, the question is whether to decentralize purchasing activities to each plant or to centralize them at the home office of the firm. There is considerable variation in dealing with this issue. The soundest procedure appears to be to centralize all policy matters and the purchase of major raw materials and equipment in the home office. The individual plants make other purchases in accordance with policies established by the home office.

However, there are reasons for a substantial amount of purchasing autonomy at decentralized locations. Most branch operations are conducted as distinct entities, and the branch manager is held responsible for the operations of his or her location. Because materials and supplies used in the plant have a direct bearing on the efficiency and economy of operations, it may be argued that the branch manager should have control over their purchase.

Another reason for decentralizing purchasing to branch locations is the probable delay if all matters must be channeled through a home office. Such a procedure requires branch plants to maintain higher reserve inventories of materials and supplies to compensate for the extra time it takes to purchase through the central office.

A third reason for decentralization is the better public relations that develop with the communities in which a firm has its plants. Local purchasing tends to be neglected in a centralized purchasing system. Such purchasing has proved to be a foundation of sound community relations for industrial plants.

In a multiplant firm in which each plant manufactures different products, the case for decentralized purchasing is even clearer since many requirements will differ for each plant. Furthermore, local conditions such as transportation facilities, storage facilities, climatic conditions, or local laws and customs are often not fully understood and appreciated by a home-office purchasing department. Even in the situations described, however, the home office should receive detailed reports of all items purchased so that contracts can be let for standard items, allowing the advantage of quantity discounts.

There are also reasons for the centralization of purchasing. Since a company is managed as an entity, its materials program should also be coordinated. In addition, centralization permits the realization of economies of scale in purchasing as well as in other areas. For instance, with home-office control of purchasing it is possible to transfer surplus materials more readily from one plant to another than when each plant does its own exclusive buying.

A centralized organization also permits a degree of specialization by buyers that is not possible in a smaller organization. Such specialization gives buyers greater knowledge of the commodities and market conditions, and they become skillful in buying.

From the point of view of suppliers, centralized purchasing is often preferable. It is costly to have sales people calling on plant purchasing managers or other prospects in branch plants who lack authority to place orders directly and therefore must work through a home-office purchasing department.

Assignment of Responsibility for Purchasing

Another organizational problem confronting the purchasing department is, "To whom should the purchasing manager report?" The answer to this question tends to define the status of purchasing in an organization. For the present we shall disregard the materials management form of organization, reserving those special considerations for later in this chapter.

Purchasing has been increasingly accepted as a major line activity in business organizations. This means that in a large single-plant company, or in the home office of a well-managed multiplant company, the head of purchasing reports to a general management executive rather than to the head of another line department. When the firm is small enough for the span of control to permit it, the purchasing executive may report directly to the president of the corporation or to the executive vice president. In a larger firm the purchasing executive may report to the vice president in charge of operations or to the controller. These executives in turn report directly to the president.

When the purchasing executive reports to a person other than the president or executive vice president, that person should have broad enough authority that he or she is not inclined to subordinate purchasing considerations to other line activity concerns. Obviously purchasing activities have implications for the finance executive or the manufacturing executive, but it would be questionable to subordinate purchasing (which typically spends about 50 percent of a company's revenues) to the limited objectives of these executives. Therefore, wherever possible, purchasing should report to the president or some executive with a broad view of corporate objectives.

Local purchasing executives of multiplant companies usually report to the plant manager, who is principally a manufacturing supervisor, in order to consolidate responsibility for the local operation.

There is some justification for having the head of purchasing report to the top financial officer in an organization that is operating under a fixed budget, as do schools, hospitals, prisons, and government units. In these institutions priority consideration must be given to purchasing within the limits prescribed by the budget.

Government and institutional purchasing departments differ significantly from those of industrial organizations in that the authority over them is multiple. Typically, supervision is exercised by a board. In government this board is usually composed primarily of elected officials, although occasionally the purchasing manager may be directly responsible to a city manager or similar appointed executive.

Tables of Organization

Figures 4-1 through 4-4 are designed to illustrate graphically the various ways a purchasing department may fit into the overall organizational structure. Later the internal organization of the purchasing operation itself will be considered.

Figure 4-1 presents an example of the type of organizational chart most frequently found in medium-sized firms. Purchasing is assigned as a direct

FIGURE 4-1. An example of an organization chart, showing purchasing's high-level position.

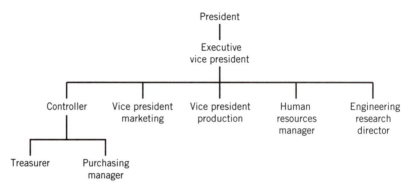

FIGURE 4-2. An example of a more complex organization chart showing purchasing's position under the controller.

line function under the control of the head of the organization. The director of purchases has status and authority equivalent to the other functional divisions of the concern.

A firm in which the head of the purchasing department reports to the financial officer is shown in Figure 4-2. As previously noted, this type of organization is occasionally encountered in industrial firms, but is most frequently found in institutions that operate under fixed budgets. Occasion-

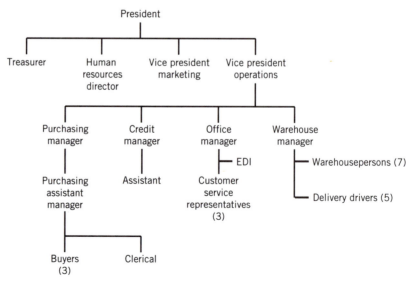

FIGURE 4-3. An organization chart depicting purchasing's position under operations.

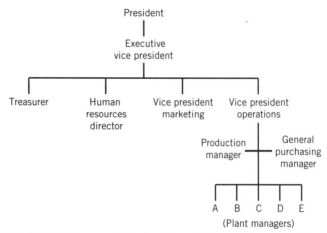

FIGURE 4-4. An organization chart for a multiplant textile goods producer.

ally, in companies in which the scope of the purchasing function is not fully understood, purchasing is assigned to the financial executive as a convenient means of eliminating friction between operating divisions and the purchasing officer.

Figures 4-3 and 4-4 illustrate the organization plans of two large Midwestern firms. In both plans the head of purchasing reports to the operations head of the concern. In Figure 4-3 purchasing is made an activity directly under operations. In Figure 4-4 the general purchasing manager operates in a staff capacity, reporting to the vice president in charge of operations. In this company each of the plant managers has a purchasing manager directly responsible to her or him. The general purchasing manager is then primarily responsible for making and coordinating company-wide purchasing policies.

INTERNAL DEPARTMENTAL ORGANIZATION

Purchasing departments are considered line operations with a purchasing manager, director of purchases, or some similarly designated person in charge. Many organizations have a limited number of people assigned to the purchasing department. In small concerns each buyer is directly responsible to the head of the department. A small clerical staff is usually assigned to the department rather than to the individual buyers. A representative internal organization chart for an average-sized firm is shown in Figure 4-5.

The usual procedure is to assign a commodity or group of commodities to a buyer who is held responsible for all related purchasing activities. This

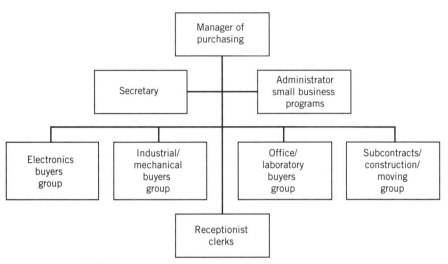

FIGURE 4-5. A purchasing department's basic organization chart.

procedure enables the buyer to become a specialist in a prescribed area. It is also desirable from the seller's point of view because most salespeople sell related products. If these products are handled by one buyer, the sales person has to deal with only one person.

Different bases may be used in grouping commodities for assignment to buyers. One common basis is similarity of physical properties; for example, nonferrous metals as one group and steel and welding supplies as another. A second common basis is similarity of use. Under this arrangement one buyer would be responsible for raw materials, another for operating supplies, and a third for tools and equipment. A third basis is similarity in sources of supply. Here all items purchased through supply houses might be assigned to one buyer and those bought directly from manufacturers to another buyer. The number of commodities assigned to a buyer depends on the complexity of the items, their variety and number, the number of suppliers, the method of purchasing (centralized versus decentralized), and the extent of the buyer's responsibility for follow-up and expediting.

As a firm grows in size, the structure of its purchasing operation changes accordingly. The subdivision of commodities is usually more extensive, and specialists in traffic, economic forecasting, expediting, specification development, and salvage reclamation are assigned to the department. These specialists assume some of the buyer's responsibility in their area of expertise.

At some stage in the growth of an organization an assistant to the head of the department is frequently appointed. This person assumes day-to-day control over the individual buyers and frequently buys some of the more important commodities. Figure 4-6 provides an example of this type of organization for a large public utility. In this organization the manager of purchasing has two staff assistants and an assistant manager of purchasing. The various buyers are in a line. Often, as the duties of a buyer increase in scope and volume, an assistant buyer is appointed. Large purchasing departments customarily assign clerical help to buying groups rather than to the entire department. The hierarchy of positions within purchasing is typically as follows: expediter, purchasing assistant, assistant buyer, junior buyer, buyer, senior buyer, staff assistant, assistant purchasing manager, purchasing manager, director of purchasing, and vice president for purchasing.

Internally, government and institutional purchasing departments are organized along lines similar to those of industrial purchasing departments. There is, however, a greater emphasis on the clerical function because more detailed procedures are needed to meet such statutory requirements as the open-bidding method of purchase.

A recent organizational development is the assignment of purchasing responsibilities for a large and special type of project to a team, usually called a project group. This group has complete responsibility for whatever is needed for its project, and consequently its buying will overlap regular purchasing assignments. This organization is appropriate only when a company wants to give a measure of priority to a major project or must meet stringent quality, cost, or time requirements for a major construction project, a new product development, or a government contract.

Examples of Innovative Purchasing

At Uniroyal a centralized purchasing council was formed, from the corporation's three major line divisions (tires, chemicals, and engineering) and three major support groups (energy, equipment and services, and planning and research). Each council member procures the materials for which its division or group is responsible, in the amounts needed by the whole company. For example, the procurer of carbon black for tires buys it for the entire Uniroyal organization. National contracts for the major raw materials are negotiated by the council and forwarded to the national headquarters. Thus each product Uniroyal buys has one manager who is responsible for its procurement. This system has enabled the company to maximize buying leverage, identify cost reductions, eliminate suppliers selling at different prices in different locations, and set clear lines of reporting. Moreover, Uniroyal has streamlined its purchasing positions throughout the company, reducing the nonpurchasing functions of purchasing personnel by 30 percent. Finally, the company has set up a task force of general managers, market researchers, engineers, and purchasing specialists from all divisions

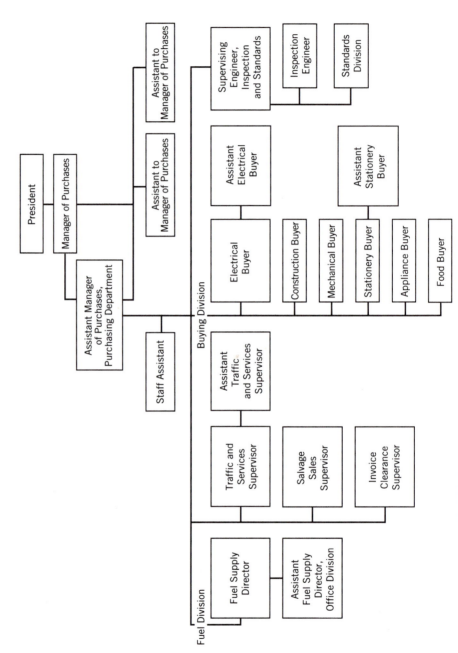

FIGURE 4-6. A complex organization chart for a large firm's purchasing department.

with a mandate to recommend a blueprint for reorganizing the company's purchasing.

Similarly, Digital Equipment has established an innovative comprehensive partnership program that stretches to all buying locations. Each plant or office is responsible for the procurement of its own manufacturing or administrative needs. However, 80 to 85 percent of the buying is done through blanket order contracts, which are negotiated by commodity steering committees. Any location can buy through these blanket agreements, but they also have the freedom not to if there is a good economic reason. The steering committee members are appointed on the basis of their expertise or buying activity in a given commodity. Each steering committee is in turn linked with two central supply-base coordinating groups, one covering production materials, and the other covering in-house administrative procurement. The small steering committees, which are the essence of Digital's purchasing reorganization, allow for a degree of decentralization in the buying decision process and simultaneously provide for coordination and integration. In addition, each steering committee writes a five-year plan outlining their expectations of the cost, availability, and capacity of their commodities. There forecasts are integrated into the corporation's master purchasing plan.

Following an innovative purchasing plan saved Dow Chemical Company, Michigan division, $100,000 the first year. It orders 20,000 items by computer from its primary supplier of office consumables, Boise Cascade. Boise helped Dow figure out how much it bought, what it bought, and who could give Dow the best value for the best buy. At stake: about $2 million yearly in office supplies.

Dow's office supplies buyer and a Boise representative put together a catalog, updated yearly, with pictures, information, and a code for ordering. No invoice arrives. Dow's warehouse generates computer information on deliveries, running 98 percent on-time. Accounts payable audits the information and accounting issues a check to Boise twice a month.[3]

Matrix Design

A kaleidoscope of matrix management systems emerges in the theory and practice of management today. Douglas McGregor devised the first matrix design—the business team concept for Union Carbide in the early 1960s to strengthen competitive impact on the chemicals market. The teams borrowed a person from marketing, one from production, one from research and process development, one from finance and accounting, and one from distribution. Each team focused totally on one family of chemical products,

---

[3] "A Penny Saved Is a Penny Earned," *Purchasing* (April 20, 1989), pp. 66–67.

like ethylene oxide and glycols. Team members took time out from their regular positions to attend team business several times a year, perhaps for a week or two near one of the sites from which one team member came.

This extraordinary organizational arrangement reduced barriers to effective communication among diverse functions. It departed from the classical model of management in favor of a multidimensional system of sharing decisions, results, and rewards in an organizational culture characterized by multiple authority–responsibility–accountability relationships.

INTERDEPARTMENTAL RELATIONSHIPS

The complexities of modern purchasing require purchasing professionals to take a sophisticated approach to their duties, especially concerning the interrelationships of distribution, forecasting, engineering, quality control, computer systems, finance, and international marketing.

The significance of interdepartmental relationships in a make-or-buy decision is shown in Table 4-1, which was compiled from a poll on the purchasing practices of corporations. The table shows the percentage of companies requiring input from the listed departments on make-or-buy

TABLE 4-1. Typical Departments Involved in Make-or-Buy Decisions

Department	Companies Requiring Input (percent)		
	0	50	100
Purchasing	---		
Manufacturing engineering	---		
Design engineering	--		
Top management	---		
Production control	-------------------------------		
Accounting	-----------------------		
Quality control	------------------		
Estimating	----------------		
Inventory control	-----------		
Marketing	-----------		
Maintenance	-----------		

Source: Unpublished research by the author.

decisions. The purchasing department almost always has major input, but the additional contributions of other departments is crucial to ensure proper quality, cost, and production capability.

Department interaction is also quite important for supplier evaluation. Purchasing has input concerning the quality of supplier items as they are used in the production process; inventory control has information concerning the timeliness of supplier deliveries; accounting and production have information on ordering patterns; engineering has opinions on the supplier's technical expertise. Smooth interdepartmental cooperation is required for most aspects of the purchasing process to function effectively. The importance of good relations between purchasing and other departments is illustrated by Figure 4-7. The figure indicates that more than 80 percent of the respondents had purchasing representatives sitting on committees with engineering or marketing representatives: proactive purchasing.

Proactive purchasing anticipates the needs for materials and services, for cost containment, and for increasing the organization's success in achieving its objectives. Its opposite, reactive purchasing, follows the traditional line of waiting for the requisitioner to request action. The availability of computer programs to handle large amounts of data required for thousands of parts has increased the popularity of materials requirements planning (MRP) that Chapter 6 discusses, involving proactive purchasing. This method for production scheduling based on derived demand has an addi-

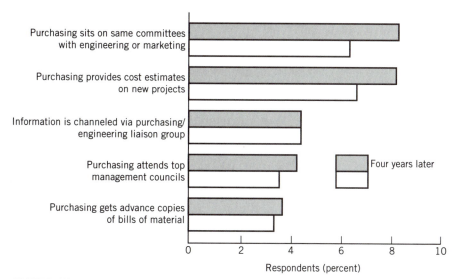

FIGURE 4-7. Increasing representation of purchasing on committees. (*Source:* ''Purchasing Better—Forged Links Bring in Better Designs,'' *Purchasing* (September 6, 1984), p. 70. Copyright © 1984, by Cahners Publishing Company.)

tional support from the just-in-time technique. As a consequence, many firms assign the production planner the task of working with suppliers on their production schedules and actually committing the firm to a purchase. The buyer-planner concept organizes the aim of closer communication and coordination with suppliers so that materials deliveries coincide with production requirements. Materials management's broad inclusive scope facilitates the buyer-planner concept to function without any department feeling a loss of prerogative to buy or to plan.

Friction may develop between purchasing and other departments because they misunderstand task assignments; or the purchasing, production, and engineering departments may have conflicting perceptions about product and supplier selection. An organization policy manual that clearly describes the duties and responsibilities of each department helps to avoid such conflicts. Adoption of the materials management form of organization also helps to minimize such friction and to improve coordination among the materials departments. The following examples of specific relationships of purchasing with other departments serve as an introduction to the materials management organizational structure.

Technological transfer in product development represents another need for excellent interdepartmental relationships. It requires moving information, technical know-how, and people through the various functions of an organization. When the firm designs the organization for integrating technological changes, it introduces research and development projects into other operations by transferring key individuals along with the project.

More and more U.S. companies turn to the team approach to project development. The project may consist of designing a new product or redesigning an existing process. The team includes persons from research and development, engineering, manufacturing, purchasing, finance, and marketing. In designing a new product, the team addresses such key product features as performance, appearance, weight, producibility, quality, cost, safety, design, reliability, serviceability, timing, and risk analysis.[4]

Ford Motor Company set out to develop a new mid-size car in the early 1980s. Ford convened "Team Taurus," an interdisciplinary group consisting of designers, process engineers, tool-builders, research and development personnel, and marketers. This cross-functional team created the Taurus that sold nearly one million units in its first four years.

The Virginia-based automotive division of Siemans, the German electronics giant, has reorganized completely into multidisciplinary teams. Increased collaboration and cooperation occur, due to people trusting one another, sharing information, and managing themselves.[5]

---

[4] "Integration: The Fire Under Technology Transfer," *Industry Week* (June 19, 1989), pp. 39–55.
[5] "Give Me a T!" *Industry Week* (January 8, 1990), pp. 62–65.

Production

Production and purchasing have the common goal of efficient and profitable operations. However, their methods of achieving this goal may conflict. A production executive typically concentrates on having on hand all the required materials in good numbers and of the best quality. Such a philosophy may lead to excessive inventories of unnecessarily high quality. The purchasing executive may end up in an unpopular position by insisting on reasonable quantity and appropriate quality. To a considerable extent, the relationships between these two departments can be harmonized through the exchange of information that each department generates in the normal course of its operations.

Production must keep purchasing informed as far in advance as possible about production plans and schedules. With such information, purchasing can plan its procurement program intelligently and efficiently, minimizing rush and emergency orders. As changes in production plans develop, they need to be communicated to purchasing so that time is available for vendor selection, negotiations, and delivery. The production department should be made aware of the lead time that must exist between the issuance of a requisition and the receipt of goods. Efficient purchasing procedures can minimize this time, but production must work closely with purchasing to make certain the minimum lead time is allowed for as needs are anticipated.

On the other hand, purchasing has certain responsibilities to the production department. Purchasing must keep production informed of expected arrivals and notify promptly of any unusual delays so that work can be rescheduled without plant stoppages.

The purchasing department's file of technical information is a valuable tool for the production department. Purchasing has the responsibility of informing production of new materials, technology, and processes that come to the attention of buyers through salespeople's visits or trade literature. A buyer is sometimes asked to secure samples for testing by the production department. At other times buyers secure samples on their own initiative and bring them to the production department for testing.

In many organizations the purchasing and production departments share responsibility for development of standards and specifications for materials and supplies to be purchased. In others, purchasing has less input in the matter, and ultimate responsibility lies with the production department. It is purchasing's concern that wherever possible standards conform to materials readily available in the market and that unnecessarily costly deviations are avoided.

In the purchase of plant equipment, purchasing and production are only two of many departments making the decision. Each, however, has a unique role to play. Production concerns itself with initiating the action and determining the kind of equipment to be purchased. Purchasing surveys the potential suppliers who will be requested to bid on the order and has an important voice in deciding which supplier gets the order. The treasurer, the engineering department, sometimes the sales department, and often the president also participate in these decisions.

Engineering

The engineering department is primarily responsible for the design and specifications of the products a company makes and the processes it uses. Engineers in such departments have definite ideas about the physical and chemical properties required and know which materials have the desired properties. Because there are frequently several alternative materials, it must be determined which may be purchased the most advantageously. This is an essential responsibility of the purchasing department.

A close working arrangement must be developed between the engineering and purchasing departments. Engineering must not be so exacting that its demands override price and market considerations, and purchasing must not stress price to the point where it interferes with sound engineering requirements. Engineering has the responsibility for setting specifications and has the final say. Purchasing can ask for and suggest changes but cannot make changes.

The two departments should complement each other in producing a product that meets company specifications with both technical and market efficiency. Such cooperation was illustrated at Admiral Corporation's plant in Galesburg, Illinois. Refrigerators were being produced using urethane insulation ingredients that were sized and then injected into the refrigerator cavities at low pressure. But the ingredients were being obtained from several different suppliers and had different cure times. Part of the urethane sometimes set up early, creating voids. To alleviate this problem, purchasing went to engineering and asked them to devise one standard optimal insulation formula. In response to this request, engineering not only produced the formula but also redesigned the refrigerator box and developed a high-pressure injection system. Purchasing then conferred with its chemical suppliers and standardized orders for the two key ingredients. The material is now more economical, the voids have been eliminated, and there has been a reduction in heat loss. Admiral's Galesburg plant now produces refrigerators that are 82 percent more energy efficient.

Sales

Purchasing can help the sales department by buying efficiently and by minimizing costs so that a company's selling prices can be competitive. This is significant because about 50 percent of a typical organization's sales are purchased from others. In turn, the sales department can help purchasing schedule its acquisitions effectively by keeping them apprised of sales quotas and forecasts. Sales can also be helpful by providing advance information regarding special orders and potential design changes.

Accounting

Every purchase transaction initiates a series of accounting transactions. In Chapter 1 examples showed how part of the accounting process may be performed by purchasing. Regardless of where particular accounting tasks are performed, close coordination is essential, because it involves substantial funds and significant discounts.

Capital purchases may be so costly that they necessitate raising additional funds. Although such transactions are financial rather than accounting in nature, the general practice of placing both financial and accounting matters under the control of a treasurer or coordinator makes this another area in which close coordination between the purchasing and accounting departments is vital.

In purchases by nonprofit institutions and government agencies, there is a clear need for a close relationship between the two departments. In such organizations, all transactions must be strictly regulated according to budget. It is routine procedure for all purchase requests to clear through the accounting department, to ensure that there is an uncommitted balance in the proper account to pay for the contemplated purchase.

Inventory Control

If the inventory control department is independent of the purchasing department, the relationship between the two is closer and more continuous than that between any other two departments. Purchase requests for all shelf stock items are initiated by the inventory control department and acted upon by the buyer. The buyer's decision takes into account such factors as stock on hand, estimated usage, and trends in usage. This information is most easily secured by consulting the records of the inventory control department. The buyer must keep inventory control informed on current lead times, minimum stocks, and reorder points in order to help keep inventories at proper levels.

CONGLOMERATE ORGANIZATIONS

Conglomerate organizations have unique problems with respect to purchasing, primarily because of the diversity of the companies that comprise conglomerates. Operating different levels of businesses may make it necessary to have larger staffs with expertise in the particular areas of business. Coordination and communication between member companies may become difficult. The parent company may not readily benefit from volume discounts because of the diversity of the various businesses. This diversity complicates the process of developing a meaningful concept of corporate purchasing.

One solution to this problem is to develop a centralized group of purchasing professionals who can act as consultants to the various business divisions when unique problems arise. Of course, it is also possible to decentralize the purchasing operation among the business divisions, but this generates greater staffing problems as well as communication and coordination problems.

INTERNATIONAL SCOPE

A large proportion of the major firms throughout the world sell to a worldwide market. An increasing number of these companies are becoming truly multinational in the sense that they look upon the entire world as their market. Any geographical location that will optimize production costs is a potential plant location, and any country that can supply reliable materials or parts at a low cost is a likely resource. Price is an important determinant in the decision to import foreign products, as indicated by Figure 4-8.

Quality and durability likewise enter the offshore purchase decision. A recent General Motors service bulletin notified Chevy dealers that when replacing defective oxygen sensors in 1990 and 1991 Geo Storms to use a replacement part made by Nippondenso rather than one supplied by the automaker's own AC Rochester division—favoring the more durable Japanese part.[6]

In a truly interdependent world, political boundaries need not be a barrier to the free flow of raw materials and supplies. However, a history of nationalism, company policies and practices based on nationalistic thinking, and certain laws and government policies often inhibit the development of certain sources of supply and the movement of supplies. A well-managed company should look upon world trade as an opportunity to improve its supply capabilities. This step often involves giving appropriate responsibility to the manager of purchasing. When this is done at an early date, it can give the company a competitive advantage.

---

[6] "Buy American? Big Three Can't Be Serious," *Purchasing* (April 2, 1992), p. 37.

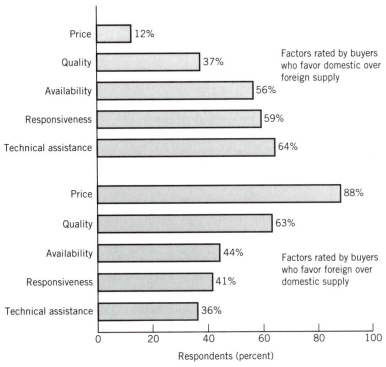

FIGURE 4-8. Domestic and foreign suppliers' ratings of price. (*Source:* ''Buyers Say Foreign Suppliers Have Better Price, Quality,'' *Purchasing* (March 8, 1984), p. 23. Copyright © 1984, by Cahners Publishing Company.)

MATERIALS MANAGEMENT

Although the concept of materials management (MM) was part of the interdisciplinary approach of the 1950s, it came into more common usage and practice in business during the 1960s. Its essential significance is that it highlighted for management the advantages of coordinating the related activities of production planning and scheduling, purchasing, shipping, storing, handling, and control of the materials used in the manufacturing process.

This coordination was achieved by placing all functions concerned with moving materials into the plant under one organizational head, called the materials manager. Whereas the specific functions vary depending on the philosophy of the firm and the type of production process, those always included under the materials manager are purchasing, inventory control, and traffic. Two additional functions often included are production control and stores. Materials management in this form can be defined as an organizational approach that brings under one organizational component the responsibility for determining the production requirements, scheduling the production process, and procuring, storing, and dispersing materials at a minimum cost.

This idea is not new. Military organizations have unified their logistical activities since the seventeenth century. In business organizations, however, the principles of specialization have caused these activities to be placed under the control of different managers who often have conflicting objectives. For example, production scheduling was under the control of the production manager, whose interest was in minimizing production costs through long runs regardless of the effects on carrying costs which were the concern of the inventory control manager.

From a company-wide point of view, it is only reasonable that decisions be made that will be in the best interests of the company as a whole. It was such trade-off considerations, and the development of operations research techniques to quantify them, that led to the adoption and popularization of MM.

Reasons for Adopting MM

The essential purpose for uniting materials departments under a materials manager is to provide improved coordination and control of the following issues in making materials decisions.

Utilizing Control Tools: One reason for the growing use of MM is management's desire to employ relatively new control tools such as operations research, electronic programming, and profit centers. The effective application of such tools to materials problems necessitates cutting across functional lines, which requires the coordination and control available with MM.

Achieving Cost Reductions: Another factor is the simple need to improve control over areas that represent as much as 50 percent of production costs. Large cost reductions are typically available in inventory reduction, transportation, and purchasing when coordination of these activities is improved.

Reconciling Conflicting Objectives: Another important reason for the increasing acceptance of MM is the realization that the materials departments often have conflicting objectives that must be coordinated to optimize results. For example, the goal of purchasing and traffic, to buy and ship in large quantities in order to cut cost, conflicts with inventory control's objective of high inventory turnover and few obsolete materials. There is the danger that conflicts of this type may be resolved by compromises more political than economic. When a decision must be made between conflicting objectives, someone must be available to make that decision; under the MM organization the materials manager performs this function.

Utilizing Automated Facilities: Companies that use automated facilities have found that these systems work best with an even and regular work flow. Exceptions must be programmed into them in advance. By providing coordination and control of all materials subfunctions, MM levels the work flow and provides the advance information necessary to allow the systems to function efficiently.

Facilitating Make-and-Hold Purchases: Buyers increasingly request suppliers like steel service centers to *make and hold* finished goods inventory; suppliers carry inventories that previously were held by the buyers. Effective utilization of this service requires that supplier inventories be closely coordinated to developments in the buying company's production and inventory control. Therefore, MM is often adopted to coordinate supplier inventory management with internal materials operations.

Behind all these reasons for adopting MM is the fundamental point that it provides improved coordination and control of the materials subfunctions by centralizing materials authority.

Organizational Variations within MM

In its purest form, the MM structure would have one organizational unit that has responsibility for buying and moving materials, parts, and supplies from

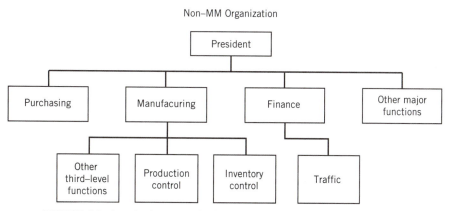

FIGURE 4-9. Organization chart of a firm without the conventional MM department.

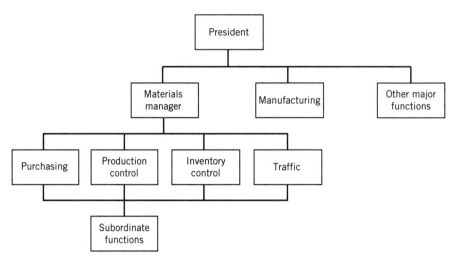

FIGURE 4-10. Organization chart of a firm with the MM concept.

outside sources; controlling them through the storage and processing stages; warehousing the finished product; and supervising its movement to the customer. This inclusive kind of logistical control may sometimes be achieved, but it often encompasses too many diverse activities to be efficiently managed by one authority. Usually the storage and shipment of finished goods (frequently called physical distribution) is excluded from MM. In a fully developed MM organization, one authority has responsibility for the movement, storage, and control functions. However, there are many organizational variations, and partial consolidations of an interim nature, that are more common than fully developed MM plans. The organizational charts given in Figures 4-9, 4-10, 4-11, and 4-12 show some commonly used alternatives.

Without a conventionally organized MM operation, the material functions could be found as shown in Figure 4-9. Figure 4-10 shows the structure after reorganization. Materials management organizations incorporating staff functions may be found in large firms (Figure 4-11). When decentralized management is used, MM reports to division managers for line responsibilities, and a separate centralized MM staff sets materials policy (Figure 4-12).

Another way of viewing the MM operation is to note the several functions that come under its purview, whatever their location within the organization. The following is a typical list of such functions.

1. Planning the types and qualities of materials and parts required by the production operations.

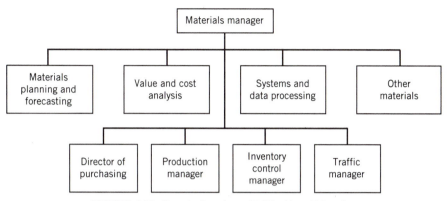

FIGURE 4-11. Organization chart of MM with staff functions.

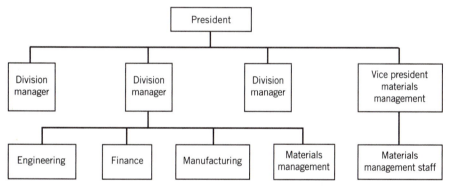

FIGURE 4-12. Organization chart of decentralized MM.

2. Planning the quantities to be purchased and controlling inventories at defined levels.
3. Acquiring the necessary materials, parts, and supplies.
4. Researching materials, sources, and methods.
5. Contracting for and supervising transport services for incoming items.
6. Checking incoming items to ensure proper quantities and conditions of goods.
7. Measuring and testing incoming items to make sure they meet contract standards.
8. Physically controlling and protecting inventories.
9. Scheduling the production time and rate, and specifying the rates at which materials and supplies will be required for production.

10. Moving goods from the point of storage or receipt to the production line.

11. Disposing of scrap materials and unneeded equipment.

Limitations of MM

Critics of the MM form of organization emphasize that it is difficult, if not impossible, for one person to coordinate and control the many variables of materials operations effectively, and that effective coordination is too difficult to achieve merely by establishing a new organizational structure. Others feel that the production control and purchasing departments will be neglected under such an organization. In a study of both users and nonusers of MM, the major limitations listed in Table 4-2 were cited.

The difficulty in obtaining personnel qualified to handle subfunction procedures, particularly the materials organization, is a significant limitation of MM. This has important implications for persons employed in the materials subfunctions; they should broaden their knowledge of the entire materials operations. The shortage of qualified personnel also indicates a need for management development programs, particularly to provide specialists in the subfunctions with total materials knowledge.

Several companies have already begun taking strides in this direction. For example, the MM concept has been successfully implemented in large organizations such as Rockwell International.

Rockwell International restructured its staff from a purchasing base to a MM base. The underlying objectives of this change were to more definitely fix the responsibilities for day-to-day and long-term operating decisions, as

TABLE 4-2. Major Limitations of MM

Problem	Cited by Respondents (percent)
Qualified personnel are too difficult to find	29.9
Coordination is too difficult	25.2
Production control is too important to be subordinated	15.7
Purchasing is too important to be subordinated	13.4
Too expensive to administer	6.0
All the above	3.0
Other	6.7

Source: Gary J. Zenz, ''The Economics of Materials Management,'' unpublished doctoral dissertation, University of Wisconsin, p. 123.

well as for inventory management. The company's 600-page purchasing manual was reduced to a 100-page basic policy guide. A materials management advisory council, comprised of the chief materials managers from each division, was formed to identify key issues affecting the corporation's materials management.

This restructuring brought about loosening of control of the purchasing function, through a "deproceduralizing of the process." The MM function was coordinated and integrated through the MM advisory council. This restructuring allowed Rockwell International to shorten its build-and-buy cycles. Production schedules can be planned a year in advance, and with this information being provided to suppliers, delivery times have been cut by a month. This shortened lead time has helped Rockwell International increase the return on its assets by lowering the asset base.

RESEARCH IN PURCHASING

The challenging events of the recent past have prompted researchers to seek better methods of making economic forecasts, demand–supply projections, and international analyses. These events involve world-class competition, the U.S. economy slowdown in the early 1990s, the vast changes in materials flow into production processes—fewer numbers of vendors, larger order quantities, deliveries just-in-time, and dock-to-stock quality making buyer inspection unnecessary.

The greater complexity of variables that figure in decisions about materials means that they need researching. This section discusses the efforts of firms to conduct research on purchasing and materials management and some of the new techniques in use.

On a customer service level, the buyer needs to ask the question, "End-user or Requisitioner, what improvement would help you in the purchasing services we provide you?"

To prepare to ask that question, the buyer may follow a three-step plan, for reviewing the end-user's case:

1. *Benchmark:*   What items do we buy for you now, in what quantities, on what delivery schedules, at what prices, with how many rejects and missed delivery promises, in what inbound freight arrangements, and from how many different vendors, by name? Which vendors have we certified?

2. *ABC analysis:*   As Chapter 6 describes, for which item do we spend most of our budget dollars, the second most dollars, and so forth, to depict a rank order that clearly distinguishes the vital few from the

trivial many? This rank order provides a priority basis for the buyer's third step.

3. *Forecast:* For the high-rank items, on which we spent the most dollars, what future spending do we project? What industry changes in prices and availability should we anticipate, so that we may time our purchases to best advantage, as Chapter 21 outlines? When will end-user's budget dollars run out under the purchase timing plan we presently follow? Overall, how well does the buyer actually help the end-user to achieve organizational goals?

Results from this three-step study should show the end-user how he or she may work better with the buyer. Can we stagger the requisitions to keep the buyer's workload level? Would standardization lead to better specifications, on which additional suppliers might bid? Would these specifications provide for safety and environmental concerns? An industry provides the trader information. The buyer and other professional people consume information. Should the buyer solicit product and price information for substitutes, their availability, and delivery dates, then ask the end-user for reactions?

ORGANIZATION FOR RESEARCH

The benefits of research efforts include improved procedures, anticipation of potential materials problems, and substantial dollar savings. Research can be conducted as an adjunct to the regular assignments of the members of a purchasing department or by specialized staff members, usually called purchasing analysts. Purchasing research can be performed best by individuals

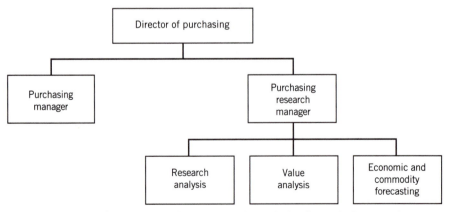

FIGURE 4-13. An example of a departmental organization for purchasing research.

who do not have primary responsibility for line buying. When research is a supplementary responsibility, there is a tendency to concentrate on the purchasing function, which often appears more urgent. Although most management personnel are aware of the benefits of purchasing research programs, most do not believe that the area is being fully utilized. One of the problems is that in many corporations, research is merely a secondary assignment to people who are already busy with purchasing. In most instances research efforts will be most productive if employees are assigned to this activity on a full-time basis.

Evaluation is also a problem when research is a supplementary activity, for it is difficult to determine the degree to which management should reward the research efforts of line employees. The preferred procedure, therefore, is to assign research as a staff responsibility to separate purchasing personnel.

In most companies, top management exercises the prerogative of evaluating and approving all profit improvement programs. It is therefore imperative that those engaged in research report to the chief purchasing officer. A preferred organizational form is illustrated in Figure 4-13.

When budget constraints preclude the use of separate staff personnel, research should be considered an important part of each buyer's assignment. Department schedules should be arranged to permit time for research, and the performance of buyers should be evaluated accordingly. Large research projects are usually instigated by the director of purchasing.

The Center for Advanced Purchasing Studies in Tempe, Arizona, began publishing the results of its purchasing research and industry purchasing benchmark studies in 1988. Corporate management finds the objective industry performance standards helpful in justifying department size, staffing, and budget requirements.[7] Figures for the petroleum, food-service, and semiconductor industries, for example, show that annual purchases per professional employee (buyers and above) amount to $13,000, $40,000, and $9000, respectively.[8]

Research projects in purchasing at academic institutions across the nation delve into the unknown to further enhance the body of knowledge for the purchasing and materials management profession. NAPM's Academic Planning Committee lists the following topics that will require study and greater understanding:

Expansion of outsourcing on a global basis
Extended intrusion of government into private sector decision making
    to influence environmental, social, and ethical issues

---

[7] "Purchasing Research: How Do You Measure Up?" *Purchasing World* (May 1990), pp. 30–33.
[8] "Performance Benchmarks: A Comparison," *NAPM Insights* (October 1990), p. 9.

Broadened basis for understanding purchasing within the context of overall corporate operations

Expanded education and skills qualifications for every purchasing person[9]

In addition to academic researchers, inquisitive purchasers conduct research to make informed purchasing decisions in such specific areas as price history and forecast, quality considerations, supplier capabilities and strategy, raw material availability, and transportation logistics.[10]

Linear programming (LP) presents a straightforward method for allocating resources. Thierfauf and Grosse (see Selected Bibliography), among many authors, show analytic geometry and algebraic techniques for helping the purchasing manager and business analyst decide how to balance resources, capacity, costs, and profit. Computer programs abound for solving resource allocation problems.

An 18-month research project at Michigan State University covered more than 50 major U.S. manufacturing companies, focusing on management and procurement strategies for the 1990s.[11] The study revealed that the most significant emphases in terms of gaining market share, improving return on investment, and raising profit margins will develop from the companies achieving low-cost producer status, world-class quality status, and the ability to move from concept to market in a short time period.

THE PURCHASING LIBRARY

Since a purchasing library provides specialized research references, many of which are unique to the purchasing functions, it should be a supplement to any central library facilities a firm may have.

Desirable types of purchasing library material include (1) technical information relating to products and materials, (2) economic data pertaining to supplying industries, (3) vendor and commercial references to sources of supply and industry associations, and (4) purchasing management literature on subjects such as job evaluation, profit centers, and organization theory. Library materials will consist of directories, magazines, handbooks, textbooks, and periodicals. People using the library should know that specific requests for information may be directed to the library of the National Association of Purchasing Management (NAPM) at its headquarters in

---

[9] "Academia Puts Purchasing Under the Microscope," *NAPM Insights* (July 1990), pp. 10–11.

[10] "In a World of Inquisitive Purchasers," ibid., pp. 12–13.

[11] "Are You Aggressive Enough for the 1990s?" *Purchasing* (April 6, 1989), pp. 50–57.

Tempe, Arizona. Appendix C lists the published items in a well-stocked purchasing library.

AREAS OF RESEARCH

Purchasing research that is designed to increase profits by improving and refining purchasing planning and procedures may be classified into four categories:

Procedural analysis
Vendor and commodity research
Economic projections
Special projects

In practice, these categories are related. A given project could conceivably include all four.

Procedural Analysis

The internal structure and flow of work within the purchasing department, and between purchasing and other departments, is studied in procedural analysis. The following is an example of interdepartmental research. The study revealed that all purchase orders were accompanied by blueprints of the purchased parts. Although this procedure was acceptable for the initial order, it constituted needless duplication for repeat orders with the same vendor. Blueprint costs and the costs of delays, of time spent waiting for blueprints, were substantial. The purchasing and engineering departments developed an improved procedure whereby repeat orders for purchased parts merely referenced the latest revision number on the blueprint already in the vendor's possession. The prevalence of Fax machines today makes it possible for the buyer to fax revised blueprints to the vendor. The vendor acknowledges receipt by fax and perhaps queries the buyer further by fax. The buyer responds by fax, and another game of fax tennis takes place.

Other typical research subjects of a procedural nature include measuring the effectiveness of the purchasing department's job descriptions and speci-fications, personnel evaluation procedures, wage payment plans, and re-ceiving and invoice procedures. A consumer products firm reported the following areas of procedural research.

1. Study of the feasibility of contract purchasing, prepaid purchase orders, systems buying, stockless purchasing, electronic data interchange, and other new purchasing techniques.
2. More effective use of blanket orders to minimize repetitive ordering.
3. Investigation of the forms generated and processed by purchasing to minimize the number and optimize their use.
4. Research into the feasibility of establishing the purchasing function as a profit center generating a target profit by measurable performance.
5. Development of a purchasing manual.

Vendor and Commodity Research

Vendor and commodity research investigates the availability of commodities and their price trends. A representative listing of such projects would include the following.

1. Development of information helpful in locating and evaluating sources of supply.
2. Traffic studies of shipments from vendors' plants, including the possibility of consolidated shipments, lower-cost freight classifications, use of company truck fleets, use of freight-forwarding companies, and so on.
3. Elimination of single sources of supply to stimulate competition.
4. Development of vendor evaluation techniques.
5. Studies of terms and discounts offered by vendors, with a view to obtaining the lowest net cost.
6. Review of new products being developed to determine whether parts should be produced internally or purchased from suppliers.
7. Review of current and long-run future commodity needs and subsequent analysis to determine whether an acquisition or internal development of a problem commodity would be more appropriate. If acquisition is viewed as the optimal strategy, purchasing should review potential companies and then conduct negotiations relating to the acquisition.

Economic Projections

Discussion appears on pages 30–32.

Special Projects

By their nature, special projects may apply any type of research to the purchasing function. Studies to determine economic order quantities, to make lease-or-buy decisions, to establish quality control procedures, and to make value analyses are examples. The benefits of such purchasing research and planning activities include greater exposure to top management through research analysis, greater awareness of potential long-range procurement problems, better inventory management, improved product design, greater coordination with other departments, better cash flow, more long-term agreements with vendors, a greater number of sources, and a reduction in paperwork.

PERT AND CPM

Purchasing planning and research can be aided by the use of program evaluation and review technique (PERT), and the critical path method (CPM) of scheduling. Both are control techniques designed to make planning more effective. Although they are principally scheduling and cost control devices, their principles can be used in other areas of purchasing research where relationships are complex. An increasing number of applications are being found in subcontracting, development work, construction contracts, and project buying.

The techniques have a number of advantages. They (1) provide a means for more careful planning by specifying all the variables involved; (2) provide a clearer understanding of the interrelationships involved in projects; (3) assure a constant review to see that projects are progressing on schedule; (4) identify potential trouble spots early so that resources can be diverted to avoid cumulative delays; (5) schedule resources in the most efficient way; and (6) make it possible to predict the completion time of projects with reasonable accuracy.

Development

As commonly used today, the techniques of PERT and CPM are almost identical, differing only in minor details of administration. CPM was originally developed by DuPont and Sperry Rand as a means of scheduling plant construction efficiently. PERT was the product of the U.S. Navy, the Booz, Allen & Hamilton consulting firm, and Lockheed Aircraft Corporation; it was designed to reduce the development time for the Polaris Ballistic Missile Program. At present PERT and CPM are used for scheduling far simpler projects than were originally contemplated, and the techniques have been correspondingly simplified.

Application

The essential part of the system is the network, which is a graphic portrayal of a sequence of tasks that must be performed to complete a project. In PERT terminology, an event, described by a noun, marks a partial completion of the total tasks, for example, the completion of a subsection. An activity, described by a verb, is the action necessary to produce an event, for example, procure steel for the subsection. The network is thus the master plan showing all events and activities and the times necessary to complete each specific task. The network, therefore, (1) lists all activities necessary to complete the total project, (2) indicates the time required for the completion of each portion of the total (called events) and the total project, and (3) establishes the necessary sequence of activities. Figure 4-14 illustrates a simplified network. In this illustration A, B, C, D, E, and F are events necessary to produce the finished task G.

It should be noted that some activities can be carried on simultaneously, such as AB, AC, and AD; however, activity DE cannot be started until both activities AD and CD are completed. Estimates are made of the amount of time necessary to complete each activity. From this information the critical path is determined. The critical path is the chain of events that takes the longest time between beginning and completion of a project. The total

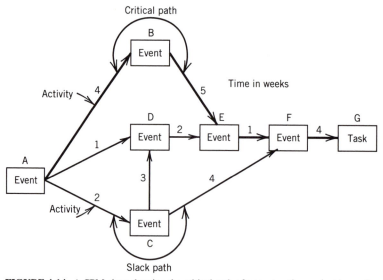

FIGURE 4-14. A CPM chart showing the critical path of a construction project in weeks.

project would be delayed if any of the critical path activities were held up. Therefore, if difficulties develop along the critical path, resources from the other activities should be diverted to the critical path activities to keep the total project on schedule.

In the illustration, path ABEFG is the critical path, as the scheduled time is 14 weeks. A delay of one week between event C and event F would not delay the total project, because the total time of ACF is six weeks, whereas ABEF requires ten weeks. Therefore, path ACFG has a slack (or leeway) of four weeks. The amount of slack is the difference between the times scheduled for the critical path and those for the noncritical path. However, if path ACFG were to develop a delay of more than four weeks, it would become the new critical path.

Were this a construction project, materials for activities AC, AD, CD, DE, and CF would not need delivery until two weeks, six weeks, two weeks, two weeks, and four weeks respectively, after the start of A. Money tied up in those materials meanwhile could serve in some other way. Table 4-3 displays a computer printout of this project, listing earliest start and finish times for each activity, the latest start and finish times so as not to delay project completion, and slack times. Critical path activities have zero slack. The project analyst would study the slack path activities to determine what resources he or she could reallocate to critical path activities if something delayed them.

Resources include materials, equipment, tools, space, trucks, money, and humanpower. Real productive hours available each workday for the

TABLE 4-3. Project Critical Path Worksheet (in weeks)

Activity	Activity Duration	Earliest Start	Earliest Finish	Latest Start	Latest Finish	Slack
AB	4.00	0.00	4.00	0.00	4.00	0.00
BE	5.00	4.00	9.00	4.00	9.00	0.00
EF	1.00	9.00	10.00	9.00	10.00	0.00
FG	4.00	10.00	14.00	10.00	14.00	0.00
AD	1.00	0.00	1.00	6.00	7.00	6.00
DE	2.00	5.00	7.00	7.00	9.00	2.00
AC	2.00	0.00	2.00	2.00	4.00	2.00
CD	3.00	2.00	5.00	4.00	7.00	2.00
CF	4.00	2.00	6.00	6.00	10.00	4.00

Project Critical Path   AB   BE   EF   FG   14 Weeks

human resources does not equal eight hours times five days a week 52 weeks or 2080 hours a year. From that figure the analyst subtracts time for vacation, sick leave, holidays, administrative meetings, education/training, breaks, and travel.

The first three items account for seven weeks a year in a typical company—280 human-hours or 13.5 percent. Allowing 1.5 hours a week for administrative type meetings, 80 hours of education yearly, and half-hour daily breaks, these items add up to another 280 human-hours for a total of 27 percent. Subtracting 27 percent of an eight-hour day leaves 5.84 productive human-hours per day as a yearly average. Persons traveling to other locations will have even less hours available. Managing human resources when not on vacation or sick, and no holiday or administrative meetings scheduled, the project leader may count on 7.5 hours of productive time for that individual for that given day. The PERT chart combines with a real calendar and personnel profile sheet to plan realistically the expected completion date for the project.[12]

The determination of time estimates for each activity is as important as properly identifying and sequencing the events. PERT uses three time period estimates for each activity, CPM only one time estimate (called normal time). The three time estimates of PERT consist of (1) an estimate of the shortest time in which the activity can be accomplished under the most favorable conditions, (2) an estimate of the longest time assuming the most unfavorable conditions, and (3) an estimate of the most likely time that an activity will take. These three time estimates may be put into the following formula to obtain an estimated time to be used for network analysis:

$$\text{Time estimate} = \frac{(\text{most likely estimate} \times 4) + (\text{shortest and longest estimates})}{6}$$

This formula weights the most likely estimate four times as much as either of the extreme estimates. Table 4-4 illustrates a list of activities, together with optimistic, pessimistic, most likely, and estimated times.

Table 4-5 shows a typical time schedule for introducing a new product, illustrating the interrelationships of a company-wide project.

When a PERT diagram becomes extremely complex, involving thousands of events, the network may be stored on a computer tape. The computer can then be used to provide printouts of segments as working documents.

[12] "Planning for Project Management," *Journal of Systems Management* (January 1989), pp. 16–20.

TABLE 4-4. PERT Time Calculations

Activity	Optimistic	Pessimistic	Most Realistic	Time Estimate Used for PERT Analysis
1	8.45	11.00	9.25	9.41
2	4.30	6.25	5.43	5.38
3	9.43	12.65	11.68	11.47
4	1.26	2.95	2.83	2.59
5	5.83	6.13	6.00	6.00
6	21.00	24.63	21.40	21.87
7	13.00	26.83	13.94	15.93

PURCHASING AND PERT

As indicated in the preceding illustrations, PERT provides a means of keeping account of critical parts and materials whose delay would hinder production schedules.

Without PERT the purchasing department may lose contact with the total project schedule and may be supplied only with specific delivery dates that must be met. When purchasing is supplied with a PERT network analysis, the most economical purchasing and traffic decisions can be made. For example, knowing how much latitude is available on delivery date, purchasing can select low-cost suppliers who may require relatively long lead times. In addition, slower but cheaper forms of transportation may be selected. PERT is also valuable in expediting because it quickly indicates when a crucial delivery deadline is missed.

In summary, the advantages of PERT in purchasing research consists of (1) careful planning of all steps, including activities that may precede purchasing; (2) an overview of the entire project; (3) a mechanism for systematic review of progress; (4) a plan for handling emergencies by diverting resources from a noncritical path to the critical path activity; and (5) a technique for using computer technology to control the myriad of interrelated events, many of which are remote in their relationships.

RESEARCH—AN EXPANDING FIELD

A few of the purchasing research techniques currently in use are discussed in this chapter. With increasing attention being devoted to purchasing research,

TABLE 4-5. New-Product Time Schedule

Activity	Date
Product Engineering	
Checklist submission	X
Product committee approval	X
Engineering release—major	2/8
Engineering release—minor	3/1
Industrial Engineering	
Complete cost estimate	4/9
Finalize make or buy	4/2
Process authorization required by	3/26
Complete processing	4/16
Complete tool design	5/14
Complete tool build	7/16
Purchased tooling in	7/9
Complete tool tryout	7/16
Finalize carton design	7/9
Production Planning	
Firm up build schedule by	3/12
Place material required by	3/19
Purchasing	
Place dies by	2/19
Samples by	6/18
Production castings by	7/9
Place all orders by	4/9
Raw material by	7/2
All purchased components by	8/6
Manufacturing	
Machining—castings:	
Start pilot lot	7/19
Start production lot	7/19
Assembly:	
Start pilot lot	9/6
Start production lot	9/13
Warehouse	
Ship salespeople's samples	9/17
Stocking quantities	10/1
Motor Schedule (Outside Vendor)	
Engineering release	3/1
Raw material in	4/23
Shafts and fans to vendor	6/4
Motors required for assembly	8/6

it is inevitable that many techniques and sophisticated methods of analysis that have been developed in other areas will be applied to purchasing problems.

Linear programming is a mathematical approach to problem solving that can be applied to some aspects of the field of purchasing. For example, a buyer faced with allocating a given volume of a commodity purchase to several vendors with delivery to more than one location can use this technique to advantage.

Electronic data processing equipment is pushing management to examine other areas of operations in which this sophisticated research tool may be efficiently utilized. Now that the pace of applying the equipment to purchasing has accelerated, it is inevitable that research will become an increasing part of the total purchasing function.

CHAPTER SUMMARY

Organizations provide clear assignment of responsibility to personnel and clear definition of authority and accountability. Communications follow clear lines of relationships across boundaries that fit particular functions into the overall company structure. A purchasing department relates with other departments in the company through organization and in turn its own personnel relate within a departmental organization.

The materials management concept brings several functions together under one organization. The benefits that result include clearer and faster communications regarding materials, less duplication of effort, less lost time and lost inventories, and greater flexibility in changing product or process to meet customers' needs.

Centralized purchasing organizations operate in the home office or at some prominent location where vendors call to negotiate the terms of major contracts. The centralized organization of experienced purchasing personnel meet their requisitioners' needs for goods and services and at the same time provide contracts under which dependent plants may order materials. Decentralized purchasing operations gives more autonomy to persons at lower levels in the firm to perform the buying function.

The head of the purchasing effort reports to a financial officer, or to a production manager, or to an accounting executive, as best suits the company's needs. Within the purchasing department, different bases exist in grouping commodities for assignment to buyers.

Conglomeration of companies, such as a multinational company, calls for centralized purchasing to coordinate the diverse parts of the vast corporation, with respect to materials.

Policies of individual firms express whether the firms conduct formal or informal purchasing research. Senior executives prefer to have research as a specific staff assignment, ensuring that it will receive proper attention. With firms devoting increasing attention to purchasing research, inevitably many techniques and sophisticated methods of analysis that have developed in other areas will find application to purchasing problems.

Linear programming (LP), for example, may work as a mathematical approach to solving problems in the purchasing field. A buyer may use LP when faced with a decision to allocate a given volume of a commodity purchase to several vendors with delivery to more than one location.

The availability of electronic data-processing equipment in more and more companies encourages management to examine other areas of their operations which use sophisticated research tools. Purchasing applications develop at an accelerated pace from those reviews. Determined managers will position purchasing research as a part of the total purchasing function.

Discussion Questions

1. What is the role, function, or purpose of organization in a company?
2. Trace the history of organizational emphasis since 1900.
3. What is over-organization? Give an example of it in purchasing. Discuss the general effects of over-organization.
4. Discuss the argument for the centralization of purchasing for branch plants.
5. How does one determine the number of commodities a buyer should handle?
6. Discuss the importance of interdepartmental relationships to purchasing efficiency.
7. What unusual problems does a multinational company face in purchasing?
8. What functions are included in materials management?
9. What are the basic reasons for adopting the materials management form of organization?
10. What basic difference in philosophy exists between production and purchasing departments? How can it be resolved?
11. What are the most important limitations of materials management as a mode of organization?
12. What purpose does matrix organization serve?
13. What is the objective of purchasing research?
14. What are the important areas for purchasing research?
15. Discuss the meaning of PERT and its application in purchasing.

Suggested Cases

Ajax Sewing Machine Company

Expediting Problems

Gamma Corporation

The Geer Company

The Janmar Corporation

John Roberts Manufacturing Company

Powers Company

Radmer County

═5

Sourcing

Wayne E. Appleby, director of purchasing at Industrial Powder Coatings, Inc, (Norwalk, Ohio) acquires materials for coating parts mainly for the automotive industry. He has two major responsibilities. He must accurately anticipate and have available the types of powder coatings needed on a just-in-time basis. Also, he has charge of the in-house fleet of tractors and trailers. Appleby finds that these two efforts go together because JIT at IPC often requires turnaround times of 48 hours, or even 24 hours. Operating its own fleet gives IPC better control over scheduling, delivery times, and costs.

In addition, picking up raw materials in company trucks improves inventory control. Appleby and his staff buy about 3 million pounds of powder per year that is used in powder coating.*

CHAPTER CONTENTS

Sourcing

Authority for Selection

Selection Procedures

Types of Suppliers

Single versus Multiple Sourcing

Supplier Evaluation Factors

Supplier Evaluation Methods

Intangible Factors in Source Selection

Supplier Certification

*Source: ''How JIT Buying Works When You're the Supplier,'' Purchasing (February 7, 1991), pp. 42–44.

> Selection of a proper source is in some respects the *most* important single factor in purchasing. (Howard Thompson Lewis, Harvard Professor of Purchasing, 1945)

In the 1980s, the supplier certification concept attained acceptance. In the 1990s, it is expanding to even wider use. It aids a firm in implementing the just-in-time idea referred to in Chapter 3. The receiving firm (the buyer's) no longer has to inspect incoming materials. Supplier certification promotes lower inventories, defect-free supplies, and elimination of wasted time, money, and labor. Thus, supplier certification leads from ship-to-stock to ship-to-WIP (work-in-process). The heightened insistence on quality focuses the purchasing manager's scrutiny on supplier selection.

Conrail, for example, makes a quality turnaround by means of supplier performance. Its formal quality program, implemented in 1987, has the supplier assume the responsibility for delivering to quality specifications on a daily basis. Conrail's Certified Quality Supplier Program requires suppliers to demonstrate their own quality assurance programs' efficacy by shipping defect-free materials over a specific time period.[1]

The selection of a vendor is the most crucial concern in the buying process. The process includes the continuing surveillance of the relationship between the supplier and the buyer to maintain mutually satisfactory conditions of cooperation and interest.

In selecting sources of supply, purchasing makes decisions that influence not only a firm's economic success, but the livelihood of the suppliers and the efficiency of the entire economy. The purchase decision directly influences the financial situation of the supplying firm and ultimately the economic welfare of employees and their families. The vitality of the entire economy is involved because proper functioning of our free-enterprise economy depends on sound product choices. Purchasing, by its dollar votes (i.e., purchases), determines the economy's production and its allocation of resources. The efficiency of vendor selection stimulates competition, which means that better products and services are developed for the economy. This chapter focuses on the principles of vendor selection—the sources of information, the factors to be considered, and the evaluation systems to assure that factors will be rationally weighed.

SOURCING

A new term, sourcing, has emerged for the supplier selection procedures. Sourcing can be defined as the strategic philosophy of selecting vendors in a manner that makes them an integral part of the buying organization for the particular component or part they are to supply. In essence, the term denotes

---

[1] "Suppliers Critical in the Quest for Quality," *Purchasing* (January 18, 1990), pp. 121, 123.

a closer relationship between suppliers and buying organizations than was traditionally the case. Some organizations have even changed the title of their top procurement officer from vice president of purchasing to vice president of sourcing.

The integration of suppliers into buying operations is in large part an outgrowth of the move toward JIT buying (see Chapter 7), whereby the production facilities of the supplier and buyer theoretically integrate. Blanket orders further integrate seller and buyer. The word sourcing also fits the current trend of reducing the supplier base, that is, reducing the numbers of suppliers. The rationale is that a closer relationship can be fostered if fewer suppliers are involved. Finally, the concept of sourcing reflects a move toward buying rather than making—on the part of organizations that previously made (see Chapter 20 for buy or make considerations) and the transfer of the technology to an outside source.

In reality, the process of sourcing is still a selection of suppliers. The concerns expressed in the remainder of this chapter are those that must be considered whatever the number of suppliers and the intimacy of the relationship between buyer and supplier. All buying personnel must give these considerations their rational attention, and see that suppliers competition—which is the lifeblood of the free-enterprise system—is maintained.

AUTHORITY FOR SELECTION

Because selection is the essence of the purchasing process, it is imperative that final authority rest with the purchasing department. If selection is improper, goods and services will be inferior and the using department may share the blame. Under these circumstances a large measure of control over purchasing is lost, competition decreases, friction develops, morale suffers, and costs rise. Therefore, proper source selection is crucial and the most important decision made by purchasing personnel.

SELECTION PROCEDURES

Source selection starts with determining all potential suppliers and continues with elimination on various grounds until the number has been reduced to a workable few. The procedure essentially searches and sorts—searches for all potential suppliers and then sorts for those with whom to do business. Source loyalty, somewhat analogous to consumer brand loyalty, often enters the retention process.[2]

---

[2] "Source Loyalty in Organizational Markets: A Dyadic Perspective," *Journal of Business Research* 16(2) (1988), pp. 117–131.

Preparing a Prospective Supplier List

The first step is to prepare an exhaustive list of prospective suppliers. The effort expended depends on the importance of the business to be transacted. Purchasing naturally weighs the value of orders to be placed against the cost of this step. In the following discussion, it is assumed that very seldom would any buyer consult all these named sources, each of which will now be evaluated. The list of potential vendors is accumulated from:

Experience
Salesperson interviews
Catalogs
Trade directories
Trade journals
Trade shows and conventions
Requests for quotations
Direct mail
Vendor monitoring

Experience. Past experience with firms is the most available and widely used source of information about prospective suppliers. Because a large amount of purchasing is repetitive, a wealth of information is available to the buyer on the basis of past performance. When a new item is under consideration, a buyer usually determines whether present or past suppliers are likely prospects.

Most purchasing departments maintain computerized vendor files with the names and addresses of past vendors and the classes of goods they handle. These records include such additional data as reliability of the supplier in meeting commitment dates, research and development facilities, and defect or reject ratios on past shipments. Computers are programmed to record this experience.

Salesperson Interviews. The salespeople who call on purchasing personnel are extremely valuable sources of information, not only about their own companies and products but also about sources for items their company does not make.

To provide visiting salespeople with the greatest possible amount of information about purchase requirements, many firms display their finished products and purchased components in reception lobbies or special display rooms. These displays provide technical assistance and are helpful in determining items that can be supplied. Supplementary information about standards of quality expected are also provided. The more a vendor knows of a prospective buyer's needs, the better the chances that he or she will be able to supply the items needed.

Because salespeople are such valuable sources of information, most buyers interview all salespeople who call. A buyer never knows when a salesperson may have either a product or information about a product that will prove beneficial.

In evaluating the salesperson as a source of information, the buyer must recognize the strong impression that is left in his or her mind by the character and personality of the salesperson. Generally the salesperson is the only point of contact between two companies, and the buyer tends to identify the company with its personnel. If the salesperson appears to be reliable, cooperative, and competent, the buyer is inclined to assume that the company represented is also reliable, cooperative, and competent. This assumption is not necessarily true; some very good companies may have poor sales personnel and vice versa. Consequently, a buyer should attempt to evaluate the factual information given by a salesperson as objectively as possible, not relying solely on his or her impressions of the salespeople in evaluating a supplier.

Catalogs. The catalogs published by vendors, in which they list and describe the various items they make for sale, are a valuable source of information about possible suppliers. For standard production items such catalogs frequently are one of the most effective and efficient sources of potential suppliers. All buyers make some use of catalogs, and a substantial percentage of buyers use them extensively. A reference system of listing the vendor's name and major product lines is often used.

Trade Directories. A trade directory is a publication that lists and classifies suppliers according to the products they make. Frequently, it gives additional information such as names of company personnel, financial status, and location of sales offices. Usually trade directories are published by private organizations as a commercial undertaking and include advertising. Some trade directories are specialized by industries (e.g., paper products). However, the better-known directories include all industries. The two best-known general directories are *Thomas' Register of American Manufacturers* and *MacRae's Blue Book*. In addition, the yellow pages of the telephone directory provide a rather complete source of local suppliers. It is also possible to find directories prepared by chambers of commerce.

The buyer may access *Thomas Register* on compact disk (CD) by company name, by product, by service, or by trademark name. The purchasing department's personal computer equipped with an optical disk drive provides the directory on disk, which is easier to use than referring to the eight linear feet of shelved printed books.[3]

Distributor giant Grainger has put its entire catalog on compact disk. The information on more than 38,000 products contains 125,000 cross-referenced terms by product and brand names, product groups, competitive products, stocking codes, and product model numbers. A separate floppy disk carries pricing data for the buyer to access through the compact disk program. An order pad function enables the user to print a purchase requisition list, to fax orders to a company location, or the nearest Grainger branch via the user's fax modem. The catalog also contains product selection guides and material safety data sheets (MSDS).[4]

Trade Journals.   Trade journals, or business magazines, are another useful source of potential suppliers. There are hundreds of such publications oriented to specific industries, such as *Iron Age* and *American Machinist.* In addition, many organizations subscribe to purchasing-oriented magazines, such as *Purchasing,* which are directed specifically to their interests. These trade journals provide general sources of information on new products and technical developments, presented in both their editorial and advertising pages.

These magazines and their ads condition buyers to give a readier welcome to the appropriate salespeople. Purchasing personnel rely on these trade journals and their advertisements for information about new products and suppliers.

Trade Shows and Conventions.   Practically all important industrial groups hold trade shows or conventions at various times during the year. At a typical trade show the members of a specific industry display their wares, attempting to attract and stimulate buyers' interest. In contrast, a convention is usually a trade association meeting designed primarily as a forum to exchange ideas. Most conventions also have display space that is rented to suppliers for the display of equipment and materials. Such conventions are ideal places for suppliers to show their lines to a concentrated group of interested prospects and offer a convenient way for a buyer to learn about new products and suppliers.

Requests for Quotations.   Information on prospective suppliers is often secured through a formal quotation request form. A written request to a supplier for price and delivery on a named part is referred to as a request for quotation. Such requests outline quality requirements and estimated usage.

---

[3] "Put a Thomas Register in Your PC," *Purchasing World* (June 1989), pp. 63/M7–64/M8.
[4] "Need a Wiggy? Grainger's Catalog Goes on Line," *Purchasing* (April 16, 1992), pp. 21, 23.

Annual quotations are usually obtained on all significant components from a minimum of three potential suppliers. Government buyers are required by law to employ open-bidding procedures.

Direct Mail.   Many suppliers write purchasing managers unsolicited, to identify product specifications, availability, and price. These letters designate shipping points where supplies await release. The letters may include multicolor brochures, tear sheets or magazine advertising reprints for filing in the buyers' catalog reference library. Purchasing managers names' come from chambers of commerce, city and state economic development councils, trade fair booths, national conference attendance, name-list dealers, or responses to advertising.

Over 8500 design engineers, purchasing people, and top management responded to the SGS-Thomson Microelectronics Inc. (Phoenix, Arizona) advertisement. Interested respondents could call or write for a free "Cream of the Crop" soup can of voltage surge protection devices. Each can contained a list of distributors and sales offices, along with a qualifying business reply card for individuals desiring a short-form catalog or a sales representative's phone call.[5] Such response builds a prospective buyer list for further contacts, especially by direct mail.

LeCroy Corporation (Chestnut Ridge, New York) needed to shift to larger companies from the narrow and stagnating market to whom it supplied electronic testing equipment for 25 years. The company used direct mail and advertising to identify buyers, then followed up with product demonstrations. Success with this strategy brought the company from $20 million to $55 million in sales in five years. The Small Business Administration named LeCroy its 1990 SBA Subcontractor of the year.[6]

The owner-manager in a small firm gets to see all incoming mail. However, in large firms mailroom employees decide who gets what mail. Such a firm needs instructions and supervision to make sure that the proper diffusion of mail occurs. Large dollar amounts may ride on the outcome. A potential supplier awaits selection.

Vendor Monitoring.   Computer-based systems can combine several purchasing techniques and apply them to specific problems. Integrated materials management systems and effective computerized purchasing application assist the buyer to make more intelligent vendor selection decisions through the use of an automated database. The buying process begins with the buyer receiving a requisition for specific goods or services, something

---

[5] "SGS-Thomson's Soup Cans Are "M'm, M'm Good," *Electronic Business* (February 20, 1989), pp. 30, 32.

[6] "When Your Customer Base Changes," *Sales & Marketing Management* (February 1990), pp. 72–74.

previously purchased, or a new item. Buying screens displayed on the computer monitor aid in making the initial buying and subsequent decisions for a repeat buy item. The delivery screen assists the buyer in reviewing anticipated stock-out situations. The vendor performance screen provides the buyer with facts to more fully understand the company's vendors. The open purchase order screen acts as a sales representative's performance review.[7]

A library departed from the normal pattern of sending orders electronically to a vendor. Instead, the vendor dialed into the library's mainframe to receive and send messages using a low-cost packet-switching network, at transmission costs of less than a postage stamp.[8] For the government or the commercial firm, the prospects of vendors dialing into the computer raises information security issues. The Foreign Corrupt Practices Act of 1977 mandates that businesses take measures to ensure the security and integrity of assets, including accounting and ledger information stored and processed on electronic data processing systems.[9]

TYPES OF SUPPLIERS

In the search for suppliers, all available types—distributors, manufacturers, and foreign sources—should be considered. The number of suppliers to be used should also be considered. Trade-offs between price, delivery, and service and community relations and goodwill must be weighed when selecting various types of vendors. This section discusses the concerns relevant to choosing types and numbers of suppliers.

Local versus National Suppliers

There are inherent natural advantages to buying from local suppliers whenever possible. Among the most significant are the following.

1. There is usually a freight savings when the distance between firms is relatively short.
2. Local vendors tend to share the same political and tax concerns as the purchaser. The tax burdens of schools and municipal services of

---

[7] "What Buyers Can Expect from Computer Assisted Purchasing," *Purchasing World* (April 1990), pp. 48–52.
[8] "Exploring Costs of Electronically Transmitting Information Between a Library and a Vendor," *Information Technology and Libraries* (March 1990), pp. 53–65.
[9] "Security Is Big Business," *UNIX Review* (November 1989), pp. 60–67.

local communities are reduced when businesses are healthy and active.

3. Close proximity permits many possibilities for communication and service; make-and-hold practices, shorter lead times, and exchanges.

There are also considerations that favor national suppliers.

1. National concerns may offer lower prices because of their ability to produce in mass quantities for large numbers of customers.
2. Technical assistance may be better from large firms that provide extensive research and development support.
3. Continuity of supply may be more certain with larger-volume producers, which exercise considerable raw material purchasing power and maintain large in-process and raw materials inventories.
4. Local branch and warehousing facilities can enhance the service provided by national firms.

Buyers are constantly weighing these alternative considerations in determining whether to use local or national vendors.

Distributor versus Direct

The buyer will often have to choose between buying through a distributor or direct from a manufacturer. Both options have their advantages and disadvantages.

The manufacturer often offers lower prices than the distributor; this difference usually depends on the volume of business. Manufacturers generally prefer large-quantity orders. They often find small-quantity purchases unprofitable, considering the expenses involved, and charge a premium price to compensate.

Thus, a distributor may offer lower prices on purchases of smaller quantities. Since the distributor's business is largely a break-bulk operation—buying in large quantities from the manufacturer and selling in smaller quantities—smaller-quantity business is appealing. Because of the large volume of purchases and the corresponding discount, the distributor often offers lower prices than the manufacturer on these small buys.

Since distributors are generally local firms, they are often able to provide better service than manufacturers. For instance, distributors are able to ship quickly and handle rush orders as well as visit the buyer's facility frequently and provide personal services.

Another factor in the decision concerns inventory levels. Buying direct usually means buying in large quantities, and the purchaser must hold these quantities in inventory. In contrast, the distributor maintains a local inventory, and the buyer can utilize it, making smaller, more frequent buys.

Furthermore, a manufacturer must first be willing to sell direct. Some manufacturers have well-established distributor networks and want to protect their distributors. When localized service is necessary, manufacturers are likely to refer inquiries to the local distributor. This policy is usually part of a manufacturer's marketing plan, which will not be jeopardized for the sake of a few scattered purchases.

A final factor in the analysis of distributor versus direct buying is local public relations. Because the distributor is usually a local firm, the company may gain community goodwill by using it.

Both alternatives should be considered when they are available. The buyer must know what each has to offer, and what factors are important to his or her company, to make an accurate and profitable decision. As indicated, although the distributor may have the higher price, the service and technical assistance may balance out the cost.

Foreign Sources

The increasing industrialization of third-world countries, coupled with lower labor costs, has made foreign purchasing increasingly attractive in recent years. The quality problems formerly associated with foreign goods have in many instances been transformed into quality standards that challenge domestic firms. However, the drawbacks of foreign sources sometimes negate the cost savings.

The first problem is long lead times. In addition to the actual travel time of the goods, time is spent in customs. A large volume of paperwork is necessary to import goods, and there is a lack of service. When a source has no domestic facilities, there are few avenues of recourse should the supplier make a mistake. Another problem is currency fluctuation. With such long lead times, the price agreed upon may rise or fall between purchase and payment simply because the foreign currency exchange rate fluctuates against the dollar.

These problems can be dealt with in many ways, and the supplier will often handle most of the import details. Information about foreign sources can be obtained from embassies or trade offices operated by various countries in major U.S. cities. Additional information is usually available from the independent import agents who act as a buyer's representative, sometimes handling everything from pricing to delivery. More than 700 such agents are located in New York City alone, and several can be found in each port city.

SINGLE VERSUS MULTIPLE SOURCING

Single Sourcing

Because of quantity discounts or low shipping rates on carload quantities, it may be more economical to concentrate purchases with a single supplier. JIT and blanket orders, as discussed in Chapter 3, lead to single sourcing. In other instances the total amount needed may be too small to justify splitting the order among suppliers because it would increase per-unit handling and processing costs.

Other purchases that encourage the use of a single supplier are those of parts made by processes employing expensive tools or dies. Since the buyer pays these costs, the tendency is to concentrate such purchases with a single supplier. Supplier service may also be a factor in favor of concentrating the order. It may be easier to plan deliveries on an orderly basis when there is only one supplier. In times of material shortage, the buyer who has concentrated purchases with a single supplier may have a greater assurance of supply.

Multiple Suppliers

In most cases, however, the buyer who utilizes multiple suppliers has greater assurance of uninterrupted supply in the event of fire, flood, or strikes, which might disrupt the operations of a single plant. Multiple sourcing also stimulates competition among vendors in price, quality, delivery, and service. Therefore, many buyers use multiple sources for most of the items purchased.

The decision to use multiple sources prompts questions about how many suppliers to use and on what basis to allocate the business. Although these questions cannot be answered universally, these decisions are influenced primarily by the amounts required, the relative size of the suppliers, and their past performances. Most buyers split orders between two or three suppliers. The evaluation plans discussed in a later section are an aid in making this determination and provide the impetus for competition.

SUPPLIER EVALUATION FACTORS

After potential suppliers have been determined and located, a qualitative evaluation and elimination process is used. This process compares suppliers in terms of their ability to provide the desired quality, quantity, price, and service.

In the purchasing context, quality refers to the suitability of an item for its intended purpose; therefore, quality must be evaluated by considering how the product is to be used. In purchasing parlance, quantity also has a somewhat specialized meaning, referring not only to the total amount required but to the schedule according to which the goods must be received. Thus, a supplier who might be able to supply the desired quantity during the time period specified (the third quarter, for example), but could not supply this quantity on specified dates (such as August 14, 21, and 28), would not be a satisfactory supplier. In purchasing, price is meaningless when considered in isolation from other factors. A price is good only if the item supplied has the desired quality and quantity and is accompanied by sufficient useful services.

In turn, many aspects of service take on meaning only when considered in connection with a specific product and its buyers and sellers. Service is often an intangible factor in supplier evaluation, including such issues as location, reserve capacity, technical assistance, quality control procedures, production assurance, and labor and financial stability.

Location

The geographical location of the supplier is an important consideration in evaluating service. Shipments from distant suppliers are subject to more and greater risks of interruption by accidents, strikes, and acts of nature. The possibility of using substitute modes of transportation is also lessened as distance increases.

Companies may overcome some of their geographical disadvantages by providing pool car shipments, branch warehouses, and make-and-hold services. The term ''pool car shipments'' refers to the practice of collecting a number of small orders from a given geographical region and combining them into one shipment, thereby economizing on freight by obtaining the full-car rate rather than the much higher less-than-carload (LCL) rate. A usual practice is to arrange such shipments once or twice each week. Pool car shipments may be used in conjunction with branch warehouses that act as distributing points for shipments originating at the home plant. For example, XYZ Company located in Waterbury, Connecticut, may utilize a branch warehouse in Chicago. Orders for customers in the Milwaukee–Chicago area are pooled and shipped on Wednesdays and Mondays to the Chicago branch, from which final distribution is accomplished. Public warehouses can be used in instances in which a privately operated branch is not economically feasible.

In make-and-hold service, the seller produces in anticipation of a buyer's needs and stores the merchandise. The seller is then ready to ship immediately upon word from the buyer, minimizing total order time. The increased flexibility in providing immediate shipments may offset the disadvantage of a geographically inferior location.

Reserve Capacity

The reserve facilities of a supplier are another consideration in evaluating service. This issue is of special importance during business booms. A supplier with an adequate reserve of productive facilities can respond to increased customer requirements. Technical and managerial skills as well as physical plant and facilities must be considered in evaluating reserve facilities. If a potential supplier's engineering and management staff is spread thin, it is doubtful that more items can be produced during a seller's market, when humanpower is often at a higher premium than goods. Thus it is important to analyze in detail the facilities various companies have to offer, in trying to determine the service they will supply.

Internal Operations

The stage of a supplier's technological development and its ability to keep up with current methods are other considerations affecting service. Technological capabilities give the buyer access to outreach research. Buyers rely on vendors to suggest design and material changes as new concepts are perfected. The buying firm often relies on the provision of such service as an extension of its own research and development facilities.

The inspection methods and quality control procedures used by the prospective supplier are also considered. A supplier who is careless about inspecting finished goods will ship items that must eventually be rejected and returned as unsatisfactory for their purpose. If such a supplier is also lax in controlling production quality, the problem is aggravated, because some imperfections may not be discovered until the item has been incorporated into the finished product.

A closely related consideration is the housekeeping or plant maintenance standards adhered to by the supplier. A supplier that is careful in its in-plant maintenance practices is likely to incur a minimal number of production disruptions from machinery breakdowns and similar mishaps. Since disruptions in production frequently cause delays in shipments, customers have less assurance of supply, an important consideration in service.

Labor Relations

Another possible source of interference with the continuity of production in a supplier's plant may be the workers themselves. If the relations of the supplier with its workers are poor, there may be strikes or slowdowns in production. The possibility of such delays can sometimes be projected by determining the morale of the workforce, reviewing the labor policies as expressed by general management, and observing the degree of responsible leadership exercised by the union associated with the plant. The history of strikes and the length of the union contract will also reflect the labor–management climate.

Warranties

Service also includes the kind and form of warranties that accompany a supplier's products. Relevant considerations include a vendor's ability to provide installation wherever necessary and to provide replacement parts as needed. The supplier should assure the buyer that the product delivered will be maintained throughout its normal life.

Vendor Sources

Vendor relations also influence a supplier's service rating. A good supplier has well-developed sources of raw materials and components that will ensure continuity of production during periods of fluctuating business conditions. The volume of raw materials carried in inventory and the relationship between direct (mill) and distributor sources affect this evaluation. To the degree that the supplier has well-developed sources of supply, the firm will be able to produce effectively during business booms and resultant shortages in materials.

Plant Visitations

Buyers perceive risk when deciding upon a choice among alternative market offerings. The uncertainty about the consequences of any given selection heightens the anxiety or stress. Hawes and Barnhouse examined how purchasing executives handle personal risk.[10] They found nine important tactics in use for handling perceived personal risk. The foremost tactic mentioned consisted in ''Visit the operations of the potential vendor, to observe its viability firsthand.'' In addition to reducing buyer stress, visits to the plants of suppliers are an important means of initial evaluation and periodic examination of existing vendors. It is often desirable for a representative of the production or engineering departments to accompany the buyer on such visits, especially if the products are highly technical. Technical associates

[10] ''How Purchasing Agents Handle Personal Risk,'' *Industrial Marketing Management* 16 (1987), pp. 287–293.

enable the buyer to make a sound judgment of the equipment and capabilities of the supplier.

Although no list can cover all factors to be considered on all plant visits, it is possible to indicate major areas of concern that should be observed and examined.

1. *Facilities:* The production facilities and overall plant layout, as well as such facilities as receiving, shipping, the internal materials-handling system, the supply and tool rooms, and the offices should all be examined.

2. *Personnel:* The degree and type of supervision should be observed, and the state of the employees' morale should be evaluated. The degree of technical competence shown by individuals whose work has any bearing on the purchased goods should be determined. Particular attention should be paid to union relations.

3. *Housekeeping:* Plant maintenance and general cleanliness are useful clues to the efficiency and reliability of output that may be expected.

4. *Procedures:* It is wise to study how the supplier processes an order, from the time it is received until the shipment leaves the plant. Such an analysis will reveal the level of efficiency that is maintained and indicate potential procedural problems that could affect service. Special attention should be paid to quality control procedures.

5. *Production specialization:* The buyer should determine, during a plant visit, the kinds of production in which the supplier tends to specialize. The supplier may be most effectively utilized as a source for such specialized products.

Financial Status

The financial status of the supplier directly affects its ability to serve and should be carefully evaluated. One way to perform this evaluation is through the analysis of credit reports. The Dun and Bradstreet (D&B) report and other similar credit reports contain information about suppliers' financial standings. These reports also provide information on the experience, management, and facilities of the potential vendor. D&B does not publish its reports but releases them only to subscribers.

A related supplementary procedure is independent analysis of the vendor's financial statements. The purchasing official can obtain information regarding the vendor's financial stability, pricing policies, and general operating efficiency by applying the tools of ratio analysis to the vendor's balance sheet and income statements. A short account of the more popular ratios and their uses follows.

The *current ratio* relates current assets to current liabilities. The usual rule-of-thumb acceptable ratio is two to one. Because current assets and liabilities are those that can be turned into cash within a short period of time (one year or less), this ratio measures the financial ability of the firm to continue in the short run. However, because in recent years companies have often maintained current ratios less than two to one to avoid having idle and unproductive assets, this ratio should not be overemphasized.

The *acid test ratio* is a variant of the current ratio in that it relates current assets, excluding inventories, to current liabilities. Inventories are omitted from current assets because they are often difficult to liquidate. An acceptable ratio here is one to one. Like the current ratio, it is a reflection of a company's short-term functioning ability.

The *sales-receivable ratio* represents sales divided by accounts receivable. It indicates whether customers are paying their bills promptly or whether too much of the vendor's assets are tied up in receivables. This ratio is related to the seller's standard terms of payment. For example, if the terms are 90 days, not much more than this amount of total sales should be in receivables. A firm with annual sales of $6 million and 90-day terms should not have much more than $1.5 million in accounts receivable.

Net profit to sales is an overall measure of the firm's profitability after all expenses have been deducted. The size of the profits gives an indication of the possibility of successful price negotiations.

Cash flow is obtained by adding net profit after taxes to depreciation charges, which are allocations against profits that do not reflect actual cash outflow. It measures the amount of dollars the firm is receiving. Cash flow assists profit evaluation because it is a measure of how much cash a company is likely to require to meet short-term expenses.

The *inventory turnover ratio* is the cost of goods sold divided by the average inventory. It indicates the degree of efficiency in inventory management and the freshness and saleability of the inventory. If the ratio is low, the firm is either over-inventoried or undersold. A high turnover ratio is usually preferable to a low one.

Supplier Goodwill

Developing supplier goodwill is a vital part of purchasing personnel's strategic planning. Goodwill benefits the organization in emergencies and helps ensure adequate levels of supply during periods of shortages.

SUPPLIER EVALUATION METHODS

Purchasing magazine found in a survey that the number of firms with formal vendor rating programs matched the number of companies without formal programs. Moreover, fully half the formal supplier evaluation programs in place in 1989 did not exist five years earlier. The quality movement throughout the United States has brought supplier evaluation into recent prominence.[11]

The measure of a supplier's value is expressed in its performance record. In recent years buyers have emphasized the setting of objective standards and procedures for evaluating and comparing existing suppliers. Three of the most popular techniques are presented here.

The Categorical Method

The least precise evaluation technique is the categorical method. It relies heavily on the experience and ability of the individual buyer. Basically, it is a procedure whereby the buyer relies on a historical record of supplier performance. Initially, a list of evaluation criteria is identified. The buyer then assigns a grade to each supplier, for each criterion, based on past experience. A simple marking system of plus, minus, and neutral grades may be used.

Evaluation lists are often provided to other departments involved, such as quality control, engineering, production, and receiving. The buyer periodically assembles the ratings from these departments and uses them in conjunction with his or her own. Vendors with composite high or low ratings are noted, and future supply decisions are influenced by them.

Although this system is nonquantitative, it is a means of keeping systematic records of performance. It is also inexpensive and requires a minimum of performance data. However, the process relies heavily on the memory and judgment of the individuals providing the ratings, and the ratings may become routine chores performed without much critical thought.

The Weighted-Point Method

The weighted-point method quantifies the evaluation criteria. A number of evaluation factors can be included, and their relative weights can be expressed in numerical terms so that a composite performance index can be determined and supplier comparisons made. For example, assume that the following evaluation criteria have been chosen: quality of shipments, accu-

---

[11] "Buyers Are Putting Guts into Supplier Rating Programs," *Purchasing* (March 9, 1989), pp. 24–26.

TABLE 5-1. Composite Rating Sheet for a Buyer Who Rates Three Vendors

Part Number _____ Month ended _____

	Total Shipments Received	Percentage with Less Than-Normal Rejects	Quality Rating (% × 40)	Percentage on Schedule	Delivery Rating (% × 30)	Useful Value Analysis Cost-Reduction Suggestions	Percentage of Total	Cost Reduction Rating (% × 20)
Vendor A	100	90	36	80	24	1	20	4
Vendor B	60	80	32	90	27	1	20	4
Vendor C	50	70	28	100	30	3	60	12

	Average Price per Unit ($)	Lowest Price/Actual Price (=%)	Price Rating (Price % × 10)	Total Composite Rating (Quality, Delivery, Cost Reduction, and Price)
Vendor A	40	40/40 = 100	10	74
Vendor B	50	40/50 = 80	8	71
Vendor C	60	40/60 = 67	7	77

Composite Rating Comparison

	Quality (40 points)	Delivery (30 points)	Cost Reduction (20 points)	Price (10 points)	Composite Rating
Vendor A	36	24	4	10	74
Vendor B	32	27	4	8	71
Vendor C	28	30	12	7	77

racy of delivery promises, frequency of cost-reduction suggestions, and price. Assuming that quality and delivery are the most significant, a point-rating system such as the following might be used: quality, 40 points; delivery, 30 points, services (expressed in useful value analysis cost-reduction suggestions), 20 points; and price, 10 points. Based on hypothetical performance figures, an evaluation might be as shown in Table 5-1.

Acceptable and unacceptable ranges are applied to the composite rating, such as excellent, 85 and above; acceptable, 84 to 70; unacceptable, 69 and below. The advantage of the weighted-point plan is that a number of evaluation factors can be used with relative weights corresponding to the needs of the firm, thereby minimizing subjective evaluation. Furthermore, if this individually assigned plan is used in conjunction with the categorical method, suppliers can be evaluated on a quantifiable basis and many of the intangible aspects of service can still be considered.

The Cost-Ratio Method

The third evaluation technique, the cost-ratio method, relates all identifiable purchasing costs to the value of the shipments received from the respective suppliers. The higher the ratio of costs to shipments, the lower the applicable rating for that supplier.

What costs categories are used depends on the products involved. Quality, delivery, service, and price are the overall categories, and respective costs are accumulated for each. Costs associated with quality normally include the costs of unusual visits to a vendor's plants, unusual inspection costs of incoming shipments, and all costs associated with defective products, including rejected parts and the resulting manufacturing losses.

Quality Cost Ratio. Quality costs can be accumulated by the quality control department with the aid of information from production on the possible costs of reworking defective parts. An alternative procedure is to have departments forward their excess costs to purchasing. Total quality costs are then related to total dollar purchases to determine the quality cost ratio, as shown in Table 5-2.

Delivery Cost Ratio. The usual costs associated with delivery include expediting, telephone, telegrams, emergency transportation (e.g., air shipments), and miscellaneous expenses. The same tabulating procedure would be followed as that described for quality costs. A typical tabulation is shown in Table 5-3.

Service Cost Ratio. Measuring the intangible aspects of service is the most difficult part of an evaluation procedure. The cost-ratio method re-

TABLE 5-2. Quality Cost Ratio

Vendor _____	Month of January, 19____
Visits to vendor plant	$ 200
Sample approval	300
Incoming inspection	75
Manufacturing losses	0
Reworking costs	0
Value of rejected parts	425
Other	9
Total costs	1,000
Total value of purchases	100,000
Quality cost ratio (total costs/purchases)	1%

duces the subjective element common to other methods by establishing a norm for supplier services and then evaluating the suppliers above and below the norm in relation to price. The following procedure is used to integrate service into the cost ratio.

1. Determine the important subjective service factors, including (but not limited to) research and development facilities, capacity for future production expansion, field service facilities, labor stability, warranty provisions, financial stability, inventory-storing service, and flexibility in meeting short lead times.

TABLE 5-3. Delivery Cost Ratio

Vendor _____	Month of January, 19____
Telephone calls	$ 300
Telegrams	175
Expediting (visits to plant)	200
Premium shipments	125
Miscellaneous	200
Total delivery costs	1,000
Total value purchases	100,000
Delivery cost ratio	1%

2. Assign numerical weights to each factor according to its importance to the buying firm.

3. Establish a premium over quoted price that the total subjective service package is worth. A firm producing highly technical electronic components might value this package at 10 percent of quoted price, whereas a buyer of standard fasteners might value it at only 1 percent.

4. Determine an acceptable norm. For example, with 100 possible service points, a score of 70 might be considered acceptable.

5. Rate the suppliers according to the service factors.

6. Determine by what percentage the supplier being rated is over or under the acceptable norm.

7. Apply this percentage to the value of the total service package to determine the cost ratio of service. For instance, if the total service package is valued at 10 percent of price, and the total possible points is 100, with 70 being acceptable, a vendor with 91 points would have a service cost ratio of -3 percent whereas a vendor with 50 points would have a service cost ratio of $+3$ percent.

This final value is obtained by relating the actual number of service points earned to the acceptable level and subtracting the result from 100 percent. In this example, $91/70 = 130\% - 100\% = 30\%$ over norm. This value, 30 percent, multiplied by 10 percent (the total value of the service package) equals the service ratio of 3 percent. As the final value is over the average, the service cost ratio is -3%. A tabulation chart such as Table 5-4 could be used.

Finally, the quality, delivery, and service cost ratios are combined with the quoted prices to determine the vendor's net cost. Assuming that the rating procedure already described has been applied to four competing firms, the comparison would be as shown in Table 5-5.

The flexibility of the cost-ratio method allows it to be adopted by any company for any product. The relation of the evaluation criteria to quoted price provides for comprehensive vendor evaluation.

All three evaluation plans are designed to aid buyer judgment and quantify what would otherwise be subjective analysis. However, these plans must be used as an aid to, not a replacement for, buyer judgment.

Even though it is desirable to evaluate prospective suppliers on the basis of the preceding considerations, such evaluation is not always practical; not all purchases warrant the expenditure in time and money required to do a complete evaluation. Small-volume purchase items do not justify the time an extensive evaluation requires.

TABLE 5-4. Service Rating

Vendor		Month of January, 19____

Maximum Possible Point Value	Factors	Rating
20	Financial stability	20
10	Field service facilities	9
15	Research and development facilities	11
10	Flexibility in providing short lead time	10
10	Labor stability	8
10	Geographical location	10
5	Potential expansion of capacity	3
5	Warranty provisions	5
5	Inventory-storing service	5
10	Miscellaneous	10
100	Total points	91

Maximum value service package: 10% of price

Acceptable service rating: 70

Present rating: 91

   Over acceptable by 30% (minus)

   Under acceptable by (plus)

Service cost ratio $= -3\%$ (30% over norm $\times$ value of package, 10%)

TABLE 5-5. Summary Cost Comparison of Four Vendors

Part					Month of January, 19____	

Firm	Quality Cost Ratio (%)	Delivery Cost Ratio (%)	Service Cost Ratio (%)	Total Cost Adjustment (%)	Quoted Price per Unit ($)	Net Adjusted Cost ($)
Z Company	1	1	-3	-1	87.00	86.13
F Company	2	2	$+3$	$+7$	83.25	89.08
W Company	3	1	$+6$	$+10$	85.10	93.61
P Company	2	1	$+1$	$+4$	85.00	88.40

INTANGIBLE FACTORS IN SOURCE SELECTION

Reverse Marketing

Emphasis in American industry has shifted from arrogant production-orientation—sell what we produce!—to customer satisfaction and service. Customer satisfaction flows through the whole organization back to the firm's suppliers. Reverse marketing ''reverses'' the standard marketing process in which the supplier takes the initiative in trying to persuade purchasers to buy. In reverse marketing, the purchaser tries to persuade the supplier to supply.

The president of the National Swedish Association of Purchasing and Logistics explains reverse marketing as:

> To give suppliers complete information of all our needs as customers, and objectively evaluate suppliers' possibility to meet our requirements and measure performance. The result should be optimal for both sides.[12]

In addition to the considerations of price, quality, delivery, and service, intangible factors must also be considered in selecting a source. These cannot be quantified but significantly influence the decision and ultimately affect wider issues concerning the organization and the economy. These intangible variables, the important gray areas of source selection, are influenced to a large extent by individual buyers' interpretations, to a lesser extent by departmental or organizational policy. These variables, which the buyer should keep in mind, include the following.

1. The extent to which minority suppliers should be given consideration or preference in source selection.
2. The extent to which the societal policies of vendors should be included in source selection and vendor business allocation.
3. Reciprocity and its influence in supplier allocation decisions.
4. The extent to which personalities are allowed to influence buyer–seller relationships.
5. The limitations that are placed on a buyer's acceptance of entertainment and gifts from vendors.
6. The relevant concerns in deciding whether to pay or protest cancellation charges.

---

[12] ''Reverse Marketing in 1991,'' *NAPM Insights* (July 1991), pp. 26–27.

Minority Vendors

Perhaps no single aspect of vendor selection has received more attention recently than the degree of consideration that should be given to minority vendors. Many people in business and government question the propriety of federal requirements that companies with federal contracts allocate a certain percentage of the purchases under the contract for minority vendors. Often, these allocations mean that an inefficient operation is preserved, which increases total costs, decreases quality, and generally complicates purchasing practices. Because purchasing officials may allocate billions of dollars, representing half the value of their organizations' sales volume, the inclusion or exclusion of minority vendors can have a make-or-break impact on thousands of such firms. The overall social, political, and economic implications of these decisions are significant. The final decision is the buyer's and usually includes an appraisal of the confidence that can be placed in the vendor relative to quality, delivery, service, and price considerations.

Societal Concerns

The extent to which a vendor is evaluated in terms of its employment practices, pollution abatement policies, and resource conservation is the most controversial and subjective aspect of vendor selection decisions.

The simple act of a buyer's asking a vendor the percentage of minorities it employs, the types and extent of pollution controls it uses, or the reclamation policies it follows, automatically arouses a high level of awareness. With the U.S. Environmental Protection Agency's (EPA) Toxic Release Inventory (TRI), the public will have access to an annual "report card" on how companies perform environmentally.[13] Whether to make these concerns into relevant factors that influence the decision to buy or not to buy is controversial. On the one hand, an argument can be advanced that the buyers should be concerned only about the lowest possible cost, after considering quality, service, and delivery. The other argument is that a purchasing firm and its buyers have a social responsibility that transcends these objective factors and requires a consideration of the relevant societal issues as decision factors.

There is no obvious decision criterion that can be applied to these societal considerations. Buyers, as they collectively allocate billions of purchasing dollars, will undoubtedly bring their individual interpretations of social justice to the buying decision. In some organizations, these societal concerns are formally included as factors in supplier selection and allocation decisions.

[13] "Environmental Performance Will Count in the 1990s," *Marketing News* (March 19, 1990), p. 22.

Legal Constraints

In government and institutional buying there is a wide divergence of policy on local purchases. Some states have so-called home-preference laws of various types.

One class of home-preference laws requires preference to be given to bidders providing services within the state. Contracting and printing in particular seem to be singled out by a number of states for such preferential laws. Several state laws direct purchasing agents to give preference to bidders from the state when the quality and price of products are approximately the same. These laws define "within the state" in one or more of the following ways: the concern (1) must have paid taxes in the state; (2) must be licensed in the state; and (3) must maintain plants or stores in the state.

A second group of such state laws outlines specific products that must be given preferential treatment. Such laws give preference to certain products that are raised, grown, or manufactured within the home state. Most of these laws provide for such purchases only in cases of "all things being equal." Seven states specify that state institutions must use coal mined in their respective states. Other products that have been singled out by particular states are limestone in Indiana, green marble in Maryland, and products of the states's own "mines, forests and quarries" in Missouri.

Reciprocity

In business, reciprocity refers to the practice of buying from a company that buys from you *because* it buys from you. The practice has some positive aspects but continues to be an area of legal and ethical concern, as it directly influences the degree of competition. When companies simply buy from each other, there is no reciprocity unless each company's buying is caused by the other's purchases. An example of simple reciprocity is a paper mill's placing an order for chemicals with a chemical producer that buys paper products from the mill. A more complicated form of reciprocity might require the chemical firm to buy the boxes it needs from one of the paper mill's customers, as a condition of the paper mill's buying from the chemical firm. Such an indirect relationship is called complex, or secondary, reciprocity. Trade relations is a phrase often used as a synonym for reciprocity. Technically, in trade relations there is a *formalization* of the planning of, and establishment of procedures for, the practice of mutual (reciprocal) buying. Formal trade relations are considered illegal, for they represent an unfair trade restriction.

In practice, the distinction between the two terms is unimportant. Both formal and informal practices are legally questionable. The Federal Trade Commission (FTC) and the Justice Department continually monitor such practices. Although the line between legal and illegal practices is very fine and will be elaborated later in this chapter, reciprocal practices are generally considered illegal if they are used with the intention of restricting competition. Merely favoring one's customers when purchasing goods of like grades, quality, and price is legal and considered by some to be good business practice.

Philosophical Considerations. From a purely tactical standpoint, reciprocity poses many questions for purchasing personnel. Decisions must be made regarding the following: whether to use reciprocity as an input to the buying equation; how to monitor the practice to be certain other purchasing variables are not compromised; how to handle the delicate interdepartmental considerations of the purchasing and sales departments, since a sales staff is not needed and there are no commissions; how to safeguard other competitors; and, of course, how to avoid any possible legal transgressions in the process.

An initial consideration is whether even to practice reciprocity. Most purchasing personnel will, if other things are entirely equal, give favorable consideration to their company's customers. It is certainly reasonable to enhance a customer's profit prospects so that it will prosper and improve as a customer. The ethics and economic validity of this pure form of reciprocity are sound. The soundness of reciprocity is a source of concern if the buyer either pays more or receives less when buying from a customer than from a noncustomer. Theoretically, the practice could be justified if the buying company gained more from the sales made to the customer (and would not have made these sales without practicing reciprocity) than it lost through the higher price or poorer quality and service. However, in a complicated business economy such proof is virtually impossible while demonstrable costs are being raised without compensating benefits.

Reciprocity is strictly a competitive device that does not increase the total demand for a product. The less efficient producers are likely to gain the most from the practice, since they may secure sales they could not obtain on a basis of quality and price. Therefore, purchasing personnel should not consider reciprocity when other considerations are not entirely equal.[14]

International Status. In the international market, reciprocity is estimated to have amounted to approximately 30 percent of world trade in 1982 and is expected to reach 50 percent by the year 2000. Reciprocity is known by a variety of names when practiced abroad. Barter, countertrade, and offset and cashless purchases are some of the most common terms used to

---

[14] "Tie-ins and Reciprocity: A Functional, Legal, and Policy Analysis," *Texas Law Review,* 58, no. 8 (November 1980): 1410–1445.

imply reciprocity. In the world market, reciprocity is most often practiced by industrializing countries that are often short of foreign currencies. They use their purchasing power to force multinational firms to engage in reciprocal practices. International reciprocity is criticized because of its inhibiting effect on competition. It may serve to prop up uncompetitive industries and hurt exporters because they must compete against these subsidized goods. No guidelines have yet been established to deal with this issue. At present, the Department of Commerce assists companies in countertrade transactions, the Departments of Treasury and Labor oppose it, and the Import–Export Bank has no policy for dealing with it.

Antitrust Laws Relating to Domestic Reciprocity. Continued use of reciprocity as a business practice has been challenged by the FTC and the Justice Department. Court decisions have indicated that in many instances reciprocal trading interferes with the successful operation of the free-enterprise system and violates the antitrust laws.

The sections of the major antitrust laws that may apply to reciprocity and the significance of court interpretations are discussed in the following paragraphs.

The Sherman Act, Section 1.

> Every contract, combination . . . or conspiracy, in restraint of trade or commerce . . . is . . . illegal.

To prove violation of this law, passed in 1890, authorities demonstrate that reciprocity practices are restraining trade—a difficult task because of the oral nature of the typical sales negotiation. Surrounding circumstances, such as the amount of competition in the industry and freedom of entry, are considered in an attempt to determine whether the practice was significantly interfering with and restraining trade.

In a suit brought by the government against General Dynamics in 1962, the use of reciprocal buying to restrain trade was evidenced by the existence of a formal trade relations department. In this case, the government proved that a special trade relations department and unusual selling practices were evidence of trade restraint. Therefore, the existence and functioning of a trade relations department constitutes restraint of trade, and any large company using such an organizational structure would be vulnerable to legal attacks. This decision caused organized trade relations departments practically to disappear and greatly reduced the extent to which reciprocal selling pressures were exerted.

Sherman Act, Section 2.

Every . . . attempt to monopolize . . . any part of trade or commerce . . . shall be punished.

This portion of the Sherman Act can be applied in instances in which the practice of reciprocity has proceeded to such an extent that monopoly effects are imminent. The Clayton Act, Section 7, specifies as follows:

No corporation . . . shall acquire . . . the whole or any part of the stock or other share capital, and no corporation . . . shall acquire the whole or any part of the assets of another corporation . . . where the effect of such acquisition may be substantially to lessen competition, or to tend to create a monopoly.

Federal Trade Commission Act, Section 5.

Unfair methods of competition in commerce, and unfair or deceptive acts or practices in commerce, are hereby declared unlawful.

Within this legal framework, it is clear why the use of formal trade relations departments and intensive reciprocal selling activities have greatly diminished. Today, informal considerations influence the buyer only if all other factors are completely equal. However, because reciprocity will always provide a temptation for sales departments and management to influence purchasing activities, it is wise to keep the possible competitive, psychological, and legal implications in mind.

Personal Influence

Personal relationships play an important part in normal business relations, but they should not become the prime basis for purchasing decisions. Sales personnel occasionally attempt to make a sale by presenting such arguments as their need to reach a quota or their participation in sales contests. Purchasing personnel should ignore such considerations.

Purchasing personnel should also attempt to avoid biases resulting from a clash of personalities with sales personnel. Everyone has likes and dislikes, but purchasing personnel should keep emotions and personal feelings from influencing their business relationships and concentrate on spending the company's money as effectively as possible.

Where personal influences on purchasing matters originate with higher levels of management, there may be serious problems of policy and internal goodwill. If outside pressures are being exerted, purchasing personnel should document the specifics of such attempts. Data relative to price, quality, and delivery should be gathered from other sources, and any added costs to the buying firm should be carefully noted and available when such questionable practices are investigated by management or stockholders. Invariably such outside influences diminish competition and either raise prices or reduce service or quality.

Partnering

Chapter 2 describes strategic partnering as part of the long-range planning for the firm's purchasing and materials management goals. World-class competition, customer insistence on quality, cost containment: these factors have led to the development of partnering as a collaborative buyer–seller relationship which sets aside traditional bid/buy methods of purchasing in favor of a problem-solving approach.[15]

The best applications include custom engineered products, high dollar high volume items, multi-item off-the-shelf products that systems contracting serves well, and services of all types. Partnering does not work well for market-driven commodity products like metals, for poorly managed firms where long-range planning means little, or firms with high personnel turnover that erodes partner relationships.

The benefits of partnering include less inventory, shorter lead times, higher quality, fewer suppliers, easier changes, easier computer linkages, faster problem resolution, lower prices, and lower total cost.

The overhead crane industry has involved itself in partnering for quite a while. Crane technology has improved through innovative thinking and creative efforts of manufacturers as well as users. Making a huge machine flexible and adaptable to changing manufacturing needs often comes about by relatively low-cost retrofitting, most often in the area of controls. Service constitutes the ultimate and oldest form of partnering. Some manufacturers recognize their own lax attention to the user's needs and have started separate organizations that offer solutions to customers' problems.[16]

Government red tape precludes defense contractors from partnering. Likewise, power utilities. The major motives for purchasing professionals developing supplier partnerships appear linked to traditional performance measurements; namely, improved delivery and quality.[17]

However, *Purchasing* magazine's 1991 survey found that only a third of the purchasing professionals polled said that their efforts to build strategic alliances with suppliers received enthusiastic backing or encouragement

---

[15] Brian G. Long, *Partnering: An Approach To Long Term Buyer–Seller Relations* (Kalamazoo, MI: Marketing and Management Institute Inc., 1990).

[16] "Partnering Gets Lift from Crane Manufacturers," *Material Handling Engineering* (January 1992), pp. 65–67.

[17] "Fork Found in Partner Path," *Purchasing* (December 19, 1991), pp. 22–23.

by top management. Price buying remains the paramount obstacle blocking the path to true strategic supply alliances.[18]

Partnerships rarely exceed three years, according to *Purchasing* magazine's ongoing survey covering strategic sourcing issues. The typical long-term business contract averages in the one to two year range. Fifty percent of survey respondents stated that they did not trust any supplier enough to enter into a five-plus year contract.[19]

Results later may reflect the staying power and effective benefits of partnering.

SUPPLIER CERTIFICATION

NAPM provides guidelines for supplier certification, along with a videotape to assist in evaluating suppliers.[20] Their five-phase program relies on time-proven techniques such as plant visits and quality inspections of initial shipments to check out a potential supplier's ability to perform under contract.

Phase One: Identify types of rejects through a review of incoming quality control history, and suggest cures.

Phase Two: Make on-site inspections to survey the supplier's manufacturing process.

Phase Three: Initiate an inspection plan until supplier completes the certification process.

Phase Four: Acknowledge supplier's achievement of qualification with a certificate or some type of ceremony.

Phase Five: Maintain an on-going audit by statistical sampling until satisfied, then shift to random audits. Disqualify the supplier if discrepancies recur with no immediate resolution. Requalify by repeating Phases Three and Four.

Buyers may list certified suppliers' products on a qualified products list (QPL). The list typically shows brand name, model number, part number, and place of manufacture. This list forms yet another method for specifying what the buyer intends to buy, as Chapter 7 describes.[21]

The National Minority Supplier Development Council has a certifica-

---

[18] "Leaders Lag on Partner Push," op. cit. (March 5, 1992), pp. 20–21.
[19] "Partners Face Early Divorce," op. cit. (June 4, 1992), p. 20.
[20] "Supplier Certification," *NAPM Program Aids Library PAL 91* (1988).
[21] Donald W. Dobler, David N. Burt, and Lamar Lee, Jr., *Purchasing and Materials Management: Text and Cases* (New York: McGraw-Hill, 1990), p. 136.

tion process to verify only bona fide minority and woman-owned businesses.

CHAPTER SUMMARY

Supplier selection impacts the entire economy because the buyer's firm succeeds in part on the quality and reliability of its supplied materials. Likewise, the supplier succeeds in part on trading with the buyer. The financial situation of the two firms ultimately influences the welfare of their communities and the nation.

The strategic philosophy of integrating vendors into the company's materials flow responds to several changes in the 1980s. The just-in-time concept caught on with more and more firms turning over the inventory function to their distributors and manufacturer-suppliers. The trend toward fewer vendors and fewer carriers made partnering with selected vendors and carriers more possible and more effective. Suppliers agreed—however reluctantly—to submit to certification by customers and their purchasing organizations. Buyers waived inspection on receiving the goods because they had certified the suppliers' quality beforehand. Computerization continued strongly such that the long-heralded buyer–supplier link-up finally took place in which computer-to-computer exchange substituted for human interaction. Several catalogs appeared on databases for buyers to use through their computers. Evaluation of vendors performance in supplying reliable quality on precise delivery schedules strengthened as a general practice, with eager competitors waiting to move into the territory.

Discussion Questions

1. Any supplier considerations that cannot be quantified are probably not worth worrying about. Discuss.
2. What are the arguments in favor of buying from a local supplier? How important are the various arguments?
3. What are the so-called home-preference laws? What variations of such laws can you identify?
4. What is reciprocity, and what degrees or kinds of reciprocity can you name?
5. What is the legal status of the practice of reciprocity?
6. From what sources may a buyer obtain infor-

mation about prospective suppliers? Evaluate these sources.
7. How could data processing equipment be useful in connection with supplier evaluation?
8. For what reasons is the geographical location of the supplier an important consideration in the selection process?
9. Explain why quality control procedures should be used in evaluating supplier service.
10. What factors can a purchasing officer learn through a plant visit that are unlikely to be learned through other means?
11. What ratios are important in judging the fi-

nancial stability of a supplier? Which of these do you consider the most important?

12. What are the advantages of the weighted-point plan of supplier evaluation? What limitations does this method of evaluation have?

13. State the advantages and disadvantages of single sourcing.

14. Why is gift giving from suppliers to purchasing personnel a questionable practice? In the end, who pays for the gifts?

Suggested Cases

ABC Corporation (A)

ABC Corporation (B)

Berg Raingear, Inc.

Evans Corporation

Household Cleaners Corporation

Howell Chuck Company (A)

Industry-Wide Pricing

MF-1

Sharpe Machine Corporation

Smith Electronic Corporation

6

Quantity and Inventory Planning and Control

Lot-sizing focuses on computing the right quantity of materials to order and to carry in inventory. Purchasing Manager Kathi knows that inventory consists of stock that the operation consumes, plus safety stock that prevents shutdown if delays disrupt the replenishing cycle.

Economic Order Quantity (EOQ) works well as a lot-sizing method, when demand remains constant and stable, and when factors change very little. She knows that the factors include acquisition cost, carrying charge (as a decimal), and purchase price (including inbound transportation)—the so-called delivered cost.

Kathi uses the EOQ computer diskette for items her shop produces as well as for items she buys on the outside. She depends on EOQ in repeated use during the year. So the speaker at her monthly purchasing management association meeting startled Kathi when he expressed strong doubts about using EOQ.

CHAPTER
CONTENTS

Managers for generations have tried to control inventories with accuracy and relative simplicity. In 1926 a General Electric industrial engineer published an article in which he developed formulas and charts to simplify the problem.[1] The formulas still apply today; a later section in this chapter describes the basic economic order quantity formula.

The 1930s–1940s brought mixed reasons to produce in economical manufacturing quantities, thereby controlling inventory. The Depression resulted in operating cash shortages and curtailed production. The World War II effort placed a heavy premium on conserving time, conserving raw materials, and maintaining enough inventory to keep war production in high gear.

The 1950s saw renewed research effort devoted to controlling inventory. The Rand Corporation and the Office of Naval Research published highly mathematical discussions, which were of little use to most managers and buyers.[2]

High interest rates in late 1979 and the 1980s galvanized concern in the business world. Management examined the impact of high interest rates on decisions affecting inventory. Closer control meant that companies operated with leaner inventories, with the excess of earlier years cut away.

Moreover, higher prices for industrial and retail goods, 30 percent higher in 1990 than base year 1982, meant that last year's materials budget did not buy as much material this year. Companies conserved their spending in order to purchase essentials and postponed buying an extra period's supply of inventory.

In addition to the high interest rates of the early 1980s and inflation-fueled higher prices, a third discovery stimulated American managers to focus close attention on inventories. The Japanese showed that just-in-time (JIT) inventories worked well for their companies. American managers pondered whether large just-in-case inventories of buffer stock had to continue as basic operating procedure.

Purchasing and materials personnel hold significant responsibilities, as well as opportunities, to affect an organization's overall performance regarding inventory. Statistics obtained from American industry's balance sheets reveal that inventories make up a sizable percentage of a company's

---

[1] Benjamin Cooper, "How to Determine Economical Manufacturing Quantities," *Factory and Industrial Management* (October 1926), pp. 229–233.

[2] Kenneth J. Arrow, Theodore Harris, and Jacob Marschak, "Optimal Inventory Policy," *Econometrica 19* (1951), pp. 250–272; A. Dvoretzky, J. Kiefer, and J. Wolfowitz, "The Inventory Problem: I. Case of Known Distribution of Demand," *Econometrica 20* (1951), pp. 187–222; and Op. cit., "II. Case of Unknown Distribution of Demand," pp. 450–466.

assets and usually the largest single current asset. Typically, firms hold from 15 to 40 percent of their total capital invested in their inventories. Many companies list inventory reduction as their first priority. Thus, inventory control becomes one of purchasing's foremost goals. Specifics behind these inventory control decisions and the variables to be considered are the focus of this chapter.

There are essentially three types of inventories: raw materials, work in process, and finished-goods or stores inventories. The finished-goods inventory represents the largest percentage of value added.

Although there is only one right quantity to buy for any given transaction, there are many different kinds of transactions; this fact complicates the determination of ideal quantity.

If too small a quantity is purchased, the unit cost will be high, shortages are likely to increase, and expediting work will be greater. On the other hand, too large a quantity causes excess inventory with attendant costs, and obsolescence becomes a problem. The need for additional storage facilities also creates investment problems. Placing orders at the wrong time can be costly in about the same ways. Keeping a tight rein on inventory expenses is one way for purchasing to fight price increases. Inventory–sales ratios have stayed near record lows during recent years. The ratio hovers around 1.50 which means 1 1/2 months of manufacturing and trade inventory to fill customers orders if new production stopped altogether.[3]

Although most costs of doing business have soared, inventory managers have contained costs. A national survey revealed that inventory costs as a percent of total stocks rose sharply after mid-1988 but still ranged between 10 and 25 percent for the largest group responding, unchanged from earlier years. During this same period, interest rates on loans to finance inventory, wages, prices, and insurance premiums were generally soaring. A combination of factors have been responsible for the steady inventory rate.

1. There was a key shift in purchasing strategy from ordering in quantity toward ordering less, but more often.

2. Ordering was tied much more closely to actual production requirements, rather than to replenishing stock levels based on historical records. This shift was possible through the use of computers, closer coordination with other departments, and purchasing's skills.[4]

---

[3] *National Economic Trends,* The Federal Reserve Bank of St. Louis (July 1992), p. 12.
[4] See also ''Inventory Levels Remain Low, But Carrying Costs Keep Rising,'' *Purchasing* (March 23, 1989), p. 24.

FACTORS AFFECTING THE ORDERING OF QUANTITIES

Special-Order Manufacturing

The amount of supplies ordered depends in large part on the type of manufacturing done. Some firms produce to order, rather than manufacturing in anticipation of orders.

When goods are made to order, it is the usual practice to prepare a *bill of materials* for the items being manufactured. This bill of materials contains a complete list of the component parts and materials required to make the finished goods, including detailed descriptions and quantities needed.

When the sales department receives an order, it notifies purchasing and production scheduling. The purchasing department then secures a copy of the bill of materials covering the order. After checking stocks that may have accumulated in the stores department, the buyer calculates how much must be ordered. When production schedules the order, the purchasing department buys and controls the quantity of goods to be purchased.

Continuous-Run Manufacturing

In contrast to special-order manufacturing, continuous-run production, which is the way consumer goods are made, consists of producing standardized goods in anticipation of orders. Bills of materials are established when the product is designed. Purchasing controls the quantity of purchase in accordance with planned production schedules for the various goods. Because of the repetitive nature of production, there is considerable latitude with respect to quantities and timing of purchases.

Maintenance, Repairs, and Operating Supplies

All manufacturing plants use maintenance, repair, and operating (MRO) items, which are regularly stocked and used. Some MRO items cannot be purchased in the most economical quantities because of the large amount of storage space required, or because of fire hazards. Examples of such items are gasoline, paint, lubricants, excelsior and other packing items, materials, and chemicals. Some MRO items are called shelf-life items—that is, they tend to deteriorate or waste away during storage. Batteries, cement, and paste are examples.

In buying MRO items, the purchasing department must consider the space, hazard, and shelf-life aspects as well as the most economical unit of purchase.

TABLE 6-1. Composition of Carrying Charges

Carrying Charges	Percentage Ranges
Interest cost	6–15
Obsolescence and deterioration	2–8
Storage	0–5
Insurance	1–4
Taxes	1–3
Total carrying charge	10–35

COSTS ASSOCIATED WITH INVENTORIES

Possession or Carrying Costs

Carrying material is expensive, with estimates varying from 10 to 35 percent depending on the type of material and economic conditions. Table 6-1 illustrates typical percentage ranges of the various cost elements included in carrying charges.

Not all inventory items are subject to the same risk. Stock bought for a single customer's requirement and parts used for a single machine are examples of high-risk inventory. In contrast, stock bought for a general line sold to many customers, or parts used on many machines, would be considered low-risk inventory. Many companies using formal economic order quantity (EOQ) procedures (described next) have established various risk categories. In initially putting a system into effect, the purchasing department should consider all items as average risk and incorporate refinements as information becomes available.

Acquisition Costs

Four costs make up the acquisition costs that the firm pays every time the purchasing department makes a purchase.

1. *Requisition:* The cost to search for specifications to describe the quality of the item that the user wants, clerical handling of the requisition form, managerial time to review and approve the requisition and to verify the availability of funds to pay for the item.
2. *Purchase and Expedite:* That portion of the buyer's time and expense to purchase and expedite the item, confirmed by clerical action on necessary forms and filed away.

3. *Receive, Inspect, and Put into Storage:* Receiving clerk's time to break open the shipping package, the inspector's time and expense to verify the item's quality, the storeroom attendant's time and expense to first put the item into storage, and the necessary forms to record these various actions, then distribute and file the resulting paper-work.

4. *Audit Invoice and Make Payment:* Clerical expense matching the supplier's billing with the correct purchase order and receiving-inspection report; and preparing and mailing a payment check.

ECONOMIC ORDER QUANTITY

After determining the marginal cost of acquiring the material and the possession costs, the purchasing department is in a position to figure the economic order quantity (EOQ) for any stock item not subject to quantity discounts. (The effects of quantity discounts will be discussed later.)

Mathematical Proof of EOQ

The least-cost quantity is the quantity at which acquisition costs equal the cost of possession, assuming that carrying costs vary directly with average inventory.[5] This is the basic principle of EOQ buying and is true regardless of the factors used. An example of this principle follows, illustrated by Table 6-2.

Assume that an order's cost is $3 and that the carrying charges are 15 percent of one-half the value of the order. Further consider that the item is used at the rate of $1000 per year. (There are no quantity discounts.) As Table 6-2 shows, if the item in question is ordered once every month, the ordering cost per year would be $12 \times \$3$, or $36. If the item is purchased once every two months, its per-year ordering cost would be $6 \times \$3$, or $18. Costs can be similarly calculated for other order frequencies, as shown in the second column of Table 6-2.

If the item in question is ordered once every month, the annual carrying charges would be 15 percent of the average inventory (one-half the dollar value of the order) or $0.15 \times \frac{1}{2}(1000/12) = \$6.25$. If it is purchased once every two months its carrying charges would be $0.15 \times \frac{1}{2}(1000/6) = \$12.50$. Costs can be similarly calculated for other order frequencies, as shown in the third column of Table 6-2.

Adding the acquisition and carrying costs gives the total annual cost of

---

[5] See Robert M. Brown, ''On Carrying Costs and the EOQ Model: A Pedagogical Note,'' *The Financial Review*, 20, no. 4 (November 1985): 357.

TABLE 6-2. Acquisition and Carrying Costs of Various Order Frequencies

Order Frequency (times per year)	Annual Acquisition Costs	Annual Carrying Costs	Total Annual Costs
12	$36	$ 6.25	$42.25
6	18	12.50	30.50
4	12	18.75	30.75
3	9	25.00	34.00
2	6	37.50	43.50
1	3	75.00	78.00

purchasing the item at different order frequencies per year, as shown in the fourth column of Table 6-2. The total annual costs for purchasing the illustrated item are lowest when it is bought six times per year. The total annual cost of this frequency is $30.50; the ordering costs are $18.00 and the carrying charges are $12.50. These cost figures are more nearly equal at six than any other order frequency.

The basic principle is also illustrated in Figure 6-1, which is based on the same values for annual usage, acquisition costs, and possession charges. The graph, unlike the table, shows that at the point where the order cost curve and the carrying charge curve intersect, the quantity to be ordered is slightly more than a two-month supply, and that at this point the total cost will be about $30. However, it is impractical to refine purchasing decisions to this point. In practice, one rounds the answers to the closest time unit with which one is working: days, weeks, or months.

The table and graph were constructed using certain assumed values for ordering costs and carrying charges. It is possible to construct other tables and graphs on the basis of different values. It is also possible to compute the correct EOQ algebraically.

If total order costs equal total carrying charges, then

$$AX = \frac{IU}{2X}$$

where

A = acquisition costs in dollars per order
I = possession (carrying) charges in dollars

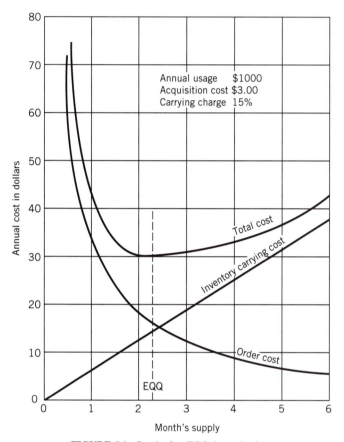

FIGURE 6-1. Graph of an EOQ determination.

U = annual usage in dollar value
X = correct order frequency per year
EOQ = economic order quantity in dollar value = U/X

Solving for X, we obtain

$$X = \sqrt{IU/2A}$$

Substituting $\sqrt{IU/2A}$ for X, we obtain

$$EOQ = \sqrt{2AU/I}$$

or

$$EOQ = \sqrt{\frac{2 \times \text{acquisition costs} \times \text{annual use (\$)}}{\text{possession charge}}}$$

Thus, the EOQ quantity does not vary directly with usage but with the square root of usage. When usage increases, supply for a shorter time is ordered. Therefore, the adoption of a rule for buying a fixed-time supply such as one or two months' usage (or sales) can result in extra inventory costs.

Shortcut Method of Calculating EOQ

For the everyday use of the purchasing department, it is possible to incorporate EOQ data into tables that show directly the amount to be ordered for items with varying rates. In order to prepare simple tables for practical use, one must depart from exact mathematics and reduce the figures to reasonable approximations. Table 6-3 is an example of such a reduction. It assumes $3 order costs and carrying charges of 24 percent.

Many companies have developed comprehensive tables or charts of this nature, and they have been used successfully. These tables utilize actual company cost figures and the basic principle that the correct ordering quantity is the amount at which order costs are equal to carrying charges. Numerous computer software programs compute EOQ.

Although the EOQ indicates the most economical quantity to buy, the actual quantity decision must consider the following additional factors.

1. If space for the item is limited, quantities must be limited as space permits.

TABLE 6-3. EOQ Table

Dollar Value of One Year's Usage	Ordering Interval	Dollar Value of One Year's Usage	Ordering Interval
0–10	3 yrs	101–200	5 mos
11–20	1 1/2 yrs	201–300	4 mos
21–30	1 yr	301–400	3 mos
31–50	10 mos	401–600	10 wks
51–75	7 mos	601–1000	8 wks
76–100	6 mos	1001–2000	6 wks
		2001–up	1 mo

2. If the item has a limited shelf life, quantities must be adjusted to this shelf life.

3. If a product is about to be discontinued, quantities obviously must be limited.

4. Calculations are based on usage or forecasts of usage, as well as on cost calculations that may be less than perfectly accurate.

Another version of the EOQ that has the same theoretical and arithmetic justification but uses units instead of dollar value is

$$\text{EOQ (units)} = \sqrt{\frac{2 \times \text{acquisition costs} \times \text{total annual usage (units)}}{\text{unit cost} \times \text{carrying charges}}}$$

Assuming a $5 acquisition cost per order, usage of 1200 units per year, a cost of $20 per unit including inbound freight, and 20 percent carrying charges per dollar of inventory,

$$\text{EOQ} = \sqrt{\frac{2 \times 5 \times 1200}{20 \times 0.20}} = 55 \text{ units}$$

A simplified version results from separating the equation into two parts, the unchanging factors making up the first part. Thus,

$$\text{EOQ} = \sqrt{\frac{2 \times \$5}{0.20}} \sqrt{\frac{1200}{\$20}} = 7.07 \times \sqrt{\frac{\text{annual usage (units)}}{\text{unit cost}}}$$

Similar calculations can be made for various units and the appropriate tables constructed.

EOQ Graphs

When purchasing a large number of items of the same category that have similar quantity discounts, it is possible to construct a graph that indicates the EOQ by direct reading. Plotting annual usage on the vertical scale and price on the horizontal scale locates EOQ points. Figure 6-2 shows such a graph used for various nonferrous materials.

When to Take Advantage of Quantity Discounts

Quantity discounts have not received enough attention as a factor in improving purchasing's effectiveness, even though they can provide significant cost reductions. (A more detailed discussion of quantity discounts will be found in

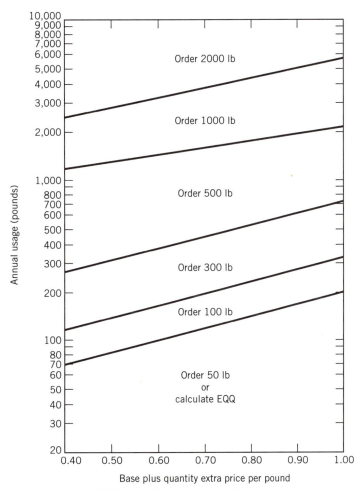

FIGURE 6-2. EOQ chart for repetitive items.

Chapter 8.) It is not uncommon to realize reductions in unit price in excess of 50 percent in exchange for agreements to purchase in increased quantities.

In the example given earlier, where the item being bought was not subject to quantity discounts, it was found that the correct ordering frequency was six times per year. At this frequency the total cost was $30.50 per year.[*] Now assume that a quantity discount of 10 percent for a $1000 purchase is available. If $1000's worth of this item is purchased once a year, the ordering cost will be $3 × 1, or $3, and the carrying charge will be 0.15 × 500, or

_____

[*] Small numerical amounts are used to simplify the presentation.

$75. Thus, the total cost for buying once a year would be $78. This is an increase of $47.50 over the minimum cost of $30.50. However, since $100 could be saved by taking the 10 percent discount, the company would spend $47.50 to save $100. This produces a net saving of $52.50, which suggests that the company should take advantage of the discount.

The basic relationship between the factors involved in the quantity discount purchasing decisions can be evaluated by analyzing the trade-off between the cost of the increased inventory investment and the unit price reduction brought about by the quantity discount obtained. Any question whether to take a quantity discount can be evaluated in this way.

Buyers traditionally have examined quantity discounts as they reduce unit price. Freight cost has a quantity discount also, resulting from scale economies.[6] Thus, buyers may compute two simultaneous quantity discounts at the same time. However, they must factor in the added carrying cost of larger inventories.

The issue of splitting a large order quantity into multiple deliveries confronts the purchasing manager and buyer, especially in the just-in-time environment. Economic models sometimes provide solutions to the decision dilemma. One such approach analyzes a deterministic order-splitting EOQ model that assumes that the gross ordering cost does not decrease with the number of deliveries.[7] For multiple sourcing, the analyst formulates and solves a mathematical programming problem to obtain the optimal selection of suppliers and the size of the split orders. For single sourcing, the analyst finds the optimal number of deliveries.

Another approach extends the conventional EOQ and economic production quantity (EPQ) to determine the optimal selling quantity and purchasing price for an intermediary firm. Such a firm purchases products from numerous independent producers and sells those products to other firms that process or use them at a given market price. The basic profit maximization model that the approach formulates can use either a fixed or a variable purchasing price as a variable. The basic economic model contains an inspection cost component that realistically fits intermediary firms. However, as this text has discussed earlier, the firm may incur no inspection cost if it receives a just-in-time delivery or delivery from a certified supplier.[8]

Yet another approach optimizes purchase order quantity. It presents a simple analytical procedure for finding the order quantity that minimizes total purchase costs that reflect both transportation economies and quantity

[6] "An EOQ Model with Quantity Discounts for Both Purchasing Price and Freight Cost," *Computers & Operations Research* (UK 1990), pp. 73–78.

[7] "Just-in-Time Purchasing: Single or Multiple Sourcing," *International Journal of Production Economics* (May 1992), pp. 175–181.

[8] "Optimal Selling Quantity and Purchasing Price for Intermediary Firms," *International Journal of Operations and Production Management* (1991), pp. 64–68.

discounts. The optimal purchase order quantity falls into one of four possibilities:

1. The valid economic order quantity (EOQ).
2. A purchase price breakpoint in excess of the valid EOQ.
3. A transportation rate breakpoint in excess of the valid EOQ.
4. A modified EOQ that provides an overdeclared shipment in excess of the valid EOQ.

An algorithm explores these four possibilities, in an effort to assist the buyer in deciding what to do.[9]

A simple formula develops from another researcher's study into the general optimal policy toward economic order quantity lot sizes.[10] An integer multiple of monthly demands constitutes the optimal EOQ, provided the capital investment component of the inventory holding charge does not exceed 30 percent of the component due to the physical holding of inventory. The optimal solution shows that the buyer should order less than a month's demand, provided that the capital investment component of the inventory holding charge does not shortfall one-fourth of the component due to the physical holding of inventory.

The Department of Defense wrestles with the continued application of strict EOQ-based quantities in the DOD purchasing process. In today's economic environment, some, if not most, of the critical assumptions do not hold true. The buyer needs to address the dynamics of the interaction of customer demand, time, and market conditions that he or she must incorporate at the line item level to make a reasoned buy-quantity decision at the time of purchase. DOD computes EOQ using a continuous review–reorder point system to manage wholesale and retail spares and repair parts. The review system considers order-cost and holding-cost figures, unit price, and an estimate of steady-state demand for the item.[11]

A survey of 44 manufacturing firms in the heavily industrialized Midwest sought to analyze the cost of ordering and the current use of this cost figure in U.S. industry. The firms utilized one of four types of inventory systems: material requirements planning (MRP), economic order quantity (EOQ), buy to order, or just-in-time (JIT). Most respondents noted that they consider the cost of ordering a significant decision variable. However, many reported that they do not calculate or even estimate a value for this variable,

[9] "Optimal Purchase and Transportation Cost Lot Sizing for a Single Item," *Decision Sciences* (September/October 1991), pp. 940–952.

[10] "EOQ Under Date-Terms Supplier Credit: A Near-Optimal Solution," *Journal of the Operational Research Society* (September 1991), pp. 803–809.

[11] "Reconciling Procurement and Inventory Management Objectives in Department of Defense Spares Acquisition," *National Contract Management Journal* (1991), pp. 1–6.

using instead a single cost to order value for all order decisions. Vendor selection represented the largest single cost. Overall, the results show that for the firms studied, little if any change in the use and determination of the order cost value has occurred since the 1913 development of the classical EOQ model.[12]

A major metal-fabricating plant adopted a simplified set of rules for the guidance of its buyers. Assuming a monthly inventory carrying cost of 2 percent applied to all purchased items, they used the following guidelines.

1. If buying an increased quantity does not reduce the price, buyers should strive for a minimum of 12 turnovers per year.
2. If the company is now buying a 30-day requirement and an increase in quantity to a 60-day supply effects a cost saving of more than 2 percent, the larger quantity should be bought.
3. If the company is now buying a 30-day requirement and an increase in quantity to a 90-day supply effects a savings of at least 5 percent, the larger quantity should be bought.
4. Order quantities should always be based on requirements for periods not exceeding 90 days.

LIMITATIONS OF EOQ

The original EOQ concept was developed to determine production quantities, and the trade-off was between machine setup costs and inventory carrying costs. Purchasing adapted the formula by substituting ordering costs for setup costs. This practice has been criticized by some who state that ordering costs are often trivial and indeterminant. In addition, the formula does not actively take account of such changing conditions as demand variations, seasonal changes, quantity discounts, freight costs, obsolescence risk, or stock-out costs. Other disadvantages of the fixed order size (EOQ) system include the following.

1. The system may be unreliable, with a high varying rate.
2. A large investment in safety stock may be required.
3. The buyer must obtain forecasts for all items.
4. The system is based on past demand data.
5. Price fluctuation for the ordered items is not provided for.

The previous discussion of the EOQ mentioned possible adjustments to

---

[12] "The Cost of Ordering," *Journal of Purchasing and Materials Management* (Summer 1990), pp. 30–36.

rectify some of these limitations. The EOQ methodology results in a single value, which implies a degree of precision that the model does not really possess. An EOQ range model can be used to help resolve this problem. Once the EOQ is calculated, the range is set by adding or subtracting 25 percent of the EOQ to that number. Studies show that a range model is applicable in all but the most inflationary times. It can still be used during such periods if some inflationary modifications are made. Such modifications help overcome some of the limitations of the classical model, but not all. Firms should exercise caution when reordering inventory and keep in mind that in some cases the EOQ model can be used as a guide only.[13]

Inventory control's growing importance has spurred rack and shelving designers and distributors to find new ways to meet customers' needs. The trend toward automated manufacturing and high-density storage requires even greater expertise. The roll-out rack pictured in Figure 6-3 gives additional storage space for structural steel or long members of steel or tubing. By using the air space above the existing floor area, the rack effectively increases the area by as much as five times. It saves labor hours by permitting the unloading of cars and trucks directly into storage without stacking or piling the steel or having to move any other bundle. The rack enhances safety by minimizing the hazard of toppling piles. Each rack stands alone, separately purchased and installed as needed. The figure shows the receptacles in their closed position, except one on the right side shown in the open position, ready for loading or unloading by the overhead crane. An attendant moves the receptacles in or out by turning control shafts with a crank.[14]

INVENTORY VALUATION

In contrast to the physical attributes (flow of goods) of an inventory, which are factual and objective, the financial characteristics (flow of costs) are more subjective and fluctuate with the accounting procedures adopted by the organization.

The inventory flow of cost refers to the manner and timing of removing items from inventory. At present four principle methods of calculation are being used. They are discussed here in order of frequency of use.

The *first-in, first out* (FIFO) method is a widely used inventory flow method. The cost of inventory is calculated on the basis of the items that have been in stock the longest amount of time. The goods bought first get used

---

[13] Gene Woolsey, editor-in-chief of *Production and Inventory Management Journal,* adds similar warnings in ''A Requiem for the EOQ: An Editorial,'' *Hospital Material Management Quarterly* (August 1990), pp. 82–90.

[14] ''The SpaceSaver System,'' catalog of Steel Storage Systems, Inc., Commerce City, Colorado, 1990, p. 2. U.S., Canadian, and British Patents cover the product.

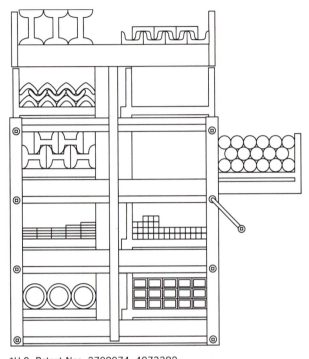

*U.S. Patent Nos. 3708074, 4073382;
Canadian Patent No. 1049938;
British Patent No. 1558294;
Other Foreign Patents Pending.

FIGURE 6-3. The spacesaver system of roll-out rack, with permission of the manufacturer.

first, goes the assumption. It is also assumed that goods remaining in stock came in at higher prices. As a result, FIFO tends to show lower costs and higher profits in times of rising prices, indicating a higher taxable income. The alternative *last-in, first-out* (LIFO) method operates according to the principle that current revenues should be matched against current costs. Therefore, items issued to users from stock are priced at the unit price of the latest items acquired or produced. In periods of rising costs, the LIFO method tends to decrease income and subsequently taxes as the actual price charged reflects the higher costs. Alternatively, LIFO will increase earnings during periods when prices are falling.

The *average unit cost* method, as an alternative to LIFO or FIFO, does not attempt to determine which item went out first or last. Instead, the average cost for all items during a specified time period is calculated.

The *specific* or *standard unit cost* method prices items received or issued using a predetermined unit cost. The specific cost used is multiplied by the number of units sold to arrive at the ending inventory cost.

The U.S. Congress on occasion examines inventory accounting reform. The Inventory Simplification and Reform Tax Act of 1981 resulted from such effort. Congress goes into immense detail in its efforts to prevent a material distortion of income from occurring. To illustrate, hearings in one congressional committee considered the suggestion for preventing the potential for tax avoidance that no purchase of inventory at year end be so great as to alter the normal rate of inventory turnover.[15]

Inventory management and valuation have received more attention and scrutiny than ever before because of the Uniform Capitalization (UNICAP) Rules of the Internal Revenue Code Section 263A. A firm must now capitalize certain previously deductible indirect costs: off-site storage or warehousing, purchasing, handling of inventory, and general and administrative costs relating to the other categories. UNICAP spurs not only tax costs but increased accounting costs associated with the complex record keeping and analysis necessary for cost capitalization.[16]

INVENTORY CONTROL

Inventory control involves the planning, ordering, and scheduling of the materials used in the manufacturing process. It exercises control over three types of inventories: raw materials, work in process, and finished goods. Purchasing is primarily concerned with control over the raw materials inventory, which includes raw or semiprocessed materials, fabricated parts, and MRO items. Figure 6-4 illustrates purchasing's major areas of emphasis in controlling inventory: actual stock on hand, monthly usage in past years, identification number, description and location in stores, unit cost, vendors, and recent purchase orders and quantities.

There are four major reasons for maintaining sound inventory control procedures.

1. *Lower unit costs:* Quantity purchases (or long production runs) permit lower unit costs.
2. *Lower operating costs:* Quantity purchases (or long production runs) permit efficient use of humanpower, machines, and facilities.

---

[15] "Inventory Accounting as a Burden on the Capital Formation Process," Report of the Committee on Small Business, House of Representatives, Ninety-Sixth Congress, Second Session, October 2, 1981 (Washington: U.S. Government Printing).
[16] "Fourteenth Annual Student Manuscript Competition: UNICAP—A Bitter Pill to Swallow?" *Pennsylvania CPA Journal* (Summer 1989), pp. 6–8.

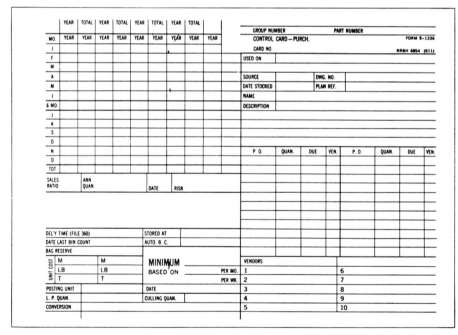

FIGURE 6-4. An inventory control ledger.

3. *Optimal customer service:*   Quantity purchases (or long production runs) assure optimal customer service and provide for efficient scheduling of internal operations.

4. *Efficient use of invested capital:*   The balancing of the three preceding elements with the cost of capital encourages good financial management of inventory.

Responsibility for Inventory Control

The broad responsibility for determining inventory policy rests with general management because inventories figure prominently in a company's financial operations. However, the actual management of inventory is usually entrusted to subordinate departments. There is considerable variation in which a department manages inventory control procedures.

The implications of inventory control for management are many. Examples include inventory control with known demand; continuous delivery (like pipeline flow); continuous outflow of product; known demand, back-ordering allowed; uncertain demand; price breaks; batch delivery and constant usage; constant delivery and batch usage; and simultaneous usage and delivery. Purchasing departments that supply offshore oil rigs face the classical newsboy or Christmas tree lot case—order a predetermined amount with no reorders possible in this time period, a single batch delivery, and use until runout.

The customer service level that the firm wants to maintain and the stockout levels that the firm tolerates require defining as part of management's responsibility for inventory control.

In earlier years the purchasing department most often assumed this responsibility. With the introduction of the materials management form of organization, inventory control increasingly becomes a responsibility of the materials manager. In Chapter 4 it was noted that a separate inventory control department is quite common under the materials management form of organization.

In a few companies an inventory control committee has been established to initiate broad control policies, with the administration of the policies left to the purchasing department. Representatives of all the company departments affected by inventory control policies sit on such committees.

Records Management for Inventory Control

One of the biggest boons to inventory management in the past decade has been the computer. The management of inventory requires the use of timely and accurate records for each item in inventory, and the process of keeping these records by hand is tedious, time-consuming, and often mistake-ridden. The computer allows inventories to be updated automatically when orders are placed and filled and when new inventory items are checked in.

Although most companies in the United States today are using computers to keep track of their inventories, a few are still holding on to manual systems. Therefore, this section surveys records management under manual and computerized systems. The reader should be aware that a totally manual system is unlikely to be encountered in any large company but can often be found in smaller operations that might be suppliers to the larger firms. As computers become increasingly affordable and necessary, it is likely that manual inventory record-keeping systems will completely vanish.

Manual System

Basic to a sound system of inventory control is the assembling of pertinent data to provide economical ordering points and ordering quantities. With a properly designed inventory control ledger card it is possible to gather the pertinent data in one place.

Inventory ledgers range from relatively simple to extremely complex forms. The nature of the business will determine the complexity of the form adopted. The form illustrated in Figure 6-4 is used by a firm manufacturing in advance of orders from customers. The data included in this form are:

1. Detailed identification of item
2. List of suppliers
3. List of open purchase orders
4. Monthly rate of usage for past several years
5. Delivery time
6. Minimum order quantity
7. Bin balance available for issue to production

In many organizations it is common practice to group inventory items into related product lines and assign responsibility for each group to an individual who concentrates on those items and becomes thoroughly familiar with their characteristics. Furthermore, it is advisable to isolate large-volume items for special consideration.

Computerized Systems

Records management under a computerized system is easier and more accurate than under a manual system. The computerized system uses code numbers that correspond to specific items. Each item in inventory is coded, and any adjustment made to the item is effected through use of the item's code number.

Most computerized systems make an inventory adjustment each time an order for a particular item is processed, for either an internal requisition or an outside sale. When the item is ordered, the amount of the item remaining in inventory is adjusted accordingly. This adjustment is a decrease in the total inventory.

Similarly, each time any amount of an item is placed in inventory, whether through receipt of an order, a return from a customer, or internal manufacture moving into inventory, the amount is noted and the item's inventory amount increased accordingly.

Reordering under a computerized system can be accomplished in two ways. With the first, there are prespecified reorder points. A reorder point for each item is established, using such factors as lead time, desired levels of service, and rate of usage. The computer is programmed to give a signal automatically when the reorder point is reached. At the end of each day, or some other fixed interval, a program is run that identifies the items that need to be reordered, giving both the ideal order quantity and the amount in inventory. This program is often written so that a purchase order is automatically written for each item required.

The second way to facilitate reordering under a computerized system is through manual perusal of the inventory levels on a daily basis. Under this plan a printout is generated of all items in inventory and is examined by the inventory manager, who decides when and how much to order based on usage rates and expected future needs. Although this system is less accurate, since it may allow an item to pass unnoticed, it can be very useful in unstable demand situations when an average usage rate and lead time are impossible to determine.

Two methods of establishing inventory review plans, ABC analysis and minimum–maximum, are discussed next. These methods are useful for both manual and computerized systems.

ABC Analysis—The Vital Few, The Trivial Many

Vilfredo Federico Damaso Pareto (1848–1923), an Italian–Swiss engineer and economist, believed that 20 percent of a country's population does 80 percent of the work. Today's inventory control manager refines Pareto's argument into three priority categories—A, B, and C. The A items may number only 10 or 20 percent of the inventory's total number of items. However, they may account for 65 to 80 percent of the dollars tied up in inventory. A items deserve executive attention, like General Electric's copper buying executive.

The B items number perhaps only 10 to 15 percent of the total inventory.

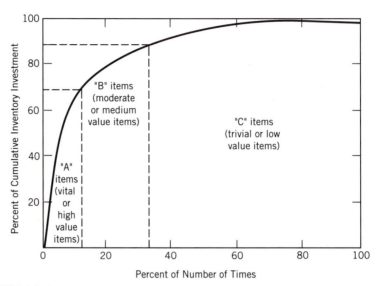

FIGURE 6-5. Cumulative inventory investment, arranged for the ABC method of inventory control.

Typically they tie up 20 to 25 percent of the dollars invested in inventory. B items deserve EOQ analysis or some other form of verifying the right quantity to buy and hold in stock. Purchasing department buyers typically compute and order the B item quantities.

The C items number perhaps 65 percent of all items in inventory. However, their combined dollar value totals only 10 percent of the entire investment in inventory. Clerical personnel or computers connected to suppliers' computers order the C items for many firms.

Because most firms find that a small number of purchased items account for the major portion of the purchased value, it is often advisable to classify purchased items according to value, a procedure generally referred to as ABC analysis. Figure 6-5 illustrates a typical classification of this type.

Other rankings help to focus attention on important decision opportunities. These rankings include the following:

Unit cost: What items will be most subject to theft and should have very accurate records?

Unit volume: What items will require the most storage space?

Dollar inventory: Where are the real reductions possible?

Shelf life: Are we watching for potential spoilage?[17]

[17] George W. Plossl and W. Evert Welch, *The Role of Top Management in the Control of Inventory* (Reston, VA: Reston Publishing, 1979), p. 22.

Typical advantages that have resulted from use of the ABC concept include the following.

1. Reduced purchase prices because efforts are concentrated on class A and B and on using larger order quantities on class C.
2. Reduced purchasing department costs through processing of fewer orders.
3. Reduced receiving and inspection costs through the elimination of the handling and processing of materials as well as the paperwork for many small-value items.
4. Reduced materials-handling and internal traffic costs because of fewer and easier loads.
5. Reduced stores costs because there are fewer receipts to handle, process to storage location, and record.
6. Reduced purchasing expediting costs because there are fewer calls for emergency items.
7. Reduced traffic costs because there is less premium freight and less need for emergency tracing.
8. Reduced accounts payable costs because there are fewer invoices to process.
9. Reduced stock-outs in stores operation through better-balanced inventory.
10. Reduced manufacturing cost through reduction of scrap and of the rework involved in the use of substitutes during supply shortages, plus more effective utilization of supervision, equipment, and production facilities.
11. Reduced costs for production control because the smoother flow of materials eliminates the need for schedule revisions.
12. Reduction in total average inventory, after the initial surge of large quantities of C items work down, and as more-concentrated purchasing generates reduced costs for A and B items.
13. General improvements in all involved departments because the elimination of much unnecessary work frees up time to concentrate on further improvements.

Minimum–Maximum

Another widely used method of inventory control involves the establishment of minimum and maximum inventory levels. Theoretically, the minimum inventory level could be zero. The last unit of inventory would be used up at the moment a new shipment arrives. The maximum inventory would then be the correct ordering quantity or EOQ.

In practice it would be unwise to follow this extreme policy, since it involves planning that is much too close for safety. In the minimum–maximum system a safety factor is established, which becomes the minimum point below which the inventory should not go under normal circumstances. The maximum inventory consists of this safety factor plus the correct ordering quantity.

The safety factor ensures against such contingencies as sudden increases in the rate of usage, failure to receive ordered materials on schedule, inbound traffic disruptions, vendor strikes, receipt of defective materials that cannot be used, and clerical errors in the records of bin balances. The size of this safety factor depends on the importance of the particular item to the process, the value of the investment, and the availability of substitutes on short notice.

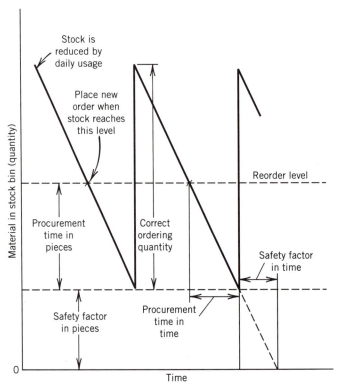

FIGURE 6-6. Graphic representation of safety stock and reorder principles.

A high safety factor is indicated for any item, the lack of which would cause production shutdowns.

Under the minimum–maximum system, the rate of use of an item is determined by past experience and forecasts, and the length of time required to obtain delivery is secured from the inventory control ledger and from studies of alternative sources of supply. An order minimum, or reorder point, is established. This point is equal to the monthly usage multiplied by the delivery time in months plus the safety factor. A graphic illustration of this concept is presented in Figure 6-6.

This system of inventory control provides a rather automatic procedure in that at a specified time, in terms of the rate of usage, a reorder is placed. This order quantity is predetermined in accordance with the EOQ procedures outlined earlier in this chapter. However, judgment is required in establishing the control and in making adjustments for changes in the size of the safety factor, usage rate, and price. No automatic system can guard against all possible changes.

This buffer system is not as popular as it once was, for it tends to encourage the maintenance of excess inventories. Most executives feel that present carrying costs of inventory make such excessive inventories unacceptable.

Just-in-Time System

Just-in-time purchasing emerges. It means the uninterrupted flow of 100 percent acceptable materials delivered on due dates at optimal costs 100 percent of the time.[18] The cited authors relate this definition to dozens of techniques including supplier certification, materials requirements planning (MRP), manufacturing resources planning (MRPII), bar coding, systems contracting, electronic data interchange (EDI), Deming's approach to quality, value analysis, and work simplification.

There is a trend toward smaller inventories to beat high holding costs and meet international competition. In this regard, the just-in-time (JIT) inventory technique made famous by the Japanese is gaining prominence in American industry. The industries making the most progress in inventory control are the industries most hard-pressed by international competition. The Japanese have an advantage over American manufacturers in that they do not have much concern about strikes that could cause shortage of materials, for their suppliers are usually nearby and under tight control.

The JIT production system reduces carrying costs by slashing production lot sizes, purchase lot sizes, and buffer stocks. This system also utilizes a

---

[18] Peter L. Grieco, Jr., Michael W. Gozzo, and Jerry W. Claunch, *Just-in-Time Purchasing: In Pursuit of Excellence* (Plantsville, CT: PT Publications, 1988), p. vii.

costing method that includes not only interest and material control costs, but also shop floor material and handling costs, work improvement costs, and uneven work load costs. JIT seeks to reduce setup and order-processing costs by cutting setup time* and by achieving frequent deliveries from nearby suppliers. The resulting reduction in optimal order quantity to the ideal of one unit will then reduce carrying costs, because storage space and storage expenses are reduced. But the JIT system will add ordering costs if an item is ordered more frequently.

Prudential-Bache's display of factory inventories ratios[19] shown in Figure 6-7, exhibit how well JIT has worked to control factory inventories. The just-in-time ratio of raw materials and supplies to work-in-progress inventories closely matches the finished goods to work-in-progress inventories through much of 1989 and 1990.

In three years the Square D Company Control Products Business (Asheville, North Carolina) reduced inventory by 40 percent. Its manufacturing philosophy closely resembles the JIT philosophy. The Square D plant developed in every employee the renewed commitment to produce the highest quality product and deliver it as promised. The plant reduced assembly operations, certified outside vendors, reduced lead times, and reduced or eliminated assembly inspections.[20]

Problems may short-circuit JIT purchasing benefits from lack of: supplier cooperation, top-management support, employee readiness and support, and support from design engineering personnel. Support problems may resolve themselves in an operating climate that encourages and promotes a consistently high level of incoming materials quality.[21]

This type of purchasing, production, and inventory control has the great advantage of locating and fixing quality problems immediately. Ingle makes the point:[22]

> It is just like large rocks under the water in a lake: If the water level is too high, one cannot see these rocks and avoid the danger. Similarly, if the inventory is small, the defects are spotted and corrected immediately. There is less scrap and rework, and quality improves dramatically.

Benefits from JIT mount up. When a Connecticut engine-brake manufacturer implemented JIT, it reduced manufacturing floor space by half, increased output 30 percent (with fewer employees), scored an 80 percent on-

---

Poke-yoka technique means "single minute exchange of dies (SMED)" for setup reduction.

[19] Prudential-Bache Securities Inc., *Strategy Weekly* (April 4, 1990), p. 9.

[20] "JIT at Square D Supports a Commitment to Quality," *Material Handling Engineering* (January 1990), pp. 40–43.

[21] "JIT Brings Problems and Solutions," *Purchasing World* (March 1990), pp. 47–50.

[22] Sud Ingle, *In Search of Perfection: How to Create/Maintain/Improve Quality* (Englewood Cliffs, NJ: Prentice Hall, 1985), p. 6.

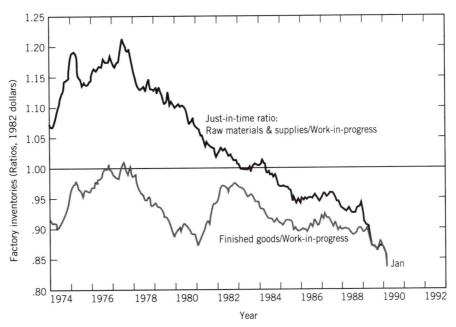

FIGURE 6-7. Factory inventory managers still making great ''just-in-time'' progress. (*Source:* Prudential-Bache Securities, *Strategy Weekly* (April 4, 1990), p. 9, with permission.

time record with customers, and reduced inventories 70 percent in dollar terms and 70 percent in rework costs.[23]

However, management has to change its relations with and attitudes towards its employees to realize the JIT approach's full potential. The traditional just-in-case approach often remains firmly entrenched in the minds of employees and managers and in their firms' procedures, supporting large inventories and safety stock. To unfreeze old habits to install JIT, some companies extend the scope of JIT implementation to cover not only raw materials and supplies, but also informational, financial, and human resources. Some firms report easier implementation when they couple JIT in terms of material as needed with total quality assurance and continuous quality improvement programs.[24]

The Norand Corporation (Cedar Rapids, Iowa) supplies portable computer systems. In 1986 it introduced JIT into its manufacturing process by using its own radio-frequency (RF) data transmission terminals and bar coding in its manufacturing resources planning (MRPII) system. The firm finds that JIT forces high-quality production because it eliminates safety

[23] ''Just in Time: Two Perspectives,'' *Industry Week* (September 18, 1989), pp. 26–29.
[24] ''Fitting Organizational Design to JIT,'' *National Productivity Review* (Winter, 1991–1992), pp. 97–104.

stocks and other inventory cushions. With the MRPII and bar coding systems in place, the addition of RF transmitters "turbo charges" their application, allowing for extensive reports on product quality and materials movement. Transmitters scan materials at the receiving dock, which automatically updates the quantity-in-stock number.[25]

Three main approaches for controlling the flow of materials into and through manufacturing organizations have developed over the past 30 years. Materials requirements planning (MRP), just-in-time (JIT), and optimized production technology (OPT) each can make a positive contribution to the organization's performance, complementing each other. In addition to these three approaches to controlling materials flow, bottleneck resource scheduling might constitute the first step in developing an integrated approach to materials control.[26]

JIT success must include carriers. Contracting between manufacturers and carriers must focus on the smaller inventory levels in JIT distribution. Manufacturers need to know the exact status of their materials at all times. Carriers need information on shipping volumes, transit time requirements, performance goals, special service needs, traffic flow patterns, equipment requirements, operating procedures, and tracking abilities.[27]

Oregon Cutting Systems (Portland) succeeded in changing from a traditional to a JIT manufacturing system. Within five years of adopting its JIT, strategy along with the interaction of employee involvement and total quality commitment, the firm reduced defects by 80 percent and scrap, sort, and rework by 50 percent. Activity-based costing shows promise of providing the company's service departments with many of the benefits that zero inventory and total quality commitment have brought to the manufacturing area.[28] The flexible mindset that integrates JIT in a positive way also remains open to other changes as well, such as accounting and even supplier relocation.

Many distribution channel members see JIT as a way to transfer the inventory burden to their suppliers and to get more favorable prices, while many suppliers see JIT as a quick fix and a way to guarantee a higher level of sales. However, when implemented correctly, JIT can reduce distribution channel conflict and improve channel cooperation. The channel leader must play a pivotal role in initiating JIT, educating channel members on the

---

[25] "RF Data Transmission Guides JIT Implementation," *Manufacturing Systems* (February 1992), pp. 20–24.

[26] "A Simulation Study of Bottleneck Scheduling, *International Journal of Production Economics* (February 1992), pp. 187–192. The reader will enjoy the novel *The Goal: A Process of Ongoing Improvement,* revised edition, by Eliyahu M. Goldratt and Jeff Cox (Croton-on-Hudson, NY: North River Press, 1986), that speaks so well to managers who struggle with bottleneck resources.

[27] "Achieving Inventory Reduction through the Use of Partner-Shipping," *Industrial Engineering* (May 1992), pp. 36–38.

[28] "Cutting Waste with JIT," *Management Accounting* (May 1992), pp. 28–32.

benefits of JIT, and minimizing the amount of conflict that may arise over changes that this system necessitates.[29]

Real estate counselors can use the JIT trend to their advantage by helping suppliers locate strategically. Decision factors for supplier location include:

1. Contract value
2. Contract volume
3. Frequency
4. Type of goods
5. Type of counterpart organization
6. Mode of interchange
7. Legal status
8. Time budget
9. Spatial dimensions

In addition to these characteristics, counselors need to know how JIT affects market segmentation regarding benefits, volume, status, and accessibility. Purchasing and materials managers stand to gain from supplier locations that actually keep inventory at a minimum, by viewing anything that does not add value directly to the product as a waste that managers must eliminate.[30]

Time management experts divide the product delivery cycle into five stages:

1. Book/bill cycle
2. Purchase/produce cycle
3. Manufacturing cycle
4. Design/develop cycle
5. Spec/source cycle

The implementation of JIT technologies traditionally has concentrated on reducing time consumed in the purchase/produce cycle and the manufacturing cycle. To reduce the design/develop cycle, firms try to develop products and manufacturing processes concurrently to collapse time and ensure manufacturability. Under simultaneous engineering, sourcing constitutes an integral part of the development process. Purchasing managers may shorten the spec/sourcing cycle by establishing price requirements as a part of this

---

[29] "The Effect of JIT on Distributors," *Industrial Marketing Management* (May 1992), pp. 145–149.
[30] "The Effects of Just-in-Time Inventory Procedures on the Locational Decisions of Suppliers," *Real Estate Issues* (Fall–Winter 1986), pp. 33–36.

phase. A product-oriented flow would likely reduce the book/bill cycle. The just-in-time (JIT) philosophy manages the most visible cycle time in the operation. Firms that reduce the consumption of time throughout the system will gain an advantage in time-based competition.[31]

Since 1987, several companies such as Honeywell and the Bose Corporation have implemented a new concept, JIT II, to improve the relationship between customer and supplier. The supplier provides full-time, on-site personnel who attend design engineering meetings involving their products and use the company's purchase orders to effect delivery. The supplier's representative within the purchasing function forges a link between the customer's planning department and the supplier's production plant. Partnering and concurrent engineering form integral parts of the JIT II concept.[32]

MATERIAL REQUIREMENTS PLANNING

Material requirements planning (MRP) is a computer-based planning and control system used to plan effectively and control internal production and materials flow. The objectives of the system are to minimize inventory and maintain delivery schedules. These steps are accomplished by using forecasts of needs, derived from a master plan and the bill of materials required, which can be used to project, release, and control orders.

The MRP system, as illustrated in Figure 6-8, is derived from four central elements: the bill of materials file containing product structure records; the inventory status file; the master production schedule; and the MRP package.

The bill of materials file contains information about every component of the end product, including its relationship to subassemblies and of finished products. The bill of materials for a given end product can be exploded and extended for the number of units to be produced. In the same manner, requirements for that particular part in all products can be summed up to obtain the total need during all operations. This explosion and aggregation process results in a great volume of data, which must be entered into a properly programmed computer to be processed for many different products.

Tied into the bill of materials file is the concept of dependent demand, whereby the demand for parts and components is directly dependent on the demand for some higher-order assembly or manufacturing step that is carried out in batches. This is the essential logic of MRP—that is, the fact that the demand for materials, parts, and components depends on the demand for an

[31] "Time-Based Competition: Challenges for Industrial Purchasing," *Industrial Management* (March–April 1992), pp. 31–32.
[32] "JIT II—More Than Just a Partnership," *NAPM Insights* (December 1992), p. 5.

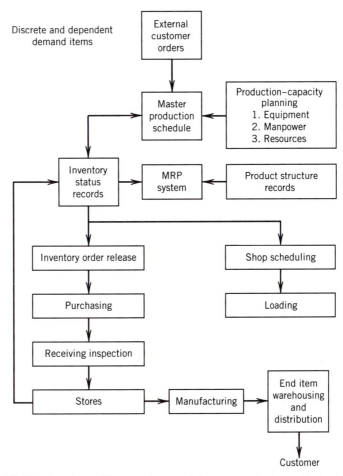

FIGURE 6-8. Flowchart for an MRP system, from receiving customers' orders to shipping to customers.

end product. If there is an independent demand for a part, the materials file indicates this fact in order to maintain the distinction between dependent and independent demand. If a demand is continuous and independent of the demand for any other item, a fixed order size (EOQ) system is utilized. The number of items that can be most efficiently controlled are substantially greater under an MRP system than under a fixed order size system.

The EOQ system discussed earlier can best be adopted for inventory items that have a continuous, uniform, and independent demand. Table 6-4 compares the fixed order size system and MRP systems. The second element in an MRP system is the inventory status file. This file contains a record of the actual inventory level and the on-order status of every item.

TABLE 6-4. Comparison of Fixed Order Size and MRP Systems

Fixed Order Size System (EOQ/EPQ)	MRP system
Part oriented (every item)	Product/component oriented
Replenish supply	Actual requirements
Independent demand	Dependent (derived) demand
Continuous item demand	Discrete/lumpy item demand
Random demand pattern	Known lumpy demand pattern
Continuous lead time demand	No lead time demand
Reorder point ordering signal	Time-phased ordering signal
Historical demand base	Future production base
Forecast all items	Forecast master schedule items
Quantity-based system	Quantity- and time-based system
Safety stock for all items	Safety stock for end items
End items/spare parts	Raw materials/work-in-process
Just-in-case	Just-in-time

Source: Richard J. Tersine, *Principles of Inventory and Materials Management,* 3rd ed. (New York: Elsevier Science Publishing Company, 1988), p. 353. Copyright 1988, by Elsevier Science Publishing Company, Inc. Reprinted by permission.

The master production schedule, the third element, drives the system by listing what end items are needed and when. Initially, this information is a forecast of sales, but as actual sales develop the master plan is altered to reflect actual sales. Changes are fed into the computer, which incorporates the revisions and prints out revised scheduling of purchases and work orders. The ability to replan and reschedule allows order priorities to be kept up to date. The master production schedule also indicates when finished products should be assembled in order to meet customer orders or finished-goods inventory requirements.

Finally, the material requirements planning package contains the necessary logic to operate the system. Once the system is tied together, MRP becomes a tool for planning and controlling a great number of products and parts that may be interrelated. MRP considers the current and planned quantities of parts and products in inventories in addition to the time element, in order to incorporate long- and short-run changes for interrelated parts and products.

All MRP has universally applicable elements for inventory control and can be most advantageously applied for items that have a discontinuous, nonuniform, and dependent demand, and for assembly, production, manufacturing, or fabrication operations. The MRP approach is not as appropriate for wholesalers, distributors, and retailers.

Properly implemented, MRP proves to be beneficial in areas such as keeping inventories low, reducing material shortages, eliminating paperwork, improving customer service, keeping priorities straight, giving early warnings about promising customers delivery dates, planning long-range operations, and planning and communicating with vendors.

MRP, as a specialized form of materials planning, requires accurate bills of materials, a well-developed realistic master plan, and inventory records that are updated on a continuing basis. Inaccurate files and records are a major reason that some MRP systems fail to live up to managerial expectations. It is also vital to have all necessary records in good database form for computer application.

Although extremely useful, MRP systems are expensive and complex and can severely strain vendor and interdepartmental relations. These problems are being addressed, however, as the system evolves.

MRP will greatly reduce inventory investment in dependent demand items. It removes the built-in risk of shortages that EOQ sometimes creates. Tersine writes:

> Independent demand inventory models when used for dependent demand items generate excessive inventory when it is not needed and insufficient inventory when it is needed.[33]

The United States has developed and implemented materials requirements planning (MRP) and bar coding systems, along with Japan's *kanban* concept. The standard *kanban* technique forms a cornerstone for JIT. It serves as a replenishing parts dispatching device, both internal to the plant and external to the supplier. By integrating MRP, bar coding, and *kanban,* a firm may significantly reduce the launching of purchase orders, the dependency on a stockroom, and the formal quality control inspection on commercial items. Proponents of the combined technique report it working well in both the job shop and the high-production environment.[34]

INVENTORY-MONITORING SYSTEMS

Essentially, either a continuous or a fixed monitoring system is employed in most inventory control procedures. The continuous system utilizes a periodic review of the stock of inventories and is accomplished by taking a periodic

[33] Richard J. Tersine, *Principles of Inventory and Materials Management,* 3rd ed. (New York: Elsevier Science Publishing Company), 1988, p. 353.
[34] "MRP, Bar Coding, Kanban Form System," *Purchasing World* (September 1989), pp. 61–67.

physical inventory and monitoring either computer or hand-calculated records of receipts and disbursements. The frequency of such inventory reviews depends on the importance and value of the specific items. The distinguishing feature of the continuous system is that it has a time orientation, rather than the quantity orientation of a fixed order size system.

The fixed order quantity system makes more direct use of EOQ levels than does a time-dictated review. The desired EOQ and safety stock is predetermined, and a ''flag'' is developed to indicate when a new order is necessary.

When usage draws down the inventory level on hand to the lead-time usage level, the reorder point ''flags'' reordering. The usage per day times the number of days of lead time equals the lead-time usage.

Cycle counting is an alternative to a periodic, physical count, which often requires an annual shutdown of the facility. Under cycle counting, a continuous count is made of selected items throughout the year. These items are selected via the ABC method. This system is useful in that there is no need for an annual physical inventory, no year-end surprises when errors are detected for the first time, and the validity of perpetual inventory records is improved.

The preceding techniques provide a variety of ways to control inventory according to the needs of the individual organization.

JIT versus MRP

JIT is a manual system that focuses on the past and serves to replenish what has been consumed. To implement it, the Japanese have adjusted their manufacturing functions and laborers' working methods to this system. Conversely, MRP is a computerized system that replenishes the supply network only if it is predicted that more will be needed. The two systems reflect a fundamental difference in manufacturing production requirements.

The Japanese are very adept at the mass production of goods requiring highly repetitive procedures. It is in this type of production that JIT is most effective. Most production methods in America, however, are geared toward a system that works well for specialized and made-to-stock items, as well as mass-produced items. Thus, MRP appears to be more suited to American manufacturing systems than JIT.

Manufacturing resource planning (MRP II) adds the financial function to MRP. Managers can know the accounts payables to vendors by studying MRP timing of purchase orders and their due dates. The schedules of outputs from the MRP system can provide information about the quantity and timing of materials delivered to customers and the resulting receivables.

Financial managers as a general rule do not accept MRP II as sufficiently accurate on which to base the quantity and timing of cash requirements.

OPPORTUNITIES FOR MECHANIZATION

During the past two decades great strides have been made in the use of electronic data processing equipment in inventory control systems. Data processing is still used most commonly in companies that have computerized control systems and to a lesser degree in companies that have implemented a MRP system.

Lipton Corporation's Ragu Spaghetti Sauce plant in Peterborough, Ontario utilizes its personal computer-based system for distribution requirements planning (DRP) and materials requirements planning (MRP). The system has reduced raw materials inventory 35 percent and finished goods inventories 8 percent in less than a year. Lipton uses modules for system control, bill of material, inventory control, MRP, manufacturing order management, purchasing, and database querying.[35]

The greatest advantage of such equipment, for inventory control purposes, is that it provides the possibility of reducing the investment in inventory.

Electronic equipment allows considerable time to be saved in determining inventory status; this reduces the size of the reserve or safety element in the inventory. Computer use can also help reduce surplus on hand, as it did for Bell Canada.

Until 1989, Canada's largest telephone company, Bell Canada, experienced problems in managing its $100 million worth of internal telecommunications resources. Any of the company's 20,000 Quebec employees would spend days triggering a paperwork process of requests for a new phone or data terminal. Then, in 1989, Bell Canada's new system TACTIQ automated and streamlined the old process, saving the company $400,000 a year. Further automation follows, to encompass budgeting, inventory control, and accounting functions.[36]

There are many opportunities, in the areas of quantity determination and inventory control, for the application of data processing equipment:

Forecasting usage rates

Measuring deviation from forecast of usage

Calculating economic order quantities

Calculating order points with the possibility of changing forecasts, deviation, and dollars of investment

[35] "PC-Based MRP, DRP Help Lipton Cut Inventories," *Modern Materials Handling* (February 1989), pp. 86–88.

[36] "A New TACTIQ for Bell Canada, *Telephone Engineer & Management* (February 1, 1990), pp. 49–50.

Scheduling and flagging overdue orders

Calculating physical inventory balances on hand, on order, and assigned

ABC inventory analysis

CHAPTER SUMMARY

Inventory-planning techniques suffer from a variety of difficulties such as vendor relations, lead-time variability, variable demand, and improper inventory record-keeping methods. Some of the current techniques do not satisfactorily deal with these difficulties. Under a reorder point system an order for a predetermined quantity is placed when a certain inventory level is reached; this system assumes continuous demand with fixed lead times. The EOQ system is also of questionable value because it also assumes constant demand and does not relate inventory control to other factors of production such as labor scheduling and lead time variations. The just-in-time (JIT) system deals well with minimizing lead times and improving vendor relations but requires the firm to sacrifice some of its independence. Thus, the firm can become locked into long-term arrangements. Moreover, the Japanese JIT system may not be as well suited to American manufacturing methods as was once thought. Finally, although extremely useful, MRP systems are expensive and complex and can severely strain interdepartmental relations.

Discussion Questions

1. In calculating economic order quantities, should the average cost or the incremental cost per order be used?
2. What is the basic principle of the relationship of order costs to carrying charges embodied in the economic order quantity?
3. Of what do MRO items mainly consist?
4. State the formula for the economic order quantity.
5. How do quantity discounts affect purchasing effectiveness?
6. What factors must be considered by a purchasing agent in modifying EOQ?
7. What are the factors that influence the size of the safety factor to be used in setting minimum–maximum inventory levels?
8. Define inventory control.
9. Discuss the four major reasons for maintenance of sound inventory control procedures.
10. What data are normally included on an inventory ledger form?
11. What is materials requirements planning?

Suggested Cases

Gamma Corporation

Gorman Products, Inc.

Exercises

1. Snow Valley Distributing Company has a total of 30 different classes of materials valued as follows. Using ABC Analysis, assign the 30 classes by numbers to executive action, middle management, and clerical-computer control.

Class 1	16983	Class 9	21155	Class 17	12986	Class 25	13174
Class 2	9588	Class 10	2300	Class 18	865	Class 26	16348
Class 3	20775	Class 11	10400	Class 19	13243	Class 27	17530
Class 4	1337	Class 12	22759	Class 20	193	Class 28	6562
Class 5	16779	Class 13	1187	Class 21	1672	Class 29	18403
Class 6	9586	Class 14	8296	Class 22	17170	Class 30	18911
Class 7	10438	Class 15	15816	Class 23	25000		
Class 8	14725	Class 16	23368	Class 24	23261		

2. Flowers Calendar Company buys paper matches for advertising distribution throughout the year. Annual demand amounts to 16,000 boxes of 24, ordering cost per order $40, carrying charge per box per year 0.30, delivered cost $3.50 per box. A recent quotation came in at $3 per box, minimum lot size 1200 boxes. Should the buyer take the discount? How often should the buyer place an order and in what quantity? What total annual inventory costs does the buyer encounter?

3. Given an order quantity of 100 units at a unit price of $100 each, what annual usage would you expect if acquisition costs $30 per order and inventory carrying charge amounts to 20 percent?

4. Becky's Bakery ships 25,000 loaves of french bread throughout the year to a New Orleans steamboat company on the Mississippi River. The customer wants steady deliveries and freezes loaves in excess of immediate need. Delivered cost per loaf $1; $20 to place the order, and 25 percent of average inventory valuation to carry inventory. Figure the optimum number of orders a year. Why not negotiate a contract?

5. An auto parts distributor offers Hillary a $0.50 discount if she will sign a one-year contract for a specialized part B-16. She sells 16,000 a year at a constant rate. She figures acquisition cost at $40 and carrying charge at 30 percent on the $3.50 item, delivered and before discount. How much would she benefit monthly by signing the contract?

=7

Managing Quality

Total quality has created the most lasting change in our culture and our approach to business that I've seen in 27 years with Procter & Gamble. . . . Quality is seen by 98 percent of our people as absolutely essential to our success. . . . During the past three years, Procter & Gamble's return on equity increased by 50 percent—to 21 percent—and profits have doubled. There are many reasons for these results, but I would list total quality management as among the three most important factors.*

CHAPTER CONTENTS

The just-in-time (JIT) movement created most of the gains made in quality by U.S. firms during the 1980s. Motorola increased quality dramatically while saving more than $250 million annually on quality-control costs since implementing JIT.[1]

Estimates suggest that defective purchased materials causes 50 to 70 percent of a company's quality nonconformances. To counteract defects, some companies hold that purchasing and engineering organizations should

---

Source: John Pepper, Procter & Gamble Company president, 1990
[1] "JIT in the '90s: Zeroing in on Leadtimes," *Purchasing* (September 12, 1991), pp. 54–57.

develop a partnership, beginning with the formulation of the initial acquisition strategies and contracting methodologies, continuing through the placement of the order and successful delivery of quality products. When successful, such a purchasing–engineering partnership exerts a pronounced influence on the finished product's quality, cost, and delivery.[2]

The so-called principle of "good enough" disturbs engineers who want fabricated items to last forever. But the purchasing manager's realistic view of quality focuses on determining the specific threshold of acceptable quality that works. Buying at or slightly above this quality level (to allow for uncontrollables) provides the firm with the needed material, conserves environmental resources by not overspecifying quality, and controls cost in a day when developing technology renders many of yesterday's product designs obsolete.

The appropriate quality of materials and components is a function of use. It is a relatively common error to specify a quality level that is higher than necessary for the end product being produced. It is as much an error to provide too high a level of quality and incur the resulting cost premiums as to use too poor a quality for a given application. In more precise terms, quality expresses the measured properties, conditions, or characteristics of a product or process. These are usually stated in terms of grades, classes, or specifications and are determined by how the product or process is to be used.

A simple example will illustrate the meaning of the term quality as it is used by purchasing personnel. When buying lumber for crating purposes, the purchaser could choose many grades that would be of straight grain and free from defects, blemishes, knotholes, and similar imperfections. Such lumber, however, would not be the best quality for crating. Instead, purchasing should buy a grade of lumber that would be considered low quality by the general public, although such lumber is suitable for the intended purpose. This concept of suitability must be kept clearly in mind when considering quality.

In the supplier evaluation plans outlined in Chapter 5, quality is one evaluation criterion. In this chapter three more basic quality considerations are discussed: (1) determining the right quality for a given purpose; (2) defining this quality in a way that is clearly understood by both buyer and seller; and (3) establishing methods of measuring quality to ensure that goods received conform to the specified quality.

Quality cannot be inspected into a product; the desired quality of purchased material must be in the material when it arrives. Careful considerations must be given to the exact quality desired, the development of adequate descriptions or specifications of that quality, clear communication with the supplier, and the application of a suitable inspection program.

---

[2] "Statement of Values—Purchasing's Role in Quality," *AACE Transactions* (1991), pp. A4(1)–A4(5).

TOTAL QUALITY MANAGEMENT

Many companies speak of adopting strategies for total quality management (TQM), but few have accomplished the goal so far. However, managers talk more and more of installing the TQM system, if for no other reason than to boast that they have installed the system.

TQM focuses on the customer and his or her needs. For the purchasing function, the customer may consist of the person or department that initiates the purchase requisition or who ultimately uses the goods and services that the purchaser obtains. The purchaser continually reviews the methods, procedures, and techniques that result in a purchase, in order to improve continually the purchasing function. This concept of continuous improvement leads to better service, better relations among people, lower cost, faster delivery, fewer delays and rejects, and greater financial returns. Returns in profits and market share measure the ultimate success of TQM.

Federal Express Corporation's philosophy simply states: Find out what the customers want and give it to them. As the human resources vice president said, "We try to communicate to our people that the purpose of a business is to get and keep customers. . . . Our corporate philosophy statement—People, Service, Profit."[3]

Initiating Quality

How is the quest for quality initiated? Ingle explains that the organizational quality improvement process can be implemented using systematic statistical problem-solving methods, basic industrial statistics for nonstatisticians (statistical process control), and vendor quality control.[4]

The European quality manager for Dow-Corning, Ltd., Brussels, recounts that the corporation's total quality management vision for overseas operations seeks to control the corporate culture, while recognizing the needs and requirements of customers and employees. Thus, the firm articulates three objectives:

1. To be the preferred supplier of customers we choose to work with.
2. To see that all employees understand what their job is and where it fits into the process.
3. To halve our failure costs.[5]

---

[3] "Federal Express Corporation," *Baldrige Winners on World-Class Quality,* The Conference Board Report No. 990, 1992, p. 17.

[4] Sud Ingle, *In Search of Perfection: How to Create/Maintain/Improve Quality* (Englewood Cliffs, NJ: Prentice Hall, 1985).

[5] John Evans, "A Three-Pillared Approach to Quality Management," *Managing Globally: Key Perspectives,* Frank Caropreso, ed. (New York: The Conference Board, Report No. 972, 1991), p. 30.

How is process quality measured? Harrington describes excellence indicators for functional areas.[6] For purchasing, he designates premium freight cost, down-time because of parts shortages, number of parts declared off-specifications to keep lines going, cycle time from start of purchase request until items in house, and excess inventory.

Participation

Companies that stand most ready for TQM regard participative management as a primary philosophy for making the best use of people. Total quality management expands that philosophy to encompass people, process, and product.

Cound states that "quality is a journey, not a destination."[7] He emphasizes the evolving authority that attracts followers to perform. Cound examines approaches and methods that create a motivational atmosphere that improves quality and reliability.

Torrington Company, a division of Ingersoll-Rand, has implemented a total quality management program that requires supplier participation.[8]

The general manager of a major aluminum foil company states that the development of TQM means getting the individuals in each department to set and strive for the corporation's continuous quality objectives, with better definitions of the specifics of corporate total management programs for both buyers and sellers.[9]

The Atlantic City, New Jersey Medical Center formed the Atlantic Alliance, a partnership with four prominent vendors that has sought to redesign the operational system linking the hospital to its vendors. Because many vendors have involved themselves in total quality management much longer than most hospitals, vendors can offer experience about what has worked in quality improvement as well as what has not worked. For example, Baton Rouge Louisiana General Medical Center collects data on the accuracy of supply shipments, verifying what it receives, and eventually eliminating the extensive receiving process and the paperwork involved with it.[10]

Management expert Peter Drucker states that obtaining major productivity gains in production-type service work usually requires contracting it out to a company that has no other business, understands this work, respects

[6] H. J. Harrington, *The Improvement Process: How America's Leading Companies Improve Quality* (New York: McGraw-Hill, 1987), p. 43.

[7] Dana M. Cound, *A Leader's Journey to Quality* (Milwaukee: ASQC Quality Press, 1992), p. 171.

[8] "Professional Profile: Richard W. Klingerman of Torrington Co.," *Purchasing* (June 6, 1991), p. 45.

[9] "Aluminum Roundtable," *Purchasing* (February 6, 1992), pp. 54–57.

[10] "TQM Shifts Hospital–Vendor Focus to Total Value, Productivity, *Hospitals* (July 5, 1992), pp. 114–117.

it, and offers advancement opportunities for low-skilled workers. In participating in the TQM process, the contract manager must work with their people and with other departments to play a role in patient/client/customer satisfaction on an interpersonal level.[11]

How do service firms improve their quality? Much of the success comes from working with their employees since the employees connect with the customers. Many service firms:

1. Hire right
2. Train their employees
3. Empower employees
4. Acquire the right technology and equipment to ensure that employees have the best tools to service customers.

The service industry uses customer retention and satisfaction as its yardstick for quality.[12]

The Chemical Manufacturers Association (CMA) designed a continuous improvement program for its members, based on the Malcolm Baldrige National Quality Award criteria. Chemical companies that adopt the CMA criteria as a means to assess both their internal operations and their suppliers' external operations may develop customer–supplier partnerships. Remaining competitive globally constitutes a primary objective of the U.S. chemical industry.[13]

From her headquarters office, Humana's director of service excellence guides the service assurance program throughout their nationwide operations. Local service assurance managers in insurance markets work on organizational quality improvement with quality improvement teams. Service assurance managers monitor the company's performance against customer requirements. They evaluate all aspects of service from the point of sale to the delivery point of patient care. Trend analysis checks the organization's continuous quality improvement process.

Origins

Historically, quality management began in the 1950s. After World War II, Japan's industrial system began rebuilding after its virtual total destruction. Moreover, Japan had to change its reputation for cheap imitation products.

---

[11] "Hospitals Look to Hospitality Service Firms to Meet TQM Goals," *Hospitals* (May 20, 1992), pp. 56–58.

[12] "TQM Gains Ground in Service Firms," *NAPM Insights* (December 1992), p. 41.

[13] "Chemical Industry Group Introduces New System for Quality Management," *Chemical and Engineering News* (December 7, 1992), p. 17.

The civil communications section of the occupation forces provided the first assistance in the form of three American engineers. They then had the good fortune to gain the services of Joseph Juran and Dr. E. Edwards Deming, two stalwarts in the field of quality management. Under their leadership, from 1951 to 1954, quality control developed rapidly in principal Japanese plants and became a major theme in Japanese management philosophy. By 1960, quality control had become a national preoccupation.[14]

Deming recognized the lack of awareness of product quality at all levels of Japanese management. He began promoting the introduction of quality control procedures in particular and an improved quality awareness in general. Deming who had followed the work of Walter A. Shewart of Bell Laboratories joined the U.S. War Department in 1941 where he taught quality control techniques as part of a national defense effort.

Juran's early empirical observations in quality control led him to write in the first edition of the *Quality Control Handbook* (1951):

> There is widespread feeling. . .that the principle cause of defects is operator carelessness or indifference. This is dead wrong. Over 80 percent of failures to meet specifications are, in the author's experience, for reasons not related to operators at all.[15]

In 1964, Juran further contributed by distinguishing between control and breakthrough in his book *Managerial Breakthrough.* He defined control as maintaining the status quo and preventing adverse changes. He specified breakthrough as the change to a new and more desirable situation.

In 1979, Philip Crosby of the International Telephone and Telegraph Company in the United States produced *Quality is Free,* recognizing that firms do not inspect quality into their products but invest quality through the work of their operators. He set up a method for measuring the status of a company's quality improvement process and showed the positive steps to take to evaluate and improve it.

Japanese management heard the messages and led Japanese manufacture to new heights of quality and reliability. The high quality of Japanese cars spurred U.S. industry just at a time—1980—when U.S. automakers entered a disastrous period. Japanese and British TQM successes propelled U.S. interests in gaining similar attainment for buyers and suppliers alike. Questionnaire data obtained from 300 United Kingdom-based suppliers to three major customers in the automotive industry and fieldwork carried out in buyer and supplier organizations identified the main barriers that hinder the development of an effective buyer–supplier relationship in quality man-

---

[14] Barrie G. Dale and John S. Oakland, *Quality Improvement through Standards* (Cheltenham, England: Stanley Thornes, 1991), p. 7.
[15] Ibid., p. 4.

agement. The barriers include poor communication and feedback, supplier complacency, buyers having poorly defined and unstructured quality improvement programs, the creditability of buyers as perceived by their suppliers, and misconceptions regarding purchasing power.[16]

Vigorous as ever, Deming advises a transformation of the American style of management. ''American Industry has just gotten used to burning toast and scraping it.'' Deming continues:[17]

> This is what I told the Japanese in 1950. If you improve your quality you improve your productivity automatically—it's a chain reaction. You do this by lowering waste, lowering restarts, lowering rework. When this finally happens you then can capture markets with higher quality, lower cost of goods and services. This will allow you to stay in business and provide more jobs. So simple. . . .

> American management doesn't want to step out and take a chance to help improve things. It's easier to do nothing. We can no longer take this route. Management at all levels must now take ownership of the process and in one small step at a time act to improve it. I think we are closer to a now or never situation than ever before. Time is running out![18]

At Deming's former Department of Defense, a commission studied defense management. The United States responded positively to the call for quality. As an inducement to quality control, Congress created the Malcolm Baldrige National Quality Award in 1987.

The Baldrige Award

The National Institute of Standards and Technology administers the award. To apply, a large company must pay a fee of $2500 and submit answers to 133 questions on a 75-page questionnaire. A small company pays $1000 and answers a 50-page questionnaire. A panel of nine judges reviews application scores and examiners' reports and submit their choices to the U.S. Secretary of Commerce.[19] Table 7-1 lists recipients of the Baldrige Award.

Examiners assess seven primary criteria: leadership, quality information and analysis, strategic quality planning, human resource utilization, quality

---

[16] ''The Buyer–Supplier Relationship in Total Quality Management,'' *Journal of Purchasing and Materials Management* (Summer 1989), pp. 10–19.

[17] Donald A. Stratton, *An Approach to Quality Improvement That Works,* 2nd ed. (Milwaukee: ASQC Quality Press, 1991), p. 4.

[18] Ibid., p. 126.

[19] Samuel C. Certo, *Modern Management: Quality, Ethics, and the Global Environment,* 5th ed. (Boston: Allyn & Bacon, 1991), p. 47.

**TABLE 7-1. Malcolm Baldrige National
Quality Award Recipients**

1991
   Solectron Corp. (manufacturing company)
   Zytec Corp. (manufacturing company)
   Marlow Industries (small business)
1990
   Cadillac Motor Car Division of GM (manufacturing company)
   IBM Rochester (manufacturing company)
   Federal Express Corp. (service company)
   Wallace Co. (small business)
1989
   Milliken & Company (manufacturing company)
   Xerox Corp., Business Products & Systems (manufacturing company)
1988
   Motorola Inc. (manufacturing company)
   Nuclear Fuel Division of Westinghouse Electric Corp.
      (manufacturing company)
   Globe Metallurgical Inc. (small business)

assurance of products and services, quality results (including supplier quality improvement), and customer satisfaction.[20]

Intel Corporation (California) uses the Baldrige criteria to measure quality awareness and performance throughout its purchasing and materials system. The maker of microcomputer components uses the 32 criteria grouped into the seven broad categories stated above as part of an overall corporate quality continuous improvement benchmarking process.[21]

The Baldrige Award has a Japanese counterpart—the Deming Prize. In 1951 the Japanese Union of Scientists and Engineers established this prize to recognize organizations that demonstrate a successful company-wide quality control program.

Benchmarking

Environmental analysis involves determining the primary opportunities and threats that the organization faces in its operating environment. Searching the environment for ways to improve product quality, a firm may undertake

---

[20] Richard J. Pierce, *Leadership, Perspective, and Restructuring for Total Quality* (Milwaukee: ACQC Quality Press, 1991), pp. 153–154.
[21] "How Do You Measure Purchasing's Quality?" *Purchasing* (January 16, 1992), pp. 85–93.

benchmarking studies of its competitors products, taking them apart piece-by-piece, to see how they work. Benchmarking's ultimate aim seeks to identify how to improve on the quality and/or price of each component. It serves as one criterion for the Malcolm Baldrige National Quality Award.

Organizational design benefits from using layer and span benchmarks to manage structure.[22] Traditional operations improvement programs differ from benchmarking, which consists of a continuous process of measuring parts, services, prices, and practices against competitors or those companies known as the best in the business.[23]

The benchmarking process helps a manager to know himself or herself, understand the competition, define the best processes, and integrate them into one's own organization. The effort supports the business process improvement concept to develop world-class goals.[24]

Purchasing and materials managers may utilize purchasing benchmarks reported for over 30 industries by the Center for Advanced Purchasing Studies, associated with the National Association of Purchasing Management. A December 1992 report on construction/engineering industry benchmarks states that 83 percent of the 12 leading firms in those industries have TQM programs.[25]

Total Quality Service

The techniques of total quality management change the way the service industry measures and improves quality. TQM simultaneously integrates customer-oriented service into both the manufacturing and service sectors. The front-line employees receive, along with training, reward and recognition that helps employees function well in the demanding TQM environment.[26]

Total quality service exists in a family of interrelated processes for assessing, defining, and improving service quality. Customer service means relating to the customer and going the extra mile to make the relationship special and valued.[27]

After a period of hesitation, American companies generally move into

[22] Allen Janger, *Measuring Managerial Layers and Spans* (New York: The Conference Board Research Bulletin, No. 237, 1989), p. 9.

[23] Kathleen H.J. Liebfried and C.J. McNair, *Benchmarking: A Tool for Continuous Improvement* (New York: HarperCollins, 1992), pp. 34–37.

[24] H.J. Harrington, *Business Process Improvement: The Breakthrough Strategy for Total Quality, Productivity, and Competitiveness* (New York: McGraw-Hill, 1991), p. 218.

[25] "Construction/Engineering Industry Benchmarks," *NAPM Insights* (December 1992), pp. 9, 29.

[26] "Total Quality Management Cuts a Broad Swath—Through Manufacturing and Beyond," *Organizational Dynamics* (Spring 1992), pp. 16–28.

[27] "Total Quality Service," *Executive Excellence* (July 1991), pp. 18–19.

customer-oriented management. U.S. businesses realize that to stay ahead in today's competitive marketplace and to gain customer loyalty they must make customer satisfaction their first priority. This new focus amplifies the need for ways to measure service worker activity. A vast range of service-oriented issues that require measuring include: (1) whether the company meets customer expectations, (2) whether knowledgeable, courteous, and efficient frontline representatives face the customers, and (3) whether they can resolve customers' complaints. Discovering customer needs constitutes the first step in service-conscious measurement. German grocer, now management consultant, Karl Albrecht believes in asking customers directly by means of focus groups, one-on-one and telephone interviews, and written surveys.[28] He asserts that because customers can make or break a business, firms must operate from the basis that every complaint has a valid point, even if the reason for the complaint may not stand.[29] "The customer is always right."

Alternatives Federal Credit Union (Ithaca, New York) developed a policy that allows employees to grasp the compensation rules and instills in new employees a sense of pride in the credit union and a commitment to total quality service. The liberal compensation policy induces credit union employers to understand that by providing slightly more than the market rate of pay they can easily measure and quantify the extra benefit. Whereas, if employees earn less than the market rate, they are demotivated and management has difficulty measuring what the credit union loses in turnover costs and member service.[30]

Total quality service earns wide recognition. Federal Express Corporation won the coveted Malcolm Baldrige National Quality Award for 1990. Revenues totaled $7 billion from its revolutionary overnight and second-day delivery service. A total of 90,000 employees at 1650 sites processed 1.5 million shipments daily that year. The firm replaced its old measure of quality performance—percent of on-time deliveries—with a comprehensive 12-component index that described how its customers viewed its performance. Federal Express employed a well-developed management evaluation system involving employee surveys, analysis of each work group's results by the work group's manager, and a discussion between the manager and the work group to develop written action plans for the manager to improve and become more effective.[31]

The Ritz-Carlton Hotel Company won the Baldrige Award in 1992. This complex service business integrated a comprehensive service quality

---

[28] "A Total-Quality Approach to Customer Service," *Incentive* (September 1990), pp. 68–76.

[29] "Customer Service Equals Profits," *Executive Speeches* (March 1989), pp. 6–8.

[30] "Liberal Compensation Combats Turnover," *Credit Union Magazine* (April 1992), pp. 42–44.

[31] Malcolm Baldrige National Quality Award announcements, undated.

program into the firm's marketing objectives. The program included participatory executive leadership, thorough information management, and a trained workforce committed ''to move heaven and earth'' in pursuit of customer satisfaction.[32]

QUALITY STANDARDS

The systematic control of quality and development of standards had their inception with the industrial revolution and the mass-production techniques that accompanied it. Before that time, it was a relatively simple matter for a single worker or a small group such as a guild to control quality by firsthand inspection of materials as the articles were being made. With the industrial revolution came the spread of machines, factories, and enterprises throughout the world, and the change of emphasis from hand methods to machine methods made it necessary to manufacture materials without the artisan's personal observation and inspection. Means of describing products precisely had to be devised, and this led to the use of samples, brands, and specifications to illustrate the quality of products.

Mass production had its origin when Eli Whitney discovered that he had contracted to deliver 12,000 muskets to the army in an impossibly short time. He found that the only way of meeting his contract would be to make all the components sufficiently interchangeable. This decision in effect created the assembly line and with it mass production became possible, placing new emphasis on rigid inspection, control, and—perhaps most important—standardization of quality.

Control of quality was no longer accomplished principally through visual inspection of raw materials and finished product. This new development opened up a broad new field to handle the sorting, gauging, metering, and various other procedures to assure that the materials and component parts conformed to preestablished standards. Because process materials needed to have a consistent quality, standards describing the chemical and physical characteristics that the buyer would accept—size, color, hardness, weight, finish, and purity—were established.

Standardization has continued to play an important role in advancing America's technical progress. It has substituted common measurement methods for rule-of-thumb criteria, and so parts made in Illinois are interchangeable with those produced in New York, and buyers have an economical means of specifying and measuring levels of quality without excessive cost.

[32] Ibid.

The Proper Quality Trade-offs

An important quality consideration is how much quality is enough. Or, put another way, ''How suitable is the quality with respect to the intended use of the product?'' These questions point up important trade-offs between the level of quality and price for any given use. For example, if a chair is built strong enough to support a 300-pound man (which is probably more than strong enough), it makes little sense to incur the extra expense and build it to support a 500-pound man. People of these sizes are exception, not the rule. On the other hand, when the situation is critical, or a matter of life and death, as it often is in hospitals, it is imperative that the equipment be of the highest quality regardless of price. Then a consideration of what is the ''best buy'' places highest quality well ahead of price. Thus, in the price–quality situation, trade-off is important and should govern the purchasing decision.

Standards Defined

A standard is a description of an acceptable level of quality, design, and composition of a particular item that has evolved through the study and experience of organizations, sometimes in cooperation with governmental agencies.

Commercial standards are compiled by the Department of Commerce, with the National Bureau of Standards as the guiding agency. Other groups develop their own standards or develop them jointly with professional engineering or testing associations.[33] Similar work is carried on at the international level in cooperation with the International Standards Association and with agencies of the United Nations.

Standards are widely publicized and are readily available to any buyer who wants to use them or to any supplier who needs them to develop a quotation. Most buyers find that they can adapt industry or government standards to their use.

---

[33] Some of these are the American Society for Testing Materials, the American Society of Mechanical Engineers, the Society of Automotive Engineers, the Institute of Electrical and Electronic Engineers, the Mining and Metallurgical Society of America, the Underwriters Laboratories, the National Safety Council, the Canadian Standards Association, Standards Engineering Society, and the Institute of Scrap Recycling Industries (Waste).

ISO 9000

The Baldrige Award has a limited appeal throughout American industry. A more global indicator of high-level quality is ISO 9000 registration. The Switzerland-based International Organization for Standardization administers the certification of companies for quality management and assurance. The standards of procedures that bring about proven results gain ever-widening acceptance as a type of "third-party" certifier that buyers can trust.

ISO 9000 registration helps on two special occasions: (1) when a company lacks the resources to put together its own elaborate supplier-quality program—ISO 9000 assures the buyer that the supplier has put in place a product quality system that reaches those standards, and (2) when a company desires quality from a nonstrategic supplier whose product doesn't affect its own product quality.[34]

Several DuPont plants already have succeeded in attaining the ISO 9000 standard, strongly emphasizing management's commitment and suggesting that everyone in the company knows the quality process.[35]

Union Carbide's "Gulf Coast Pipeline" received the country's and the world's first recognition for compliance with the International Standards Organization's quality standards criteria for transportation and distribution of ethylene product. The ISO 9002 registration resulted from the year-long efforts of a quality improvement team. The cross-functional team included representatives from purchasing, product scheduling, pipeline operations, product analysis, metering, drafting, and several maintenance support groups. Such registration becomes an essential tool for doing business with the European Community.[36]

Quality audits make excessive drains on the resources of smaller companies. For instance, a Midwest electronics company experienced 21 different audits, causing an inordinate amount of digging and presentation of quality data. Suppliers need to limit the endless quality audits and, as a consequence, will select customers who cooperate with them in recognizing ISO 9000 registration.[37]

During the 1980s the ISO developed a series of five standards (ISO 9000–9004) to document, implement, and demonstrate quality assurance systems. The standards do not refer to specific products and services, nor do

---

[34] "Is Baldrige the Right Way to Go?" *Purchasing* (January 16, 1992), pp. 79, 81.
[35] "Prepping for ISO 9000," ibid. (June 18, 1992), p. 29.
[36] "ISO Registration for Pipeline," *UC World* (Winter, 1992), p. 7.
[37] "World-Class Customers," *NAPM Insights* (May 1992), p. 8.

they guarantee that a manufacturer produces "quality" products. They apply to the systems that produce them.

Under ISO 9000, a company assures that it has a quality system in place to meet those standards. A mix of internal and external audits verifies the quality system. Maintenance audits regularly ensure that the firm's quality system stays on target. A registrar or lead assessor from outside the company conducts the audits. The assessor qualifies for the task by means of work experience, a five-day course, and a four-hour examination. The American National Standards Institute (ANSI) and the Registrar Accreditation Board (RAB) jointly direct the accrediting of U.S. assessors or registrars.

ISO 9000 applies to purchasing activity as well as to the actual production process. An audit documents and verifies that the purchasing function (1) assures that purchased products conform to specific requirements, by inspection and test, and (2) assesses suppliers and subcontractors. American companies may find help on ISO 9000 from The U.S. Department of Commerce's Single Internal Market Information Service (SIMIS), the American Society for Quality Control (ASQC), the American National Standards Institute (ANSI), and the National Institute of Standards and Technology (NIST).[38]

ISO 9000 registration becomes important especially in Europe as a marketing tool. Some companies require suppliers to attest that they have an approved quality system in place as a condition for purchase. Purchasers pressure for ISO 9000 registration in aerospace, automobiles, electronic components, measuring and testing instruments, and chemicals.

Experts estimate that more than 20,000 companies from European Community countries have registered under ISO 9000, the greatest number from the United Kingdom where more than 16,000 businesses have registered to the standards. This number encompasses 80 percent of the largest employers—payrolls of over 1000. In the service industry, ISO 9000 registration has been given to car dealers, garages, hospitals, legal practices, transportation companies, warehousing, and computer services.[39] If firms presently do business with the EC, their customers may soon direct them to register, as a commitment to quality and a promotion of customer confidence.

A paltry 621 U.S. companies have registered as of December 1992.[40] Preparing for registration can take as long as two years and can cost into the hundreds of thousands of dollars. However, the firm that uses total quality

[38] "ISO 9000 and the European Community," *NAPM Insights* (August 1992), pp. 22–23.
[39] "ISO 9000: Outside U.S. Borders: Status and Trends," *NAPM Insight* (November 1992), pp. 26–27.
[40] "U.S. Firms Lag in Meeting Global Quality Standards," *Marketing News* (February 15, 1993), pp. 1, 6.

management may find that ISO registration contains far simpler procedures than some of the more technical aspects of TQM.

The registration process for UNC Manufacturing Technology, a single-site facility with 40 employees, took about eight months. The firm had operated for over 35 years as a military specification for quality program requirements house with the vast majority of documentation and systems that the ISO 9000 system requires. Its procurement manager said, "The small operation without a well-developed purchasing system requires considerably more effort to achieve registration."[41] The J. E. Baker Company took about 16 months to achieve registration at its 500-employee site in York, Pennsylvania. DuPont has registered more than 100 of its sites and plants in Europe, and more than a dozen domestically. It estimates that it cost $250,000 and nine months to certify one European site employing 300 workers. However, payback from registering turns up: on-time-delivery increased from 70 percent to 90 percent in one plant, and at another, cycle time decreased from 15 days to 1.5 days.[42]

More than 50 countries around the world officially recognize the ISO 9000 series that ISO first published in 1987 under the title, *ISO 9000 Quality Management and Quality Assurance Standard Series.* As countries adopt the ISO 9000 series, they develop their own nationalized version and assign a number that relates to their own standards. A few examples follow.[43]

United Kingdom	BS 5750
Hungary	MI 18990
Denmark	DS/EN29000
European Community	EN29000
United States	ANSI/ASQC Q90-1987 series

America's Version

America's version consists of five documents. Q90 (ISO 9000) provides guidelines and definitions, an overview of the standard, its concepts, and a "road map" to the other standards. Q91 (ISO 9001) provides a quality assurance model for assuring conformance in design, development, production, installation, and servicing. Intended for the firm that designs and

---

[41] "Understanding ISO 9000," *NAPM Insights* (September 1992), pp. 28–29.
[42] Ibid.
[43] "Understanding ISO 9000," *NAPM Insights* (September 1992), pp. 28–29.

develops its own products, it utilizes all of the standard's 20 areas that need satisfying:

1. Management responsibility
2. Quality system
3. Contract review
4. Design control
5. Document control
6. Purchasing
7. Purchaser–Supplied product
8. Product ID-traceability
9. Process control
10. Inspection/testing
11. Inspect, measure, and test equipment
12. Inspection/test status
13. Control of nonconforming status
14. Corrective action
15. Handling/storage/package/delivery
16. Quality records
17. Internal quality audits
18. Training
19. Servicing
20. Statistical techniques[44]

Major purchasing topics of Q91 relate to assessment of subcontractors, purchasing data, and verification of purchased product.

Q92 (ISO 9002) provides a quality assurance model for conformance in production and installation, for companies that do little product development. Q93 (ISO 9003) supplies a model for conformance in final test and inspection standards. Q94 (ISO 9004) furnishes guidance in establishing and documenting a quality system. It identifies relationships between inputs needed to assure quality and supplies a large amount of guidance in ''quality in procurement.'' It encourages a close relationship with suppliers and feedback to them to support planned and controlled purchasing of supplies. The standard exalts the close purchaser–supplier relationship as supportive of continuous improvement—a tenet of total quality management.

---

[44] Ibid.

Q94 provides the quality standards that the procurement process requires, on the following topics:

Specifications, drawings, and purchase orders
Selection of qualified suppliers
Agreement on quality assurance
Agreement on verification methods
Provisions for settlement of quality disputes
Receiving inspection planning and controls
Receiving quality records[45]

In all the standards, only Q94 mentions possible quality control techniques, as follows:[46]

Design of experiments/factorial analysis
Analysis of variance/regression analysis
Safety evaluation/risk analysis
Test of significance
Quality control charts/Cusum*
Statistical sampling inspection

In sum, ISO 9000 documents that a firm has accepted quality as part of its culture.

Savings

The company's ability to meet international standards for quality assurance constitutes a prerequisite to global competition. Voluntary ISO 9000 standards provide a "license to compete," as some managers state it. Most chemical industry quality managers lean toward the view that within a few years ISO 9000 will carry the weight domestically as it presently bears internationally. ISO 9000 certification requires companies to document processes to such a degree that if a company replaces all personnel the process could continue with the same level of quality assurance. Finally, direct savings in time and money accrue from the reduced frequency of individual customer audits and fewer audits of the company's own suppliers.[47]

[45] "ISO 9000: The Purchaser's Role," *NAPM Insights* (October 1992), p. 28.
[46] "ISO 9000: The Positives and Negatives," *NAPM Insights* (December 1992), pp. 42–43.
* Cumulative Sum Technique.
[47] "Value of Global Quality Standards Becomes Clear to Chemical Industry," *Chemical and Engineering News* (March 1, 1993), pp. 12–17.

STANDARDIZATION AND SIMPLIFICATION

Standardization is the process of establishing agreement on quality, design, and composition, the end result of which is the standard.

Simplification, in an industrial sense, is reducing the number of sizes and types of parts used. It is, therefore, a sorting and selection process that is usually carried on as part of an organization's overall standardization program.

An attempt to simplify and standardize is illustrated by the programs of classified parts specifications developed by various industries. Classified parts and materials are commercially available and standard in an industry. They consist of items that can be described without the use of drawings or blueprints, such as brand-name items, standard raw materials, hardware, and pipe fittings. As the need for new items develops, their specifications are checked against the classified parts list before new part numbers are assigned to them on the list.

Informal standardization programs are carried on by all firms. Sometimes such efforts are the responsibility of buyers, inventory control, production control, quality control, and engineering personnel. However, in many firms formal standardization programs have been reported ranging from $3 to $12 for every dollar spent on informal standardization efforts. Regardless of whether the effort is formal or informal, purchasing employees should be alerted to examine every requisition to see whether a standard item, with its usual lower purchase price and greater availability, can be substituted for a so-called special.

Sometimes a user must develop individual specifications because the commercial standards are so broad that they do not meet the particular requirements. However, some standards can be used even when certain features require unique specification. For example, a firm may find that a specially threaded bolt is required in a certain application to withstand excessive vibration. The bolt will be a special because of its unique threading, but the material composition standards can be used in describing it. For this bolt a standard steel, such as #1010, can be specified to indicate temper, hardness, and composition.

Hartford headquarters officials of Connecticut Bank & Trust worked with an architectural and design firm to create a plan to renovate 150 branch banks—50 a year, over a three-year span. Together they established a corporate design standard that specified colors, materials, furnishings, plantings, and accessories in every branch. Standardization speeds up construction. It facilitates advance purchase of materials and interchangeability of furnishings.[48]

[48] "Standardization Is Key to Bank's Renovations," *Office* (June 1989), pp. 90, 94–95.

Metric Measurement

The customary units of standards and measurement used in the United States have been undergoing a radical change to the Système International (SI) of metric units, which is the international system of units. Its adoption reflects the desire to have a common, universal worldwide measuring system, thereby facilitating worldwide communication and trade.

The United States and Britain have customarily used a measurement system that is essentially fractional in character and is identified as the English or customary system. Elsewhere in the world, for almost 200 years, developing nations have been adopting the metric system, which is based on the use of decimals.

The limitations of the English system primarily hinge on its imprecision, particularly when products and their components must be duplicated. Fractions beyond one sixty-fourth prove unwieldy to use or communicate.

The meter (39.37 inches) is generally assumed to be one ten-millionth part of a quadrant of the earth's meridian extending between specified points north and south of the forty-fifth parallel. The system uses seven basic units which are interrelated; all other units derive from them and are expressed in multiples of ten.

The conversion to the metric measurement will be gradual and extend over a long period of time, with the federal government providing guidance and assistance. Certain segments of the business community have already converted. The automotive, steel, computer, and other basic industries are using metric dimensions, and others are in the process of conversion. Large numbers of capital equipment that use the English system will continue in service for perhaps another 50 years before being replaced by metric machines.

METHODS OF DESCRIBING QUALITY

There are several ways in which a purchaser can describe the quality of product desired. The description may be simply a brand name or market grade. For specialized or intricate articles, it may be detailed specifications or a blueprint. In some instances it may be necessary to use a sample. For basic products, market grade may occasionally be used to describe quality. We shall consider these methods individually with their advantages and disadvantages.

Brand or Trade Name

A brand name is the mark or designation a manufacturer uses to distinguish a product and to identify its origin. In putting a brand name on a product, the manufacturer wishes to secure proper credit to the product for any goodwill developed in satisfied customers. To build and retain this goodwill, the manufacturer must provide consistent quality.

In ordering by brand, the purchaser depends on the integrity and reputation of the supplier. If a first purchase has proved satisfactory for the intended use, it is reasonable to expect that subsequent purchases of the same brand will prove equally satisfactory. When the manufacturer with an established record of quality can provide satisfactory materials and products, the purchaser is saved the trouble and cost of writing specifications. In addition, there are situations in which it is desirable or necessary to purchase by brand.

Purchase by brand is necessary if an essential part or material is patented. It might also be desirable if a product to be used as a fabricated part has been so successfully advertised that its inclusion in a finished good makes that good more salable. For example, a small appliance company purchases General Electric cord sets for use on appliances because the sales department could use the GE name in its selling efforts. Goods may also be purchased by brand when the brand represents a clearly superior product. The superiority may lie in labor skill or extreme care in manufacture, and these elements cannot be reduced to specification or be duplicated by other producers. Purchase is also by brand when the quantity to be bought is so small that preparing a specification would incur undue cost.

The buyer purchasing by brand may encounter some difficulties. First, because there are many customers for any particular branded item, the supplier may alter quality slightly from time to time to meet specific needs of users. These variations may aid some buyers but cause difficulties in other buyers' operations because of different processing procedures. A second, related difficulty is the fact that the buyer's inspection department normally will not put branded items to rigorous tests. If a specification names a brand, the inspection department may merely assume that the brand received is satisfactory.

The price of branded products may be so high that the purchaser is induced to seek unbranded substitutes with a lower price or to establish individual specifications. A purchaser buying by brand should attempt to develop alternative sources of brands of equal quality in order to maintain flexibility and price competition.

Specifications

Specifications are made up of a detailed description or listing of the characteristics of a particular item. Compiling specifications often requires considerable time and may prove costly compared with other methods of communicating to the supplier what is desired. Nevertheless, buying by specifications is common because the great majority of business purchases require its use.

Dimensional and Material Specifications. Specifications may be a listing of the physical or chemical properties desired in a product. These are called dimensional specifications because they state the desired properties in measurable terms. Commodities such as metallic raw materials, oil, and paint are typical items for which this type of specification is used. Dimensional and material specifications can usually be checked quite simply for conformity.

Another form of specification is the precise prescription of both the material and method of manufacture. This method is sometimes used in military purchasing but rarely in industry except when the requirements are unique. Ordinarily vendors are in a better position than buyers to determine what materials and methods of manufacture are necessary. Buyers assume a heavy responsibility under this procedure and have no recourse if the products are unsatisfactory, assuming the specifications are met by the suppliers. Buyers incur the further risk of not benefiting from new improved methods of production, with which they are unfamiliar. Finally, costly inspection at the vendor's plant may be necessary.

Performance Specifications. Specifications may detail the performance or use of the purchased item. The purchaser indicates the use or application of the product and tests the product for appropriate performance. In accepting the specifications, the vendor assumes the responsibility for a satisfactory product. For example, a part may be specified as capable of being bent to a 90° angle and subjected to a temperature of 180°F. Performance specifications are the simplest specifications to formulate and are especially suitable when the purchaser has little technical knowledge. The seller is less free to utilize the most modern, economical production techniques. Effective use of performance specifications requires adequate competition to avoid the possibility of sellers suggesting more expensive items than are needed.

Drawings. The blueprint, engineering drawing, or dimension sheet is an important corollary of many specifications. The blueprint usually accompanies some descriptive text in the purchase order. It is the most precise and probably the most accurate of all forms of description and is applicable when close tolerance or a high degree of mechanical perfection is required. The blueprint is expensive to use, not only because of its cost but also because it usually describes an item of special design that is costly to manufacture. However, for items that require extreme accuracy, such as castings, forgings, and machine parts, it is the most feasible method of description. Blueprints also provide the basis for an accurate check against specifications by the inspection department when material is received, or by the using department when the construction project stands erect and complete.

Specifications should be revised as conditions change. In one instance a situation developed in which a purchasing agent and supplier informally agreed that steel supplied under certain specifications could vary from the specifications. The specifications called for a thickness tolerance of ± 0.003 inch. The informal agreement was that the supplier would aim at this tolerance but that actual shipments might actually vary up to ± 0.005 inch. The agreement worked successfully for eight years, but a new buyer, apprised of the agreement of the supplier and seeking formal recognition of the agreement, was unable to get the using department to accept the terms of the informal agreement. After considerable time, however, the specifications were changed because adherence to the stated requirements threatened to raise the cost so much that the company would have been unable to compete in the sale of the final product. All this could have been avoided if the informal agreement had been expressed in revised specifications.

Advantages and Disadvantages of Specifications.   The main advantages of specification buying are the following.

1. Drawing up specifications requires careful thought and a review of the buyer's needs. This action frequently results in a simplification of the variety of products purchased and often reveals the possibility of using less costly items. Both factors result in economies.
2. Buying according to specifications frequently induces more vendors to bid because many suppliers bid on identical items. This increased competition may result in lower prices.
3. Specifications ensure the identical nature of items purchased from two or more sources.
4. Purchasing to specifications provides an exact standard against which to measure incoming materials, which makes accurate inspections easy, and assures a uniform quality of materials.
5. Specification buying is a necessary step toward industry-wide standardization, with attendant economies.

The principal disadvantages of specifications buying are:

1. It is expensive to prepare specifications for small-lot purchases.
2. Specification buying increases the purchaser's responsibilities. The supplier's obligation extends only to complying with the specifica-

tions; if the product does not perform satisfactorily, the responsibility rests with the buyer.

3. In specification buying, the cost of inspection is greater than in purchasing items by brand.

4. Specifications may be overly refined and as a result more costly than necessary.

5. Once specifications are established, they are difficult to revise. Unless specifications are periodically reviewed, there is the chance that product improvements will be overlooked.

6. Some products defy specification buying because they depend so heavily on the unique skill of the maker that specifications are inappropriate.

Market Grade

Another method of describing quality is by market grades. This method is largely confined to primary, raw material commodities such as cotton, steel, and lumber. The market grade indicates the relative purity, lack of defects, or differences in quality of a particular class or kind of material. For example, a purchaser knows that when "No.1 pine" is the specification, the lumber differs from the other grades in that it has fewer knots and imperfections. The accuracy of the grading and confidence in the ability of those responsible for grading and of those ascertaining differences in grade during inspection are all important factors in determining the suitability of this method.

Commercial Standards

The conversion of market-grade commodities into commercial products such as nuts, bolts, plywood panels, and shirts calls for specifying quality by commercial standards. Again, governmental agencies and trade associations define these standards.

Samples

When none of the preceding methods of defining quality is satisfactory, the purchaser may submit a sample of the item desired. There may be difficulties if the sample is subject to physical or chemical change. The suitability of the sample description obviously depends on the ability of the supplier to ascertain and duplicate the sample.

A large proportion of commercial orders employ a combination of the various methods of describing quality. The method used depends on the product and the importance of quality in the item being purchased.

Responsibility for Quality Control

The responsibility for defining the quality of purchased materials should rest with the department that establishes the standards of quality to be maintained in production. Ordinarily, this is the engineering or production engineering department. When the decision concerns equipment and supplies not involved in production processes, the responsibility usually lies with the department that will use the material. For example, office equipment and supplies are largely the concern of the office manager, whereas laboratory equipment and supplies are of primary interest to the laboratory director; thus these officials are responsible for defining quality for their own equipment.

In large companies where responsibilities may be divided among several departments, the joint interest of sales, research, production, purchasing, inspection, and engineering may enter into the decision.

Service and Quality

An important ingredient in most purchasing decisions, with respect to quality, is the level of service provided by the vendor. This can range from no service to 100 percent service, and each level is appropriate for a given item or situation. Certain raw materials that go into the manufacturing process require no service, and service obviously should not enter into the quality decision. At the other extreme, some highly sophisticated manufacturing processes utilize highly sophisticated machines and instruments. In these instances, service is very important to maintaining overall quality and in fact may require the use of special service contracts to ensure that quality is maintained on a timely basis. This factor is particularly important if the purchasing company lacks the internal expertise to perform such service work.

Motorola uses quality function deployment to diagnose customer preferences and translate those choices into design, material, process, and production requirements.[49] The company set two goals to reach: 100-fold quality improvement by 1991, and 99.9997 percent error-free performance by 1992.

Motorola achieved both goals, according to a spokesman,[50] saving $3.4 billion in manufacturing costs over a six-year period and doubling employee

---

[49] "The Service Imperative," *Personnel Journal* (March 1990), pp. 66–74.
[50] Author's telephone interview, June 17, 1993.

productivity. As incentive, the company crafted the term "Six Sigma" to represent 3.4 defects per million parts or opportunities or about 99.9997 percent defect-free manufacturing, for its own finished goods output and for vendor-supplied items that become components of that output.

Some of Motorola's vendors objected to the standard as unrealizable in such items as machined parts.[51] However, Motorola persisted in-house where it could and realized savings of some $2.2 billion per year from teamwork-focused quality programs.[52]

The defect level of the average United States company is 67,000 to 6,200 parts per million (ppm). Motorola's Six Sigma concept sets the target at 3.4 ppm. The true statistical calculation of 6 sigma is 2 parts per billion (ppb). One analyst explains the comparison as follows:

> If there is one transaction every second, with Motorola's definition of 6 sigma, there would be one defect every 3.4 days; with the true statistical 6 sigma, there would be one defect every 15.9 years.[53]

The American Express Co. Traveler's Cheque Group (TCG) has utilized the six-sigma concept as a total quality service goal—99.9997 percent compliance or three errors for every 1 million customer interactions.[54]

Buyers have access to another data source on vendor performance. The U.S. Environmental Protection Agency's Toxic Release Inventory annually reports on how companies fulfill the public's desires for good environmental stewardship.[55] The report focuses on positive actions taken and constitutes another expression of service and quality rendered by the vendor.

DETERMINING QUALITY: INSPECTION

Once the proper quality has been determined, concise definitions of quality have been made, and an order has been placed with the chosen supplier, it becomes the responsibility of the inspection department to ensure compliance with the standard of quality. Inspectors monitor incoming material to ensure that it is of the proper quality.

[51] "Six Sigma: Realistic Goal or PR Ploy?" *Machine Design* (September 10, 1992), pp. 71–74.
[52] "At Motorola, Quality Is a Team Sport," *The New York Times* (January 21, 1993), p. C1.
[53] "Inside the Baldrige Award Guidelines, Category 5: Management of Process Quality," *Quality Progress* (October 1992), p. 78.
[54] "Service Quality Measurement at American Express Traveler's Cheque Group," *National Productivity Review* (Autumn 1992), pp. 463–471.
[55] "Environmental Performance Will Count in the 1990s," *Marketing News* (March 19, 1990), pp. 22.

Places of Inspection

Inspectors' responsibilities sometimes include visits to the vendor's plant. If a product is complicated and manufactured to precise standards, its high cost may justify stationing an inspector in the vendor's plant to oversee the production process. If the cost of transportation is high in relation to the value of the goods, inspection may be made in the plant before shipment to avoid return transportation costs in the event of rejection. Some large companies find it economical to maintain inspectors at or near the source for subcontracted items, special items such as heavy forgings and castings, and goods bought in large quantity. The most extensive use of inspection at the source is for military purchases by the Department of Defense.

Where conditions dictate inspection at the source, independent testing laboratories or inspection agencies can sometimes be employed. The cost involved in hiring the agency and the level of quality needed are the determining factors in deciding whether to employ this method.

In the usual situation, purchased material is inspected when shipments arrive at the purchaser's plant. The details of the inspection vary depending on the nature of the product and the production processes.

Benefits of Quality Control

An effective quality control system benefits both the buyer and the seller. Effective quality control by the vendor reduces the inspection costs of the buyer. Zero-defect programs discussed in the next section depend on excellent quality control programs. The use of scientific sampling methods that are based on the laws of probability cut inspection time and effort for both purchaser and vendor and minimize inspection costs.

A mutual interest in quality control methods improves user–supplier relationships. The user occasionally provides quality control assistance to the supplier. In one instance in which there was such cooperation, rejects were originally 16 percent; when quality control was applied in the vendor's plant, they were reduced to 2.5 percent. By reducing the number of rejects and the amount of rework, the supplier effects savings that may result in better prices for the purchaser.

INSPECTION METHODS

Certified Quality Control

The vendor may issue a statement certifying that the shipment meets the specifications set forth in the purchase agreement. Thereafter only periodic inspection need be made of shipments for assurance and to prevent a major slip in quality. This practice is called "certified quality control" or "quality certification." The basic objective is to have quality control procedures performed by the vendor and eliminate the traditional inspection procedures used by the buying firm's inspection department.

This program is best applied to precision components whose large volume and critical tolerances make inspection costs significant. Naturally, a high degree of correlation between buyer and seller is required, including an interchange of inspection tools and techniques. However, when effectively executed, the purchaser's inspection department is relieved of the need for duplicating work already performed by the vendor's inspection department. If vendors were generally to adopt satisfactory programs of production quality control, incoming inspection could be greatly reduced in importance.

Zero Defects

A program that originated in the missile-producing industry, aptly called a zero-defects program, is based on the premise that no defects are permitted. It aims to prevent defects by developing a deep concern and personal awareness on the part of each employee, in most cases by employee identification with each unit produced. Although all firms would naturally prefer to have such a program, the intense concern for quality and in-process safeguards make it most appropriate for industries in which defects can cause huge losses and malfunctions can put human beings at high risk. These are conditions found in the missile and aerospace industries.

Statistical Quality Control—Acceptance Sampling

The widespread use of statistical methods of quality control and acceptance sampling plans in inspection is a reaction to the inadequacy of rule-of-thumb methods of inspection, such as a flat 5 percent or 10 percent of receipts, and the impossibility, because of time and expense, of 100 percent inspection. Even 100 percent inspection does not eliminate all defective items because monotony and inspection fatigue set in, and because there is some ineptitude on the part of the sizable staff necessary for the task. The basic goal of statistical sampling is therefore to inspect a minimum sample characteristic of the entire lot.

To use statistical (acceptance) sampling, the practitioner needs to understand only the underlying assumptions. The purchaser, buying on the basis of the samples, assumes the risk that the sample does not contain defects that are in fact present in the lot. This risk is called the consumer's risk. On the other hand, some defects may show up in the sample that are not present in the remaining lot, and the buyer might therefore reject the lot unjustly. This is aptly identified as the producer's risk in sampling. These risks notwithstanding, sampling statistics are based on the law of large numbers and instances of these types of error are correspondingly rare.

Sampling inspection tables prescribe for various lot sizes the size of the sample that enables the buyer to limit risks. Although lot sampling does not provide absolute certainty, it does prescribe the dimensions of the sampling plan, which keeps the sample size to a minimum and correspondingly reduces inspection costs.

When incoming material arrives, the receiving department first checks the quantity and condition of the shipment. If the shipment is in good order, the next step is to determine the quality. Where acceptance sampling is used, the inspector will be guided by commercially prepared sampling tables. Four facts are needed to utilize the predetermined acceptance procedure.

1. *Lot Size:* Number of parts in the shipment.
2. *Acceptable quality level (AQL):* Lowest lot quality that can be accepted.
3. *Sample size:* Number of pieces drawn from the lot that will be inspected to determine the quality of the entire lot.
4. *Acceptance number:* Maximum number of defective pieces allowed in the sample if the lot is to be accepted on the basis of the sample.

For example, to judge a lot of 75 pieces with an AQL of 0.3 percent, the table shows that 20 pieces would have to be inspected. The acceptance number is 0, because in order to accept the lot at 0.3 percent defective AQL, no defectives may appear in the sample of 20 pieces. If one or more defectives were found in the sample, the entire lot would be rejected. This procedure is called single sampling and is employed mainly on small lots which must be maintained at a very high quality level.

Double Sampling.   On the basis of the four facts listed, the sampling tables may call for double sampling, a procedure similar to single sampling except that a decision can often be made with much less inspection. In double sampling the sample can be smaller, but the tables safeguard against accepting or rejecting a doubtful lot by using a second sample to prove the quality of the doubtful lot.

In single-sampling plans the decision to accept or reject a lot is based on the results of inspection of a single group of specimens drawn from the lot. In double-sampling plans, a smaller initial sample is drawn, and a decision to accept or reject is reached on the basis of this group if the number of defectives is either quite large or quite small. A second sample is taken if the results of the first are not decisive. Since it is only necessary to draw and inspect the second sample in borderline cases, the average number of pieces inspected per lot is generally smaller with double sampling.

For example, to judge a lot of 4000 pieces that is to be accepted only if the AQL is 1 percent or less defective, the first sample size is 150 pieces with 3 defectives permissible. The second sample size is 300 pieces with 7 defectives permissible. Thus, if 3 or fewer defectives appear in the check on the first 150 pieces, the entire lot will be accepted. If 8 or more defectives appear, the lot will be rejected. Should 4, 5, 6, or 7 defectives be found in the first sample, the second sample of 300 pieces is drawn from the lot and the number of defectives in it is added to the defectives found in the first sample. With total of 7 or fewer, the lot is acceptable; 8 or more, the lot is rejected.

Sequential Sampling.   Another procedure for acceptance inspection is called sequential sampling. Here the decision to accept, reject, or continue inspection is made as the test or observation of each piece is performed. Where lots are comparatively large and homogeneous, less inspection may be necessary with sequential sampling.

If single sampling requires 100 pieces, double sampling will ordinarily accomplish the same result with 74 pieces, and sequential sampling with 55 pieces. However, when sequential sampling is used, the shipment must be homogeneous and have a uniform distribution of defects. The smaller sample size could cause acceptance of a shipment whose defects were segregated in a portion of the lot not included in the sequential process.

Sample Selection.   Obtaining a truly representative sample is an important part of the sampling procedure. Since many materials are received in cartons, crates, and boxes, a part of the sample should be taken from each container. Skimming the top may give an untrue picture of the lot. A random sample, in which each unit has an equal chance of being included in the sample, is the ideal objective of inspection by sampling.

The acceptability of a part may depend on several distinct features of the part. For instance, a rocker arm for a tractor must have correct bore size, correct overall width, parallel surfaces, polished surface on an adjusting screw, and a certain degree of hardness. A particular piece may have more than one defect when all these requirements are checked. However, it is only considered one defective in the count of the sample. Thus, a defective is a part that has one or more defects.

Figure 7-1 illustrates how one company records the results of an inspection of a rocker arm. The inspector enters the total quantity received in the shipment as well as the sample size called for by the sampling table. As the

Dwg. No. 54369				Part Name Rocker Arm			Sample Lot	Total Pcs. Rcd.	Date	OK or Reject
Vendor Howadore Company										
Critical Requirements Bore 0.811	Width 0.946	Parallel 0.003	Finish	Hardness Rockwell 54c min			Sample Lot	Total Pcs. Rcd.	Date	OK or Reject
0	0	0	0	0			35	300	6/10	OK QR
0	0	0	1	0			35	300	6/19	OK QR
0	0	0	0	0			35	300	6/26	OK QR
2	0	0	0	0			105	302	7/6	OK QR
0	0	0	0	0			35	300	7/14	OK QR

FIGURE 7-1. Sample form for quality control inspection and sampling procedures.

pieces are checked for the critical requirements, the number of defects is listed under each heading. A copy of this form is retained in the inspector's file.

After several lots have been received from a supplier, it is possible to compute the average quality of the lots received. This represents the supplier's process average, which can be used as a guide in determining the degree of inspection needed for that supplier's later deliveries. If the average is good, less inspection may be necessary, saving time and reducing costs. If the average is bad, tighter inspection may be called for. The compiling of all this information into graphs and charts provides pictorial data for easy understanding. Organizations with data processing equipment store inspection results in computers from which they can draw a variety of reports for the purchasing department and the supplier.

When the cost of inspecting each piece is substantial, the goal of reducing the number of pieces inspected may justify the use of sequential sampling, despite its greater complexity and higher administrative costs. However, the sequential process requires holding the entire lot of parts while sampling and inspection are going on.

If the full number of items that may need to be inspected are to be set aside before the inspection begins, single sampling is preferable. A single-sampling plan is simplest to train for, set up records for, and administer. However, double-sampling plans have proved to be useful in a wide variety of conditions, are economical in cost, and are psychologically acceptable to both producer and user.

The need for close cooperation between inspection and purchasing has been mentioned. The following is an example of the type of information that inspection can make available on vendor performance.

During the year Company X had purchased 94,318 magnet coils from four vendors. Table 7-2, submitted by the inspection department, shows the results of these purchases. Vendor A furnished more coils than vendor B, but fewer types. Therefore, the percent requiring inspection and the percent rejected should be lower. The quality of work of vendor A was excellent, and it was considered the preferred source of supply.

Vendor B furnished a large percentage of small-lot business, but the quality of product was not equal to that of vendor A.

Vendor C furnished only two types of coils, each in reasonable quantity. However, the figures were considered of little value in determining the overall quality that might be expected were vendor C furnishing the same variety and quantities as vendor B.

Vendor D had furnished coils largely on rush orders and in small quantities; therefore the rejection rates could not be considered conclusive. A careful study of one coil furnished in quantity showed results comparable to those for vendor A, and it was known that the vendor was furnishing a large quantity of coils to another local manufacturer at a very low rejection rate. It was believed that further study of this vendor's quality or purchases in quantity during the next year would determine vendor D's suitability as a regular supplier.

This type of information is a valuable guide for the purchasing department in its consideration and selection of suppliers.

In 1983 Eaton Corporation formed the Eaton Quality Institute. Eaton's 43,000 employees, and in many cases its suppliers, have a selection of some 14 workshops held for the company's 39 divisions and 117 plants around the world. The Institute first aimed to introduce statistical process control in all divisions and plants. Now, and over the next few years, it aims to improve supplier quality by integrating supplier procedures into Eaton's operations.[56]

The Operating Characteristic (OC) Curve of a Sampling Plan. Every sampling plan will incorrectly accept some lots and reject others. By mathematical formulas, once the inspection—lot size, sample size, and acceptance and rejection—numbers are determined, it is possible to compute the percentage of inspection lots of any given quality that will be accepted.

This information is presented in graphic form referred to as the operating characteristic (OC) curve. The OC curve tells the user how effectively the sampling plan discriminates between good and bad lots.

Figure 7-2 illustrates an OC curve for a lot size (N) of 2000, from which samples (n) of 300 are drawn containing (c) 11 or fewer defectives.

Using probability mathematics one can compute the probability that 11

---

[56] "Quality Training: Eaton's 'University without Walls' Aims at a Complete Culture Change," *Purchasing* (January 19, 1989), p. 96B23.

TABLE 7-2. Inspection Statistics for Four Vendors

Vendor	Total Purchased(%)	Coils Furnished Requiring Inspection(%)	Coils Furnished Rejected(%)
A	58.0	24.3	0.85
B	32.5	53.8	3.06
C	7.1	38.3	1.45
D	2.4	94.9	22.4

or fewer defects will be drawn from the lot in a random sample of 300 if there are a known number of defective items in the lot. Using this sampling plan, if the incoming lot contains 4 percent defective items, there is a 90 percent probability that the sample will contain 11 or fewer defectives, thus indicating acceptance of the entire lot. There is also a 10 percent probability that the sample will contain more than 11 defectives, indicating rejection of the lot.

Every combination of lot size, sample size, and allowable number of defectives has a different operating characteristic whose values are usually plotted in the form of a curve.

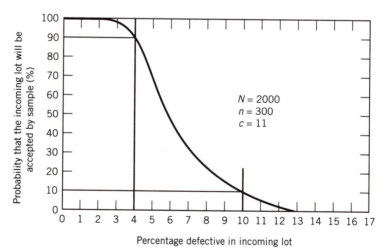

FIGURE 7-2. Operating characteristic curve.

REJECTION PROCEDURES

When inspection determines that incoming material does not comply with the purchase order, further shipments are temporarily suspended. Notices of rejection are immediately sent to the departments involved in the procurement, use, control, or disposition of the material.

There is the possibility that the rejection decision might be reversed if the sampling showed the lot to be closer to the borderline of the allowable tolerance. Time may be a factor, since the demands of the buyer's production schedule may not permit the delay caused by returning the material. In an emergency, reworking, sorting, or both, may be done by the purchaser's inspection department, or arrangements made for defectives to be set aside as the material is used in production.

Rejection may take different steps:

1. The firm may send back the rejected goods to the supplier without advance approval. However, confusion may arise on the supplier's dock and return credit never posted to the buyer's account. The prudent buyer, therefore, obtains supplier's approval to return rejected goods. The supplier usually issues return shipping instructions.

2. The firm may keep the rejected goods and attempt to negotiate a settlement. The cost of rework may fix a goal for the buyer's negotiation. The goal may include a penalty dollar amount for delaying the buyer's production.

3. The firm may determine that rejection steps cost more than the goods cost in the first place. The buyer issues an exception notice for in-house understanding that the buyer accepts the rejected goods. The notice authorizes payment and the rejected goods go directly into scrap.

4. The firm may store the rejected goods in an empty closet or bin until some possible use arises in the future.

The accounts payable desk needs the buyer's instructions relating to paying the supplier's invoice, not paying it, or if already paid, deducting payment from the supplier's next invoice. The buyer should remind the supplier of the rejected goods incident the next time a purchase is presented to that supplier.

Negotiations with the vendor regarding rejections should be handled through the purchasing department for several reasons.

1. Purchasing is in the best position to protect the goodwill existing between the firms by diplomatically appraising the vendor of the rejection and negotiating the terms of replacement.
2. Purchasing has the ultimate responsibility for obtaining materials of proper quality, which naturally includes replacement of rejected shipments.
3. Purchasing has the perspective of the overall material requirements of the organization and must utilize this knowledge in negotiating replacements.

When rejection is necessary, a clear statement of the reasons is vitally important, along with all pertinent facts and data, in order to minimize the possibility of arguments. Protracted discussions over unpleasant aspects may cause ill will on both sides and may jeopardize future relationships.

THE COST OF QUALITY

For many years the conventional wisdom concerning quality held that as product quality increases, the cost of manufacturing increases exponentially. Crosby in 1979 debunked this contention with the statement, "Quality is free." Other analysts followed his lead and proved that the cost of quality increases up to a point, then the net costs decrease dramatically, as the benefits of good quality exceed the costs. Conventional wisdom overlooks both the costs of poor quality and the value of good quality. Corporate management must give top priority to quality to make the difference.[57]

An effective quality system requires that the supplier consider costs due to marketing and design deficiencies, and nonconformances—including unsatisfactory materials, rework, repair, replacement, reprocessing, loss of production, warranties, field repair, and product recall campaigns. The buyer needs to consider costs such as safety, acquisition, operating, maintenance, downtime, repair, and disposal.[58]

CHAPTER SUMMARY

A slogan grew up with the quality control movement—"Quality cannot be inspected into a product." When the purchased material arrives, it must

---

[57] Donald W. Fogarty, John H. Blackstone, Jr., and Thomas R. Hoffmann, *Production and Inventory Management*, 2nd ed. (Cincinnati, OH: South-Western Publishing Company, 1991), pp. 594–595.
[58] Barrie G. Dale and John S. Oakland, *Quality Improvement through Standards* (Cheltenham, England: Stanley Thornes Ltd., 1991), p. 56.

contain the desired quality. Reasonable assurance of this precondition comes through careful attention to all responsibilities in the purchaser's organization. The buyer gives careful consideration to the exact quality desired by developing accurate descriptions or specifications of that quality, by making certain that the supplier understands what the buyer needs and has the equipment to do the job, and by applying a suitable inspection program. There remains little possibility of failure to achieve the desired results.

Standardization and simplification contribute strongly to the description of quality desired. The buyer may describe quality desired in one or more of several methods: brand name, dimensional and material specifications, performance specifications, drawings, market grade, commercial standards, samples, or a combination of two or more of these methods.

Statistical quality control (SQC) has grown into a highly profitable industrial element. Most of the large companies have well-developed programs. Since the pioneering work has resulted in a substantial body of knowledge, well-managed smaller companies can follow similar procedures to equal advantage. Widening the practice of SQC will heighten the quality level of industrial production and will increase the nation's productivity.

Discussion Questions

1. A buyer who specifies the material and method of manufacture assumes what responsibilities relative to possible rejection if the items prove unfit in the production process?

2. It has been stated that use of performance specifications can result in a supplier's presenting goods of excess quality. Explain.

3. Indicate the alternative methods available to define the quality of a purchased item.

4. What is the basic objective and economic justification for use of certified quality control procedures?

5. What are the disadvantages of using brand identification to ensure purchase quality?

6. Indicate the proper use of a simplification policy in conjunction with an overall standardization program?

7. What is the essential difference between the English and metric systems of measurement?

8. Under what circumstances might a buyer decide to utilize incoming goods that could actually be rejected and returned to the vendor?

9. What are the benefits of buying by brand name?

10. Which department should handle negotiations or notification of the vendor when items are to be rejected? Why?

Suggested Cases

ABC Corporation (B)

Ajax Sewing Machine Company

Selma Instruments Company

8

Principles of Price Determination

Henry wants to write a good textbook on determining price. With a Master's degree in economics and 25 years' commercial buying experience for a not-for-profit institution, he teaches evening classes in a local college. He wants an organized and systematic text on private sector pricing methodology from the buyer's perspective. "Not a how-to-text but a philosophical approach," he states. He finds no book that satisfies him, so he intends to write one himself. He knows the ins and outs of public sector pricing practice. However, *How does private sector pricing differ?* he wonders.

CHAPTER CONTENTS

Why do prices rise as demand slows? What happens to prices when the Federal Reserve eases credit? How does a buyer in a highly competitive arena know when to buy and how much to pay? Is he or she a price taker or will sellers negotiate better prices? The Austrian economist Hayek argued that, "We must look at the price system as. . . a mechanism for communicating information." What information does the buyer perceive in the seller's offered prices?

The process of price analysis as a standard practice as well as a crucial prerequisite to negotiation sessions receives increased attention from purchasing executives. The professional pricing deliberation used by many organizations today is not only to analyze components of a price quotation but to make suggestions for ways of reducing costs and for what to avoid. For example, a purchasing executive might direct the supplier "to produce the entire lot with only one setup cost, then to ship to us as we release." By this process purchasing has taken a proactive posture in negotiations and correspondingly suggests what it deems proper price levels. This step is in marked contrast to earlier reactive roles in price analysis and subsequent negotiations.

This chapter provides an overview of various approaches to price determination as well as of the philosophies of pricing. Significant legal considerations that affect pricing practices are also examined.

PRICING ECONOMICS AND THE CIRCULAR FLOW

Two principal forces operate in the free-enterprise system. Business, by providing the means of production, supplies goods and services. The means to produce, the so-called factors of production, are labor, land, capital, and managerial talents. Factors of production are defined as a society's means of sustaining itself, by providing shelter, food, and clothing. The second force consists of those who own the factors of production. In the United States, ownership of these factors of production is private. The two forces interact in a circular flow.

As shown in Figure 8-1, the owners of the factors of production provide their labor, land, capital, and managerial talent to businesses, which in turn pay for them in the form of wages, rents, interest, and profits. These payments constitute the basis of society's demand, which is met by business's provision of goods and services.

In this system, motivation for all parties is the reward system called self-interest; people look out for themselves and conduct their activities in order to maximize their self-interest position. The regulator that controls self-interest motivation and assures that unfair advantages are not taken is the force of competition. Competition is the only regulator in the free-enterprise system.

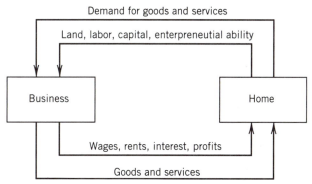

FIGURE 8-1. Circular flow diagram of the free-enterprise economy. The regulator is competition, the motivation self-interest.

The workings of these forces can be illustrated in an example. Suppose one firm has the only means to produce a given product such as motors. Without any competition we can assume that they would price these motors as high as possible to maximize their self-interest. However, the workings of competition brought about by other firms producing similar motors see to it that the final offered price is reasonable.

In the purchase–selling relationship, wherein sellers interact with purchasing personnel, the competitive process works to keep prices (self-interest) at a reasonable level.

MARKET CONDITIONS

The market condition under which a particular product is produced and sold is distinguished by the number and types of producers and buyers and the resulting competitive scale. Economists refer to three fundamental types of competition in markets: pure, monopoly, and oligopoly. Pure competition, in which the forces of demand and supply freely set the price is one extreme.* Buyer and seller do not control price in the pure competition model. At the other extreme is a monopoly, which consists of a single seller controlling the market and extracting a high price because there is no regulator (i.e., no competition) to its self-interest. An oligopoly is the market condition between the extremes, one in which a few sellers operate. Examples are the aluminum, steel, and automobile industries. The amount of competition existing in an oligopoly depends on the aggressiveness of its few firms.

*Pure competition assumes (1) a large number of buyers and sellers, (2) perfect knowledge of all actions, (3) homogeneous products, and (4) freedom of entry into the industry.

In practice, there are no clear lines of demarkation between these three market structures. Buyers are primarily concerned with the degree of competition existing in the production and distribution of the particular commodities they are purchasing.

SELLERS AND MARKETS

Reviewing the market structure leads to a consideration of the pricing process from the seller's (i.e., the price maker's) perspective.

Cost Approach

Two basic approaches to price determination are the cost approach and the market approach. The cost approach is the most common one and has a very simple central idea—the price maker adds together the individual cost items. These unit costs include raw material, direct labor, indirect labor, machine time, factory overhead, warehousing, sales, advertising, transportation, office costs, general overhead, and profit. The individual cost items are usually grouped into the following file categories: material, labor, manufacturing overhead, general and administrative overhead, and profit. These cost items are discussed in detail in the following chapter.

At times, the cost approach to pricing is reduced to a formula. The price maker observes a definite, rather permanent relationship between certain items of the costs and the previously set prices. For example, the price may have been approximately twice the raw material and direct labor costs. Therefore, instead of assessing the individual costs, a formula of doubling the raw material and direct labor costs may be used. As long as the relative importance of the cost categories does not change, the method is a simple variation of the cost method of pricing. However, as cost relationships change over time, adherence to formula pricing will ultimately lead to noncompetitive pricing.

Although the cost method of pricing is quite popular, it is not always economically sound. In the long run the prices a company receives for its products must necessarily equal or exceed total costs, but a price less than full average costs does not necessarily mean that a company should decline an order. A seller may be better off selling at lower than full cost for a while, in order to carry a part of the overhead, rather than refusing to sell below total cost. When a company produces a line of products, it may even be advisable to sell one or more of them permanently at less than cost if their sale would aid in selling other products that are profitable. Furthermore, the cost approach fails to consider the possibility that a product may be distinctive or of a quality that makes it worth more than its cost plus a reasonable profit. And a price based on cost cannot succeed for long in a competitive market if it is out of line with value, for competitors will force the price down to the value level. Thus, although the cost approach to pricing is popular and justifiable under certain circumstances, it should not be used inflexibly or under all circumstances.

The cost approach is often a beginning step in the pricing process, with the final price being modified by the conditions just outlined.

Market Approach

The market approach to pricing emphasizes the price the market is willing to bear. The methods of determining this price vary. It may be done on the basis of market research or market testing to determine what volume can be sold at various possible prices. Theoretically, this approach would indicate what price is the most desirable in producing maximum sales volume. However, this approach is quite costly to the individual firm.

The most common approach to market pricing is the reactive strategy technique known as *follow the leader*. Here a company selects a strong competitor and aims to keep its prices in a certain relationship to those of its competitor. This approach recognizes that products must sell competitively and that price differences can succeed only if they measure differences in quality or service.

A third method sets a price that will give the seller a certain desired volume of business. This process cannot completely disregard cost considerations, but it explicitly recognizes that increasing sales that utilize existing facilities may be more important than maximizing profit on every sale. This method has its principal application to heavy fixed-cost industries in which net profit is highly dependent on large-volume production.

Another technique for pricing according to the market is to set prices in relation to the price of related products. With the growth of interindustry competition this means of pricing is quite common. Glass containers, for example, cannot be priced effectively without taking into account the prices of tin, paper, and plastic containers.

Pricing to the market has a sounder economic basis than cost pricing and has become increasingly popular in recent years. It recognizes that price must reflect conditions of demand as well as of supply and assures that the significance of cost in the process of pricing will not be overemphasized. If market pricing were perfectly done, prices of all products would be set with a view to their worth to the consumer.[1]

A specialized pricing question arises in purchases of specially made

---

[1] For an approach to measure and evaluate purchasing price performance, see "Controlling Purchasing Price Performance," *Journal of Purchasing and Materials Management* (Fall 1988), pp. 36–39.

parts and subassemblies. Often there is only one buyer and there may be no seller offering the precise item. Then the buyer must judge whether the price offered is reasonable. A procedure for judging the price in this situation is known as the in-plant estimate. Here the buyer has internal specialists plan the part or subassembly in terms of materials cost and the manufacturing operations that must be performed. Costs are then determined for each step of the process. A target price is developed and the buyer negotiates with one or more suppliers. Frequently the buyer's specialists assist the supplier in planning production methods to meet the target prices. This procedure is a by-product of value analysis.

Buyers need to assess their company's immediate and longer term needs before making a purchase decision. Without this critical step, almost any purchase could be wrong. A complete and accurate needs assessment is an important first step to price determination.[2]

ADMINISTERED PRICING

The term "administered pricing" was first used by some economists during the depression of the 1930s in an attempt to explain why prices of certain basic materials did not drop enough to stimulate the demand for greater volume and thereby initiate recovery from the depression. Such industries were assumed to be controlled by a few suppliers who "administered" the prices rather than allowing the free play of supply and demand to determine the level of price. The issue of administered pricing was later revived because of the government's attempt to hold down prices in the face of rising inflation. Charges are made that such industries as steel, aluminum, or automobiles are raising their prices through administrative action rather than in response to market pressures. The government has been inclined to put the blame on management for administering prices to keep them high, whereas management explains the situation by pointing out that costs, made up largely of labor costs, have risen and thus have forced them to maintain or raise prices.

The question raised by the controversy over administered pricing is essentially misleading. It assumes that the significant issue is whether large companies today set their prices or have their prices set for them by the impersonal forces of supply and demand. No one can seriously doubt that management sets its prices. In fact, it is doubtful that any industrial economy (as opposed to an agricultural economy) could operate by trying to wait for supply and demand to set prices for all the infinite variety of products manufactured. The theory of impersonal supply–demand price

---

[2] "Opening the Door to Office Productivity," *Purchasing World* (October 1989), pp. 26–32.

setting was meant to apply where many small producers all manufactured a few basic, homogeneous products. The U.S. economy has many large companies trying to manufacture unique products. Under such conditions the manufacturer must name the price. The pertinent issue is whether in doing so that manufacturer is being responsive to the needs of the market and the value of the product to its users. A manufacturer who thinks too much in terms of unit cost and unit profit, as opposed to total cost and profit, may set prices that restrict production and retard the growth of the economy.

PRICE CONTROLS

During war periods, the federal government has imposed price controls in an attempt to prevent inflationary price advances. Except for such national emergencies, the United States has depended on competition to regulate prices and price levels.

Although the issue is debatable, controls may moderate the pace of inflation. Wage and price restraints are similar to the quasiformal plans called income policies that have been tried in western European countries and Canada and have failed to halt long-run inflationary trends.

Price controls affect purchasing in a number of ways. First, since prices will usually be pushing against the ceilings, a seller is much more likely to have one price for all buyers. Second, the seller will be less inclined to negotiate prices with a buyer because there will not ordinarily be enough slack in the profit margin to give the seller the required leeway for negotiating. Third, since the buyer can rely less upon price as an indication of value, the responsibility for measuring quality objectively will be greater than usual.

PSYCHOLOGICAL CONSIDERATIONS

One of the fundamental psychological factors bearing on price is the prediction of future supply–demand relationships. At any given time there is, in addition to the offers and orders that influence price, a market undertone of confidence or uncertainty that has a decided influence on prices. A particular supply–demand relationship coupled with confidence about the future may result in advancing prices, whereas the same supply–demand relationship in an atmosphere of pessimism may bring about declining prices. This attitude about the future cannot be measured, either quantitatively or qualitatively. Through experience, purchasing personnel develop the economic expertise and sixth sense that enables them to project and evaluate this intangible element and act accordingly.

Other psychological considerations in price determination are nonbusiness factors such as entertainment, gifts, or actual bribery. These factors should not be a part in the buyer–seller relationship and are rarely found in modern organizations.

DISCOUNTS

The discounts available on given purchases are an important part of determining price. The primary discounts available from suppliers include cash, trade, and quantity discounts.

Cash Discounts

Suppliers offer cash discounts that vary in both the amount of discount allowed and the period during which it can be taken. The most common cash discount is stated as 2/10, net 30. This means that, if the purchaser pays for the goods within 10 days of the date of shipment or date of invoice, a 2 percent discount may be deducted from the amount of the invoice. If, however, payment is delayed beyond 10 days, the face amount of the invoice must be paid. If the buyer delays payment beyond 30 days, the seller may institute collection procedures and, in some cases, will add interest for the extended period. Receiving a 2 percent discount for anticipating the final due date of an invoice by 20 days is equivalent to earning interest on the amount involved in the transaction at the rate of about 36 percent each year, since there are approximately 18 periods of 20 days each in a year. A 2 percent discount for anticipating payment by 20 days is therefore equivalent to a rate of 2 percent multiplied by 18 periods, or 36 percent. Thus, the annualized cost of not taking the discount is 36 percent.

Cash discounts do not usually vary among the several suppliers of a given type of industrial product. However, there is some variation from industry to industry according to the practice established in the particular industry. The buyer must be familiar with these discount practices. Cash discounts should be thought of primarily as a reward for prompt payment and not figured in the price.

Trade Discounts

In some industries it is customary to quote prices to the customer in the form of a price list, from which one or more trade discounts are deducted before the actual selling price is established. Ordinarily, the list price is considerably higher than the actual selling price. A trade discount represents the compensation to the buyer who assumes certain distribution functions for the seller.

Here is a typical illustration of how a trade discount is rationalized. A manufacturer sells mainly through wholesalers or mill supply houses but occasionally sells directly to large industrial users. The wholesalers are expected to sell to the small customers in their area and are granted a substantial discount to compensate them for storing goods close to the customers and for handling small-sized orders. The buyer who purchases directly from the manufacturer may expect a discount from list price that nets a lower price than would be obtained through a wholesaler; however, the buyer should not expect a discount as great as that granted to the wholesaler, who performs many additional distribution functions for the producer of the goods.

Trade discounts are usually granted for the purpose of protecting a particular channel of distribution. This is accomplished by making it more economical for certain classes of customers to buy from the distributor instead of directly from the manufacturer. If a manufacturer has found that wholesalers provide more efficiency in the handling of goods than does direct sale, a discount schedule will be established to induce customers to patronize wholesalers.

Frequently a seller employs what appears to be a discount plan but is in fact merely an alternative method of quoting price. The seller issues a catalog illustrating products and indicating prices that are set significantly higher than the prevailing level. An accompanying discount sheet notifies buyers what discounts or series of discounts to apply in calculating the true price. The discount may run as high as 65 percent or may be a series such as 40 percent–20 percent–10 percent. When prices are changed by the seller, only the discounts on the accompanying discount sheet need be changed. This can be done in less time and at much less cost than reissuing the entire catalog. Such discounts are sometimes called arbitrary discounts.

Quantity Discounts

Quantity discounts are granted by sellers to customers who purchase in larger quantities than those to which the regular trade discount applied. They may be calculated on the basis of individual transactions or on the basis of a series of transactions over a period of time. The former are called noncumulative and the latter cumulative quantity discounts.

The seller usually justifies such discounts on the basis of savings realized from selling in large quantities. Savings are realized on marketing expenses because costs do not increase in proportion to the size of an order. The paperwork is the same, and the increased costs of packing and shipping are not significantly larger. There may also be production savings on large orders, especially if they are placed well in advance of delivery and thus permit more orderly production planning and scheduling.

From the buyer's point of view, the quantity discount is closely related to internal inventory control policies. The costs of carrying the larger inventory must be compared with the savings realized through the quantity discount.[3]

Single Discount Equivalents of Multiple Discounts

Discounts represent special inducements to encourage a buyer to purchase. The seller affords the discounts as a promotional expense or as payment to a buyer who assumes one or more of the seller's tasks. For example, a retail filling station may sell its gasoline for a certain charge card price and for four cents a gallon cheaper if bought for cash. In one case, the seller has to process the charge slips and wait for reimbursement; in the other case, the seller has cash in hand and offers the buyer a discount to attract cash and to disburse savings.

An industrial buyer who receives suppliers' prices quoted with multiple discounts may compute single discount equivalents for comparing the various offers. Computing a single discount equivalent folds 40–20–10 or any other string into a single figure. To compute a single discount equivalent, add the first two discounts as decimals ($0.40 + 0.20 = 0.60$), then subtract their product ($0.40 \times 0.20 = 0.08$) ($0.60 - 0.08 = 0.52$). To that difference then add the next quoted discount ($0.52 + 0.10 = 0.62$), then subtract their product ($0.52 \times 0.10 = 0.052$) ($0.62 - 0.052 = 0.568$). Thus, 40–20–10 folds into a single discount equivalent of 56.8 percent. Thus, a list price of $100 less 40 less 20 less 10 computes to $43.20 net price ($100 less 56.8 percent of $100).

PRICE INFORMATION AND DETERMINATION

Purchasing personnel should indicate a specific price on the purchase order. There are a number of sources from which such prices may be secured; the choice depends on the time available and the type of organization represented.

---

[3] "Evaluation of Quantity Discounts Considering Rate of Return," *Production and Inventory Management Journal* (Second Quarter, 1989), pp. 68–71.

Published Price Lists

For items that are bought frequently, price information can be maintained in the purchasing files of the company. These are standard production items for which catalogs and price lists are prepared.

Salespersons

A second important source of information about price is salespersons. They can supply information regarding price changes or revisions in the price lists and can also secure quotations on modifications of standard stock items.

Published Market Data

Most raw materials are traded on well-organized central markets. Business publications such as *Iron Age* and *The Wall Street Journal* publish price information on raw materials that is current, complete, and reasonably accurate. However, since these prices tend to fluctuate, published figures are used mainly as a basis on which to begin price negotiations.

The most important factor in determining the price to be paid for raw materials is the price trend of the commodity. Since purchases of raw materials can usually be delayed or advanced to take advantage of a favorable price trend, purchasing is interested not only in current price quotations but also in price projections. It is, therefore, vital that a buyer of commodities sold on organized markets be versed on both market prices and market trends.

The fact remains that not all suppliers sell at market prices. Some regularly sell above the market, believing that their quality and service are better than average and, therefore, worth more than market price. Others either regularly or occasionally sell under the market for the opposite reasons or because they are especially anxious for business. If a preferred source is found to be above the market without good reason, competitive bids or bargaining may be effective in reducing the price.

Negotiations

When a usual source is found to be higher in price or to offer delivery terms less desirable than those offered by a competitor, the buyer will frequently negotiate with that source for better terms. Negotiations are also frequently used for nonstandard items that have to be produced to the buyer's specifications.

Negotiations permit a more personalized approach to the problems of agreeing on the terms of the sale than does the formal bid invitation method described in the following section. Negotiations are useful whenever compromises are likely to be necessary in arriving at any of the terms of the contract.

Competitive Bids

Still another method of determining price is to secure competitive bids from potential suppliers. Most buying by government and other public agencies is done almost exclusively by this method because of statutory requirements. Exceptions are sometimes permitted in emergency situations when time is of the essence or when patented or proprietary items are required. Industry, by contrast, resorts less often to the competitive bid procedure and usually only for certain special purposes.

Bids may be used by a company as a means of developing a list of suppliers for a product not previously purchased or to secure alternative sources of supply. The competitive bid is frequently used by industrial firms in buying special, nonrepeat items such as heavy equipment or machinery. Competitive bids may also be used for term-contract purchases of fabricated parts of materials (items to be incorporated into the buyer's finished product with little or no further change). In some instances, industrial firms making goods under government contracts must use the competitive-bid process in order to establish costs to the satisfaction of the government.

Bids are obtained by buyers through the use of a special form usually called an invitation to bid or a request for quotations. Although the form is not a purchase order and usually explicitly states that it is not, it is similar to a purchase order in form. It describes in detail the item on which bids are sought giving an accurate description, the quantity to be purchased, conditions of delivery, the end use of the item, and terms of the transaction. Bid requests generally have a statement appended that clearly states the manner in which the bids will be handled, the time during which they will be accepted, and other conditions deemed appropriate.

The use of a standard bid request form is necessary in order to secure all quotations on a comparable basis so that accurate comparisons can be made. Since all sellers are equally informed of what is desired and the conditions involved, the buyer may presume that all bids are comparable. However, a careful buyer will make it a practice to verify any bids that seem too high or too low in relation to the other bids received.

In industrial buying, bid requests are usually sent to a representative list of qualified sources. The buyer should request bids only from sources with whom an order might be placed. From either an ethical or practical point of view, bids should not be requested from suppliers to whom there is no intention of awarding a contract.

The buyer for a public agency is in an entirely different position in the securing of bids. Statutes, ordinances, and local rules of agencies that award contracts generally specify the procedure to be followed. In most instances public agencies are permitted to establish certain standards that bidding firms must meet before their bids will be considered.

When the bids are received from the prospective suppliers, they are listed and tabulated to facilitate comparison. In most public buying, all bids are opened at a stipulated time, and the award made to the lowest responsible bidder whose bid conforms to the conditions stated on the request. Invitation-to-bid forms of public agencies frequently include a provision that reserves to the buyer the right to reject all bids if the price is considered excessive. (Government purchasing and contracts are discussed in Chapter 12.)

A buyer is under no obligation to accept the lowest responsible bid. The purchase decision is likely to be made on the basis of a comparison of service and quality considerations as well as price. Sound policy suggests that all quotations be kept confidential; particularly, they should not be disclosed to competitors of the bidding firm. The practice of allowing rebids may undermine the integrity of the bidding process since the preferred supplier is not likely to put in the lowest price originally, and the other bidders may bid perfunctorily. If the buyer suspects that a bidder has made an honest error in computations, it would be ethical and proper to call this fact to the attention of the bidder and request verification of the original bid.

A buyer is not obligated to accept any of the bids submitted if they are too high or if, because of an apparent uniformity of bids, collusion is suspected. In either of these cases, new bids may be requested or direct negotiations with one or more of the bidding firms may be used to arrive at a satisfactory contract.

If the bids seem to be in order, the buyer completes the transaction by accepting one. Bids submitted in compliance with a request for quotations have the legal status of an offer. The offer is binding on the seller if it is accepted within a reasonable period of time. The buyer sends the successful bidder a purchase order with the notation that it is in accordance with the seller's quotation of a certain date. There is then a legally binding contract between the parties.

Since the industrial buyer does not necessarily accept the lowest responsible offer submitted in answer to a bid request, evaluating the bids in terms of quality, price, and service is difficult. Each buyer is likely to have an individual approach to this problem, but the following list includes most of the aspects to be considered.

1. Are the specifications identical on all bids submitted?
2. Do all suppliers comprehend the manufacturing requirements?
3. Are the specifications accurate and complete?
4. How anxious are the bidders for the business?
5. Have former dealings with the vendors been satisfactory?
6. How long have the suppliers been in business?
7. Do all the suppliers have technically qualified personnel?
8. Is time of delivery important?
9. Is the proximity of sources a significant factor?

Unpriced Orders

There may be items of small value that do not warrant the expenditure of much time or effort to determine their price. One way such items may be priced is for the buyer to add a clause to the purchase order stating that the latest price paid prevails. Here the buyer relies on the supplier to adjust when there has been a downward revision in price. Many of these small-value purchases are made locally with prices spot-checked by telephone.

Special Price Clauses

In some situations it is necessary to put special clauses in contracts or purchase orders to permit later changes or revisions in price. The two most common types of clauses are the escalator clause and the clause guaranteeing against a price decline. Under normal business conditions such clauses are not widely used. However, market conditions may dictate such clauses.

Escalator Clauses. Suppliers may adopt escalator clauses during periods of rising costs and prices. Such clauses permit upward revision of a contracted price in accordance with some preestablished formula, to protect the seller from having to comply with a contract signed during a period of lower prices. When estimating price the seller is governed by current costs and, to a limited extent, future price trends. In a competitive industry, protection against extreme price fluctuations may be needed. If all suppliers bid on the basis of current costs and include an escalator clause, the seller has protection against inflated cost and the buyer has the dubious assurance that the sellers bid on the basis of known rather than assumed costs.

If the escalator clause is adopted, problems to be solved are the establishment of a basis on which price revisions are to be made (indexes of prices and wage rates), limitations on the number of revisions possible, and determination of the time at which revisions can be made. From a legal point of view, a contract must have a definite price, or a means of determining one, in order to be enforceable. There has been considerable litigation concerning the acceptable wording of a contract on this point. No one acceptable clause has yet been developed.

Guarantee Against Price Decline. During a period of slow business and general price declines, the buyer occupies the dominant position in any transaction. He or she may demand and receive from the seller assurances that any decline in the price of the commodity during the life of the contract will be passed on. In order to attract business, the seller will frequently offer buyers such price protection for other reasons. The seller finds that a guarantee against price declines keeps buyers from holding back orders in the hope of further price declines. Some sellers are also able to stabilize their production cycle by using such clauses to secure orders in advance of the season. A seller may find that a guarantee against price declines brings in larger orders and fewer cancellations than if no such guarantee is given. Some also contend that, in the long run, such clauses tend to lessen extreme price fluctuations by encouraging the maintenance of demand.

From the buyer's point of view, in addition to preventing loss resulting from price declines, such clauses encourage placing orders earlier, thus ensuring supply, avoiding shipping delays, and building goodwill with the supplier. Buyers quite naturally encourage clauses guaranteeing against a price decline whenever possible because these clauses have no inherent disadvantages to them.

Cancellation Charges

Contracts are likely to be canceled when the buyer's production plans have changed or when a substantial decline in price levels has put the buyer at a competitive disadvantage. If prices have declined, the buyer is likely to look for a loophole that will allow cancellation of the contract. The seller may be willing to renegotiate the contract if costs have gone down substantially.

When contracts are canceled because of changes in plans, it is customary to reimburse the seller for the time and materials already expended on the contract. Such reimbursement is sometimes provided in the contract itself, which may set forth the cancellation charges to be levied. If it has not been included in the contract, the buyer and seller must negotiate a mutually satisfactory arrangement. Few sellers will hold the buyer to a contract when the reasons for cancellation are other than a price decline.

LEGISLATION AFFECTING PRICE

Robinson–Patman Act

In interstate commerce the Robinson–Patman Act makes illegal those quantity discounts that for "commodities of like grade and quality" are not based on "differences in the cost of manufacture, sale, or delivery resulting from the differing methods or quantities in which such commodities are to such purchasers sold or delivered." The law provides not only that a seller who offers quantity discounts that cannot be justified under its provisions is in violation of the law, but also that the buyer who knowingly accepts such discounts is guilty.

Under a provision of this law it is legal for a seller to meet in good faith an illegal low price offered by a competitor. This good faith defense against price discrimination is legal as interpreted by the U.S. Supreme Court. Congress has made repeated attempts to limit the seller's right to meet the low prices of competitors to cases for which meeting such prices would not substantially tend to lessen competition. Such a change would prevent large companies from meeting lower prices of small competitors. This change in the law is opposed by the executive branch of the federal government, and by a large segment of business, and thus is not likely to be made.

Although the primary burden of justifying discounts as legal rests with the seller, a buyer who knowingly induces the seller to grant a discriminatory discount may be held responsible. After 1953, when the *Automatic Canteen Co. v. FTC* case was decided, it appeared that the courts would virtually absolve buyers from their responsibility under the law. However, recent cases are tending to place more responsibility upon buyers who are strong enough to influence prices. Therefore, buyers should be cautious in dealing with sellers who are greatly in need of their business.

A discount does not necessarily have to equal the full savings accruing to the seller by reason of the buyer's order. It must merely be no more than the saving. Although one of the purposes of this law was to eliminate price discrimination among buyers on the part of the seller, purchasing personnel should not rely on the law to guarantee this nondiscrimination. Enforcement of the law has not been entirely effective.

What can a buyer do under the Robinson–Patman Act if victimized by unfavorable price discrimination? The following quotation from "Small Business and Regulation of Pricing Practices," prepared by the U.S. Department of Commerce, clearly sets forth the possible courses of action.

   1. *Informing the Seller:* The fact that you are charged more than someone else for an item is not in itself proof of illegal discrimination.

You may be able to get your supplier to eliminate discrimination or to show why he is not discriminating against you.

2. *Reporting to the Federal Trade Commission:* The Federal Trade Commission carries the major burden for enforcing the Robinson–Patman Act. Its normal procedures include investigation, complaint, hearing, and—if the facts seem to warrant—a cease-and-desist order. Orders may be appealed to the Circuit Court of Appeals and finally to the Supreme Court. Procedure is normally slow because the seller does not have to change the pricing practice until an order against that seller becomes final. Buyers' complaints to the FTC are treated in confidence. Matters are expedited if letters to the commission give definite information about specific violations of the law.

3. *Reporting to the Department of Justice:* Since the antidiscrimination section of the Robinson–Patman Act is a part of the Clayton Act, Clayton act procedures can also be set in motion. U.S. district attorneys in the various districts can bring suits for injunction.

4. *Bringing Private Suit:* You can ask the courts for injunctive relief against threatened damage from illegal price discrimination. You can also bring suit for triple damages for a loss you have sustained because of a discriminatory high price. The courts have ruled that a buyer who is injured by discrimination can collect three times the actual amount of the discrimination. This means that, if you were charged $1 more for an item than a competitor and bought 10,000 items, you can collect $30,000 if you win the case.

The best remedy for a suspected discrimination against the buyer is to discuss the matter with the seller. Often the seller can explain the reasons for apparent discrimination or take corrective action if discrimination exists. If the discrimination is not intentional, this method enables both parties to avoid the difficulties and costs of legal proceedings and, in the long run, may result in better relations between the buyer and seller.

Sherman Act, Clayton Act, and Federal Trade Commission Act

The antitrust laws affecting interstate commerce have established the principle that business practices that hinder competition or tend to restrain trade are illegal. These acts are of interest to purchasing personnel concerned with prices, in that they apply to cases in which a number of sellers, through collusion, quote identical prices.

Sherman Antitrust Act (1890). Monopolies, contracts, combinations, and conspiracies that restrain trade are outlawed by the Sherman Antitrust Act.

Clayton Act (1914). Price discrimination, tying contracts, exclusive dealing arrangements, requirements contracts, reciprocal deals, and acquisition of the trade of another company are regulated by the Clayton Act. There are several amendments of the Clayton Act.

> The *Robinson–Patman Act (1936)* regulates seller-induced price discrimination and price discounts.
> The *Celler–Kefaurer Amendment (1950)* regulates the acquisition of assets and stock of one company by another.
> The *Hart–Scott–Rodins Antitrust Improvement Act (1976)* requires large firms to notify the Federal Trade Commission of intentions to merge.

Federal Trade Commission Act (1914). The FTC Act declared unfair methods of competition to be illegal and established the Federal Trade Commission. The FTC Act has three amendments.

> The *Wheeler–Lea Act (1938)* prohibits deceptive acts and unfair methods of competition.
> The *Alaska Pipeline Act (1973)* increased the penalty for violation of a cease-and-desist order and allows for injunction ratification.
> The *FTC Improvement Act (1975)* expanded the power of the trade regulation rules and remedial powers of the FTC.

When a buyer suspects that quoted prices have been the result of collusion, there are several possible courses of action. The buyer may accept the situation temporarily, in the belief that there is nothing that can be done about it in the short run, and meanwhile initiate action on the part of the production and engineering departments to develop acceptable substitute materials that may be secured from other sources. Legal action, a second alternative, is seldom used because of the time and cost involved. The buyer may select one of the collusive bidders and exert pressure to reduce the price.

Basically, the antitrust laws are based on the assumption that competitively determined prices will be lower than those resulting from monopoly or collusion.

Dual Prices

As an outgrowth of FTC and court action, purchasing personnel who are buying items both for original equipment use and for resale through company branches as service parts are faced with a dual price problem. It is legal to charge different prices for original equipment and replacement, but it is illegal to allow the lower-priced original equipment to be placed in the replacement market where it could compete unfairly with like items bought at the higher equipment replacement price.

In fields in which dual use is common, suppliers insist that the purchase order contain a phrase identifying the end use for the item ordered. In this way they can comply with the requirement that prices of original equipment and replacement parts be different. Since automotive parts bear a federal excise tax for automotive use but not for nonautomotive use, the purchase order for them must also identify the end use.

The article, "Pricing Your Products and Services Profitably," in the U.S. Small Business Administration booklet *Management Aids* Number 4.014, undated, specifies how to figure costs and profits for a consulting service.

Some managers confront the issue of how best to order purchased materials in material requirements planning (MRP) environments when vendors make discounts available.[4]

CHAPTER SUMMARY

Buyers and sellers communicate information through price. They determine price by either the cost approach or the market approach. With the cost approach, the price maker adds the individual cost factors and includes a target profit. In the market approach, the price maker follows the leader, or studies what happens in the market relating to price, or adjusts price to sell a designated volume.

The competition in the market influences price. In the pure competition market, buyers and sellers do not control price; supply and demand set price. In the monopoly market, the single seller controls the market and exacts whatever high price he or she wants. In the oligopoly market, the few sellers who make up the supply side watch each other's prices, and meet or match competitors' prices. The sellers keep prices very stable or else they imitate the leader who tries to improve the cash situation by changing price.

---

[4] "An Experimental Comparison of MRP Purchase Discount Methods," *Journal of the Operational Research Society (UK)* (March 1991), pp. 235–245.

Discounts extend the seller's offers. He or she may offer cash, trade, or quantity discounts.

Discussion Questions

1. Explain the cost method of pricing. Contrast it with the market approach.
2. How do psychological factors enter the pricing process?
3. Discuss the pros and cons of buying on the basis of the lowest price.
4. Indicate the method by which you think a firm should establish its price.
5. What can a buyer do when all vendors quote identical prices?
6. Distinguish clearly between a trade discount and a quantity discount.
7. Name the sources from which prices may be secured.
8. Under what conditions might a buyer expect the seller to insist on an escalator clause? Under what conditions would a guarantee against price decline be appropriate?
9. When should cancellation charges be paid? When should they not be paid?

Suggested Cases

Golden City

Hearons Company

Household Cleaners Corporation

Industry-wide Pricing

Italiana, Inc.

Jones Price Analysis

Space Systems, Inc.

Warehouse Steel Company

Exercises

1. Vendor A offers discounts of 25–15–10–5 on a list price of $100. Vendor B quotes $70 less 5–5–5–5. Vendor C would have to come in with what maximum price to win the bid, within pennies?
   Figure the discount equivalent for (a) 15–10–5; (b) 40–15–5; (c) 10–10–2.
2. Flowers Calendar Company distributes paper matches for advertisers to use for promotional purposes. Flowers offers discounts for quantity, seasons, buyer's trade level (retailer, discount house, manufacturer), and cash.

For maximum discount, Flowers quotes list price less 20 less 10 less 5 less 2. Compute the single discount equivalent. Recommend whether Flowers should quote the string of discounts or the single equivalent.

9

Negotiation and Cost–Price Analysis

The Japanese Mazda assembly plant in Flat Rock, Michigan rolled off the first MX6 automobiles in September 1987. Since then, purchases of parts and materials from North American suppliers increased from $400 million to $1.6 billion in 1992. This brings the domestic content of each car produced at the Flat Rock facility close to the 75 percent mark.

Richard heads Mazda's purchasing department. He has almost as many engineers as production buyers. Besides assisting suppliers in technical matters, the engineers give high priority to reducing costs through value engineering.

Rose, a graduate of a first-rank engineering school, sees that the persons who get ahead in the department effectively use negotiating skills with vendors and with in-house customers of the purchasing department. Rose speaks to Richard:

"In engineering school I studied nothing about negotiating. Now I see it used all the time. Should I take a short course or buy a book to cover the principles? Just how important to my career should I consider negotiating skills?"

What should Richard tell Rose?

**CHAPTER
CONTENTS**

Negotiation

Cost–Price Analysis

Price Analysis

Cost Analysis

Learning Curve

Direct Material Costs

Direct Labor Costs

Overhead Costs

Overhead Analysis

General and Administrative Costs

Profit Analysis

The objective of negotiation is agreement regarding what is fair and reasonable from both the buyer's and the seller's point of view. Of primary importance in successful negotiation is proper preparation, including knowledge of cost–price analysis, the capabilities and needs of the vendor, and the needs of the purchaser. Any item for which alternatives exist can be negotiated, including payment terms as well as delivery and production schedules and the services needed.

A knowledge of the learning curve concept can help determine whether the price charged is reasonable. In addition, it can form the basis for successful negotiations with suppliers.

Cost–price analysis is a technique used by purchasing to ensure fair prices. Every element of the cost incurred by the supplier in manufacturing the needed item must be examined—the manufacturing processes and accounting procedures, as well as direct costs, overhead expenses, and profit levels desired.

NEGOTIATION

Negotiation is one of the most important tasks of purchasing professionals. It is also the most delicate and difficult. It is delicate because it involves dealing with a seller whose primary aim is to maximize profits, hence price. The buyer, on the other hand, has the opposite objective, to hold seller's profits and prices to acceptable levels.

Negotiation is particularly difficult under these circumstances, for two diametrically opposed forces are at work. These forces must interact and be resolved to a middle ground with professionalism and finesse in order to leave both parties with a good feeling and attitude at the conclusion of the negotiations. A good attitude is essential because after negotiations are completed, other aspects of the seller–buyer relationship are just beginning. The supplier has yet to furnish quality goods, deliver them, and give good service.

The final goal of negotiations is therefore an acceptable level of price and related conditions of sale, and two parties who leave with ''smiles on their faces'' and feelings of mutual respect and goodwill. The buyer's accomplishment of this task is an art and is the focus of this section.

Definition

The word negotiation, as derived from Latin and from civil law, means tradings or deliberations leading to an agreement. Negotiations refer to more than just price discussions. Although it is true that price looms large in any procurement negotiation, it is but one of many elements subject to discussion between the parties. Legally, any contract must involve agreement by the parties on all aspects of the contract. Thus, negotiations should include discussion of the quantity, quality, and service elements of the transaction as well as price.

Types of Negotiation

There are essentially three items of purchasing price negotiation—specially made products, industry-wide products, and services. Specially made products are products that are made specifically for and purchased by many organizations, but are not yet purchased industry-wide.

Examples of specially made items include screw machine products, castings, and specialty extruded products. Examples of industry-wide products are steel, cartons, motors, and cord sets. Services include accounting, consulting, and similar tasks. Negotiations for particular products and services require essentially different approaches, as will be discussed. Negotiations concerning quality, delivery, and service are somewhat the same for all types of products and services.

When to Negotiate

Not all purchase–sale transactions require negotiations. Small-value branded items that are part of the shelf stock of the supplier and are catalog-priced are seldom subject to negotiations. As a rule, negotiations should be limited to purchases requiring significant dollar expenditures and in which compromise or change is possible. Buyers should prepare to negotiate any time they suspect that the prices quoted may not be reasonable. Negotiations are also recommended when the buyer suspects that truly competitive bidding did not take place, when purchases include a multiplicity of terms and conditions of sale, when the supplier may have included an excessive factor for risk protection, and when purchases require high tooling or setup costs.

Objectives

Obtaining a fair price is the most common but not the only objective of negotiation. Related issues include delivery schedules; particular quality levels; service ingredients such as technical assistance, stocking, and make-and-hold provisions; and terms and methods of payment.

Preparation

Purchasing personnel engage in short-term as well as long-term negotiations. Usually a series of short-term discussions precedes more complicated negotiations involving quality standards, sales and service considerations, prices, or vendor stocking. Negotiations are most often conducted at the buyer's place of business, but they may also be carried out during a visit to the supplier.

The purpose of negotiation is to improve the position of a company with a vendor, so that the lowest possible ultimate cost for the right products and services can be achieved. Accordingly, the buyer must plan extensively before the negotiation process begins. The buyer who is well prepared has the maximum advantage in negotiation sessions. Planning for negotiation includes the following steps.

1. *Industry and Product Analysis:* Review all background facts regarding the industry and products involved. This step means reviewing the present pricing along with demand–supply projections about the number and types of future competitors.

2. *Internal Buyer Organization Analysis:* In this step the buyer's needs and background are thoroughly reviewed.
   a. What are the analytical volumes involved?
   b. What are the quality levels needed?
   c. What quality variances are permissible?
   d. What stocking and delivery requirements are desired?
   e. What departments are involved and what are their concerns?
   f. What cost–price and make-or-buy analysis figures are available?

3. *Supplier Analysis:* A thorough review of the supplier would ask the following questions.
   a. What personalities are involved?
   b. What quality, delivery and service capabilities exist?
   c. What does the negotiated item mean to the vendor relative to other customers?
   d. What specific managerial talents are available?

4. *Review of Generalized Background Data on Actual and Potential Seller–Buyer Relationships:* This step requires a brainstorming of all potential issues of concern, including issues uncovered during steps 1, 2, and 3. The issues will vary with the extent of past experiences and types of buying organization. The following are typical background concerns.

a. What is the total quantity of business expressed in dollars?

b. How important is this quantity of business to the vendor?

c. What is the extent of competition for the business?

d. How much time is available for negotiations? Is either party facing deadlines?

e. Is the buyer prepared with a comprehensive knowledge of the cost–price analysis of the supplying firm's proposals?

f. Is the negotiator aware of the concessions each party can make?

g. Can the negotiator appeal to the vendor as a prestige account?

h. Are buyer requirements so critical that a high rate of waste would occur in production to meet the standards?

i. Is there any way that one can work out major production requirements to coincide with relatively slack schedules of the producer?

j. Is the buyer prepared to see that the buying company performs properly in receiving shipments, rendering prompt inspection, and promptly pointing out deficiencies if any, as well as promptly paying for acceptable merchandise received; and that personnel inspect to the agreed-on standards?

k. The buyer must be satisfied as to the ability and stability of management and ownership, as well as the operating people through whom the vendor will be handling the business.

l. The buyer must be satisfied that the vendor is financially stable and has good labor relations.

m. Has the buyer who is to engage in team negotiations selected others from the company who can contribute most to the negotiation? Do they understand who will take the lead and has authority to actually conduct the negotiations and bring them to fruition?[1]

n. Does the buyer know when to adjourn negotiations for future research by the company with whom negotiations are being conducted, or by the buyer's own company?

o. Do all members of the team understand that overbargaining and seeking ''to squeeze the last drop of blood out of the turnip'' can result in less than adequate performance for a contract?

---

[1] ''The Size and Composition of the Buying Firm's Negotiation Team in Rebuys of Component Parts,'' *Journal of the Academy of Marketing Science* (Spring 1989), pp. 121–128.

p. Has the buyer or others in the organization negotiated with people in the vendor firm?

5. *Projected Negotiation Topics and Strategies:* In this step the specific goals of the negotiation session and the types of strategies to employ are determined. This step is the heart of the negotiation process and is discussed in detail next in this chapter.

Topics

Any element of a transaction that needs to be discussed and for which there are alternative choices is an appropriate issue for negotiations. It was pointed out earlier in this chapter that the cost upon which a seller bases a price quotation is composed of a number of different elements, many of which are not precisely attributable to a given unit of production. Thus, any aspect of cost—particularly overhead, and to a lesser extent profit—is negotiable.

The required quality of a product, previously defined as suitability for the intended purpose, can be met by using different material. A change in a raw material, in the composition of a chemical, or in methods of packaging are all potential negotiation topics.

Similarly, the quantities to change hands in the transaction are negotiable. Quantity discounts, commitments to supply quantities over an extended period of time, blanket contracts, and the possibility of future orders may be discussed and negotiated.

Finally, the service aspects of a transaction are negotiable. The handling of rejects and defective materials, involvement with intermediaries such as service centers, use of technical services, and make-and-hold provisions are all negotiation topics.

Strategy

Both strategy and tactics are important aspects of negotiations. Strategy concerns the planning and directing of the negotiations to achieve the negotiator's goals and objectives. Tactics are the moves and maneuvers employed to implement strategy.

As an illustration of a strategy, consider the positions of buyer and seller with regard to downward pressure on prices during a negotiating session. The seller has limited strategic strength when the product under consideration is a product readily available from many sources; when the selling industry is composed of sellers who are smaller and financially weaker than the buyers; when it is relatively easy for new firms to enter the field; and when there are few artificial impediments to price bargaining such as laws, restrictive industry pricing practices, and strong industry or trade associations.

The reverse is also true. The vendor can resist downward pressure when the product is unique or available from a limited number of sources; when the industry is dominated by a few large sellers; when it is not easy to enter the field because large amounts of capital or specialized technical skills are required; and when there are strong impediments to free and open price negotiations.

The topics covered during the negotiation process take a certain path. For example, the objective of a given negotiation might be to obtain a concession from a steel mill to make and hold three months' inventory of 18-gauge terneplate. The strategy might include a discussion at the steel mill between the sales vice president and the buyer, during which the buyer will initially bring up the possibility of a price concession, fully expecting to be turned down. This presupposed condition, the turning down of a price concession, would have been assumed in the careful planning stages during the preparation for negotiation. The strategy would be to go for the price issue, be turned down, in the hope that an apparent compromise, the service of making and holding three months of inventory, would be obtained.

Cost Savings

Selling to today's purchasing agent does not draw on long-standing personal ties where prices make up the principal point of negotiation. Purchasers look for salespeople who have a thorough knowledge of what their customers produce and who have the ability to offer powerful insights into helping them make things better, faster, and cheaper. Those insights consist in translating the product's high specifications into cost savings or by demonstrating how the products low specs achieve proportionate results while reducing costs.[2]

Better Relationships

To attain world-class competitive status, U.S. manufacturing companies have begun to create a new order in buyer–supplier relationships. The new order calls for a new philosophy in negotiating, replacing the adversarial method wherein one party does whatever it takes to obtain the desired result without regard for the needs of opponent. The 1992–1993 NAPM President Richard Auskainis asserts the new philosophy:

---

[2] "Salesmanship: A View from the Other Side," *Sales & Marketing Management* (June 1990), pp. 108–120.

> The sophisticated purchasing professional of the 1990s recognizes the obligation of negotiating the best deal, while at the same time being sensitive to the needs of the other party and the effect of the final agreement on long-term relationships.[3]

Auskainis acknowledges the concept of principled negotiating as described by Roger Fisher in his book *Getting to Yes—Negotiating Agreements Without Giving in.* To NAPM's president, the phrase ''principled negotiating'' applies quite appropriately to the partnering, integrated supply, and team concept environment of today's purchaser, that places a premium on mutual trust and respect. Principled negotiating allows purchasers the opportunity to negotiate successful agreements with suppliers and, at the same time, develop long-term positive working relationships with those suppliers.

Cooperative negotiation may constitute the new negotiating style—one demonstrably superior from the standpoint of overall cost reduction.[4] Each party of cooperative bargaining has a detailed and complete breakdown of all its costs, and releases them to the other party in the negotiation.

Tactics

As previously stated, the tactics of negotiation are the moves and maneuvers that will be taken to implement the strategy. Much has been written about negotiation tactics. They include, but are certainly not limited to, the following.

1. *The Physical Arrangement of the Negotiation Site:* For example, some negotiators feel they have an advantage if their seat is higher than that of the opposite party.
2. *The Amount of Listening versus Talking:* Some negotiators stress the skill of listening versus talking as a means of obtaining rather than giving information.
3. *The Use of Body Language:* Some negotiators use eye contact to continue negotiation sessions, and drop this contact as a means to stop the session when the advantage is on their side. Other aspects of body language include types of handshakes (firm versus limp) and position of feet (flat on floor versus slightly jiggling).
4. *Tactics for Closing.* Many tactics have been suggested for stopping the negotiation when deadlocks are perceived or when a maximally advantageous position is obtained. Rising from the negotiating table,

[3] Richard J. Auskainis, ''President's Outlook,'' *NAPM Insights* (September 1992), p. 2.
[4] ''Joint Optimality in Buyer–Supplier Negotiations,'' *Journal of Purchasing and Materials Management* (Spring 1990), pp. 20–26.

use of body language (such as dropping eye contact), and changing voice inflections are some of the many tactics available.

It is beyond the scope of this book to identify more than a few tactics of negotiation. Purchasing personnel may or may not elect to use planned tactics in their negotiations. Many buyers consider the use of tactics unprofessional and prefer to be sincere and direct in their negotiation sessions, armed simply with the knowledge that they have carefully analyzed the negotiation issues, stated their objectives, prepared thoroughly, identified relevant topics, and, finally, developed the appropriate negotiation strategy.

The Law

The Robinson–Patman amendment to the Clayton Act has long been excessively feared by purchasing personnel as a restriction on negotiations in interstate commerce. This law prohibits preferential pricing and requires that buyers of like commodities purchasing under like conditions be quoted like prices. It does not prohibit all price differentials among buyers.

Price differentials are legal if the following conditions are met:

1. Such price differentials are offered because of savings in costs of manufacture, sale, or delivery by means of variations in quantities sold.
2. The transactions concern different grades of quality.
3. The differentials do not substantially lessen competition.
4. The price differential was made in good faith to meet competition.

Although this law prohibits buyers from knowingly accepting discriminatory prices, one should recognize that it is unusual for a buyer to *know* that a price is discriminatory because such knowledge implies access to the records of the competitors, which is clearly illegal under other provisions of the antitrust laws. This provision of the law is not likely to be invoked against a buyer who is bargaining hard but honestly.

Sellers may legally depart from the prices that are normally charged in order to keep customers, when forced in good faith by competition. Sellers may also negotiate lower prices by lowering quality specifications. Finally, sellers may quote lower prices to buyers whenever cost savings on the transactions can be proved.

Besides considerable amounts of planning, preparing for negotiation requires cost–price analysis, the subject of the remainder of this chapter.

COST–PRICE ANALYSIS

A crucial part of the negotiating process is cost–price analysis. As Chapter 8 indicates, cost and price data obtained through research set the stage for subsequent negotiations of specially made products. Cost–price analysis is therefore an attempt to ensure that the final price is reasonable in terms of the use to which the material is to be put and the competitive situation faced by the buying and selling firms. The objective of cost–price analysis is not to get the lowest price, but to obtain the lowest fair price—fair to both the buyer and seller.

Figure 9-1 demonstrates how price can respond to the economic power of the bargaining parties. Cost represents the actual costs to the producer of making and selling the item. Frequently these costs are not known exactly but are estimated. Value represents the utility (in the economic sense) of the item to the buyer. Price falls somewhere between these two levels. The seller tries to push price as close to the value level as possible whereas the buyer has the opposite motivation. Their relative pressure on price reflects their competitive strength and their bargaining skill.

Some knowledge of the seller's costs is important to the buyer prior to negotiation. The process of exerting downward pressure on price is economically, legally, and ethically sound. Such bargaining by the buyer, and resistance by the seller, are fundamental assumptions underlying the marketplace method of price setting. Cost–price analysis offers several economic benefits to a firm. There is the obvious possibility of a reduction of the price that will be paid for materials and supplies. In addition, information about production methods, materials used, and improved inventory policies developed in the course of such analyses may be shared with the supplier to the mutual benefit of both firms.

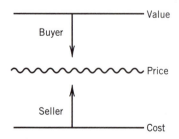

FIGURE 9-1. Cost, price, and value forces at work to determine a final price.

PRICE ANALYSIS

A price quoted by a vendor reflects more than merely costs and profit. Price is subject to many other influences. Particularly pertinent is competition among both sellers and buyers of the commodity. The seller who faces only limited competition from other sellers will react differently in pricing from the seller who faces active competition from many sellers. The number of prospective customers is also an influence on pricing strategy.

Sources of price information such as requests for quotations were indicated in the preceding chapter. Published data on prices, by trade journals, and government publications provide additional information for specific commodities on a regular basis. However, these data are of a conglomerate and average nature and may not reflect the local conditions an individual firm faces.

The buyer should also attempt to ascertain from the potential supplier the various cost components that are included in the supplier's price. As will be pointed out in succeeding pages, the buyer attempts through cost–price analysis to establish the proper level of costs for the various components of total cost. Through such analysis the buyer may detect means of lowering costs that had not occurred to the seller. Sellers in turn can use this information on all of their production, not just that sold to this buyer.

Why are businesses so slow to change their prices? A Princeton University economist found in an extensive study that when faced with strong demand, businesses tend to cut back on extra services to customers or to delay delivery, rather than raise prices to take advantage of the strong demand.[5] Moreover, the researcher found that businesses show reluctance to raise prices because they aren't certain what competitors will do. In addition, the respondents reported that their businesses base prices on costs— not on demand for their goods—and it takes awhile for cost increases to work their way from supplier to manufacturer to wholesaler to retailer. Finally, the study results showed that businesses have "an invisible hand-shake" with their customers to keep prices steady.

COST ANALYSIS

Costs are composed of different classes, the most common classification being direct and indirect. *Direct costs* are those that can be readily attributed to specific units of production, such as direct material cost and direct labor cost. *Indirect costs,* on the other hand, cannot be directly or accurately

---

[5] "The Price Is Wrong, and Economists Are in an Uproar," *The Wall Street Journal* (January 2, 1991), pp. B1, B6.

attributed to specific units, since they tend to be incurred for general purposes and to apply to the entire population of the firm. Property taxes, executive salaries, and machinery depreciation are such examples.

Another classification system uses the terms fixed, variable, or semivariable. For purposes of cost–price analysis, this classification has the serious drawback that it is not always possible to differentiate costs as clearly as is implied by the threefold classification.

If a plant were operating at capacity, it is apparent that it would be using such utilities as heat, light, and power to the maximum extent. However, if the plant were completely idle, there would still be need for some utility services, hence some of these costs. Therefore, one would have to classify utility costs as semivariable. Furthermore, accountants have traditionally treated production supplies, such as cutting oils and grinding wheels, as overhead rather than variable expenses because of the cost of identifying the unit of production for which they were used. Logically, however, they are variable costs.

Because of such problems, it is common to approach cost–price analysis on the basis of a narrower classification of the elements of cost:

Direct materials
Direct labor
Factory overhead
General overhead
Other costs
Profits (Although not usually a cost element, by accounts profit is an economic cost and must be considered in a cost–price analysis.)

Before these classes of cost are discussed, it will be helpful to introduce the learning curve concept, since this concept has direct application to many of the cost elements.

LEARNING CURVE

The learning curve is a formalization of the commonsense realization that the per-unit cost of production of a new item decreases as additional units of the product are manufactured. The labor cost should decline with each succeeding unit produced as the supplier becomes more skilled or learns how to make the product. The more a worker repeats an operation, the more that worker improves in speed and efficiency until reaching an optimum. This reduces labor costs. The more complex the process, the greater the reduction and the longer this "learning" will continue.

The same reasoning applies within limits to materials used in the product. With experience there is less waste or scrap in the process. Scheduling becomes more efficient. Executive supervision is reduced. Tooling improvements may be expected. In fact, all elements will be lowered according to some learning curve.

Although the concept was developed in connection with new products, one might expect that to a lesser extent the learning curve also exists for products in which a company has had a long history of production. The American productive genius has always prided itself on constantly improving efficiency. A series of synonyms for learning curves have been developed, including improvement, progress, cost, experience, time reduction, and efficiency curves, and production functions.

The learning curve concepts originated during the mid-1920s in connection with cost studies of aircraft production.[6] Researchers developed the hypothesis that as the production quantity of an item was doubled, the worker hours required per unit declined by a constant percentage. Initial studies of aircraft production during World War II found a curve with an 80 percent slope;[7] later studies arrived at comparable conclusions.[8]

In adapting the learning curve concept to an analysis of costs, one must first identify the factors that bring about a lowering of costs (i.e., factors that affect the slope of the curve) and then determine the importance of each of these factors.

The factors most commonly found in such analyses are the following:

1. Job familiarization and task learning (workers and supervisors)
2. Improvement in shop organization and production control
3. Type of work and methods in use
4. Product (stage of development and complexity)
5. The ratio of assembly hours to machine hours
6. Tooling quality and coordination
7. The extent of preproduction planning

Although it is evident that one can resort to computer analysis in order to arrive at the slope of the learning curve, the problem can be resolved more pragmatically.

By way of illustration, if the buyer knows that it takes a supplier 100

---

[6] T.P. Wright, "Factors Affecting the Cost of Airplanes," *Journal of the Aeronautical Sciences* (February 1936).

[7] J.R. Crawford and E. Straus, *World War II Acceleration of Airframe Production* (Air Material Command, Dayton, Ohio, 1947), pp. 9–10.

[8] Werner Z. Hirsch, "Firm Progress Ratios," *Econometrica* (April, 1956), p. 139; Reno R. Cole, "Increasing Utilization of the Cost–Quantity Relationship in Manufacturing," *The Journal of Industrial Engineering* (May–June 1958), p. 175; and *The Improvement Curve Trainees Manual,* (Air Material Command, Dayton, Ohio, 1958), p. 12.

hours of direct labor to make the first unit of a new item and 90 hours to make the second unit, the average labor hours would be 95 hours. When production doubles to four units, the third unit requires 84.6 and the fourth unit 81 hours; the average labor for the four units is 88.9 hours. If each time production doubles the labor hours decline by 10 percent, this product has a learning curve of 90 percent.

It is possible to plot the data on regular graph paper or on double logarithmic paper (see Figure 9-2). When the rate of change remains constant, the logarithmic plot is a straight line, which is easier to read. The

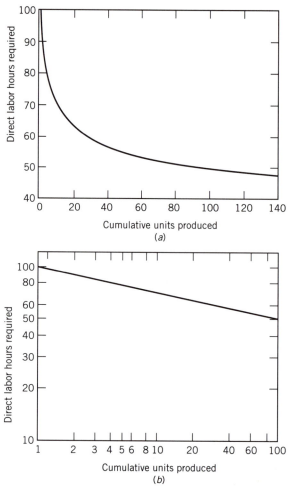

FIGURE 9-2. The learning curves derived from lower cost after experience in production.

learning curve depicted in the first graph shows that learning improvement gradually flattens as the number of units increases. When large volumes are produced, the reduction of labor hours ultimately becomes negligible. Because of this tendency, the learning curve concept has its greatest application in cost analysis of new products.

The learning curve is very valuable as a negotiation tool for several reasons. First, it provides a starting point for pricing new products; second, the negotiator should use the learning curve concept in renegotiation after initial production runs have been completed.

Using a learning curve approach, Teplitz suggests using the seller's given discount schedule and interpolating from that a model for their approximate cost structure.[9] He bases this method on the assumption that the prices given for various quantities reflect the vendor's minimum expected profit at the price-break quantity.

Implications

Purchasing and operations managers find several implications of learning curve theory:

1. Buyer and seller productions increase with no change in resource capacities—the same machines, the same plants, the same workers as before the learning improvements begin.
2. Costs of labor and manufacturing overhead decrease.
3. Seller's product price adjusts downward as a result of decreasing costs; lower materials prices lead buyer's firm to offer finished goods at lower prices.
4. Finished goods become ready for shipment sooner, since it takes fewer hours to produce the output.
5. Buyer's sales force realistically can promise earlier delivery, at lower price, promoting increased sales. If sales increase, the buyer should expect more frequent requisitions, larger quantities to purchase, and larger quantity discounts.
6. Raw materials may stockout sooner, because workers produce at a faster rate.
7. Apparent capacity of the plant increases without investing more money in the plant.
8. The trend toward single-supplier systems enhances productivity improvements from the learning curve concept. The supplier can make

[9] ''Negotiating Quantity Discounts Using a 'Learning Curve Style' Analysis,'' *Journal of Purchasing and Materials Management* (Summer 1988), pp. 33–40.

longer runs between interruptions in production and can produce more output to a buyer without changing specifications or setups.

DIRECT MATERIAL COSTS

The costs of direct materials, those that go directly into making finished goods, can generally be estimated with a high degree of accuracy. The bill of materials, a listing of all materials and parts included in a finished product, is the basic source of buyer's information about materials. However, the quantity of materials used will normally exceed the quantity shown in specifications. An excess is needed in most manufacturing processes because some materials are lost to scrap. The buyer should include a scrap and a possible spoilage factor in the cost–price analysis of direct materials.

In addition to establishing the quantity of the materials to be used, it is necessary to establish a price per unit or pound, before the direct material cost is computed. Furthermore, the analyst must recognize that the scrap and spoiled material will generally have some residual worth when disposed of (see Chapter 19), and this amount must be deducted from the direct material costs to arrive at a net cost figure.

DIRECT LABOR COSTS

The analyst often finds it more difficult to estimate direct labor costs than material costs because knowledge of production processes or methods is often limited. Engineers can measure materials, but at best they can merely approximate the production time required by an outside supplier.

Direct labor costs involve two elements: hours per unit of output and wage rates per hour. Even when the prospective supplier provides a cost breakdown for labor, it is important to separate this figure into its two component elements and then compare the results, as shown in Table 9-1.

Although the second supplier is quoting a lower cost per unit, the hourly

TABLE 9-1. Labor Cost Breakdown—Hours and Hourly Rate

	Supplier 1	Supplier 2
Labor hours	7	3
Rate per hour	$ 6.00	$ 7.00
Direct labor cost	$42.00	$21.00

pay scale is higher. Perhaps in the negotiation process the buyer will be able to convince the supplier that workers with less skill than those performing the job at present can do it. On the other hand, in dealing with the first supplier, the buyer may be able, on the basis of the analysis, to show how hours per unit might be reduced. Either approach could result in a lowering of the costs of procurement.

As mentioned earlier, the learning curve has its greatest application to labor hours and should not be overlooked by the analyst. The analyst should observe in particular whether the supplier appears to use an average wage rate in making cost estimates. It may be that the item can be made by less-skilled workers at lower wage rates and lower cost. If production of the item will entail overtime labor, the analyst should be apprised of this fact and treat it accordingly in estimating direct labor costs.

Most cost–price analysts devote more attention to direct labor costs than to any other category of cost. The reason for this attention is the commonly accepted accounting practice in many firms of computing overhead costs as a percentage of direct labor costs. Thus, when the final price is determined, a reduction in direct labor costs reduces total costs by an amount far in excess of its own amount.

OVERHEAD COSTS

Overhead costs are costs of an indirect nature that are attributable to the manufacturing, engineering, and research activities of a firm. Sales and administrative costs are generally treated as a separate category in cost–price analysis.

Overhead costs are partially fixed, partially variable, and seldom directly attributable to a given unit of production. Overhead costs tend to be recorded and accumulated for specific time periods, such as annual insurance premiums and monthly utility charges. These are costs that must be shared among all the customers of a supplier and completely covered before a profit is earned. There is no completely fair method of spreading such costs, because there are inadequacies in the cost allocation process.

Table 9-2 illustrates some of the most common methods of allocating overhead costs and points out the advantages and disadvantages of each method.

The cost–price analyst must determine which, if any, portion of the overhead costs were incurred for the buyer's benefit. If elements of a supplier's overhead costs are not pertinent to a specific procurement, a buyer should attempt to negotiate them out of the price. For instance, some companies include their research and development costs as a part of overhead. If a given procurement is based on the buyer's own engineering

TABLE 9-2. Methods of Allocating Overhead Costs

Method	Ratio	Allocation	Remarks
Direct Labor Dollar	$\text{Total overhead} \div$ Total direct labor hours	Percent application of direct labor cost	This is the most popular technique. *Advantages* Easily developed. Simple application, plus greatest familiarity. *Disadvantages* Does not consider value added by any factor other than labor. Penalizes operations using highly paid employees over those performed by employees, paid low wages.
Direct Labor Hour	$\text{Total overhead} \div$ Total direct labor hrs	$/hr addition to job costs	Advantages and disadvantages same as Direct Labor Dollar method.
Machine Hour Rate	$\text{Overhead expense/ machine} \div$ Estimates hours of operation (each facility)	Operating time multiplied by machine hour rate added to prime costs	*Advantages* Each machine is a separate entity and can be evaluated as such. Inaccurate gross application of overhead can be minimized. *Disadvantages* Requires detailed analysis of overhead factors by machine, e.g., power, space.
Unit of Product	$\text{Total overhead} \div$ Number of units produced	$/piece addition to unit prime costs	*Advantages* Most direct method. Useful where similar products are made with common factors, i.e., weight, volume. *Disadvantages* Relies on historical base that could be quite misleading.
Prime Cost (total of direct labor and direct material	$\text{Total overhead} \div$ Total prime costs	Percent application of prime costs of order	*Advantages* Easily developed. Simple application. *Disadvantages* Overhead expense relationship to material or labor content (or both) may be poor. Possible inequitable distribution.
Material Cost	$\text{Total overhead} \div$ Total material	Percent application of prime material costs of order	*Advantages* The listed advantages plus particularly useful in bulk industries with uniform product. *Disadvantages* Can result in severe distortion of allocation.

specifications and drawings, one should question the inclusion of seller's research and development costs in the price.

Start-up costs, and occasionally tooling costs, are treated by some organizations as overhead and are thus allocable. The preferred treatment would be to regard them as direct costs chargeable to a given procurement, but this may not be possible if more than one buyer is buying the same item. Furthermore, such costs tend to decrease and may even disappear on future purchases of the item. It is therefore important to identify start-up and tooling costs so as to be in a position to negotiate them out of the cost of subsequent purchases.

OVERHEAD ANALYSIS

Overhead is by far the most negotiable aspect of a vendor's costs. Because overhead is an allocation of many costs, a large number of which are only tangentially related to a given product, there are specific areas that a buyer should investigate.

Essentially, the buyer should investigate overhead by asking the following questions.

1. What is included in the overhead?
2. How is overhead accumulated?
3. How is overhead allocated?

In analyzing what is included, one will often find heavy research and development costs included in the overhead figures. If the buyer requires such research and development in the product being purchased, the inclusion may be warranted. However, if the product is a standard off-the-shelf item requiring no special applications, this expense should not be paid. In summation, the buyer should pay only for the overhead items associated with the research and development needed for the product involved.

Second, the manner of accumulation should be investigated. Some suppliers accumulate the overhead expenses for several product lines; that is, a firm could produce operating tables and conference tables and accumulate the overhead on a total basis. In addition, some vendors might include different plant locations in their overhead accumulation; that is, plants could be located in New York City and Peoria, Illinois. The point is, the actual amount of specific overhead expense will vary with the type of products and the locations. It is logical to assume that operating tables have more specific overhead costs than conference tables, and that costs in New York City are higher than those in Peoria. The important point here is that the buyer would ideally pay only for the costs incurred at the production location of the product in question.

Finally, the method of overhead allocation must be considered. One of the most common approaches is to allocate overhead on the basis of direct labor costs. The ratio of overhead to labor has often been established at some past time or date. Given a long-established relationship or formula, such as, two of overhead to one of direct labor, the amount of overhead charges will be increased every time the direct labor cost increases. In reality, the amount of overhead would be relatively independent of this wage rate times hours worked, which may fluctuate often; the alert buyer negotiates a separate overhead.

To summarize, the buyer should investigate overhead and pay only the charges that are useful to the product being purchased. Second, the overhead accumulation should be predicted at the production site of the product, and the allocation should be based on a relevant, current factor.

GENERAL AND ADMINISTRATIVE COSTS

General and administrative costs resemble overhead costs in that they include elements that are fixed, variable, and direct. However, these costs are seldom tied to a given unit of production. They usually are grouped into one large pool and allocated at the end of a given time period. Typically, they are allocated as a percentage of total manufacturing costs.

To the extent that individual items in a supplier's general and administrative expense are identifiable, there is the possibility of negotiating some of them out of the price. Advertising and certain sales expenses are two items that are likely to be negotiated if it can be shown that neither cost will be incurred in a particular purchase.

PROFIT ANALYSIS

Profits are a normal and necessary part of business transactions. In the short run, a supplier may forgo profits for tactical reasons, but ultimately a profit factor must be included in the price. The cost–price analyst, therefore, should consider the reasonableness of a supplier's profits along with the other elements of cost.

As a rule, if effective competition exists in the supplier industry, the analyst need make no detailed study of profits. Competition will exert pressure to keep profits at a reasonable level. The following are considerations helpful in judging the reasonableness of profits.

1. Competitive prices—are they in line?
2. Initial orders (may have unusual profits depending on repeat projections).
3. Size of order (profit per unit varies inversely).
4. Amount of value added to a product (the more value added, the more justifiable a profit).
5. Kinds of management talent demanded (direct relationship).
6. Risks involved in the production (direct relationship).
7. Efficiency of the vendor (influences costs, prices, and profits).

If effective competition exists, the profit is a reward for efficiency. On a first procurement it may be necessary to allow the vendor a higher than average profit to induce the firm to assume the risks and problems associated with new production.

The profit on small orders will usually be high in order to induce the supplier to accept them. A manufacturer who functions mainly as an assembler of components should expect to receive lower profits than a manufacturer who produces the component elements of the finished product.

If a supplier contributes a high degree of technical design and engineering skill or assumes especially difficult production problems, the firm merits higher profits than a firm engaged in routine production. Similarly, if a supplier assumes unusual risks because of the nature of the product or a long delivery schedule, a higher rate of profit should be paid.

A supplier who has demonstrated extreme reliability in past performance can command a higher profit. An unreliable or unproved supplier may have to prove credibility before earning the same profit rate.

Large increments added to the volume of a supplier will justify a lower profit to that supplier. A buyer who furnishes tooling, equipment, or other services to a supplier should pay a lower profit rate than a buyer who does not supply such aid. Finally, previous experience with a supplier's accuracy in estimating costs is a factor in judging the profit allowance. A supplier whose record shows a tendency to inflate cost estimates may be presumed to be trying to increase profits again.

New Stance

Three basic negotiation strategies characterize the stance that industrial buyers adopt in negotiating the rebuy of component parts, according to a 1991 report. A national field study of more than 300 purchasing agents uncovered their reliance on problem solving, manipulating perceptions about competition, and tough tactics.[10]

The report came at a time when some buyers were experiencing the most trying times of their professional lives. An authority on negotiating observed a huge number of skilled buyers who had not experienced hard times during which they had to negotiate rigorously.[11] The general weakness of the economy and the foreign competitive pressures on sellers during the 1990s require purchasing to take on a much tougher role in negotiations. Moreover, forming better partnerships with sellers may strengthen purchasing managers and buyers' efforts to contain costs.

CHAPTER SUMMARY

Negotiation seeks as its objective an agreement regarding fair and reasonable dealings from both the buyer's and the seller's point of view. Successful negotiation requires proper preparation, including knowledge of cost–price analysis, the capabilities and needs of the vendor, and the needs of the purchaser. Parties can negotiate any item for which alternatives exist, including payment terms as well as delivery and production schedules and the services needed.

A knowledge of the learning curve concept will help determine the price's proper value. In addition, it can form the basis for successful negotiations with suppliers.

Purchasing managers use cost–price analysis as a technique to ensure fair prices. The technique examines every element of the cost incurred by the supplier in manufacturing the needed item—the manufacturing processes and accounting procedures, as well as direct costs, overhead expenses, and profit levels desired.

Discussion Questions

1. Define negotiation as related to purchasing.
2. Identify the various types of negotiation and their applications.
3. What are the objectives of negotiation?
4. What are the important topics in negotiation?
5. Discuss the techniques used in successful negotiations.
6. When should negotiation be used?
7. How should one prepare for negotiation?
8. Relate strategy to the negotiation process.
9. Explain why cost–price analysis is frequently slighted by some purchasing managers.
10. Explain the difference between cost and value.

---

[10] "Purchasing Agents' Use of Negotiation Strategies," *Journal of Marketing Research* (May 1991), pp. 175–189.

[11] "Karrass: If You Think Negotiating Was Hard. . ." *Purchasing* (April 4, 1991), pp. 19–22.

11. What arguments should buyers present in trying to convince sellers to disclose their various cost elements?

12. Describe the various elements of total cost that should be included in cost–price analysis.

13. Explain the learning curve and how it is used in cost analysis.

14. How do you judge the reasonableness of a supplier's profits?

Suggested Cases

Berg Raingear, Inc.

Hearons Company

Household Cleaners Corporation

Industry-wide Pricing

Italiana, Inc.

Jones Price Analysis

McKeough vs. Negotiation Case

MeKeough's Learning Curve

MF-1

Nelson Auto Parts Corporation

Road Equipment Manufacturing Company

Space Systems, Inc.

Warehouse Steel Company

=10

Purchasing in a Global Marketplace

American businesses engaging in international commercial transactions should take note of a new law—the United Nations Convention on Contracts for the International Sale of Goods. In general, the convention applies to contracts for the sale of goods between commercial buyers and sellers located in different convention countries. Under the convention, as is generally the case under the Uniform Commercial Code, the parties to a sales contract are free to agree on any terms they wish or to exclude the application of the convention altogether, in favor of the law of a particular country or state.*

CHAPTER CONTENTS

*Source: "New Taboos on the International Sale of Goods," *Management Review* (July 1991), p. 33.

Purchasing managers' pursuit of excellence in the workplace means that they must search worldwide for materials and occasionally play by foreigners' rules. This reality places American buyers in special circumstances at times, with special fees being the only way to get a cargo moving. The European Community (EC) confronts traders with over 300 directives with its public procurement rules that contain a 50 percent local content requirement, for example.[1]

Trading with Japan, Eastern bloc nations, and the Pacific Rim of southeast Asia have distinct differences that severely challenge purchasing managers.

During the last decade the world has "shrunk" as far as purchasing is concerned. Buyers look to international firms as regular sources of competition, supply, and technological assistance. In the process, unique purchasing concerns regarding tariffs, currency fluctuations, cost components, and political implications present themselves. This chapter presents the relevant issues to be considered by the professional buyer engaged in the international buying arena.

THE STAGES OF CORPORATE INTERNATIONALIZATION

Companies engaging in international trade generally go through four phases of internationalization, beginning with international purchasing and culminating in foreign production operations.

In the first phase, the organization buys or sells sporadically, often using buying and selling agents or brokers. In the second stage the relationship between sources and customers developed in stage one, become continuous. In stage three the organization locates its purchasing or selling personnel abroad, permitting on-location trading relationships. In the fourth stage full-scale production, sales, purchasing, and related facilities are permanently located on foreign soil. Thus, the entry by purchasing personnel into the international market is often the initial inroad of an organization's international involvement, which may eventually become a very extensive international relationship.

Buying American

The Buy American Act of 1988 encourages free trade in government procurement and at the same time urges strict compliance with the International

---

[1] "Europe 1992: The Blueprint for Change," *Marketing Communications* (March 1989), pp. 22–25.

Agreement on Government Procurement. The two positions conflict and therefore freer trade in government procurement may never occur.[2]

The Crafted with Pride in the USA Council joins other ''Buy America and Americans work'' efforts to reduce the job-loss toll. During the past decade, 14 percent of the apparel manufacturing plants in the country have closed. Consumer attitudes toward buying foreign fashions change in response to extensive advertising campaigns like the ''Look for the Made-in-USA label.'' No such response occurs, however, among industrial buyers to the same extent.

THE RATIONALE FOR INTERNATIONAL SOURCING

Historically, the major motives for international purchasing were price–cost advantages. Certain countries have had a comparative advantage in international pricing because of lower wage rates, technological advantages (such as the Japanese electronic advantages of the late 1970s), or abundant supplies (such as sugar). Each of these comparative advantages have, on occasion, meant reduced prices for foreign sources.

Buying Abroad

Purchasing managers buy from foreign sources for product quality, service, price, availability, or compatibility with existing products. The United States bought internationally (i.e., imported) $508.97 billion (including cost, insurance, and freight) in 1991, of such commodities as crude and partly refined petroleum, machinery, automobiles, industrial raw materials, food, and beverages.[3] The U.S. trading partners consisted primarily of western Europe (21.5 percent of U.S. imports in 1989, and 27.3 percent of U.S. exports in 1989), Japan (19.7 and 12.1 percent, respectively), and Canada (18.8 and 22.1 percent, respectively).[4]

Japan will soon dominate international trade and politics as the next global superpower, according to many economists, who refer to the twenty-first century as the Pacific Century. The world's 13 largest banks fly the Japanese flag. A single Japanese company—Nippon Telegraph & Telephone—possesses more worth than IBM, AT&T, General Motors, and General Electric combined. Japan's net foreign assets exceeded $290 billion

---

[2] ''The Buy American Act of 1988: Legislation in Conflict with U.S. International Obligations,'' *Lay & Policy in International Business* (1989), pp. 603–618.

[3] *International Financial Statistics,* International Monetary Fund (September 1992), p. 538.

[4] *The World Factbook 1991,* Central Intelligence Agency, Washington, D. C.

in 1990, the most ever accumulated by one country.[5] Some Japanese business leaders have suggested that, since their investors purchase 30 percent of the U.S. Treasury's securities, the U.S. should consider denominating them in yen rather than dollars.[6]

Endaka (literally, "appreciation of yen") refers to the current purchasing power of the yen compared with the U.S. dollar. In 1983, one U.S. dollar bought 237 yen; in mid-1993, it bought less than 110 yen. *Endaka* makes Japanese goods more expensive in the United States and American goods less expensive in Japan.[7]

In the 1970s, Japanese industry shifted from labor- and energy-intensive manufacturing toward technology-intensive industries such as semiconductor chips, computers, robotics, machine tools, videocassette recorders, and fax machines.

The president of Nippon Steel USA stresses mutual dependence between Japan and the United States:

> Our countries need each other more than ever. Our economies are forever intertwined. The United States needs Japan for its economic and financial strength, and Japan needs the United States to continue its world leadership and umbrella of military strength.[8]

In a rigorous study of European and Japanese multinationals, two researchers concluded that:[9]

> global sourcing appears to be strongly supported by standardization of the components and the product. . . .Standardization enhances the ability to integrate the resources of developing countries into a global sourcing strategy.

New Trading Partners

Several nations now overshadow the U.S. industrial dominance that lasted 100 years. Substantial changes took place in U.S. trade between 1970 and 1988, including a shift of trade to the Pacific, particularly to Southeast Asia. The Federal Reserve Bank of Chicago senior economist points to events in the late 1960s, when the European Community and the European Free Trade Association developed. At that time, the U.S. dollar and investments abroad dominated international exchange. However, these events had the

---

[5] "Reflections on Leadership," *World* (KPMG Peat Marwick, Montvale, NJ), 1990, pp. 6–7.

[6] "U.S.–Japanese Trade Relations," *Vital Speeches* (May 15, 1989), pp. 450–454.

[7] "Endaka in Japanese Means Change," *Chemical Engineering* (November 7, 1988), pp. 33–38.

[8] Op. cit., footnote 5.

[9] Masaaki Kotabe and Glenn S. Omura, "Sourcing Strategies of European and Japanese Multinationals: A Comparison," *Journal of International Business Studies* (Spring 1989), pp. 113–130.

net effect of eliminating "the U.S. trade surplus and shifting the U.S. trade balance into negative territory."[10]

The abrupt rise of Southeast Asia as a trading partner has surprised many purchasing managers. Singapore, Hong Kong, Taiwan, and South Korea form "a new trading bloc that exceeds in volume the combined trade with the United Kingdom and Germany."

Corresponding changes occurred in commodities traded, as Table 10-1 shows. Compared to 1970 imports, the 1988 import figures show that purchasing managers bought machinery and transport equipment internationally in massive volume.

To a much lesser extent, buyers may be prompted to engage in international purchases to "barter" their firm's sales to given countries. A U.S. firm may sell a large quantity of a given product to a certain country and, as a part of the sales agreement, be required (requested) to return the favor by purchasing materials and components from organizations in that country. This practice is often referred to as countertrading.

COUNTERTRADE

A U.S. purchasing manager orders materials from a supplier located in a third world country. Under countertrade the supplier takes something in return from the U.S. customer instead of cash. The supplier then sells it in his or her domestic market or in some other country. The proceeds constitute the transaction's sales revenue.

Multinational corporations find themselves increasingly obliged to become involved—almost entwined—with their third world and socialist business partners. The trend started with huge offsets and coproduction deals in the 1970s between American arms manufacturers and the NATO countries. The trend continued with numerous buybacks with Eastern Europe, the USSR, and China.[11] Estimates of countertrade now range from 1 percent to 40 percent of world trade.[12]

Forms of Countertrade

> *Barter:* An even swap of goods; the direct exchange of goods for goods of equal value.

[10] "Southeast Asia Seen as New U.S. Trade Area," *Chemical & Engineering News* (April 23, 1990), pp. 12–13.
[11] Kenton W. Elderkin and Warren E. Norquist, *Creative Countertrade: A Guide to Doing Business Worldwide* (Cambridge, MA: Ballinger Publishing Company, 1987) describes the topic fully.
[12] "Beyond Barter," *Chief Executive* (March 1990), pp. 72–75.

TABLE 10-1. Various Commodity Classes Show U.S. Export/Import Shift

$ Billions	Exports		Imports	
	1988	1970	1988	1970
Manufactured goods	$22.75	$ 5.07	$ 61.78	$8.44
Machinery	88.43	11.37	117.38	5.28
Transport equipment	46.78	6.52	79.87	5.88
Chemicals	32.36	3.83	19.86	1.44
Petroleum products	3.52	0.47	38.39	2.76
Crude materials	24.99	4.60	13.24	3.32
Food and live animals	26.27	4.34	20.29	5.40
Miscellaneous manufactures	24.67	2.56	70.61	4.84
Other	50.53	3.79	20.74	2.60

Source: Federal Reserve Bank of Chicago.

Buyback: The U.S. provides equipment or a turnkey plant in exchange for manufactured products shipped at a later date, perhaps over 15 years.

Compensation: Offset; cash plus goods from Country A's company to Country B's company that then ships its products to Country A's company; one party pays for the raw materials with the goods produced.

Counterpurchase: Exchange of unrelated goods associated with a third party inside the host country; one party agrees to buy a similar value of the other party's goods after receiving payment.

Switch: Enlarges the trade area by using at least one third party outside the host country.

Barter and countertrade arrangements increase due to the lack of hard currency in many Eastern European countries. Dismantling the extensive 40-year legacy of centralized planning and overregulation has slowed the increased trade that many Eastern and Western nations desire. Closed economies have instilled lower expectations of quality in workers and management than the expectations of the Western world.[13] Low quality swaps may find no other outlets in a strictly competitive marketplace. A survey of 25 United Kingdom firms engaged in countertrade activity with Eastern bloc

[13] "Eastern Europe's Changing Face," *NAPM Insights* (April 1990), p. 4.

nations revealed as the major problem the lack of in-house use for goods offered in countertrade.[14]

The global countertrade service industry has emerged to assist international marketing managers in marketing a wide range of commodities that they had to accept in payment for the goods that they sell. Ninety-three organizations providing countertrade services constitute this industry.[15]

Loans based on commodity swaps may greatly assist U.S. and Western European countries that strive to open trade in Eastern Europe and the former USSR. Swap-based loans could provide capital, and move the Soviets and others in the East bloc closer to convertible currencies. Small businesses especially stand to benefit by sidestepping the currency problem.[16]

Eastern Europe and the former USSR have opened their doors to Asia and want Asia to take part in their economic reconstruction. However, since Eastern Europe's currencies do not convert, Asian countries must learn the elements of countertrade if they want to win business there.[17]

Japan, Germany, and other European countries have many foreign trading companies in their private sectors; the United States has no U.S. government trading company.[18]

SPECIAL CONSIDERATIONS

International operations differ from an organization's traditional domestic ones because there are three environments: domestic, foreign, and international.

The domestic environment consists of these issues that exist in the host country, such as tariffs and export–import policies, currency fluctuations, and strikes. The issues may vary slightly for each foreign country.

Each particular foreign country has the special implications of its domestic situation. For example, the export–import policies of a democratic country such as England have implications different from those of an authoritarian country such as China.

Finally, the international aspect consists of the interaction of the domestic country's policies and procedures with those of other countries involved

[14] "Empirical Insights into British Countertrade with Eastern Bloc Nations," *International Marketing Review (UK)* (1990), pp. 15–31.

[15] "Worldwide Network of Countertrade Services," *Industrial Marketing Management* (February 1990), pp. 69–76.

[16] "Swaps II: Trading for a Convertible Currency," *Futures: The Magazine of Commodities & Options* (June 1990), pp. 42–44.

[17] "The Soviet Bloc: Open for Business," *Asian Business (Hong Kong)* (February 1990), pp. 20–31.

[18] "Countertrade as an Export Strategy," *Journal of Business Strategy* (May–June 1990), pp. 33–38.

in international trade. Included are groupings of countries, such as the European Common Market and the Organization of Petroleum Exporting Countries, which collectively set trade policies and must be considered accordingly. In addition, the international nature of such issues as the cold war, embargoes, and regional hostilities have a distinct effect on buyer–seller relations.

ECC

The 12-nation European Economic Community expanded from the original six-nation economic alliance created in March 1957. Plans for trade barrier removal by 1992 focused attention on a need for quality standards, inspection procedures, and a common currency. When national pride preserved the individual currencies, the nations adopted freer exchange for each other's currencies. These actions bear out the Single European Act aim: creation of "an area without internal frontiers in which the free movement of goods, persons, services and capital is ensured."[19]

Euro-consumers could become the largest single market in the industrialized world, 30 percent larger than the United States. The market's 340 million people could exceed the United States by 60 million and Japan by 216 million. The European Community gross national product for 1991 exceeded $8.5 trillion at the current exchange rate.[20] In comparison, the U.S. 1991 gross national product exceeded $5.685 trillion.

The European Economic Community nations include Belgium, Denmark, France, Germany, Greece, Ireland, Italy, Luxembourg, the Netherlands, Portugal, Spain, and the United Kingdom.

STRATEGIC MATERIALS

For generations, strategic materials have come from abroad. By definition, the term "strategic materials" refers to those elements, minerals, and substances that the United States needs for defense, and that do not exist abundantly in the United States. Geopolitics shift occasionally, disrupting supplies. Disruptions provoke American buyers to curtail production or to introduce substitutes. To locate supplies, U.S. and Canadian buyers sometimes work through intermediaries who know how to find the materials and keep them moving to the North American continent.

The National Defense Stockpile holds strategic materials that the United States might not find available during a full-scale conventional war. Im-

---

[19] *The Europa World Year Book 1990* (London: Europa Publications Limited, 1990), p. 141.
[20] "One Big Currency—And One Big Job Ahead," *Business Week* (December 23, 1991), pp. 40–42.

ported stockpiled strategic materials include chromium, manganese, cobalt, platinum, phosphate, and crude oil.

Economic modeling provides government and private planners with tools for simulating market disruptions. The expected results include stability solutions and surprise-free projections.[21]

The United States needs to adjust to a world based on interdependence. Efficient recycling, the development of various synthetic materials, and the international processing of raw materials are helping the United States to shift from its traditional dependency on raw materials from abroad.

NATIONAL VENTURING

Buyers of new or scarce materials look at home or abroad to tap the supply. They find the supply in those nations that venture successfully. The supply of new products and the outflow from new processes occur when nations harness the forces that build and sustain enterprises. Cash starts the cycle. Cash finances research and development laboratories and inventor staffs and later finances production and distribution. Cash ends the cycle. It refunds the initial investments and rewards the investors. Venture capitalists hunt for ideas that pay off after exposure to some amount of risk. A national mood supports venturesomeness, if it has the cash. At other times the mood discourages venturing, as a faithless public mocks eggheads and the intellectual elite.

Eastern Europe finds itself short of cash as its new freedoms begin. Therefore, it cannot start the cycle that engages R&D to create marketable products.

For many nations the number of R&D scientists and engineers per million population trends upward since 1969, as Figure 10-1 shows.[22] The U.S. decline until the mid-70s reflects the general malaise toward science and scientific education following the "flower-people" generation and the war in Vietnam. Japan's sharp rise results in part from the U.S. education of Japanese scientists and engineers and the Japanese pride in its professional people. Other nationals avail themselves of U.S. educations. In fact, almost a third of 1988's science and engineering graduate students in U.S. schools came from abroad.[23]

Five countries in 1988 spent more of their gross national product (GNP)

---

[21] "A Dynamic Nash Game Model of Oil Market Disruption and Strategic Stockpiling," *Operations Research* (November–December 1989), pp. 958–971.

[22] *Statistical Yearbook 1987* (United Nations Educational, Scientific and Cultural Organization, Paris, 1987), pp. 5–14.

[23] *Chemical and Engineering News* (August 20, 1990), p. 52.

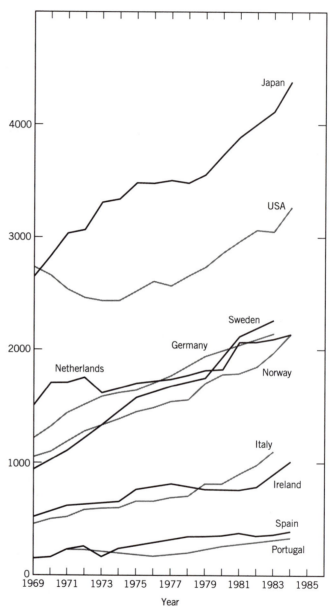

FIGURE 10-1. Number of R&D scientists and engineers per million population in 10 selected developed countries; trends since 1969.

on R&D than the U.S.'s 2.8 percent, namely Sweden (3.1 percent), Israel (3.0 percent), Japan (2.9 percent), Switzerland (2.9 percent), and West Germany (2.8 percent).[24]

A national pride in quality output, the rise from poverty and disrupted lives following World War II, and the fire-from-within to venture, form immense motivational power factors. These factors create Japanese and West German supplies of goods and services that attract U.S. and Canadian buyers. Natural resources and venturesome spirits do the same for the Pacific Rim of Southeast Asia.

GATT

The General Agreement on Tariffs and Trade (GATT) since 1948 has governed in part international traders. It has witnessed a ten-fold increase in world trade volume since 1950. Its guidebook specifies how companies in different countries should buy and sell their products.

World-trade ministers among the 98 members meet about once every five years to renegotiate the agreement's rules. Typically, the reforms encourage nations to stop placing taxes on foreign goods and to avoid preparing technical specifications that create international trade obstacles.

Since 1981, the Government Procurement Code, negotiated under GATT, allows U.S. suppliers to sell goods to foreign governments on an equal par with domestic suppliers.[25]

The Free Trade Agreement between Canada and the United States finds a parallel with the borderless Europe of 1992.[26] However, many environmentalists, labor and human-rights activists and Third-World leaders strongly oppose the free trade concept. They argue that it permits international corporations to operate in any place on the globe with as little government interference as possible. Much of the authority to protect the environment, food, labor and small businesses would shift from communities, states, and nations into government-appointed trade ministers, multinational corporations, and international agencies.[27] For example, the UN's Codex Alimentarius Commission based in Rome would create uniform global food standards. Historically low standards set by Codex would allow importing, for example, bananas containing up to 50 times the DDT amount that the

---

[24] Ibid., pp. 55–56.
[25] "Procurement Code Gives U.S. Suppliers 'Level Playing Field,'" *Business America* (November 21, 1988), pp. 6–7.
[26] "The U.S.–Canada Free Trade Agreement," *Business America* (January 30, 1989), pp. 2–27. Effective January 1, 1989, expected to eliminate all tariffs on U.S.–Canada trade by 1998.
[27] "Trading Away the Planet," *Greenpeace* (September–October 1990), pp. 14–16.

U.S. Food & Drug Administration permits. If Texas, for further example, tried to restrict imports of food contaminated with pesticides that the United States now bans, foreign governments under GATT rules could sue the United States for setting nontariff barriers to trade. GATT rules could make it extremely difficult for countries anywhere to develop their raw materials and natural resources.

Under the Omnibus Trade and Competitiveness Act of 1988, the U.S. Trade Representative (USTR) identifies countries that violate the GATT rules or that support them. In this latter regard, the USTR recently reported on foreign governments that have strengthened intellectual property rules. Examples included Saudi Arabia's new copyright law and Portugal's increased penalties for audio piracy.[28]

North American Free Trade Agreement (NAFTA)

Contentious debate may keep the U.S. Congress from approving the North American Free Trade Agreement that was finalized in August 1992 after 14 months of almost nonstop negotiations. The pact would bind 363 million consumers into the world's largest trading zone with a combined gross domestic product of more than $6 trillion. Mexico could gain 600,000 primarily industrial jobs by 1995 as the agreement rolls back tariffs and reduces restrictive quotas that hobble the country's exports. The United States and Canada could profit from an explosion in sales to the Mexican market.[29]

Manufactured goods comprise nearly 75 percent of U.S.–Mexican trade. Advantages of expanding facilities with the 82-million-people Mexican market include low wages, a relatively well educated work force, proximity, ample energy reserves (twice U.S. crude reserves), and political stability. However, risks include nationalistic policies regarding industry and a vastly different legal system. Two other obstacles appear: Canada's sensitivity to preserving advantages gained in the 1988 free-trade agreement with the United States and opposition in the U.S. Congress.[30]

The International Purchasing Challenge

Ongoing changes in the world scene challenge purchasing people to broaden all aspects of their concept of buying. Purchasing in the international marketplace requires a view of the entire world as a potential source

---

[28] "USTR Issues Reports on Procurement and Intellectual Property Protection," *Business America* (May 21, 1990), pp. 15–16.
[29] "The Barriers Come Tumbling Down," *Time* (August 17, 1992), pp. 15–16.
[30] "The Mexico Variable," *Purchasing* (December 12, 1991), p. 22.

for raw materials, components, services, and finished goods. The customs regulations on international trade firm up around tradition, custom, and cultural values that may look on bribes in commerce as a manner common among business people; on the other hand, customs officials may impound the shipment. The ramifications of failing to comply with import regulations may lead to criminal penalties.[31]

Understanding exchange rate fluctuations and knowing how to pay for a product internationally could play an important role in getting the right product at the right quality and price.[32]

Assistance to professional purchasing people to meet the international purchasing challenge has also grown. The United Nations' International Trade Commission gives specific directions to buyers in locating sources, as does the U.S. Department of Commerce, the Small Business Administration, the U.S. Agency for International Development, and local trade groups. The National Association of Purchasing Management assumes leadership in international purchasing development and frequently assesses conditions.[33] For instance, NAPM's 1991 survey of about 800 U.S. purchasing professionals found that only one-fourth of the responding firms have well-defined international purchasing strategies that apply consistently from one buying situation to the next. The respondents indicated a strong tendency toward avoiding risk in making international sourcing decisions.[34]

A decisive no vote in Quebec during August 1992 boosted an independence movement there. That attitude strengthens the position of a majority of Canadians who oppose both the 1989 U.S.–Canada Free Trade Agreement and NAFTA.[35]

Other problems arise. The disparity between U.S. and Mexican judicial systems creates a problem of commercial dispute resolution, one that disgruntles U.S. exporters. These traders may withstand heavy losses because of widespread corruption and the lack of a reliable Mexican court system to which to address commercial disputes. Capitol Hill free-trade proponents readily acknowledge the disparity between U.S. and Mexican systems and say that people with legitimate claims must sue their customers or partners in Mexican courtrooms.[36]

Despite problems, already many major U.S. companies such as Sears, PepsiCo, Compaq Computer, and Microsoft have expanded their Mexican operations. Likewise, many large U.S. and Canadian companies have al-

[31] "Avoid Customs Hassles, Know Your Import Regulations," *NAPM Insights* (August 1992), p. 9.

[32] "Forecasting Currencies," op. cit. (August 1990), p. 5.

[33] "NAPM's International Mission," op. cit. (May 1990), p. 2.

[34] "International Purchasing Strategies of Multinational U.S. Firms," *International Journal of Purchasing and Materials Management* (Summer 1991), pp. 9–18.

[35] "Northern Disorder," *Business Week* (November 9, 1992), pp. 58–59.

[36] "Disorder South of the Border," *World Trade* (November 1992), pp. 38–41.

ready laid the groundwork for the official advent of the North American Free Trade Agreement, which will create the world's largest free-trade zone.[37]

To control the potential environmental impact of NAFTA, Mexico, Canada, and the United States have summarized key environmental provisions, including:

1. The trade obligations of NAFTA countries regarding endangered species, ozone-depleting substances, and hazardous waste will take precedence over NAFTA provisions.
2. NAFTA countries will work jointly to enhance the protection of human, animal, and plant life, and health and the environment.
3. NAFTA permits the parties to impose environmental standards on new investments, including the requirement that prospective investors submit environmental impact statements.[38]

Most U.S. shippers and transportation executives say they stand to benefit tremendously from NAFTA. U.S. manufacturers of finished goods and food products gain the most. Freight transportation constitutes the key to increasing trade between NAFTA nations. Under NAFTA, Mexican truckers will have immediate access to the United States. American truckers will have access to Mexican states contiguous to the United States in 1995 and all of Mexico in 1999.[39]

The Canadian Free Trade Agreement (CFTA)

The Canadian Free Trade Agreement (CFTA) includes trade in services, the first trade agreement to do so. The CFTA ensures that companies in over 150 service sectors can provide their services in the partner country without discrimination. Moreover, CFTA streamlines border-crossing procedures for business travel and removes barriers to trade in energy; in fact, it provides secure access to energy. NAFTA extends coverage to nearly all service sectors and eliminates existing federal and local regulations restricting partner country access to service markets.[40]

A Jakarta, Indonesia court has judged illegal two contracts between a

[37] "Free Trade? They Can Hardly Wait," *Business Week* (September 14, 1992), pp. 24–25.
[38] "Environment Gains an Edge: NAFTA Adds an International Dimension to Environment Regulation," *Business Mexico* (October 2, 1992), pp. 38–39.
[39] "After NAFTA: Shippers Examine Its Dollars and Sense," *Global Trade (GTR)* (October 1992), pp. 10–13.
[40] "NAFTA Improves Trading Opportunities with Canada," *Business America* (October 19, 1992), pp. 30–32.

United Kingdom businessperson and an Indonesian businessperson. The contracts allegedly violate Indonesian restrictions against importing sugar. Appeals failed. The court's decision represents a setback to Indonesia's efforts to expand world trade.[41]

SPECIFIC CONCERNS IN EVALUATING SOURCES

In a general sense, the process of evaluating an international source is quite similar to the evaluation of a domestic source. The potential is considered in relation to quality, service, price, and delivery—with the important modifications described here.

First of all, quality becomes an important variable because the buyer cannot expect U.S. standards and specifications to prevail for an international source. Particular attention must therefore be given to clear communication between seller and buyer, a task that is naturally more difficult when different languages must also be considered.

The service aspect of an international source is generally less significant than with a domestic source. Service concerns such as engineering assistance and research and development efforts, although not unknown, are not as likely to be major considerations in evaluating an international source.

Price takes on new dimensions, since foreign currencies must be considered relative to the value of the dollar, and the future relationship of the foreign currency to the dollar must be considered and projected. For example, a purchase of steel on July 1 may be quoted on the basis of an exchange rate of 2.5 yoiks to the dollar, with shipment scheduled for December 1, to be paid with currency in effect at time of shipment. If the yoik strengthens relative to the dollar during the six-month period so that the relationship becomes 2.0 yoiks to the dollar, the relative currency change has resulted in a 25 percent increase in price. Therefore, currency hedging using the futures market becomes an important tool in safeguarding price levels in international trade.

Delivery also takes on a new light because international shipping procedures and in-transit time variables complicate inventory planning and necessary safety precautions. Special consideration must also be given to the following factors.

1. *Political Situation:* Is the host country of the international source projected to be stable? Changes in political structures can obviously alter trade policies and even international source ownership.

---

[41] "Jakarta Court Declares Standard International Sales Contract Illegal," *East Asian Executive Reports* (March 15, 1990), pp. 6, 13–14.

2. *International Source Commitment to the Export Market:* Is the choice of source part of a long-term exporting policy or the result of a temporary recession or cyclical deviation in the source's industry?

3. *The exporting expertise of the international source:* Relevant considerations include transportation and financing abilities, international trade, internal sales organization and experience of personnel, familiarity with the United States, ability to provide short-term delivery, and international legal considerations, among others.

REQUIRED BUYER EXPERTISE

International buyers must develop specific expertise in the following areas: financing alternatives, shipping and transportation, and international agents or intermediate coordinators. The following discussion highlights the major concerns in each of these areas.

Financing

Domestic purchases have terms such as 1–10–30, or net-30, to which buyers must calculate effective rates of return in deciding whether to pay early to take the discount. (See Chapter 8 for a translation of 1–10–30 to an annualized rate.) International purchases can be made on the basis of open accounts, letters of credit, documentary drafts, or compensatory trade arrangements.

Open-Account Purchase. In an open-account purchase the buyer pays for the material after it has been received and inspected at the buyer's location. The seller assumes all the risks and has capital tied up for long periods of time. Consequently, open-account financing is limited to a few close buyer–seller transactions.

Letter of Credit. A document issued by the buyer's bank, a letter of credit guarantees payment of a specified amount to the international source when the bank has received specified documents within a specified time. Figure 10-2 is an example.

In effect, the bank has substituted its credit for that of the buyer, providing much more safety to the seller. Naturally, fees are charged by the bank. The exporter can tie this letter of credit to a draft (see following section) to obtain funds earlier than would be possible through other methods of sale.

There are variations in the usual five points of letters of credit; some are revocable (i.e., they are not guarantees but merely facilitate payment) whereas others are irrevocable (i.e., once the letter of credit is issued it cannot be canceled).

The letter of credit is the most widely used method of finance in international trade because it provides latitude for most specific contingencies between the buyer and the seller and substitutes third-party financial credibility (the bank's) to ensure the transaction.

Documentary Draft. A documentary draft does not provide the same assurance that a letter of credit does—the assurance that payment will be made. As its name implies, it requires documents to be provided before payment is made. Made by the seller (exporter), it directs the bank of the buyer (importer) to pay a third party (either the exporter or its bank) when specified documents (usually proof of receipt of acceptable materials) are presented.

Drafts that are payable upon presentation are called sight drafts; those payable at some specified period after presentation (e.g., 30 days) are called time drafts.

A draft is commonly used with a letter of credit. The letter of credit is a strong promise to pay but of and by itself is not the means of payment. It merely substitutes the bank's superior credit for that of the buyer. A draft usually directs the bank to review the letter of credit and the stipulated documents and then issue the draft. The executed draft then becomes a negotiable financial instrument that can be sold by the exporter (usually at a discount) to obtain immediate returns.

Compensatory Trade. A barter-type transaction, compensatory trade entails the transferring of assets as a condition of the contract. It is used primarily when volumes of trade are large and to influence the value of one country's trade relations. It is a means of balancing imports and exports by an exchange of goods in order to avoid complete dependence on currency transfers.

Transport

The alternative modes of international shipping are primarily air and water travel. Air freight is the most rapid but also the most expensive and therefore is usually limited to high-value, low-bulk products. Water or ship transportation, slower and cheaper, is the most widely used form of international transportation. In dealing with transactions on an international scale, buyers must have a basic understanding of the ground rules of international transportation and the legal considerations involved.

OUTGOING TELEX INSTRUCTIONS

THIS MESSAGE IS TO BE SENT AS A

INTERNATIONAL TELEX NO: 9999999999999

DATE: SEPTEMBER 19, 199X
TEST 999999

TO: BEST CORREPONDENT BANK
    BIG CITY
    SELLER'S COUNTRY

WE OPEN IRREVOCABLE LETTER OF CREDIT NO. 123456789
EXPIRY: DECEMBER 20, 199X IN SELLER'S COUNTRY
AMOUNT: YEN 115,300,000 (ONE HUNDRED FIFTEEN MILLION THREE
            HUNDRED THOUSAND NO/100 JAPANESE YEN
FAVOR: FAR EAST TRADING CO.
            INTERNATIONAL DIVISION
            FOREIGN CITY
            FOREIGN COUNTRY
APPLICANT: BIG TIME US IMPORT CO.
            500 MAIN STREET
            AMERICAN CITY, STATE, USA
AVAILABLE WITH/BY   YOU/NEGOTIATION
  DRAFT AT/DRAWN ON   SIGHT/YOURSELVES, INDICATING NUMBER
                                  AND DATE OF THIS CREDIT
—SIGNED COMMERICAL INVOICE   2 ORIGINALS AND 3 COPIES
—PACKING LIST   2 ORIGINALS AND 3 COPIES
—CERTIFICATE OF ORIGIN   1 ORIGINAL AND 2 COPIES
—INSURANCE POLICY/CERTIFICATE FOR 110 PERCENT INVOICE VALUE, COVERING
  ALL RISK, BLANK ENDORSED 1 ORIGINAL 2 (COPIES)
—FULL SET CLEAN ON-BOARD OCEAN BILLS OF LADING, DATED NOT LATER THAN
  NOVEMBER 20, 199X, CONSIGNED TO THE ORDER OF SHIPPER, BLANK ENDORSED,
  MARKED "FREIGHT PREPAID" AND NOTIFY ACCOUNT PARTY AND CANDO
  CUSTOMS BROKER, 100 MAIN STREET, AMERICAN CITY, STATE, USA, TELEPHONE:
  222-8888
—BENEFICIARY'S WRITTEN STATEMENT CERTIFYING THAT EACH CONTAINER IS
  MARKED WITH LC AND P.O. NUMBERS
—CERTIFICATE OF ACCEPTANCE ISSUED BY MR. TOSHIO KUMISURU, BUYER'S
  QUALITY ASSURANCE REPRESENTATIVE
COVERING SHIPMENT OF 10,000 WIDGETS AS PER P.O. NO. 444; CIF
FOREIGN CITY

FIGURE 10-2. A letter of credit. Reprinted by permission of the Nations Bank, San Antonio, Texas.

SHIPMENT FROM FOREIGN PORT TO US PORT
PARTIAL/TRANSHIPMENT   PERMITTED/PERMITTED IN US. ONLY
SPECIAL INSTRUCTIONS:
COMBINED TRANSPORT DOCUMENTS ARE ACCEPTABLE
UCP 400 APPLIES
MAIL DOCUMENTS IN ONE LOT TO   NATIONS BANK, 100 MAIN STREET,
AMERICAN CITY, STATE, USA., ATTN: INTERNATIONAL DEPT.
ALL CHARGES OUTSIDE OF USA FOR ACCOUNT OF BENEFICIARY.

THREE DAYS AFTER RECEIPT OF YOUR TESTED TELEX NOTIFYING US THAT YOU
HAVE NEGOTIATED DOCUMENTS IN STRICT CONFORMANCE WITH CREDIT TERMS, WE
WILL REIMBURSE YOU IN ACCORDANCE WITH YOUR INSTRUCTIONS
THIS IS THE OPERATIVE INSTRUMENT AS NO MAIL CONFIRMATION WILL FOLLOW.
PLEASE ADVISE THE BENEFICIARY.

TKS/BEST REGARDS
NATIONS BANK, AMERICAN CITY
JOE GOODGUY, MANAGER
LETTER OF CREDIT DEPT.

FIGURE 10-2. (Continued)

Price Quotations. The most common means of price quotation used by overseas suppliers are those that provide for "cost, insurance, and freight" (CIF) or "cost and freight" (CF). The CIF contract is an agreement by the supplier to pay the total costs of transportation, insurance, and freight to the destination. Though both contracts include freight, they are considered not destination contracts but shipment contracts; the title and the risk of loss are the buyer's, once the goods are delivered to the carrier.

Rules of Shipping Contracts. International trade shipping contracts have five basic customary practices. Since the United States ratified the Convention on International Sales of Goods (CISG), these customary practices would require the supplier to perform the following:[42]

1. Deliver goods to the carrier and obtain a negotiable bill of lading that covers the agreement all the way to the destination.
2. Load the goods and obtain a receipt that shows the freight has been paid or provided for.

---

[42] United Nations Convention on Contracts for the International Sale of Goods (1980) (Doc. A/Conf. 97/18, Annex I). Treaty drafted by UNCITRAL—the United Nations Commission on International Trade Law, ratified by the United States effective January 1, 1988.

3. Obtain a policy or certificate of insurance payable to the buyer or "to whom it may concern."
4. Prepare an invoice and obtain other required shipping documents.
5. Forward all documents to the buyer with any necessary endorsements for the buyer's rights.

Greater Flexibility

The CISG now provides for greater flexibility in the contracting of international sales, to depart from prior law of various nations and have a uniform international sales standard.[43] However, in the customary transaction, the bill of lading that covers the entire transaction provides the buyer with the most complete protection possible. It gets the goods moving in commercially available shipping channels and enables the buyer to deal with the goods while they are still in transit. The bill of lading must therefore cover only the quantity of goods specified in the contract. The buyer is not obligated to accept a bill of lading for a greater quantity than contracted for or to accept goods not covered in the bill of lading for the contracted quantity.

The supplier is not permitted to ship "freight collect" unless the contract specifies otherwise. The supplier must either pay the freight or provide for its payment through means such as an open account extended by the carrier. The supplier must obtain a receipt to assure the buyer that payment of freight is not required.

It is customary procedure for the supplier to obtain normal transit insurance, at the point of shipment, for the particular type of goods being shipped. Also to be considered, if they affect the degree of risk, are the carrier's equipment and any peculiarities of the destination facilities. However, the applicable law does not require that the insurance cover all risks to which the goods might be exposed during shipping. Furthermore, the amount of insurance need cover only the value of the goods at the time and place of shipment; in-transit market value increases and the buyer's anticipated profit from resale or use are excluded. It is also required that the proceeds of insurance be paid in the currency agreed on in the contract.

As specified by the UCC, the supplier's invoice is an important document. This invoice usually describes the goods and states their quality, information not readily available in any other documents. The supplier is obligated to forward all documents immediately so that if the goods are lost

---

[43] For an in-depth treatment of the international sales transaction, see Folsom, Gordon, and Spanogle, *International Business Transactions* (St. Paul, MN: West Publishing, 1986), Chapter 4, p. 32.

or destroyed during transit, the buyer may take action against the carrier or insurer.

CIF and CF contracts require that the buyer provide payment to the tender of the required documents before inspecting the goods. However, this does not amount to an obligatory acceptance of the goods and does not impair the right of the buyer to subsequent inspections. Suppliers utilize CIF and CF contracts primarily as a protection against unjustified rejection of goods by buyers at distant destinations.

Intermediaries

In international shipping circles there are a number of facilitators who give considerable assistance in the preceding and other aspects of the physical flow of goods. These parties act as agents of buyers, sellers, and shippers and provide technical expertise that assists the flow of goods between exporter and importer. Some American companies use intermediaries initially, then set up a direct purchasing situation. Others continue to use intermediaries.

Foreign Freight Forwarders. The intermediaries forwarding freight do not take possession of the goods; they merely handle paperwork necessary to ensure proper shipment. Their specific responsibilities usually include the original bookings on the primary carriers, providing for port transfers, arranging for packing, translating foreign correspondence, and tracing shipments.

They are used on most overseas shipments and provide a valuable service requiring specialized expertise. Their fees are usually based on a percentage of the actual charges of the primary freight movers and the number of intermediate steps from the point of shipment to the destination.

Import Agents. Representing foreign sellers, import agents are in effect commissioned salespeople for the selling firms. They can negotiate all conditions of sale between buyers and sellers and are primarily located in major trading cities. They tend to specialize in certain lines of commodities, for example, raw materials and cloth products.

Shipping Brokers. Shipping brokers, as their name implies, are intermediaries who deal in space on ships for the transportation of materials. Paid on a commission basis and located in major shipping centers, they can alleviate most of the concerns in contracting for specific transport carriers.

INFORMATION SOURCES

To assist buyers in contacting knowledgeable sources, the *Global Guide to International Business* provides information on trade under several categories, as follows:[44]

Transportation, Shipping and Forwarding Information Sources

Air Freight Forwarders Association of America
American Institute of Marine Underwriters
The ICC Publishing Corporation, Inc.
International Traffic Services, Inc.
National Cargo Bureau Inc.
National Customs Brokers and Forwarders Association of America
National Export Traffic League, Inc.
Trade Information Service, The Journal of Commerce
American Shipper
Brandon's Shipper & Forwarder
Export–Import Traffic Management and Forwarding
Export Shipping Manual
Handbook of World Transport
The Journal of Commerce Export Bulletin
Shipping Digest
Transportation Telephone Tickler
Transport Laws of the World
World Shipping Laws

Importing and Purchasing Information Sources

American Association of Exporters and Importers
Compliance Office, Import Administration, International Trade Administration, U.S. Department of Commerce
Export Information, Organization of American States
Foreign Trade Zones Staff, Import Administration
Public Information Office, U.S. Customs Service
Directory of United States Importers

[44] Facts on File Publications, 460 Park Avenue South, New York, NY 10016, 1983, pp. 129–133, 137–141.

Handbook of International Purchasing
The Journal of Commerce Import Bulletin
The "How-to" Guide for Importers and Exporters
U.S. Import Weekly
World Industrial Reporter

Customs and Tariffs

Custom House Guide
Customs Regulations of the United States
Tariff Schedules of the United States, Annotated

Hazardous Waste Cleanup

Internationally, stricter laws and controls have made the removal of waste and hazardous materials one of the business environment's fastest-growing segments. Areas with the greatest potential and opportunity include Mexico (a $2 billion agreement to clean up the 2000 mile U.S. border, another $4.6 billion to cut air pollution by 1994), Eastern Europe, the European Community, and Southeast Asia. The worldwide environmental market, estimated at $200 billion, may go beyond $300 billion in the decade.[45]

Purchasing and materials managers concern themselves with hazardous materials, including transport, as Chapter 18 discusses. In the global marketplace The International Maritime Dangerous Goods code regulates more than 1000 commodities—not lethal chemicals but consumer items like cosmetics, adhesives, and garden supplies. The burden of complying with a seemingly bewildering array of regulations falls on the manufacturer. Violators risk not only having shipments rejected by a carrier or turned back at a distant port, but also face the prospect of large fines, lawsuits, and criminal penalties in case of an accident.[46]

Trading with Japan

Purchasing executives in over 300 manufacturing companies make up the Business Survey Committee for the National Association of Purchasing Management. Seventy-seven percent of committee members report that they import amounts averaging 12.9 percent of their annual overall weighted dollars of total domestic requirements.[47]

---

[45] "Profiting from the Global Cleanup," *International Business* (June 1992), pp. 36–42.
[46] "Tough Laws Strand Cargo," *International Business* (July 1992), pp. 19–22.
[47] "Insights on Imports," *NAPM Insights* (March 1992), p. 13.

Traders report that Japan experiences difficulties due to weaknesses in management style, friction in international trade, high living costs, poor housing conditions, expensive education for children, and a poor social infrastructure. Japanese manufacturing industries now pay much attention to technological innovation for both products and processes,[48] which offers a boone to American purchasing managers.

The Japan Institute of Plant Maintenance observes American practices such as Tennessee Eastman Company's use of Total Productive Maintenance (TPM) at its Kingsport facility that has accumulated savings of over $24 million. Reengineering the Japanese company with TPM and other innovations from around the world represents the challenge for the 1990s.[49]

Trading with Russia

The advantages of buying manufactured goods from the former USSR include dramatic cost savings and easier access to the imminently lucrative foreign market comprising the Commonwealth of Independent States (CIS). Sourcing in the CIS nevertheless presents a daunting task. In addition to language and geographic barriers, the Russian business culture operates on connections. U.S. buyers should plan on almost a month for shipping.[50]

CHAPTER SUMMARY

In a global marketplace, buyers of materials and services search worldwide for better quality, better delivery, and better prices. Tariffs, currency fluctuations, cost components, and political implications complicate the purchase transactions. Firms place purchasing executives in foreign branches or employ agents in those countries that produce materials.

Buyer–seller transactions become complex in light of different quality standards, different customs, different languages, and different national values. U.S. firms buying internationally provide currency to fuel the foreign economy and to finance their buying America's goods and services. International purchasing reaches higher prominence as the United States grows more dependent on foreign sources for goods that domestic mines and plants no longer produce.

---

[48] "Present Trends and Issues in Japanese Manufacturing and Management," *Technovation* (April 1992), pp. 177–189.

[49] "Time Bomb or Profit Center?" *Industry Week* (March 2, 1992), pp. 52–57.

[50] "Sale Days—Russian Style!" *Purchasing* (August 13, 1992), pp. 20–21.

Discussion Questions

1. What are the four stages of corporate internationalization?
2. What is the rationale for international sourcing?
3. Discuss the special considerations relevant to international business organizations.
4. Delineate the specific concerns of international sourcing and explain their importance.
5. What areas of expertise are required of the international buyer?
6. Discuss the various types of financing available for foreign purchases and their applicabilities.
7. What is the difference between a shipment contract and a destination contract?
8. What are the basic rules of shipping contracts in international trade?
9. Discuss the individual functions of each of the intermediaries discussed in the chapter.

Suggested Cases

Italiana, Inc.

Stith Foreign Steel

Purchasing Performance Measurement with Internal Audit and Feedback

Motorola, Inc. spent a decade of concentrating its own energies on quality procurement. The company won the 1988 Malcolm Baldrige National Quality Award; now it demands that its suppliers put themselves in a position to apply for the award. Annual Motorola sales in 1989 exceeded $9.6 billion, with roughly 40 percent earned outside the United States.

The company derives value from the award by being involved in the examination, which constitutes a quantifiable, impartial, and rigorous quality assessment process. The award covers the range of requirements necessary to achieve total quality management, namely, prevention, effective policies, and measured results.*

CHAPTER CONTENTS

Evaluation Objectives

Evaluation Criteria

Evaluation Standards

Evaluation Methods

Management by Objectives and Results

Purchasing Manuals

Evaluation of Materials Management

Control and Audit

Auditing of Organizational Structure

*Source: "Quality 1991—Buying Quality: Why Reinvent the Wheel?" *Purchasing* (January 17, 1991), pp. 89, 91.

Outstanding performance needs encouraging. In rushing to fight daily fires and to meet deadlines, managers sometimes overlook subordinates' outstanding performances that make the organization better. The evaluation process requires that managers determine what they expect, communicate those management expectations to subordinates, and then compare performance to expectations.

Managers increasingly find themselves setting objectives for their entire organization and for functions such as marketing, production, finance, and accounting.[1] The matrix management style of organizing the enterprise brings together managers from those various functions, who can describe the trends within their environment and relate those trends to the owners' and shareholders' desires for profit, market share, or dominance in the field.

Many senior managers measure the productivity of purchasing departments today on the basis of total cost management.[2] Cross-functional teams, sometimes including representatives from external customers and suppliers, allocate a portion of the cost savings or return-on-investment improvement to each purchasing department member who contributed to the gain. This gain-sharing constitutes a new recognition of purchasing as a value-adding, cross-functional process.

Measuring feedback takes the form of managers discussing with subordinates their contribution to increasing shareholder value.[3]

Purchasing's potential for making significant contributions to an organi-

[1] Samuel C. Certo, *Modern Management: Quality, Ethics, and the Global Environment* (Boston: Allyn & Bacon, 1992), p. 116.

[2] "Productivity Measurement: A Shifting Paradigm in Purchasing," *NAPM Insights* (February 1992), pp. 10–11.

[3] "The New Math of Performance Measurement," *The Journal of Business Strategy* (March–April 1992), pp. 33–38.

zation means that its performance should be measured to ensure that it is meeting expectations. The task is a complicated one because purchasing as a function must deal with people and ideas; many of its efforts involve interpersonal relations with sales, engineering, and other departments within both its own and supplying firms. In contrast, other business functions are more amenable to objective measurement. The production department, for example, can be evaluated by units of output, worker hours of labor, power consumption, rejection rates, and technical product tests.

Any evaluation of purchasing must recognize the difficulties of using subjective performance measures. For example, it is difficult to quantify supplier development, interdepartmental relationships, and negotiation skill, to name a few. Furthermore, the results of evaluation should be interpreted with caution.

Every management function, including purchasing, must be measured in terms of its contribution to the basic objectives of the firm. The evaluation process consists of developing measurement criteria and then measuring performance against them. The task of evaluation is difficult even in the simplest case because few functions can be accurately or completely measured in quantitative or objective terms.

EVALUATION OBJECTIVES

Improvement of Performance

Perhaps the most fundamental reason for evaluating any department is a desire to improve its performance. But first it is necessary to ascertain the current level of performance in order to have a basis for suggesting improvements. After the level of performance has been determined, it is possible to discern the points that need improvement and to set goals of expected attainment.

The abilities and capacities of purchasing personnel are also evaluated and used in establishing policies on hiring, training, compensating, and promoting personnel.

Improvement of Morale

Evaluating purchasing performance is likely to improve morale and increase the efficiency of purchasing personnel. Employees work better and take a greater interest in their jobs when they know that their efforts will be recognized.

An Aid in Organization

Evaluation aids management in internal reorganizations and in assigning functions to departments. Earlier chapters indicated the substantial variation in the number and kind of activities assigned to purchasing departments. Through evaluation it is possible for management to determine how effectively a given activity is being performed and whether related activities should be assigned to the purchasing department.

Facilitating Coordination

A multiplant company that has decentralized purchasing within its several plants will find evaluation an effective tool for controlling and coordinating the purchasing function throughout the company. Through uniform evaluation techniques it is possible to compare the performance of the various purchasing departments. Moreover, evaluation will provide a flow of information from the several plants and allow improved methods and techniques in one plant to be transferred to others.

EVALUATION CRITERIA

The difficulty inherent in evaluating people, as opposed to other elements that are part of an operation, has been mentioned. This section considers some of the more common evaluation criteria and the problems that arise in using them. Although no one formula exists for measuring every facet of purchasing performance, specific aspects of the function can be evaluated and then combined for an overall picture of purchasing performance.

Cost–Purchase Comparison

A common measurement device relates the dollar volume of purchases to the dollar cost of operating the purchasing department. The figure obtained indicates how much it costs to spend a dollar. It is calculated by dividing the annual cost of operating the purchasing department into the dollar volume of annual purchases.

This ratio of department costs to purchase volume has significance for evaluating a single department over time, provided that its responsibilities have remained fairly constant. The greatest limitation of this criterion is that it represents a measure of total department performance and does not indicate points of strength or weakness within a department. In growing companies, constant change may make comparisons irrelevant.

Cost–purchase comparisons between purchasing departments of different companies are not likely to be revealing, since there usually are substantial variations in both factors of the ratio. Particular companies buy different proportions of raw materials and processed goods, and this significantly alters the dollar volume of purchases. Companies also assign quite different responsibilities to their purchasing departments, which affects the costs of running the departments. Thus, there is likely to be little common basis for comparing companies on this criterion.

Cost per Order

Attempts are often made to evaluate purchasing departments in terms of their cost per order placed. The calculation is made by dividing total purchasing department costs by the number of orders placed. This measurement may be criticized because it can so easily be manipulated by those being evaluated. They could greatly improve their showing by ordering smaller quantities more often. The cost-per-order approach is even less useful when open-end and annual contracts are used. Under such contracts, materials are released at specific times—sometimes on an automatic basis—replacing formal orders for individual shipments. Then the higher cost per order denotes increased rather than decreased efficiency.

Return on Investment

Another way of employing cost data is to calculate the net savings per dollar spent on purchasing, called the return on purchasing investment. Figure 11-1a illustrates such a calculation. In this illustration the return is derived by multiplying the degree of effectiveness (purchasing savings minus departmental operating costs divided by total purchases) by dollar disbursement (dollars spent per dollar of operating costs). Dollar disbursement can be misleading, since one could cut operating expenditures and thus increase the dollars spent per dollar of operating costs, but departmental efficiency might be seriously curtailed. Return on invested capital (the lower portion of the figure) is a more significant measure of purchasing performance. Return on invested capital (investment turnover times profit margin) emphasizes purchasing's contribution to profits rather than its expense. Figure 11-1b illustrates the effect of a 3 percent savings for a firm with $20 million in sales and an initial profit margin of 5 percent. Purchases are reduced to $10.3 million, profits increased by $300,000, profit margin increased to 6.5 percent, and return on invested capital improved by 28 percent (10.5 percent to 13.6 percent).

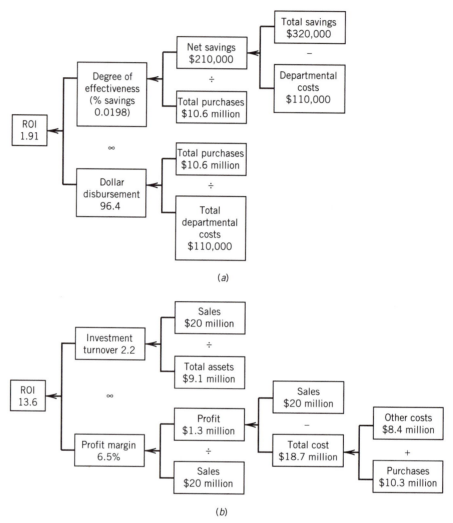

FIGURE 11-1. Two comparative methods of measuring return on investment.

Index Numbers

An index number indicates a change in magnitude compared with the magnitude at some specified time, usually taken as 100. Index numbers are useful in purchasing to analyze cost changes, price changes, and the relationships of both to generalized economic measures. As such they provide a means to measure purchasing performance.

When the cost of specific commodities over time is related to a base period, a useful quantifiable measure is obtained. The procedure to transform absolute prices to relative figures is as follows:

$$\frac{\text{Current Price}}{\text{Price in Base Period}} \times 100 = \text{Index Number for the current year}$$

Table 11-1 shows this relationship, using 1992 as the base year and expressing a 50-cent price increase over a four-year period as index numbers.

In this example, the product has experienced a 16 percent increase over the actual four-year period. By putting a price on this type of relative basis, comparisons between widely different commodities can be made and appropriate attention given.

Index numbers of general price levels such as the wholesale price index, retail price index, and commodity indexes provide an overall measure of price changes. Purchasing personnel can compare their commodity prices and, indirectly, their buying performance to their index. For example, assume the wholesale price index is as follows:

1992:1.00
1993:1.05
1994:1.15
1995:1.20

The relative relationship in 1995 is established as follows:

	Commodity Index	Wholesale Price Index	Relative Relationship
1995	1.16	1.20	$\frac{1.16}{1.20} = 0.97$

TABLE 11-1. Commodity-Price Changes, 1992–1995

Year	Price	Index
1992	$3.05	1.00
1993	3.15	1.03
1994	3.33	1.09
1995	3.55	1.16

The buyer in this case was able to key price increases slightly below the overall inflation rate.

Indexes can be similarly applied to group prices for parts, and thus highlight total price changes, as illustrated in Table 11-2. From Table 11-2, the product index may be calculated as

$$\text{Product Index} = \frac{147.80}{98.00} \times 100 = 150.82$$

Thus, the overall product prices collectively increased 51 percent, and prices of motors and blades were the most volatile.

The application of indexes allows individual prices to be expressed in a relative basis and permits comparisons between commodities and both overall price movements within commodity classes and macroeconomic variables.

Quality Criteria

Quality achievement may be measured in terms of the number of rejections of incoming shipments. Defects discovered during the production process should also be considered. The responsibility for defective items must be assumed by the purchasing department because it selected the supplier.

Quantity Criteria

Quantity performance can be measured in different ways. One criterion is the amount of downtime resulting from a shortage of materials. Another criterion is the amount of rescheduling of production caused by lack of materials. The extent of forward buying to cover production needs and the cost of such

TABLE 11-2. Prices of Grouped Parts

Item	1990 Prices	1995 Prices	Relative Price Index	Quantity 1992	1990 Price and 1990 Quantity	1995 Price and 1995 Quantity
Fan belts	1.00	1.10	110	3	3.00	3.30
Motors	22.50	41.50	184	1	22.50	41.50
Blades	4.25	6.50	153	2	8.50	13.00
Remainder	16.00	22.50	141	4	64.00	90.00
					98.00	147.80

coverage are both quantity factors that should be considered in an appraisal of purchasing performance.

Another quantity factor is the relation between inventory and use. This relation is known as the turnover rate and is calculated by dividing the value of purchased materials, parts, and supplies by the average investment in such items during a certain time period. A related measure is the inventory losses occurring through spoilage or obsolescence. A low level of spoilage and obsolescence is a reflection of purchasing efficiency.

A final quantity variable concerns the number of new vendors used and the number of new quotations solicited during a specific time period. This measure reflects efforts to maintain a strong competitive environment.

Price Criteria

Purchasing performance can be measured by evaluating prices. The long-term relationship between the price paid for purchased goods and the price secured for a company's finished product is an important benchmark. Over time, the typical company will find that a reasonably constant proportion of its sales dollar is spent for purchased goods. Short-term performance can then be measured against the long-term standard.

A comparison of the price index of company purchases with one of the standard price indexes can help in appraising price performance. A comparison of the market price at the time of use with the price that was actually paid for the item measures how well a purchasing department is anticipating price changes. Discounts obtained may also be considered in evaluating price performance, but it is difficult to find any basis for comparison other than the past performance of the department.

Time and Place Criteria

Many of the criteria that measure quantity performance are also applicable in determining performance with respect to time and place. In addition to quantity measures, however, it is desirable to compare suppliers' delivery dates with promised shipping dates and to evaluate the amount of follow-up required.

Other Criteria

In addition to the foregoing measures involving dollars spent and saved and quality, quantity, price, time, and place considerations, performance can be evaluated by analyzing the specific steps in the purchasing process.

Completion of Orders. One such criterion is the total number of purchase orders issued, which is an indication of the work load of the department. One might subdivide this figure into the number of local and nonlocal purchases, small and large orders, rush and regular orders, and single-item and multiple-item orders.

Interviews Conducted and Processing Times. The number of salesperson interviews conducted, the average time per interview, and the length of time that salespersons are required to wait before seeing the buyer are other factors that can be used in evaluating purchasing performance. The average time required to process an order, from recognition of need to the mailing of the purchase order, can be measured. The time taken to clear invoices for payment and the number and amount of discounts lost because of delays in clearing invoices are significant measures of purchasing performance in companies in which invoice approval is a purchasing department responsibility.

Administrative versus Operational Allocations. Some companies use still another approach in measuring purchasing performance. They evaluate the department in terms of the performance of the head of the department. An attempt is made to classify the department head's work week into the proportion of time spent on administrative matters compared to that spent on direct participation in actual purchasing. Frequently, such companies tend to overemphasize the administrative aspects of purchasing on the assumption that a well-run purchasing department requires the head of the department to concentrate on administrative matters. Overemphasis on administration is unwise in that it may divert the department head's efforts from productive to bureaucratic activities.

Image with Vendors. An important but difficult aspect of purchasing that should be considered in evaluating performance is the standing of a company with its vendors. This matter must be judged subjectively, since it is one of the intangibles that can be measured only by executive judgment, wherein management surveys vendors. Its importance should be recognized, because good vendor relations directly influence purchasing performance.

Interdepartmental Relations. The relation of purchasing to other departments should also be evaluated. Especially important are the relations between purchasing and the production, quality control, and engineering departments.

Cooperation with these departments is vital. Decisions affecting specifications, alternative materials, and quality of receipts all interface with the cost of materials and require a mutual attitude of respect and the cooperation of department employees.

Finally, the assistance given to management in such areas as economic and price forecasts, projections of material supply-and-demand conditions, new product developments, and related areas should be included in the evaluation process.

The purchasing manager who wishes to use different criteria for evaluating buyer performance may turn to a study that resulted in a final list of 10 measures as follows:[4]

1. On-time delivery
2. Incoming quality assurance acceptance rate
3. Actual vs. target cost
4. Commodity knowledge
5. Purchase order cycle time
6. Qualified suppliers cultivation
7. Workmanship error rate
8. Bottom price knowledge
9. Commodity complexity
10. Timely response to inquiries

EVALUATION STANDARDS

Additional difficulties are encountered in determining how specifically to evaluate purchasing performance. Basically, however, what is being done is compared with one of four possible standards:

Past performance

Budgeted performance

Performance of departments in other companies

An ideal or norm of performance

Past Performance

Perhaps the most widely used standard is to compare the current performance of the department with its past performance of the parts of the purchasing function that can be statistically measured. This approach is of particular value when the size of the department and its assignments are relatively

---

[4] "A Model for Professional Productivity: Evaluating Purchasing Performance," *National Productivity Review* (Autumn 1988), pp. 285–297.

stable from year to year. Table 11-3 shows a data chart covering 21 objective criteria over a five-year span. Comparisons are readily made by noting year-to-year changes.

Budgeted Performance

If past data are not available, or if procedures or scale of operation have changed considerably, performance can be evaluated against budgeted goals.

At the beginning of the budget period, purchasing objectives are established in view of the firm's total objectives. For example, the plans for a purchasing department of a manufacturing enterprise organized for profit might include the following objectives.

1. Reorganize the flow of paperwork to reduce clerical effort, with anticipated expense reduction of $100,000 annually, to be accomplished by December 1, 199X.
2. Value-analyze our line of pumps during the month of April, with a target of 5 percent reduction in material cost and a potential savings of $75,000 annually.
3. Negotiate annual agreements for aluminum casting requirements, with a cost-reduction target of $35,000 annually, to be accomplished by February 1, 199X.
4. During the month of June, acquire an additional nonferrous metals buyer to satisfy the increased demands for this class of material.

These purchasing objectives will presumably contribute to the profit objectives of the company and can be objectively measured. Evaluation by objective can include numerous budgeted criteria. It provides a goal and an incentive for personnel in addition to concrete evaluation of data.

Types of Budgets. Two general types of budgets are used for purchasing activities. One is the purchasing or materials budget, the other the department's operations budget. The materials budget is an estimate of the amount of materials, parts, and supplies to be purchased during the budget period and is derived from production schedules. The operations budget deals with the estimated costs of running the department.

Although many companies do not employ budgets, a number of reasons can be advanced for doing so. An operating budget establishes a standard of performance—at least, a standard of a very general nature. A materials budget enables other departments in the concern to coordinate their activities with those of the purchasing department. For example, the materials budget provides the financial division with information on the funds needed to meet

TABLE 11-3. Data Chart Showing Typical Indicators of Purchasing Efficiency

No.	Factor		Year				
			1	2	3	4	5
(1)	$ purchases per year (millions)		12.4	16.6	20.4	16.8	18.0
(2)	$ sales per year (millions)		24.3	33.0	41.5	33.6	35.7
(3)	$ purchases/$ sales ratio (%)	$(1) \times 100 \div (2)$	51.0	50.3	49.2	50.0	50.4
(4)	Purchase orders per year		24,909	25,530	25,655	26,230	26,000
(5)	Number of purchasing employees		19	23	25	24	22
(6)	Ratio of purchasing employees/total employees		1/124	1/122	1/126	1/131	1/146
(7)	Purchase orders per purchasing employee per week	$(4) \div (5) \div 52$	25.2	21.3	19.7	21.0	22.7
(8)	$ purchases per purchasing employee per year	$(1) \div (5)$	653,000	722,000	816,000	700,000	818,000
(9)	Average $ value per purchase order	$(1) \div 4)$	498	650	795	640	692
(10)	Purchasing employees per $ million purchases	$(5) \div (1)$	1.53	1.39	1.23	1.43	1.22
(11)	$ cost of purchasing per year		120,000	140,000	153,500	150,000	152,000
(12)	$ cost per purchase order	$(11) \div (4)$	4.82	5.48	5.98	5.72	5.85
(13)	Cost of purchasing as % of purchases	$(11) \times 100 \div (1)$	0.97	0.84	0.75	0.89	0.84
(14)	Cost of purchasing as % of sales	$(11) \times 100 \div (2)$	0.49	0.42	0.37	0.45	0.43
(15)	$ saved per year		125,200	127,000	321,000	353,000	295,000
(16)	$ saved as % of $ purchases	$(15) \times 100 \div (1)$	1.01	0.77	1.58	2.10	1.64
(17)	Interviews per week		235	217	196	214	225
(18)	$ telephone expenses per month		265	326	369	315	380
(19)	Purchased material price index—% increase (base-100)		50.1	51.2	55.3	58.1	61.0
(20)	$ direct labor (millions)		1.82	2.07	2.09	2.15	2.25
(21)	Ratio of purchases to direct labor	$(1) \div (20)$	6.8	8.0	9.8	7.8	8.0

the commitments that will be made, and it gives the receiving and stores departments the pattern of their work during the coming period.

Another advantage of budgeting flows from the manner in which the budget is prepared. Implicit in its preparation is planning, and planning encourages coordination and cooperation. In addition, budgeting means that plans have been formalized to the extent of being put into writing and thus have become a matter of record. This can be important as a means of avoiding mistakes in subsequent periods.

Disadvantages of Budgets. Although the advantages of budgeting are significant, there are some difficulties in using them as a control device in purchasing operations. This is much more the case for the materials budget than for the operations budget. The principal difficulty is that purchasing personnel should buy what is needed rather than what has been forecast. Strict adherence to a budget could lead to overbuying, with its attendant costs. In other instances, adherence to the budget might lead to shortages and work stoppages in the plant. In both situations the department would be given a high rating on the basis of adhering to the budget, but it could hardly be considered to be performing its functions well.

Comparison with Other Companies

Associates in other companies may share performance data that show how well a purchasing department performs. One benefit to purchasing executives of participating in civic and professional groups is that they become acquainted with purchasing executives in other companies.

The Center for Advanced Purchasing Studies (CAPS) reports on the results of benchmarking studies on purchasing performance for the petroleum, foodservice, and semiconductor industries.[5] CAPS plans to identify and compare purchasing trends across industries as it benchmarks purchasing performance in more industries.

Norms

The use of nonbudgetary purchasing norms as standards for purchasing performance has not been very common, primarily because there is such a wide variation in the specific duties assigned to individuals within purchasing departments and in the ways they perform these duties. One has only to consider the variation in salespersons and their concept of how to deal with buyers to understand the difficulty in developing a norm for evaluating a buyer's interview performance.

---

[5] "Performance Benchmarks: A Comparison," *NAPM Insights* (October 1990), p. 9.

What is true with respect to the development of norms for comparing buyer performance is even truer of developing norms for the head of a purchasing department. Not only are the duties and responsibilities more diverse, but they are also more individual in nature. A major consumer goods manufacturer has prepared the following list of performance standards for its director of purchases.

1. Successful planning establishes and achieves management-approved goals and programs that (*a*) improve purchasing operations within budget limits; (*b*) produce profit for the company; or (*c*) increase the ability of the division to meet new and emergency situations expeditiously.

2. Materials, equipment, and supplies are being purchased at prices resulting in the lowest ultimate cost consistent with required quality, delivery, and established policies; late deliveries and rejections for quality do not exceed agreed-on levels.

3. Competition between suppliers is encouraged, and buying is competitive whenever possible. Whenever competition is not possible or practical, careful negotiation is practiced, and adequate precautions are taken to ensure that the best interests of the company are served.

4. Management is adequately informed of purchasing activities, significant market conditions, and trends affecting the company's operations. Recommendations for action are promptly made.

5. An active personnel-training program is in force, as well as counseling and a periodic assessment of the abilities and performances of buyers and purchasing agents. A satisfactory number of employees are able to assume greater responsibilities when there are vacancies.

6. Purchasing activities are effectively coordinated within the purchasing division and with other company activities resulting in the smooth integration of all functions related to purchasing. Purchasing of items used at various locations is consolidated, and the interpretation of purchasing policies and procedures is uniform.

7. Purchasing policies that are fair to all vendors assure the ability of the company to make the best purchase possible and promote good relations with vendors and other outside contacts as well as other company divisions.

8. Written procedures are established and revised to ensure a standard and efficient handling of purchasing operations.

9. Working relations with the divisions served ensure effective communication and mutual cooperation and understanding. The divi-

sions have confidence in purchasing's ability to provide the services required.

10. Vendor relations are based on mutual cooperation, confidence, and respect. Consequently vendors provide high levels of quality, service, and technical information and offer new product as they are developed.

11. When requested, surplus or salvage materials and supplies are disposed of promptly and at favorable prices.

12. There is active participation in purchasing and industry associations.

It is evident that these standards are *qualitative* rather than *quantitative* and that norms in the usual sense of the word cannot be developed.

EVALUATION METHODS

A large number of methods are being used for evaluating the purchasing function. Although no one method is universally preferred, the following discussion presents considerations that are found in one form or another in most evaluation plans.

Internal Audit

Since Chapter 11 discusses the internal auditing of the purchasing department, it will only be mentioned here that many companies conduct an internal audit of their purchasing department, as they do of other departments, to measure conformity to established procedures and acceptable business practice. Evaluation in the usual sense is not involved, in that the internal auditor is not concerned with how well purchasing is functioning but only with whether it is following established procedures.

Quite often an accountant in the organization's accounting department conducts the internal audit, thereby assuring that an independent person evaluates purchasing's objectives and standards of performance.

Purchasing Department Savings

The savings achieved in the course of purchasing operations are rather commonly used as a means of evaluating performance. These savings accrue because costs of materials, supplies, and services being purchased are lower. Some companies refer to these savings as cost reductions; others call them profit improvements.

Determining what is a savings is a problem. If a buyer through negotiations secures a price lower than originally quoted, should this be considered a savings? Is a quantity discount a savings? How does one measure savings brought about through changes of materials or design for which purchasing department had little responsibility?

Notwithstanding these questions, most savings can be analyzed, and portions of them can be attributed to the purchasing department and used to evaluate its performance; this is the most widely used evaluation method.

Variance from Standard Cost of Materials

Some companies establish a standard cost of the more important materials they purchase, which is derived from the record of prices paid for such materials in the past. Evaluation of purchasing performance then consists of comparing actual costs with this standard cost for the period under evaluation. This method of evaluation is commonly found in companies that employ standard costing as a control over manufacturing operations.

Outside Audit

The outside audit is conducted by a person who is not employed by the company whose purchasing department is being evaluated. Management consulting firms typically are employed, although occasionally the company's certified public accountants may conduct the audit.

Auditors usually start with the purchasing procedures or policy manuals, if they exist, and measure adherence to such guides. They attempt to ascertain the extent to which the purchasing department is operating by commonly accepted sound management methods.

Variance from Operating Budgets

Companies that prepare operating budgets, as opposed to materials budgets, may use these budgets as the basis for still another method of evaluating performance. If the operating budget has been realistically prepared, if purchasing has had a significant voice in its preparation, and if the department has the resources to do what management expects, judging in terms of compliance with the operating budget is fair and reasonable.

Vendor Performance

Evaluating a department in terms of the performance of the vendors is yet another evaluation method. Methods of evaluating vendors have been described in previous chapters. Such evaluation should consider quality, quantity, price, time, and place, with appropriate variations in the importance of each relative to the commodities being purchased and their importance to the production process.

Appraisal of Personnel

Most organizations use job evaluation and merit rating systems for evaluating purchasing and all other personnel. Each person's performance is reviewed by one or more supervisors using an established form. Although such a process may be sound for evaluating individuals in a purchasing department, it is not adequate for the evaluation of an entire purchasing department's performance.

Inventory Performance

A purchasing department's performance may be evaluated in terms of inventory levels and turnover. This method should be used only when the purchasing department has major responsibility for determining inventory levels and quantities to be bought. Most companies do not give such blanket responsibility to their purchasing departments.

Frequency of Reports

A final concern is the combinations of reports and their frequency. They naturally depend on the peculiar requirement of the individual firm. Table 11-4 is a possible record showing type of report and frequency.

MANAGEMENT BY OBJECTIVES AND RESULTS

The process whereby a manager and employees outline objectives to be accomplished in a given future period of time is called management by objectives (MBO). Management by objectives and results (MBOR) extends the MBO concept by specifying objectives and performance results. The concept of MBOR is especially well suited to purchasing and other functions wherein a substantial amount of the efforts made must be subjectively measured. Improved vendor image, increased utilization of the service capabilities of vendors, and improved interdepartmental relations are mainly subjective in nature, hence handled well by the management-by-objectives-and-results process.

TABLE 11-4. Reporting Frequency for Various Evaluations

Topic	Annual	Semiannual	Quarterly	Monthly
Total dollar value of purchases	✔	✔	✔	✔
Dollar purchases by commodity class	✔	✔	✔	
Dollar purchases by major item	✔			
Dollar purchases by major suppliers	✔	✔		
Dollar volume of cash discounts	✔	✔	✔	
Dollar value of lost discounts	✔			
Standard cost variances	✔	✔		
Inventory levels and turnover rate	✔	✔		
Scrap and surplus sales	✔			
Number of salespersons interviewed	✔			
Total purchasing department expense	✔	✔		
Purchasing department expense by class	✔			
Total cost savings	✔	✔	✔	✔
Cost savings by buyer	✔			
Cost savings by type	✔	✔		
Long-term contract changes	✔	✔		
Supplier performance	✔	✔		
Problem solving				✔
Current objectives	✔			

The Process

The MBOR process is quite simple. The employee is asked to develop specific objectives for a specific period of time (usually 6 to 12 months) that coincide with the organization's overall goals.

The key to this approach is to involve the employee in the process of setting individual goals, including performance evaluation measures that can be applied during and at the end of the period. The essential steps of MBOR are as follows.

1. Overall organizational goals are identified and communicated to the employee.
2. The employee develops an introspective attitude toward all the facets of his or her position.
3. The employee identifies areas of performance output and possible improvement.
4. The employee translates these areas into specific, stated objectives or goals.
5. A reasonable time frame for accomplishments is identified.
6. The methods of evaluation are determined.
7. The employee reports results to his or her supervisor.

Obviously, quantifiable objectives such as a percentage decrease in material costs or a percentage increase in new vendor quotations are part of the MBO process. However, an introspective attitude toward the task and the evaluation process carried out by the self-motivated employee are particularly helpful in identifying important subjective areas of purchasing.

An objective might arise under the general topic, Buyer's Professionalism. The objective perhaps would read, ''Show more professionalism.'' Specific action steps might include, ''Join the local purchasing management association,'' ''Attend monthly meetings of the local purchasing management association,'' and/or ''Take a college course in negotiations and contract administration.'' At year's end, the buyer and supervisor talk over the results of taking one or more of these action steps and identify action steps to follow the next year.

As the specimen executive management appraisal (Figure 11-2) shows, the evaluation confirms results. This actual specimen displays midyear results. Incumbent and supervisor might make mid-course corrections to increase I-B Project Cost Compliance over the remainder of the year. It may call for allocating more resources to achieve the desired results, or finding what causes cost overruns and eliminating those causes.

Management by objectives and results extends MBO as a tool for improving organizational performance, focusing as it does not just on goals and objectives but especially on results.

PURCHASING MANUALS

Purchasing manuals aid evaluation by specifying policies and procedures to be followed by purchasing personnel. The policy manual contains statements of the policies under which the department operates. The procedures manual

**Executive Management Appraisal
for Period JAN 9X thru DEC 9X**

Individual's Name:	Adam Smith

Position Goals: Objectives in this section establish requirements to assure that individual's functional responsibilities are integrated with organization goals.

Goal—Expected Result—Date	Evaluation

Goal—Expected Result—Date					
I. *Service Objectives*		*1st Qtr.*	*2nd Qtr.*	*YTD*	
A. Project Schedule Compliance. On time implementation of:	A.				
a. 95% of all 148's	a.	98.3% (57/58)	100% (49/49)	99.1% (106/107)	
b. 95% of regulatory 148's	b.	100% (36/36)	100% (30/30)	100% (66/66)	
B. Project Cost Compliance. Implement 75% of all 148's within 130% of manhours estimated at SES	B.	72.4% (42/58)	69.4% (34/49)	71% (76/107)	
II. *Quality Objectives*					
A. Discrepancies—Maintain	A.				
a. The number outstanding at or below 125	a.	104	67	83.5	
b. The average age at or below 75 days	b.	31 days	44 days	41.5 days	
B. Production Failures—maintain rerun costs at or below 0.8% of production costs	B.	0.48% ($1266) (261,490)	0.36% (2075) (581,386)	0.40% (3341) (842,876)	
III. *Management Objectives*	A.	(4.48%)		0.17%	(2.18%)
A. Stay within approved budget (unless excess is approved)		Budgeted Actual	694,733 633,612	701,672 702,388	1,396,405 1,366,000
B. Compliance Rate—Maintain	B.	99.1%	99.1%	99.1%	
a. 98% with use of CPU standard for testing	a.	(19912) (20099)	(18825) (18997)	(38737) (39096)	
b. 90% with use of output lines standard for testing	b.	96.3% (19348) (20099)	95.4% (18137) (18997)	95.9% (37,505) (39,096)	

FIGURE 11-2. Management by objectives and the results of a mid-year evaluation.

contains the procedures to be followed by the department in conducting its activities. Because policies should not be changed frequently, whereas procedures are subject to frequent changes, separate manuals are advisable.

The specific benefits derived from the compilation of a purchasing policy manual are as follows.

1. A manual eliminates questions about the position of management on important issues in the administration of the purchasing function.
2. New personnel can be quickly taught the policies under which they are expected to act.
3. A manual can serve for continued training.
4. A manual tends to ensure greater consistency in the handling of controversial matters such as reciprocity.
5. A manual may be used to inform suppliers of what they can expect in dealings with the company.

The subjects that should be included in a purchasing policy manual will vary with the company. Inasmuch as a policy is a prescribed method of handling a type of situation, matters of a nonrepetitive nature are not included. Policy manuals must have the approval of management.

The procedures manual, in contrast, is primarily an internal matter for the purchasing department. These manuals are frequently prepared in loose-leaf form, which makes it possible to insert the frequent changes to which procedures are subject, and to separate portions of the manual for forwarding to interested departments without burdening them with details of no interest to them.

EVALUATION OF MATERIALS MANAGEMENT

In earlier chapters the interrelationship of the activities of purchasing, inventory control, and traffic and production control were cited, and the organizational concept of materials management was presented. It was pointed out that the major function of a materials manager, who supervises these subfunctions, is to promote their coordination and integration. The major benefits are assumed to be

1. Reduced interdepartmental conflicts
2. Reduced inventory levels and greater assurance of materials availability
3. Reduced materials-handling costs

4. Increased knowledge of total corporate operations by materials subfunctions

5. Improved vendor relations

6. Reduced paperwork

7. Improved customer service

Because of the diverse (though related) subfunctions involved, the process of evaluating the materials manager must be considered in the broad terms of planning, integration, and performance of subfunction. The following discussion examines these tasks and suggests a specific evaluation process.[6] This evaluation process sets budgets of performance and compares the results against them. The qualitative and quantitative measurement factors are then used collectively, so that the MM contribution to total organizational effort can be evaluated.

The Materials Management-Evaluation Process

First, the extent of MM's responsibilities must be clearly defined. An exhaustive listing of all MM operations is required, and then these operations must be assigned to departments (e.g., value analysis to purchasing, control of finished goods to inventory or stores). This procedure will ensure that no duties are neglected and will highlight any significant areas of authority that have an influence upon MM performance but have been assigned to other departments. If, for example, production planning is assigned to manufacturing, the accountability of MM will be greatly affected.

Thus, we can establish the areas of accountability for the MM effort and the materials manager. The choice of which measurement to use is an individual decision based on the particular corporate operation. Balance, depth, and appropriate weighting must be considered, however, in setting criteria. The suggested major categories of MM responsibility are

1. Planning and forecasting

2. Integration of MM with total company operations

3. Carrying out individual functions

For each of these responsibilities performance should be budgeted, and actual results compared against the budget.

Planning and forecasting responsibilities of purchasing to be evaluated are:

---

[6] Most of these concepts were originally identified by the author in "Evaluating Materials Management," *Journal of Purchasing and Materials Management* (Fall 1975), pp. 15–18.

1. Success in planning and meeting overall material dollar budgets
   a. Actual versus budgeted ratios for budgets involved

2. Accuracy in forecasting
   a. Commodity prices
   b. Interest rates
   c. General economic activity
   d. Specific corporate assignments

3. Organization and training
   a. Degree to which clear lines of responsibility and authority were established within the MM operation
   b. Degree of personnel turnover
   c. Success in implementing training and rotation plans for personnel
   d. Degree of self-development by subordinates, such as attendance at lectures, conferences, seminars, and association memberships
   e. Rating of morale of subordinates

Integration with total operations would include developing good relations with and providing service to other departments and management personnel. Specific evaluation would consider success in providing

1. Interfunctional management meetings
2. Understanding of MM principles throughout the company
3. Significant reports to management directed to proper audiences and providing usable information

Performance measurement of subfunctions—inventory control, production control, purchasing, and traffic, which are the most common—would cover the following.

Inventory Control

1. Ratio of inventory investment to sales.
2. Inventory turnover ratios for raw, in-process, and finished goods inventory.
3. Relation of direct materials cost to costs of finished goods.
4. Changes in ''make or buy'' (dollars of this year's purchases which were ''make'' last year and vice versa).
5. Performance in establishing reorder points, that is, predetermined inventory levels at which additional purchases or production should be instituted.

6. The utilization of economic order quantities.
7. A ratio of inventory control salaries and expenses to total manufacturing salaries and expenses.

Production Planning and Control

1. Percentage of promises kept: (*a*) customer shipments, (*b*) shipments to finished stock, (*c*) shop operations.
2. Establishment of a direct materials price index, using an appropriate base year, showing changes in internal and production costs.
3. Changes in make or buy (dollars of this year's "make" that were "buy" last year).
4. Amount of dollars of indirect materials cost reductions.
5. Ratio of production planning and control salaries to their expenses.
6. Changes in the average production cycle time for representative models or products (including new models, standard models, and repairs).

Purchasing

1. A quantitative measure of machines and personnel idled through a shortage in purchased supplies.
2. A measure of the success of substituted materials and parts.
3. Ratios of total purchasing salaries and expenses to total purchases and total manufacturing salaries and expenses.
4. The value of purchase orders subjected to competitive bidding, as a percentage of total orders placed.
5. Number of rush orders.
6. Quantitative measures of expediting expenses.
7. Ratio of rejected purchases to total purchases.
8. Savings on discounts and quantity purchases.
9. Measure of the extent of supplier technical assistance.
10. Measure of vendors keeping delivery promises.

Traffic

1. Ratio of the cost of inbound freight to total purchases.
2. Packaging costs, expressed as a percent of hundredweight of shipments.
3. Ratio of cost of outbound freight to total hundredweight of shipments.
4. Trend of total transportation costs.

5. Cost reduction.

6. Measure of average in-transit time of incoming and outgoing shipments.

7. Ratios of total traffic expenses to value of total manufacturing salaries and expenses.

Alert management assesses the purchasing and materials management departments' internal performance as well as external factors that involve their operations. Assessing takes the form of audits. An operational internal audit includes an evaluation of such purchasing issues as: accounts payable, receiving, inventory control, make-or-buy decisions, demand forecasting, and production scheduling.[7]

A supplier quality audit serves to verify that adequate quality systems exist in a supplier's operation and that those systems function well. Before the audit, the purchaser develops a statement of requirements and communicates that statement to the supplier. The purchaser monitors the supplier's performance and improves his or her company's internal procedures affecting raw materials. The supplier audit focuses on maintaining a productive relationship between the supplier and the purchaser.[8] Reports to upper management transmit the audits' conclusions.

CONTROL AND AUDIT

The discussion that follows concentrates on the procedures and principles of three types of in-house audits used by purchasing departments. The first, the accountant's audit, is designed to assure that the purchasing department follows the procedures and controls generally accepted by the accounting profession in formulating certifiable financial statements and reports. The second, the internal audit, is designed to evaluate specific job descriptions and employee performance within the purchasing department. The third, the management audit, evaluates the integration of the department in the total corporate organization and its goals.

Because the major purpose of the management audit is to determine whether the firm is functioning as an efficient whole, it is necessary that someone outside the purchasing department view it objectively. In short, for an audit to be effective, each function must be evaluated by someone who has a concept of the entire operation and can detect strengths and weaknesses that may not be apparent to one confined to a single operation.

---

[7] "Operational Audits of Purchasing," *Internal Auditing* (Summer 1990), pp. 3–14.
[8] "Develop a Consistent Supplier Audit," *Purchasing World* (April 1990), pp. 54–56.

In practice, outside consultants with varied training are often charged with the management audit task. The consultant may be a management consulting firm or an internal audit team from the public accounting firm handling the company's account. When the audit is performed by the company itself, the responsibility tends to be assigned to an internal auditing section of the controller's division of the company.

In general, the audit studies the organization, policies, procedures, and evaluation and reporting of the purchasing department.

In auditing it is customary to employ sampling procedures. The selection of an adequate sample is important if an auditor is to secure a true picture of the operations of the department. The auditor must examine both usual and unusual purchase transactions. There must be enough transactions to enable the auditor to verify that established procedures and policies are being followed or to reveal situations that call for more intensive examination.

AUDITING OF ORGANIZATIONAL STRUCTURE

The effective performance of any function requires good organization, including clearly defined responsibilities accompanied by commensurate authority. Both internal department and interdepartment organization should be considered in evaluating purchasing.

Intradepartmental Organization

Within the department the auditor should check to see that there is a defined hierarchy of authority running from the director of purchasing through to the lowest-ranked clerical employees. Typical questions of concern in such an analysis would be:

1. Are line and staff functions clearly defined?
2. Does each department member know his or her immediate supervisor?
3. Are supervisors given sufficient authority over conditions of work, specific job assignments, and related salary evaluations?
4. Are consistent lines of work assignments established—for example, are buyers assigned by products, such as steel and aluminum, or by service areas such as engineering supplies and tool-and-die requirements?
5. Does the organization promote high morale and a feeling of group cohesiveness (often a by-product of definite job promotion possibilities and clearly defined responsibilities)?
6. Are interplant purchasing responsibilities clearly defined?

Interdepartmental Organization

Because purchasing's efforts are so interwoven with those of other departments, it is imperative that its responsibilities be clearly defined. The following questions are representative of those guiding the auditor.

1. Is departmental authority concerning what to buy clearly understood?
2. Is authority for determining quantity clearly understood?
3. Which department controls choice of vendor? Are approved source lists clearly defined?
4. Are any purchasing responsibilities assumed by other departments?
5. Is purchasing consulted by other departments on procedures or changes that affect vendors, order quantities, or specifications?

The auditor should be certain that the internal and interdepartmental organizations have sound procedures, thereby avoiding ''management by crisis.''

AUDITING OF POLICIES

The auditor should begin the audit as a whole by determining whether there are policies to cover all important aspects of the purchasing process. A normal starting point would be the published purchasing policy manual. Such a manual, if it exists, will reflect what aspects of purchasing are considered important enough to be covered by stated policies. The policies should bear the approval of the top management of the company and be binding on all personnel. Included should be policies for

1. Challenging specifications or requisitions
2. Investigating, approving, and selecting vendors
3. Obtaining bids
4. Awarding contracts
5. Handling conflict of interest, gifts, and entertainment

Auditors should concern themselves with whether policies are clear, workable, and enforced. Each audit must cope with the situation that exists in a given company. No standard audit questions can be formulated that would apply to all companies or all the topics that might be covered by a policy statement.

AUDITING OF PROCEDURES

An auditor should ascertain that adequate procedures are established to carry out management and purchasing policy, clarify responsibilities, provide and standardize routines, and provide standards of performance. Because a procedure audit often covers the area of greatest concern, the following discussion will be quite detailed.

Requisitions

Analysis usually starts with a review of the formal purchase requisition. Auditing will determine who has the defined authority to initiate a purchase requisition and whether the prescribed procedure has been followed in transmitting it to purchasing. The examination may not extend back into determining the effectiveness in planning the requisition, but focuses rather on the mechanics and the defined authorities. The requisition will also be examined to determine whether it includes enough information to allow an intelligent approach to the purchasing transaction.

Purchase Order Control

Control over the issuance of purchase orders or purchase order numbers should be of concern to auditors. They should ascertain whether a prenumbered purchase order system or other control procedure has been established, so that it is not possible for unauthorized people to issue purchase orders.

Included in a procedures audit should be unusual types of purchase orders, such as the following:

1. Blanket or continuing orders requiring a number of deliveries made over a certain period
2. Orders where in which the specification of item, quantity, or price is not definite
3. Orders placed under long-term purchase contracts

Vendor Investigation

Auditors may examine the apparent ability of vendors to perform, as well as general procedures for selecting vendors. Financial stability, technical proficiency, and apparent favoritism in the selection of vendors should be reviewed. Management constraints or trade relations considerations that may limit purchasing personnel when selecting vendors should be noted.

A supplier quality audit referred to earlier emphasized the 1980s' and 1990s' insistence on high quality. W. Edwards Deming, the statistician who helped Japan to create an economic comeback after World War II, said:

> American management thinks the way to increase profits is to cut costs. How ridiculous. If you concentrate on building quality and eliminating mistakes, your costs will go down automatically.[9]

Auditors verify supplier quality.

Transportation and Price

The purchase order should be reviewed by the auditors for decisions that have been made with regard to transportation and prices. The auditor should investigate the procedures followed in deciding how materials are to be brought into the plant—FOB points, freight terms (prepaid, collect, or freight allowed), and methods of determining specific routings, as Chapter 18 details. Auditing should ascertain whether the transportation cost is included in the bid prices received and whether the appropriate freight terms have been clearly stated on the purchase order. If freight calculations are required in determining the cost of the material, auditing should review the role of the traffic department in verifying freight rates to assure that the proper economies are enjoyed and that the least expensive shipping mode has been used.

In pricing, the auditors should review the bidding procedure to determine whether competitive bids are solicited and from an adequate number of suppliers. Comparative prices should be examined, as well as the reasons for selecting a specific bidder, particularly if it appears that orders have been awarded to other than the lowest bidder.

There should be an analysis of situations in which price is omitted from the order. Under certain circumstances (e.g., systems contracts) the omission of price may be necessary; individual cases should be reviewed to determine the reason. Similar analysis should be made of cost-plus-fixed-fee or other flexible pricing arrangements to assure that all relevant facts have been considered and that the agreements are clear enough to avoid misinterpretation at some later time. In some situations the cost-plus approach may be desirable, although it is usually wise to include a maximum allowable price.

Discounts

Trade and cash discounts should be checked to see that they have been received at the time of final payment, that they have been properly recorded

---

[9] "W. Edwards Deming: Shogun of Quality Control," *Financial Executive* (February 1986), p. 27.

on the orders, and that they are being realized through the proper handling of approvals. Such items as taxes should be spot-checked by the auditors to determine whether sound procedures are being followed in their handling.

Adjustments

Auditors should examine the method of handling adjustments with vendors when defective materials are returned or when it becomes necessary for the buyer to perform additional operations on purchased parts. Auditors should determine who has authority to authorize such returns or reprocessing, how this is communicated to the vendor, what controls are maintained over the material during its reshipment or reworking, and how the transaction is consummated. Since these can be costly situations, there should be complete coordination within the firm with responsibilities clearly defined.

Make or Buy

Auditors should also examine the procedures established to evaluate make-or-buy decisions. This phase should include a study of what items are analyzed; the financial considerations, such as the value of money used in the calculations; and other relevant considerations, including future production plans and the possible effects on future labor negotiations.

Surplus Sale

Since in many companies the sale of scrap and reclamation material is handled by purchasing, the auditors should review the method of weight control, the method of establishing a price for the material sold, and the control of inventories being held until sale. The auditors should also make sure that material is not being scrapped when it might be returned to a vendor, or that material is not being scrapped by one department when it might be used in another department performing a different operation or making different parts.

Off-Plant Inventory

In some situations a company may have an off-plant inventory; that is, inventory of material owned by the firm but in the possession of a vendor for storing, processing, or conversion. It is important that the shipment and receipt of such material be closely controlled and that a procedure be established for ascertaining the accuracy of the physical and the book inventories of such material. Auditors should confirm the existence and suitability of these procedures.

Petty Cash Purchases

Local purchases through a petty cash fund or charge account are common. The control of these purchases to assure proper receipt and lowest cost is a matter for examination.

Receipt Procedure

Among associated procedures that should be examined by an auditor are the receipt and inspection of incoming material. Here the auditor is concerned with such matters as whether quantities are checked at some point other than the initial receiving station, the procedure for moving material into and out of the storeroom, the procedure followed in handling receiving reports, and the procedure by which differences between quantities received and billed are handled.

More companies discover the need for developing long-term, mutually beneficial relationships with fewer but better suppliers through just-in-time (JIT) purchasing.[10] A JIT purchasing operation impacts audit testing and internal control. Changes in receiving procedures and eliminating individual purchase orders call for providing a suitable audit trail.[11]

Vendor Payment

The authorization for payment of vendors is sometimes approved by purchasing; however, many companies have an accounts payable section that assembles the documents relating to the purchase, the receipt of the material, and the amount owed for the transaction. Whatever the organizational pattern, auditors should make sure that the necessary checks and balances exist to guard against collusion, missed discounts or slipshod operations.

Ethics

In examining purchasing, auditors should always be on the alert for unusual situations that might indicate ethical problems. Large gifts or unusual entertainment is often evidence of an undesirable situation. Discussions with personnel, examination of records, and spot-checking of vendors are steps taken by auditors to inquire into such situations.

The Ernst & Whinney survey that Chapter 22 refers to alerts auditors to recognize that the willingness to accept vendor-supplied gifts has increased

---

[10] "Just in Time—Managing Your Suppliers," *Purchasing World* (January 1990), pp. 40–47.
[11] "The Impact of Just-In-Time on the Audit of Purchasing," *Journal of Purchasing and Materials Management* (Fall 1989), pp. 26–30.

in recent years. In addition, "buyers" outside the purchasing department have become a serious problem. A further survey finds that management guidance on ethical practices has diminished.[12] While the survey states that the great majority of purchasing people are ethical, auditors face formidable tasks to verify this.

DETERMINATIONS OF PURCHASING PERFORMANCE

The final function of an audit is to determine whether objective standards of purchasing performance exist and adequate provision is made for reporting of this performance to management. Even though a department is organized soundly and proper policies and procedures exist, there is no assurance that they are being followed unless the performance of the personnel is periodically reviewed and evaluated.

Specifically, a personnel audit should address the following questions.

1. Are personnel evaluated regularly on objective bases?
2. Is the department as a whole objectively evaluated in relation to clearly established goals?
3. Do periodic reports present the individual and departmental performance to management, and do such reports highlight the significant areas of evaluation?

TYPICAL AUDIT PROGRAM

A typical audit program of the Institute of Internal Auditors would include the following items.

1. Company policy and organization
   a. Place of purchasing department in organization
   b. Purchasing responsibility and authority
   c. Physical facilities used
   d. Main and branch-plant purchasing relationships

2. Departmental operations connected with basic purchasing activities
   a. Procedures
   b. Forms
   c. Audit sampling procedures

[12] *Purchasing Ethical Practices*, Ernst & Whinney and NAPM Center for Advanced Purchasing Studies (December 1988), p. 7.

3. Other purchasing activities
   a. Inspection
   b. Invoices
   c. Receiving and storage
   d. Surplus and scrap disposal
   e. Transportation
   f. Purchases for employees

4. Records and reports
   a. Departmental records
   b. Internal reports
   c. External reports

THE PURCHASING MANAGER'S ROLE

Since an internal audit should and will usually be conducted either by a company internal auditor or by the public accounting firm with which the company has a relationship, one might think that the purchasing department manager would have little responsibility for the audit. This should not be the case. The manager should be aware of what information the auditor will be looking for and should take the necessary steps to make such information readily available. In some purchasing departments, an individual within the department may even be charged with the responsibility of making periodic informal internal audits to ensure that the department's affairs are ready for a formal internal audit.

The results of audits go to management in reports. Purchasing reports are of three types: (1) intradepartmental reports designed to inform the head of the department about departmental matters, (2) interdepartmental reports directed to other departments, and (3) reports directed to higher levels of management. Informative reports extend the service of the purchasing department to the company by improving interdepartmental efforts and interpreting purchasing's role to management. Electronic data-processing equipment can be programmed to provide information promptly and in a form that facilitates the preparation of reports.

PRIMARY PURPOSES OF REPORTS

Reports serve three purposes: They provide information, assist evaluation, and aid self-analysis.

Information

A report is an instrument of managerial control providing information on which to base a decision or judge an activity. Top executives must make decisions on subjects of which they personally have little knowledge. Consequently, they must receive a condensed explanation of the significant factors affecting the decision at issue. The purchasing department's reports to management interprets its actions, motives, and plans. Procurement difficulties and market conditions are explained to enable management to make the adjustments necessary to coordinate the efforts of all departments toward common goals. An important by-product of this informational flow is the cooperation resulting when the operations of the purchasing department are understood by all.

Evaluation

A second reason for management reports is to evaluate the performance of the department. By the submission of such reports, purchasing managers educate management about their activities and the contribution of purchasing to organizational profits and goals, gaining appropriate recognition in the process.

Self-Analysis

An important by-product of reporting is that the preparation tends to improve performance. To prepare a report, the department must, in addition to gathering data on its performance, analyze and interpret the data. In the process of such an analytical review, the purchasing manager often uncovers practices and procedures that can be changed to improve the overall efficiency of the purchasing department.

PRINCIPLES OF REPORT PREPARATION

Because a report is basically a means of communicating information, the writer should avoid extravagant expressions. A report should be as brief and to the point as possible. The report's recipient will often be a busy person, and the report will compete for attention with other administrative matters and with other reports. The following principles will help accomplish this end.

1. *Direct the Report to a Specific Person.* Every report will be of primary interest to some particular person even if it is addressed to several.

Prepare the report with this person in mind, considering appropriate motivations, needs, and time limitations.

2. *Be Objective.* Emphasize the facts and conclusions presented in the report. When personal opinions are expressed they should include only minimal emotions. Undue emotion puts the reader on guard against a hidden bias on the part of the writer and reduces the report's effectiveness. All facts should be logically arranged for easy assimilation.

3. *Be Specific.* The report must distinguish the relevant from the irrelevant facts, since the reader wants only what is essential. The writer should try to tell all that the reader will want to know, not all that the writer knows.

4. *Save the Reader's Time.* It was mentioned previously that a report is competing for the executive's time, often at a disadvantage. The resulting need for the writer to make the report inviting can be accomplished to a large extent through form. If the report contains a summary and conclusions section, the busy executive can read this over quickly and get the highlights of the report. The report that uses titles and subtitles generously allows the reader to refer from the summary to other sections of the report for supporting facts.

5. *Interpret Data.* Raw statistics, even when reduced to charts and tables, are hard to interpret for someone remote from the operations of a department. Significant facts and relationships should be pointed out to the reader. Whenever possible, comparisons should be made with the figures for previous periods. Frequently the trend is more important than the present status.

6. *Do Not Draw Unwarranted or Unnecessary Conclusions.* It is usually better strategy to understate than overstate an issue. Do not say "the facts prove" something unless they do so beyond reasonable doubt. A report is not a sales presentation, and the writer should not endeavor to force a decision by the way the evidence is marshalled. Further, the writer should not draw more conclusions than are necessary. The report is supposed to provide the evidence on which the reader can reach conclusions.

7. *Keep the Number of Reports at a Minimum.* In most organizations the number of reports have a tendency to increase. Therefore, all reports should be reviewed at stated intervals to see whether they are still being used and whether they are serving their intended purpose. Reports should be meaningful and should cover the significant exceptions rather than repeating information already being received through other channels. It is as important to eliminate reports that have outlived their usefulness as it is to create new ones.

TYPES OF REPORTS

Oral and Written

A report of consequence should be put into written form to become a part of the department's records. However, much of the day-to-day business of a company is conducted orally. A superior may ask for an offhand opinion on some matter of purchasing policy or procedure, requiring an immediate reply. It is also common practice to have reports that are prepared in written form delivered orally before the interested officials. Such an oral presentation gives the officials a chance to discuss the subject while it is fresh in their minds and permits them to question the reporter on points requiring elaboration. The popularity of oral presentation of written reports highlights the importance of effective speaking abilities. The possibility of an oral presentation also influences the way in which written reports are prepared, particularly the statistical material, which must be organized so that it can be summarized for a group. This often means arranging figures in the form of graphs, bar charts, pie charts, pictographs, and so on. Often special graphic materials are prepared for the oral presentation.

Formal and Informal

As to form, reports may be classified as formal or informal. The informal report follows no prescribed pattern, is frequently written as a memorandum, and is often prepared in response to a specific request for information on a point of sufficient importance to warrant some investigation and a memorandum of record. The format for the formal report appears later in this chapter.

Periodic and Special

Reports may be periodic, submitted regularly, or they may be special reports. The special report may concern a particular subject the department wishes to bring to the attention of management. For example, the purchasing manager may feel that prospective price and market conditions warrant a reduction of forward purchases from those suggested by current policy. A special report would set forth views with a supporting rationale. More frequently, special reports are initiated by management asking for specific information. An example might be a request to evaluate the advisability of changing from natural gas to coal as a fuel source.

As the term implies, the periodic report is submitted at specified intervals. In contrast to the special report, which deals with one particular subject, the periodic report discusses a variety of subjects. Furthermore, the special report is usually analytical in nature and is based on the results of some special study or investigation. The periodic report is in the nature of an interpretive history of the operations of the department during the period immediately preceding. This is not meant to suggest that the periodic report may not be analytical. However, the analysis is likely to be in the nature of interpretation rather than research. The annual or six-month reports of purchasing department activities are typical examples of periodic reports.

Although the need for reports varies from firm to firm, the following types are indicative of the periodic reports a purchasing department might present.

1. Analysis of general business conditions and their probable effects on the company. Included would be suggestions regarding hedge buying, inventory levels, and rescheduling alternatives.
2. Performance evaluation of purchasing personnel, including suitability for existing work assignments and qualifications for promotion. Also included would be an evaluation of training and improvement techniques for personnel.
3. Vendor reports, including analysis of plant visitations, delivery performance, price reductions, and rating programs.
4. Interdepartmental relations describing significant joint efforts directed toward profit improvement, including value analysis projects.

Because periodic reports are common to most purchasing departments, it is possible to discuss them in more detail than special reports.

THE PERIODIC REPORT

The significant facts in a periodic report have to do with the trend of the department's performance over a period of time, thereby permitting evaluation of present performance.

Topics

The first step in the preparation of the periodic report is the gathering of the data, which are usually available from departmental records. Periodic departmental reports usually cover the following phases of purchasing activity.

1. *Price performance:* direction of price changes, savings, transportation, and related costs
2. *Administrative performance:* department operating costs, relevant ratios, department activities, cost reduction, dollars saved

3. *Inventory performance:* dollar value of inventory, relevant ratios to operating results
4. *Procurement performance:* new sources developed, relation of delivery to requested dates
5. *Economic and market conditions:* supply, demand, delivery implications

Most organizations have particular needs that are reflected in the specific content of their respective periodic reports.

The National Institute of Governmental Purchasing advises purchasing managers to furnish two reports to management. The first report, Vendor Performance, cites complaints on late delivery, unauthorized substitutions, and poor quality. The second report, Management Information, recapitulates workload summary, vendor summary, class-item summary, bidder analysis by vendor, and bidder analysis by class.

Statistical Presentation

Much of the data in a periodic report will be statistics, which are difficult to present interestingly and accurately. Diagrams such as bar charts, pie charts, and graphic curves are very helpful in making such statistics comprehensible. Statistical measures are also a means of summarizing material for presentation in a report. Frequently a mass of statistics can be greatly simplified for the reader by combining them for an average.

Averages.   Three alternatives are available when an averaging process is desired: the arithmetic mean, the median, and the mode.

Mean.   The *arithmetic mean* is computed by totaling the quantities of individual items and dividing this total by the number of individual items. The mean is the most commonly used method of averaging. It has the disadvantage of being influenced by extremes in the values of the individual items. Therefore, when there are large variations in the data, either the median or the mode may be a more representative figure.

Median.   If a few of the items differ from the rest by substantial amounts either above or below, the median may be preferred. The *median* figure is an *average of position;* that is, half the observations are above it, and half are below. The median is computed by arranging the items to be averaged, and taking the item at the midpoint of the total number as the average value of the group. This method of averaging is most applicable when there is an extreme range in the magnitude of the items. If the arithmetic average of such a series were used, the few extreme items would have disproportionate influence on the average. With the median, these extreme items are each counted as only one item and therefore do not unduly distort the final average.

Mode. The third method of averaging is to arrange the items into several small groups or classes. This is done by dividing the range from the highest to the lowest item into equal-sized group intervals and then recording each item in its proper group. The group that contains the largest number of items is then taken as the average, called the *mode*. This method is most applicable to a situation in which the items, by their very nature, fall into certain sizes. It provides a measure of which size is the most frequently used. An arithmetic average would probably give a figure that did not conform to any standard size. The median, by summing several groups that were not large in themselves, might indicate the average to be a size used infrequently. The modal average would reflect the most popular group or class interval.

Dispersion.   Although averages describe the tendency of data to cluster in the middle, they are not complete descriptions. It is helpful to know how widely the observations are scattered away from the average. The scatter of data away from the measure of central tendency is called dispersion. There are several measures of dispersion: the range, the variance, and the standard deviation.

The Range.   The *range* is defined as the difference between the smallest and the largest values in a statistical distribution. It is a measure of difference, which is used in a report to represent dispersion of the data. When a range is small, the mean is a close representation of the population, but a wide dispersion unduly influences the value of the mean as a true representation of the population.

The Variance and the Standard Deviation.   The variance and the standard deviation are the most commonly used measures of dispersion, to accompany the mean. The process of squaring the distance of each observation from the mean, summing the values, and dividing by the number of observations produces a measure called the *variance,* the square root of which is the *standard deviation.* Both the standard deviation and the variance are measures of distance from the mean and provide an indication of the dispersion in the original data.

Index Numbers.   As described earlier, an index number is a means of comparing numerical changes (usually prices) in percentage form over a period of time. One of the two numbers is used as the base from which the percentage is calculated. When used for a comparison of prices, the index compares prices in period 1, called the base period, with those of period 2. The result indicates how much prices have increased or decreased relative to what they were in the base period. The calculation in formula form is

$$\text{Price Index} = \frac{\text{Price in any given period}}{\text{Price in base period}} \times 100$$

The price comparison is multiplied by 100 in order to express it as a percentage. Suppose that product X sells for $10 in year 1, $20 in year 2, and $25 in year 3. Using year 1 as the base, the price index for year 2 would be $20/10 \times 100 = 200\%$, and for year 3, $25/10 \times 100 = 250\%$.

Logs. Logarithmic comparisons are helpful in graphic presentations, particularly when the rates of growth of two series of widely different magnitudes are computed over a period of time. If two such series are compared pictorially, it will appear that the larger magnitude series has grown at a faster rate, simply because it deals with larger figures. What is needed is a comparison of percentages of growth of the two series. This can be accomplished by plotting the data logarithmically rather than arithmetically. The log comparison shows the percentage of growth between the two series of different magnitudes.

Analysis and Interpretation of Data

Because undigested facts and figures do not communicate effectively to a reader who is not in daily contact with an activity, a report should point out the significant relationships and trends, comment on their significance, and offer possible explanations.

FORMAT FOR REPORTS

The principal objective of form is to secure the initial attention of the recipients and hold their interest throughout the report. One way of achieving this is to make a report appear light and easy to read. Short sentences, short paragraphs, wide margins, and a liberal use of headings and subheadings all work toward this objective.

Contents

Titles. It is usual practice to begin a presentation with a clear and descriptive title. Because long titles tend to discourage prospective readers, it is suggested that a short title with longer and more complete subtitles be used when relatively long descriptions are required. The name of the reporter should appear on the title page.

Summaries. The first part of the report proper should contain a summary and conclusions. This is an important, but often neglected, part of the report. The summary should contain all the important points of the report in highly condensed form. Subjects should appear in the summary in the same order in which they will be found in the report, to facilitate reference from the summary to the report. The summary should contain no material that does not appear in substance in the report proper; it is not a place for postscripts and afterthoughts.

Text. Following the summary the main body or text of the report should be presented. The report proper should be clear, logical, complete, and interesting. This is the part of the report that calls on the writer's ability, originality, and conscientiousness.

Recommendations. The recommendations should appear at the end of the body of the report if they have not been made a part of the summary. They should be a part of the summary if management has specifically requested the report and has asked for recommendations.

Appendix. After the body of the report should come the exhibits and appendices used to support the statements, conclusions, and recommendations reached in the report proper. Properly referenced in the text, they provide the background data that the reader may need for review.

Illustrative Techniques

Illustrations allow the reader to grasp significant changes and trends without having to analyze detailed figures. Very often the essential points of a report can be summarized in one or two diagrams. There are six basic illustrative alternatives: picture diagrams, pie diagrams, bar graphs, line graphs, maps, and flowcharts. Which device to use depends on the material to be presented and the intended reader.

Picture Diagrams. The picture diagram has the advantage of being nontechnical while still achieving a strong presentation. In general, pictures are used to portray changes in quantity by their relative sizes or numbers. Figure 11-3 uses two numbers of stick figures to illustrate a reduction in the number of vendors over a two-year period.

Picture diagrams often include geometric figures such as cubes, triangles,

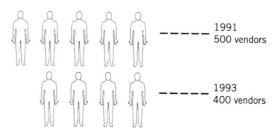

FIGURE 11-3. Example of a picture diagram used in reports.

and rectangles in addition to representations of people, buildings, and so on, to illustrate the data. When pictures are used, care must be exercised not to create optical illusions. Picture diagrams are not normally used when precision in reporting of facts is desired. A pictograph uses symbols to help answer questions like, *How much? how often?*

Pie Diagram. Pie diagrams are frequently used to show the distribution of purchasing expenditures or to express a whole and the sum of its parts. Pie diagrams should be used only when the number of divisions is relatively small. Figure 11-4 is a pie diagram showing the amounts of a purchasing dollar spent on particular factors.

Bar Chart. The bar chart is one of the most effective ways to compare quantities. The length of the bar represents the quantity, and the variations in length provide instant comparisons. A bar chart comparing the on-time performance of vendors for two time periods is shown in Figure 11-5.

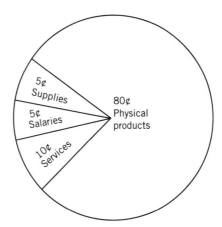

FIGURE 11-4. Pie graph, showing relative size of various factors.

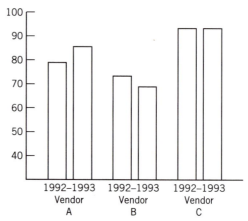

FIGURE 11-5. Bar graph, showing changes by periods and comparing vendors.

Line Chart. A line chart is particularly useful in presenting data that vary over a substantial period of time. Quantity and time are represented on the vertical and horizontal axes, respectively. Figure 11-6 is a line chart showing a hypothetical relation between sales revenues and material costs over time.

Line charts are very useful when an attempt is made to project the future on the basis of the past. Such estimates generally use the statistical least-squares line to project future estimates. Line charts offer the reader easy

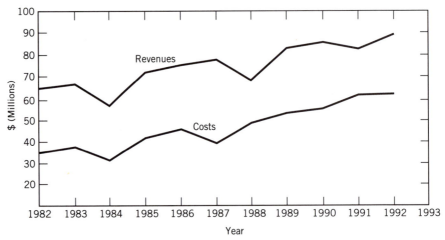

FIGURE 11-6. Line chart, contrasting revenue changes with cost changes.

FIGURE 11-7. Map segments showing vendor locations within the state of Wisconsin.

comprehension of the relative sizes and the relations between as many as three or four sets of data.

Maps. Maps, as an illustrative technique in reports, are used when the data to be presented follow some geographical division. When data appear on a map, the visual effect is instant and clear. Figure 11-7 is a map indicating the distribution of vendors within a state. Variations can be achieved by letting each dot represent more than one vendor and by expanding or contracting the size of the maps.

Flowcharts. A flowchart can be used to indicate a sequence of operations, series of work procedures, or any similar presentation that involves a series of stages. Figure 11-8 is a flowchart indicating the route followed by an incoming purchasing invoice.

Properly used, these illustrative techniques can add clarity and vividness to any report. Because illustrations summarize in a clear and succinct manner, they should be used wherever possible to portray the important data of a report.

Sample reports have not been included in this chapter, because each department will find it necessary to vary its reports in accordance with its objectives and policies. The contents of reports, their frequency, and type depend on the needs of the organization. In general, however, purchasing reports are provided monthly, quarterly, semiannually, or annually.

CHAPTER SUMMARY

The multitude of factors that purchasing and materials management involves enable managers to incorporate a large number of variables into meaningful

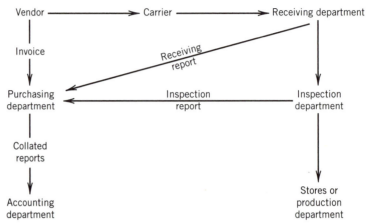

FIGURE 11-8. Flowchart showing sequence of activities.

evaluations of purchasing performance. Management first determines what it expects, expresses those expectations to subordinates, and then compares performance with expectations. The resulting improved performance leads to lower materials and transport costs, punctual delivery in dependable quality and quantity, and stronger relationships with selected vendors.

Cost per item takes on meaning when compared to the total volume of dollars that the purchase entails. The annual dollar purchases of all items compared to the total cost to operate the purchasing department reflects a ratio that management may compare year-by-year. Also, the National Association of Purchasing Management surveys provide industry-wide figures for comparison. The net savings per dollar spent on purchasing reflects the return on purchasing investment.

Evaluation standards include past performance, budgeted performance, comparisons with other companies, and norms of performance. Methods comprise internal auditing of performance and external comparisons with known leaders in the field, identified by trade associations and by the literature.

Management by objectives and results (MBOR) offers purchasing managers a tool for engaging subordinates in focusing on the important work aspects that contribute to bottom-line profits.

Evaluating the materials management effort calls for examining the total range of services that the department renders in meeting the firm's need for materials and services. Such evaluations encompass performance reviews for several functions in addition to the purchasing function. The objective: improved performance.

Managers audit the policies, procedures, and performance of their purchasing and materials management departments. Audits examine such factors as accounts payable, receiving, inventory control, make-or-buy decisions, demand forecasting, and production scheduling.

Similarly, managers audit supplier's performance, especially regarding quality and on-time delivery. The managers strive to strengthen the buyer–seller relationship, so that a long-term partnership continues. Therefore, audits observe complaints on late delivery and unauthorized substitutes.

Purchasing and materials management departments issue reports to higher management for information and evaluation. Self-analysis improves the performance. Report information includes workload summaries, vendor summaries, and bidder analyses.

Discussion Questions

1. What are the objectives of evaluating a purchasing department's performance?
2. How is the cost–purchasing comparison obtained and what is its primary weakness in evaluating the purchasing department's performance?
3. Why do open-end and annual contracts negate the usefulness of cost-per-order comparisons?
4. Why is return on capital a more significant measure of purchasing performance than return on purchasing investment?
5. What is the rationale for comparing actual purchasing performance with budgeted performance?
6. What is the essential distinction between policy and procedure manuals?
7. In what ways can quality of performance be measured?
8. Compare and contrast the materials budget and the operating budget.
9. What is the principal difficulty of using budgets?
10. Discuss the outside audit.
11. What are the principal benefits of materials management?
12. Discuss the process of materials management evaluation.
13. What are the major categories of materials management responsibility?
14. Discuss the applications of management by objectives and results.
15. List the major areas of a purchasing audit.
16. What aspects of purchasing policy should auditors review?
17. What should be included in a procedure audit?
18. How does an auditor check for accuracy?
19. In audits of interdepartmental activities, what areas are investigated?
20. What is the auditor's concern regarding trade and cash discounts?
21. Define off-plant inventory.
22. What role, if any, does the purchasing manager have in the internal audit?
23. State and discuss the principal objectives or purposes of reports.
24. Name the types of purchasing reports and indicate their use.
25. What principles should be observed in making reports as easy to read as possible?
26. What various aspects of purchasing should be included in a periodic report to ensure its completeness?
27. What basic illustrative techniques are commonly used in reporting? Give an example of the kind of data that would be presented by each of the techniques.
28. Oral reports are quite common in business.

What advantages can you see in oral rather than written reports?

29. Occasionally it is a good idea to omit circulating a periodic report to see who misses it. Discuss.

30. The report may not be an ideal communication device, but it is one of the few ways of communicating upward in a formal organization. Discuss.

Suggested Cases

Ajax Sewing Machine Company

Davis Mills, Incorporated

Landis Evaluation

Pressure Tanks, Inc. (A)

Sharpe Machine Corporation

Smith Electronic Corporation

=12

Purchasing and Materials Management in the Public and Nonprofit Sectors

State highway officials suspended business with three contractors and announced changes in bidding procedures Friday in response to bribery charges against a former employee and a contractor. The charges relate to an investigation on bidding procedures to hire contractors to remove fuel tanks from sites slated for road improvements.

The probe uncovered "a serious flaw" in which highway officials who invited bids also determined who got the job. The bidding process was kept hidden from other department employees who should have known what was happening. Steps have been taken now "to ensure it is a competitive process" by advertising the work instead of relying on staff solicitation. The indictments are the latest black eye for an agency battling legislative charges of inept management.*

CHAPTER CONTENTS

*Source: From *The Greenville News* (October 19, 1991), pp. 1A, 14A.

State and Local Purchasing

The Model Procurement Code

Quasi-Public Purchasing

An angry public and a responsive Congress sharply attack the federal procurement system. Waste, fraud, and abuse issues plague the system. Attempts to overhaul the procurement system find roadblocks: inside inertia and outside lobbies for keeping favored relations. Cheap substitutes go undetected. Whistle-blowers—persons who inform the public, the press, or Congress representatives—bring to light frightening news, such as defective fasteners that may fail in flight on 70 percent of America's airliners and military planes. Whistle-blowers typically face company dismissal for their efforts.

State and local governments spend more money on purchasing goods and services than the federal government. Here, community groups' watchful eyes and voting strengths nearer home keep abuses to lower levels.

Public sector purchasing managers face enormous challenges of rising costs, constricting budgets, and the public's watchful eye. The nonprofit sector faces similar challenges, as this chapter will show.

The movement toward government involvement in the economy is associated with the 1930s and referred to by economists as the Keynesian Era. Basically, the philosophy involved government taking an active role in helping the economy toward the goals of full employment and price stability. During the ensuing years many programs developed that altered prices, demand, and supply and affected the freedom of the traditional marketplace. Coincidentally, state and federal agencies were increasingly thrust into the market as purchasers of goods and services to bolster economic as well as social goals. The 1980s witnessed somewhat of a departure from this governmental influence, on the premise that adjustments should be handled by free-market demand–supply adjustments of prices, wages, and interest rates.

This shift of attitude has had an impact on the amount and nature of government purchasing, resulting in a greater emphasis on state rather than federal buying and altering the emphasis of nonprofit purchasing efforts. These agencies have had to revise their procurement practices, responding to a need to minimize costs because revenues are uncertain and often declining, and new forms of competition emerge. This chapter presents the dimensions of procurement in these sectors, highlights the unique characteristics of their procurement concerns, and examines corresponding practices.

PUBLIC PURCHASING–AN OVERVIEW

Federal, state, and local government purchases of goods and services reached a record dollar level in 1989. They exceeded a trillion dollars and continued to rise, as Table 12-1 shows. Of those sums, state and local governments spent for goods and services almost twice the national defense purchases of goods and services, and five-to-six times the federal nondefense expenditures.

Gross domestic product (GDP) came into use in January 1992 as the primary measure of U.S. production, with revisions to earlier years' national income and product accounts as shown in Table 12-1. Federal, state, and local purchases of goods and services as a percent of gross domestic product reveal remarkably stable levels over the years that Table 12-2 covers. Out of every dollar spent in the United States, 26.1 cents goes to purchase goods and services for federal, state, or local needs.

GDP does not include receipts by U.S. residents of interest and dividends and reinvested earnings of foreign affiliates of U.S. corporations. It does not include payments to foreign residents of interest and dividends and reinvested earnings of U.S. affiliates of foreign corporations. Thus, it tends to slightly shortfall gross national product (GNP). Gross domestic product plus receipts of factor income from the rest of the world, less payments of factor income to the rest of the world equals gross national product.

Purchasing and materials managers adjust for inflation when comparing economic data over a time span of five years or more. They relate dollar figures to base years—like, for example, 1987 or 1982—thereby comparing constant dollars. The U.S. Department of Commerce Bureau of Economic Analysis explains the laborious process of adjusting purchases to constant 1982 dollars in *Government Transactions Methodology Papers: U.S. Na-*

TABLE 12-1. Government Purchases of Goods and Services (in billions of dollars)

	1969	1979	1989	1990	1991	1992
Federal	100.0	178.0	401.4	424.9	447.3	449.1
National defense	78.9	121.9	300.0	313.4	323.8	315.5
Nondefense	21.1	56.1	101.5	111.5	123.6	133.7
State & Local	107.2	289.9	570.1	618.0	643.2	655.7
Total	207.3	467.8	1,372.9	1,467.8	1,532.0	1,554.0
Gross Domestic Product			5,244.0	5,513.8	5,677.5	5,945.7

Source: Survey of Current Business, February 1991, p. 12 and January 1993, Tables 1.9, 3.2, 3.3, and 3.7B.

TABLE 12-2. Government Purchases of Goods and Services (as percentage of gross domestic product

	1989	*1990*	*1991*	*1992*
Federal	7.7	7.7	7.8	7.6
National defense	5.7	5.7	5.7	5.3
Nondefense	1.9	2.0	2.2	2.2
State & Local	10.9	11.2	11.3	11.0
Total	26.2	26.6	27.0	26.1

Source: Calculated from Table 12-1.

tional Income and Product Accounts, Government Printing Office, November 1988.

Federal cost analysts enlist manufacturers' and shipyards' aid to price in 1982 terms the earlier and later years' purchases of aircraft, missiles, ships, vehicles, electronic equipment, petroleum products, weapons, ammunition, and military and other structures. In this manner, the 1982 adjustments occur, corrected for characteristics changes, quality changes, and learning curve effects—as Chapter 9 describes. For example, the design of a specific ship (usually the second ship) in a class—for example, the design of a nuclear submarine in the Los Angeles class—becomes frozen. A shipyard that has produced this class of ship then reprices the design using the current-period wage structure and technology. Any change in the price calculated for the ship constitutes a price change. These estimates form the basis for constructing a price index. The sample comprises five frozen ships. Price indexing forms the basis for recovering overcharges and for negotiating new contracts. Purchasing managers and all citizens benefit from the careful work of federal auditors, although the audit burden continues years afterward for enterprises that supply the federal government.

The federal government in 1992 spent a total of $449.1 billion for purchases of goods and services. This sum amounted to 38.7 percent of federal revenues, as Table 12-3 shows. Since 1979, this percentage has flattened at the upper thirties.

The growth in public purchasing spending has increased concern about the methods adopted by government agencies in their purchasing functions. Organizational adaptations exemplify this concern. The Office of Federal Procurement Policy (OFPP), created in 1974, standardizes policies for all governmental agencies. The major result of analyzing policies has been a move away from in-house production and toward contracting out to minimize government cost. The Federal Acquisition Act of 1977 attempted to professionalize governmental purchasing. It assimilated some practices used

TABLE 12-3. Federal Purchases and Receipts (in billions of dollars)

	1969	1979	1989	1990	1991	1992
Purchases of Goods and Services	100.0	178.0	401.4	424.9	447.3	449.1
Receipts	199.7	505.0	1,055.2	1,104.8	1,122.2	1,160.0
Ratio (P/R) $\times$ 100	50.0	35.2	38.0	38.5	39.9	38.7

Source: Survey of Current Business, February 1991, pp. 12, 29, and January 1993, Table 3.2.

in the private sector. The Federal Acquisitions Institution was established to centralize policymaking and to simplify purchasing procedures, in addition to promoting professionalism in federal procurement.

In light of these developments, prime contractors as well as organizations involved in subcontracting efforts need to understand federal purchasing regulations and procedures.

The CALS Initiative

The U.S. Department of Defense (DOD) in 1985 developed a government and industry initiative, Computer-Aided Acquisition and Logistic Support (CALS). The program uses automated digital technical data instead of paper for weapons systems acquisition, design, manufacture, and support.[1]

DOD's director of CALS predicts that a widely used CALS program could save $580 million during the life of a typical weapons system.[2] Savings would accrue in automated engineering drawings, electronic publishing of technical manuals, and productivity gains in computer-integrated manufacturing. A Pentagon official foresees world-scale industrial networks by the year 2000.[3]

DOD expects CALS to reduce lead times, cut costs, and improve the delivered weapons systems' quality. CALS' Phase I, implemented in 1988 to 1992, delivered digital information along with the usual paper-based documents. Phase II, 1991–1995, has engaged contractors in establishing databases that the government and other vendors may access.[4]

[1] "The CALS Initiative: Creating a Standard Digital Format," *Inform* (January, 1990), pp. 31–33.
[2] "DOD Wants to Throw Tons of Paperwork Overboard," *Electronic Business* (February 5, 1990), pp. 15–16.
[3] "Digital Data System Expected to Benefit Defense and Industry," *Aviation Week & Space Technology* (February 5, 1990), pp. 66–70.
[4] "Data Exchange: Standards for Documentation Management," *CAE* (August 1989), pp. 52–55.

COMPARISON WITH PRIVATE SECTOR PROCUREMENT

In a general context, government and private purchasing are quite similar. Both are purchasing for use and processing rather than resale, and both involve substantial quantities and large individual transactions. Both have the objectives of minimum cost. But there are also some significant differences.

Source of Authority

Authority for government purchasing is derived from laws. These include federal and state laws and constitutions as well as local laws and ordinances. The laws not only create the buying agencies but also levy taxes to secure the funds to provide for their functions. Therefore, the government purchasing manager is responsible to a legislative body and ultimately to the voters who elect that body. By contrast, the private industrial purchasing official has no responsibility beyond that to the corporation's executives.

Legal Restrictions

Most of the laws that establish the public purchasing agencies also prescribe the regulations under which they must operate. These regulations are intended to protect both the public for whom the buying is being done and the vendor.

The regulations are designed to prevent personal favoritism on the part of public officials and to assure all qualified vendors an equal opportunity to bid on government business. Usually they require an agency to advertise for bids. In addition, bids must be publicly opened and the award made to the lowest responsible bidder. Industry, by contrast, may negotiate secretly, buy without competitive bidding, award contracts to any vendor, and not divulge information concerning its purchases.

Prices

All public purchasing records are open to the scrutiny of interested parties. All actions taken must be defended against any challenge, necessitating full and complete records. Such a "fishbowl existence" sometimes forces government buyers into paying higher prices for comparable goods than industry does. Vendors know that quotations to governmental agencies are publicly posted, revealing their offers to all competitors. Consequently, they are less inclined to cut prices to secure government orders than they are to secure industrial orders. However, prestige, pride, and advertising value accrue from the use of a firm's products or equipment by a government agency. This is a silent testimonial, and attractive bids are sometimes submitted to public agencies with the price reduction charged to advertising.

The rather common industry practice of granting vendors a second chance to bid in order to meet lower prices quoted by competitors may also lead to industry's paying less than public agencies for comparable items. In public buying, unless all bids are rejected, the first bid submitted by each vendor is final.

Absence of Interest Cost

In private purchasing one of the considerations in determining the size of the reserve inventory of materials and supplies is the total cost of maintaining that inventory. In public purchasing, not much thought is usually given to the cost of carrying inventory, since funds come from taxes that are collected annually. However, as public agencies increasingly invest unspent tax receipts in short-term securities, they are beginning to see the advantage of operating on minimum inventories. In government purchasing the major considerations are still the favorableness of the quoted price and whether budgeted money is available to pay for the purchase. Of course, when government agencies buy major capital items for which interest-bearing bonds are issued, they factor the interest into their cost considerations.

The necessity of operating within a budget occasionally hinders the governmental buyer. It may restrict purchases to goods that will be consumed within the fiscal year. The prices for goods bought under two-year or three-year contracts are typically lower. Toward the close of the year, after the succeeding year's budget becomes available, purchases for stock can be made. Without this limitation many purchases would be made toward the close of a fiscal year to obligate the unexpended funds that had been allocated. Because of the large amounts involved, examinations of proposed budgets for public agencies and supervision of their operations are becoming more severe and of wider scope.

Other Significant Differences

A public agency purchases against a budget and must commit funds for each purchase made against the budget. The private counterpart buys against production schedules that have been established by other departments.

The public buyer cannot practice reciprocity, whereas some private buyers scan the expenditure from various points of view, including buying from customers.

The private buyer regards sources of supply and prices paid as trade secrets. By contrast, tabulations of bids received on public purchases are posted for general information. These become sources of competitive information for people in the selling field. Public buyers readily exchange price and source information, but private buyers do not. The posted information is one of the prime sources of information for federal and state authorities charged with detecting and prosecuting instances of concerted action to regulate prices and apportion markets. Patterns of collusion are investigated to protect both the private and public consumer.

Although public buying procedures assure free competition, broad exploration of the market, pressure to lower price, and equal opportunity for suppliers to compete, there are certain inherent disadvantages. These are:

1. Inability to deviate from established procedures when time is important.
2. Reluctance of suppliers to furnish technical advice and service, since they cannot be assured of compensation for their efforts.
3. The inability to favor a deserving supplier who has performed exceptionally well.

DOES COMPETITION EXIST?

Tax-supported agencies and institutions usually are required by law to request formal bids whenever the amount of a transaction exceeds the established statutory limit of $50,000. The Armed Services Procurement Act of 1947, now Title 10 of the U.S. Code, liberalized procedures by stipulating 17 exceptions to the advertised sealed-bid procedure. Negotiations can be used in such cases.

One of the premises underlying the sealed-bid procedure is that it fosters competition, for awards must be made to the lowest qualified bidders. It is assumed that all bidders will behave competitively in setting their price, since no influence other than price can be brought to bear.

Studies of competition in federal purchasing have indicated that prices tend to cluster around the level of the last government purchase. During periods of oversupply, when sellers are particularly interested in the business and are willing to sell at less than full cost, direct out-of-pocket costs may be used as the bid floor.

Competition in government buying is influenced by the various reporting requirements and by interaction with the Renegotiation Board. This board is an outgrowth of concerns first established by law during World War II to ensure that excessive profits were not being made through contracts that, because of wartime conditions, could not be priced as carefully as desired. In 1948, several years after the war ended, renegotiation was reimposed on a limited basis. The Korean War prompted enactment of the Renegotiation Act of 1951, which with amendments has been temporarily extended many times. The history of renegotiation legislation makes it abundantly clear that major considerations in enacting it were past difficulties in arriving at proper pricing when necessary data were unavailable and when procurement of military supplies and equipment during wartime was urgent.

AUTHORITY TO PURCHASE

The Constitution of the United States authorizes action to ''pay the debts and provide for the common defense and general welfare of the United States.''[5] This provision is the constitutional authority for federal purchasing. To implement it, Congress passes laws that authorize purchases either directly or indirectly through the creation of agencies and bureaus that are given authority to engage in the activities required to carry out their prescribed functions.

Authority for purchases at the state level stems from state constitutions, supplemented by laws passed by state legislatures. Some states have established central purchasing agencies. In many states, however, the purchasing function is left to the various departments, bureaus, and institutions of the state.

In most states authority to create purchasing agencies is delegated to counties, cities, towns, and other subdivisions, and the exercise of this right is optional for the local governments. In states where home rule is granted by law to cities, the right to establish purchasing agencies is implied in the grant.

Education is the legal responsibility of the states, and state laws establish the rules and procedures under which schools shall operate at the local level. Authority is usually given to local boards to operate the schools within the framework of the regulation established by the state. Corresponding power to purchase is delegated to these local boards.

The laws establishing purchasing authorities vary considerably and lack uniformity. Much study has been given to the formulation of a uniform law. From these attempts two generalizations may be drawn:

1. The law establishing a purchasing agency should conform to local conditions.

[5] *U.S. Constitution,* Act. I, sec. 8, cl. 1.

2. The law should be broad enough to permit details to be worked out by the local agency.

The American Bar Association has drawn up a model procurement code for state and local governments, that a later section in this chapter describes.

Public purchasing officers use the following processes to obtain needed products and services:[6]

1. *Small dollar purchases*—beneath the dollar threshold to obtain competitive quotes or bids.
2. *Request for quotations (RFQs)*—above the dollar threshold to obtain competitive quotes, yet below a dollar amount that would require issuing a formal bid solicitation.
3. *Invitations for bids (IFBs)*—above the dollar threshold to issue formal bid solicitation, normally involving the purchase of a product or contractual (nonprofessional) service.
4. *Request for proposals (RFPs)*—over the threshold to issue a formal bid solicitation, to obtain professional services and/or high-tech needs.
5. *Emergency purchases*—used only for the immediate protection of public health, life, and/or property.
6. *Sole source purchases*—to purchase a unique product or service.
7. *Negotiated acquisition*—usually a part of RFP or sole source purchases, or to acquire any exempted services such as power, utilities, or landfills.

FEDERAL PURCHASING—CONSIDERATIONS

Budget limitations often restrict the extent of federal purchasing. Procurement and related laws enacted by Congress are unique to federal procurement and are calculated not only to safeguard the expenditure of public funds, but to fulfill other missions in the public interest. Federal procurement considerations include encouragement of small business, nondiscrimination in employment, research, and the national defense, the use of American-made products, the employment of surplus labor, and purchasing the products of federal prisons and of the blind.

Many of the federal procurement considerations and techniques are not sufficiently different from the considerations and techniques of industrial buying to warrant separate notice. However, considerations that are unique

[6] "Purchasing in the Fishbowl," *NAPM Insights* (March 1990), pp. 21–22.

to the federal purchasing program are important and deserve the following attention.

Publicizing Procurement Actions

Bids exceeding specified amounts must be published in *Commerce Business Daily,* except for perishable subsistence requirements, utility services, classified restrictions, and emergency purchases. Defense procurements also must be included in this centralized publication, which is issued by the Department of Commerce.

Business concerns may communicate with the buying agency to secure further information on bid specifications. This is allowed in order to increase competition and broaden industry participation in government procurement. All bid notices, regardless of dollar volume, are forwarded to the agency's local post office for public posting.

Protest of Contracts

Suppliers who fail to secure a contract with a government agency have a well-defined right to protest and can hold up a procurement for months or even years through the General Accounting Office and the courts. The advantage of this is the discouragement of political pressure in contract bidding. In contrast, the government contract officer, to avoid possible protest, often finds it safer to award the contract to the lowest bidder regardless of the questionability of the product or past performance of the supplier.

Standardization

The standardization program of the federal government establishes standardized procurement forms and specifications for products. These standards are designed to reduce purchasing costs, lower capital investment in inventories, and enhance effective control.

Federal procurement agencies employ standardized forms for use in formal bids, informal quotations, construction contracts, blanket orders, and imprest funds (cash transactions). These standardized forms are economical, and their uniformity facilitates the objective of offering all responsible suppliers an equal chance to bid on federal requirements. Federal specifications are intended to be clear and accurate descriptions of requirements for materials, products, and services. They establish minimum requirements for quality and construction of acceptable products.

Specifications are developed by the Federal Supply Service (FSS) with the assistance of the agency that has the primary interest in the product. The cost of the FSS has been questioned by the General Accounting Office, which has indicated that the cost of creating specifications may exceed the product cost. Another criticism points out that specifications may lag behind current market conditions, causing agencies to purchase obsolete or costly products. As a result, federal agencies are phasing out some government specifications and shifting to commercial specifications, such as those of the American Society for Testing and Materials (ASTM).

Federal Procurement Reform

In order to promote further economy, efficiency, and effectiveness in the procurement of property and services by the executive branch of the federal government, Congress passed Public Law 96-83 in 1979.[7] This law sets the stage for the future refinement of federal procurement regulations by mandating the Office of Federal Procurement Policy to develop and implement both a uniform procurement system and a central management system. In addition, the administrator is directed to consult regularly with executive agencies and Congress regarding the development and implementation of these systems.

In March 1982, Executive Order No. 12352,[8] which attempted to reform federal procurement practices in a number of additional ways, was implemented.

1. Heads of agencies engaged in procurement are required to establish programs to reduce administrative costs, balance individual programs, needs against mission priorities and available resources, improve the effectiveness of procurement systems, simplify small purchases, and establish career management programs for federal purchasing personnel.

2. Common procurement regulations must be consolidated into a single Federal Acquisition Regulation.

3. Personnel policies and classification standards must meet the needs of executive agencies for a professional procurement workforce.

4. Government-wide procurement systems criteria must be identified, conflicting views among different agencies resolved, procurement processes streamlined, criteria for procurement career management programs developed, and major inconsistencies in law and policies

[7] Public Law 96-83, October 10, 1979, 93 Stat. 648.
[8] Executive Order No. 12352, March 17, 1982, 47 F.R. 12125, Federal Procurement Reform, 41 USC Section 401.

relating to procurement identified. Agency implementation of the provisions of this executive order is to be reviewed.

The Office of Federal Procurement Policy developed additional changes. On April 1, 1984, the Federal Acquisition Regulation (FAR) established a single regulation for use by the Department of Defense, the General Services Administration, and the National Aeronautics and Space Administration. The FAR replaced earlier systems regulating the acquisition of supplies and services with appropriated funds and stresses market competition as the way to improve quality and lower costs.[9]

Action to reform the federal procurement system encounters difficulties, with little purchasing research to help. A study that reported on a survey of purchasing directors of the 46 largest U.S. counties outside Florida noted the absence of purchasing research in mainstream public administration journals and public financial management textbooks.[10]

For example, the General Accounting Office, Congress' investigative arm, studied failures to streamline the Department of Agriculture's field structure and management after repeated reform attempts that extended over 45 years. The problems involve 36 agencies employing 110,000 full-time persons in more than 15,000 places around the world at a 1988 cost of $44 billion.[11]

The Carlucci Initiatives and the 1984 Competition in Contracting Act (CICA) fueled competition and required procuring agencies to use commercial products wherever feasible. The Public Information Act describes what records the public should find available and mandates procedures for their availability.

New approaches appear from time to time. For example, five prime contractors submitted an interim teaming agreement to the U.S. Air Force. General Dynamics, McDonnell-Douglas, Rockwell International, Rockwell's Rocketdyne Division, and Pratt & Whitney participate in the National Aero-Space Plane (NASP) program. Their agreement would allow the contractors to end competition among themselves and unite them into a team for developing an X-30 hypersonic research vehicle.[12]

Despite some progress, government-wide procurement statutes remain restrictive, such as the Federal Property and Administrative Act, the Armed Service Procurement Act, and the Small Business and Federal Procurement

[9] *Federal Register* 48, no. 182, Washington, D.C., September 19, 1983.

[10] "Procurement Policy: The Missing Element in Financial Management Education," *International Journal of Public Administration* (1990), pp. 155–179.

[11] "Watchdogs Snapping at Heels of USDA," Associated Press release April 8, 1990.

[12] "Contractors Agree to Unite NASP Development Efforts," *Aviation Week & Space Technology* (January 29, 1990), pp. 21–22.

Competition Enhancement Act. This latter act eliminated business opportunities for small businesses by demanding compliance to size standards and other stipulations.[13]

Prompt Payment Act

In 1982 Congress passed the Prompt Payment Act. Formerly, suppliers of goods and services to the federal government suffered long delays in receiving payment. Now suppliers report much-improved attention to the payment of invoices by federal procurement agencies as they seek to avoid the interest penalties imposed by the act on late payments.

Small Business Preferences

It is the policy of the government to aid, counsel, assist, and protect the interests of small business firms and to place with small businesses a fair proportion of government purchases and contracts for goods and services. This policy was established by legislation when the Small Business Administration (SBA) was created.

For the purpose of the Small Business Act, a small business concern is deemed to be one that is (1) independently owned and operated, and (2) not dominant in its field of operation. In addition to these criteria, general size standards are specified for business groupings within the individual categories of wholesale, retail, construction, and manufacturing.

The SBA has functioned as a lending institution; however, a number of its other activities are quite important and have a direct bearing on procurement activities at the federal level.

First, there is the Prime Contracts Program. Many proposed governmental purchases are beyond the capabilities of small business. To promote small business participation, the SBA developed, in cooperation with various procurement agencies, a set-aside program. Major government purchasing agencies set aside contracts or portions of contracts for small business bidding. Through its own procurement representatives stationed in major military and civilian procurement installations, the SBA recommends additional set-asides, suggests the relaxation of unduly restrictive specifications, tries to discover small business competition, closely watches the Certificate of Competency (COC) program to ensure its application when appropriate, and in general determines ways and means of increasing the amount of business that small firms may transact with government agencies.

Under the program, if a contracting officer proposes to reject the bid of a small business firm that is a low bidder because the officer questions the

---

[13] "The Problem in Government Procurement," *Purchasing World* (April 1989), pp. 35, 38.

ability of the firm to perform the contract on the grounds of capacity or credit, the officer refers the case to the SBA. Upon receipt of the case, the SBA contacts the rejected bidders, advises them of the impending decision, and affords them the opportunity to apply for a COC, which if granted would require the contracting officer to award the contract to the firm. Upon receipt of the COC application, the contracting officer of the procuring agency is notified, and a team of financial and technical personnel is sent to the firm to survey its potential. After the survey is completed, and if the SBA concludes that the company can fulfill the contract successfully, the SBA issues a COC attesting to these facts. The certificate is forwarded to the procurement officer, and the contract is awarded.

The following are basic guidelines that can help small businesses in obtaining federal contracts:[14]

1. Understand exactly what business line the company wants to pursue.
2. Learn the process for submitting a bid to the government and avenues of appeal if problems develop.
3. Get to know the agency the company will deal with and the particular contracting officer.
4. Know the company's limits.

Recognizing the necessity of ensuring that "a fair proportion of the total purchases and contracts or subcontracts for property and services for government" is placed with small business enterprises, Congress in 1961 passed Public Law 87-305. Under this law the Small Business Administration, the Defense Department, and the General Services Administration were required to develop jointly and cooperatively a small business subcontracting program. Under the Armed Services Procurement Regulations (ASPR) provisions, contracts in amounts ranging from $5000 to $500,000 must contain a so-called best-efforts clause, which states that the contractor agrees to accomplish the maximum amount of subcontracting with small businesses that he or she "finds to be consistent with the efficient performance of the contract." In procurements over $500,000, the contractor is required by a mandatory contract clause to undertake a full business subcontracting program.

As previously indicated, the Public Works Act of 1977 requires 10 percent of all federally funded construction contracts to go to minority companies. The law applies to federally funded programs, including the activities of general contractors who do work for a client who in turn holds a federal contract. In the future, minority buying percentage requirements

---

[14] "A Demanding Customer," *Nation's Business* (March 1990), pp. 29–30.

are likely to be questioned on the basis that such provisions represent reverse discrimination against nonminority firms.[15]

Disadvantaged Business Development

Another ongoing program is the Disadvantaged Business Development Program, section 8(a) of the Small Business Act. To assist eligible disadvantaged firms to compete effectively in the economic mainstream, section 8(a) authorizes the SBA to channel government purchases of them. The SBA accomplishes its goals under this program by negotiating contracts with federal agencies for supplies, services, and construction and then subcontracting to the disadvantaged firm. In effect, the SBA acts as prime contractor.

Labor-Surplus Areas and Prevailing Wages

It is the policy of the government to relieve labor-surplus areas by placing contracts with firms in such areas, whenever such purchases are consistent with broader procurement objectives and do not result in prices higher than those obtainable in other areas. Under this regulation, tie bids may be awarded to concerns in labor-surplus areas and some government requirements may be "set aside" for firms in labor-surplus areas. The Bacon–Davis Act requires payment of "prevailing" wages in the area under all government construction contracts of public works or public buildings. The Department of Labor has ruled that the wage rate paid to at least 30 percent of the workers in one category in the area is termed prevailing. Before the contract is awarded, the contractor is told precisely what rate must be paid to employees. During the life of the contract, the contractor is required to submit weekly payroll reports to assure compliance with the specified rate.

The Buy-American Act

Federal contracts may be awarded under the Buy-American Act, to other than the lowest bidder if the bid of an acceptable domestic concern does not exceed the lowest acceptable foreign bid by more than 6 percent, or 12 percent if the domestic bidder operates in a labor-surplus area.

Sale of Federal Property

There are three categories of disposal property offered for sale by the United States when they are no longer needed by any agency of the federal

[15] See Britt Robson, "Ohio Law Challenged," *Black Enterprise* (May 1983), pp. 20–21.

government: personal property, real property, and strategic materials no longer vital to the national interest.

Disposal sales are planned to have minimal effect on the market. For the same reason products of the Federal Prison Industries are used by the federal government. Prison-made products, with low labor costs, would unfairly compete with products produced at full labor and capital cost.

Unique Requirements of Federal Purchasing

Purchasing departments of federal agencies perform duties in every area of procurement. Departments buy items of rare, exotic, and even secret composition as well as ordinary items. They buy every type of equipment manufactured and some that are still in the research and development state. They become involved in construction contracts for roads and buildings that employ unique nomenclature and trade practices. Some federal purchasing departments specialize in one method of contracting, but many departments are challenged by the need to use all purchasing methods for a wide variety of goods and services.

CIVILIAN PURCHASING

The historical development of procurement for the civilian agencies of the federal government dates back to 1792, with relatively recent organizational revisions.

Alexander Hamilton, the first secretary of the Treasury, was given responsibility for procurement of supplies for the federal government in the first law pertaining to government procurement in 1792. Procurement responsibility remained with the Treasury Department until 1949.

In 1861 Congress recognized the need for additional statutes dealing with federal procurement. At that time a law was passed requiring at least three bids on each purchase. In 1868 Congress established a procedure for the public opening of bids and awarding of contracts. In 1949 a committee known as the Hoover Commission made recommendations for specific purchasing practices. This report led to, among other things, the passage of Public Law 152, the Federal Property and Administrative Services Act of 1949.

Under this law the General Services Administration (GSA) was established with authority to develop and organize a method of central buying for most of the civil departments of the federal government. The GSA maintains centralization responsibility today. Before GSA, the bulk of buying for civil divisions of the federal government had been handled by the individual bureaus, departments, and administrative agencies. This division of responsibility resulted in duplication, overbuying, and general inefficiency.

Under the present system, the administrator of the GSA has authority to buy for almost all other agencies of the government, to set standards and specifications, to buy and warehouse for future use, and to draw back, store, and transfer supplies and equipment from one department to another in the event of nonuse or oversupply.

In 1978 the GSA, which buys $5 billion in goods and services each year, was involved in a major scandal of collusion between government employees and private contractors. This scandal prompted investigation into the purchasing activities of all government agencies, and legislation was passed to make the process simpler, more flexible, more competitive, and easier to regulate.

Much of today's government purchasing is based on contracts covering periods of time rather than individual orders for immediate delivery. The GSA enters into contracts with vendors to supply the needs of departments for stipulated periods of time at prices that have been established through bids or negotiations. All using departments are notified of the contracts that have been placed, and when they need goods, they place their orders directly with the contract vendors.

Most agencies have their own procurement activities in addition to the purchasing done by the GSA. These purchases are usually of items peculiar to the agency's needs. Civil agencies with extensive purchasing programs include the Atomic Energy Commission, the Departments of Agriculture, Commerce, Health, Education, and Rehabilitative Services, Interior, Justice, and the Treasury; the Federal Aviation Agency; the National Aeronautics and Space Administration; the Postal Service; the Tennessee Valley Authority, and the Veterans Administration.

MILITARY PURCHASING

Historically, the army and navy were assigned responsibility for their own purchases. The Navy Department was given this authority in 1795, and the army was given similar authority in 1799.

Before World War II the total purchasing by the military services was not so large as to have much effect on the economy. Consequently, even though there was waste and duplication, little was done to improve methods of purchasing. In succeeding years, with defense playing a large role in the economy, the reorganization of military procurement procedures became imperative.

Two laws were particularly designed to remedy the situation. The Armed Services Procurement Act had the following main features:

1. Provision for exceptions to the standard method of purchasing through advertising for bids
2. Elimination of cost-plus-percentage-of-cost contracts
3. Assignment of a proportion of contracts to small business

The National Security Act as amended has two main provisions bearing on military purchasing.

1. The establishment of an Office of Procurement Methods charged with (*a*) purchase assignment, (*b*) procurement regulation, (*c*) contracting, (*d*) pricing, (*e*) cost analysis, (*f*) contract termination, (*g*) renegotiation, (*h*) inspection, (*i*) standardization, (*j*) cataloging, and (*k*) the small business program.
2. The establishment of a procurement policy council, with the responsibility defined in the following paragraph, from section 213-c of the act:

It shall be the duty of the board, under the direction of the Secretary of Defense, to recommend assignment of procurement responsibilities among the several military services, and to plan for the greatest practicable allocation of purchase authority of technical equipment and common-use items on the basis of single procurement.

As a result of these laws, most military purchases are now made by a single department for all three military departments. Basic differences in the procurement practices of the three departments remain. The army has decentralized purchasing to the technical services and field offices, with policy control centralized at the general staff level. The navy has delegated purchasing responsibility only as far as its bureaus in Washington and maintains policy control in the Office of the Chief of Naval Material. The air force has assigned purchasing responsibility to the Air Material Command in Dayton, Ohio, with control of policy retained by the Director of Procurement in Washington, D.C.

The Department of Defense (DOD) has reoriented its procurement practices to bring them more into line with industry. For instance, in 1988 the Secretary of Defense made Total Quality Management (TQM) official policy of the Department of Defense. Emphasis has been placed on introducing more active competition, starting with ideas for alternative items and extending into production. Profit and other incentives have been emphasized to motivate industry to self-manage rather than rely on regulations, as it has done in the past. An additional change is the creation of an office separate from the SBA, which will deal specifically with minority and small businesses by providing advice on DOD procurement opportunities.[16]

Within DOD, the majority of procurement decisions are arrived at by negotiations rather than through sealed bids. Negotiations have become almost inevitable because of the rapid increase in technology, which frequently requires the military to solicit proposals for items that have never been made. The military specifies what it wants the item to do. The proposals submitted by prospective suppliers suggest the nature of the item they propose to supply to meet the performance requirements and the price.

Standard procedure on negotiated purchases is to solicit proposals from a number of sources. After the proposals are evaluated, the procuring officer calls in the most likely contractor and negotiates the entire procurement, including the price.

Types of Contracts

There are four types of contracts in common use in military procurement, and one of these is adopted as a result of the negotiations.

Cost-No-Fee Contract. Contracts made with educational and other nonprofit organizations, primarily for research, pay them costs but no fee or profit.

Cost-Plus-Fixed-Fee Contract. Contracts for cost plus a fixed fee tend to be used for research performed by industrial concerns and for the procurement of new products requiring considerable developmental work. Such contracts frequently include a ceiling price.

Incentive Contract. In incentive contracts the producer is given an incentive to meet or beat specified targets. A target price is established and includes an allowance for profits. When production is completed, the actual costs are compared with the target. If they are lower than target, the profit allowed is higher by a predetermined percentage of the cost reduction. If the costs are higher than target, the producer's profit is lowered by a predetermined percentage. These contracts are designed to lower costs by the incentive of additional profit and to penalize inefficiency.

Firm-Fixed-Price Contract. A price is agreed upon in a firm-fixed-price contract, with no provision for adjustment. The contracts are comparable to most industrial purchase contracts and are used for standard items.

[16] Slava W. Harlamor, ''Defense Department Procurement Procedures,'' *Aviation Week and Space Technology* (April 17, 1978), p. 56.

An important difference between federal and industrial procurement is the required adherence, in government purchase contracts, to certain laws governing wages, hours, and nondiscrimination. Frequently, prime contracts must make adherence to these provisions a condition of any subcontracts they place under a government contract that they hold.

If a firm violates these laws, it is placed on a blacklist and for a time is not permitted to bid on government contracts. The Secretary of Labor maintains a list of ineligible firms. Ineligibility lasts for a period of three years.

STATE AND LOCAL PURCHASING

Organization

Most state and local government units today have organized purchasing departments. There is considerable variation in the extent of authority and the amount of the purchasing done by these departments. In some states the purchasing agent buys almost everything used by the state agencies and institutions. In other states the purchasing agent buys for only a few designated departments, and such agencies as highway departments, airports, prisons, and educational institutions are exempted from centralized purchasing.

There is a trend to centralize purchasing at the county level, even though counties lag behind both cities and states in this respect. Through the efforts of the National Association of Purchasing Management, the National Institute of Governmental Purchasing, and other civic-minded bodies that are constantly striving for more efficiency in the spending of taxpayers' money, the number of counties that have centralized their purchasing activities has increased greatly.

In the larger cities purchasing is almost always centered in a department organized to buy for most of the bureaus and divisions. A few departments may be permitted to do their own buying because of the specialized nature of their activities. Libraries, museums, hospitals, schools, and water and transportation utilities are examples of such departments.

There is a growing trend to set up legislatively some advisory body, such as the county board, the common council, the village board, a commission, committee, or board of top officials, to serve the purchasing agency in an ex officio capacity. This advisory body usually has five or seven members. The legislation specifies the composition of the group and its authority and function in directing the public buying agency. Such a body is invaluable in insulating the purchasing agent from many pressures and in providing experience and mature judgment in making major decisions.

The group usually formulates objectives and procedures to guide the purchasing department, using bylaws that cover all the phases of public buying. These bylaws also designate committees that function in specific areas.

When many makes or brands have been requested by the various departments, a standardization committee is frequently established with authority to rule on simplification issues. The requests need to be reduced to one or a few acceptable items in order to achieve savings through quantity purchases. This committee might also approve purchases of items for which standards do not exist.

A specifications committee may review proposed specifications with prospective bidders to determine whether the specifications will unduly restrict competition and whether they will meet the requirements of the agency. Controversial specifications may also be reviewed by the committee with the interested parties.

A valuable authority for a public buying agency to have is the right to call on other departments, boards, and commissions to assist in technical matters. With the growing variety of materials, supplies, and equipment to purchase, the drawing up of specifications, inspection, and quality checking often require technical assistance.

The National Association of State Purchasing Officials (NASPO) assists state purchasing officials in improving the quality of purchasing through exchange of information and cooperation to attain greater efficiency and economy.[17] States tend to purchase more consumer-oriented goods than does the federal government. Suppliers can rely on the state to pay for products or services and the state could end up as a company's largest customer.

Cooperative Purchasing

The advantages of cooperative purchasing are the greater economy and efficiency inherent in the process, especially for the smaller units of state and local governments. The larger quantities obtained through combined purchasing lead to lower unit costs, and standardization of requirements provides further savings. The smaller participating units can also share the technical skills, buying skills, and testing facilities of the larger agencies. Finally, better buyer–vendor relationships are likely to be developed.

Certain legal and political obstacles have inhibited the growth of cooperative buying, although experience indicates that legal barriers can usually be overcome in time. Political obstacles, such as the desire to favor local merchants, the fear of loss of autonomy, the difficulty of settling on stan-

---

[17] "States: A Mother Lode Ripe for Mining," *Industry Week* (June 17, 1991), pp. 79–83.

dardized items acceptable to all, and the feeling of the larger participants that their savings will be less than those of the smaller units, are more difficult to overcome.

A supplementary purchasing technique available to most state and local governmental units is joint purchasing. This technique permits two or more distinct agencies to achieve together the advantages of centralized purchasing, which may not be available to them as separate buying jurisdictions.

The various forms of joint buying can be divided into the following categories.

1. Joint buying by various independent public agencies within a specific metropolitan area.
2. Participation in state contracts by governmental agencies within the state.
3. Utilization by member cities of contract prices negotiated by state municipal leagues.
4. Use of commercial buying services that perform the buying functions for small governmental units on a fee basis.
5. Utilization by educational institutions of contract prices negotiated by national educational associations.

Many systems called joint purchasing systems are, in reality, cooperative pricing systems. Often a lead agency, basing its actions on requests from other participating local government units, solicits bids from various vendors on behalf of the group. The lead agency then awards a contract to the vendor, and it becomes a master contract setting forth the standard unit price and the specifications against which other participating government units may write their own purchase contracts.

There are approximately 81,000 governmental units below the state level that can utilize cooperative purchasing arrangements. Such arrangements are also applicable for other types of nonprofit agencies such as private schools, hospitals, and religious organizations.

Successful cooperative agreements should follow at least a few of the following guidelines.

1. Initially only a smaller number of units should participate.
2. The initial commodities covered should be used by participants (e.g., gasoline, heating fuel, road salt).
3. All participants, regardless of size of unit, should have equal status.
4. State legislation should allow cooperative arrangements.

5. Committees should be developed to address specific areas of concern.

6. Purchasing in the individual cooperating units should be centralized, with an administrative system favorable to the concept.

Purchasing Procedures

State and local governmental purchasing follows a fairly standard procedure. Small purchases and emergency purchases may be negotiated over the telephone. One or two local sources of supply are called.

Larger purchases are usually made only after a written solicitation of bids. The law or the regulations of most buying agencies specify that all purchases above a certain dollar amount must be bought through public advertising and public opening of bids. Award of contracts is usually made at a public meeting where bidders or interested persons may be heard.

To encourage bidders, the buyer must state precisely what he wishes to buy so that all bidders can quote on equal terms. The specifications required for this procedure can ordinarily be obtained from the U.S. Bureau of Standards. It has hundreds of specifications covering almost every item purchased by local governments. The National Institute of Governmental Purchasing and the National Purchasing Institute also maintain libraries of specifications contributed by members; the libraries are available to members. Many public purchasing agents start with these basic specifications and change them to meet their needs.

Another common method of specifying quality is to name some product by brand and request the bidder to quote on that item ''or equal.'' Although this practice has desirable features, particularly for special equipment, it also has disadvantages. Few companies will admit that their product is not the equal of their competitor's product, and one may find it difficult to prove it inferior, even if it may be so regarded.

A third type of specification buying is called performance specifications. This method sets forth in general what is desired and the use to which the product will be put. Bidders are asked to submit a sample of their standard product that comes closest to meeting the general performance requirements. The request for bids states that the samples will be evaluated by a committee, which will report on the suitability of the items for the intended use. This method has been used by the board of school directors of Milwaukee for buying such items as school desks, pianos, film projectors, and phonographs, and it has worked very well.

When specifications are properly drawn, it is usually a simple matter to determine the winner. The lowest-cost responsible bidder meeting the specifications obtains the contract. Responsibility, in this sense, is determined on the basis of past dealings, through information from other purchasing agents, or through prequalification of bidders. Prequalification means that the supplier has convinced the buyer of appropriate reliability in advance of bidding.

When specifications are inadequate, or when performance tests are needed to determine the quality of the items offered, a greater element of judgment is required in awarding a contract. In order to justify buying from a bidder other than the lowest, the public purchasing agent must be able to substantiate the choice made. The agent is on the firmest ground if the bids or samples submitted are examined by a committee of experts, composed in part of those who are to use the goods.

Often in public purchasing more than one bid is required before an award can be made. However, a single bid may be accepted if the law governing the agency so permits. Single bids become fairly common during periods of scarcity. Single bids are also common in the purchase of patented or proprietary articles made by only one concern.

The state or local purchasing agent is usually authorized to permit using departments to make emergency purchases necessary to maintain essential services. These cases are usually limited to true emergencies, with a maximum expenditure specified. Written reports justifying the emergency's procedure are usually required.

Most state and local purchasing departments also permit using departments to make small cash purchases when the amount involved is small. Since it costs from $15 to $50 to issue and pay a purchase order, it is advisable, where permitted by law, to give each department a petty cash fund out of which to make these minor purchases.

Fiscal Aspects

Most public purchasing agencies work under a regulation that prohibits issuing a purchase order unless funds to cover the payment are on deposit with the public treasury and have been appropriated for the purpose. It is, therefore, customary for orders to be cleared through the proper accounting or fiscal agency before being placed. This permits the funds to be encumbered and held for payment of the invoice when due. This clearance is especially important toward the close of the fiscal year when the budget may become exhausted.

In most state and local governments the purchasing departments must obtain the invoices, check them, and then pass them to the auditing department for further checking and payment. Some government purchasing departments require that invoices be on their own forms for simplicity of handling and filing. Public agencies have often used procedures that hamper efficiency and competition in purchasing. An example is the now-obsolete practice of requiring a notarized statement of a vendor's invoice, indicating that it is a true and correct copy of the amount due.

State and local governments are exempt from federal taxes as well as state and local sales taxes, and the federal government is exempt from state and local taxes. This exemption requires constant checking on the part of the purchasing department to make sure that taxes are not included in invoice totals by vendors who are unfamiliar with the facts. There may be confusion concerning taxes paid at the point of manufacture and added by the manufacturer to the price charged to dealers. Not knowing what taxes they have paid, dealers have trouble getting refunds from manufacturers. Standard forms of tax exemption certificates are available and should be included with government purchase orders for any item subject to excise or sales taxes that do not have to be paid by the government.

Internal Revenue Service regulations permit each exempt agency to assign a number to itself that may be used without an exemption certificate if the purchase is made directly from a manufacturer.

Warehousing

Efficient centralized purchasing requires storage facilities. Widely and frequently used materials and supplies are stored and distributed to using departments as needed. Central warehousing permits quantity purchases at lower prices, allows the buyer to make purchases when the market conditions seem most favorable, facilitates inspection and testing by providing sufficient reserve stock for use during the process of rejection and replacement, and provides a reserve stock from which goods are available when needed.

A perpetual inventory control should be maintained for all stock items so that the supply is never exhausted. Deliveries are usually made to using departments at stated intervals, varying from daily to monthly, and pickups at the warehouse are permitted. Some purchasing departments charge the cost of storage and distribution to the general overhead of their department. Others add a small markup to the cost of the goods in order to make the service self-supporting.

Inspection

Where the volume of purchases warrants it, government purchasing departments have their own testing laboratories. Sometimes these may be maintained jointly by several departments. In smaller governmental units it is possible for the buyer to conduct simple tests and inspections to determine whether the goods delivered are as ordered.

Manufacturing, Repairing, and Printing

Some manufacturing processes are conducted, or at least supervised, by the purchasing department. New York City, for example, manufactures drugs and medicines, roasts coffee, and cans food from its own farms. In other cities such items as soap, floor seal, waxes, traffic lights, and street signs are manufactured. Usually such manufacturing is limited to items that require little equipment and a small capital investment.

A service frequently provided by state and local purchasing departments is the repair and maintenance of equipment. In some cities purchasing is responsible for shops that repair motor vehicles, water meters, typewriters, office machines, and so forth. This organizational structure has proved efficient, for many items are kept in service that otherwise would be scrapped or traded sooner than necessary.

Many governmental units have long maintained departments for printing and duplicating under the control of the purchasing department. This practice developed as agencies found that large savings in printing and duplicating were possible. Centralized printing and duplicating promote standardization, reduce the number of items to be duplicated, and allow for longer press runs with consequent savings. Service is also usually faster than can be secured from outside sources.

Salvage Control

There is probably no better place to centralize the control of salvaged materials and equipment than in the purchasing department. The buyer, who knows the market, is the logical one to assume responsibility for the sale of items a governmental unit no longer needs. Salvage control includes the transfer of equipment as well as its sale. If one department has materials or equipment it no longer needs, they sometimes can be transferred to another department. Centralizing this transfer authority in purchasing prevents using departments from viewing equipment as their own rather than belonging to the public. Most city purchasing departments now have the power to transfer surplus material or equipment between using departments.

When material or equipment ceases to be usable by any governmental unit, the purchasing department uses it as a trade-in on a new purchase or sells it for cash. Sales of such items are generally handled through competitive bids in the same manner as purchases.

Supplies and equipment declared surplus by federal agencies are often offered to state and local units of government for use in health, welfare, education, and civil defense. Such items are usually distributed through a state surplus property agency, often under the state educational system.

THE MODEL PROCUREMENT CODE

The American Bar Association (ABA), responding to a perceived need to assist states in setting up purchasing operations, developed its Model Procurement Code in 1979.[18]

The code's purpose was to provide:

1. Policy guidelines for managing and controlling the purchase of items for public contracts.
2. Ways of resolving controversies about public contracts.
3. Ethical guidelines for public purchasing personnel.

The code consists of twelve parts, covering general provisions, organization, service selection, specifications, legality, costs, and related topics. In 1982 a revised document was published by the ABA consisting of a similar outline for local governmental units.

At present it is estimated that 10 states have code-based legislation. Kentucky was the first state to adopt legislation based on the code in March 1978, and it has had no court challenges to the validity of procedure or policy on procurement methods.

The Georgia legislature adopted sections of the code pertaining to postbid negotiations and competitive sealed proposals. South Carolina not only implemented part of the code in its Consolidated Procurement Code but added its own related provisions. Finally, in Tennessee the legislature revised state law so that approval of procurement contract specifications by the State Board of Standards is no longer required. The Tennessee Purchasing Division is now authorized to issue invitations to bid without prior approval from the board. This is consistent with the philosophy stated in the code that an oversight board should not, as a general rule, involve itself in day-to-day operations. Rather, such a board should develop policies and criteria and review compliance.

It appears that states that have adopted the code or parts thereof have benefited from the decision. By helping to standardize the language and

---

[18] *The Model Procurement Code for State and Local Governments* (Chicago: American Bar Association, Fourth Printing, December 1987), p. vi.

policies of procurement on a national basis, the Model Procurement Code offers innovative approaches for government procurement.

QUASI-PUBLIC PURCHASING

Certain types of agencies such as schools and hospitals, may be either public institutions or private, nonprofit institutions. Occasionally they may be operated for profit. Because of their functions, all these institutions are quasi-public.

Purchasing officials in such institutions have some of the characteristics of both private and public purchasing personnel. Their responsibilities tend to resemble those of the public buyer. Generally they are responsible for ordering, pricing, specifications, quality control, value analysis, materials' control, central storerooms, printing departments, mailrooms, and often auxiliary enterprises such as bookstores and gift shops. Because their institutions are private, they are not hampered by the restrictive legislation that controls the public buyer, but being supported by many, they have a responsibility to their supporters. Generally they do not open bids in public but do make vendor and price information available when this is not detrimental to the institution.

Often these institutions spend funds as an agent of the government. Many research and support programs of the federal government are administered by these institutions and are subject to government audit. In such instances the programs must comply with the regulations and policies of the supporting government agency.

Purchasing personnel in quasi-public institutions recognize that there are differences in the objectives and philosophy of a profit and a nonprofit institution. Emphasis tends to be more on service to the requisitioning individuals and departments than on purely economic considerations.

CHAPTER SUMMARY

Public purchasing carries a very large accountability for properly spending the nation's money—over a trillion dollars spent in 1992. States and local governments spend more than the federal government. Together with the federal government, they apply the whole range of purchasing and materials management concepts that private sector procurement employs. They operate under more legal restrictions and more open to outside scrutiny than does the private sector.

Federal procurement personnel lead the way in buying from small businesses and from minorities. Military procurement negotiators develop worldwide sources to meet enormous needs for goods and services.

Smaller units of state and local governments sometimes combine their purchasing efforts with larger agencies in a technique named cooperative buying. Under this technique, smaller governmental units share the technical skills, buying skills, and testing facilities of the larger entities. The combined quantities lead to lower unit costs. Officials in the smaller units sometimes object to cooperative buying because they can't favor local merchants with contracts, nor can they hold out against standardization of materials.

Joint purchasing operates like centralized purchasing in a large corporation. A number of small governmental units band together to pool their requirements for goods and services, which leads to lower unit prices. No joint partner dominates.

Quasi-public agencies like schools, hospitals, museums, civic symphonies, and research institutes may operate for profit or not-for-profit. Their purchasing efforts resemble the economic sector's procedures in the former case and the regulated approach of a government agency in the latter case.

Discussion Questions

1. What are the significant differences between government and industrial purchasing?
2. Describe the responsibilities of GSA.
3. Does competition exist in governmental procurement? Discuss.
4. What is the role of the SBA in federal procurement?
5. What is meant by contract renegotiation?
6. The lowest responsible bidder is awarded government purchase contracts. What is meant by responsible bidder?
7. What is the difference between cooperative and joint purchasing at the local level?
8. What are the advantages of cooperative purchasing for local units of government?
9. Does nonprofit agency purchasing differ from other types of purchasing? Explain.
10. How can a government purchasing agent buy on a brand basis when the law requires free and open bidding for all vendors and a given brand can be had only from one vendor?
11. Discuss the advantages of central warehousing.
12. Discuss the Model Procurement Code and its purpose.
13. Discuss the reforms of federal procurement implemented in the last decade.

Suggested Cases

Golden City

King County

Megalopolis City

Parktown

Radmer County

Utopia School District

Human Resources Management in Purchasing and Materials Management

Bankers Trust Company (New York) has begun contracting many jobs ordinarily done by the bank's own employees out to private vendors. The bank primarily has decided to contract out its more mundane functions in order to focus management attention on strategic business issues. As a result of such outsourcing or vending, the bank employs about 500 fewer people. The growing popularity of outsourcing provides Bankers Trust with more vendors from which to choose. Bankers Trust has installed numerous controls for monitoring performance in order to keep track of this abundance of outside vendors.

Bill, the materials manager for Giant Paper Company, put down the magazine article and pondered what outsourcing would do for his 62-person setup.*

**C H A P T E R
C O N T E N T S**

*Source: "Are They or Aren't They Bank Employees?" *United States Banker* (January 1991), pp. 49–52.

Many persons assume that the purchasing department consists of a staff of clerks who simply place orders that commit the firm to a purchase. Some persons assume that they know best what they want and who should supply it; they assume that the commercial factors of purchase economy, optimum timing, and delivery control pertain to persons in other departments, but not to them. Since World War II, the college-educated, executive-type purchasing manager serves the firm as a professional profit-generator who doubles as a kind of missionary to save persons from such false assumptions.

The purchasing manager operates in close contact with all of the organization's functions in a sort of internal partnering. Moreover, he or she links the company to the supplier world in a sort of external partnering. The purchasing manager's efforts coordinate the relationship between each outside supplier and each inside employee who requisitions goods and services for use.

Probably no area of business has more interdepartmental interaction than purchasing. The effectiveness of the purchasing professional depends on harmonious relations with production, engineering, and quality control, to name a few. The buying process itself necessitates a working knowledge of the concerns of finance, traffic, inventory, and inspection. Correspondingly, the purchasing manager needs the breadth and depth of multiple technical personal qualifications in order to capitalize on the many opportunities and challenges of the position.

This chapter examines the human resources management function of purchasing. It discusses the types of positions available in purchasing, the qualifications for them, work performed within the purchasing department, and the sources, selection, and compensation of purchasing personnel.

CLASSIFICATIONS OF WORK PERFORMED IN PURCHASING

As the size of the organization increases, there is a need to delineate the functions performed within the purchasing process. In a small firm, one person may be responsible for the entire purchasing department. In a larger organization, four functions are ultimately distinguished—buying and negotiation, follow-up and expediting, clerical, and purchase research.

Management-Administration

Management of the purchasing function involves all of the tasks associated with the management process, with the emphasis on the development of policies, procedures, controls, and the mechanics for coordinating the purchasing activities with those of the other departments. In addition, it involves the management of suppliers and commodity problems.

Buying and Negotiating

Personnel who buy and negotiate have the responsibility of locating and selecting potential suppliers with the capabilities of meeting the organization's needs. These personnel must also negotiate prices, terms, and conditions of vendor agreements. Buying and negotiating may be further specialized, depending on organizational needs and individual capabilities.

Follow-up and Expediting

The vendor's performance, in meeting its commitment to the delivery requested on the purchase order, is monitored by follow-up and expediting personnel who attempt to ensure the smooth flow of materials through the organization. Should problems arise, they have the responsibility of ensuring that the vendor meets delivery requirements. This goal is achieved by applying pressure, through frequent contacts with the vendor, and by giving the vendor any assistance that is within the reasonable power of the expediter.

Clerical

The responsibility of administration is primarily one of maintaining records. Administration personnel prepare and route the formal purchase documents and are in charge of storage and retrieval of data necessary for the operation of the department. The preparation of periodic reports to upper management and other materials management personnel is handled at this level.

Purchase Research

Personnel doing purchase research try to improve the quality of buying in the purchasing department, as Chapter 4 discusses. This responsibility includes overseeing projects for the collection, classification, and analysis of data in order to maximize correct decision making. Specific responsibilities usually include macro (national and international) economic forecasting, projections of demand, supply, and price for commodities and component purchases, and vendor analysis.

POSITIONS IN PURCHASING AND MATERIALS MANAGEMENT

The number of positions in a purchasing department varies greatly among companies and industries. The chief variables accounting for this variation are (1) the size of the firm, (2) the degree of centralization, (3) the variations in responsibilities, and (4) the differing production processes. When the purchasing activities of a multiplant firm are centralized, the number of people in the central department naturally increases. However, with a centralized operation the total number of employee hours spent on purchasing activities will be lower than in a company that decentralizes its purchasing responsibilities. Centralized control leads to the efficiencies that come from specialization.

Variations in purchasing responsibilities account for differing department sizes. In some organizations the purchasing department has responsibility for buying all materials and services, expediting, reclamation, traffic, and related responsibilities. In others the purchasing department is limited to buying, and the related functions are performed in other departments.

The nature of the production process also affects the size of the purchasing department. In a company making a simple product on a high-volume basis, material for a year's operation may be purchased on a few blanket orders or systems contracts, with delivery specified at regular intervals. On the other hand, a company producing complex made-to-order units must go through the entire buying routine for each unit, which requires more personnel.

Research has indicated a significant growth in personnel within purchasing departments. Organizations reported a 10 percent annual growth rate of purchasing personnel during the 1980s, and by the end of that decade 28,000 new purchasing positions had been created. Factors contributing to this growing demand included general business growth, retirement of current purchasing personnel, and the need to meet high standards in purchasing performance. Although studies have been made of the sizes of purchasing departments in relation to total workforce or dollar volume of purchases, the figures do not constitute a sound basis for comparison for the reasons just cited.

Among the titles in a typical purchasing department are director of purchasing, purchasing manager, assistant purchasing manager, senior buyer, junior buyer, expediter, production coordinator, price clerk, materials controller, and clerical worker. In smaller companies, the duties and responsibilities of two or more of these positions are frequently assumed by a single person, who customarily carries the title of the highest-ranking position.

No detailed job description of the various purchasing positions is applicable to all companies; however, generalized descriptions of the most common duties and responsibilities of those occupying the listed positions are given in the following sections.

Director of Purchasing (Department Head)

A 1967 article reappeared in 1989 posing the query, "What kind of executives are the men [sic] at the top of the purchasing group in a large corporation?" The reported study found that purchasing managers hold very similar values to general managers, "except for the Economic values which dominate more clearly the values of purchasing executives."[1]

Who heads the personnel in the purchasing department? Typically, the purchasing manager heads the human resource or personnel function because he or she stands fully accountable for the department's timely and effective performance. The purchasing manager may delegate the authority and responsibility to make decisions. In so doing, the manager multiplies personal effort. However, he or she cannot evade the final accountability.

Some companies use the executive committee approach to clear vital communications lines and to bring managers of related functions into closer harmony. The committee may act as decision makers or purely as advisers. For example, Intel corporation's vice president for corporate administration carries responsibility for information systems, purchasing, personnel, and facilities planning. She shares management responsibilities with Intel's chief financial officer, under a "2-in-a-box" management structure.[2]

The purchasing officer may entrust the purchasing department personnel function to an assistant or to a senior buyer who has learned company policy, training methods, benefit programs, and performance evaluation.

The duties and responsibilities assigned to the director of purchasing depend to a considerable extent on the nature of the organization's product and the type of management. In many of the largest companies the head of purchasing is a high-level official, frequently a vice president. The primary functions of such an official are to formulate and supervise purchasing policy. A subordinate, often called assistant director of purchases or purchasing manager, has the operating duties and responsibilities that more closely correspond to those of the purchasing manager in a smaller concern. These duties and responsibilities generally include the following.

1. Establishment and supervision of purchasing procedures in keeping with overall company policies.
2. The internal organization and personnel program of the purchasing department, including selection, training, and compensation. In

---

[1] "Purchasing Executive: General Manager or Specialist?" *Journal of Purchasing and Materials Management,* 25th Anniversary (1989), pp. 22–25.
[2] "Open Doors on Silicon Valley—Profile: Carlene Ellis," *Computerworld* (December 25, 1989–January 1, 1990), pp. 59–60.

larger companies the personnel department usually works with the purchasing department in these matters.

3. Supervision of department activities, such as the selection of vendors, placing of orders, expediting, storekeeping, and the approval of invoices for payment. The operating head of the purchasing department frequently assumes direct responsibility for the purchase of major raw materials or other important purchases.

4. Cultivation of sound supplier relationships.

5. Coordination with other departments of the company. The head of the purchasing department frequently serves on company committees dealing with product development, value analysis, budget, and similar concerns.

6. Preparation of forecasts of supply conditions and price trends. The purchasing manager usually has responsibility for establishing forward-buying policies in light of these trends and serves as a member of the committee that establishes these policies.

7. Such auxiliary activities as reclamation and disposal of scrap and surplus materials, inspection of incoming shipments.

8. Simplification, standardization, and specification of purchased materials and supplies.

Assistant Purchasing Manager

The assistant purchasing manager, as the title implies, is assigned to as many of the duties and responsibilities of the purchasing manager as can be delegated to lighten the load of the department head. Depending on company size, policies, and the nature of the product, there may be one or more assistants. One may supervise the activities of the buyers and another the clerical activities. Another division of responsibility may find one assistant responsible for procurement of raw materials and another for processed materials. The assistant purchasing manager generally is a buyer of certain materials.

Companies that are major suppliers to the federal government must comply with the multiplicity of government regulations relating to materials control. The responsibility for soliciting federal and state authorities, maintaining records, preparation and allocation of priority applications, and compliance with other requirements contained in government contracts may be delegated to an assistant purchasing manager in these companies.

Senior Buyer

The buyer reports to the purchasing manager or assistant purchasing manager, depending on departmental organization. Although the duties and responsibilities of buyers vary, the following list of duties, with the percentage of time devoted to each, presents a portrait of a typical buyer.

1. *Checking Requisition—5 Percent.* Examining and checking the accuracy of an average of 25 orders per day for correctness of description and manner of disposition.
2. *Placing Orders—47 Percent.* Obtaining quotations, selecting vendors, and interviewing sales representatives.
3. *Making Adjustments—3 Percent.* Checking for discrepancies in invoices and arranging satisfactory adjustments when required.
4. *Following up on Delivery—35 Percent.* Checking on the progress of all orders overdue, or about to become due, and reporting to the personnel concerned.
5. *Filing Reports and References—2 Percent.* Maintaining lists of products, prices, vendors, and other reference material.
6. *Writing Blanket Orders—3 Percent.* Making partial releases on large coverage orders.
7. *Maintaining Correspondence—5 Percent.* Keeping in contact through correspondence with vendors and interplant personnel as required.

Junior Buyer

Duties of a junior buyer are in general the same as those of a senior buyer. Commodities purchased by the junior buyer are for the most part lower value, standard "shelf" items covered by published price lists and readily available for prompt delivery. The junior buyer reports to the purchasing manager or assistant purchasing manager.

Assistant Buyer

The assistant buyer, in companies that have this position, is generally assigned to the more routine aspects of buying, both as a means of lightening the work of the buyers and training the assistant. The assistant buyer often serves as an expediter in the smaller purchasing department and may also perform follow-up duties. The assistant buyer is under the jurisdiction of the buyer.

Expediter

The duties of the expediter depend largely on the method and the degree of expediting employed. In many companies this position is primarily clerical, involving the maintenance of tickler files and the follow-up of purchase orders to secure acceptance copies with promised delivery dates. In some companies, especially during periods of short supply, the duties of the expediter are enlarged to include field-expediting. This involves contact with suppliers at their plants and may even include contacts with the suppliers of the vendor.

Production Coordinator

The production coordinator is the link between the purchasing and production departments, correlating purchase orders with manufacturing schedules. By comparing delivery promises with required production dates, the coordinator is able to advise buyers when follow-up efforts are necessary to assure that production schedules are met. A production coordinator usually reports to the assistant department head or to the materials manager.

Price Clerk

The price clerk maintains price record files, posts prices, vendors' acknowledgements, and other pertinent information.

Materials Controller

The materials controller has physical responsibility for all reserve stocks of materials, supplies, and equipment. He or she is accountable for their issuance on proper authorization and in some cases for the maintenance of inventory records. The controller is generally responsible for initiating requisitions that lead to the purchase of stock items. This position usually reports to the materials manager.

Clerical Employees

The lowest-ranking positions in a purchasing department are the clerical positions. A wide variety of activities are performed by such personnel. Among them are the typing of purchase orders and other correspondence with vendors, and the maintenance of vendor lists, requisition files, purchase order files, correspondence files, a vendor catalog library, and inventory records in companies in which this is a responsibility of the purchasing department.

QUALIFICATIONS FOR PURCHASING POSITIONS

The qualifications of persons who succeed in purchasing may be conveniently grouped into three categories: personal characteristics, business experience, and educational background.

The personal characteristics that promise success in purchasing are similar to those in other fields of business; any differences will probably lie in the relative importance attached to the characteristics. The following list of personal traits cites the more important ones, with some indication of the reasons for their importance. Probably no experienced purchasing manager would agree precisely with this list of traits or the order of importance assigned to them. Rather, the list is meant to represent a general consensus on the subject.

1. *Integrity:* Purchasing personnel expend huge sums of money. Therefore, they must be impervious to the financial temptations that accompany such a position of trust, whether in the form of an inordinate gift, a secret "kickback," or outright bribery. Employees must also have the personal integrity to avoid making unwarranted promises to potential suppliers in order to secure preferential treatment.

2. *Dependability:* Dependability is important in purchasing personnel, for the continuity of operations of an organization frequently depends on the reliability of the purchasing department in following through on requisitions until goods are delivered according to specifications.

3. *Initiative:* Purchasing personnel are constantly faced with situations that demand initiative and imagination. The continual search for alternative sources of supply or alternative materials is but one area in which initiative is important. It frequently happens that to meet unexpected need for materials and supplies, personnel must locate them in unusual places and on short notice.

4. *Industriousness:* Knowledge of materials and sources is acquired only after extended training and experience. Because of this fact, a heavy burden tends to be thrown on experienced personnel during periods of rapid business expansion, a burden that cannot be relieved until new personnel are trained. During such times the industriousness of purchasing personnel is tested by long working hours.

The person who is unwilling to work long hours when the occasion demands is lacking an important trait for success in purchasing.

5. *Cooperation:* Purchasing personnel must possess an unusual ability to cooperate, since almost every item bought is for the use of some other department of the company. Cooperation is essential to minimize the many potential points of friction in such situations. Cooperation is also important because purchasing personnel must serve on many policy committees.

6. *Tact:* Many purchasing managers consider tact the most important single personal characteristic, because maintaining sound and friendly vendor relations is of such crucial importance. A tactless person may inadvertently antagonize a supplier whose goodwill and cooperation have been cultivated over many years.

7. *Ability to learn:* Purchasing personnel must have inquiring minds. They must be seeking information continually about their company's products, materials, and processes and must study the suitability of every supplier's offerings. They must constantly learn more about the organization's requirements and the availability of alternatives for meeting those requirements.

8. *Technical skills:* Purchasing personnel must possess basic data processing skills. They should be able to operate a microcomputer as well as have a working knowledge of standard spreadsheets and word processing packages.[3]

A survey of purchasing personnel recruiters found that the ability to communicate was the most important personal qualification sought in entry-level purchasing personnel.[4] Self-motivation was ranked second in importance, followed by maintaining a good attitude, maturity, and a good grade-point average.

The study also listed undesirable traits for entry-level purchasing personnel. Among these were evasiveness, lack of self-confidence, a narrow range of interests, and little community activity on the part of the candidate.

When the factors that make for success in the purchasing field are reviewed, it is easy to see why recruiters focus on these personal traits. A purchasing manager who cannot communicate thoughts or company needs effectively is of little help to either the company or its suppliers.

[3] "Profile of a Purchasing Pro: A Look at Yourself at the Start of the 1990s," *Purchasing* (March 21, 1991), pp. 30–39.
[4] Guinipero, "Entry-Level Purchasing—Demand and Requirements," *Journal of Purchasing and Materials Management* (Summer 1982), pp. 10–17.

TABLE 13-1. Characteristics Considered Important for Hiring to Purchasing Positions

Rank Order	Characteristics
1	Business experience
2	Business education
3	General education
4	Personality
5	Technical education
6	Appearance
7	Tests

Source: Unpublished survey by the author.

Business Experience

Business experience is almost universally considered a necessity for high-ranking positions in purchasing. This is not surprising. People in these positions must be knowledgeable about both company affairs and general business practices so they can deal effectively with other departments and outside suppliers. A somewhat more surprising fact was revealed by a survey of the members of 12 associations of purchasing managers. Respondents were asked to rank the importance of seven criteria in hiring to fill purchasing positions. Table 13-1 shows how the criteria were ranked.

Significantly, business experience is rated one rank higher than the next most important characteristic, business education. It should be noted that this ranking is for initial hiring into the field. As the next section indicates, increasing emphasis is being given to education as a prerequisite for purchasing, and this may mean a gradual deemphasis on earlier experience as the chief prerequisite for entry into a purchasing department.

Education

Today, some college education has become a virtual necessity for anyone expecting to be successful in the purchasing field.[5] The preceding survey of 12 associations of purchasing managers showed that, of the 214 respondents, 85.5 percent had some college education, 32.7 percent had completed a degree program, and 15.9 percent had graduate education. The fact that

---

[5] "Profile of a Purchasing Pro," op. cit.

about half the members of a group of purchasing employees had completed college or beyond indicates the advisability of higher education for anyone seeking managerial positions in this field.

The study also showed that 58.4 percent of the respondents who had gone to college majored in business administration, whereas 16.9 percent majored in engineering. The remaining 24.9 percent had studied in a variety of fields. These percentages suggest that a general business education offers the likeliest entry into the field. An engineering education is probably best when purchasing is for highly technical products.

The previously cited research done in 1982 by Guinipero indicated that most senior purchasing managers (35 out of 56 respondents) preferred entry-level purchasing personnel to have undergraduate business degrees.[6] The rationale for hiring college graduates included: (1) the person holding this degree is considered more likely to have an interest and aptitude for purchasing; (2) the candidate has a well-rounded background; and (3) the degree places emphasis on commercial consideration. Moreover, of all the undergraduate business degrees received by candidates, respondents preferred concentrations in purchasing and materials management.

SOURCES OF PERSONNEL

Company founders still run many companies. Problems, however, often arise in finding and keeping a qualified "number 2" executive. When the founder retires, the company may need to assist the "number 2" officer in structuring a buyout,[7] so that operations may proceed as before. Moving up to head the purchasing department does not require a buyout. However, the department should provide a clearly recognized "number 2" person who has the training, experience, and capability to take over when the time comes.

Sources of purchasing employees may be grouped into two categories. Internal candidates include employees from other departments of the company and employees recommended by present members of the purchasing department or other members of the company. External sources include all those outside the organization. Some of the more important ways to access these are classified and display advertisements, college and university placement offices, employment agencies, direct solicitation by prospective employees, and recommendations by outsiders.

The data in Table 13-2 indicate the relative importance of these various

---

[6] Guinipero, "Entry-Level Purchasing," op. cit., p. 16.

[7] "The Buy-out of a Sole Shareholder by a Designated Key Employee," *Tax Adviser* (January 1990), pp. 30–36.

TABLE 13-2. Percentage of Employees Hired from Various Sources by a Selected Sample of Firms

	Clerks	Assistant Buyers	Buyers	Assistant Purchasing Agent	Purchasing Agent	Total
Transfers within organization	11	42	48	54	63	35
Classified advertisements	51	32	20	16	12	33
Solicitation by employee	13	19	17	11	25	15
Employment agencies	9	7	6	7		7
School placement office	8		4	5		5
Other	8	—	5	7	—	5
Total	100	100	100	100	100	100

Source: Unpublished study under the direction of the author.

sources of purchasing employees. The response to a survey showed that larger firms tended to rely on classified advertisements to a greater extent than smaller firms. The two most important sources were transfers within the organization (35 percent) and classified advertisements (33 percent). When the same data are analyzed to determine the source of purchasing employees above the clerical level, a different pattern emerges. For these higher-level positions, internal transfers account for 50 percent of all placements and classified advertisements for only 21 percent. The more recent survey of 12 associations generally confirms the figures in Table 13-2.

Recent college graduates are the most popular source of purchasing personnel for entry-level positions. Table 13-3 shows promotion from

TABLE 13-3. Methods Used in Filling Entry-Level Purchasing Positions

Recent college graduates
Promotion of existing personnel from within purchasing
Transfer from related materials functions (inventory, traffic, etc)
Transfer from other functional areas (engineering finance, etc.)
Transfer from other operating units within the corporation
Plant employees with seniority (clerical or direct labor)
Hiring experienced personnel from another corporation

Source: Guinipero, "Entry-Level Purchasing," p. 12.

within the purchasing department second to hiring recent college graduates, followed by a variety of internal transfers.

Internal Transfers

Hiring from within an organization has many advantages, especially when a transfer can be made from a closely related department. Training time is reduced because there is no need to cover such general matters as company history, organization, and policies. The internally transferred employee's knowledge of the company's products and familiarity with personnel with whom the employee must work are also advantages. If the transfer is from the production department, the new member of the purchasing department brings considerable knowledge that will be an aid in buying. Finally, it is universally recognized that internal transfers build morale within an organization, especially when the new position is of higher rank than the one from which the person was transferred.

Recommendations

Purchasing personnel hired through the recommendations of present purchasing employees or others within the company occasionally prove successful. Employees in the department are aware of the characteristics and qualities that are desirable for purchasing work, and if they are persons of sound judgment, their recommendations are likely to have merit. Unfortunately, it is often found that through recommendations friends and relatives are often hired without regard to their ability. It is extremely difficult for a company official to know whether a recommendation is being made in the interest of the company or the individual.

Newspapers

Advertisements furnish the majority of recruits from external sources. Classified advertisements in local newspapers are of particular value for the lower-ranking positions. Such advertisements generally bring in a large number of responses, but frequently not many promising prospects. Even when great care is exercised in preparing the advertisement to describe the job and the necessary qualifications with precision, there will be a large proportion of unacceptable applicants. Some companies have found that display advertisements are more selective, since specifications can be stated in greater detail. Display advertisements are most widely used for higher-ranking positions and are frequently run in distant metropolitan newspapers.

Display advertisements in newspapers, magazines, and trade journals enable a company to reach persons who are currently employed and cannot take the time to solicit new employment. Advertisements also reach employees of competitors without the personal solicitation that might be considered improper. The "situations wanted" columns of a newspaper will occasionally obtain a good employee. People placing such advertisements have shown the strong desire for employment that suggests initiative.

Colleges and Universities

The use of college and university placement offices for securing purchasing personnel is increasing in importance as the trend toward employing college graduates in purchasing positions continues. This is a highly specialized form of recruiting, and most of the larger companies that now use this source recruit simultaneously for a number of different divisions within the company. College recruiting is frequently handled by the personnel department of a firm. Many colleges and universities have aided the recruiting of employees by establishing placement bureaus, providing facilities for interviews, securing recommendations of faculty members, and compiling records of the scholastic achievements of applicants. A number of secondary and vocational schools today provide similar services for their students. These two sources are especially valuable in recruiting clerical and lower-ranking personnel.

Temporary Workers

Temporary workers may provide another recruiting source. Temporary services listed in telephone book yellow pages supply temporary workers for special assignments, work overloads, jobs with high turnover, vacancies, and substitutes for sick or vacationing personnel.[8]

SELECTION OF PERSONNEL

Forms

Application forms are almost universally used in the selection process. These forms contain a number of questions designed to obtain background information that will be useful in evaluating the applicant's qualifications for the position under consideration. These questions relate to such matters as the applicant's personal and family background, health, education, and work experience, and current family and living conditions. Correctly de-

[8] "Shorthanded? Hire a Temp," *Purchasing* (March 22, 1990), pp. 70–76.

signed questions, when properly interpreted, aid immeasurably in the evaluation of an applicant.

The use of application blanks before interviews enables a company to weed out applicants who are obviously not qualified for the position. They further serve as a good starting point for the interviews and provide a basis for verifying the honesty of the applicant. This is accomplished by formal or informal checking on some of the statements made on the blanks and by consulting the references given. Application blanks should not be used as the sole basis for the decision to hire. They are but one of three tools that should be used in the selection process: forms, interviews, and tests.

Many companies use a form letter to communicate with character references given by the applicant. There is much difference of opinion among experts about the value of information secured by this means. Most people asked for a reference believe that in the interest of giving everyone another chance they should not report derogatory information. A person skilled in the process of selection will, therefore, study a report from a reference for its omissions rather than its explicit statements. A reference letter may also uncover misrepresentations by the applicant about previous employment or similar pertinent facts. Thus, its role in the selection process should be to supplement the application blank.

Interviews

The interview is even more widely used than the application blank. A common practice is to hold a preliminary interview that, together with the application blank, is a part of the screening process for eliminating those who do not merit further consideration. Frequently this preliminary interview is conducted by a member of the personnel department. The second and succeeding interviews are conducted by the purchasing manager. These interviews are much more extensive than the preliminary interview and furnish most of the information on which the final decision is based.

The purpose of interviews is to allow the employer and the applicant to get acquainted so that each can judge whether they have further interest in the other. When conducting an interview, the purchasing manager should remember that it is also important to sell the company to the prospective employee. An important element in a fruitful interview is a detailed plan of the ground to be covered during the interview. Experienced companies prepare interview patterns or guides to aid the interviewers in this matter. It is also important to record all pertinent information as soon as the interview is over. Interviewers should not trust their memories, especially if several applicants are to be interviewed for the same position.

Tests

Many companies use psychological tests as a third tool in the selection of employees. There is a wide difference of opinion among employers concerning the value of tests, and a great diversity of tests is available. All psychological tests used for selection may be conveniently divided into three categories: (1) intelligence tests, (2) personality and interest tests, and (3) aptitude or trade tests.

The use of intelligence tests is based on the assumptions that intelligence can be measured and that there is some relationship between intelligence and success in purchasing. It should be understood that neither of these two assumptions has been proved. There are a number of different tests that can be used for measuring intelligence. Some measure mechanical intelligence (the ability to manipulate objects), others measure abstract intelligence, and still others measure the ability to understand people (the so-called social intelligence tests).

Personality tests are used to rate an applicant on such traits as self-confidence, temperament, emotional maturity, and other personality traits that would appear to be important as a measure of success. Interest tests are designed to reveal the extent to which an applicant's interests coincide with those who have been successful in the field. Aptitude tests are designed to measure the natural ability of an applicant in the field and inherent fitness for the work.

Aptitude tests have been found to be quite reliable in measuring mechanical or clerical abilities, but in testing for positions requiring judgment and mental abilities the aptitude tests have not proven reliable.

The selection of personnel through psychological tests is imprecise at best. Such tests, therefore, should be viewed as a supplement to established procedures, and the results should be correlated with later success. If conducted over a sufficiently long period of time, with validation at a future date, such tests may become a more reliable selection device.

The lie detector, or polygraph, has lost its popularity as a means of verifying the information that a prospective employee gives on the application blank. Many persons will not submit to a lie detector test because they perceive the use of polygraphs as invasions of privacy. Moreover, the Employee Polygraph Protection Act of 1988 prohibits most private employers from using lie detector tests either for pre-employment screening or during the course of employment. However, inventory shortages, for example, qualify as a "specific incident" permitting polygraphs for testing purposes.[9]

---

[9] "Application of the Employee Polygraph Protection Act of 1988: Final Rule," Department of Labor, Employment Standards Administration, Wage and Hour Division, in *Federal Register* (March 4, 1991).

TRAINING

The training approach that best serves the department may focus on two different types of personnel and their training needs:

> On the one hand, older people with limited formal education but extensive purchasing experience and capabilities in specialized fields compose one group. On the other hand, a second group consists of younger personnel who typically have bachelors or masters degrees that provide a broad academic preparation for business, but who have limited practical procurement experience.[10]

There are three types of training for purchasing personnel. First, education by schools—particularly universities and their continuing education divisions—can be adapted to the training needs of beginners as well as practicing purchasing personnel. Second, a company may train its own beginners, generally called job training. Third, in-service training, is designed primarily as a means of continuing training after employees have progressed beyond the beginning stage. The subject matter peculiar to each of these three types of training will be considered after a brief discussion of training methods.

One method of training a new employee is by trial and error. Although no accurate method of measuring the costs of such a training method has been devised, it is probable that the costs are disproportionate to the amount of useful knowledge produced.

A second method is the apprentice technique, whereby the new employee is assigned to an experienced employee in the department. The employee starts with routine tasks such as clerical and filing; progresses to invoice checking, requisitions, and stock record checking; and is next permitted to make routine repeat-order purchases to gain buying experience.

A third method of training involves semiformal classes or seminars. The seminar method is usually best for handling the continuing training of experienced personnel, works best with small groups of 5 to 25 trainees, and relies heavily on group participation rather than on the lecture method of teaching.

University Education and Training

The training afforded both potential and actual purchasing department employees by universities is of three types. First, the full-time student can

---

[10] "Developing a Procurement Training Program," *Journal of Purchasing and Materials Management* (Summer 1989), pp. 26–34.

pursue a program leading to a degree with specialization in the field of purchasing. The second type of training for purchasing sponsored by colleges and universities consists of extension courses, normally run during the evening hours and designed to attract inexperienced employees in the field. Third, many universities also offer management development seminars designed specifically to meet the needs of experienced purchasing personnel. These programs tend to deal more with policy matters than the procedural aspects of purchasing.

Job Training

The vast majority of training that a firm undertakes occurs on the job and is, therefore, informal. Some companies refer to on-the-job training as vestibule training because it takes place as the new employee enters the company. Casual coaching by more experienced employees orients the trainee to company mission, rules, facilities, health and safety factors, and organization. Job skills such as using the desktop computer and printer and filling out forms comes after an introduction and some practice.

A new buyer may get a small number of commodities assigned to him or her for purchase and expediting, as a prelude to in-service training. After proving worthy, the trainee may attend formal sessions as an in-service trainee and begin job rotation. Companies that participate in formal training report a lower labor turnover rate than companies that give no instruction at all.

In-Service Training

A program of progression through various purchasing duties until a satisfactory degree of competence has been acquired by the trainee is generally called in-service training. Job training is supplemented by written materials and contracts with other departments in the company to provide the trainee with familiarity with organization, policies, and interrelationships. In-service training is an effective means of increasing the skills and abilities of buyers and assistant buyers to qualify them for advancement to higher-ranking positions within the department. Continued training is also frequently provided through staff meetings held throughout the year. Another technique of in-service training is job rotation. With this method an employee learns the duties and responsibilities of several positions through actual experience and thus becomes better qualified for promotion.

One study examined the activities being emphasized by in-service training in today's organizations. It found that the following, ranked in descending order, are stressed in training:

1. Negotiations
2. Vendor analysis
3. Bid analysis
4. Contracts
5. Expediting
6. Purchasing policies
7. Minority purchasing
8. Price–cost analysis

Westinghouse offers a typical in-service training program. First, the new purchasing employee is oriented to the company, its subsequent training program, and the resources available for personal growth and development. Next, the individual is assigned to a division for 12 weeks. The new employee learns about the fundamentals, interfunctional relationships, and the opportunity to create a profit for Westinghouse. Finally, the new employee goes to corporate headquarters and works with purchasing people from several different divisions. In addition, Westinghouse provides its new purchasing personnel with a variety of formal courses taught at the Westinghouse Education Center. They include an introduction to purchasing (the basic tools of the trade), negotiations training, and problem solving and decision making.

NAPM's PHRASE

NAPM's national office provides a service to identify purchasing department personnel training needs. The program entitled PHRASE (Purchasing Human Resource Audit System Evaluation) uses three stages for providing the service.[11] Step one conducts a job analysis for each position in the department; as to duties, knowledge, and skills, and the importance of, and time spent on, each duty. Step two undertakes a diagnostic evaluation, including such factors as individual strengths and weaknesses and acute company training needs. Finally, step three leads to an employee professional development training proposal conforming with the company's training requirements. This phase includes consultation with NAPM's educational staff to assist with professional development programs that meet specific needs.

[11] PHRASE pamphlet in NAPM correspondence (March 19, 1990).

COMPENSATION

The purchasing department and the materials management group endeavor to ensure that their members receive internally equitable and externally competitive compensation levels—that is, base salary and benefits. These levels should reward high-quality and completely ethical performance.

Details listed in Table 13-4 add to Chapter 1's overall statements about compensation.

The straight salary method of compensation is almost universally used to pay employees of purchasing departments. Employees are paid per unit of time worked rather than per unit of work performed. Upward revisions in the rate of compensation depend on improvement in the quality of the employee's work, company policy, and economic conditions.

In many organizations employees are classified into various wage-level groups, with steps in each group denoting the individual's relative proficiency. Improvement in proficiency, gained through application and experience, advances an employee through the steps of one wage-level group and into a higher group, with a higher rate of compensation at each advance in level.

Because purchasing responsibilities are difficult to measure, and because the salary of each employee in each level should reflect relative proficiency in the level, it is important that the ability and performance of each employee be rated periodically. From these ratings the employee should be advised of shortcomings and rewarded for improvements.

Purchasing executives will normally be included in organization-wide incentive or bonus plan. Such plans are almost invariably related to company profits. The financial opportunities and rewards in the field of purchasing are increasing as greater recognition is given by management to the importance of this business activity. The *Purchasing* magazine salary survey cited in Chapter 1 reports that 35 percent of the survey respondents received part of their compensation in the form of bonuses, amounting to about 11 percent of base pay.[12]

Employers often buy corporate-owned life insurance (COLI) to fund various compensation and benefit plans for employees. The employers retain beneficiary rights and actually own the policies as investments of corporate assets. Proceeds pay for the benefits when the employee dies.[13]

Rising health-care costs have prompted some employers to form coalitions for controlling benefits costs. The health-care purchasing coalitions

[12] "Salary Survey," *Purchasing* (December 10, 1992), p. 77.
[13] "How to Evaluate COLI Proposals," *Pension World* (January 1990), pp. 42, 44.

TABLE 13-4. Salary by Title

Title	Average Salary	Highest 1991 Salary	Percent Receiving Bonus
Buyer	$31,300	$75K	23
Purchasing agent	37,800	85K	32
Senior buyer	40,400	95K	23
Purchasing manager	48,800	142K	40
Subcontract administrator	49,300	83K	23
Materials manager	52,900	240K	43
Purchasing director	68,500	175K	61
Materials director	81,000	160K	74
VP-purchasing	87,200	200K	76

Source: "Salary Survey," *Purchasing* (December 10, 1992), p. 84.

endeavor to manage care networks, negotiate provider fees, and stress quality services for their members.[14]

Ford Motor Company, Hewlett-Packard, and many other corporations support national health-care system reform. At Ford, health-care costs account for 15 percent of payroll. Through cost-containment efforts in 1989, Ford achieved a $145 million (12 percent) reduction in health-care expenses.

Intangible Compensation

Any discussion of compensation for purchasing should also mention the intangible rewards. First, there are the challenging and rewarding interactions with salespersons and other representatives of sellers. Another intangible reward is the satisfaction associated with the allocation of large sums of money. The conscientious fulfillment of this trust is a source of inner satisfaction. Another benefit of purchasing is the opportunity to gain an overview of a firm's operations and the interrelationships and interactions of its various departments. Because purchasing is closely allied with production, engineering, and sales, it is constantly enlisted by these departments in finding new or alternate materials, securing technical assistance, and determining sales and marketing trends. This variety of endeavors and the feeling

[14] "Controlling Benefit Costs: Employer Coalitions Offer Purchasing Clout," *Business Insurance* (February 19, 1990), pp. 3, 22–26.

of accomplishment gained by sharing in the planning of products and production are interesting, challenging, and rewarding.

PROFESSIONAL CERTIFICATION

The concept of certification of the individual as a professional has long been a goal of special-interest groups in various areas of business. Today there are varied certifications, such as Certified Public Accountant and Certified Professional Casualty Underwriter. In the field of purchasing and materials management, six programs leading to certification have been established, one implemented by the National Association of Purchasing Management (NAPM), which has set the pace for the field.[15]

The aim of the NAPM certification program is to evaluate knowledge in four areas: purchasing, administration, organization, and education. A written examination is required. The certification procedure is open to all engaged in purchasing or materials management, but it does require a minimum of five years' experience in the field or a degree from a recognized college plus three years of vocational experience. Successful completion of the examinations earns the applicant the designation of Certified Purchasing Manager (C.P.M.).

The attainment of the C.P.M. designation provides evidence to management of the professional interest, motivation, and capabilities of the purchasing employee. One recent study showed that 14 percent of purchasing personnel who earned their C.P.M.s received raises immediately upon receiving the designation. The program formulated by the National Institute for Government Purchasing (NIGP) requires completion of a general academic curriculum, a public curriculum, a written examination, and an oral examination by a three-member board of examiners. There are additional age and experience requirements.

The popularity of these certification programs has sharply increased during the last few years. Since the inception of the C.P.M. program in 1974, 21,847 professional purchasing personnel have been certified, as of March 1993.

The C.P.M. written examination has a multiple-choice format and is divided into four modules. Through arrangements with the American College Testing Program in Princeton, New Jersey, a candidate may take the examination on a computer, assisted by a professional tester who scores the exam and reads the results at once. Topics covered are the purchasing, administrative, and organizational functions of a procurement manager. The

---

[15] "An Overview of Certification Programs in the Purchasing and Materials Management Field," *International Journal of Purchasing and Materials Management* (Winter 1992), pp. 34–39.

fourth module is devoted to alternative subjects. This module stresses a functional understanding of economics, so that the purchasing manager will be able to understand analysis trends and events in terms of the firm, the nation, and the world market. Also, Module 4 covers forecasting and strategies, external/internal relationships, computerization and environmental issues.[16]

NAPM's 28,000 members formed an alliance in 1992 with the American Production and Inventory Control Society's (APICS) 72,000 members to share resources. The alliance prompted a joint review of the Certified in Production and Inventory Management (CPIM) and Certified in Integrated Resource Management (CIRM) certification programs that APICS conducts and the Certified Purchasing Manager (C.P.M.) certification program that NAPM administers. Both organizations want to develop jointly educational materials, identify comparable examination modules, and develop a procedure where credit in one program receives credit in the other program.[17]

Regardless of their certification status, purchasing personnel can do much to increase the stature of their occupation. They can encourage better performance through higher educational attainments for themselves and their subordinates. They can also foster high ethical standards and condemn the few who do not follow such standards.

CHAPTER SUMMARY

The personnel of purchasing and materials management departments work in contact with people in all departments inside the company and with many people outside the company. Persons inside the company requisition goods and services, which purchasing personnel order from outside sources and arrange for inbound transportation. Other materials management department personnel receive and inspect the incoming items and either deliver to the requisitioner or put directly into storage for later use. Still other personnel audit the vendors' invoices and transportation companies' billings and authorize payment.

Purchasing department personnel represent the company outside the firm. Buyers look for sources of materials and services; they may visit vendors' plants to verify performance capability and negotiate terms with the vendors. As representatives, they must understand their own company's policies regarding ethics and vendor relations. They must master the technical knowledge concerning the materials and services they buy. They build relations with suppliers to encourage them to take the order in the first place

---

[16] NAPM correspondence (March 19, 1992).
[17] "NAPM and APICS Form Alliance," *NAPM Insights* (September 1992), p. 35.

and to ship the order in the second place. Close contacts may come in handy when sudden changes occur at the buyer's plant, necessitating vendors to change the order quantities up or down.

Sources of personnel include transfers within the organization and classified advertising. In-service training provides the basis for competent performance. Compensation recognizes the professional status of many positions in the purchasing and materials management fields. Certification by national associations further recognize the performance capability to generate bottom-line profits.

Discussion Questions

1. What are some of the changes in business methods that will require more highly skilled personnel in the purchasing department?
2. What factors influence the size of the purchasing department of a particular company?
3. What two activities take the major share of a buyer's time? Are these also the buyer's most important activities?
4. From what source do most of a purchasing department's personnel come?
5. What use or uses should be made of the application form in hiring for the purchasing department?
6. How would you distinguish between interest tests and aptitude tests? How useful is each in the hiring process?
7. In what part of the training process is the seminar approach usually recommended? What are its advantages?
8. What form of compensation is most appropriate for purchasing? Why?
9. Name and discuss some of the intangible rewards of purchasing.

Suggested Cases

Ferner Company

Powers Company

Pressure Tanks, Inc. (B)

Testing and Psychological Assessment

The Wagner Corporation (B)

14

Legal Considerations

Grace liked her job with the State Attorney General Office. She probed such issues as kickbacks involving suppliers to retailers, financial institutions, hotels, and restaurants.

Her good friend and lunch companion, Sally, bought tires for a regional trucking firm. At lunch one day, Sally told Grace that several automotive parts suppliers complained of not receiving orders from her company.

Grace knew that the incidence of kickbacks had increased since the beginning of the 1981–1982 recession. She also knew that corrupt employees sometimes give themselves away by their behavior. So she made some discreet inquiries. She discovered that the automotive parts division head of Sally's company demanded kickbacks from suppliers. Grace prepared the case. Her actions led to convicting the division head on six charges of accepting secret commissions. He received a three-year prison sentence. The court fined one supplier $100,000 for paying secret commissions.*

CHAPTER CONTENTS

*Source: Based on ''The Kickback Boom and How to Fight It,'' Canadian Business (November 1991), pp. 78–81.

RICO

Foreign Corrupt Practices Act

Purchase Order Clauses

JIT Influence

Some firms move toward fewer suppliers and fewer freight carriers, closer to the buyers' plants. Other firms deal with suppliers after deciding which state's laws apply for buyers' best advantage. This practice favors selecting suppliers out of the diversity that exists in products liability based on negligence. Many state-to-state differences center on statutes of limitation, limiting the right to sue to a given period. When this period starts also varies.[1]

On January 1, 1988, the United Nations Convention on Contracts for the International Sale of Goods (CISG) became a part of U.S. law. The convention represents an effort at unification of international trade law across economic, legal, developmental, and political barriers.[2]

Purchasing managers and buyers face reality despite paradoxes, relying on legal counsel, their own experience and training, and trustworthy suppliers. This chapter describes some of the legal considerations they face.

Purchasing has received much legal attention in the last decade. Issues such as contractual disputes, reciprocity, state and international law, and the effects of the Motor Carrier Deregulation Act of 1980 have had significant impact upon the purchasing practices of today's manufacturers and distributors. Normally, procurement practices and the buyer–supplier relationship are predicated upon good faith between the parties and are not dependent on legal considerations. However, the purchase–sale interchange does give rise to legal and binding commitments. The dominant legal areas involved are those concerning the laws of agency and of contracts. The legal considerations afford protection, and in many instances monetary recompense for nonperformance, but are relied on only as a last resort. The primary concern of purchasing personnel in legal matters is to use a knowledge of the basic principles of law to avoid litigation.

When legal action becomes necessary, the outcome depends principally on two factors: (1) the lawyer's ability to resurrect, in a form permitting proof in court, a precise and detailed record of the transaction, including every tacit understanding, conversation, proviso, fact, and circumstance involved; and (2) the conformity of the company's conduct and procedure,

---

[1] "State Laws Can Play Big Roles in Timing of Various Lawsuits," *Purchasing* (May 3, 1990), pp. 84A9–84A10.

[2] "The United Nations Convention on Contracts for the International Sale of Goods," *Syracuse Journal of International Law & Commerce* (Spring 1989), pp. 361–389.

in the transaction in question, to legally established standards of proper performance.

BASIC ASPECTS OF THE LAW

Sources of Law

There are five important documentary sources of modern law.

1. Court opinions, reported and published over the years, deciding literally hundreds of thousands of prior legal controversies. Together, these are sometimes referred to as common law.
2. Federal and state constitutions, including their various amendments.
3. Federal, state, and local legislative enactments (called statutes and ordinances) governing a great variety of subjects. When grouped by subject, these enactments are sometimes referred to as codes, such as the binding code, the criminal code, or the commercial code. Especially in the commercial area, there has been a strong effort, not only to codify the law, but to codify it uniformly throughout the country. The Uniform Sales Act, originated in 1909, was for many years the prime source of law relating to purchases and sales of goods. Its principal weakness was its failure to cover a number of collateral subjects such as the credit, shipping, inspection, and security terms of the sales transactions. In 1958, the Uniform Commercial Code was produced to supplement the Uniform Sales Act and more than a dozen earlier codifications of commercial law subjects. The Uniform Commercial Code (UCC) has become the commercial law of every major business center of the country, except New Orleans.
4. Published general orders and rulings of public regulatory or administrative boards, commissions, agencies, and departments.
5. Secondary sources, consisting of writings on legal subjects, prepared by attorneys, judges, professors, and the editorial staffs of legal publishing houses, primarily for the continuing education of lawyers.

Substantive and Adjective Law

It is not always possible to distinguish completely between the definition of a legal right in the abstract and a statement of the procedures and processes by which that right is enforced. Nevertheless, the abstract definition is called the substantive law of the subject, and the forms and procedures of enforcement are called adjective (or procedural) law. This text largely ignores adjective law and provides a survey of the substantive principles that have frequent impact on purchasing.

Elements of Legal Claim

There are three basic elements in every legal claim.

1. A factual relationship of the parties, by which each party is entitled to have the other *act or refrain from acting* in a certain way. This is called the right–duty relationship.
2. *Conduct* of one or both parties that violates the right–duty relationship. This is called the breach.
3. *Injury or damage* to one or both parties resulting from (caused by) the breach.

Kinds of Right–Duty Relationships

Legal rights and duties are classified according to the relationships from which they spring. The two basic relationships are public (the relationship between a citizen and an agency of government) and private (the relationship between two citizens).

Public relationships give rise to rights of government against the citizen (requiring the citizen to act or refrain from acting in certain ways) and to rights of the citizen against the government. In the first group, there are two major subclasses: (1) criminal laws and public regulatory laws, and (2) revenue (tax) laws.

Constitutional and political guarantees are of fundamental importance among the laws defining the rights of citizens against their government; however, a host of other rights of the citizen persist, ranging from police protection to social security.

AGENCY

The overwhelming majority of the right–duty relationships in modern commercial law arise *vicariously*—that is, through the agency of representatives rather than direct dealings between persons on their personal accounts. Purchasing personnel do not ordinarily buy for their own account, nor do selling agents ordinarily sell for their own account. Before examining the specific rights and duties that arise out of the typical purchase transaction, therefore, the basic rules by which an agent can effectively bind a principal—that is, hold someone liable—should be examined.

The question generally arises in one of three basic patterns. First, there is the case of the general officer of the selling or buying organization, whose authority is very broad but not unlimited. Second, there is the limited agent or employee whose authority to represent the principal is, by definition, relatively specialized. Finally, there is the problem of the broker, distributor, or commissioned salesperson, who may represent a seller in a still more limited manner.

In order for an agent to operate effectively in binding a principal, two factors are necessary. The agent's authority must have been *broad enough* to cover the transaction in question, and the agent must have *exercised* that authority in negotiating the particular transaction.

Authority to act in the name or on behalf of a principal most commonly arises by *express* authorization. The principal tells the agent to undertake transactions of a given description in the principal's name, usually as a matter of job assignment. Every express authorization gives rise to a number of implied authorizations that empower the agent to do those things that are reasonably necessary or customary to carry out the expressly assigned job. No implied authority can rise, however, in direct contradiction of an *express limitation* of the agent's authority. Thus, if a salesperson is expressly prohibited from signing contracts, or from granting credit terms or other concessions not stated in the principal's published lists, or from negotiating with certain buyers, or from handling certain lines, the power of the salesperson in these respects is limited, regardless of how necessary or customary a broader authority might be.

Both express and implied authority are legally classified as forms of *actual* authorization. Their basic weakness, in everyday practice, lies in the fact that a person dealing with such an agent has no way, other than by direct inquiry of the principal, of knowing just how far the actual authority extends. The agent's own assurance may not be used to prove actual authority unless the principal has somehow *seconded* those assurances.

The last-mentioned possibility—that the principal has *apparently* authorized the agent to contract in the principal's name—represents the most common ground upon which a third party, dealing with an agent who is exceeding the actual authority, can nevertheless hold the principal responsible. The keynote of apparent authority is the third party's *reliance* appearances of authority for which the principal was responsible. A supplier who, for example, gives a freelance commissioned salesperson a set of the supplier's order forms or other restricted sales materials, or who gives such a salesperson an office at the supplier's place of business, or who rather regularly receives and fills orders written by such a salesperson, may well create an appearance of agency despite the fact that the salesperson has no actual authority to bind the supplier. Furthermore, a principal who knowingly accepts the product (sometimes called the fruit) of an unauthorized transaction *ratifies* the transaction and becomes bound as thoroughly as though the principal had originally authorized it.

Obviously, however, a person claiming either implied or apparent agency cannot ignore a plain contradiction of that claim, which the purported principal has taken pains to circulate. Printed sales materials often contain statements that directly deny the authority of any but certain designated agents to represent the seller, the most common clause being one that states, in effect, *"No obligation shall rise against the seller unless this order is accepted at the principal office of the seller."*

In summary, purchasing personnel should be aware of the agency problem in two respects, First, they should recognize company limitations on their own authority to obligate their own companies and should take pains to inform suppliers' representatives of these limitations in transactions where they may apply. Second, they should routinely verify the authority of purported suppliers' agents, especially where the agents' connection with the supplier is indirect, indistinct, or doubtful. A fully authorized agent will usually have no difficulty in producing satisfactory credentials and will not take offense if asked to do so. Representatives who resent having their authority questioned are often attempting to work both sides of the street, as it were, legally representing no one.

CONTRACTS: EXPRESSED AND IMPLIED

"Claims sounding in contract," as the lawyer often expresses it, are those that arise from rights and duties that the parties have voluntarily undertaken by the terms of an agreement. They arise because one party has either not done something that was agreed upon or has done something that was not agreed upon. Implicit in the concept is the idea that, aside from the agreement, there was no legal obligation for the claimant to act or not to act in a particular way. The agreement, then, is the heart of contractual liability, constituting its source, its definition, and its limitation.

However, one must be careful not to exaggerate the coverage of the contract itself. Unless the agreement specifically and expressly calls for a given detail of performance, the performance is not required. And every specific and express stipulation to which the parties agree does not invariably raise a corresponding duty of performance in that regard.

Some contracts arise without any express agreement whatsoever. They are totally implied and arise out of the conduct of the parties, rather than from their verbal or written agreements. If a supplier, for example, delivers goods that a customer has not ordered, but the customer receives and uses the shipment, a contract to pay for the shipment arises by implication.

Under some circumstances, the law will also imply certain stipulations not mentioned by the parties in their express agreements. Such implied stipulations are of two kinds: those implied in fact and those implied in law. Agreements are implied in fact when reason and common sense indicate that the parties probably took the matter for granted and simply failed to say anything about it. To determine what terms, conditions, and stipulations are implied into an agreement in this way, we must consider all the circumstances under which an agreement was made, at least so far as these circumstances were known to both parties. These circumstances include (1) the terms of the express agreement; (2) the terms that are standard or customary, either in past dealings between the same parties (called a course of dealing) or generally in the industry (called a course of trade); and (3) any legal rules of interpretation that may have been established, by statute or judicial decision, to govern questions of that kind.

Stipulations implied in law consist of the terms and agreements that the law itself imposes on all contracts because, without them, the agreement would violate public law. For example, an agreement to construct a bathroom implies that the plumber will be licensed, that building and plumbing permits will be obtained, and that the work performed and the materials will comply with applicable codes. An agreement for transport by rail, road, or air implies a stipulation that all applicable regulatory rules will be observed, including those requiring licenses and permits, and further implies that the rates are in accordance with approved tariff schedules.

Matters implied in law into a given agreement, unlike matter implied in fact, may override even express stipulations to the contrary. Put another way, the law will not insist that the parties intended a certain point of agreement, which they expressly stated differently or to the contrary, *unless* the point was on which they had no real choice because public law permitted them only one possibility. For example, tariff schedules control the rates that public utilities and regulated passenger and freight carriers may and must charge. Even though a contract stipulates a different rate, it is implied in law that the parties intended to contract at the legal rate.

The line between statutes and other laws that are merely interpretative of private agreements and those that are aimed at public regulation sometimes becomes extremely fine. As a result, it may occasionally become a delicate matter to distinguish between contract terms that are inescapable, because they are implied in law, and those that are *disclaimable,* because they are implied only where the agreement is not expressly to the contrary. This problem is present when a contract, by its express terms, attempts to *exculpate* (i.e., declare blameless) conduct that is *tortious.*

Torts

Private rights and duties sounding in tort, as it is called, are legally *imposed* on all persons who stand in a certain relationship to each other and in that sense arise without regard to any voluntary agreements. Tortious conduct is conduct that violates the legally protected interests of another, either by act or by failure to act.

Many acts that violate public law are also tortious when regarded from the standpoint of their private victim. Indeed, the act may also constitute a breach of contract. For example, a drug supplier contracts to deliver a shipment of penicillin. Federal and state pure food and drug laws prescribe certain standards of quality and purity for such drugs, which the supplier violates. The customer, a retailer, resells half the lot before the deficiencies are discovered, and several consumers are injured because of the poor quality. By one act, the supplier has breached:

1. The public duty, which is punishable by fine, imprisonment, or other penalty.
2. The contract duty to the customer, which may require payment of damages to the customer.
3. The tort duty to the retailing customer.
4. The tort duty to the injured consumers even though there was no direct contract.

It is erroneous to conclude, however, that tort duties are limited to cases in which the prohibited conduct constitutes a violation of public law. There is a vast area of tort law that is strictly private in its applications.

Intentional Torts. Torts are classified into three groups: intentional, unintentional, and strict. Intentional torts are those in which the invasion of another's interests is more or less deliberate. Most of the intentional torts have close parallels in public law crimes such as theft, embezzlement, obtaining money or property under false pretenses (confidence games), assaults, and various types of fraudulent schemes. But a number of other torts are classified as intentional principally because they are not clearly unintentional. These are less commonly proscribed as crimes but may have considerable importance in the commercial world. They include the following:

1. Conversion—the assertion of ownership in the property of another. The subtlety of this tort lies in the fact that an *innocent* mistake about rightful ownership is not a complete defense.

2. Patent or copyright infringement, of which a person may be guilty despite the fact that the infringing product or process was purely a new invention.

3. Misrepresentation and deceit, which do not necessarily require that the false statement be uttered as a deliberate lie but include a number of cases in which one falsely certifies to the truth or accuracy of a matter on which one is innocently mistaken.

4. Defamation (libel and slander), to which the defense, ''I honestly believed it was true,'' is very rarely available. Parenthetically, one should note that the reputation of a company or business may be tortiously defamed as easily as that of an individual, and this often involves substantially greater damages.

5. Tortious interference with contract, which consists, essentially, of inducing another to violate contractual obligations with a third person, the claimant. The battle among business competitors comes under severe restrictions after a contract has been made.

6. Conspiracy to fix prices or control markets, and unlawful price discrimination. Since these are almost purely statutory torts, they merit separate consideration.

Unintentional (Negligent) Torts. Negligence is defined as a failure to exercise *ordinary care* to avoid *unreasonable* risks of harm to the interests of another. Ordinary care is such care as the *ordinarily prudent and careful person* would be expected to exercise *under the same or similar circumstances.*

It is a rare case in which accidents happen without someone having been in a position to prevent them by stronger precaution. Nevertheless, one of the more difficult elements to satisfy in a claim based on negligence and arising out of the accidental failure of a product, is proof of foreseeability: for example, that the supplier should have anticipated that the product would be used under the particular conditions and circumstances in which it failed. The defense, in essence, is that the supplier took no greater precautions because the necessity for greater precaution could not reasonably have been foreseen. The supplier would probably claim that the product met the specifications of the purchase order and also measured up to the standard of ordinary care.

Whose fault, then, is an accident by which someone may have lost life, limb, or fortune? No blanket answer is possible. But it is possible that, if the purchasing office had managed to gather more information about the intended use of the supplier's product and had passed that information on to the supplier, the *unavoidable accident* would have been avoided. At very least, the *unforeseeability* defense would have been effectively nullified.

It is important to understand that, though failure to fulfill a contract specification often constitutes negligence, adherence to contract specifications does not necessarily constitute ordinary care. In one case, a purchase order for industrial aprons did not, either expressly or by implication, specify that they be treated for flammability. Yet the supplier of such aprons was held liable for tort to a workman injured when his apron burst into flames. Before assuming that negligence shifts all liability to the supplier, one should realize three things. First, the purchase order should have specified nonflammable materials; second, the purchaser's company itself ultimately absorbed a generous portion of the liability; and third, the litigation expense alone far exceeded the cash of the entire order.

Strict Liability Torts.   Until fairly recently, most claims arising out of various types of product failure were based either on breach of contract (including the closely related breach of sales warranty) or on negligence. Today, a sizable segment of product liability cases—those involving personal injury or property damage caused by defective products—are being brought on a developing tort theory, that of *strict liability*.

The legal and commercial implications of this doctrine accentuate the need for careful purchasing practices. This is true primarily because of the heavy inroads that the doctrine of strict liability makes into traditional privity limitations. Privity refers to the direct connection between persons under contract for some transaction, such as the customer and the distributor.

For example, assume the case of a motorist injured because of a defective brake cylinder. Conceivably, the manufacturer of the defective cylinder could be liable to the consumer for negligent design or manufacture; but in contract or warranty, under traditional sales law, liability could also extend to the automobile manufacturer to whom the cylinder was sold. Traditional privity does not reach beyond the immediate contract relationship. The automobile manufacturer, in turn, might conceivably be liable to the consumer for negligent inspection but ordinarily cannot be liable for negligent design or manufacture except to the distributor to whom the car was sold. The result is that in the past the consumer's warranty claim was not enforceable beyond the person from whom the purchase was made, and the negligence claim required proving the particular *want of ordinary care.* Strict liability or to use its misleading title, implied warranty, makes each member of the manufacturing and distributing chain liable to the injured user—irrespective of contract, warranty, or negligence—provided the defect was present when the product changed hands. Lack of privity is no defense against such liability.

Section 2-715 of the UCC, covering incidental damages resulting from the seller's breach, includes reasonably incurred expenses as may occur in inspection, receipt, transportation with care, and custody of goods rightfully rejected, as well as any reasonable expenses or commissions in connection with effecting cover or incidental to the breach or delay. Effecting cover means that if the seller breaches by not delivering the goods, one of the buyer's remedies is to "cover"—that is, purchase equivalent goods from another source—even though they are higher in price. The buyer may recover the difference between the contract price with the original seller and the purchase price from the second seller as part of her or his, the buyer's, damages.

Warranties

There is a new movement to secure punitive damages against vendors who knowingly supply defective parts or products and fail to notify the buyer. Many such cases have gone to trial. A particular case is *Cantrell* v. *Amarillo Howard Company* (27VCC Rep 1276), in which the court awarded punitive damages in addition to breach of warranty damages to the buyer.

When a purchased item breaks prematurely and fails to fulfill its purpose, someone must absorb the resulting loss. Potential loss extends beyond the cost of repair or replacement of the item and is not eliminated simply because the purchaser manages to pass the item to third parties before it goes bad. The claim can also return (as breach of warranty, misrepresentation, negligence, or strict liability) from the damaged consumer.

In sales law, as in contract law generally, warranties may be either express or implied. Express warranties arise from direct negotiations between seller and buyer and indirectly from statements in catalogs, advertising, brochures, or labels. Intention to make a warranty in a formal sense is not required to establish legal responsibility. Statements in letter, conversations, or other communication will suffice.

Express warranties are generally preferable to implied ones because they are more precise and detailed. Express warranties do not easily yield to standard disclaimer clauses and because they tend to be filed or noted, they are more easily proved. The chief difficulty with express warranties is that they take time, effort, and skill to formulate and negotiate.

Oral warranties can also be important and enforceable. In a recent court case, a company had recorded a salesman on tape when he made an oral guarantee that exceeded the written warranty of the product. This oral agreement was found to be legal and subsequently served to expose the supplier to further liability when the product failed.

Implied warranties arise whenever the seller is considered a dealer in the goods or services. These warranties, collectively called the warranty of merchantability in UCC 2-314, require that the goods or services:

1. Pass without objection in the trade under the contract description.
2. In the case of fungible goods, are of fair average quality within the description.
3. Are fit for the ordinary purposes for which such goods are used.
4. Run, within the variations permitted by the agreement, of even kind, quality, and quantity within each unit and among all units involved.
5. Are adequately contained, packaged, and labeled as the agreement may require.
6. Conform to the promises or affirmations of fact made on the container or label, if any.

Implied warranty is based on the premise that a product is reasonably fit for a particular purpose. If the product is properly used, yet still causes loss or harm to the user, there has been a breach of warranty, making the supplying firm liable. To help avoid this, the purchasing firm must continually review their contracted responsibilities and their suppliers' compliance with these contracts. They must also inspect orders received for defects of manufacturing and damage from shipping. This effort may even require a materials tracing system to recall merchandise if and when the purchasing firm is informed by the suppliers that their goods are defective (strict warranty). These necessary courses of action illustrate the importance of dealing with reputable vendors as well as the need for close ties among all the firm's departments in order to minimize communication problems should a tracing system be needed.

Offer and Acceptance

The *meeting of the minds* that is the legal keynote of every contract is usually arrived at by the process of offer and acceptance. Not all promises that may be termed offers and acceptances can be made enforceable by law. In order to separate enforceable from unenforceable promises, the law recognizes the principle of *consideration* as the primary agent of determination. Consideration occurs when the promisor obtains some legal right or detriment from the party to whom the promise is made, in exchange for the promise. Basically, consideration is the value received in exchange for a promise, and it makes the promise enforceable. A gratuitous promise (a promise to make a gift) is not an enforceable promise unless it is combined with some reliance of a substantial nature. This is the theory of promissory estoppel (detrimental reliance), and when used with a gratuitous promise, the contract will become binding.

Mirror Image

Prior to the UCC, conventional sales law declared that no enforceable sales contract could arise until offer and acceptance were in substantially complete agreement with each other, without any variation of material terms between the two. This rule, often called the *mirror image* doctrine, treated a number of common mercantile contract procedures quite unrealistically. Whenever an attempted acceptance or confirmation added a detail of specification not stated in the offer, substituted one detail for another, proposed alternates, or deleted or qualified a term, the nominal acceptance or confirmation was treated as a rejection of the original offer *in toto* and as a counteroffer that required a mirror image acceptance of its own.

The mirror image rule thus requires the parties to agree on 100 percent of the terms and specifications of a given transaction before the law will recognize an agreement. So long as any detail remains unsettled, the transaction cannot move out of the negotiation stage. Such a rule is not necessarily a bad one, but it is unrealistic and impractical if applied in blanket fashion. It works especially badly when standardized forms of purchase and sales orders are used. Rarely, if ever, will all clauses of one company's purchase order conform to another company's sales order clauses.

The disagreement may be purely a disagreement of forms. The actual meeting of the minds may be fully present on all substantive matters. In such cases, an inflexible mirror image requirement may deny legal support to agreements that both parties regard as complete. It is likely that a large percentage of routine sales transactions are completed without a legally enforceable mirror image contract having been concluded.

The UCC relaxes the rigidity of the mirror image doctrine, permitting the parties to contract either strictly or liberally, as they prefer. In the absence of express stipulation by either party that no contract will arise except upon the terms that party states, or expressly agrees to, a legally enforceable agreement may arise, at least to the extent of the terms upon which offer and acceptance correspond, even though other terms remain open to further negotiation. Furthermore, in the absence of such stipulation, *failure to object within a reasonable time to certain terms* introduced incident to an acceptance or confirmation makes those terms a part of the contract, even though there may be no affirmative assent to them.

There is one exception to this principle of *assent by silence:* it does not apply to *material alterations* of the contract. Unfortunately, the distinction between material alterations and mere additional terms is not entirely clear. A good rule of thumb is that any significant difference between the *express* specifications of offer and acceptance relating to parties, price, quantity, quality, or credit terms is probably material. But it is bad practice to depend on any such rule of thumb in purchasing practice. The only safe practice is to examine documents of acceptance of confirmation for nonconformity and to send prompt and pointed notices of objection with respect to any non-conforming term that is objectionable.

The other alternative is to state expressly in advance that the other party's nonconforming or added terms are rejected. A clause in the purchase order form, for example, might read, "This order may be accepted only in strict and total conformity with its terms and specifications, without variance, addition, or limitation, and no contract shall arise upon any different terms unless this company expressly assents thereto." Although in solving the problem of material alterations, such a clause requires full mirror image procedure and subjects the transaction to the objectionable aspects of that procedure.

Time of Legal Contract

Precisely when a transaction leaves the negotiation state and becomes a contract is a matter of great importance, since no legal rights or duties of a contractual sort can ordinarily arise out of mere negotiations.

As a general rule, a contract arises at the moment when a conforming acceptance of an unrevoked offer is *communicated* to the offerer. Communication of acceptance, therefore, generally marks the point of no return in purchase negotiations, after which neither party is entitled to back out of the transaction by withdrawing or materially changing either an offer or an acceptance without the other's consent.

Under common law, the rule of *deposited acceptance,* or the *mailbox rule,* was most often followed. Under this guide, an acceptance became good when the offeree placed it in the correct communication medium even though it was never received. The risk of transmission was borne by the offeree. The two tests used to determine the correct medium were (1) the one expressly dictated by the offer, or (2) the medium used by the offerer. This means that an acceptance of an offer received by mail became effective as soon as the offeree mailed it back, unless the offer stipulated another method of communication to be used. The UCC continues to recognize the deposited acceptance rule, but it also adds another possible communication method: "whatever is reasonable." Specifically this means that acceptance may occur in any reasonable manner by any reasonable medium unless the offer clearly indicates by language and circumstances that a particular manner of acceptance is demanded. An acceptance may arise without any oral or written expression, in some cases by shipping the goods and in other cases by commencing to produce or acquire the goods. The confirmation in such special cases may follow the offer by a matter of days or weeks and operate retroactively.

UCC 2-205 now confirms the mercantile practice of making firm offers, which, unlike the usual offer, cannot be withdrawn during the period the offerer has promised to hold them open. Two technical requirements should be noted in this regard. The assurance that the offer will be held open must be written and signed; and it is not binding for longer than three months.

Terms Remaining Open

Traditional contract law explicitly condemned practices by which one or more of the material terms of an agreement were either deliberately left open for later settlement or stated indefinitely in some respect. UCC 2-204 liberalized that traditional rule to allow commercial standards of dealing, rather than unyielding legal technicality, to control the question of whether or not a contract has been reached. Basically, therefore, the UCC provides that a contract indefinite in reference to some terms is still binding if (1) the parties involved intended that a contract should arise, and (2) current commercial standards indicate that a reasonable basis for a legal solution exists. When negotiations are not intended to create a contract until all details of the transaction have been clearly settled and stated, special care may be required to guard against a possible opposite claim. Therefore, preliminary inquiries and contingent understandings should be plainly labeled as such.

Requirements Contracts

In a requirements contract a supplier agrees to sell all the goods of a certain kind that a buyer may require. UCC 2-301 provides that requirements contracts are enforceable if the buyer is seen to have made its requirements in good faith and there are no stated estimates or unreasonable disproportionate quantity requirements. The consideration received by the supplier is the implied promise that the material or supplies "needed" or "required" by the purchaser will be ordered from the supplier. Recent court cases support the UCC doctrine that a requirements contract can be implied from the facts and the circumstances of an agreement even though specific terms are not included in the negotiated document.

IMPORTANCE OF WRITTEN COMMITMENTS

Must It Be in Writing?

Human memory is fallible, and misunderstandings are inevitable if contracts are not recorded. There are at least two legal reasons why a written record of a purchase transaction is necessary. The first was mentioned earlier in this chapter in the discussion of the importance of proof of contract. The second is the Statute of Frauds, which operates to deny legal enforceability to oral agreements in certain cases.

Whether a written record is needed depends on the type of transaction. The requirements of the UCC relating to contracts for the sale of goods should not be mistakenly applied to contracts for services or real estate.

Where UCC 2-201 is in force, contracts for purchase and sale of goods for a price of $500 or more are not enforceable unless some writing "sufficient to indicate that a contract has been made between the parties" is signed "by the party against whom enforcement is sought or by his authorized agent or broker." Even a scratchpad memorandum may be sufficient under this requirement, provided that it (1) names a seller and a buyer; (2) is signed, initialed, or otherwise authenticated by (or on behalf of) at least one party; (3) specifies a quantity of goods; and (4) in some manner indicates that it is a memorandum of sale. Of course, such a memorandum would ordinarily be binding only on the party who prepared it, since it would not contain a signature of the other party. Such a situation, where one party is bound and the other is entitled to withdraw, rarely becomes a matter of practical significance, unless one of the parties seeks to repudiate what the other insists was a firm verbal agreement. A sufficient memorandum or confirmation letter will block the escape of the party who prepared it in such cases.

There are several exceptions to the rule that a party whose commitment is oral can legally repudiate the deal. The UCC has introduced some significant changes in this regard, not all of which have been entirely clarified at this time. The new rules include the following provisions.

1. It is still true that a contract for less than $500 need not be in writing; but to what extent it is possible to divide a given transaction into two or more component parts, so that some or all of the parts are under $500, is less clear.

2. Nonresponse for 10 days after receipt of a written confirmation that binds the sender also binds the silent party; but this rule applies only "between merchants," and there is some doubt (especially concerning purchasing agents) about precisely when a party qualifies as a merchant.

3. Contracts for goods that are manufactured especially for the buyer, and are of custom design or utility, require no writing when the seller has substantially begun manufacture or procurement before the buyer repudiates.

4. Payment for or acceptance of goods sold under oral contract waives the rule, at least to the extent of the goods paid for or accepted.

Acceptance of part of a "commercial unit" is acceptance of the entire unit.

5. Admission in court that the oral contract was, in fact, made forecloses the admitting party's right to insist upon the statute. In practical terms, then, the requirement of a signed writing has no significance unless the nonsigner claims, under oath or affirmation, that the parties did not come to terms in the first place.

One cannot emphasize too strongly what was previously stated about so-called open-price and other open-term contracts. A *sufficient* written memorandum or confirmation need not state any price at all. Businesspersons trained under earlier law and practice may fail to realize that now a casual letter *confirming our discussions* can give rise to a fully enforceable contract. Even memoranda prepared and kept in one's own file, for one's personal use, may acquire strong, and perhaps unintended significance. Important as it is to be careful of what is said in negotiating a transaction, it is even more important to scrutinize what is written. If a matter is only tentatively settled, subject to further negotiations, every notation of the transaction should expressly say so.

Inspection, Acceptance, Rejection, Returns

Except in rare cases, a purchaser is entitled to inspect goods before paying for them to determine whether they conform to contract specifications. If the contract includes terms prescribing the method, place, or time of inspection, such terms control the inspection. Expenses of inspection are the purchaser's responsibility unless the goods prove to be nonconforming and are rejected.

Nonconforming goods may be rejected *in toto,* accepted subject to correction or price adjustment, or accepted in part and rejected in part. The last-named alternative is not available, however, if it requires the splitting of a commercial unit; that is, leaves what is regarded in the business as a broken lot. To whatever extent a shipment is rejected for nonconformity, the purchaser must (1) notify the seller of rejection within a reasonable period of time, (2) hold the goods for seller's disposition, and (3) follow the seller's reasonable instructions with respect to disposition or return. The purchaser is entitled to be paid for expenses incurred in connection with rejected goods, as well as for damages.

The notice of rejection should specify every way in which inspection has revealed the goods to be nonconforming. Failure to specify can waive the unspecified defect. This suggests the advisability of making a complete inspection of any shipment that a purchaser intends to reject. If the principal ground for rejection is clear and uncorrectable, there is no great risk in only specifying it, but should the principal ground be disproved or corrected, the other defects may be needed to justify the rejection.

Whether or not the shipment is inspected, acceptance waives any complaints that a reasonable inspection would have disclosed. An accepted shipment cannot always be rejected on subsequent discovery of defects. Furthermore, a purchaser has only a reasonable time to reject a shipment before being presumed to have accepted by silence.

This is not to suggest that a purchaser who accepts a shipment has no recourse for subsequently discovered nonconformity. If the defect or deficiency of the goods is one that is not reasonably discoverable by ordinary commercial inspection, purchasers are entitled to claim damages if they notify the seller of the problem promptly upon its discovery.

In three cases, an accepted shipment can be subsequently rejected for nonconformity that "substantially impairs its value" to the purchaser. One is the case in which the original acceptance was made upon the reasonable assumption that the seller would correct the nonconformity. A typical case would be one in which a machine arrived without specified motors and the purchaser assumed that the motors would follow from a different source. The second situation is one in which the deficiency is not discoverable by ordinary processes of inspection. The third is the case in which a seller's pointed "assurances" induced the purchaser to take the shipment on faith. In no case, however, can an accepted shipment be rejected after its condition has been substantially changed by use. Then the purchaser is limited to a claim of damages.

Some of today's purchases are made on approval, sale-or-return, or consignment. On-approval arrangements permit the purchaser to return even conforming goods if, after a reasonable period of trial, he or she decides not to accept. Both shipment and return of such goods are, in the absence of a different point of view, at the seller's risk and costs. From a purchaser's point of view this arrangement seems ideal, but it has its legal and practical limitations. Few sellers are willing to do business on approval without extensive contractual safeguards. The purchaser who accepts part of the goods, by using or consuming more than a trial amount, accepts all of them. The purchaser who delays decision beyond a reasonable time has accepted goods. In addition, purchasers are inclined to relax their specification standards too far in buying on approval and therefore are without remedy for nonconformity discovered after acceptance.

Purchases on a sale-or-return or on a consignment basis are usually purchases for resale. Broken lots are not subject to return under these arrangements, the return is ordinarily at the buyer's expense, and the buyer is responsible for the goods if they are not returned. Beyond those restrictions a sale-or-return follows the pattern of outright sales, except that commercial units are subject to return if unsold, and special legal consequences for the buyer's creditors arise under a sale-or-return arrangement.

PATENT RIGHTS

UCC 2-312(3) provides some protection against patent infringement in contracting for goods and supplies. Under this section a merchant seller, whose contract does not specifically provide otherwise, warrants against patent claims by third parties, unless the buyer furnished the infringing specifications. There is no necessity for an express provision that the goods be sold free of patent claims. Nor is the seller's warranty against infringement one that a general disclaimer will eliminate. Under UCC 2-605, should an infringement claim arise against the purchases, the seller must be promptly notified. If the seller demands in writing the right to settle or defend against the claim, the buyer must conform.

Assuming the seller's financial ability to pay damages, these provisions should protect purchasers against infringement claims that do not arise out of their own specifications. Contract language suggesting any disclaimer of the seller's full patent right to the product should be scrutinized with extreme care and usually rejected. Purchasers should be as suspicious of buying an item without guarantee against infringement as they would be if the seller refused to guarantee title.

Protection of the buying company's trade secrets and patentable ideas may occasionally become a responsibility of the purchasing manager. This presents a problem of special delicacy where a supplier is required to develop a new product meeting functional specifications described in the purchase contract. When the purchaser's development of the idea has not yet progressed to the point where formal patent or copyright protection can be applied for, there is real danger that the supplier will claim the fruit of research suggested by the purchase order. The purchaser may lose rights to the idea. Where it is necessary to solicit a number of potential suppliers on such an order or where subcontractors are involved, the problem is compounded.

ANTITRUST LAWS

The individual states of the United States have laws regulating monopoly and prohibiting unreasonable restraint of trade. A purchasing manager should be familiar with these state laws in the state where the organization is located and in states where major purchases are made. These laws vary significantly in their provisions and the vigor with which they are enforced.

Historically, the state laws have not been the source of as much litigation as the federal laws, but recently the more industrial states have become increasingly active in prosecuting restraint-of-trade offenses. Since a company indicted under such laws not only runs the risk of heavy fines and the imprisonment of its responsible officers, but also suffers a form of unfavorable publicity difficult to counteract, a purchasing executive should be very careful to avoid antitrust involvement.

The federal antitrust statutes apply to transactions that involve interstate commerce. With the broadened definition of interstate commerce, these laws can be invoked in almost any situation in which the federal government wishes to intervene. Of the many types of transactions with antitrust implications, the following are the ones with which a purchasing executive is most likely to be involved.

Price Fixing and Agreements Not to Compete

The first section of the Sherman Act prohibits contracts, combinations, or conspiracies in restraint of trade. Any kind of an agreement among competing buyers or sellers is such a conspiracy and represents the commonest violation of Section 1 of this act. Many companies do—and all companies should—have firm rules against their executives talking with executives of competing companies about pricing and related matters. Fixing prices; allocating customers, markets, or territories; monopolizing a market; and boycotting a customer are all per se violations of the law and not defensible under any conditions.

Boycott. Although a purchaser may ordinarily buy from anyone, an agreement with others not to buy from a particular seller may not be made without serious danger of violating Section 1 of the Sherman Act, since a boycott is clearly a combination on conspiracy in restraint of trade.

Price Discrimination

The Robinson–Patman Act not only prohibits sellers from charging different prices to purchasers of goods of like grade and quality, subject to certain limited exceptions, but also prohibits purchasers from knowingly inducing or receiving an illegal discriminatory price in interstate commerce.

Aside from bona fide general price changes and distress sales, the only exceptions to the prohibition against price discrimination among competing customers for comparable goods are, for all practical purposes, those permitting differences in price that (1) merely reflect differences in the seller's costs of dealing with the favored customer resulting from differing methods or quantities in which the goods are manufactured, sold, or delivered to such a customer, or (2) are granted to meet (not beat) a competitor's bona fide offer to a favored customer.

Discriminatory pricing practices have been detected in various forms of concessions, beyond the obvious practice of shading—that is, lowering, the price itself. Although none of these concessions is illegal in itself, they are illegal if given under circumstances that tend to produce the prohibited result, that is, injuring a competitor of the buyer or seller without cost justification. The common forms of illegal concession are:

1. Quantity differentials not based on demonstrable cost savings.
2. Cumulative volume differentials, in which purchases are aggregated over a period of time, with increasing discounts being granted as the volume rises.
3. Geographical differentials, based on adjustments for shipping and delivery costs, in which the favored purchaser is given a concession on delivery cost not accorded competitors.
4. Trade and functional discounts based on a system of customer classification that essentially distinguishes the consuming purchaser from the purchaser for resale, and further arbitrarily distinguishes between classes of purchases for resale. Trade and functional discounts are of doubtful legality if they are arbitrary and are merely designed to preserve a channel of distribution.
5. Locality differentials, often used as part of a seller's localized promotion campaign and having overtones of predatory price cutting for the purpose of hurting a competitor.
6. Carrier option discounts, which discriminate between customers served by different modes of shipment (e.g., by rail and by truck) to a degree not justified by the differences in cost.
7. Pooled-order discounts, in which a number of buyers combine their orders but for all other purposes act as independent buyers. The legality of these cooperative purchasing schemes has not been finally settled, but it is fairly well established that when the pooled orders produce no significant savings to the seller, the arrangement is suspect.

Exclusive Dealing and Supply Contracts

Section 3 of the Clayton Act, another of the federal antitrust laws, prohibits a sale or lease of goods conditioned upon the purchaser's agreeing not to use or deal in the goods of a competitor of the seller where the effect of such arrangement "may be" to lessen competition substantially or tend to create a monopoly in any line of commerce. An exclusive dealing arrangement that ties up a large dollar amount of business or involves a dominant member of the industry will ordinarily be considered to have the necessary adverse effect on competition. Common examples of exclusive dealing arrangements that violate Section 3 of the Clayton Act are (1) agreements to supply all of a purchaser's requirements of a particular commodity for a substantial period of time and (2) tie-in sales or leases under which the purchaser of one product is also required to purchase a related product from a seller or lessor. These practices are prohibited if the sales substantially lessen competition or have a tendency to create a monopoly. The legal rationale behind the prohibition of tie-in sales is that (1) the buyer is prevented from obtaining alternative suppliers for the tied product and (2) sellers attempting to compete are shut out of part of the market, thereby conferring monopoly power on one seller and lessening competition.

Unfair Competition

The Federal Trade Commission Act, Section 5, makes unlawful certain methods of competition and unfair or deceptive acts or practices. The law is vaguely worded, but it has been interpreted to reach activities that do not clearly fall within the prohibitions of other antitrust laws. Antitrust violations can have serious and far-reaching consequences. In addition to severe criminal fines and imprisonment for individuals, violations can result in the invalidation of contracts and destruction of patent rights, as well as injunctive decrees and cease-and-desist orders that may jeopardize an entire business operation and cripple a business's ability to react in a changing market. If the government does win an antitrust case, it opens the way for civil suits from private parties who have suffered damages. Claimants are entitled to three times the amount of their actual damages, plus court costs and reasonable attorneys' fees. Therefore, even minor questions of legality under the antitrust laws deserve cautious handling and early consultation with legal counsel.

OSHA

The passage of the Occupational Safety and Health Act of 1970 and the creation of the Occupational Safety and Health Administration (both known under the acronym OSHA) have created additional problems for purchasing personnel. Previously, the purchasing manager was concerned only with the value, service, quality, and price of the goods or services. The passage of OSHA has added another item to this list of concerns, the quality of safety. Every item that is bought must have been produced under guidelines set forth in OSHA and administered by the Department of Labor.

Some buyers have attempted to protect themselves and at the same time to shift responsibility to suppliers for compliance by including in their purchase orders a clause somewhat as follows:

> Seller agrees to comply with the provisions of the Occupational Safety and Health Act of 1970 and the standards and regulations issued thereunder. Seller certifies that all items furnished and all work performed hereunder will comply with said standards and regulations. Seller further agrees to indemnify and hold harmless Buyer for any loss, damages, fine, penalty, or any expense whatsoever as a result of Seller's failure to comply with the act and any such standards or regulations issued thereunder.

Buyers must also be alert for attempts by suppliers to include a disclaimer for any liability for damages suffered as a result of the failure of its products to comply with OSHA standards. This might be stated in the following terms:

> The warranty of merchantability and fitness for a particular purpose as well as any other express warranty are hereby disclaimed. Furthermore, seller does not warrant or represent that the goods supplied herein comply with the provisions of any law, including but not limited to the Occupational Safety and Health Act of 1970 and any standards or regulations issued pursuant thereto.

If the seller's own form conspicuously contains this and the buyer accepts (which constitutes a counteroffer) goods shipped under this provision, the buyer would be bound by the seller's terms and the seller's disclaimer would be effective.

Whether such clauses are included in purchase agreements seems to depend on the relative bargaining position of the buyer and seller while the contract is being negotiated. Even if there is no OSHA clause in a purchase contract, it is possible that the buyer will have recourse under the implied warranty of merchantability, UCC 2-314. The buyer could argue that failure to comply with OSHA standards that the seller could have discovered is a breach of warranty since goods that do not comply with OSHA standards are not *merchantable* goods.

RICO

The Racketeer Influenced and Corrupt Organizations Act of 1970 (RICO)[3] has evolved into a private civil law quite different from the U.S. Congress' original conception.[4] The broad scope of the act has brought individuals—

---

[3] Chapter 96 of Title 18, U.S. Code of the Organized Crime Control Act 1970, Public Law No. 91-452, 84 Stat. 941 (Title 18 United States Code, Secs. 1961–1968).
[4] Professor Clayton Trotter, Trinity University unpublished manuscript, *RICO Revived: The Need for Congressional Action.*

CPAs, lawyers, and brokers—who wouldn't be considered traditional mobsters, into the net of zealous prosecutors and private parties seeking damages. For example, RICO has turned up in oil business prosecutions involving violations of oil price-setting standards,[5] in business take-over cases where target companies, in their efforts to ward off a takeover, allege violations of security laws by the company seeking to take them over,[6] and commercial commodity trading cases where unauthorized trades (churning) have taken place.[7]

Purchasing managers have witnessed with alarm that a dishonest firm, alleging RICO violations, may unleash the broad discovery tools available under RICO to access records and internal memoranda.

In addition to fines and imprisonment, RICO's forfeiture clause provides that anyone convicted under the act shall forfeit to the United States the following:

> any interest he has acquired or maintained in violation of section 1962, and any interest in, security of claim against, or property or contractual right of any kind affording a source of influence over, any enterprise which he has established, operated, controlled, conducted, or participated in the conduct of in violation of section 1962.

FOREIGN CORRUPT PRACTICES ACT

The U.S. Foreign Corrupt Practices Act (FCPA) empowers the U.S. government to deter corrupt practices by U.S. multinational companies. The FCPA resulted from efforts to promote an international free market not distorted by bribes and to protect and enhance the U.S. image abroad. Enacted in 1977, the law imposes strict accounting standards and antibribery proscriptions. The Omnibus Trade and Competitiveness Act of 1988 amended the FCPA to narrow its scope and to establish specific business community standards to determine permissible conduct under the act.[8] However, the amendment adds little to the statute, and the ambivalent and unstructured environment in which foreign business often takes place demands clearer definitions of unlawful acts.[9] The law's reach will not broaden. The United

---

[5] *United States* v. *Uni Oil, Inc.,* 646 F.2nd 946 (5th Circuit 1981).

[6] *Spencer Companies* v. *Agency-Rent-A-Car, Inc.,* [1981–82 Transfer Binder] Fed. Sec. L. Rep. (CCH) Sec. 98,361 at 92,214 (D. Mass. November 17, 1981).

[7] *Taylor* v. *Bear Stearns & Co.,* 572 F. Supp. 667, (N.D. Ga. September 30, 1983).

[8] "Complying with the Amended Foreign Corrupt Practices Act," *Risk Management* (April 1990), pp. 76–82.

[9] "Foreign Representatives: Saudi Law and the FCPA," *Middle East Executive Reports* (May 1990), pp. 16–19.

States will likely undertake criminal prosecutions involving foreign representatives only in cases of straight bribery and fraud.

The growing public pressure for greater corporate accountability brings more demands for fraud prevention, detection, and disclosure, and for early warnings of possible business failure. The Commission on Fraudulent Financial Reporting—the Treadway Commission—calls for mandatory independent audit committees for all public firms. The Foreign Corrupt Practices Act uses internal controls as an accounting mechanism. Therefore, any revival or expansion of FCPA, also known as the Internal Audit Full Employment Act, places greater emphasis on internal auditors as experts in detecting and preventing management fraud.[10] Internal auditors hold strong organizational standing to warn officers or employees, and persons acting on their behalf, from giving or offering to give anything of value to any foreign official for influence.

The law specifically condemns payments to officials to ease routine government action, ranging from processing visas and licenses to providing water, electricity, telephone service, police protection, and mail delivery.[11]

So far, no other governments have followed the U.S. lead in passing antibribery laws regarding foreign officials, although nearly all countries have laws against the bribing of their own officials. Nevertheless, western business style encourages bribery in developing countries that take advantage of visiting executives who show little patience with local bureaucratic rules.[12]

Analysts study three categories of bribes to determine their ethics:

1. *Utilitarian:* Ethical conduct produces the greatest net benefits for society.
2. *Moral Rights:* Conduct that does not interfere with another's rights nor coerce another party.
3. *Rights or Fairness:* Transaction bribes (made to secure or accelerate the performance of an official's duties) can be ethical or unethical, while variance (pay to secure the suspension or nonapplication of a legal norm) and outright purchase bribes (made to get the favor of a foreign employee) are unethical.[13]

---

[10] "Auditing, Directors, and Management: Promoting Accountability," *Internal Auditing* (Winter 1990), pp. 3–9.

[11] "When Somebody Wants a Payoff," *Fortune* vol. 120, Issue 13 (Fall 1989), pp. 117–122.

[12] "Business Bribes: On the Take," *The Economist* (UK) (November 19, 1988), pp. 21–24. Dominique Lapierre's *The City of Joy* (Doubleday & Company, 1985) describes Calcutta's bureaucratic mire that American purchasing managers find pervading many overseas markets.

[13] "Foreign Corrupt Practices Act: A Legal and Moral Analysis," *Journal of Business Ethics* (Netherlands, October 1988), pp. 789–795.

Purchasing managers during the 1990s will likely see Congressional efforts to define foreign corrupt practices more clearly, to give American businesspersons a cleaner image. Internal auditors will serve leadership roles in establishing and monitoring ethical standards. As protection, an estimated 85 percent of the 2000 largest U.S. companies now have codes of ethics, while 35 percent have ethics training for their managers.[14]

PURCHASE ORDER CLAUSES

Many companies, in order to avoid legal entanglements with respect to purchase of materials, include on the purchase order form carefully worded phrases regarding the requirements placed on the seller. The seller in return usually sends an acknowledgement of the order containing fine print and various clauses in an attempt to secure a favorable position. The two parties then proceed as if there was a contract. If problems develop, the legal issue becomes "a battle of the forms." Before the UCC became effective, the seller was usually legally correct. This was based on the reasoning that the purchase order form was an offer, but since the seller's acknowledgement form did not exactly match the terms of the offer, it was not an acceptance but a counteroffer. This counteroffer thereby nullified the original offer in the purchase order form and when the buyer accepted the goods after receiving the counteroffer, the seller's terms became dominant under law.[15]

The UCC has attempted to resolve contractual problems involving fine print, which the law recognizes may not be read but merely filed away. UCC 2-207 stipulates that if a vendor wishes to make a counteroffer, any different terms in their acknowledgement forms must be carefully spelled out for the buyer. Inserting different terms in fine print will not necessarily be legally effective. Nevertheless, the buyer must continue to be alert in this nebulous area for clauses making the seller's acceptance conditional on the buyer's acceptance of the seller's terms, as well as for changes in forms that may be conspicuously added and therefore considered enforceable.

Purchase order clauses almost always include items such as cash discount terms, billing procedure, number of copies of invoices, bills of lading required, and mailing instructions for such documents. Such clauses, although technically a part of the contract when properly accepted, generally are considered informative and to some extent instructive and may not have legal significance.

Particular concern must be exercised when purchase orders are used to

---

[14] *The Economist*, op. cit.

[15] "The Battle of the Forms, Part I," *Purchasing* (January 16, 1992), p. 39, conveys a strong statement concerning this perennial buyer–seller problem.

communicate offers by the buyer or to confirm oral agreements. If an offer is to be made using a purchase order, the intention to do so must be clearly indicated on the form. If the desire is to accept an offer, the purchase order form should be changed to state that it is an acceptance of an offer. To confirm an oral contract, the order should clearly state that it is sent as a confirmation, not an acceptance and not an offer. This can be accomplished by having forms available for separate purposes or one form with different purchase order clauses to identify the buyers' intentions in each particular purchase.

Other clauses, however, that relate to such matters as patent protection, proper insurance protection, and percentage of overrun have considerable significance and should be prepared in good legal form. Typical purchase order forms include clauses on:

Patent infringement
Inspection
Packaging charge
Change without written authority
Verbal understanding
Fair labor standards
Price
Time of shipment
Billing and bill of lading
Replacement of defective goods
Payment
Acknowledgement
Routing
Insurance and overrun of quantities

Although it would be desirable to have a standardized set of purchase order contract clauses for use by purchasing departments, such a set does not appear feasible. There is a wide divergence of opinion among both purchasing and legal personnel on the means of affording a company protection in its dealings with suppliers. As a result, most companies employ purchase order clauses that they have developed through experience over a period of years and that afford them the protection they desire.

JIT INFLUENCE

Changes could affect the way industrial buyers operate. Just-in-time (JIT) dictates that companies reduce the number of vendors they work with in order to develop strategic alliances with each one. The vendor–manufacturer relationship relies on stable production scheduling, efficient communication, quality control, and large volumes of business. These same principles apply to suppliers of transportation and to distributors.[16]

JIT distribution for maintenance, repair, and operating goods has undergone a period of rapid and fundamental change. Much of the change has involved the structure of the industry; a lot also involves the industry's relationship with its suppliers.[17] Some analysts state that American industry has too many distributors, perhaps as a response to JIT's insistence on punctual delivery from a well-stocked inventory. Manufacturers have treated their distribution base as a customer base, resulting in too much inventory parked at the distributor level in the supply chain. Distributor consolidations have contributed to glut situations. While many of these mergers have resulted in fewer names, stocking locations have not shrunk correspondingly; rather, territorial expansions fill out the surviving distributorship's added geography.

Knowing the subtleties of the Robinson–Patman Act can help purchasers safely avoid price discrimination. JIT's severe requirements for precision scheduling require that the buyer give close attention to subtle differences in delivery requirements that may affect price.[18]

The just-in-time philosophy can reduce distribution channel conflict and improve channel cooperation if implemented correctly. Channel members' predisposition towards JIT has a large impact on how they perceive the process. Many channel members see JIT as a way to transfer the inventory burden to their suppliers and to get more favorable prices. Many other suppliers see JIT as a quick fix and a way to guarantee a higher level of sales.[19] Buyer awareness protects self and company against legal hazards.

CHAPTER SUMMARY

Common sense and evenness must temper the application of the rules of law. For example, custom or established practice within an industry or

---

[16] "Achieving Inventory Reduction through the Use of Partner-Shipping," *Industrial Engineering* (May 1992), pp. 36–38.

[17] "MRO Distribution—An Industry in Transition," *Purchasing* (May 21, 1992), p. 50.

[18] "Purchaser Liability Under Robinson–Patman," *NAPM Insights* (September 1991), p. 8.

[19] "The Effect of JIT on Distributors," *Industrial Marketing Management* (May 1992), pp. 145–149.

between the parties may make rejection of goods once each year a reasonable arrangement, although by other standards parties would hold it unreasonable. The printed provisions of a seller's acknowledgement form may provide that his or her salesperson's representations will not bind the seller. However, previous practice may express otherwise. Even though a seller suffers substantial damages as a result of a buyer canceling an order, the seller may not recover those damages if the industry follows the custom of allowing only the recovery of nominal damages.

A purchasing manager may understand better the rules of law and their exceptions applied to purchasing routines when he or she recognizes that they grew out of a long-term effort of the courts to establish the "intention of the parties."

Therefore, when entering into a contract one should leave no room for doubt as to intentions. The written contract must include every important feature of the intention. A complete and clear statement of intention gives the purchaser a positive assurance of avoiding legal difficulties.

Knowing and understanding the basic laws that govern purchasing activities provides the purchasing manager with the best assurance of avoiding or minimizing legal difficulties. The manager will have to seek legal counsel whenever questions arise that require legal skill.

Discussion Questions

1. How much knowledge of law is required of the industrial buyer?
2. What is meant by implied authority?
3. What are the specific legal principles to be considered relative to signing a purchase contract?
4. What are the three basic elements to every claim?
5. Name and discuss the three classifications of torts.
6. What should a purchaser do when rejecting a shipment for nonconformity?
7. List the types of transactions that have antitrust implications to a purchasing agent.
8. What is OSHA and how does it affect purchasing?
9. What is meant by purchase order clauses? Are they important?
10. Is it necessary for all contracts to be in writing? Why?

Suggested Cases

ABC Corporation (A)

American Arbitration Association

Court Decisions on Purchasing Issues

Industry-wide Pricing

Utopia School District

═15

Health-Care Purchasing

Director of Materials Management Job Description: Responsible for the effective management of the purchasing, storage and delivery of equipment and supplies required by all hospital departments and activities. Directs the activities of Central Supply including Sterile Processing (other than Surgery) to meet all departmental needs, including property control and accountability as well as processing of patient charges related thereto. Responsible for operation of the Print Shop to include forms preparation, forms control, and forms issue. Responsible for storage, control, and disposition of excess property and equipment.*

CHAPTER CONTENTS

Source: Large U.S. hospital, asset size half a billion dollars, annual budget $50 million.

Serious problems in the United States have beset health care, the most essential of a society's services. Expenditures for health care increased to 13 percent of gross national product in 1991. Outpatient and ambulatory services expanded to encompass a seemingly "drive-through" mentality.[1] Meanwhile, many conventional hospitals have had to struggle for survival and have come to advertise and compete openly for patients.

The age wave brings the fabled baby boomers closer to the high-consumption years of health care. The acquired immunodeficiency syndrome (AIDS) crisis, with roughly 40 percent of AIDS patients on Medicaid, has forced hospitals to provide care often with below-cost reimbursement. New technology has become commonplace but very costly. Thus, home care may resume its role as the health-care delivery center, leaving the hospital for the very ill or for short-term outpatient care.

HEALTH-CARE PURCHASING DIFFERENCES

Purchasing in the health-care field differs from industrial buying in a number of ways. First of all, the field has grown more rapidly in expenditures than any other economic field. The national health-care expenditures in 1960, $27.1 billion or 5 percent of the gross national product, exploded to 1991's estimated $723 billion or 13 percent of GNP.

Second, because government benefits and health insurance companies, as third-party providers, cover 70 percent of United States citizens' health-care costs, the actual consumer of health care does not feel the pinch immediately and directly and does not complain effectively. Of course, public alarm and Congressional outcry focus attention on the need for cost containment; as a member of the alarmed public, the actual user may clamor for cost containment. Yet, as an individual patient, he or she makes no cost-cutting impact. As a shopper of industry's goods, however, the consumer complains against high prices by buying the low-cost producer's goods, typically.

And third, in hospitals, doctors and surgeons decide what high-cost technology they want with little resistance from hospital administrators, whereas industry executives budget and monitor purchase dollars tightly. This difference further involves administrators. A trend has started that eliminates hospital purchasing managers from many transactions in favor of chief financial executives and chief hospital administrators as negotiators of large purchase contracts. In addition, the trend toward fewer vendors for

[1] The Changing American Hospital: Back to the Future," *Hospital Materiel Management Quarterly* (February 1991), pp. 1–5.

longer time periods commits extremely large dollar amounts that require administering by executives above the purchasing manager's level.

A further difference emerges from the life-and-death nature of hospitals. The purchasing manager who wants to contain costs may face an overpowering demand to buy the best quality without delay, intolerant of standard procedures, commonly accepted substitutes, or good business practice.

These differences create the need for alert, well-informed purchasing and materials management personnel to meet the challenge by using effective negotiating techniques, value analysis, inventory control, and supplier selection and evaluation methods.

HOSPITAL MATERIALS MANAGEMENT

The voluntary efforts of the American Hospital Association, the American Medical Association, and the Federation of American Hospitals to contain costs have led to widespread adoption of the materials management concept by hospital administration as a key element in cost containment. Materials management goals must remain organizational, not departmental or individual. The materials manager must organize different groups within the hospital toward a common goal, such as standardization.

In 1988 hospitals spent $30.4 billion on medical and surgical supplies and instruments.[2] Until recently the management of these dollars was given relatively low priority in hospital organization. This priority status is changing as cost containment and avoidance are receiving increased attention through the growth of private health-care facilities and public concern with the inflationary aspect of health costs.

A study identified the following key areas for potential savings in health-care materials costs.[3]

1. More sophisticated price negotiations
2. Effective use of economically sized reorders
3. Obtaining volume-based price discounts when possible
4. Sizing inventories at optimal levels
5. Control of inventory damage, waste, and obsolescence
6. More efficient use of storage space

[2] *Hospitals* (March 20, 1990), p. 14.
[3] David S. Greisler and Sumer C. Aggarwal, "Hospital Materials Management: Potential for Improvement," *Journal of Purchasing and Materials Management* (Spring 1985), p. 21.

7. More effective use of price lists approved by Hospital Shared Services

8. Greater accuracy of inventory records; error rate below 5 percent

9. Minimization of materials-handling costs by conducting materials flow analyses

10. Improved paperwork processing and better use of humanpower by making methods studies and process analyses of materials management operations

11. Improved training for materials management personnel

Most of the procurement techniques adopted in health-care materials management are similar to those of industry, but there are some peculiarities. Common functional aspects include purchasing, inventory control, and storage. The processing function, however, is not as complex, and there is little high-volume production. Hospitals have a wide variety of processing categories, and distribution is complex and costly. Furthermore, inventory management must include hygienic control of the supplies and environment.

Some hospitals include only the functions of purchasing, central stores, and central supply in their concept of materials management. Others include the additional functions of supply, process, distribution, pharmacy, printing, and linen distribution.

COMPUTERIZATION

Huge investments in automation have achieved limited results in hospital administration. When installing systems, hospitals often have made the mistake of over-rating system capabilities.[4] However, the development of networking standards holds promise to improve the effectiveness of purchasing and planning. The Open Systems Interconnection (OSI) provides a means of linking admitting, emergency rooms, bed assignment, pharmacy, medical records, and accounting. Computers help develop the standards by which PCs may tie together disparate health-care information systems.[5]

[4] "Vendors Must Make Good on Automated Medical Records," *Modern Healthcare* (April 2, 1990), p. 29.

[5] "The Networking Standards Evolution: Toward a Real Electronic Medical Record," *Computers in Healthcare* (February 1990), pp. 18–21.

Systems Concepts

Systems approach can help to administer material in a multihospital complex. A computer model based on a total systems approach can help to organize evaluation about how material and its use affect the organization's objectives.[6] Strategic planning led the material management departments in one hospital complex to formulate goals regarding computerization, prime vendor contracts, elimination of the central warehouse, inventory control, and performance standards. Using the systems theory model, the organization recognized that material management involves more than purchasing; it involves procurement, transaction, and quality.[7]

Warehousing

Space is a major problem in all hospitals. The average hospital requires 10 square feet of storage space per bed; in nursing homes, 5 square feet per bed is needed. Industry remedies to this problem have been initiated—stockless purchasing, random warehousing, off-site warehousing, and stockless inventories.

In *stockless purchasing,* central stores consist of only standardized items that are used by several units in the hospital—such as intravenous solutions, used by every nursing unit including the emergency room, surgery, and recovery. These standard products usually account for 50 percent of all supplies. The other 50 percent are unique to one department, such as laboratory reagents and serums, which need refrigeration, or x-ray film, which must be stored in conditions providing proper light, humidity, and temperature. In stockless purchasing these items are stored within each department, to avoid costly replication by stocking in central stores.

Random warehousing is a stocking technique that allows for bulk storage of pharmaceuticals, supplies, and equipment. Supplies are stored in any available space with the location and date stored in the computer. The computer then produces an order for the supplies needed, based on first in, first out (FIFO) and giving the location of the supplies.

A related stocking technique that facilitates a smaller central store is the *off-site warehouse.* Particularly for a hospital using many disposables, off-facility warehousing can save on costs. This procedure allows for the consolidation of the subactivities of the purchasing department, frees space for

---

[6] "The Baptist Medical Centers' Model: A General Systems Approach to Managing Materiel in a Health Care Organization," *Hospital Materiel Management Quarterly* (February 1990), pp. 12–19.
[7] "Strategic Planning for Materiel Services in a Multihospital System," ibid., pp. 1–11.

clinical use, and facilitates use of the economic order quantity (EOQ) concept.

Stockless inventories involve still another technique. Medical centers can effectuate large savings from using the stockless inventory approach, reflecting just-in-time delivery support. Vendors bring ready-to-use supplies directly to closets, nurses' stations, and operating rooms. Hospitals keep just a 24-hour reserve, instead of large warehouses. They send orders electronically to one or two vendors, who deliver 95 percent of supplies within 12 to 18 hours. By contrast, the typical 500-bed facility may spend a million dollars on supplies, but stock as much as six times that amount of inventory throughout the hospital, while using an excessive number of vendors. For example, using the JIT approach, Vanderbilt University Medical Center (Nashville) slashed inventory by almost $3 million and significantly reduced operating costs by eliminating 27 supply positions.

Despite these gains, relatively few U.S. hospitals now use JIT or some form of stockless inventory. Analysts estimate that only one-third of the nation's hospitals can make the switch, because many function too far from major distribution centers, lack sophisticated computers, or can't develop the appropriate suppliers.[8]

British practice cross-fertilizes ideas and technologies between distribution in the health-care sector and retail superstore chains.[9] Large, centralized warehouses emerge as regional distribution centers, replacing small stores and warehouses. Economies of scale allow authorities to use more advanced technology, resulting in shorter lead times, lower stocks, and reduced head counts. Handheld data recorders, capable of storing large amounts of data, transmit orders directly to warehouses from pharmacies or retail outlets where a clerk can pick the product immediately and, if necessary, dispatch it by courier.

Disposals and Reusables

With an increase in the cost of labor in health care as elsewhere, the use of disposables instead of reusables has increased tremendously. Besides cost savings, other advantages include (1) patient safety, since the need for sterilization and quality control is eliminated; (2) availability of the product when it is needed; (3) protection against obsolescence; and (4) sharing of the legal liability for the product with the producer.

---

[8] "Sometimes Less Is More in Hospital Storerooms," *The Wall Street Journal* (August 23, 1990), p. B1.
[9] "Ways Forward in Warehousing," *Health Service Storage and Handling (UK),* undated article by Touche Ross Management Consultants.

INVENTORIES

Many hospital administrators are unaware of the value of the inventories they carry, even though inventory carrying costs are often 15 to 20 percent per year. Many of the supply systems in use today rely on central supply rooms as well as additional storage throughout the hospital. In such cases the only means of determining the actual inventory on hand is to conduct a physical count, which often results in discrepancies.

In two otherwise well-managed institutions in Cleveland, Ohio, a physical count of certain consumables such as sutures and syringes uncovered a stockpile throughout the institution that amounted to three or more years' supply.

The reasons for the excessive inventories in the health-care field are the low priority given to inventories, the lack of inventory controls, duplication (owing to multiple-ranking requests by personnel), little or no standardization, and the general overprovision of the health product. There is little accountability and an overemphasis on so-called safety stock. However, the health-care industry does have unique needs in that people may live when supplies are available and die when they are not. Some hospitals use the prime vendor concept, which is really dependence on a single source.

The prime vendor concept means locating a supplier who is capable of meeting most or all of the organization's needs. Most of the hospital's business is then directed to this vendor for as long as it continues to perform satisfactorily. An obvious disadvantage of this procedure is that competition is minimized and prices can be adversely affected.

Distribution

Distribution is an integral part of the supply process and is of vital importance to the safety of the patient.

The traditional distribution process, in which the using department goes to the central store for restocking, is proving to be costly and inefficient. The alternative process is the supply cart system. In this system a materials distributor restocks each department from a supply cart via the central store.

Cooperative Health-Care Purchasing

The Hospital Cost Containment Act is designed to keep communities from creating unneeded and redundant hospital facilities and services. Through this bill and the voluntary efforts of the hospital associations, the sharing of services and cooperative purchasing have increased.

Related or nonaffiliated hospitals, nursing homes, clinics, and related health institutions usually establish a legal organization to do their cooperative purchasing. This organization attempts to secure lower prices and acquisition advantages through group negotiation and consolidation of purchase orders.

Cooperative buying originated among the New York City hospitals that are publicly owned. After much debate, group purchasing by hospitals is now becoming an accepted principle, with more than 70 percent of voluntary hospitals in the United States having membership in an affiliated group.[10] Pressures to reduce costs and to share services have led to this growth.

Health Progress lists a comprehensive directory of group purchasing organizations prepared by the Catholic Health Association of the United States.[11] The SMG Marketing Group, Inc., Chicago, reports that nearly three-fifths of all hospitals that belong to group purchasing organizations affiliate with more than one group.[12]

According to *Modern Healthcare*'s 1991 group purchasing survey, purchasing groups and alliance purchasing programs accounted for $11.1 billion in goods and services bought by hospitals in 1991.[13]

Although different techniques are employed, a major objective of all group purchasing associations is to save through volume buying. There are three common methods of organizing group buying: centralized, decentralized, and selective purchasing. In the *centralized* purchasing programs, anywhere from 50 to 90 percent of all purchase orders are sent to a central office that acts as the hospitals' major placement source. Sources are determined by a consensus of the purchasing managers of all the hospitals. Purchasing and billing are done through the central office, which sends invoices to the individual hospitals on a monthly basis.

In a *decentralized* purchasing program, a central office negotiates contracts and establishes major sources of supply, with each hospital purchasing directly from the selected sources. Individual hospitals receive the volume discounts without going through a central office.

A *selective* purchasing arrangement is much like the centralized system logistically, except that each member hospital selects from preestablished lists of potential group items. This program is usually a supplement to major procurements by the hospital staff.

---

[10] J. H. Holmgren and W. J. Wentz, *Material Management and Purchasing for the Health Care Facility* (Ann Arbor, MI: AUPHA Press, 1982), p. 276.

[11] *Health Progress* (December 31, 1989), pp. 9–13.

[12] *Hospitals* (April 20, 1988), p. 82.

[13] "Groups See More Use of Pacts, Targets, Alternate Sites," *Modern Healthcare* (November 11, 1991), pp. 38–47.

COST CONTAINMENT

Effective purchasing administration can bring about significant savings. An Atlanta hospital effectively used a linen vendor to suggest alternative products for six different items, including knitted contour sheets, drawstrings, towels, scrub suits, patient gowns, and isolation gowns. To overcome the traditional reluctance of hospital staff to accept changing products, they implemented a selective evaluation program. Specific departments test the products, experience the benefits, and offer product evaluations.

Forms control may also lead to reduced costs. Representatives from medical records, information services, nursing, and laboratory made up one hospital's committee oriented to reducing paperwork. They selected one vendor to work on a stockless purchasing system.[14]

Housekeeping and dietary departments encounter similar significant price increases for patient care products.[15]

Some of the greatest challenges in lowering operating costs lie within hospitals' purchasing functions. More than 20 percent of the nation's total health-care expenditures go for supplies.[16]

A *Hospitals* magazine survey revealed that a majority of respondents expect purchasing budgets to rise through the early 1990s, with capital expenditures accounting for a large portion of the increase. These expenditures will likely emphasize equipment that replaces labor-intensive activities.[17]

NATIONAL HEALTH EXPENDITURES

The growing concern with health has created one of the largest, most expensive, and fastest-growing segments of the United States economy. National health expenditures as a percent of gross national product have climbed steeply, as Figure 15-1 shows. Spending for health care amounted to 13 percent of the 1991 GNP and exceeded 170 other nations' GNPs for that year. Such spending rose sharply from earlier years—the 1960 national health expenditure amounted to $27.1 billion and $74.4 billion in 1970.[18] The Congressional Budget Office charted the 1991 spending for health at $723 billion.

---

[14] "Purchasing Management Section Perspectives," *ASHMM*, vol. 7, no. 1, undated.

[15] "Annual Forecasts Show Where to Beef up Budgets," *Hospitals* (February 20, 1989), pp. 68–69.

[16] "CEO Looks to Vendors for Savings," *Hospitals* (January 5, 1990), pp. 60–61.

[17] "Survey: Executives Expect Increases in Purchasing Budgets," *Hospitals* (November 20, 1990), p. 50.

[18] Health Care Financing Administration, Office of the Actuary, in *Health Affairs* (Summer 1990), p. 172.

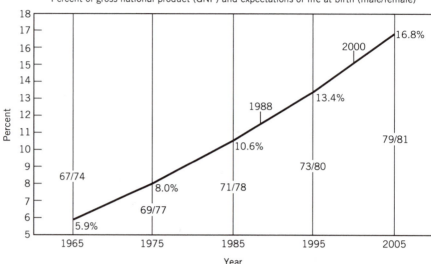

FIGURE 15-1. National health expenditures. *Sources:* HCFA, Office of Actuary No. 12 and Statistical Abstracts of the United States 1990, p. 72.

Life expectancy at birth continues to lengthen, as Figure 15-1 reveals. Projections to 2005 show a continual incline in life expectancy.

The American Hospital Association predicts that expenditures will total 15 percent of gross national product by 2000, as Figure 15-1 shows. The hospital unit continues to serve as the core institution for health-care activity although an estimated 18 percent fewer hospitals (from 2000 in 1987) will furnish health care by the year 2000.

The increased expenditures, reduction in numbers, and changing levels of competitive health-care institutions have made hospital administration including the purchasing function a matter of crucial concern.

RESTRUCTURING

The U. S. health-care delivery system appears headed for structural changes.[19] Congress adopted a dramatic change in the way physicians starting in 1992 receive Medicare reimbursement for health services. This change, called the resource based relative value scale (RBRVS), constitutes a new system for measuring the value of physicians' services. It offers

---

[19] "Resource Based Relative Value Scale: A New Challenge and Opportunity for Health Care Cost Management," *Employee Benefits Journal* (March 1990), pp. 2–5.

opportunities for trust funds and corporate plans to negotiate more aggressively with providers of care. Physicians expect a major income shift, as Table 15-1 predicts.

Some health experts propose putting price controls on health-care procedures and products. Others propose managed competition, relying in part on market forces to save money in the health-care system. The United States is moving towards a national plan to insure the 37 million Americans without health insurance and to contain the costs that everyone faces for health care.

COMPARISON WITH OTHER COUNTRIES

Health-care expenditures do not correlate necessarily with life extensions. As the figures in Table 5-2 show, the United States health expenditures per capita amounted to one-and-a-half times Canada's expenditures, while life expectancies remained identical. The United Kingdom's health expenditures amounted to a third of that of the United States, with nearly the same life expectancies, while the United Kingdom has the highest population per physician, eight times the U.S. rate. Japan's gross national product per capita exceeds the other countries in this trading partner list. Yet, Japan posts the lowest death rate per 1000, the lowest population per hospital bed, and the highest life expectancy, 75/80, male/female respectively.

Japan provides national health insurance for the entire population and free medical care for the elderly with 80 percent of hospitals and 60 percent of beds functioning under private ownership.[20] To improve efficiency Japanese hospitals have introduced highly efficient state-of-the-art medical equipment, have used outside contractors to provide many aspects of medical services, and have controlled materials inventory.[21]

STANDARDS

Incorporating standards and professional association guidelines provides policy and procedural direction in the design, organization, and administration of the materials management department. Standards and regulations from the following references furnish that direction.[22]

---

[20] "Japan Undergoes a Period of Transition in Medical Care," *Japan Hospitals: The Journal of the Japan Hospital Association* (July 1986), pp. 9–13.

[21] "Trend of Hospital Management in Japan during the Period of Slow Economic Growth," ibid., pp. 29–33.

[22] "Is Materiel Management the Beast in the Basement?" *Hospital Materiel Management Quarterly* (February 1991), pp. 80–83.

TABLE 15-1. U.S. Health Care Expenditures

				CGR	
	1965	*1987*	*2000*	*'87/'65*	*'00/'87*
Average Revenues					
Per physician	$29,000	$185,000	$459,000	+8.8%	+7.2%
Per hospital	$2.5 MM	$34 MM	$135 MM	+12.7%	+11.2%
Base					
Physicians	288,700	548,500	696,500	+3.0%	+1.9%
Hospitals	5,736	5,671	4,659	-0.5%	-1.5%

Source: HCFA, Office of Actuary, No. 13; Dept. of Health & Human Services, No. 11, AHA Hospital Statistics.

Joint Commission on Accreditation of Health-care Organizations (Joint Commission)

American Society of Hospital Material Managers (ASHMM)

American Society for Health-care Central Service Personnel (ASHCSP)

American Operating Room Nurses (AORN)

Centers for Disease Control (CDC)

Association for the Advancement of Medical Instrumentation (AAMI)

Health-Care Material Management Society (HCMMS)

National Association of Hospital Purchasing and Material Management (NAHPMM)

TABLE 15-2. Health Issues in Trading Partner Countries

	USA	*UK*	*Japan*	*Germany*	*Canada*	*Mexico*
Life expectancy, male/female	72/79	72/77	75/80	67/73	72/79	67/67
Death rate/1000	8.7	11.6	6.2	11.2	9.9	6.3
Population per hospital bed	185	133	87	88	143	1240
Population per physician	593	4632	760	427	604	2646
GNP/capita in US $	18,951	10,556	23,616	18,569	14,586	1880
Health expenditures/capita US $	2051	723	1347	1502	1376	N/A

Sources: Statistical Abstract of the United States 1990 and *The World Almanac and Book of Facts 1991.*

THE AMERICAN SOCIETY FOR HOSPITAL MATERIALS MANAGEMENT

The American Society for Hospital Purchasing Agents changed its name to The American Society for Hospital Materials Management (ASHMM), representing the interrelationship of purchasing management, logistics management, and inventory and distribution management. The society seeks to increase knowledge, develop competence, and promote professionalism among its several thousand members. It partly achieves these goals by library and staff services, annual conferences and conventions, professional achievement awards, and monthly and quarterly publications.

The Society and the health-care profession face unique needs in waste disposal, as few environmentally-conscious options exist.[23]

CHAPTER SUMMARY

Purchasing in the health-care field differs from industrial buying. Doctors and surgeons dictate what high-cost technology they want and administrators defer to their requests. The patient typically protests very little, since a third party pays the bill. The life-and-death mission of hospitals overpowers the buyer's efforts to take the time to shop around for new sources, better service, and lower prices.

Mounting national health-care expenditures defy administrators best efforts to contain costs by traditional methods. Therefore, many hospitals join the industrial sector's trend toward longer contracts with fewer vendors. However, longer contracts in larger dollar amounts with fewer vendors bring upper-level hospital executives into the buyer's role. The will to respond effectively creates a need for purchasing personnel to know and effectively use negotiating techniques, value analysis, inventory control, and supplier selection and evaluation. In short, sharply rising health-care expenditures summon assertive buyers who use the best procedures of the profession.

Discussion Questions

1. Discuss particulars of purchasing in the health-care field.
2. Define three types of cooperative purchasing in the health-care field.
3. Discuss materials management in relation to procurement in the health-care industry.
4. Discuss the problems of hospital inventories.
5. What is the prime vendor concept and why is it important to the health-care industry?
6. How do international health data impact the U.S. purchasing manager?

---

[23] "Environmental Challenges in Healthcare," *NAPM Insights* (March 1991), p. 6.

7. Why have national health expenditures increased so sharply in the 1990s?
8. Describe restructuring in the health-care delivery system.
9. Discuss the advantages of various warehousing techniques.

10. What cost containment efforts might a hospital materials manager attempt?
11. What computerization problems arise in the health-care field?
12. Describe how to start value analysis in health-care materials management.

Suggested Cases

Golden City
King County
Megalopolis City

Parktown
Radmer County

=16

Acquisition and Disposal of Capital Equipment

Ever since high school days, you monkeyed around with electronic equipment. So, now that you are the buyer for the county hospital, you figure it makes sense to save money when purchasing laparoscopic systems: Just start with the video equipment; modify existing equipment used in orthopedic procedures at a fraction of the cost for new equipment; buy video equipment from a local distributor to cut costs further. The hospital budgeted to spend about $30,000 for one set of laparoscopic instruments, not including the video equipment, to perform one of the latest surgical procedures, the laparoscopic cholecystectomies. The minimally invasive gall bladder surgery cuts inpatient recovery time to a couple of days from a week and reduces full recovery to a week from four-to-six weeks for standard open abdominal surgery. You expect approval on your plan.

C H A P T E R
C O N T E N T S

Business owners in small companies and appropriations committees in large firms deliberate the many aspects of acquiring capital equipment. Then they make their decision, perhaps months or even years in advance of receiving and installing the equipment. When the purchasing manager or buyer takes part in deciding, the purchase of capital equipment comprises one of the greatest challenges to a purchasing department. Engineering talent within or outside the purchasing department plays an important role in the typical acquisition of plant equipment. Such acquisitions usually require detailed specifications, involve large dollar expenditures, and last for a long time before they are replaced with new equipment.

The capital equipment of an organization consists of its permanent physical fixtures and components. Included are such items as conveyors, steel-rolling equipment, boilers, railroad cars, and so on. They include items that are peculiar to one industry only (e.g., steel-rolling equipment), which are called special-purpose equipment; and others that are used in many industries (boilers), referred to as general-purpose equipment.

The purchase of capital equipment usually involves substantial sums of money and therefore involves senior purchasing personnel. Accounting practices depreciate these pieces of equipment over a period of years, and their value is indicated on the balance sheet, in contrast to materials and supplies, which are immediately charged to expenses on the profit-and-loss statement.

DISTINGUISHING CHARACTERISTICS OF CAPITAL EQUIPMENT PURCHASING

Extended Negotiations

The purchase of capital equipment differs from that of other items in that each purchase involves substantial sums of money and is concluded after extended negotiations, requiring the consideration of more vendors than is usual for other purchases. With raw materials such as coal or chemicals, after the vendor has been selected—on the basis of price, quality, location, and similar factors—subsequent purchases are often made from the same vendor until there is some reason for change. With major equipment, however, each transaction is likely to result in separate and extended negotiations. Occasionally, satisfactory experience with the first purchase may result in an automatic reorder, but this is the exception.

Lead-Time Requirement

Another distinguishing characteristic concerns lead time. Lead time—the interval between the placing of an order and the delivery date—is much greater for capital equipment than for other materials and supplies. This is particularly true for equipment that is special or custom-built and for which considerable engineering is required. Even though the item is of standard design, there are usually options available for the buyer to select. Standard equipment is of such size and value that it is often impracticable for it to be made up and stocked by the manufacturer.

Involvement of Other Departments

Because of its importance to the manufacturing process, large dollar value, and uniqueness, a capital equipment purchase involves the interaction of several members of the buying organization. Primary interest is centered in the using department, with inputs from top management as well as engineering and financial personnel.

For example, the purchase of a new turbine generator generates widespread interest. Top management will first consider the matter based on reports it has received of the need for the equipment, its estimated cost, and the savings to be expected. Finance must consider the availability of funds because large cash outlays are usually required. After the purchase is authorized, engineering work must be done to determine the exact size of the unit, the particular type to be bought, its location, its installation, and similar matters.

To further illustrate the importance of engineering decisions, consider, for example, the selection of air compressors. Improper selection of air compressors may cause future problems, including insufficient pressure or flow, excessive operating costs, excessive moisture in air lines, high maintenance costs, and lack of expansion capacity. The prudent purchasing manager would do well to check these five common mistakes in the selection process for any equipment type:[1]

1. Selecting equipment too high or too low in capacity to meet system requirements.
2. Selecting equipment on price alone.
3. Failing to account for environmental factors.
4. Neglecting to make a thorough evaluation of supplier bids.
5. Failure to include essential system components.

[1] "Avoiding Mistakes in Air Compressor Selection," *Plant Engineering* (January 25, 1990), pp. 36–39.

Flexible Specifications

The specifications for standard capital equipment are frequently more flexible than those for other types of purchases. One reason is that the equipment available for the same purpose from alternative sources may vary significantly in characteristics. Manufacturers of pumps, for example, tend to offer pumps with common capacities and heads, but with related specifications that vary. Buying organizations must consider the alternatives in relation to specific needs. To insist on rigid specifications would reduce competition and probably result in a higher price.

For example, emerging specification trends in U.S. lift-truck manufacturing include an increased emphasis on operator safety and comfort, and on automation. Most major lift-truck manufacturers provide some form of operator restraint system as either standard equipment or as an option.[2]

Detailed Records Requirements

A further difference between capital equipment and most other purchases is that the identity of major equipment items must be presented in detailed records. This equipment record is used as a basis for depreciation, for ordering spare parts, and for operating and servicing needs.

High Value

The unit value of capital equipment is high because producing such equipment requires a higher ratio of labor to raw material than almost any other kind of purchase. Moreover, the supplier in fabricating the equipment must probably make, at added cost, detailed engineering drawings of the design according to the purchaser's specifications. Finally, the equipment may require large quantities of construction materials, even special materials such as tantalum or high-grade stainless steel, and components such as electronic instruments. The high unit value requires extensive budget and financial planning.

The manager needs to examine his or her equipment and determine the equipment's average expected life. The U.S. Treasury publishes guidelines on average expected life, gathered from Internal Revenue Service filings. Equipment manufacturers may furnish life expectancies on their equipment; their customers may share such data with buyers who deliberate replacing such equipment. The buyer's own company may accumulate files that contain experience data on average expected life. When the equipment

---

[2] "Industrial Trucks: The Workhorse Rears Up for the '90s," *Purchasing* (January 18, 1990), pp. 180–181.

nears the end of its life, the manager should establish a schedule in the budget for replacing it. He or she should price new equipment, including installation costs, and determine the old equipment's value. The difference between the two establishes the amount to budget.[3]

Nonrecurring Purchases

Most pieces of capital equipment are purchased at infrequent intervals. This infrequency of purchase necessitates a careful evaluation and study of each transaction. The history of previous purchases usually provides little guidance for a new purchase. In addition, purchasing must be alert to changes and new developments in the field.

There is also the possibility of purchasing many pieces of capital equipment from foreign firms. Points in favor of domestic purchasing include the creation and preservation of jobs, the preservation of buying power for domestic products, and the payment of domestic taxes that otherwise would have to be borne by fewer firms. On the other hand, the price of foreign-made equipment may be lower and quality is often comparable. But emergency repairs may not be possible; difficulty in securing qualified service personnel and costly communications are other disadvantages of purchasing foreign-made equipment.

Government Inducements

The federal government often seeks to encourage investment in capital equipment as a means of stimulating productivity or influencing the level of economic activity. Accordingly, liberal provisions that permit depreciation of capital equipment at an accelerated rate are often available. An example is the investment tax credit, which permits an investing company to deduct a percentage of the value of the investment from taxable income in the year of purchase. The government can regulate the amount of the tax credit or even suspend it entirely to stimulate or curb economic activity and inflation as the situation warrants.

Capital investment has lagged as a result of frequent changes in U.S. macroeconomic policies, which have led to investor uncertainty. The Brookings Institution, Washington, D.C., states that to promote long-term investment, the United States must adopt policies to:

1. Stabilize monetary and fiscal policy.
2. Increase savings.

[3] "Making Allowances," *Equipment Management* (February 1990), pp. 33–35.

3. Lower interest rates.

4. Remove tax biases against savings and investment.

5. Increase research and development expenditures.

6. Reduce inefficiency in the financial and legal systems that retards investment in the most productive sectors.[4]

Allied Purchases

Another factor distinguishing the purchase of capital equipment is that related equipment, materials, or supplies frequently must also be purchased. The purchase of one new machine may make some other piece of equipment obsolete and necessitate its replacement. It may also be necessary to find a substitute raw material in order to utilize the new machine, or new supplies may be needed for its operation. Therefore, the purchase of a major piece of equipment may start a chain reaction. If the persons responsible for buying capital equipment are not those who buy the related materials, good interdepartmental coordination is required.

SERVICE AS A FACTOR

Service is a factor in the purchase of materials and supplies, but it is a particularly important consideration in the purchase of capital equipment. There are four varieties of service available to a buyer, and their relative importance varies with the type of equipment involved. Often the service is as important as the equipment.

Prepurchase Survey by Vendor

Because equipment for a particular job may vary in its characteristics when bought from different manufacturers, it is frequently necessary to have each potential vendor make a survey of the buyer's needs. Such surveys also have legal significance, since the responsibility for correct application can be placed with the vendor. The purchase of a pump in the chemical industry illustrates the benefits of prepurchase surveys. The materials used in making a pump are important because of the chemical and physical properties of the substances to be moved. Manufacturers have varying metal alloys to handle the different chemicals, and special names are used to designate these alloys. The material to be moved is studied, and these varying alloys are

---

[4] "Capital Investment: Key to Competitiveness and Growth," *Brookings Review* (Summer 1990), pp. 52–56.

considered in relation to the capacity of the pump, its head, and related specifications. Such prepurchase surveys often find ways of improving the equipment.

Installation Service

The installation of a large machine is often handled by personnel from the buyer's plant under the supervision of the vendor's representative. The cost of this supervision is normally included in the purchase price. However, when supervisory installation service is optional, charges may be assessed on the basis of the actual time and expenses incurred.

Training Service

The training of operators may also be an integral part of the installation service. Such training is important to the buyer because vendors frequently include a provision in their warranty relieving them of responsibility for damage to equipment caused by improper operation.

Postsale Service

Service on equipment after it has been installed and is in operation is of two types, service during the warranty period and service after the warranty period. On most items of capital equipment there is a written guarantee against failure of the equipment from faulty design or defective parts or assembly for a stated period, frequently one year. During this period the buyer can obtain free service on the equipment if any trouble develops.

After the warranty period the buyer must usually pay for service calls on the basis of the hours spent and the travel and living expenses of the service representative. Sometimes, in order to build or preserve goodwill, a seller will give free service after the guarantee period is past. If trade practice necessitates that a seller perform a large amount of such postguarantee service, the price will have to cover these costs. Ultimately all customers will be paying an average share of such costs, and those who use less than an average amount of service are penalized. In view of this inequity, it is better for both buyer and seller to have a reasonable guarantee period and to adhere strictly to its terms.

An unusual failure may present a problem. Managers may avoid unusual claims by understanding normal industry practices and by examining the terms of a specific warranty before signing a purchase agreement. Sellers and buyers alike should pay particular attention to the applicable equipment categories and models, the warranty period, the components covered, and whether dealers may transfer the warranty over to other dealers. Prudent equipment buyers may want to negotiate certain terms into the contracts, including the use of loaners, extended coverage periods, and more comprehensive coverage.[5]

PROCEDURE FOR PURCHASING CAPITAL EQUIPMENT

Because of the nature of equipment purchases in terms of sums involved, relative infrequency of purchase, and capitalization of the purchase, detailed procedures have been developed to facilitate and control such purchasing. Some organizations utilize the critical path method (CPM), explained in Chapter 4, to ensure that each step in the process is handled properly.

Need

Evaluation of need is the first step in the purchase of capital equipment. The determination of need originates with the using department. The evaluation includes a study of alternative methods and their relative costs, location of sources for the equipment, and a feasibility study of projected benefits from the equipment. Relevant departments cooperate in this evaluation, including purchasing, which provides information on available equipment, its cost, and the probable delivery schedule.

Specifications

After the need has been confirmed and the basic type of equipment determined, it is necessary to establish the specifications. It is preferable to use equipment that is standard or common to an industry. Such standard equipment is readily available, requires no engineering modifications, and has a minimal purchase price. When it is necessary to customize otherwise standard equipment to meet the specific needs of the buyer, there will be additional engineering expense and customizing cost. However, this alternative is preferable to the purchase of specially designed equipment, which is the most expensive of the available options.

Negotiation

At the negotiation stage, purchasing chooses vendors to solicit for quotations, presents specifications, and requests quotations. Negotiations on prices, service, and equipment follow, culminating in the selection of a

---

[5] "Parts and Labor Included...," *Equipment Management* (January 1990), pp. 39–42.

particular vendor. Payment options, transportation terms, and warranty provisions are all included in the negotiation process.

Follow-Up

Because the delivery of capital equipment involves many variables and usually covers an extended period of time, follow-up is an important responsibility. Engineering work often precedes fabrication, and needs the buyer's approval early in the transaction.

The various intermediate stages of the transaction must be outlined and followed prior to delivery and installation. A CPM analysis is often used to verify each of the steps in the process and to pinpoint potential bottlenecks.

NEW VERSUS USED EQUIPMENT

When major equipment is required, the possibility of buying used equipment should be considered. The used-equipment market is large; every industry has firms specializing in the used-equipment market.

Few end users in the telecommunications market actively use the secondary market to satisfy their equipment needs. They show concern over product quality, warranty, service, and support. Large companies may resolve these concerns by forming partnerships with smaller, established secondary marketers, with a continued focus on service.[6]

The secondary market has grown as a result of increased competition among equipment resellers and increased supply of used equipment. Some *Fortune 500* companies sell their used equipment to recoup a portion of their recyclable and surplus assets. Buying surplus military equipment avoids broker and dealer markups. This equipment sells at the regional level by sealed bids or negotiated sales; at the local level, equipment sells by auction, spot bids, sealed bids, or retail sale. One sale of $750 million worth of used buses, cafeteria furnishings and fixtures, and office furniture sold for $250 million, elating whole communities, school districts, and church groups. Sources of used equipment include: (1) the Investment Recovery Association, (2) the Machinery Dealer's National Association, (3) Source Telecommunications, Inc., (4) The Surplus Record, (5) the Used Equipment Directory, and (6) The Source.[7]

---

[6] "In Telecommunications: Civilizing the Used Equipment Market," *Purchasing World* (March 1990), pp. 52–53.
[7] "Used Equipment Can Be a Profitable Buy," *Financial Manager* (March–April 1990), pp. 63, 67.

Considerations Favoring the Purchase of New Equipment

Long Life Expectancy. One of the obvious advantages of new equipment is its long life expectancy. If the equipment is a substantial item that will be needed for many years, purchase of a new machine is advisable. Items of equipment that are subjected to extremely hard use, such as earth movers and construction equipment, are usually bought new because their life expectancy is relatively short at best.

Uniform Life Expectancy. The nature of the related facilities will influence the new versus used decision. For example, when modernizing an entire department or plant, it is important that all components of the process have a uniform life expectancy. It would be unwise to install an item of used equipment with an uncertain life expectancy that could cause a shutdown of operations.

Technological Innovation. New equipment naturally includes the most recent technological innovations. When such innovations are meaningful to the buyer's applications, new equipment may be the more rational alternative.

DuPont has tested process control equipment for decades. The Engineering Test Center evaluates process instrumentation and manual valves and then furnishes the results to DuPont plants worldwide. It now sells its test results to other firms as individual reports or as an annual subscription service. Although the DuPont Performance Reports list equipment performance by brand name, the reports do not endorse products. Vendors may view test results and offer their comments in the final report.[8]

Reduced Maintenance. New equipment quite naturally requires less maintenance than used equipment. This is a major consideration, for over a period of time maintenance costs can exceed the original purchase price.

A firm has to pay a maintenance and operation cost to obtain a fixed level of equipment service. Analysts study those evolving costs as descriptors of a piece of equipment's deterioration and replacement state. The optimal replacement policy emerges from using differential calculus, according to one report.[9]

---

[8] "Consumer Reports for the Chemical Process Industry," *Chemical Engineering* (January 1990), pp. 37, 39.

[9] "Optimal Replacement Policy with Stochastic Maintenance and Operation Costs," *European Journal of Operational Research (Netherlands)* (January 5, 1990), pp. 84–94.

Lower Parts Inventory. Related to the lower maintenance cost for new equipment is the fact that a smaller stock of spare parts is needed. The cost of inventory for spare parts and the associated capital investment, storage space, and accounting needs can represent a sizable expense.

Bid Comparisons. It is much easier to evaluate competitive bids for new equipment than those for used equipment. Items of used equipment are rarely in exactly the same basic condition or state of repair.

Specification Considerations. Specifications play a very important part in the purchase of major equipment. Because the only used equipment that can be considered is what is available for sale, it is difficult to match the available equipment with a set of specifications. As one departs from specifications, it becomes increasingly difficult to evaluate the competitive bids.

Warranties. It is difficult to secure a performance guarantee with the purchase of used equipment. By contrast, most manufacturers guarantee new equipment to produce up to a specified level of performance, an obvious advantage.

Considerations Favoring the Purchase of Used Equipment

Cost. The major consideration favoring the purchase of used equipment is its lower cost. At times, substantial savings can be made by purchasing such equipment.

Delivery. Sometimes a compelling reason for the purchase of used equipment is its immediate availability. When equipment would have to be produced on short notice, the only possible alternative may be the purchase of used equipment. When one unit of an elaborate manufacturing process breaks down, the cost of shutting down the entire process, even for a short time, is often much greater than the purchase price of a used unit.

Design Considerations. At times equipment presently in the plant must be duplicated. When there are several of the older designed units in service, the addition of a similar used unit minimizes the need for spare parts inventory, and allows all maintenance of the plant to be synchronized.

Temporary Need. On occasion used equipment is advisable because the need for the equipment is only temporary.

Difficulties in the Purchase of Used Equipment

One of the major problems in buying used equipment is assessing its physical condition and estimating its future useful life. Determining why the equipment was withdrawn from its former service will aid in this decision. Mechanical assessments of wear and tear and potential difficulties are usually imprecise and uncertain.

The terms of sale for used equipment are usually restrictive. Most sales are on an as-is and where-is basis, with terms of net cash. This means the machine is purchased where it stands and in its present condition. The buyer must arrange for transportation, which often adds as much as 10 percent to the purchase price. If the equipment must be dismantled before moving and assembled when received, the extra cost may run as high as 20 percent. The net cash terms are often supplemented with a sight draft bill of lading, which requires the buyer to pay the draft before securing delivery of the equipment.

Because buying used equipment often necessitates dealing with unfamiliar sources, even when guarantees are extended, the buyer must carefully evaluate the guarantor as well as the equipment.

LEASING

Many pieces of major equipment may be leased instead of purchased. A principal difference between the two types of transactions is that under leasing arrangements title to the equipment remains with the original owner. A primary advantage is that a minimum capital investment is required.

Lease accounting departments in banks work diligently to survive and prosper. By rescinding the investment tax credit, the federal government placed the equipment leasing industry at a higher risk for lower returns. Many major lessors have reassessed their presence in this business, with more caution than before.[10]

Leasing provides alternatives to firms searching for ways to acquire capital equipment in the face of diminishing budgets. Most large firms use economic models to closely examine lessors' offerings in order to obtain the best and most cost-effective agreements. Models combine depreciation schedules, tax rates, lease costs, and interest percentages to derive bottom-line charts and tables comparing the cost of leasing and purchasing. Equipment residual value forms the most important forecast—the resale value after the lease expires or after the equipment's useful life at the corporation

---

[10] "Equipment Leasing in the 1990s," *Journal of Commercial Bank Lending* (January 1990), pp. 24–27.

ends. Competitive lessors show more willingness to supply companies with more data that they need to make informed decisions.[11]

Reasons for Leasing

A common reason for leasing equipment is the temporary nature of the need. For example, construction work may require metal scaffolding, as well as air tools whose life is longer than the particular project and for which the user has no need after the construction is completed. Under these conditions, leasing is more economical.

Sometimes leasing may be the only alternative. A seller with unique items of equipment may decide to offer only the lease option, thereby maximizing income and giving the seller control over the supplies and resale market as well. The refusal to sell equipment outright may be a violation of Section 3 of the Clayton Act, if such a policy would, in the words of the act, ''substantially lessen competition.'' However, small companies would not risk that danger and, therefore, could legally lease their products rather than sell them.

When sophisticated equipment is subject to frequent redesign, a user might hesitate to purchase and incur the risk of the item's becoming obsolete soon after purchase. In such situations the buyer may prefer a lease arrangement, which in effect transfers the obsolescence risk to the producer.

Another reason for leasing is the buyer's desire to shift responsibility for service to the lessor. This is particularly true of equipment requiring frequent adjustments and preventive maintenance by skilled personnel.

Sometimes the nature of the equipment may make outright purchase impracticable. For example, a company requiring a railroad tank car to operate between its own plants would probably not have facilities for maintaining the car and, furthermore, the car will be on the road and out of the buyer's direct control for most of its active life. Since there are companies that own large fleets of tank cars, it is a simple matter to lease a car and have the lessor take care of all the details of repair, maintenance, and accounting necessary in conjunction with its movement over various railroads.

The fact that certain equipment has a high rate of depreciation is another reason for leasing. Companies operating fleets of trucks and passenger cars often resort to lease for this reason. It has been found that, because of the high depreciation, it is often more economical to rent the fleet and leave the problem of replacement to the lessor.

Some companies formerly kept trucks and cars for three or four years because their mileage was low. When these units were replaced, the trade-in

[11] ''Concerns Spur Pursuit of a Golden Lease,'' *Computerworld* (February 26, 1990), pp. 67, 70.

allowance was smaller than was thought fair, in view of the low mileage, because the age of the vehicle was the determining factor in the trade-in. Under a lease arrangement the owner can transfer cars among users to keep their age and mileage at the level that will secure the highest trade-in value.

Many firms lease other items with a high unit value because of income tax advantages. The total leasing charges are deductible as an expense, whereas a purchased item can only be depreciated gradually over time. Therefore, deductions permitted under a lease arrangement may be more liberal than those permitted if equipment is owned. The applicable depreciation regulations (e.g., investment tax credits) fluctuate with economic conditions and public policy.

Leasing equipment obviously requires a smaller cash outlay than an outright purchase. This is an important consideration for companies with limited working capital, or for those with other favorable opportunities for investment.

FMC Corporation has turned to vehicle leasing to reduce debt load rather than buying vehicles. Further, the fleet and corporate purchasing manager finds it best to give one automotive company the entire order. He obtains a considerably lower leasing cost—the negotiated interest rate—by dealing with one supplier. At the lease's end, FMC has the option of selling the vehicle to the public or to dealers.[12]

Considerations whether to purchase equipment or to lease include the impact of tax rules and the impact on the company's debt structure. The lease-versus-purchase decision involves selecting the alternative with the lowest negative present value. The four alternatives include cash purchase, purchase with 80 percent financing, five-year true lease, and five-year conditional sales lease. The purchase option involves less favorable return on investment, return on assets, return on equity, earnings per share, and debt–equity ratios. With certain equipment like computers, operating leases should contain reasonable upgrade clauses.[13]

Limitations of Leasing

There are some unfavorable aspects of leasing that should be considered before a decision is made. Over an extended period of time, leasing costs usually exceed outright purchase costs. This is generally true because the lessor expects to make a profit proportionate to the cost and the risk inherent in leasing.

A lessee must grant the lessor access to equipment for repair and main-

---

[12] "Fleet Buying: Not for the Timid," *Purchasing* (February 22, 1990), pp. 44–47.
[13] "The Lease vs. Purchase Decision," *Management Accounting* (March 1990), pp. 42–46.

tenance. Such access may be undesirable when secret production processes are involved.

Another consideration is that the lessor may use leased equipment as a means of inducing the purchase of supplies for the equipment. Although it is illegal to force the use of such supplies through a so-called tying contract, alternative supplies may be difficult to obtain or use.

Leasing Contracts

Equipment for lease may be available directly from the manufacturer, outside sales agencies, or firms specializing in financing and leasing equipment. The lease contract defines the duration of the lease, sets the rental rate and terms of payment, and defines the responsibility for maintenance. Frequently, the lease agreement includes an option of outright purchase with the provision that rental payments may be applied against the purchase price.

Types of Leasing Sources

In general there are four types of leasing sources, each varying according to structure. These include the full-service lessor, the finance lease company, captive leasing, and bank participation.

In full-service leasing the lessor generally performs all needed services, purchases the equipment, and provides its own source of financing. This type of lessor is generally found in the automotive, office, and industrial equipment fields.

The finance lease company does not own or maintain equipment. Instead, its function is to provide funds to companies so that they may lease from the manufacturer.

In captive leasing a subsidiary or division sells the parent company's equipment to a lessor at a given transfer price.

In bank participation, a bank may generally provide financial assistance to a lessor with a solid credit rating. In return the lessor takes care of the purchasing, servicing, and the disposal of the equipment.

FINANCING MAJOR EQUIPMENT PURCHASES

The financing of purchases of major equipment requires such large amounts of money that special methods of payment are often used.

Financing by the Vendor

Frequently the financing of the high unit price of a piece of equipment is handled directly with the vendor. A common financing method is the payment of a percentage of the purchase price when the order is placed, with the balance payable at the time of shipment. An alternative is an installment plan, with payments beginning when the order is placed and continuing until shipment is made. The total price of the equipment is divided into an equal number of periodic payments.

Financing through Outside Agencies

The high cost of equipment may necessitate outside funding. The simplest method is a direct loan from a bank or insurance company.

An alternative originated by the railroad industry is the issuance of equipment trust certificates. The buyer gives a mortgage on the equipment to some financial institution, which advances the purchase funds. An identifying device is often attached to the equipment showing to whom it has been mortgaged. This financing arrangement is also often used by commercial airlines to finance planes.

Another financing alternative is a rental agreement with an insurance company. The insurance company actually purchases the equipment according to the buyer's specifications and leases the equipment to the buyer on a long-term rental agreement. Usually these agreements provide that the rental payments shall be applied to the purchase price, so that at the expiration of the term the buyer takes title to the equipment. This method of financing has a tax advantage, in that the full amount of the rental paid can be deducted from income as an expense. Its status appears to be the same as that of the lease in this respect.

Financial options carry different tax, use, cash-flow, and ownership advantages. The primary option, debt financing, consists of a down payment and installment payments. The finance lease features the benefits of a lease structure (no money down), but permits the lessors to retain equity in the equipment. The operating lease features low monthly payments, but has a very high fair-market purchase option. The tax lease must meet certain Internal Revenue Service requirements, which the Tax Reform Act of 1986 makes unfeasible.[14]

[14] "Taming the Financing Jungle," *American Printer* (January 1990), pp. 36–40.

DISPOSAL OF SURPLUS OR OBSOLETE EQUIPMENT

Commonly the responsibility of the purchasing department, the disposal of surplus or obsolete equipment can be accomplished in several ways. First, it is sometimes possible to trade old equipment in for new equipment, with the vendor taking responsibility for the disposal of the old. Second, it may be possible to sell the old equipment for scrap or to an individual in the used-equipment business. Lastly, it is sometimes possible to sell the equipment directly to another company that can use it. Of course, various mechanisms can be used to dispose of this equipment by sale, such as brokers or auctioneers.

One of the easiest methods of disposing of surplus equipment is by sale to used-equipment dealers, who often specialize in equipment for specific industries. Other obvious prospects are companies in the same field. For certain types of equipment, the disposal is made as a trade-in on new equipment. If new equipment is purchased directly from the producer, it is likely to be more difficult to negotiate a trade-in than if the purchase is made from a dealer. Manufacturers usually are not organized to handle used equipment.

ECONOMIC ANALYSIS

This chapter has indicated the need for careful cost analysis to compare the feasibility of proposed equipment purchases. Because of the large dollar expenditures involved, most firms use detailed economic analysis procedures to calculate the expected return from the purchase against the expected cost. The validity of these calculations can strongly influence a firm's future profitability.

Blind adherence to traditional models, such as payback and discounted cash flow, may stand as the greatest single barrier to implementing advanced manufacturing systems. Errors in applying the traditional economic decision models include:

1. Arbitrarily high hurdle rates, such as high interest rates and abbreviated project lives, that restrict the number of feasible investments.
2. Comparison with the status quo—new investment models implicitly compared to doing nothing.
3. Insufficient benefits analysis in terms of dollars.[15]

---

[15] "Persistent Pitfalls and Applicable Approaches for Justification of Advanced Manufacturing Systems," *Engineering Costs and Production Economics (Netherlands)* January 1990), pp. 247–253.

Payback Period

The most widely used method of analyzing the economics of major equipment purchases is the payback method. The objective is simply to determine
the number of years required before the cost of the equipment is recovered
from the savings generated.

In its simplest form, the yearly savings is assumed to be constant. No
allowance is made for depreciation and the return is computed by equating
annual operating savings after taxes with the net investment. A commonly
used payback target period is three years. If the equipment does not pay for
itself within that time, the purchase will not be made. The specific time
periods used vary with the organization and economic conditions.

There are two advantages, in addition to simplicity, of the payback
approach. It emphasizes the rate of cash flow associated with the equipment
purchase. In addition, where rapid obsolescence is likely, it provides the
necessary short-run emphasis to the investment decision.

A criticism of this approach is that it does not consider the total
profitability of the equipment investment that accrues after the payback
period. The method also makes it difficult to compare equipment alternatives with varying useful lives.

Present Value

Essentially any investment calculations involve two factors: (1) the expected payoff, or savings, which extends over many years; and (2) the cost of
the capital invested. Because capital equipment will usually produce savings
over a long period of time, it is desirable to determine the worth of the
future savings today. The so-called present value of anticipated savings can
be used in this analysis. The simplest present value calculation is:

$$V = \frac{R_1}{1 + i} + \frac{R_2}{(1 + i)^2} + \cdots + \frac{R_n}{(1 + i)^n} + \frac{s}{(1 + i)^n}$$

where

$$V = \text{present value}$$
$$i = \text{the interest rate on capital}$$
$$R_1, R_2, \ldots, R_n = \text{cash inflow after taxes in years } 1, 2, \ldots, n$$
$$n = \text{life of asset}$$
$$S = \text{salvage value in year } n$$

If the present value of the investment, V, exceeds the cost of the
equipment, the purchase is economically sound. The difficulties in this

approach include the problems of accurately estimating the life of the equipment and the amount of the cash inflows.

If the annual return amounts to 24 percent and the total value of the projected net cash flow at a certain term's end totals $780,000, the current value amounts to only $302,000, according to one study.[16] This 61 percent differential comprises the real justification for the investment.

Internal Rate of Return (r)

The internal rate of return refers to the rate of discount that, when applied to the future cash flows, will equate their sum to the cost of the assets. It is the discount rate that makes the present value equal to the cost. It is given by the following formula:

$$C = \frac{R_1}{1 + r} + \frac{R_2}{(1 + r)^2} + \cdots + \frac{R_n}{(1 + r)^n} + \frac{S}{(1 + r)^n}$$

where

$$r = \text{internal rate of return}$$
$$R_1, R_2, \ldots, R_n = \text{cash inflow after taxes in years } 1, 2, \ldots, n$$
$$n = \text{life of association}$$
$$S = \text{salvage value}$$
$$C = \text{cost}$$

After the internal rate of return on the investment has been calculated, it is compared with the cost of the capital to be invested. If the return is greater than the cost, the purchase is economically sound, because the expected return is greater than the return that could be obtained from the invested capital in alternative uses. This approach again requires that estimates be made of future returns and the estimated life of the equipment. The limitations in accurately making these determinations have already been presented.

Return on Assets

The projected savings resulting from the purchase can be related to the amount of money invested. Simply stated, this ratio is:

$$\frac{\text{Present Value of Savings}}{\text{Dollar Investment}} \times 100$$

[16] "Case Study: How Much to Pay for a Business or Any Capital Investment," *Business Owner* (January 1990), pp. 12–13.

The result is an estimate of the proposed equipment's profitability that can be compared to alternative investments.

Current liabilities are sometimes deducted because they are a normal source of short-term funds for any business and are not considered a part of the investment base by some managements.

This approach is subject to all the conceptual difficulties already mentioned: estimated life of equipment, estimated future returns, and so forth. However, it is a simple approach and does allow comparisons of alternate investment possibilities.

Illustrative Problems

Payback. Angus decides on payback as a proper decision method for new capital equipment he has to buy. Three bids came in on the equipment, all the same at $15,000. Suppliers made rough estimates of salvage value: $2000 after 5 years, $2300 after 7 years, and $1900 after 8 years. The finance department calculate cash flow amounting to $19,500 for each machine over their economic life. Which should he purchase?

$$\text{Payback} = \frac{\text{Investment} - \text{Salvage Value (if any)}}{\text{Profit/year}}$$

$$\frac{\$15,000 - \$2,000}{\$19,500/\,5} = 3.33 \text{ years}$$

$$\frac{\$15,000 - \$2,300}{\$19,500/\,7} = 4.56 \text{ years}$$

$$\frac{\$15,000 - \$1,900}{\$19,500/\,8} = 5.37 \text{ years}$$

Internal Rate of Return. Angus considers investing $89,000 in a new project using the new machine. Only an internal rate of return of 9 percent or better will pass his company's test. After two years the worth of the project will amount to $100,000, Angus believes. What internal rate of return will this investment generate? (Omit salvage)

$$\text{Initial Investment} = \text{Present Value of the future cash flows}$$

$$\$89,000 = \$100,000 / (1 + i)^2$$

$$= 0.05999 \text{ or about 6 percent, which shortfalls the company policy.}$$

$$\text{Net Present Value} = \$89,000/2 \text{ years} = \$44,500 \text{ per year.}$$

$$\$44,500 (1 + 0.09) = \$48,505 \text{ first year}$$

$$\$48,505 (1 + 0.09) = \$52,870 \text{ second year, net present value}$$

$$\text{Return on Asset} = \$52,870 \times 100 / 89,000 = 59.405 \text{ percent.}$$

Guaranteed Maintenance (Life Cycle Costing)

Because capital equipment costs large sums of money and is used for a long period of time, purchases are capitalized and depreciated over a period of years. Usually alternative pieces of equipment are available with differing projected lives, different features, and varying prices. The concept of life-cycle costing was developed to provide comparable evaluation of these alternatives.[17] The total costs of all alternative pieces of equipment for their entire projected life are estimated and compared. Included is the initial cost plus the cost of maintenance and service during the projected lives.

This type of evaluation has been considered the prompting force leading to the development of guaranteed maintenance contracts, which place the responsibility for servicing and maintaining equipment, during a predetermined life cycle, with the manufacturer or seller. The seller establishes the price quotation as a composite of the original cost of the equipment and the cost of maintaining it.

A price for equipment that is based on guaranteed maintenance makes alternative pieces of equipment easier to compare. It has the further advantage of bringing into consideration all the costs of equipment, both ownership and maintenance.

Limitations of Formula Analysis

A wide variety of economic analysis techniques are available to evaluate the alternatives in equipment purchases. This chapter has presented a few of the basic approaches to acquaint the reader with the techniques and provide a

---

[17] Leenders, Fearon, and England, *Purchasing and Materials Management* (Homewood, IL: Richard D. Irwin, 1989), p. 554.

departure point for future study. There are many refined approaches available; to be useful, they must be tailored to the needs of individual companies.

It is well to keep in mind the following points in evaluating any replacement formula. The comparisons that are made must be reasonable; for example, a formula that compares the performance of new and old machines over the estimated life period of the new machine is unreasonable because the old machines will probably not last that long.

The obsolescence factor of an old machine can usually be estimated, but it is difficult to establish the future obsolescence of a new machine. To some extent the same is true of salvage values. However, both of these factors may be included as inputs of a formula approach.

Sometimes replacement analyses are made on the assumption that the services rendered by the new and the old machine are identical or that the quality of the output of the two machines is the same. This frequently is not the case, and minor differences can be expected. The problem is one of assigning a dollar value to such differences.

The validity of any formula or computed approach to equipment analysis is directly related to the accuracy of the inputs. Many of these inputs are difficult if not impossible to estimate. Therefore, the calculated results must also be tempered by subjective analysis.

CHAPTER SUMMARY

Acquiring and disposing of equipment challenges purchasing personnel in a number of ways. It brings them in contact with major production executives and accountants of their own firm and the fabricators. It introduces buyers to the big league of negotiating practice. It calls into question whether used equipment would substitute well. It presents the possibility of leasing instead of buying. Finally, it focuses on economic analysis of alternative equipment and alternative methods of acquiring the equipment.

Discussion Questions

1. Discuss the ways in which the purchase of capital equipment differs from other types of purchases.
2. What are the advantages of maintaining an equipment record?
3. What are the advantages of purchasing new equipment?
4. Discuss the difficulties of purchasing used equipment?

5. What are the advantages to the lessee in leasing equipment?
6. Why has leasing not made much headway in the machine tool field?
7. Discuss the various means of financing major equipment purchases.
8. What are the means available for the disposal of used equipment?

9. Discuss the payback approach to analyzing the purchase of equipment.

10. Describe the life-cycle costing concept.

11. Describe the four types of leasing companies—full service, finance, captive, and bank participation.

Suggested Cases

=17

Value Analysis

Doesn't anyone around here care what things cost? (Larry Miles, 1947)

According to Polaroid Corporation, purchasing's most important contribution to a firm's bottom line consists in finding the lowest all-in cost. The film and instant camera firm avoids ongoing costs and saves by:

1. Monthly reviews of suppliers
2. Guidelines around overshipments or undershipments
3. Coordination with suppliers to direct-ship exact-order quantities
4. Statistical quality control
5. Coordination with suppliers on substitute materials

To stay competitive, Polaroid maintains a constant emphasis on reducing costs while maintaining high quality by strengthening its use of supplier partnerships to assure consistent quality and delivery.

CHAPTER CONTENTS

With a world war raging and many materials in short supply, Larry Miles had a hunch that substitute materials would not only save money for his company, General Electric. They would provide better quality as well. His hunch launched value analysis.[1]

The analysis of the value of purchases is a basic and continuing part of the process of professional buying. However, because of the many facets of the buying process, the responsibility for specialized concentration on and analysis of value has evolved as a separate and distinct entity, engaging not only purchasing but also the related departments responsible for specifying, testing, and using purchased products.

Because of the high cost of purchased items, value analysis initially applied as a part of the purchasing function. In this context, the objective of value analysis is to find lower cost alternative ways of performing the functions of currently purchased items.[2] However, value analysis' scope now ranges far beyond the purchasing function.

DEFINITION

Value analysis is the organized, systematic study of the function of a material, part, component, or system to identify areas of unnecessary cost. It begins with the question, *What is this item worth?* and proceeds to an analysis of value in terms of the function the item performs. For example, the function of a fastener is to join two or more parts. Value analysis compares the alternative methods of joining parts, such as welding, taping, stapling, or gluing, in view of the stresses and vibrations to which the means of fastening is subjected in a specific application.

The definition of a function is as simple and brief as possible, such as "indicates temperature" or "controls humidity." Once the function has been determined, the appropriateness and cost of the possible alternatives are considered.

Value analysis therefore consists of (1) analyzing the function, (2) considering designs to accomplish this function, and (3) analyzing the costs of alternatives. In practice, value engineering is sometimes part of the design analysis phase of value analysis.

---

[1] "Better Value, Bigger Profits," *Purchasing* (June 8, 1989), p. 58.
[2] Donald W. Fogarty, John H. Blackstone, Jr., and Thomas R. Hoffmann, *Production and Inventory Management,* 2nd ed. (Cincinnati: South-Western Publishing Company, 1991), p. 504.

HISTORY

Organized value analysis can be traced to the late 1940s, when the ending of wage and price controls brought in a substantial escalation of prices. Although its development is generally credited to efforts at General Electric and the Ford Motor Company, purchasing professionals throughout the country were critically examining functional alternatives and supplier alternatives as a means of combating rising prices. These procedures had always been followed by alert buyers, but now value analysis came to center on a special use of a part. This would assure that performance, as contrasted to the part itself, receives adequate attention, and would allow the regular buyers to concentrate on such operational responsibilities as vendor selection and price negotiations. Today, value analysis is practiced by most organizations.

General Electric's approach under Larry Miles' guidance took the form of the famous Tests for Value, in part as follows:[3]

Does use of material, part, or process contribute value?

Is cost proportionate to its usefulness?

Do we need all the features?

Can a usable part be made by a lower-cost method?

Is anyone buying it for less?

PURPOSE

The purpose of value analysis is to bring together periodically the combined talents of purchasing and its vendors as well as engineering, production, and other operating personnel to review the components and materials used by the organization on products or processes already in place. It is intended to provide a means of considering all possible alternatives in an atmosphere of open thinking and analysis.

Value analysis recognizes the fact that new production techniques and materials are continually being developed and need to be considered as possible means of redesigning existing products. It also recognizes the fact that earlier design decisions must be evaluated after the products have been used by customers. Evaluators may suggest revisions of components, an entirely different method of manufacture (e.g., casting versus forging), a new material (e.g., rubber versus copper), or eliminating the component altogether and regrouping other components.

[3] "The VA Payoff: Greater than Ever," *Purchasing World* (February 1989), p. 22.

Value analysis (VA) has mutated into value engineering (VE) and more broadly into value management (VM). Conducted in the product design/development stage before making the product, value engineering evaluates a product or service by defining its ultimate function to the customer. It then goes on to examine the processes and technology that produce the product or service. The 33 countries that now use value engineering reinforce the value of VE as a management tool.[4]

Value management organizes the steps of identifying and eliminating unnecessary costs to provide the required function at the lowest cost. The Department of Public Works Canada and Correctional Services Canada have implemented the concept, as have a small group of United Kingdom construction contractors and consultancy firms.[5]

The current U.S. construction environment can save between 5 percent and 25 percent on construction costs when managers apply value engineering properly. It takes cooperation among the project owner, designer, and constructor to create a project that functions more effectively. It also requires recognizing that cost-cutting measures have little to do with assuring value. Truly, value engineering's goal remains concise: to find a better way to accomplish something for less.[6]

APPROACHES TO VALUE ANALYSIS

Organization

The typical organizational approach to value analysis involves two main areas for research—product improvement and new product design (the latter was previously called value engineering). The typical value analysis program is operated at a decentralized division or plant level, not under centralized control from corporate headquarters. Local control allows value analysis efforts to focus on the projects with the most likelihood of significant results. Depending on individual company differences, there are four basic ways of establishing a group to do value analysis.

1. Choosing personnel from interested departments to form a committee to discuss value considerations.

---

[4] "Value Analysis Evolves into Value Management," *Purchasing World* (February 1990), pp. 32–38.
[5] "Organizational Responses of Public Sector Clients in Canada to the Implementation of Value Management: Lessons for the UK Construction Industry," *Construction Management & Economics (UK)* (Autumn 1989), pp. 203–216.
[6] "Value Engineering: Searching for a Better Buy," *Engineering News Record* (March 15, 1990), pp. 32–36.

2. Establishing a permanent staff group to support line purchasing.

3. Training operating personnel to be conscious of value analysis opportunities.

4. Setting up a quality circle program.

Value engineering works as a kind of preproduction value analysis. It applies end-product principles at the design and manufacturing stages, basic value analysis principles that initially applied to purchased products.[7]

Philips Industries Inc. manufactures components for the residential, commercial, and industrial building industries. The company enjoys product enhancement, growth in market share, cost reduction, and profit improvement from implementing value analysis and value engineering.[8] Philip's successful value analysis program has the commitment and active support of management at all levels. The firm uses VA/VE teams or committees made up of members from different disciplines for all its projects.

Committee.   A committee is most often used by companies practicing value analysis. Usually a coordinator is appointed to direct the efforts of a four- to eight-person team. The team is usually composed of representatives from the following departments: purchasing, manufacturing, engineering, quality control accounting, and marketing. On important value analysis projects, the departmental operating personnel make investigations in cooperation with their committee member. Results of an investigation are presented to the value analysis committee by the department member.

The most serious weakness in the committee arrangement is the difficulty in reaching decisions. Departmental self-interest or a lack of vigorous leadership by the coordinator may stand in the way, or perhaps no one accepts personal responsibility for a joint decision. A related difficulty is the problem of implementation in the fact of operating personnel's resistance to change. These defects can be partially overcome by a strong coordinator. Therefore, although the committee approach is a simple and inexpensive method of implementing value analysis, the committee may be limited in its ability to reach decisions and put them into action. The most effective committees are usually supported by a small permanent staff, which prepares data for discussion and follows up on committee decisions.

Permanent Specialized Staff.   A highly trained staff assigned to the purchasing department is another widely used type of organization for value analysis. Most large organizations use this approach. In this form of organi-

---

[7] "The VA Payoff: Greater than Ever," *Purchasing World* (February 1989), pp. 20–23.
[8] Ibid.

zation the staff members concentrate on the research aspect of value analysis while regular purchasing personnel perform the operational functions.

Relating staff specialists to the operating personnel is the key to successful functioning of this form of value analysis program. Of necessity, the staff will participate in studies that involve purchasing procedures. The problem is to determine the respective authorities of the staff and the regular purchasing personnel. If the staff analyst is given too much authority over operating matters, a feeling of inferiority may undermine the operating personnel.

Cooperation can best be assured by putting value analysis investigations on an advisory basis and encouraging line personnel to implement the findings on their own initiative. If a firm is organized into divisions, completed value studies can be turned over to the division manager, who is given responsibility for seeing that the division complies with recommended changes. Staff personnel also secure the cooperation of department personnel and encourage them to accept recommendations by providing them with information. They keep department personnel up to date on prices, new products and fabrication methods, as well as suggested design procedures to reduce cost.

Staff Training. The third way of installing a value analysis program is to instill an awareness and appreciation of value analysis principles within the existing organizational structure. It is hoped that an understanding of the concept and its techniques by the personnel who purchase, specify, and use production materials will encourage them to employ value analysis in their day-to-day routines. Most companies using this approach do not have a value analysis staff but rely on personnel performing each function to conduct regular value analysis sessions. On occasion, outside consultants may be employed to introduce recent advances and to act as a source of outside stimulus. Although the content of value analysis training programs varies according to a firm's needs, such programs generally provide information regarding techniques, cases illustrating successful cost-reduction applications, and recognition to individuals who have been responsible for successful projects, as well as fostering a cost-reduction attitude and a cooperative approach to value analysis.

In sum, the staff training approach is an attempt to make the objective critical thinking used in value analysis a continuing part of operating personnel practices.

Quality Circles. Borrowed from the Japanese, the quality circle is a process for involving all workers in the work environment, including the operational and decision-making processes. A quality circle is a group of workers who have volunteered for work improvement projects. These projects may tackle a range of problems, from improving worker morale to design of the production process. The groups are generally made up only of workers and their immediate supervisors, but they receive technical assistance from company engineers or other departments when needed.

Originally, the concept was used primarily at the operational, factory level where the focus was on improving quality through worker participation.

The worker involvement aspect of the quality circle has been applied to purchasing personnel as they participate in the value analysis program, particularly when the staff training approach is used. The infusion of objective, uninhibited thinking about the design, cost, and improvement of production materials through training may make purchasing personnel able to carry out the corollary of the Japanese quality circle, "progressive management."

PROCEDURES AND TECHNIQUES

The specific procedures and techniques for determining the value of a given component's function to the total assembly vary with the type of organization approach used. However, all approaches usually include (1) a design analysis of the total assembly, (2) a panel board component analysis, (3) a review of other organizations' similar experiences, (4) a brainstorming session, (5) a cost–price functional analysis, (6) supplier review and inputs, and (7) a conclusion and report.

As indicated earlier, the basic question asked in value analysis is *What is this part worth?* To answer this question, the evaluator relates function to price. Continuing with the earlier example, two pieces can be fastened together by welding, taping, stapling, or gluing. The most desirable alternative for a given application depends on the intended use of the product and the attendant conditions of use. The best product is the one that will perform satisfactorily at the lowest cost. In the value analysis process, substitutions, consolidations, eliminations, simplification, and standardization obviously are considered. The following discussion examines some of the value analysis procedures.

Design Analysis

As a starting point for value analysis, the total functional product and its components must be visualized. A panel board assembly is often used to mount each component adjacent to its mating part. Such an exploded* assembly often provides the first opportunity to view each component objectively in relation to the function it performs. During initial design and development, components are often developed by designers working individually. Now a value analysis team, made up of employees from different departments, view each of the subassemblies in relation to one another and to the total product.

Panel Board Component Analysis

With the panel board as the basic point of reference, the value analysis procedure usually starts with a detailed checklist to make certain that every pertinent question is asked about each component. Checklists vary in details, but their basic purpose is to assure that a careful investigation is made. The following questions are indicative of those included in such checklists.

1. What is the precise function of the item?
2. Can the item be eliminated?
3. If the item is not standard, can a standard item be substituted?
4. Are there any similar items used by the company that can be substituted?
5. Can the item be redesigned to allow greater tolerances?
6. Will a design change permit the item to be made from a lower-cost process or material?
7. Could the item be produced within the firm at less cost?
8. Are the finishing requirements greater than necessary?
9. If different sizes of the item are stocked, can some of these be combined to reduce inventory and take advantage of quantity buying?
10. Is there difficulty in obtaining the part at present?
11. Are there ways of economizing in packing or shipping techniques?

Other Organizations' Experiences

Potential problems may arise. The original designers of a product or process may resent greatly the intrusion of a value analysis team that works on ''their'' project without the time or budget pressures that the originators faced. However, pressure to get the product produced may build again to the

---

* A term used to denote the breaking apart and pictorial display, for analytical purposes, of all an item's individual elements.

point that insufficient time remains to incorporate design changes that value analysis conceived.[9]

At Danbury (Connecticut) Hospital, value analysis figured heavily in reducing product costs by more than $360,000 annually and freeing an additional $616,820 from funds formerly tied up in inventory. A representative of Medline Industries introduced consignment purchasing to the hospital. The hospital selected 100 inventory products for value analysis and invited prime vendors to develop procedures comparable to the Medline sample consignment program. As a consequence of the overwhelming response, the purchasing department buys 85 percent of the hospital's supplies on consignment.[10]

Value analysis has served since the early 1960s as Mazda's "secret weapon" for reducing costs. It has transformed the automobile maker from one of the highest cost to one of the lowest cost auto producers in Japan. In Flat Rock, Michigan, Mazda speaks of value analysis as the most practical tool yet devised for finding and eliminating all of the unnecessary factors that contribute to product cost. Suppliers in one year contributed a total of 926 VA ideas; Mazda engineers accepted 268 of them and split savings 50–50 with suppliers.[11]

Brainstorming

The BBDO advertising agency developed brainstorming in the 1920s to generate ideas for advertising campaigns. In the creative phase, members contribute whatever ideas pop into their heads. This free-wheeling, often humorous, stream of ideas provokes other ideas that may lay hidden behind inhibition. Finally, the judicial phase takes the creative ideas through rigorous examination—appropriateness, cost, benefit, ease of implementing, and practicality. The results may mean better, simpler, and more functional designs and methods, from the contributions of value analysis.

3M company provides an environment that not only welcomes but protects creativity in its research laboratories. The company encourages creativity through entrepreneurial policies and procedures that provide budget latitude in the expenditure of time and money toward new ideas.

For positive results, the value analysis task group should feel free to work on various studies and experiments with relatively free rein.[12]

---

[9] Jay Heizer and Barry Render, *Production and Operations Management: Strategies and Tactics* (Boston: Allyn & Bacon, 1988), p. 263.

[10] "Looking Back at Danbury Hospital: A Multiproduct Program Continues to Produce Dramatic Savings for a Hospital on 85 Percent Consignment," *Hospital Materiel Management Quarterly* (August 1991), pp. 56–61.

[11] "Using VA to Drive Out Costs," *Purchasing* (June 6, 1991), pp. 56–59.

[12] Fogarty et al., p. 506.

Cost Price Functional Analysis

Although cost is related to all phases of value analysis procedures, it is advisable to include an intensive price analysis as a distinct phase of the procedure. Essentially the questions to be asked are: (1) *Under optimal conditions, what is the cost to the producer of the item being purchased?* and (2) *In view of this estimated cost, how much is the functional value to our organization?* The cost of producing the item is established on the assumption that the supplier is thoroughly efficient, equipped with modern facilities, and allowed to make a reasonable return on its investment.

Price analysis must include a thorough study of methods of manufacture as well as prevailing business conditions. Factors such as the following must be considered to arrive at a realistic figure.

1. Industry wage rates
2. Rates of operation of suppliers
3. Excess capacity and its effect on overhead costs
4. Amount of engineering services required
5. Managerial skill and capability required
6. Degree of competition in the industry
7. Rates of profit in the industry
8. Age and condition of industry facilities
9. Changes in productivity and methods of manufacture that may reduce cost

If the conclusion of the price analysis study is that the price being asked for the item is too high, the company may decide to make the item instead of buying it. In other circumstances the company may decide that it would be preferable to show the supplier how the item might be profitably produced at a lower price. Organizations that have expert engineering and administrative talent often find it possible to counsel smaller suppliers to the advantage of both parties.

Supplier Review and Inputs

Most value analysis groups enlist the support of present and potential vendors during the evaluation process. Vendors are often in a position to give technical assistance in their areas of specialized competence.

In one instance, a supplier had a suggestion for improving a small rubber bumper, used on crop choppers and harvesters, to cushion the shock of a roll coming back on a hard surface. It was proposed that urethane be used instead of neoprene to make the bumper. Although the initial price went up 15 percent, the service life of the part increased by 400 percent.

Figures 17-1 and 17-2 illustrate forms for eliciting a vendor's suggestion on specifications, materials, use of substitute parts, and standardization, to name a few elements.

Digital Equipment Corporation's president states that getting a product to market on time serves as the most important factor in determining a product's ultimate profitability. NCR's vice president for purchasing asserts further that the chances of bringing innovative solutions to the marketplace depend on suppliers. By integrating suppliers so thoroughly into the product development and production process, they become, in effect, extensions of the original equipment manufacturer's internal activities.[13]

Manufacturing competitiveness must begin with product design, declares an Institute for Competitive Design spokesperson. He further states that eliminating or simplifying the process at the early design stage prescribes the cure for poor-quality manufacturing process on the factory floor.[14] Value analysis/value engineering/value management contribute to the method.

Purchasing magazine's special projects editor predicts that in the 1990s value analysis will occupy a part of the product planning stage. He warns that value analysis becomes a tool only when a dedicated supplier base supports the firm's value analysis efforts.[15]

The following checklist sums up what buyers will need to concentrate on in building supplier support for value analysis:[16]

1. Make sure that suppliers understand the principles.
2. Provide suppliers with the means to update their knowledge of value analysis techniques and how to apply them to the firm's products.
3. Authenticate the buyer's interest in value analysis and make it apparent to suppliers.
4. Make it easy for suppliers to submit value analysis ideas.
5. Prompt suppliers with ways they can help.
6. Include suppliers in make-or-buy discussions.
7. Assign value analysis projects to promising suppliers.
8. Recognize the limits of supplier expertise.
9. Rate suppliers on value analysis contributions.
10. Give adequate rewards for value analysis help.

[13] "Design 1990: Quality Alone Isn't Enough," *Purchasing* (February 8, 1990), pp. 46–51.
[14] Ibid.
[15] "Can Your Suppliers Meet Your Value Analysis Needs?" *Purchasing* (June 8, 1989), p. 17.
[16] Ibid.

REQUEST FOR QUOTE ADDENDUM   ANDREA RADIO CORPORATION

IMPORTANT! In order for your quote to be considered, this form MUST BE COMPLETED and returned with your quotation.

ANDREA PART NUMBER

SUBJECT: VENDOR VALUE ENGINEERING

We are Value Engineering all items used in the manufacture of our products; therefore, you are requested to supply the following information. Please give full consideration to known factors so that your suggestions will not adversely affect the function or reliability of this item.

QUESTION	YES/NO	BRIEF DESCRIPTION OF SUGGESTION	Approximate savings if suggestion is approved
1. Would a relaxation of any tolerances result in lower manufacturing costs?			
2. Can you suggest any design changes that will lower the cost of the item?			
3. Is there any part of this item that can be produced as a casting, forging, or extrusion, in lieu of machining?			
4. Can you suggest any material substitute?			
5. Are there any finish requirements that could be eliminated, or relaxed?			

FIGURE 17-1. A supplier cost-reduction checklist form.

6. Are there any test or qualification requirements that appear unnecessary?		
7. Have you any other suggestions which might save weight, simplify the part, or reduce the cost?		
8. Do you have a standard item that can be satisfactorily substituted for this part? What is it? _____ What does it cost? _____ Is it qualified? _____ What would qualification test cost? _____		

Are you willing to attend a meeting at Andrea to discuss your ideas, if requested?   Yes
                                                                                     No

The above information submitted by

Very truly yours,   Company name

                                     Signature

P. SAUNDERSON, Director of Purchases   Date

FIGURE 17-1. Continued

NEW HOLLAND DIV. OF SPERRY RAND CORP. NEW HOLLAND, PA. 17557	SUPPLIER CHECK LIST FOR VALUE ANALYSIS STUDY

N. H. part name and number_____

Buyer _____

In order to assure the functional usefulness of the above part, we solicit your help through answers to the following questions:

QUESTIONS	CHECK		SUGGESTIONS
	Yes	No	
1. Do you understand part function?			
2. Could costs be reduced by relaxing requirements: Tolerances? Finishes? Testing? By how much?_____			
3. Could costs be reduced thru changes in: Material? Ordering Quantities? The use of castings, forgings, stampings, etc.? By how much?_____			
4. Can you suggest any other changes that would: Reduce weight? Simplify the part? Reduce overall costs? By how much?_____			
5. Do you feel that any of the specifications are too stringent?			
6. How can we help alleviate your greatest element of cost in supplying this part?			
7. Do you have a standard item that could be substituted for this part?			What is it?_____ What does it cost?_____
8. Other suggestions?			

SUPPLIER: ADDRESS:

SIGNATURE   TITLE   DATE

* If "No," functional information can be obtained from Buyer involved.

FIGURE 17-2. A form requesting supplier assistance in value analysis.

Procedural Model of Value Analysis

As a help in understanding the overall process of value analysis, one can look at the procedural model shown in Figure 17-3.

Reporting

The teamwork that is needed for value analysis to be successful presents a significant political problem when the results are to be reported to management and corresponding credit is to be given. If results are credited to the group rather than to individuals, morale and subsequent performance is likely to benefit. However, when a major individual effort has brought about substantial savings, the group should obviously take secondary credit.

Most organizations attempt both to recognize outstanding individual accomplishments and to provide merit recognition to all group members. Singling out these individuals to their satisfaction while still maintaining

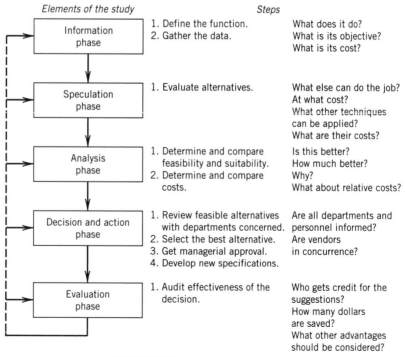

FIGURE 17-3. The value analysis process.

group momentum and morale is one of the most significant determinants to whether a value analysis program will be successful in the future.

When suppliers' contributions to value analysis sessions produce significant cost reduction and savings, the reward system is quite simple. Most organizations channel additional volume to the contributing supplier as a reward. Very few suppliers are ever granted specific cash rewards.

In addition to the concerns of recognition, value analysis reporting must consider the definition of savings. A suggested policy in this regard would include:

1. Any added costs of effecting a cost reduction must be deducted from this reduction.
2. Reductions in costs cannot be claimed retroactively.
3. Change in materials or processes must produce savings that can be measured with reasonable accuracy.
4. The existing materials or processes must have been acceptable or in use at the time the change is made.
5. All reductions in costs are subject to a complete audit.

EXAMPLES OF SAVINGS RESULTING FROM VALUE ANALYSIS

The literature abounds with examples of cost reduction and consequent savings attributed to value analysis. *Purchasing* magazine annually devotes the majority of one issue to value analysis concerns and has made an annual value analysis contest winner award since 1977. The following are a few examples of cost reductions made possible by value analysis programs.

Packaging

Packaging consumption naturally reflects industrial activity.[17] Value analysis can be used to change packaging and shipping, as an old but still relevant account illustrates. Certain delicate equipment was fixed to undergo a complicated packing procedure before it could be shipped out. With the original method of packing, the piece of equipment was bolted to a plywood board, steel-strapped, put on a rebonded urethane foam cushion, and wrapped in a triple-walled inner pack. This entire assembly was then placed in a corrugated carton, covered with a layer of polystyrene, and sealed. With the assistance of a supplier, a value analysis program was conducted, and a

---

[17] "1990 Packaging Outlook: Savings Are in the Cards," *Purchasing* (February 22, 1990), pp. 50–52.

form-in-place installation process was devised. Semigrid polyurethane cushions are molded in the plant, and the entire process—including production of the cushions. insertion of the equipment into the carton, and sealing—takes five minutes (see Figure 17-4). This represents an 80 percent saving in labor time. In addition, the cost of the pack has been reduced from $10.00 to $2.74 per unit. Other benefits include a 95 percent reduction in the space required for shipping material in inventory.[18]

Another example of how value analysis has been successfully applied to packaging is provided by the Holley Carburetor Division of Colt Industries. The company was having test problems with its carburetors, which were showing up in the final testing stage with blocked ports, as indicated at step 6 of Figure 17-5. Investigation showed that fine particles, which were rubbing off the cardboard shipping containers in which Holley received its initial castings from outside foundries, were causing the problem.

A value analysis team was assigned to the problem and came up with an answer that not only solved the inspection problem but also saved money. The team's solution was to unpack the castings from the cardboard boxes after their initial cleaning and place them in large wire baskets. The effect of this seemingly simple procedure was to cut the inspection rejection rate to under 1 percent, eliminate five steps in the materials handling process at the plant, and save approximately $100,000 per year in packaging costs.[19]

Raw Materials

There are many accounts of finding, through value analysis, lower-priced raw materials that can be substituted for those being used without sacrifice of quality.

The total costs of an air shutoff valve disk used in sewage aeration tanks were reduced by 88 percent by switching from cast bronze to molded plastic. A value analysis study began by brainstorming alternatives to the bronze valve. Using plastic allowed the mold to provide the hub threads and a fine finish. Then, as an additional bonus, the plastic supplier suggested changing to a molded-in wave design instead of the former cast straight-rib design, which provided equal strength with thinner material. The molded parts cost $0.97 each, compared to a per-unit cost of $5.66 for the formerly cast parts. The eliminated machining cost per unit was $2.30.[20]

Another example of savings on raw materials was the substitution of

---

[18] "A Better Package Can Cost Less, Too" (VA/VI Ideas Section), *Purchasing* (March 28, 1979), pp. 89–90.

[19] "Tisket a Tasket," *Purchasing* (March 29, 1984), pp. 133–136.

[20] "Shift to Plastic Saves Machining" (VA/VI Contest Winners), *Purchasing* (March 29, 1978), p. 163.

FIGURE 17-4. An example of value analysis applied to packaging. (*Source:* Reprinted from "A Better Package Can Cost Less Too," (VA/VI Idea Section), *Purchasing* (March 28, 1979), pp. 89–90. Copyright © 1979, by Cahners Publishing Company.)

plastic for glass made by Duncan Enterprises of Fresno, California.[21] Duncan is a manufacturer of paint for hobbyists, the type commonly used for painting model cars and airplanes. The move was not cut and dried, however, and the value analysis team looked at two alternatives. The first requirement was that the jars look the same as the glass jars formerly used. This point was insisted on by marketing. Second, Duncan wanted to gener-

[21] "A Tale of Two Jars," *Purchasing* (March 29, 1984), p. 143.

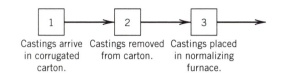

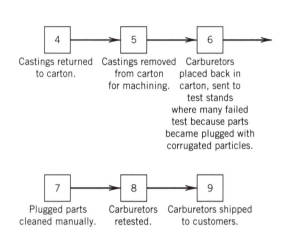

Solution: Switch to wire mesh containers, eliminating materials handling
steps 2, 4, 5, 6, 7, and 8.

FIGURE 17-5. The steps at the Holley plant for machining, testing, and shipping carburetors.

ate some type of freight savings, since the company paid freight on all
shipments and shipped over seven million jars per year. The choices narrowed down to two plastics that could fit the requirements: solid polypropylene and foamed polypropylene.

The first choice was to go with the foamed polypropylene since the air
present in the material made it lighter, taking one entire gram off the weight
of the jar. However, this decision was reversed when the team began to
investigate the costs of the materials required. Material costs represented
over 50 percent of the total cost of the jar.

The value analysis team decided that if the walls of the jar could be
made thinner, material could be saved without sacrificing the functionality
of the jar. However, the foamed plastic supplier said that the reduction
would require substantial retooling of the production facilities. The value
analysis team then turned to Owens-Illinois, which was able to manufacture
the thinner-wall jars in solid polypropylene in half the time it took to make
the foamed jars. The end result of the change from glass to plastic jars was

to save $85,000 per year on materials, *after* an initial 18-month payback period for tooling costs, and $2000 per year on freight (see Figure 17-6).

Production Parts

Savings in production parts and fittings are illustrated in the following example. One company producing gas igniters instituted a value analysis study to refine the design of the igniter shield. The old shield had been produced in two identical halves on progressive die-stamping machines; the two parts were then welded together, and the igniter was inserted into the shield and welded closed. A radical design change was proposed, fabricating a one-piece shield on a multislide stamping machine. This completely eliminated any need for welding, as the igniter would be held in place by the spring tension in the shield. The new design used approximately half as much material as the original shield, and the supplier was able to produce in one week what formerly took a month. The total savings was $324,630, with even greater savings projected.[22]

The Society of American Value Engineers defines value engineering in these terms:

> Value Engineering is the systematic application of recognized techniques which identify the function of a product or service, establish a monetary value for that function, and provide the necessary function reliably at the lowest overall cost.[23]

The following examples illustrate the nature of value engineering in solving specific problems:

A clear plastic report binder provides a fully visible cover page without overprinting or pasting labels on the binder's cover. Regular binders cost at the time 79 cents in minimum lots of 5000 binders; a year's supply averaged 4000 binders. The alternate see-through binder, 13 cents each, no minimum, provided protection and provided cover-letter advertising, the two functions that users sought.[24]

A U.S. machine manufacturer wanted to ship 16 large machines to Great Britain. Each machine weighed 28,000 pounds. Special crating, loading, and unloading six times would cost $3500 for each machine. Competitive bids from land–sea container services solved the problem at a cost of $1550 per unit, a 55 percent savings.[25]

Buying distilled water in returnable carboys became a fixed plant prac-

---

[22] "Igniter Shield Proves Hot Item for VA Team," *Purchasing* (March 28, 1979), p. 117.
[23] Arthur E. Mudge, *Value Engineering: A Systematic Approach* (New York: McGraw-Hill, 1971), p. 5.
[24] Ibid., pp. 267–268.
[25] Ibid., p. 279.

Foamed
polypropylene
jar

Solid
polypropylene
jar

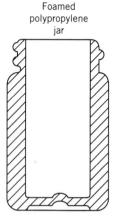 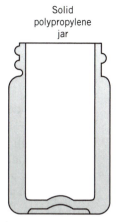

Savings of $85,000 per year over
glass after 18-month payback
period for tooling (includes
raw material costs and freight
savings resulting from lighter
weight of plastic jar). Current
cost for 7-million jars:
$314,000.

Solid polypropylene jar could
be molded with thinner walls
in half the cycle time required
to mold the foamed plastic.
Cost to make 7-million jars:
$253,000. Lighter jar also nets
freight savings of
over $2000 per year.

FIGURE 17-6. A comparison of the costs and the savings in costs of using foamed polypropylene and solid polypropylene for paint jars. (*Source:* ''A Tale of Two Jars,'' *Purchasing* (March 29, 1984), p. 143. Copyright © 1984, by Cahners Publishing Company.)

tice for use in electric trucks and in blueprint and photographic laboratory equipment. Then someone asked, ''How pure does the water have to be for use in industrial batteries?'' No one knew the answer. So the cost improvement team contacted a battery company in Boston. The battery company advised that the local plant water tested quite pure; the blueprint and photographic laboratory equipment supplier said the same. The plant stopped buying distilled water; annual savings, $250.[26]

These examples vary in dollar savings and simplicity. However, they serve to show how improvements may spring from very little investigation and no implementation cost. The firm needs a continuing improvement-minded attitude.

Toyota prepares for the twenty-first century, producing customized products quickly in short runs. It uses a flexible press system that consists of three major processes:[27]

---

[26] Ibid., p. 280.
[27] ''VA Case Histories—Toyota's Flexible Press Trims Manufacturing Steps,'' *Purchasing* (June 7, 1990), pp. 110–111.

1. A newly developed liquid-pressure press-forming method. The process accurately yields quality outer hoods, front fenders, and quarter panels, with 50 percent deeper drawing and less surface deflection compared with conventional metal upper and lower dies.
2. A high-speed three-dimensional carbon dioxide laser cutter. The laser cutter quadruples "the trimming capacity: 1.5 minutes per fender in contrast to six minutes with trimming dies."
3. A multidirectional press-forming method which applies pressure simultaneously from six directions. This method provides a number of simultaneous forming processes, such as flanging and cam flanging. It has "simplified operations, enhanced product accuracy, and reduced the number of press dies required for production."

Will U.S. value analysis/value engineering/value management keep pace with Toyota's efforts?

Benefits beyond Purchasing

One of the most important reasons for the success of value analysis is the psychological attitudes it promotes. Value analysis instills an awareness of change as a way of life for an organization. Individuals on the value analysis team go into their assignments with review, objectivity, and change as their goals. Consequently, value analysis procedures allow individuals and departments to free themselves from earlier design and material specification decisions. Without a value analysis program, these same individuals and departments will often fight even needed changes to save face.

Thus, value analysis has an important psychological ingredient that contributes to its amazing success and correspondingly takes its benefits beyond the realm of professional purchasing.

SELECTED REFERENCES—OLDIES BUT GOODIES

Robert H. Clawson, *Value Engineering for Management* (Princeton: Auerbach Publishers Inc., 1970), 144 pages. Selected chapters: "Who Needs Value Engineering?," "Organizing for Value Engineering," "Applying Value Engineering," and "Communications in Value Engineering." The book stresses attitude and function thinking; for example, the Chicago, Burlington, and Quincy Railroad president said in 1967, "We're not in the railroad business; we're in the distribution business."

William D. Falcon, ed., *Value Analysis Value Engineering: The Implications for Managers* (New York: American Management Association, 1964), 128 pages. Selected chapters: "When Is a

Company Ready for Value Engineering?," "Enlisting Suppliers in a Company's Value Program," "Value Analysis as a Sales Tool," and "The Future of the Value Profession." Appendix contains specimen wording, "Value Engineering Incentive for Firm Fixed-Price Contracts."

John H. Fasal, *Practical Value Analysis Methods* (New York: Hayden 1972), 263 pages. Selected chapters: "Decision-Making Analysis," "Predictability and Probability," "Statistical Evaluation of Design," and "Organizing a Value Engineering Program." Appendices include "Typical Value Engineering Workshop Seminar Curriculum," "Typical Job Description for a Value Engineer," "Typical VA/VE Design Review Check List," and "Tally Sheets Used to Calculate Savings." The book illustrates uses of monograms, human-movement charts, gozinto charts, CPM, PERT, line-of-balance charting techniques, utility curve for rating vendors, linear programming for allocating resources, Pareto–Lorenz Maldistribution Curve for concentrating on principle elements of bidding, quality control, defect isolation, and management schedules, 2×2 factorial tests with hill climbing toward optimum value, and overstress multiple environment analysis.

David Fram, *Value Analysis: A Way to Better Products and Profits* (New York: American Management Association, 1974), 18 pages. Selected chapters: "How Extra Costs Creep in," "The Potential of Value Analysis," and "How to Get Started."

Arthur E. Mudge, *Value Engineering: A Systematic Approach* (New York: McGraw-Hill, 1971), 286 pages. Fundamentals and theory, value engineering job plan application, and cases that illustrate the VE technique.

James J. O'Brien, *Value Analysis in Design and Construction* (New York: McGraw-Hill, 1976), 301 pages. Selected chapters: "Functional Analysis," "Typical Project Cycle," "Cost Estimating," "Design Phase," "Construction Phase," and "Value Analysis in the Construction Context," Cases. Specimen wording for contracts. Public Building Service/GSA Manual references.

CHAPTER SUMMARY

Value analysis aims as a technique to find new ways to get equal or superior performance from a product or method at lower costs, while retaining quality, function, and reliability. Moreover, value analysis examines alternative ways of achieving the functions that purchased items perform. This concerted effort to meet the organization's material needs focuses on cost reduction, at the same time supporting the quality requirements for purchased products and services.

Value engineering evaluates a product or service by defining its ultimate function to the user. Its study at the preproduction stage applies the same kind of basic principles that value analysis applies to studying purchased products. Value engineering leads to alternative designs.

Value management organizes the steps of selecting projects for improvement per cost and time involved, data gathering, and analysis to eliminate unnecessary costs while still providing the required function at the lowest cost. It fashions a system in the organization and a mindset in which value analysis works. The creative brainstorming that induces new ideas typically runs into the familiar discrediting outlook expressed as ''That won't work!'' Value management's task consists of encouraging creative searches for new ways of designing, producing, and supplying the user's needs, by keeping people's minds open to new options.

Organized value analysis may use a committee approach or specialized staff or an entire workforce trained in value analysis methods. Alert purchasing managers strongly encourage vendors to use value analysis of the products or services they provide.

Discussion Questions

1. Define value analysis.
2. What are the problems in the committee approach to value analysis?
3. Describe the staff-training approach to value analysis.
4. Discuss brainstorming and its application to purchasing decisions.
5. How can a supplier become involved in a company's value analysis program?
6. What are the various ways a supplier can be rewarded for aid in value analysis?
7. What are the various policies a company can adopt to account for savings achieved through value analysis?
8. Differentiate value analysis, value engineering, and value management.

Suggested Cases

Ajax Sewing Machine Company

Gamma Corporation

Megalopolis City

MF-1

Powers Company

Warehouse Steel Company

=18

TRANSPORTATION AND TRAFFIC MANAGEMENT

Midwest Corporation's director of purchasing Bill Kenny buys railroad rails from rolling mills worldwide, acquires capital goods, purchases maintenance, repair, and operating supplies, and handles negotiations for domestic inbound shipping. He views purchasing as the critical link between suppliers and the company's customers. Purchasing plays a major part in balancing sales projections with the current demands on suppliers' capacity. Offshore buying creates concerns such as shifting exchange rates, manufacturers stifled by import quotas, and long, unstable lead times. Bill Kenny places particular importance on remote inventories, stored near suppliers' mills. What do you admire about Bill Kenny's job?*

CHAPTER CONTENTS

Source: "Professional Profile: Bill Kenny, Midwest Steel," *Purchasing* (February 21, 1991), p. 31.

America's transportation industry in the 1990s gives better service, provides closer customer relations, makes available more customized service, and exchanges more information electronically than ever before.[1] Computer-to-computer exchange of business documents between shippers, carriers, and customers occurs by electronic data interchange for 46 percent of surveyed firms. A *Traffic Management* 1500-reader survey (37 percent response) identified the six most frequent electronically exchanged information types as follows:[2]

Tracing information	52 percent
Purchase orders	43 percent
Shipping information	35 percent
Bills of lading	32 percent
Transportation rates tariffs	31 percent

Carriers implement a variety of techniques to improve their ability to keep track of freight and to communicate with customers. In addition to using EDI, they employ laser bar coding, satellite tracking, real-time computer updates, and advanced image processing.[3]

Just-in-time production methods have redefined freight carriers from a simple delivery business to the manufacturer's warehouse on wheels. As a value-added service, JIT increases transportation costs but leads to substantial savings in inventory.

The far-ranging deregulation of air, rail, and motor freight carriers has generated new challenges and opportunities for purchasing managers who buy transportation. Transportation charges represent a major cost element of materials, with estimates ranging from 10 to 20 percent of total cost, depending on the type of goods involved.[*]

Purchasing personnel must choose carefully among the alternative transportation systems—truck, rail, air, pipeline, and water. Furthermore, there are numerous rate alternatives available within a given transportation system, depending on the materials, their form, and their packaging. These alternatives are increasing as the federal government promotes competition among carriers through deregulation of the transportation industry. Certain significant legal ramifications, which influence the manner in which the

---

[1] "Quick Guide to Quick Response (and EDI)," *Chain Store Age Executive* (October 1990), pp. 8B–9B.
[2] "EDI: The Wave of the Future," *Traffic Management* (August 1989), p. 50.
[3] "Making the Grade: Truckers Think They Can," *Purchasing* (March 23, 1989), pp. 66–69, 73.
[*] The nations freight bill runs about 10 percent of the gross national product or in excess of $300 billion.

transportation terms are presented on the purchase order, must also be considered.

With the advent of the materials management form of organization, traffic has become a function of the materials department. Purchasing personnel who aspire to the position of materials manager must therefore be prepared to assume transportation responsibilities.

In the past traffic has often been neglected, and responsibility shifted to the vendor for determining traffic routes and shipping methods. This neglect was to a large extent the result of a mistaken assumption that choices were few because rates were fixed by the Interstate Commerce Commission (ICC). As previously indicated, such regulation has been substantially reduced in recent years. This chapter demonstrates the fallacy of assuming that there are few choices by presenting the methods used in setting rates, carrier freedom in determining rates, the various class and commodity rates, rates relating to shipping practices, and rates relating to commodity descriptions. The reader should gain a greater appreciation of the challenge presented by the management of transportation.

ORGANIZATION FOR TRANSPORTATION

Because of the complexities of transportation, responsibility for it is often placed in a separate department called the traffic department. This department's responsibilities generally include incoming freight, outgoing freight, and often internal plant transportation. The traffic matters of greatest concern to purchasing include:

1. Ascertaining rates
2. Selecting carriers and routings
3. Auditing freight charges and preparing claims
4. Tracing lost or overdue shipments
5. Determining cost-reduction possibilities by consolidation of shipments and the many special arrangements available from shipping concerns
6. Preparing rate evidence for hearings with the ICC and rate and service negotiations with carriers

When a firm does not have a separate traffic department, many of these transportation responsibilities fall on purchasing personnel. Even when there is a separate traffic department, purchasing often shares a portion of these responsibilities.

In the mid-1980s a *Purchasing* magazine survey revealed that 83.5

percent of the purchasing respondents actively involve themselves in their companies' transportation decision making.[4]

Partnering, discussed in Chapter 5, has a transportation industry equal; partnershipping. The partnership concept involves a buyer and carrier relationship that shares benefits and burdens over a specified time period. Chevron USA experimented with the concept in 1989. It trimmed over eight carriers serving the Los Angeles area to one. The partnership carrier lowered its rates and obtained additional business with a multiyear contract. Chevron USA simplified its operations and cut its administrative costs.[5]

Similar response appears in the small business field. A small manufacturing firm's purchase of motor carrier service constitutes a major decision. According to one study, environmental factors, such as the decision maker's multiple responsibilities and frequent less-than-truckload shipments, compose critical issues in determining motor carrier selection by small manufacturers. Motor carriers, the study concludes, should emphasize frequent pickup, time-in-transit, low number of damage claims, infrequent interlining with connecting carriers, points served, and their rates.[6]

Vendors are frequently of little assistance to purchasing personnel in obtaining economical traffic services. They will often ship in whatever manner will get the shipment out most easily. Many vendors assign the traffic function to persons who have several other duties and little expertise in traffic. Consequently, purchasing personnel should route all incoming shipments. Because the responsibility for transportation often cannot be shifted to vendors, purchasing personnel must become familiar with how traffic rates are determined, the many carrier alternatives, and related considerations, which are discussed in the following pages.

TRANSPORTATION RATE DETERMINATION

The factors that determine freight rates, the government's role in rate regulation, and the flexibility of rates are some of the least-understood areas of purchasing and traffic management. There is a tendency to view traffic as a maze of tedious facts that cannot be influenced by the individual firm. The basic principles on which freight rates are predicated are quite simple, even though their application may at times be surprising. Firms do have opportunities to influence the rates they pay.

---

[4] "The Purchasing Interface with Transportation," *Journal of Purchasing and Materials Management* (Winter 1988), pp. 21–25.

[5] "Putting Partnering and Shipping Together," *Purchasing World* (March 1990), pp. 36–42.

[6] "Purchasing Motor Carrier Service: An Investigation of the Criteria Used by Small Manufacturing Firms," *Journal of Purchasing and Materials Management* (Winter 1988), pp. 39–47.

In the days of this country's economic development, railroads played the major role in transportation. Because they had so little competition, they could and usually did follow the pricing policy of charging what the market will bear. This is still a starting point in rate making today. The what-the-market-will-bear policy is related to other variables, however, making it more tolerable; the most important of these is the degree of competition among transportation agencies available to users. In fact, charging what the market will bear is only sound as a procedure for setting the upper limit on rate determinations. For the protection of all parties, such factors as the following must also be considered.

1. The value of the product: the more valuable the item the higher its rate can be. The rate of transporting gold can be higher than that of transporting coal, partially explained by the risk involved in handling the higher-value item.

2. The cost of hauling, which in turn is related to the following:
   a. Density of product. Product density is related to the ability of the carrier to obtain complete loads. The denser a product is, the easier it is to load a carrying vehicle completely and, therefore, the lower the corresponding rate. For example, a shipment of women's hats may occupy 300 cubic inches but weigh only 1/2 pound. For rating purposes their weight is assumed to be 2 pounds.
   b. Packaging requirements. The greater the requirements, the higher the rates.
   c. Experience of past insurance claims on the commodity.
   d. Space required. Lampshades require a great deal of space and, therefore, carry relatively higher rates.
   e. Geographical factors. Considerations such as traffic density at origin and destination and the terrain between origin and destination influence costs and, therefore, rates. The distribution of the volume of traffic moving through the territory and physical considerations—for example, overhead or bridge traffic—are included.
   f. Volume of traffic moved. Quantity discounts are universally applied. The type and seasonal movement of traffic are also considered.
   g. The distances goods must be transported.
   h. Special services required, such as special connection and stopover privileges.

3. Competition, which consists of the following:

    a. Intermodal competition; that is, railroads versus trucks.
    b. Intraindustry competition; that is, number of truck lines.

4. Government regulations, including the following:
    a. The opinions of the ICC.
    b. Policies of state and federal governments with respect to the regulation of transportation.
    c. The economic policy of the carriers or government in the development of industries or regions.

5. Other considerations:
    a. The *rule of analogy.* Used for rating a product that has not been classified previously, this rule simply states that similar items should have similar rates.
    b. The mixture or combination of materials. When an article includes materials of high and low value, the rate tends to reflect the high-value component.

In summary, established freight rates reflect many variables, and charges will vary with the relative importance of the many considerations listed. List rates in more cases than not comprise just the starting points for serious negotiations. More than three out of every four queried transportation managers report paying less-than-published tariffs, discounts often running more than 30 percent.[7]

REGULATION AND DEREGULATION

The first federal regulation of interstate commerce came with the Interstate Commerce Act of 1887, which established the Interstate Commerce Commission. The initial authority of the ICC, to determine whether rates were "just and reasonable" was broadened by the Hepburn Act of 1906 to establish maximum rates for nearly all forms of rail, water, pipelines, and highway transportation, including surface freight forwarders. The Civil Aeronautics Act of 1938 assigned regulatory control of airlines to the Civil Aeronautics Board. Later legislation, the Transportation Act of 1958, extended ICC jurisdiction to rule on the reasonableness of *proposed* rates and to establish minimum as well as maximum rates. The first move toward deregulation of transportation came in 1977 when air cargo was deregulated. This allowed greater freedom of entry into the market and gave air carriers the authority to establish freight rates as long as they were not

---

[7] "Transportation Buyers Benefit," *Purchasing World* (September 1989), p. 30.

discriminatory. Airline passenger service followed the deregulation trend in 1978. The Motor Carrier Act of 1980 articulated as its goal "the promotion of competition and efficient motor transportation." That same year Congress passed the Staggers Rail Act, allowing rates to increase slightly and progressively. The Surface Transportation Assistance Act of 1982 concerns the kind of equipment that will move over the rails and highways. The industry supports the Commercial Motor Vehicle Act of 1986. Among its provisions, it outlaws the practice of drivers holding licenses from several states, a ploy that some drivers use to spread their driving violations. Most major carriers have safety departments that work to prevent highway accidents, 94 percent of which occur from driver failure by one or more drivers.[8] Further deregulation may occur.

The ICC has considerable leeway in determining whether a proposed or actual rate is reasonable, as evidenced by the vagueness of this portion of the Transportation Act of 1958. "In determining whether a rate is lower than a reasonable minimum rate," the act states, "the ICC shall consider the facts and circumstances attending the movement of the traffic by the carrier or carriers to which the rate is applicable.[9] The statutes merely state that rates must be "just and reasonable," without defining the meaning of the terms. The law also states that rates shall be uniformly applied; that is, no common carriers shall receive a greater or lesser compensation for services from one shipper than from another.

The jurisdiction of the ICC is broad and includes authority for the following regulatory actions.

1. Grant carriers operating authority, which for railroads includes constructing or abandoning lines.
2. Govern rates and determine the reasonableness of new or changed rates.
3. Authorize consolidations and mergers, and the issuance of securities of carriers.
4. Oversee accounting procedures to evaluate returns to the carriers.
5. Regulate the publication and filing of claims.
6. Prescribe and regulate insurance coverage of carriers.
7. Prescribe and regulate safety provisions to be followed by carriers.

The ICC also hears complaints of any alleged rate irregularities and, in general, is charged with enforcing the Interstate Commerce Act and succeeding statutes.

---

[8] "Trucking Industry Concerned about Safety," *Purchasing World* (August 1987), pp. 42, 44.
[9] *Interstate Commerce Act, Section 15a(3)*, as amended by the Transportation Act of 1958.

In addition to considering the variables listed earlier in evaluating rates, the ICC also gives some thought to assuring carriers a return on their investments that is consistent with the growth and welfare of the industry and the economy. In 1977 the ICC ruled that the trucking industry rates can yield no more than a 14 percent return on investment. This ruling cut the rate from 23 percent, allowing for about a one-third reduction in trucking rates.

When the ICC regulates rates there is a tendency for shippers to develop a hands-off attitude regarding the possibility of changing rates. In the past, carriers had considerable freedom in instituting rate changes, and the ICC usually acted on the basis of the carrier's requests. However, recently the ICC has developed a more restrictive policy. In early 1979 the commission suspended a 4 percent rate hike by the Pacific Inland Tariff Bureau and a 3 percent general rate increase proposed by the Midwest Freight Bureau, warning carriers it will no longer automatically pass through rate increases to offset higher expenses.

A fact that encourages rate differentials among carriers is that all intrastate common carriers, private carriers, specialized-commodity carriers, and contract carriers are to a certain extent exempt from ICC regulation. The American Trucking Association (ATA) estimates that 44,414 regulated trucking operators account for $55 billion per year in revenues, about 25 percent of the total trucking revenue for 1990. The other 75 percent are not regulated by state commissions. Carriers are often very influential in setting their original status. In addition, those that are exempt from ICC and state regulation are subject to the same type of competitive price bargaining that characterizes the remainder of our free-enterprise economy.

The Motor Carrier Act of 1980 directs the ICC to grant a certificate of operation to anyone that ''is fit, willing, and able, and is willing to serve a useful public service responsive to public demand or need.'' As a result, the number of regulated motor freight carriers has more than doubled in the 1980s, growing from 17,721 in 1979 to 25,999 in 1983, reaching 36,000 in 1987, 44,414 in 1990, and 46,389 in 1991.[10]

VARIATIONS WITHIN ESTABLISHED RATE STRUCTURES

In addition to the differences in the rates of different carriers, there are also rate variations, which can be classified as (1) class and commodity rates, (2) rates related to specific shipping practices, and (3) rates relating to commodity descriptions.

---

[10] ''Trucking Industry Structure,'' *Standard & Poor's Industry Surveys* (October 22, 1992), p. R46.

Class and Commodity Rates

Class rates are overall rates set by grouping commodities into a limited number of classes, to which rates are then applied. The result of this process, a freight classification, is an alphabetical list of articles, together with each commodity's rating. The rating is the class into which the article is placed for rate purposes. The use of this classification system greatly reduces the number of freight tariffs in which rates are published. Tariff is the term used for a schedule that contains rates and charges, as well as special conditions governing the movement of products or persons by commercial means.

A commodity rate, by contrast, is a special rate on a specific article. It is a rate quoted directly instead of through a system of freight classification. Commodity rates are lower than class rates and are the means whereby carriers quote special prices to meet particular conditions—for example, special rates on frequent shipments between two points to meet the needs of a particular buyer and seller or a community, or to meet some competitive situation. Commodity rates, then, are established to facilitate the heavy movement of goods, and most repetitive shipments move under commodity rates. A buyer anticipating such a movement should apply through a regular carrier to have a commodity rate established. The ICC will eventually determine whether the rate request will be granted. Thus, commodity rates represent a possible cost reduction available to the transportation buyer under certain circumstances.

Shipping Practices Related to Rates

Quantity Discounts.   A commodity will have a lower transportation rate if the quantity shipped meets the carload (CL) or truckload (TL) weight limits. It carries a much higher rate if a less-than-carload (LCL) or less-than-truckload (LTL) quantity is shipped. The minimum rates vary with the cubic densities of the commodities and the specific modes of shipping. For example, for steel the truckload weight is 32,000 pounds and the carload weight is 80,000 pounds. Often intermediate-quantity rates are also allowed for shipments that reach certain amounts that are less than the full-load quantities; for example, steel shipments have intermediate-quantity breaks at 20,000 and 40,000 pounds for truck and rail hauls, respectively.

Trainload or Multiple-Car Rates.   On occasion rail rates have been established that give discounts for weights in excess of a carload. Iron ore is an example of such a commodity. These rates are usually established to meet competition from other carriers such as water carriers or trucks.

Pool Cars. If a shipper has a number of small shipments going to the same general destination, it may combine them into one carload and consign the car to an agent for final distribution. Such a combined shipment is called a pool car. The total weight of the combined orders is used to justify quantity rate differentials. Although there are distribution costs for dispersing the goods from the agent to the final customers, the quantity rate reduction normally represents a significant savings.

Commodity Consolidation. A shipper having several different commodities going to one destination may combine them to meet the minimum weights for carload lots. The applicable rate will be that applying to the commodity with the highest CL rate. Shipments may be made to one or more consignees.

Special Shipping Facilities. In recent years, transportation companies, especially the railroads, have been developing special shipping equipment as a means of holding or regaining traffic. One of the first of these developments was "piggyback" service, in which truck trailers are carried on special railroad flatcars. On high-density routes these flatcars are made up into special trains that leave at fixed times, run at high speeds, and bypass switching yards. This service combines the low-cost services of the railroad with the flexibility of truck pickup and delivery. Piggyback service was initiated in 1926 on the Chicago, North Shore and Milwaukee railroad but did not become popular until after World War II. This service is sometimes referred to as TOFC—trailer on a flatcar.

A related and even more significant facility development has been containerization. Containers are boxes, usually of metal, that are 8 feet wide, 8 feet high, and 20, 30, or 40 feet long. They can be loaded at the point of origin, closed, locked, shipped by truck, transferred to rail, to ship, to truck, and delivered at destination. They obviate the necessity of rehandling the individual pieces of freight and greatly speed the process of loading and unloading. One other big advantage is that containers minimize possible substantial losses from pilferage in transit—especially at dockside. At present, ship lines are adding specially designed container vessels as rapidly as possible. The United States, Japan, and European countries have ports with container-handling facilities, and this capability is being expanded at a rapid pace.

The unit train is another relatively recent innovation. A railroad supplies a customer, such as a utility power plant, with an entire train to carry a full load from origin to destination. This procedure greatly speeds shipment and cuts costs. Between one-third and one-half of the coal in the United States is now shipped in this manner, and other products are beginning to use unit trains.

The railroads have also been active in designing special cars for particular uses. Special automobile-carrying, three-deck cars have been so successful that the railroads have recaptured most of the long-haul automobile deliveries. Special larger cars for carrying grain from terminals to ports have been designed and are gradually gaining acceptance. New whale-shaped tank cars that hold 30,000 gallons are now in service, as well as high cube-shaped box cars and special hopper cars designed to carry large loads of bulk products. With these innovations the railroad freight industry has begun to grow again.

Freeze Rates.   Many trucking companies employ what are known as freeze rates or rate stops. These terms mean that a company quoting such a rate will not, for example, carry shipments of fourth-class or lower freight for less than the third-class rate. The term *freeze* here means that the trucking company has frozen its rate at the third-class rate. Since many manufactured articles are subject to less than the third-class rate, a shipper should inquire about freeze rates before employing truck transportation. One should not assume that because a trucking company did not employ freeze rates on one date this will continue to be true. Trucking companies change their practices in respect to such rates, depending on the availability of different classes of freight.

Shipper Associations.   For shippers who do not have an adequate volume to obtain minimum rates, shipper associations exist to combine shipments into carloads or truckloads. The shipper receives an intermediate rate from the association, and the shipment moves under the association's name.

Through Rates.   A through rate is the rate from point of origin to destination. A long-haul rate is less per mile than a short-haul rate. It is therefore an advantage to the buyer to get a rate on one long haul rather than on two short hauls. For this purpose railroads have developed various forms of through rates, with the privilege of interruption. This means that a commodity can, for example, be shipped from Milwaukee to New York with a break at Pittsburgh, with the basic Milwaukee to New York charges being applied. Through rates are obtained as a result of direct negotiation with the carrier. There are three principal forms of rates with interruption privileges.

Diversion and Reconsignment.   Rail carload shipments may be diverted or reconsigned while in transit. Diverting a car means giving the carrier a new destination at some specified point before the car reaches its original destination. Reconsignment is the practice of naming a new party as the consignee of the shipment while the car is en route. Frequently diversion and reconsignment are both involved. When a commodity is sold while it is in transit, the shipment must often be both diverted and reconsigned.

There are a number of commodities that frequently move to market on a diversion and reconsignment basis. For example, lumber, fresh fruits and vegetables, and grain handled by commission merchants are commonly shipped with the knowledge that they will be sold while in transit. New orders must be given to the carrier in time to allow the car to move by the most economical route. Freight carriers assess a moderate charge for allowing the privilege of diversion and reconsignment.

In-transit Privileges. A substantial amount of freight cost can be saved by a proper use of the *fabrication-in-transit, milling-in-transit,* and *storage-in-transit* privileges allowed by carriers. Each of these privileges is granted under defined conditions by the carrier, permitting the shipper to stop the shipment at some intermediate point without treating the shipment as though it consisted of two separate movements. Thus a shipper can stop a shipment at an intermediate point for fabricating, milling, or storage and then, at a somewhat later date, move an equivalent tonnage to a market beyond the stop-off at the lower long-haul rate and enjoy a significant cost saving.

These in-transit privileges are available only to industries and products for which an agreement exists between the carriers and shippers. They are not blanket rights for all products. Fabrication in transit is quite generally accorded to processors of iron and steel. Milling in transit is most commonly permitted for the malting, milling, and mixing of grain and for the milling of forest products. Storage in transit applies to a large number of heavy commodities but to grain in particular.

As an example of fabrication in transit, steel plates and related articles were shipped from a steel company to a processor to be made into small bridges for delivery at various destinations. The processor paid the railroad the full amount of freight for shipping the steel from the mill to its plant, and the shipper registered the freight bill with the Western Weighing and Inspection Bureau (an agency supported by the railroads). When the fabricated article was delivered to the buyer (which might happen up to one year later), the freight cost was calculated between the steel company and the ultimate destination, as though the shipment had not been interrupted. The processor subtracted the amount it had paid previously, and the balance was the amount due, plus a nominal charge by the carrier for the privilege of fabricating in transit.

In order to take advantage of fabrication-in-transit rates, the processor's location must be considered to be intermediate between the point of origin of the raw material and the destination of the fabricated product. However, intermediate should not be understood literally, since steel shipped from

Chicago may be fabricated in Milwaukee and shipped across Lake Michigan to eastern destinations. Steel plates from Pennsylvania may be shipped first to Milwaukee via car ferry and, after processing, to southwestern destinations. In both these examples Milwaukee is considered an intermediate point, although it is not geographically between the points of origin and destination.

The principles of in-transit operation are the same for milling and sorting as for fabrication. Although these special privileges were originated by rail carriers, it is possible today to make similar arrangements with motor carriers.

Stop-off Privilege. The stop-off privilege allows a shipper to distribute merchandise along the carrier's route. Although the rate is based on the maximum weight of the shipment, there still are substantial economies over the alternative costs of small-lot shipments. The privilege may also be applied to shipments of merchandise that are picked up rather than distributed. One firm reports that under a stop-off arrangement negotiated with a truck line, castings are picked up at three suppliers' plants on the day before the truckload is assembled. The combined shipments are above the minimum truckload weight and thus at the lowest rate. There is also a saving in dock space at the buyer's plant, with only one truck making delivery.

Rates Relating to Commodity Description

Changes in materials or a regrouping of commodities often makes transportation economies possible. The following rate negotiation opportunities are available to all shippers.

When components are redesigned to incorporate different materials, the new materials may allow either higher or lower rates. In one example, fittings originally made from iron and steel were changed to zinc. The initial effect was to increase the freight charges by raising the LTL classifications from Class 50 to Class 85. However, by appealing to the motor freight classification board, the manufacturer was able to hold the old classification on the ground that the zinc part was actually cheaper to make.

Some products carry a higher freight classification than necessary because they are designated by their trade name rather than a classification description. The garment hanger industry is an example of the difficulty encountered in classifying products. If a garment hanger manufacturer ships pulpboard hangers, the correct classification is LTL 55. If they are shipped ''garment hanger'' rather than ''hangers, garment, pulpboard,'' the rate goes all the way up to LTL 100.

When various materials or components are included in a shipment, the highest commodity rate will apply for the entire shipment. Lower rates can often be obtained by careful separation of materials.

Responsibility for Correct Rates

Anyone using common carriers is assumed to have a knowledge of freight classifications and rates. Carriers are not legally responsible for erroneous quotations of freight rates. For example, if a buyer in deciding between two carriers on the basis of their delivered cost relied on a carrier's erroneous rate quotations, the carrier could not be held responsible for the wrong decision. This is true even though the error might have resulted in a large loss to the purchaser. For this reason tariff schedules are on file in freight stations, and those using common carriers are well advised to be familiar with the rates.

As indicated, freight rates are subject to varying degrees of flexibility, depending on many variables. Rate economies can be achieved through a careful classification of goods. Buyers should be familiar with the various truckload and carload minimum weights and compare the advantages of buying in small quantities with the freight savings possible from larger unit shipments. In addition, they should realize that it may be possible to negotiate with the carrier and the regulatory agencies for a commodity rate that may be much lower than the class rate on which the goods otherwise move.

CARRIER ALTERNATIVES

Essentially there are three types of carriers: common, contract—sometimes referred to as for-hire carriers—and private. The extent to which each class is regulated varies.

The preponderance of freight in the United States is shipped by common carriers. They serve the general public by providing service either for all commodities or for specified types of commodities. A contract carrier is an independent contractor who operates under individual contracts, providing specialized service for selected commodities to a limited number of shippers. The private carrier provides transportation using privately owned or lease equipment.

Common carriers and contract carriers are regulated by the ICC if they are involved in interstate commerce. The regulations pertaining to contract carriers are less stringent than those for common carriers. Both must obtain ICC certification in addition to filing their rates. The ICC authorizes the geographical area in which they may operate and approves their rates. State agencies regulate the contract and common carriers that are involved only in intrastate commerce. Private carriers are regulated only in matters pertaining to safety and insurance.

FREE-ON-BOARD ALTERNATIVES

The designation free on board (FOB) indicates the point from which freight charges are calculated. The routing of shipments has economical and legal significance to buyers, carriers, and shippers. In general, the designated FOB point determines who pays the freight charges as well as who has legal title to the merchandise while it is in the hands of the carrier.

Technically, FOB has no meaning unless a phrase is added to indicate the point at which the goods are free on board, such as FOB shipping point or FOB destination. It is at the FOB point where title changes hands and from which freight charges accrue to either buyer or shipper. For a shipment proceeding FOB shipping point or origin, title passes to the buyer at the shipping point. (Ninety percent of buyers ship FOB origin.) Thereafter, the carrier acts as the agent of the buyer, who is responsible for damage, freight claims, and other complications that may arise during shipment and for paying freight charges. For a shipment made FOB destination, these responsibilities fall on the seller. If no qualifying phrase is added, FOB is generally understood to be at the point of origin.

The following outline indicates the respective responsibilities of the seller and buyer under various FOB terms. The seller, Adams Company, is assumed to be located in Milwaukee, Wisconsin, and the buyer, Baker Company, in New York City.

I. FOB named point of origin (e.g., FOB Adams Company, Milwaukee, Wisconsin, via ABC Transport).
  A. Seller must
    1. Place goods on or in cars or vehicles.
    2. Secure receipted bill of lading from carrier.
    3. Be responsible for loss and damage until goods have been placed in or on cars or vehicles at point of origin and clean bill of lading has been furnished by carrier.
  B. Buyer must
    1. Provide for the movement of goods after they are on board.
    2. Pay all transportation charges to destination.
    3. Be responsible for loss or damage or for filing claims with carrier for loss or damage to shipment while in transit.
    4. Pay any demurrage* and storage charges.
  C. Title passes to buyer when shipment is turned over to carrier.

II. FOB named point of origin with transportation charges allowed to destination (e.g., FOB Adams Company, Milwaukee, Wisconsin, Freight Allowed, via ABC Transport).

---

* A demurrage is a charge assessed for detaining a freight car, truck, or other vehicle beyond the free time stipulated for loading or unloading.

A. Seller must
  1. Place goods on or in cars or vehicles.
  2. Secure receipted bill of lading from carrier.
  3. *Pay transportation charges from point of origin to destination.*
  4. Be responsible for loss and damage until goods have been placed in or on cars of vehicles at point of origin and clean bill of lading has been furnished by carrier.
B. Buyer must
  1. Provide for the movement of goods after they are on board.
  2. Be responsible for loss or damage or for filing claims with carrier for loss or damage to shipment while in transit.
  3. Pay any demurrage and storage charges.
C. Title passes to buyer when shipment is turned over to carrier.

III. FOB named destination (e.g., FOB Baker Company, New York city, via ABC Transport).
  A. Seller must
    1. Place goods on or in cars or vehicles.
    2. Secure receipted bill of lading from carrier.
    3. *Pay all transportation charges until goods have arrived at destination.*
    4. *Be responsible for loss or damage or for filing claims with carrier for loss or damage to shipment while in transit.*
  B. Buyer must
    1. Provide for any movement of the goods after arrival at named destination.
    2. Be responsible for any loss and damage incurred after arrival of goods at named destination.
    3. Pay any demurrage and storage charges.
  C. Title remains with seller until the shipment is delivered to buyer.

To avoid retention-of-title problems, United Kingdom companies may retain ownership of goods delivered to the buyer's factory until the buyer pays for them.[11]

IMPORT SHIPMENTS

An understanding of FOB terms on import shipments is of greater importance than an understanding of these terms on domestic shipping because

---

[11] "Retention of Title: A Practical Guide," *Accountancy (UK)* (February 1989), pp. 114–115.

additional insurance coverage is required if the goods are purchased FOB a foreign point of origin. Domestic common carriers are required by law to insure all goods carried up to a prescribed minimum value. Thus, domestic shipments have a certain insurance protection whether they have been sold FOB point of origin or FOB destination. The only differences is that in the first instance the buyer must file a claim with the insurance company, whereas in the second the seller must file the claim. Of course, if the goods have a value greater than is covered by the carrier's insurance, the seller or buyer may well take out additional insurance on the shipment.

The carrier does not insure shipments aboard an oceangoing vessel, and it is vital, therefore, that the buyer provide adequate insurance coverage where the purchase terms are FOB point of origin. The marine freight term, cost and freight (C and F), is similar to the domestic term FOB point of origin with transportation charges allowed to destination. Here again it is the buyer's responsibility to cover the shipment with adequate insurance, since neither the seller nor the carrier will provide insurance. Another common marine freight expression is (cost, insurance, and freight)—(CIF). This is similar to the domestic term FOB destination. If a sale is made CIF, it means that the seller will provide the insurance, and the buyer has only limited responsibility for the goods before they are landed in the country of destination.

It is significant that under CIF terms, title to goods passes when they are delivered to the carrier. After that point in time, any losses are the responsibility of the buyer. Most buyers, therefore, prefer C and F terms because under them buyers have the choice of insurance companies; that is, they can choose the coverage that best meets their requirements and arrange for payment of claims to be made in their own country, in their own currency. With large insurance companies in the United States specializing in marine insurance, it is no longer desirable to have foreign shippers select insurance coverages under CIF terms.

Purchasing personnel should also know that in marine insurance two kinds of coverage are available. One is against general average loss and the other is against particular average loss. A greatly simplified explanation of a general average loss is that a ship's captain may, when faced with a peril of the sea, decide to sacrifice a specific shipment or part of the shipment in order to save the remainder. When such a sacrifice is made, marine law holds that all who had a financial interest in the voyage must contribute even though their own shipment was in no way harmed by the peril. Insurance against general average loss assumes the insured shipper's contribution.

Insurance against particular average loss protects the insured person against such things as loss or water damage that may befall the shipment, endangering the entire venture. Imports should be protected against both types of risk.

ROUTING INCOMING SHIPMENTS

The buyer has the right to specify the route and carrier on goods purchased FOB shipping point. By utilizing a particular routing, the buyer can minimize cost; or the buyer may be able to arrange joint routing, as previously discussed. The practice of specifying carriers allows the buyer to obtain loyalty from these carriers, which can be helpful in negotiating rates, providing services such as back hauls, and expediting shipments when needed. This carrier's loyalty can also be called on in altering rates with the ICC, as joint appeals may be presented.

It is good practice for a buyer who permits the vendor to route a shipment to put a notation of the purchase requisition, "Ship via best and cheapest." If the vendor then ships by a carrier who does not quote the lowest available rate, the purchaser is in a position to charge the vendor for the difference between the actual and the lowest freight rate applicable.

Railroads have had no success in winning business off the roads. Truckers have innovated like the railroads. A decade-long battle for market share has kept rates down. Shippers benefit from the partially deregulated marketplace but insist that truckers provide accurate estimated times of arrival, customer service, and single carrier service.[12]

There are more compelling reasons for a purchaser to route truck shipments than railroad shipments. Since rail carriers are usually larger and financially sounder than truckers, the risk of the carrier not making good on claims for loss and damage is much less with a railroad. It has been accepted practice for the receiver or trustee of a bankrupt railroad to pay loss and damage claims as well as claims for overcharges without requiring the claims to be filed through court procedure. When a trucking company goes into receivership, however, it is frequently necessary to file claims for loss and damage as well as for overcharges through the court. Claims will then be given consideration based entirely on the assets and the liabilities of the trucking company. With railroads rarely is a properly substantiated loss and damage claim not paid. The ICC and various state commissions require trucking companies to carry insurance to cover both cargo and injury to persons or property. The insurance required of a trucking company, however, is a much more limited amount.

Despite this help, hundreds of trucking companies have folded and

---

[12] "The Railroads Get Better, but Shippers Still Prefer Trucks," *Purchasing* (February 8, 1990), pp. 27–30.

others have reeled under the pressure to offer deep discounts to maintain market share.[13]

Strong innovative firms succeed. Yellow Freight Systems implemented a formal quality program in its attempt to become the largest, highest quality, and lowest cost carrier. A pilot program at Yellow's Memphis hub achieved a 3 percent improvement in on-time delivered services, a 4000-pound load average increase, a reduction in claims ratio, and a four-hour reduction in time through break. Key elements of the quality program include statistical quality control to identify the cause of problems, quality teams focused on particular issues, and a process driven by management.[14]

EXPEDITING AND TRACING CONSIDERATIONS

The terms expediting and tracing are not synonymous. *Expediting* consists of selecting the most direct route in view of prevailing traffic conditions, following through with the vendor to assure shipment, and following through with the carrier to be certain delays are not encountered. *Tracing* is a traffic function that is resorted to after the shipment has had sufficient time to reach its destination but has not arrived.

Tracing shipments is relatively simple. A person requesting that a car be traced should inform the carrier of the date of shipment, the trailer or car number, and the complete routing. If several carriers' roads are involved in the routing, the time that has intervened between the date of shipment and the date of tracing will indicate whether the request should be taken up with the initiating, intermediate, or delivering carrier.

AUDITING AND PAYING FREIGHT CHARGES

ICC rules require that freight charges be paid to railroads within 48 hours of the receipt of the goods, and to truck lines or freight forwarders within seven days. Companies having a high credit rating may be granted 96 hours by the railroads. Failure to adhere to these regulations subjects both the shipper and the railroad to a fine.

---

[13] "Transportation News," *Purchasing* (January 19, 1989), p. 39.
[14] "An Inside Story: Quality Process Grows from Within," *Purchasing* (January 18, 1990), pp. 117, 121.

Demurrage Charges

Demurrage charges are penalties assessed by carriers when cars or vessels are held by or for a consignor or consignee beyond a stipulated free time provided for loading or unloading. Two days' free time is usually permitted before demurrage charges are levied. During periods of railcar shortages, demurrage rates are made punitive so that cars will be unloaded faster. Most business concerns operate under what is known as an average agreement, whereby a receiver is given a credit for each car released before the expiration of the 24 hours of free time. This credit can be used to offset a debit of one day's demurrage.

Adjustments and Filing of Claims

When a shipment arrives, an immediate inspection should be made by the purchaser. If loss or damage is discovered, a notation to that effect should be placed on the freight bill by the carrier's agent or by a representative. The agent or the representative will then present a loss or damage report. Later, when the purchaser files the claim for loss or damage, the carrier will refer to this report and the claim can be settled in a relatively short time.

A properly presented and documented claim will eliminate the need for much unnecessary correspondence. The claim form should be accompanied by the following supporting documents: the original bill of lading, the original freight bill with loss or damage notations, a certified invoice, and a report by the carrier.

Claims must be filed within nine months after delivery of a damaged shipment, or, if the shipment is presumed lost, within nine months after a reasonable length of time has been allowed for the shipment to arrive. If it is impossible to file a claim because certain supporting documents are not available, the receiver must notify the carrier within the nine-month period of the intention of filing a claim. A claim may be filed with either the originating carrier or the delivering carrier, but usually it is filed with the delivering carrier.

Overcharge Claims

Claims for freight overcharges may be filed within three years of the payment of the charges. Errors noted during the month in which they occurred may be referred to the carrier's agent, who often can make the refund locally. However, claims for overcharges filed after the month in which they occurred must be filed with the auditor of freight overcharge claims, who is usually located at the general office of the carrier.

It should be recognized that a carrier is permitted to collect freight undercharges that have occurred during the same period of time. The carrier not only is permitted to collect such undercharges, but must do so, even to the point of bringing suit, or the amount of the undercharge would be considered an illegal rebate.

Numerous specialized audit bureaus and traffic consultants will audit their customers freight bills for accuracy. They charge a 50 percent commission for errors found resulting in overcharges by the freight companies.

Transportation Quality

Enormous gains in productivity (as well as fierce competition) have kept rate hikes in every mode of transportation well below the rate of inflation. Carriers have developed systems for tracing and tracking and for electronic communications that reduce delays and errors and shrink the paper trail.

In the evolution of quality programs in the United States, manufacturers looked first at their own processes, then at their materials suppliers', and only then at their service suppliers'. Coincident with that evolution, carriers emerged from a tightly regulated world into one where the old ways of doing business would no longer suffice. Many carriers indicated their intention to pursue dramatic improvements in on-time deliveries. However, measured by such standards as Motorola's goal of six sigma—3.4 errors per million—goals of errors in the 2 to 3 percent range miss the improvements target. Even a 1 percent error rate translates into 10,000 errors per million. Yet transportation buyers accept far worse. A consulting group's recent study found that shippers on average require 97 percent on-time delivery; they receive not even that.[15]

AT&T spends in excess of $350 million on transportation every year. Transportation quality process (TQP) forms the core of AT&T's transportation management. Their TQP focuses on three areas: transit interval, billing accuracy, and loss and damage claims. Managers consider transit interval— essentially on-time performance—most important, accounting for 70 percent of the weight in AT&T's rating system.[16]

JIT Influence. The inventory liquidation of the 1990s predicates U.S. producers converting new order growth into production growth. Approximately 50 percent of respondents to *Purchasing* magazine's recent poll described their inventory strategy as driven by long-term goals such as JIT (down impact), improving responsiveness to customers, or more proficiency in production and materials planning.[17]

---

[15] "The Drive for Transportation Quality," *Purchasing* (January 16, 1992), pp. 106–113.
[16] "Getting Better All the Time," *Purchasing* (June 4, 1992), pp. 57–60.
[17] "Inventory Drawdown Wanes," op. cit. (April 16, 1992), p. 18.

Measuring purchasing performance in an organization that utilizes a JIT system requires a broader view of quality than in a non-JIT operation. Experienced JIT managers track quality costs and their impact on scrap and rework, plant efficiency, and customer return costs, as well as the traditional incoming inspection costs.

A somewhat nontraditional yardstick of customer service measures the impact of poor quality on missing shipments to customers, the cost of premium transportation, and the cost of personnel assigned at suppliers' operations to maintain shipping schedules. Successful implementation of the JIT concept requires more involvement and dedication by a wide range of operating personnel than in a conventional operating system. Many firms evaluate purchasing departments on their ability to reduce the supplier base, and to manage lead times, supplier quality, and delivery. Most of those firms have adopted a broader view of quality, realizing that supplier quality impacts production efficiency, administrative costs, and ultimately the firm's customers.[18]

Distribution Requirements Planning (DRP). The DRP constitutes the time-phased replenishment needs of branch warehouses quantified by periods. Managers compute these requirements as the difference between customer demand and the on-hand and in-transit inventory. In a branch warehouse environment, DRP provides a solid link between distribution and manufacturing by providing a record of the quantity and timing of likely orders.[19] Transportation management amplify the search for total quality service by proximity planning—by using the control that DRP affords them.

HANDLING HAZARDOUS MATERIALS

Materials management must consider the titanic issue of hazardous materials—buying, storing, transporting, and disposing of them. More than 33,000 commodities have some sort of hazardous classification, all requiring safe handling.[20] The purchasing manager needs to stay informed about hazardous materials from a consultant or from local, state, or federal groups like the National Safety Council.

Buying hazardous materials involves selecting vendors who have

---

[18] "Motivating and Monitoring JIT Supplier Performance," *Journal of Purchasing and Materials Management* (Summer 1990), pp. 19–24.

[19] Donald W. Fogarty, John H. Blackstone, Jr., and Thomas R. Hoffmann, *Production & Inventory Management,* 2nd ed. (Cincinnati, OH: South-Western Publishing, 1991), p. 18.

[20] "Safe Handling," *NAPM Insights* (July 1992), pp. 10–11.

knowledge and experience with those particular materials. Substitution of less hazardous substances may work well for the user. The purchaser needs to understand the most important hazardous materials laws, such as:

1. The Hazardous Materials Transportation Uniform Safety Act of 1990.
2. The Resource Conservation and Recovery Act of 1976, which established a regulatory system permitting the states to track hazardous materials from the time of generation to disposal.
3. The Comprehensive Environmental Response, Compensation and Liability Act of 1980, or Super fund, that provided the needed authority and established a trust fund for federal and state governments to respond directly to any problems at uncontrolled hazardous waste disposal sites.[21]

Before buying hazardous materials, the buyer must plan for its transport, storage, and disposal.

The American Warehouse Association tracks information on hazardous substances; it therefore serves as a valuable resource. One beginning step in safe storage consists in proper labeling and separation of various goods. Other steps include a sound fire prevention and safety program for the warehouse, and liaison with the fire department and other local emergency response agencies.[22]

The Occupational Safety and Health Administration (OSHA) focuses considerable attention on the proper handling of toxic and hazardous materials, as well as on the reporting of all work-related injuries and illnesses. Employers must provide information and training on hazardous chemicals in the employers' workplaces. OSHA also mandates employers to keep all medical records of employees who have suffered exposure to toxic substances or harmful physical agents for 30 years after the employees have left the workplace.[23]

OSHA publishes lists of set, permissible exposure levels for nearly 500 hazardous substances. The warehouser's first line of defense in handling hazardous materials includes checking the accuracy of the shippers' documentation and watching for proper packaging.[24]

Changes in building codes and the increasing cost of compliance have

---

[21] Theodore H. Allegri, Sr., *Handling and Managing Hazardous Materials and Waste,* Chapter 18, ''Super fund, A Remedial Response Program'' (New York: Chapman and Hall, 1986), pp. 344–345.
[22] ''How to Control Warehouse Losses,'' *National Underwriter* (August 10, 1992), pp. 13, 16.
[23] ''Employer Compliance with OSHA,'' *Supervision* (August 1992), pp. 5–6.
[24] ''Hazardous Material: Protect Your Environment,'' *Material Handling Engineering* (July 1992), pp. 43–45.

complicated the construction of hazardous-materials storage facilities. Builders must provide containment for spills and fire hazards and a drainage system that protects the environment.[25]

Transporting hazardous materials brings the issue home to the American public. The federal government estimates that more than 4 billion tons of regulated hazardous material moves over U.S. highways each year, with approximately 500,000 shipments occurring each day. Legislation to safeguard the national interest against hazardous material exposure anticipates a time when many people will need protection. The National Industrial Transportation League president states that because of funding constraints the Department of Transportation's regulations on proper safety handling and transportation of hazardous material have come slowly, but purchasers should feel the changes over the next two years.[26]

The Department of Defense (DOD) has more than 1300 hazardous waste (HW) generators in the continental United States that produce more than 150 million pounds of HW each year. Private industrial contractors provide practically all of the DOD's HW disposal.[27] Materials managers in firms and institutions should follow the DOD's lead in soliciting the help of private industrial disposal contractors.

CHAPTER SUMMARY

The high cost of transporting products and the deregulation of the transportation industry over the last two decades has spurred company management to devise better traffic management. Customers demand good service and will take their business elsewhere unless sellers can arrange prompt delivery at a reasonable cost.

Computerized purchasing, leading to electronic data interchange, has improved communications among buyer, seller, and carrier. Partnering has reduced buyers' lists of active vendors and transport companies. Buyers now tend to place larger orders and contracts with fewer suppliers and transportation companies for longer periods of time. The reduced sales effort costs less and the buyer gets the savings in lower delivered prices.

Discussion Questions

1. Which of the traffic matters of greatest concern to the purchasing agent do you consider to be the most important?

---

[25] "Step up to the Challenge: Hazmat Storage," *Chemical Engineering* (June 1992), pp. 118–119.
[26] Fogarty, Blackstone, Jr., and Hoffmann, op. cit, p. 11.
[27] "Disposal: Using a Program that Works," *NAPM Insights* (July 1992), pp. 12–13.

2. Distinguish clearly between class rates and commodity rates. Which comes first? What brings about the change from one type of rate to the other?

3. What is the role of the ICC in rate setting?

4. Under what conditions should a buyer specify routing instructions and choice of carrier for incoming shipments?

5. Explain the difference between expediting and tracing as these terms are used in traffic management.

6. What do the abbreviations FOB and CIF stand for? Explain the importance of these terms for import shipments.

7. Describe some of the special shipping facilities that have developed in recent years.

8. What is meant by a pool car, and in-transit privilege, and demurrage?

9. It is widely held that, when truck carriers are used, buyers should insist on their right of routing and carrier. Why?

10. What are some of the ways in which a purchasing manager and traffic manager working together can save money for their company through good traffic management?

Suggested Case

Bielaw Company

19

Reclamation and Salvage Procedures

There is an economic rule of thumb: whatever we tax, we tend to get less of; whatever we subsidize, we tend to get more of. Currently, we tax work and we subsidize the depletion of natural resources—and both policies have contributed to high unemployment and the waste of natural resources. What if we lowered the tax on work and simultaneously raised it on the burning of fossil fuels? It is entirely possible to change the tax code in a way that keeps the total amount of taxes at the same level, avoids unfairness . . . but discourages the constant creation of massive amounts of pollution.*

CHAPTER CONTENTS

The purchasing department has primary responsibility for spearheading efforts to provide the most efficient utilization of and returns on materials reclaimed or salvaged from operations. Purchasing sells such materials in a market where the buyer of scrap typically knows much more than the seller. Hence, the purchasing manager turns for assistance to specialists who advise on how to recapture value.

The matter involves the world situation. Potential depletion of the world's landfills and resources, coupled with skyrocketing raw material

*Source: Senator Al Gore, *Earth in the Balance: Ecology and the Human Spirit* (Boston: Houghton Mifflin, 1992), p. 348.

517

prices, have contributed to a shift in attention to the reclamation and utilization of surplus materials. High energy costs, and the fact that primary materials consume more energy per ton of production than recycled materials, reinforce the financial and social importance of such materials.

The flow of scrap steel from metalworking plants back to steel-producing mills is an example of the efficient redistribution of materials. Because scrap is the metallic equivalent of pig iron, every ton of it used in making steel conserves up to one and a half tons of iron ore, a ton of coke, and half a ton of limestone—all of which are natural resources in limited supply. Furthermore, energy costs drop dramatically when scrap is used as the raw material. Steel energy costs can be reduced by more than 50 percent when 100 percent scrap charges are used. Aluminum has an even greater savings. If a ton of aluminum pig or ingot is recycled from scrap, the energy needed is only 5 percent of that needed to produce an equivalent quantity of virgin metal.

Normally, purchased scrap comprises 40 percent of the copper, 40 percent of the steel, 50 percent of the lead, 30 percent of the nickel and nickel alloy, 20 percent of the zinc, and 30 percent of the aluminum and paper produced in the United States.[1] It is even more significant, however, that when demand for these basic commodities rises rapidly, the producers use extra scrap as an incremental source of raw materials.

The generation of surplus materials is at least in part a price paid for the changing nature of American business. For example, an engineer may discover a new production technique requiring the use of different materials. Although overall it is economical to use the new material, the old raw material inventory is made obsolete. Or, after a new product has been on the market for a short time, design improvements may render obsolete existing finished goods and some raw material inventory. Finally, production innovations that become possible through technological advances almost always make former equipment and materials obsolete. In short, surplus is one of the prices of progress.

Other surpluses are created through human errors, such as an overly optimistic market projection. The resulting production schedule proves to be excessive. Or there is an overextension of buying for the future, and excessive inventories that may then deteriorate are accumulated.

Finally, the regular manufacturing process produces scrap residues and spoiled or damaged materials. On the average, approximately 15 percent of all finished-steel products such as sheets, plates, or shapes, and 5 percent of the original weight of all castings, eventually end up as scrap during processing.

In many ways, scrap and surpluses are a paradox. The world does not

---

[1] "Scrap: The Hidden Source of Metals," *Purchasing* (October 13, 1988), p. 48B4.

want to produce them, yet does so constantly. They are virtually the only resources that are never depleted but constantly replenish themselves and, with proper processing and redistribution, are a perpetual source of some raw materials vital to the continued existence of our industrial society.

CATEGORIES OF DISPOSABLE MATERIALS

Several terms are used to distinguish the types of disposable materials commonly comprehended under the broad term *scrap.*

Spoilage refers to items of production that are found to be defective during the manufacturing or inspection process. Such items are also called rejects or waste. The term *waste*, however, should be reserved for materials that are lost in the manufacturing process or that have no significant recovery value, such as gases, smoke, dust, and unsalable materials.

Scrap, in the narrow sense, consists of the residue of materials left by a manufacturing operation. This residue might include such materials as the turnings from a lathe, sprues and "flash" from the foundry or molding process, and paper cuttings from a book bindery. Worn-out equipment and parts are also considered scrap. More recently, the terms secondary materials or reclamation materials have been used to identify collectively all such reusable products.

Industry generally recognizes three categories of scrap. *Home scrap* is produced in the mills of the basic industries: trimmings from steel ingots, slag, and skimmings from molten metal are all scrap that can be immediately recycled. *Prompt-industrial scrap* is what is left over from the manufacturing process: skeleton sheets after stampings have been made from them, paper trimmed in the manufacture of envelopes, turnings and borings from machine shops, and so forth. The term is derived from the fact that the manufacturer must dispose of such scrap promptly to avoid being inundated by its large volume. Prompt-industrial scrap is a highly desirable commodity because it is likely to be free from contamination (mixture with other materials). The third type of scrap, *obsolete scrap,* consists of items that have been used and are basically worn out: automobile hulks, appliances, old industrial machinery, and so on. According to a recent study by the Institute of Scrap Iron and Steel, home scrap accounts for 35 percent of total scrap accumulation, prompt-industrial scrap for 25 percent, and the discarded products constituting obsolete scrap account for the remaining 40 percent.[2]

Another category of disposable goods consists of equipment, materials, and supplies that have become obsolete. An item is considered obsolete

[2] Institute of Scrap Recycling Industries, Inc. letter to the author July 11, 1990.

when the greater efficiency made possible by using a more modern item exceeds the added costs of replacing the old. An item that is obsolete for one company, however, may still be useful to another firm.

Recycling is a way of using solid waste materials in which their basic chemical and physical properties are returned as productive inputs to the production process.

In the remainder of this chapter the term surplus is used inclusively to indicate all classes of scrap, spoiled material, or obsolete material that still have economic worth.

MANAGEMENT OF SURPLUS DISPOSAL

The management of surplus is sometimes treated as a secondary management concern. The main concern of companies is the production of a marketable product. The surpluses originating as by-products of this process are often regarded as a necessary nuisance to be handled as quickly and simply as possible. It is estimated that fewer than one-third of all U.S. companies give adequate attention to the possible economic benefits of surplus goods and used machines. They are not usually thought of as a source of supplementary income. Their value is seldom, if ever, shown as a separate item on a company's income statement or balance sheet. Usually the income they generate is buried in the "other income" category or treated as an offset to the cost of raw materials. Since the variety of surpluses is great and the amount of each type is likely to be relatively small, the seller does not usually become an expert in the business. In fact, surplus material is one of the few items in the world of business about which the buyer is ordinarily better informed than the seller.

Purchasing and Surplus

The disposal of surplus is a selling rather than a buying activity, but this responsibility is usually assigned to the purchasing department, for certain positive reasons. First, it is the responsibility of purchasing to have comprehensive knowledge of price trends. Prices of scrap and surplus materials fluctuate more than the prices of most raw materials because of the changing supplies and the derived nature of their demand. For example, if steel output is reduced when scrap dealers have large inventories of scrap, the steel mills will make sharp reductions in the prices they offer for scrap. On the other hand, the demand for scrap may be exceptionally strong when its supply is low, causing the price to rise rapidly. Although no one within a typical manufacturing firm is an expert on the prices and grades of scrap, purchasing personnel should have the best insight.

The Salvage Department

When the amount of scrap and surplus generated by operations is substantial, the establishment of a separate scrap and surplus department may be considered. Of major importance in receiving administrative acceptance for a separate department is an accurate accounting of the economies to be made from the operation.

The head of the salvage department must be in a position to demonstrate the direct cost versus the return of the operation. Profit is usually demonstrated by the ratio of scrap return to sales; a rule of thumb is that a dollar returned to profit through salvage is equal to the profit generated by $100 of outside sales. This figure naturally varies with the prices and profits of the organization. A separate surplus department is justified only when the amount of savings warrants the additional cost.

Production and Surplus

Another way to organize the disposal of surplus is to assign it to production. Because most scrap and surplus originate in the production process, responsibility could be assigned to the production department. The argument against this is that the production department may be so dominated by its interest in producing the end product that the surplus program would be neglected.

Segmentation and Segregation

Because of the wide range of surplus materials, often in small quantities of each, proper preparation and segregation are major factors in obtaining maximum return from their sale. When the amounts of a particular surplus are large, a firm may semiprocess the material—for example, performing its own bailing. Then the material can be sold directly to a user rather than through an intermediary.

Segregation is the sorting of scrap surplus by type, alloy, grade, size, and weight. One can begin to understand the magnitude of the segregation task by noting that there are 27 grades of aluminum scrap, 44 of copper and brass, 46 of commonly traded wastepaper, and 105 of iron and steel. The specifications for various types and grades of scrap materials are established by trade associations and specify the maximum and minimum size as well as the type of material required to meet the standards for each category.

If sizes are mixed or several categories of scrap are combined, the return is considerably reduced. Frequently scrap that has been mixed commands an even lower price than that paid for the lowest-value item in the mixture. The reason for this is the high cost of separating a contaminated mixture. The scrap dealer must perform this segregation in order to dispose of the scrap to a user. This cost will be passed back to the seller of the scrap in the form of a lower price. The slight additional cost of proper segregation at the point of origin will usually be more than compensated for by the increased return.

Valuable stainless steels are reduced in value by 80 percent if they are mixed with other steel scrap. In general, ferrous scrap mixed with nonferrous scrap lowers the value of the nonferrous component sharply; steel scrap mixed with aluminum, for example, cuts the value of aluminum scrap 60 percent. It is therefore profitable to establish an in-plant system of scrap segregation, preferably giving the production department safety and maintenance responsibilities.

Some materials have a much higher rate of reclamation than others. Differences in the rate of recycling are related in part to the difficulties of sorting and collecting the metals once they become part of a complex system. For example, zinc has a low recovery rate because of its heavy use in galvanizing, a process from which it is not recoverable. A great deal of copper is used in a magnet wire, from which it is very difficult to recover. Other reasons for differences in reclamation rates include inequitable freight rates and depletion allowances, a need for specialized labor and equipment for reclamation, and the varying pollution codes of the states.

Plastic recycling from the waste stream probably will grow faster than metal or glass recycling during the 1990s. A Norwalk, Connecticut market research firm anticipates a 9 percent increase in the rate of metals recycled from waste between 1989 and 1994 compared with a 31-percent jump in plastics recycling. Currently about 2.6 million tons of all metals in the waste stream—about 19.5 percent—get collected for recycling. By 1994, that amount will likely increase to about 4 million tons, or almost 26 percent.[3] The firm projects that glass recycling will grow by almost 18 percent. Researchers expect the total amount of all waste recycled to surpass 35 million tons, almost 35 percent of all waste, by 1994.

Scrap material and small subassemblies should generally be distorted or dismantled before sale and removal from the seller's premises. Some sellers have been surprised to find their scrap items appearing on the market and competing with their products. However, protection may be obtained by specifying as a condition of the sale that the subassembly or part be destroyed or not resold as a usable item.

---

[3] "Metals Recycling Will Only Grow 9 Percent in 1989–1994," *American Metal Market* (November 20, 1989), p. 8.

DISPOSITION OF SURPLUS

The various ways in which surplus materials are disposed of influence the rate of return. For example, sale through a surplus dealer will usually bring 15 to 35 percent of original cost, whereas return of the material to the original supplier typically brings 90 to 95 percent of original cost. In the following paragraphs the various disposition alternatives are considered.

Use within the Firm

The greatest value is obtained from surplus if it can be reclaimed for further use. One form of reclamation is the reuse of what are called off-falls. Careful study frequently shows that a smaller piece can be stamped or pressed from an off-fall, as shown in Figure 19-1. The saving is equal to the difference between the price of raw material and the price of scrap. Although there may be extra incidental costs of processing from scrap instead of from new raw material, the overall savings are usually substantial. In the auto industry, reuse of sheet steel shearings, to make such things as flanges and washers, is estimated to save enough metal to make an extra car for every 50 produced. Other industries report similar savings.

Reprocessing is another means of reclaiming scrap materials for reuse. Sometimes this can be done by welding or the use of mechanical joints. Short ends of pipe and bar stock can be joined into working lengths by this process. Defective or spoiled castings and metal parts often can be reclaimed at minimum expense by welding.

When a careful study of the surplus material indicates that it cannot be reclaimed, a further effort should be made to determine whether the material can be modified in a way to make it suitable for some purpose other than that for which it was intended. Such analysis often reveals a part similar in shape and size can be made from the scrap material after inexpensive modification. A related possibility is for parts that have been damaged or spoiled to be reworked. One firm cited success in reconditioning old valves: as scrap they were bringing $18 per gross ton, but as usable valves they were worth $5050 per ton. Another firm had a damaged piece of equipment it had planned to sell for a net gain of $1500. Instead, the equipment was reconditioned and sold for a net gain of $18,000.

Remanufacturing consists of disassembling an equipment's component, salvaging parts worth saving, and replacing unusable parts with new ones. Original equipment manufacturers and independents who remanufacture use the term ''core'' to refer to the worn assembly with certain salvageable

Eight new parts at the price of scrap

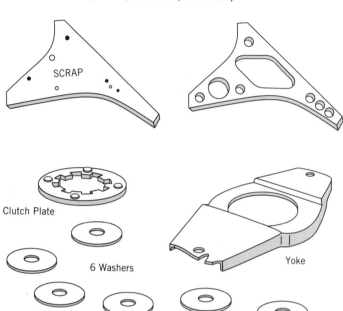

FIGURE 19-1. An example of utilizing scrap for the production of new parts. (*Source:* "Good Feeding Can Make Presses More Productive," *Iron Age,* July 13, 1978, p. 98.)

parts. Remanufacturing has economic value if the core carries a value at least 40 percent of a new assembly's value.[4]

Tracom Inc. (Fort Worth, Texas) buys used diesel engines and sells the engines and parts to remanufacturers. The company uses a truck dealers directory to find engines and engine parts in thousands of scattered salvage sheds and scrap yards around the United States. Foreign customers tend to rebuild engines again and again rather than buy new ones. Some 40 percent of the firm's revenues come from exports.[5]

Most large firms periodically circulate a list of surplus equipment and usable materials to all departments and branch plants. Often the surpluses can be used profitably by other units of the firm with little or no reprocessing costs. Figure 19-2 is a typical surplus equipment form used to inform departments and plants of available stock.

[4] "Purchasing Remanufactured Assemblies," *Purchasing World* (September 1988), pp. 79–80.
[5] "The Accidental Trader," *Inc.* (March 1990), pp. 84–89.

SEE BACK OF THIS
FORM FOR
INSTRUCTIONS

SURPLUS PLANT EQUIPMENT   No. 0177

WORKS AND LOCATION			DATE
MFG. NAME		MODEL NO.	ASSET NO.
NAME OF EQUIPMENT			
SIZE OR CAPACITY		SERIAL NUMBER	

OPERATING CONDITION (SEE INSTRUCTIONS)	▶	EXCELLENT	GOOD	FAIR	POOR

ADDITIONAL DESCRIPTION AND MOTOR SPEC., STARTERS, ACCESSORIES, SPECIAL SPARE PARTS

YEAR PURCHASED	PURCHASE PRICE $	PRESENT BOOK VALUE $	ESTIMATED WEIGHT

WHY IS EQUIPMENT NO LONGER NEEDED?

IF OBSOLETE—ESTIMATED COST TO MODERNIZE $	DATE EQUIPMENT AVAILABLE	ESTIMATED COST TO PLACE IN ORIGINAL CONDITION $	CAN NEW PARTS BE PURCHASED AT REASONABLE COST

ESTIMATED COST TO LOAD ON CARS $	ESTIMATED COST TO SCRAP $	ESTIMATED VALUE AS SPARE PARTS OR SCRAP $	RECOMMENDED METHOD OF DISPOSAL →	HOLD FOR FUTURE PROJECT	TRANSFER	DONATE	SELL	SCRAP

REVIEWED BY		REMARKS:
STOREKEEPER	DATE	
PROPERTY ACCOUNTANT	DATE	
REPORT BY	DATE	
DEPARTMENT HEAD	DATE	
CHIEF WORKS ENGINEER	DATE	
WORKS MANAGER	DATE	
DIVISION MANAGER	DATE	

FINAL DISPOSITION	PURCHASE ORDER NO.	DATE

FIGURE 19-2. A form to advise other departments and plants about the availability of surplus equipment.

Return to Supplier

Surplus material often can be returned to the original suppliers, either in the same form in which it was purchased or as scrap residue. As previously noted, when the material is returned in its original form, returns may be as high as 90 to 95 percent of the purchase price.

When the scrap is copper and other nonferrous metals, arrangements can often be made to return the off-fall material at a favorable price. Whether the original processor will be interested in the return of the uncontaminated scrap from metal sold depends on conditions of supply. During periods of shortage the seller may go so far as to put a clause in the sales contract requiring the return of scrap. Even when supply conditions are favorable, a seller will usually accept the scrap from customers; but when surpluses exist, a seller may discourage returns by refusing to take more than a certain percentage of its sales in the form of returned scrap.

Precious metals such as silver, copper, and their alloys can be returned to their original processors for reprocessing into their original form. A charge, commonly called a toll, is made for such processing.

As-Is Sale to Other Users

Scrap material may be sold to another company that can use it in its existing condition. Such sales usually bring the highest prices, and thus this possibility should be explored before it is decided to sell the material as scrap to intermediaries. Such sales are usually on an as-is basis; that is, the selling firm makes no express or implied warranty as to the fitness of the products.

As-is transactions are usually effected through the medium of trade journal advertising or through direct exchanges of information between firms in the same or similar industries.

Sale to Intermediaries

Dealers or brokers are specialized intermediaries who collect, sort, and process surplus materials, especially surplus scrap. When it has been determined that scrap cannot be used or salvaged and that the quantities are too small to justify direct sale to the supplier, these buyers are normally utilized for disposition. There are three types of scrap intermediaries: the scrap peddler, the scrap dealer, and the scrap broker.

The *scrap peddler*, with the smallest operation of the three types, collects various kinds of scrap from homes, merchants, and very small manufacturing plants but does not maintain scrap yards. Peddlers dispose of the scrap to a dealer.

The second type of intermediary is the *scrap dealer,* who maintains one or more yards in industrial centers to accumulate various classes of scrap. The scrap dealer utilizes specialized materials-handling equipment and may furnish trailers for scrap collection. Dealers have three objectives in operating a yard. They accumulate enough of a certain class of scrap so that it can be transported to the user economically. They reclassify the scrap in a way that raises its grade and price, by segregating it or cutting it into smaller sizes to increase its utility to the potential user. Finally, a dealer may hold the scrap until it brings a more favorable price. This speculative function serves the useful purpose of balancing supply and demand. Most manufacturing plants utilize scrap dealers.

The third type of intermediary is the *scrap broker.* The broker's function is to negotiate sales between scrap dealers or between scrap generators and scrap users. Their profit comes from differences between the purchase price and the selling price. Because brokers do not operate yards, only very large manufacturers with their own scrap-handling facilities deal directly with them.

Pricing Practices

Various types of sales agreement covering pick up arrangements and price calculations can be established with intermediaries. In all cases the volume of scrap offered affects the price. Infrequent collections of substantial scrap volumes are obviously more economical than frequent small pickups, and the return to the seller will be proportionately greater.

Under a variable price contract, the price may be established as that in effect at time of pickup, with provisions for the sale covering periods varying from one month to one year. The price is the market price at time of removal, less a stipulated percentage. Prices are stipulated to be those quoted in such trade publications as *Iron Age, Steel,* or *American Metal Market.* From such price quotations a dealer will deduct an allowance or margin that represents cost and profit.

Fixed-price agreements utilize a set price established by negotiation between the seller and the buyer. The dealer furnishes a trailer or container and provides periodic pickups, and weighing is usually conducted on the seller's premises. Terms range from months to one year.

The principal advantage of term contracts is that the intermediary is obligated to accept scrap regardless of market conditions. This stipulation is of particular advantage when conditions are such that mills are not buying. During these periods intermediaries accumulate substantial scrap inventories.

Other arrangements with intermediaries include (1) the bid or negotiation methods, whereby each lot of scrap is offered to intermediaries either by sealed bids or through negotiations; and (2) the commission method, whereby the intermediary periodically removes the scrap and sells it for the highest price obtainable, out of which a commission is paid.

Scrap Consultant

It was mentioned earlier in this chapter that scrap is one class of commodity about which the buyer is usually better informed than the seller. This factor is almost universally true because, though important as a source of revenue, the volume of scrap sales is small in comparison with the sale of a company's regular product line. Furthermore, the kinds and grades of scrap are so numerous as to be bewildering. There are more than 500 kinds of scrap, including 75 recognized grades of ferrous scrap alone. In order to offset the scrap buyers' expertise, some companies employ the services of a scrap consultant.

The scrap consultant is paid a commission on sales of scrap as reimbursement for services. Such services consist of an initial survey of the plant and its scrap-handling procedures. The consultant then makes a report to management, recommending a program for segregating, grading, handling, weighing, and accounting for the company's scrap. If a contract is signed, the consultant proceeds to negotiate the most advantageous sales possible. Thereafter, the service may include audits of scrap sale invoices and periodic surveys of the plant to see that the recommended procedures are being implemented.

Other Scrap Disposition Procedures

Surplus and Waste Exchange. The surplus exchange market is a relatively recent and rapidly growing innovation among buyers, with volume estimates ranging from $8 to $12 billion annually. Generally, a list is circulated of members' needs and available items, a central computer is used to match potential buyers and sellers, and a commission is paid to the sponsoring organization.

Direct Sales to Scrap Consumers. Another alternative available to the scrap-generating firm is to process the scrap by compressing and baling it and then selling it directly to scrap users. However, few firms dispose of their scrap in this manner because the volume of scrap generated by a typical plant is not large enough to warrant the substantial expense involved in such specialized equipment and employees.

THE ECONOMICS OF THE SCRAP INDUSTRY

The market of the scrap industry is in many respects unique. It is said that scrap is bought rather than sold. For practical purposes, demand cannot be created; the usual tools of advertising, styling, and so on do not apply to this industry. The demand is a derived demand completely dependent on the sale of final products and the derived need for the raw materials. Therefore, unlike manufacturing firms, which manage to achieve high rates of inventory turnover, the typical scrap dealer must usually maintain large inventories. Such dealers are dependent on the mills and foundries, which do not respond to sales, bargain prices, or hard-selling efforts. When scrap is in demand, however, it must be readily available.

The long ton of 2240 pounds is the basic unit of measurement in the industry, although some dealers quote on the basis of a short ton (2000 pounds). The scrap user's weights govern and the scrap must be suitable and acceptable to the customer. A few large firms buy scrap on the basis of standards established by the Institute of Scrap Iron and Steel and the National Association of Waste Material Dealers. The specifications are quite loose, and because scrap is a low-priced commodity not readily subject to detailed measurements, few scrap shipments are rejected.

There are thousands of dealers and other intermediaries selling undifferentiated products to relatively few large buyers. Therefore, the selling of scrap takes place in a market that resembles perfect competition on the selling side, which means that profit margins often are low.

Usually the performance of a contract is considered complete when the carrier issues a bill of lading rather than upon receipt of the material. A leeway of 5 percent is usually accepted in determining tonnage.

The scrap industry association, known as the Institute of Scrap Iron and Steel (ISIS), is composed of the large dealers in the field. A dealer must be approved by the local ISIS chapter before being admitted to membership.

The principal scrap markets are located in Boston, New York, Philadelphia, Buffalo, Pittsburgh, Cincinnati, Detroit, Chicago, St. Louis, Birmingham, Los Angeles, San Francisco, Seattle, Portland (Oregon), Dallas, and Houston. Prices established in these centers form the basis for trading throughout their areas.

Scrap dealers vary in size from a one-person operation to a venture like Proler International Corporation (1988 revenues $240 million).[6] The chairman's parents founded the Houston company six decades ago. Revenues come from his major site on the Houston Ship Channel and nine joint venture recycling plants around the country. To even out the scrap metal price cycles, the firm operates the world's largest detinning plant. The plant

---

[6] "Scrapman," *Forbes* (October 30, 1989), pp. 205–206.

can process 2.8 billion tin cans a year. The company built virtually the entire plant with used parts.

Scrap dealers' unabashed generosity during holidays puts many buyers in embarrassing situations. However, purchasing managers and buyers appreciate the vital role that scrap dealers play in recycling the estimated 60 million tons produced annually in the United States for sale to others.

THE CURRENT SCENE

America, the throw-away society, pitches about 160 million tons of municipal refuse each year, or almost four pounds per person daily. Landfill disposes of about 80 percent, incineration 9 percent, and household refuse recycling 11 percent. Nearly 70 percent of the nation's landfills will heap to capacity by the year 2004 at the present dumping rates. Without replacement, 90 percent of existing landfill capacity will fill up by the year 2009.[7] Managers know what limited capacity means—hundreds of industrial firms operate their own landfills on company property or on nearby leased lands with "no more space" signs appearing soon.

Materials Recycling Facilities

Materials recycling facilities (MRFs) is a growing industry, for sorting landfill garbage to recover space and to recover recyclables.[8] Recycling implies reuse and useful application; not all recovered items have a useful form. However, landfill mining as a component of solid waste management produces good results in some cases. At a Kingston, New Hampshire site, for example, combining and regrading the landfill area cost $1.2 million. The town saves $1.4 million over site closure and gets to use the reclaimed land.[9] Of course, few managements know accurately the cost of landfill maintenance and eternal aftercare.

The scarcity and cost of landfill space and the expense of hauling debris increasing distances has lead some demolition firms to recycle demolition debris. Other demolition contractors pay to take down a structure, then try to make a profit on the scrap steel. This plan works when no environmental remediation work arises for asbestos, industrial solvents, and other hazardous wastes. Construction contractors work on 3 percent margins, but demo-

---

[7] "America's Going to Waste," *Industry Week* (November 6, 1989), p. 63.

[8] *Adweek's Marketing Week* (October 16, 1989), p. 47.

[9] "Buried Treasure: By Mining Their Landfills, Communities Can Keep Sites Open Longer and Reduce Ultimate Closure Costs," *Civil Engineering* (April 1990), pp. 52–54.

lition contractors work on 30 to 40 percent margins due to the risk involved.[10]

Granulator manufacturers build machines to meet critical requirements for reclaiming municipal scrap. Conair-Wortex plans four machines with cutting chambers for such products as trash cans, computer cases, and bottles.[11]

Polychlorinated biphenyl (PCB) program management has challenged electric utilities for decades. PCB-tainted mineral oil in transformers requires either on-line detoxification or retrofilling.[12] For many decades electric utilities have restrained from resorting to landfill disposal of scrap transformers and transformer-oil.

Purchasing and materials managers move into a new era of protecting the earth from contamination.

Waste Management

The potential for groundwater contamination exists when volatile organic chemicals (VOC) contaminate the soil. Soil vapor extraction for VOC removal has grown in popularity as a cost-effective method. Soil vapor extraction works in conjunction with groundwater pumping and treatment as an inexpensive alternative for cleaning up petroleum and solvent spills.[13]

Groundwater contamination from a variety of sources poses significant health risks to large elements of the population. Between 1500 and 3000 U.S. public drinking water supplies that use groundwater have not met the Environmental Protection Agency's standards for safe water over the last decade. Recent surveys show that 30 states have drinking water wells contaminated with one or more of 60 different pesticides.

Europe, with less wide open spaces than America and with longer histories of dense populations, has shown leadership in resource recovery. A polyvinyl chloride (PVC) supplier operates industrial and post-consumer plastics recycling.[14] Plastics waste management covers such areas as waste collection and treatment, material recycling, and energy recovery.

[10] "Hard-Ball Business Becoming Even Harder," *Engineering News Record* (March 1, 1990), pp. 38–46.

[11] "Granulators Move Deeper into the Processing and Recycling Mainstream," *Modern Plastics* (May 1990), pp. 49–51.

[12] "Eliminate PCBs from Mineral-Oil Transformers," *Electrical World* (March 1990), pp. S39–S41.

[13] "Vaporizing VOCs," *Civil Engineering* (April 1990), pp. 57–60.

[14] "European Resin Suppliers Take Lead in Industrial, Post-Consumer Recycling," *Modern Plastics* (January 1990), pp. 144–145.

The Netherlands' waste policy has prevented and recycled waste, with these noteworthy improvements:

95 percent of the total quantity of coal fly ash now serves as raw material.

85 percent of the total quantity of waste oil recycles as fuel.

65 percent of the total quantity of sewage sludge becomes fertilizer.

Over 50 percent of the waste paper and glass in household waste collects separately for reuse.[15]

Despite such progress, the United Nations Environment Programme points to many obstacles that prevent nations from using environmentally sound technologies. These obstacles include not enough awareness of the environmental effects of production processes, especially transboundary movements of hazardous wastes, lack of understanding waste management's true costs, no access to technical advice, insufficient knowledge to carry out new technologies, lack of financial resources, or simply management inertia and resistance to change.[16] Most developed nations, now at a post-industrialist stage, are witnessing the decline in the value added to their gross domestic product by the manufacturing sector, while the information sector expands rapidly and does not pollute the environment.

Water Management

The United States society benefits from irrigation agriculture. Irrigated areas in the United States now exceed 54 million acres. Drainage water from irrigated lands, however, carries salt that requires treatment and disposal. Irrigation management monitors and reduces the mass of salt discharged in the drainage water.[17] Still, irrigation management uses traditional end-of-pipe approaches to pollution control instead of pollution prevention and waste minimization. As a consequence, pesticides and fertilizers endanger wells, springs, aquifers, and downstream runoffs from agricultural land.

The federal Clean Air and Water Act of 1978 considers all agricultural users as point sources of pollution. The act stipulates that all waters flowing out will be as clean as they came in. Feedlots began capturing their waters and in so doing recovered valuable by-products. Packing plants and dairies have long attended to controlling effluent water quality.

Irrigation management also challenges waste such as in the Colorado

---

[15] "An Approach to the Prevention and Recycling of Waste," *UNEP Industry and Environment* (January–March 1989), p. 25.

[16] Ibid., "Waste Minimization," p. 1.

[17] "America's Irrigation: Can It Last?" *Civil Engineering* (March 1990), pp. 67–69.

River's upper basin, where water gets pumped uphill over long distances to irrigate land that yields only low-profit crops.[18]

Over 70,000 chemicals find worldwide use today, with 500 to 1000 new chemicals introduced each year. The "green shopper," the environmentally informed customer, keeps pressure steaming at city hall, the statehouse, the Congress, and the marketplace to focus management's attention on pollution prevention and waste minimization. Meanwhile, he or she may buy recycled motor oil at discount stores.

Warner-Lambert Company has developed a degradable plastic wholly derived from starch, at a time of peak consumer interest in degradable plastics.[19] Exxon derives an amorphous polymer as a by-product when it manufactures polypropylene. The firm has begun recovering and selling the waste by-product and will more than recoup its investment by reducing the waste disposal cost. Savings: $8.7 million annually, by not having to incinerate the polymer.

Dow used to burn 150 million pounds of specialty chemical by-products each year. Now it ships them to its plants in the United States, Canada, Germany, and Brazil for converting into dry cleaning fluid. Dow saves on lower waste disposal bills and lower raw material costs for its cleaning fluid operations.[20]

AT&T's copper recycling subsidiary generates roughly $400 million in annual revenues by pulling gold from circuit packs, silver from solder, palladium from printed circuit boards, zinc from old telephone switch hooks, lead from casings stripped off copper wires (that is sold to battery makers), and scrap plastic from wire, telephone, and computer housings that go into fence posts and flowerpots.[21]

Finally, recycling efforts strengthen in America's neighborhoods as curbside recycling collection programs expand. This effort has helped the used aluminum beverage can (UBC) market, and the recycling of glass, plastics, steel cans, and newspapers.[22]

Purchasing managers turn to consultants and specialty contractors for reclaiming land affected by spills. Industrial purchasers watch the current scene develop into better environmental control, deeper public understanding, and new sources of recovered raw materials. It is a global reclamation and salvage endeavor.[23]

---

[18] "America's Rivers: Till the River Runs Dry," *Economist (UK)* (January 13, 1990), pp. 31–32.
[19] "Degradable Resin Is 100 Percent Starch-Based," *Modern Plastics* (March 1990), pp. 22, 24.
[20] "Alchemy, 1990s Style," *Forbes* (July 24, 1989), pp. 92, 94, 96.
[21] Ibid., p. 94.
[22] "The UBC Market Is Changing," *Beverage World* (October 1989), p. 222.
[23] "Risk Assessment of Pesticides," *Chemical and Engineering News* (January 7, 1991), pp. 27–55.

CHAPTER SUMMARY

The purchasing department carries the full accountability of salvaging and disposing of scrap that the company generates in its normal operations. A vast industry of scrap dealers reclaims scrap and returns it to the manufacturing sector.

Typically, the purchasing department negotiates contracts for waste disposal, giving particular attention to toxic waste and to the problem of diminishing landfill space for dumping.

Surplus equipment may serve the firm if again placed into service. Many purchasing departments serve as clearing houses to describe accurately the equipment, its condition, its location, and its remaining dollar value, in order that other plants within the company may get first rights to the surplus item. If no internal demand is found, the purchasing department may market the item through mass media.

Discussion Questions

1. Why are surplus and obsolete materials sometimes labeled as the price of progress?
2. Distinguish between spoilage, waste, and scrap as applied to the production process.
3. Why is the responsibility for scrap disposal typically assigned to the purchasing department?
4. In what ways can scrap be used within the plant?
5. What are the various disposition alternatives used for surplus?

6. What is an as-is sale?
7. What is the contribution of scrap dealers in the sale of scrap?
8. How is price determined in scrap disposal activities?
9. What is the role of the scrap consultant?
10. How does a firm determine whether an item is obsolete? What is a surplus item?
11. What are the arguments voiced for and against assigning the surplus disposal activity to the production department?

Suggested Case

Megalopolis City

20

Make-or-Buy Decisions

Company president Randy knows that a make-or-buy analysis computes the break-even point if the shop runs at full capacity. So he calculates the cost-to-make by adding fixed cost to the multiplication product of average variable cost times quantity needed. Randy calculates the cost-to-buy as quoted price times quantity needed. If the cost-to-buy exceeds the cost-to-make, he then decides to make the product in-house, otherwise he buys. If the cost-to-make is essentially the same as the cost-to-buy, then Randy reviews other potential benefits on which to base his decision.

When the shop operates at excess capacity, Randy excludes fixed overhead cost from fixed cost in the make-or-buy analysis. He reasons that other production departments already bear the fixed overhead burden and likely will continue to do so during the near term. After then, the new product that he *makes* as a result of this analysis, must bear its full burden of fixed cost, including fixed overhead cost. The fixed overhead cost includes items such as insurance, rent, general and administrative expenses—items the firm must pay for during the near future regardless of quantity produced and sold.

CHAPTER CONTENTS

535

Service firms and manufacturing firms often find it difficult to utilize fully their producing capacity. The firms may have bought and installed equipment to meet rising demand, but once the output demand ceases, what happens to the excess capacity? Make-or-buy decisions involve calculating when to make and when to buy. Purchasing managers confront all sorts of arguments from operating managers, engineers, and vendors, justifying the make-or-buy decision.

In recent years the make versus buy decision has become a major area of discussion. During the late 1980s, there was a trend toward more vertical integration within firms. This trend supported a rationale for more in-house production, which was reinforced by the 1990 downturn. The changed economic climate and increased efficiencies resulting from specialization, however, have led to the beginning of a long-term trend that favors outside buying. A *Purchasing* magazine survey shows that 42.6 percent of the responding purchasing professionals outsource more; that is, buy rather than make.[1]

Many organizations have the capabilities to produce and assemble their required components within their own production facilities. Most of such components, however, are purchased from outside sources that, taking advantage of mass production, specialization, and the resulting economies, can offer the components at a lower overall cost than would be incurred with internal production. However, the decision to make or buy is a major one. Significant price variables in many departments figure in the decision, and therefore a thorough evaluation by procurement personnel is required.

Although the final decision on a make-or-buy question is made through the joint efforts of several departments, the purchasing department will always play an active role in the determination. Generally the purchasing department provides the essential cost data, exercising close coordination between departments on such matters as available production facilities, quantities required, production schedules, capital availability, and returns on capital.

This chapter studies the various issues that must be considered before reaching a decision to make or buy. No simple rule can be applied in all cases. Some decisions are major, as when a paper-manufacturing firm decides whether to build or buy a pulp mill to supply its own raw material. Others are minor, as when a metal products firm ponders whether to make or purchase a small fitting. Each instance must be decided on its merits, and the relevant issues may be quite different in the two cases.

[1] "Outsourcing Solving More Supply Problems," *Purchasing* (May 18, 1989), p. 21.

THE INITIATION OF MAKE-OR-BUY INVESTIGATIONS

The procedure of evaluating whether to purchase from oneself (make) or purchase from outside vendors (buy) is a continuing process. The initial make-or-buy investigation can originate in a variety of ways.

1. Vendors may propose the alternative and request permission to submit quotations on components that they are capable of producing.
2. The question may arise because of unsatisfactory vendor performance, such as an emergency created by delivery problems or poor quality.
3. Unreasonable vendor price increases can trigger an investigation.
4. The addition of a new product or substantial modifications to an existing one typically require make-or-buy analyses; many firms include these studies as an integral step in all new-product development decisions.
5. A value analysis study of an existing product may necessitate a make-or-buy evaluation.
6. Changes in sales volume and related variations in plant capacity raise make-or-buy concerns. Reduced sales and idle equipment or personnel may prompt the firm to consider making items that were previously purchased from outside vendors.
7. Conversely, during periods of rising sales, pressure on the existing facilities often prompts management to seek external assistance from outside suppliers, and a make-or-buy investigation is required.
8. Capital equipment costs after amortization schedules may lead firms to purchase on the outside at less cost.
9. A decline of skilled labor in some localities may force firms to outsource more.[2]

In all companies, make-or-buy studies should be conducted periodically. Earlier decisions should be reviewed at least once every three years, for the factors involved in the decision are fluid and frequently changing.

In broad terms, the relevant considerations in make-or-buy decisions are the same as those involved in all purchasing decisions: quality, quantity, cost, and service. An added variable is the expense of tooling. When tooling costs are high, flexibility in changing from make to buy or vice versa is limited unless such tools can be transferred to accommodate the production facilities of the vendor or producer.

---

[2] *Ibid.*

In the sections that follow each of these factors will be discussed in the make-or-buy context to indicate how they might bear on the decision.

QUALITY VARIABLES THAT FAVOR MAKING

Lack of Supplier Quality

There are sufficient quality differences between the make-or-buy alternatives to warrant weighing the quality factor in making the decision. An extreme example of quality requiring the producer to select the make option might be a nuclear reactor whose conventional manufacturers have not made certain critical parts to the necessary high-quality and tolerance requirements. Although initially this appears to be a compelling argument for making the item, certain questions should be raised. Why is no supplier making the desired quality? Is the particular quality specified by the engineering department really necessary? Is the failure to find the desired quality on the market a temporary situation that will soon change? Is the company sure that it can produce the desired quality in its own plant?

If no producer is making the desired quality, suppliers may not have had requests for such quality. Most producers will respond to new quality specifications if they have reasonable assurance that the demand is sound and likely to recur. However, if no producer seems willing to make the item, it may be that the demand is not sound, and questions should be raised whether the user could economically and technologically produce the desired quality in its own plant.

Perhaps the specifications drawn up by the engineering department are more exacting than necessary for the proper operation or the expected life of the item. The dimensions or tolerance may be more rigid than the commonly accepted commercial standards. A review of these concerns by the proper departments may remove this impediment to purchasing from outside suppliers.

Occasionally, such rigid inspection standards are set for a purchased item that suppliers cannot reasonably comply. Considerations then include whether such high standards are necessary, and whether they can be met if the item is made internally.

The lack of the desired quality in the product of a supplier may be a temporary situation, especially if the item is a new product, and especially if it is being made by a new industry. Once a decision to manufacture rather than to buy is reached, it can be changed only at great cost and after a period of time. Therefore, it is important to ascertain that the condition is not temporary.

Finally, a thorough investigation should be undertaken to make certain that one's own plant can produce to the desired standard. If the supplier who is a specialist in making the item will not produce to a given specification, there is a reason to question whether the buyer, who may be inexperienced, can do any better.

Higher component part standardization has gained importance as a means of reducing safety stock requirements, planning larger lot sizes, and decreasing planning complexity through reducing the number of items that need planning. The degree of commonality index (DCI), the traditional measure of component part standardization, feeds into the make–buy decision. The DCI may tip the decision either way.[3]

Warranty Provisions

A manufacturer of an advertised line of baby furniture stressed the guarantee provision. As a protective device the written guarantee contained a clause excluding parts not of the firm's own manufacture. It was discovered that the company was incurring much ill will when the non-guaranteed parts manufactured by outside suppliers failed. As a consequence, a policy of making rather than buying in order to ensure warranty policies was adopted.

Maintaining Design and Process Secrecy

A reason for making that is sometimes encountered is the need to protect an unpatented process or design secrets. Design secrets will be exposed for copying when the product reaches the market, so that a buying company is risking the loss of the design at a slightly earlier date. With an unpatented process secret the owner has more at risk. If the process is confined to internal use, it may be kept from competitors indefinitely, whereas the risk of losing the secret is greatly increased if it is shared with suppliers.

Unreliable Suppliers

At times, firms choose to manufacture a particular part because available suppliers are unreliable. When the buyer generates only a small percentage of the supplier's volume, deliveries may be late or incomplete during the supplier's peak periods. In many such cases the make option is the only alternative. When the buyer needs a slightly higher volume, the firm may opt to both make and buy to ensure its supply. Thus, a reliable secondary source of supply is always available.

[3] "Component Part Standardization: An Analysis of Commonality Sources and Indices," *Journal of Operations Management* (February 1986), pp. 219–244.

Maintenance of a Stable Workforce

Another factor favoring the make decision is the desire to maintain a stable and reliable workforce. Fluctuating employment levels make it difficult for a firm to maintain a loyal and efficient workforce. Thus, many firms choose to produce as much in house as possible while varying the size of purchase orders, which causes the supplier to bear production fluctuations.

The United Auto Workers (UAW) and Ford Motor Company made an agreement allowing the union to express its viewpoints in make-or-buy decisions. The UAW's goal was to prevent nonunion or foreign purchasing by Ford and to prevent plant closings. By maintaining a stable workforce, Ford can, on its side, often secure concessions that will make a distressed plant viable.

QUALITY VARIABLES THAT FAVOR BUYING

Certain positive reasons can be advanced for buying, reasons having to do with quality and based on the assumption that other considerations of quantity, price, and service are equal.

Specialization Promotes Perfection

The strongest reason for buying is that a producer is likely to be particularly skilled in the manufacture of items that constitute its regular line. Thus, in buying one receives the benefits of specialization, whereas making the item may be a sideline operation in one's own plant. Furthermore, since the new item is likely to remain of secondary interest to the maker, there will not be the strong inducement to keep up with technological changes relating to the product. A company organized to make the item as a part of its regular line is likely to devote considerable managerial effort to research and technological improvement of the product and process.

Patent Protection

The choice in favor of buying may be necessary because the supplier controls certain patents or production methods. Occasionally a license can be obtained from the patent holder that authorizes production by the user upon payment of a royalty to the patent holder.

Flexibility

Another reason for buying rather than making is the increased quality flexibility that buying permits. It is a relatively simple matter to change suppliers as quality needs are altered. However, if the company is making the part, it is not nearly as simple to alter its production facilities to permit such changes.

Managerial Control

Finally, some firms buy components as a means of checking their managerial control systems. The utilization of suppliers' costs and quality data in this manner can often uncover internal production inefficiencies.

QUANTITY CONSIDERATIONS

Considerations of quantity differ from those of quality, because although quality can be accurately set forth, quantity is much more variable and must be considered in relation to time. The correct quantity at a given time and circumstance will not be correct at another time under changed circumstances. Thus, how much to buy is a variable, whereas what to buy is a constant.

Small Volume Requirements

When a firm uses a particular item in small quantities, it can often realize greater savings by buying from an outside supplier that produces in large quantities. This option becomes even more desirable as the part becomes more standardized.

Too-Small Orders

Regarding quantity, the most common reason for making rather than buying is that the order would be too small to interest a supplier. Before deciding to make for this reason, a buyer should consider whether buying a sufficient quantity and carrying an inventory for a longer period of time would be feasible. Consideration should also be given to possible specification changes so that several small-use items could be included under a common specification.

Another reason sometimes favoring a make decision is that, since it is difficult to forecast needs accurately, the adjustment of supply to demand as demand shifts can be made more readily if one has control over the production scheduling.

Large Orders

The need for large quantities may be a reason for either making or buying. If no supplier is able to make the item in the large quantities required, it becomes necessary either to make the item internally or to split the order among suppliers. Splitting the order often is not practicable if the parts are made with dies or patterns. The cost of furnishing separate dies or patterns to each supplier might be prohibitive. Thus requiring large quantities of an item sometimes means making rather than buying.

On the other hand, if the quantity required is so large that to make it would interfere with production of the regular line of products, it becomes highly desirable to buy.

COST CONSIDERATIONS

If quality, quantity, and service factors are equal, the cost considerations in a make-or-buy decision become a comparison of a known cost, the price charged by a vendor, with an unknown, estimated cost, that of making the item. Therefore, it is possible to generalize that if all other factors are equal, and there is only a slight cost advantage in favor of making, the item should be purchased. A known cost is usually preferable to a slightly lower estimated cost.

Estimating the Cost to Make

The accuracy of the estimate depends on the skill and care with which it is compiled. The smaller the item, in terms of either value or quantity, the more difficult it is to arrive at an accurate cost figure.

The problem of estimating accurately is compounded by the nature of overhead costs. If the make-or-buy decision concerned an item that was clearly separate and apart from all other items made in the plant, the allocation of overhead would be a simple matter. However, the item is usually produced in a multiproduct plant using common materials and machines. For example, a firm would be better able to make accurate cost estimates for a decision whether to set up a foundry to make castings, than for a decision whether to make a certain type of casting in its foundry or buy it outside.

Another variable is the current level of production in the plant relative to its total capacity. The fixed costs of a plant operating below capacity are a relatively high percentage of total costs. Therefore, additional production can be undertaken with only a small increase in total cost. On the other hand, a firm operating at capacity can take on additional production only at substantially increased costs.

Fixed versus Variable Costs

Fixed costs do not vary with output and are referred to as overhead or unavoidable costs. They include such items as management salaries, taxes, depreciation, and insurance. Variable costs fluctuate with output and are often referred to as direct costs. Examples include the direct labor and raw materials required to produce additional units of output.

A plant with excess capacity can increase production by merely adding incremental costs that are variable in nature, whereas a plant being fully utilized can increase production only by increasing its capacity, thereby adding incremental costs of both a fixed and variable nature. This point is diagrammed in the break-even chart shown in Figure 20-1.

A firm that increases production from 100 to 110 percent incurs incremental costs of $31 ($119 to $150 per unit), because of the increase in fixed and variable costs. However, the same firm could have increased production from 70 to 80 percent and incurred incremental costs of only $11 per unit

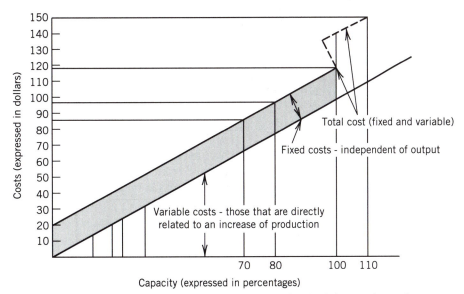

FIGURE 20-1. A graph of cost versus capacity for evaluating the choice to make or to buy.

($87 to $98), because in the latter range of output, fixed costs are constant and only direct costs are increased.

When facilities are being employed at less than capacity, the cost of making should be determined by dividing the estimated volume into the increased variable costs. The item then would be purchased only if its unit purchase cost was equal to or less than the unit increase in variable costs. At any higher price the item should be made, because it would be contributing something toward overhead costs.

When the facilities are being operated at capacity, the choice is between expansion of the facilities or an outside purchase. In such a case the company is justified in purchasing on the outside at any price less than the unit total costs of making the item. If the amount required is small, the buyer may even consider paying a higher price rather than assuming an investment in facilities that might not remain fully utilized.

VARIABLES IN COST ACCOUNTING

Although the preceding analysis implied a relatively simple approach to make-or-buy decisions, in reality, to determine costs requires difficult calculations. A first consideration is the period of time in question. A firm with a plant operating at 70 percent of capacity would make a mistake in changing from buying to making if the projected sales of its products will require capacity production within a few years. Second, the calculations already discussed assume that cost can be neatly classified into fixed and variable.

A company that wants to examine the feasibility of buying an item from a supplier instead of manufacturing it in-house can use a spreadsheet program to develop a discounted cash-flow analysis. Use of a computerized spreadsheet permits simulation by changing any variables that estimate the rate of return, after taxes.[4] Break-even analysis may also help.

Break-even Analysis

Promotion to Senior Buyer empowers Terry to try economic analysis that may reduce her company's outlays for materials bought instead of made in-house. Break-even analysis shows Senior Buyer Terry the vendor's break-even point, with no profit or loss, where total revenue (TR) equals total cost (TC) for a product that she intends to buy instead of make. The computer disk that accompanies this text computes the break-even quantity (Q) at the break-even point.

Terry pulls figures from the vendor's financial records. In the break-

---

[4] "Using Lotus 1-2-3 for Make/Buy Decisions," *Purchasing World* (November 1986), pp. 84–86.

even analysis program, she enters fixed cost (*FC*) for facilities including overhead expense to make this product, the vendor's average variable cost (*AVC*) to make this product, and the selling price (*P*) that the vendor quotes.

Selling price (*P*) times the break-even quantity (*Q*) that the program computes, equals the fixed cost (*FC*) that Terry already entered added to the product of average variable cost (*AVC*) times the break-even quantity (*Q*). The program solves for break-even quantity (*Q*).

$$\text{At break-even, } TR = TC$$
$$TR = P \times Q$$
$$TC = FC + AVC \times Q$$
$$\text{Thus, } P \times Q = FC + AVC \times Q$$
$$\text{and } Q = FC \div (P - AVC)$$

If Terry wants to find the vendor's profit (*PR*), she enters a quantity (*Q*∗) also into the program, which returns a computed value for profit (*PR*) at the quantity (*Q*∗) she intends to buy.

Fixed cost—such as land, building, machinery, lights, heat, insurance, employee benefits, and food service—does not change with quantities of products produced or sold. Variable cost includes the materials and labor directly involved in making this product—for example, the electric power to run the machines and the maintenance and repair that producing the product incurs. Average variable cost (*AVC*) puts it on a per unit or per piece basis.

Terry needs to know at what revenue and cost point the vendor operates. If the vendor operates at a loss, the situation cannot last long, otherwise the vendor will go out of business. Taking Terry's order may break the vendor. The sales representative may not know the figure or may not divulge it anyway. Therefore, Terry makes an estimate and computes from scanty data, sales brochures, and general knowledge.

Figure 20-2 illustrates a typical break-even diagram with example data. Figure 20-3, a profit–volume diagram, applies the same example data to show more clearly the sunk cost nature of fixed cost (left of break-even point) until revenue levels rise enough to begin recovering fixed cost. The diagram also shows profits rise as quantity and revenue volumes increase.

Raw Materials and Equipment Costs

If raw materials or supplies that have not previously been purchased are required for making items, the costs of buying them in the short run will be relatively high. New sources must be developed and evaluated. Additional personnel may be required for receiving, handling, and storing the materials. If the item to be made is somewhat different from regular production

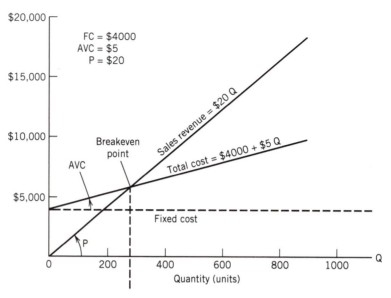

FIGURE 20-2. Break-even diagram.

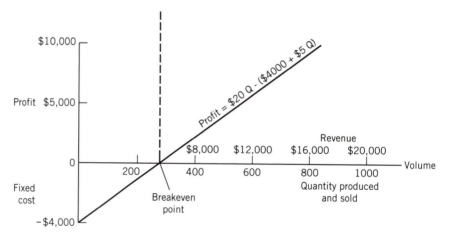

FIGURE 20-3. Profit–volume diagram.

items, it may require new machines or personnel, or at least additional training of present personnel to manufacture it properly.

An adequate return on investment should be a consideration because money invested in raw materials and equipment is tied up and is therefore a real cost, since other opportunities must be forgone. Management should ask itself: If, as a result of a buy decision, we can free money, what return can we expect from it? On the other hand, if a make decision requires an increase in investment, what will be the cost of this money?

A firm that produces for itself may have only itself as a customer, and its production runs must be large enough to take advantage of economies of scale. An outside supplier may have many customers for the same item and therefore be able to enjoy production cost advantages. In addition, increased inventory (both raw material and finished goods) results when an item is made internally.[5]

Use of the EOQ Formula

The difference in ordered quantities can be illustrated by the use of the economic ordering quantity (EOQ) formula. When EOQ is applied to a make decision, the previously used formula for purchased parts,

$$EOQ = \sqrt{\frac{2AC}{B}}$$

where

A = order costs
C = annual usage in dollar volume
B = carrying cost

is adapted to read

$$EOQ = \sqrt{\frac{2US}{ID}}$$

where

U = expected usage in units over time
D = cost per unit (direct manufacturing costs when in-plant production is involved)
I = inventory carrying charge as a percentage (including value of money invested, insurance, and other overhead items over the same time as usage)
S = setup costs or purchase costs (materials and supplies).

[5] See "A Dynamic Lot-Size Model with Make-or-Buy Decisions," *Management Science* (April 1989), pp. 447–458, for mathematical considerations when production level may not exceed a given capacity but the purchase has no restrictions.

The only difference in the two formulas is that in the second costs are changed to setup costs, usage in dollar volume is now expressed as usage in units, and the carrying charges are separated into inventory carrying charges and cost per unit.

Assuming no significant discount for volume and the same cost, regardless whether the item is purchased or manufactured, the most economical number of parts to be manufactured will be greater than the number to be purchased, resulting in a heavier carrying cost for the "make" item. The following example illustrates the higher EOQ quantity required for an item with the same purchased cost and make cost.

Economic Lot-Size Calculation
Annual Usage: 100 pieces
Purchase Price: $10
Cost to Make: $10

Manufactured Lot
  Carrying Charge: 25%
  Setup Costs: $100

$$EOQ = \sqrt{\frac{2 \times 100 \times 100}{0.25 \times 10}}$$

$$EOQ = 89$$

Purchased Lot
  Carrying Charge: 25%
  Purchase Costs: $10

$$EOQ = \sqrt{\frac{2 \times 100 \times 10}{0.25 \times 10}}$$

$$EOQ = 28$$

The higher the setup costs to prepare for production, the greater the disparity between the quantities for making versus buying. The smaller the EOQ, the better.

Transportation Costs

Another cost element that may be higher in making than in buying is the cost of transportation. Because of the greater bulk of raw materials, their transportation costs may be higher than those for finished parts. One offsetting consideration is the fact that the transportation rate per 100 pounds of raw material is usually less than the rate for processed goods.

SERVICE AND OTHER CONSIDERATIONS

To all the known costs that must be included in arriving at a reasonable estimate of the cost of making an item, there must be added a number of variables whose value can only be estimated. Although they are imponderables, these factors must be considered before a decision is made.

In purchasing parlance, service includes a wide variety of intangible factors that add to the buyer's satisfaction.

The assurance of supply is an important service consideration. In general, assurance is better when a company makes an item than when it buys it. This concern is of particular note to large mass-production firms for obvious reasons.

Making rather than buying items may enable a firm to give more assured and regular employment to its employees and, in effect, enable a company to stabilize its organization.

Another situation that may lead a company to make rather than buy is the suspicion of collusion among suppliers. Although collusion is illegal and evidence thereof should be reported to the Department of Justice or the Federal Trade Commission, a company's first reaction to its discovery will usually be to seek alternative sources of needed supply. One likely alternative is the decision to make the item.

Closely related to the collusion issue is the concern felt when only one or two suppliers are available. A buyer may not have much confidence that they will compete actively. The existence of such monopolistic conditions provides an incentive to make rather than buy.

A similar situation exists when the buyer is faced with what may be termed a legal monopoly; that is, an item is protected by patents. Here a buyer may try to develop a substitute that can be made without patent infringement, in order to protect against the monopoly power of the supplier's patent.

A decision to make an item will certainly give suppliers of other purchased items pause. When a company begins to make items that it formerly bought, its other suppliers begin to wonder whether their items too will eventually be made by the buyer. When a supplier questions the continuity of relations with a customer, the quality of service and the assurance of supply may be impaired.

Another service factor is the buyer's flexibility. When an item is purchased, the buyer is in a favorable position to negotiate with various suppliers. Competition is keen, and movement can be made from one supplier to another as the occasion demands, in order to secure the right quality at the right time and for the right price. Once a company is committed to making an item, this flexibility is lost and it becomes difficult to adjust quantity, quality, or price (cost).

Miscellaneous Considerations

A number of miscellaneous factors have a bearing on make-or-buy decisions but cannot logically be classified under one of the four main headings: quality, quantity, cost, and service considerations. Like service, they are difficult to measure quantitatively but are nonetheless significant to the decision.

The first miscellaneous factor is a proper evaluation of the know-how required to make the item in question. It is, of course, possible for a company to hire or train personnel to produce almost any item. However, the feasibility of doing this depends on the cost of acquiring the necessary competence in the form of the supplier's organization.

The contingency of war is a consideration bearing on the make-or-buy decision. International hostilities disrupt normal sources of supply, particularly of items purchased abroad. During such periods, if no acceptable domestic source of supply can be located, it becomes necessary to make the item formerly purchased.

Another consideration is the age of the firm. In general, a new company that is still growing will tend to buy more items than a company that has reached maturity. New companies tend to concentrate on increasing output by buying components from suppliers. The mature company, on the other hand, tends to have extra facilities, capital, and personnel that can be used for making rather than buying. Actually both companies are expanding in the way most appropriate to their circumstances.

The emotional element cannot be measured but is nevertheless a powerful motivating factor. Management may decide to enlarge by making items it formerly bought, in order to have the satisfaction of managing a larger concern.

The increased importance of unions in labor–management relations is reflected in make-or-buy decisions. Unions may attempt to include in their contracts clauses that prohibit management from buying or subcontracting items that can be manufactured in its own plant. In such cases the unions are given the privilege of overruling previous management decisions to purchase. On the other hand, because strikes in vendor plants can cause serious production tie-ups, an unstable history of labor relations in a given industry may dictate making rather than buying.

SUBCONTRACTING

Subcontracting is a business practice under which a producer hires another firm to perform some of the manufacturing process or to furnish subassemblies that will be incorporated into the end product. Since subcontracting is simply one method of buying instead of making, many of the factors previously discussed influence the subcontracting decision. The term subcontracting has come to be associated in particular with contractual arrangements between industrial concerns and government agencies, especially during war or active defense periods, and it is used here in this sense.

During national emergencies, large orders are placed by government buyers with large suppliers, because it simplifies the process of awarding and administering the contracts. When such prime contractors farm out some of the components to other suppliers who have available facilities, the prime contractor has in effect chosen to buy rather than to make the items subcontracted. Many government contracts favor the use of small businesses, identified as those firms employing 500 or fewer employees. Large companies that are prime contractors to the government receive special considerations if certain proportions of the price contract are subcontracted to small businesses. The government also gives extra consideration in making awards to companies subcontracting orders in so-called labor distress areas.

There are certain other advantages to subcontracting. Usually subcontracting is the fastest method of increasing output. It is a procedure that often enables the prime contractor (the buyer) to use the workforce where it is located instead of shifting it into its own plant. Subcontracting enables utilization of engineering and management skills already existing as a functioning unit instead of developing such facilities. It may also avoid the need for new plants and equipment on the part of the buyer.

Another benefit of subcontracting is in avoiding the unnecessary overexpansion of productive facilities. Expanding to meet an abnormal demand may subject a firm to heavy fixed charges in the future when such facilities are not needed.

There are several practical questions that must be raised by a company considering the possibility of subcontracting. To what extent should the subcontractor permit facilities to be committed to one prime contractor? To what extent should a prime contractor aid a subcontractor in procuring materials, supplies, and tools? To what extent should engineering assistance be extended? To what extent should a subcontractor be financed? These and many similar concerns must be settled.

The degree of subcontracting a prime contractor should undertake is influenced by a variety of factors. One of these factors is time. Subcontracting will generally take less time than production in one's own plant, because the subcontractor presumably has a background of skill, equipment, and general know-how already developed.

Subcontracting will generally reduce investment costs in specialized machinery and tooling. However, since the subcontractor does incur such costs, prices may reflect them, and the savings may be more nominal than real.

CHAPTER SUMMARY

The make-or-buy decision arises when the firm introduces new products, when vendors perform poorly or demand unreasonable prices, when rising sales create overloads on producing facilities, when reduced sales bring about idle equipment, or when a shift occurs in the supply of skilled labor.

Factors favoring the decision to make an item instead of buying it include lack of supplier quality and reliability, secrecy to protect the firm's design, and, unfortunately, the managerial ego that boasts, ''By golly, we can make the product cheaper and better than anyone else can.''

Factors favoring buying instead of making the product include the supplier's specialization that results in a superior product at lower price, the supplier may control the patent, the order may be too small or too large for one's own firm to make, or the managerial attitude that ''We can buy everything we need.''

Break-even analysis and economic order quantity calculations provide numbers to guide the make-or-buy decision makers.

Discussion Questions

1. What are the most compelling reasons advanced for buying rather than making?
2. What quality considerations dictate making rather than buying?
3. If all other factors are equal, but there is a slight cost advantage in making rather than buying, what action is recommended? Why?
4. When facilities are being operated at capacity and a make-or-buy decision is being made, what costs (fixed, variable, total) are relevant?
5. Define a *legal monopoly.*
6. What negative supplier reaction can be expected to result from a make decision?
7. How do tax laws affect the make-or-buy decisions?
8. Indicate the advantages of subcontracting to a prime contractor.
9. What conditions determine the influence of the purchasing agent in make-or-buy decisions?
10. Indicate how the traditional EOQ formula can be adapted to make-or-buy decisions.

Suggested Cases

ABC Corporation (B)

The Anson Company

Berg Raingear, Inc.

Road Equipment Manufacturing Company

═21

Forward Buying, Speculation, and Hedging

The flour mill has bought wheat within 200 miles of the mill for nearly 200 years. Mr. Samuel, purchasing agent for 25 years, has placed contracts for grain delivery a year in advance. He knows that the big cooperatives combine to reap the season's harvest and ship at a price negotiated with considerable experience. They reckon the prospect of weather changes; natural disasters; sales to Russia, Egypt, and China; wars; insect pestilence; and transportation strikes.

Last year the mill was sold to new owners. The new management reassigned forward buying of grains to the chief financial officer, leaving Mr. Samuel mad and hurt.

CHAPTER CONTENTS

One person or one firm typically makes little, if any, impact on the nation's financial system. Inevitably, the system makes its own rules and ploughs along toward the future. Does the purchasing manager who takes part in financial futures markets to avoid the risks of price fluctuations make any impact on commodity prices? Typically, he or she goes where the market goes, and pays the market price or negotiates a better price. Purchasing managers conduct only about 20 to 30 percent of potential hedging. However, hedging constitutes one of the largest possible improvements in the future.

Management of the risk of price fluctuation has long been one of the primary concerns of purchasing. Initially the practice of buying ahead, or forward buying, was the main method of safeguarding buying agreements when price increases were anticipated. More recently, the sophisticated use of organized futures markets has allowed the hedging of transactions to minimize price fluctuation risks with minimal cash investment. This chapter discusses purchase timing and the concept of forward buying and presents the speculative elements of buying beyond actual needs. The practice of avoiding price fluctuation risks via the hedging process is then examined in detail. The chapter concludes with a review of the many possibilities of avoiding risk through the use of financial futures.

PURCHASE TIMING

Purchase timing involves risk management. The purchasing manager contemplates action on a request for materials or services. He or she selects a vendor, negotiates terms of quality, delivery, and price, and advises persons in-house when to expect delivery. Little risk occurs here.

Or, the purchasing manager observes rising prices in the marketplace, or perhaps major events about to happen to make materials scarce. He or she contemplates ordering goods beyond current needs, for future delivery, so as to lock in prices before they rise. Risk management comes importantly into the picture.

The purchasing field recognizes four time-types of buying:

Type of Buying	*Covers Requirements for*
Hand-to-mouth	Up to 30 days[1]
Buying to current needs	30, 60, or 90 days
Forward buying	3–12 months
Speculative buying	Beyond 12 months

---

[1] The National Association of Purchasing Management uses a value of five days for hand-to-mouth buying policy. ''Report on Business,'' *NAPM Insights* (May 1990), p. 18.

Production cycles dictate the requirements for hand-to-mouth buying and buying to current needs. The purchasing manager gauges supply availability, on-hand inventory levels, in-house storage capacity, budgeted funds available to use for purchases, and the firm's risk-bearing–risk-aversion attitude. When prices are rising, he or she buys larger quantities for longer periods of need—90 days or even longer. When prices are falling, he or she shifts to buying for the next 30 days.

Forward buying, speculation, and hedging come into use with "futures" and "options" strategies. Table 21-1 identifies industries, commodities, futures/options, and the market exchanges that trade such strategies.[2]

FORWARD BUYING

Forward buying involves all purchasing in excess of the usual minimum stock after normal output and delivery requirements are considered. It excludes advance purchases made with the object of realizing speculative profits. Some of the more common objectives of forward buying include:

1. Providing a margin of insurance against possible supplier or carrier interruptions.
2. Taking advantage of quantity discounts.
3. Minimizing transportation costs by consolidating shipments.
4. Protecting against the risks of potential shortages of materials.
5. Securing materials of desired qualities when they are available.

The standard unit of order must consider such factors as the storage space required and available for use, the amount of funds available and the cost of money, the risk of physical deterioration during the period of storage, the cost of placing orders and receiving the goods, the quantity discounts available, and the applicable freight rates covering various weights and quantities.

Some of these considerations conflict with others. For example, the largest possible quantity discount will require the largest investment and require the most storage. The most economical shipping quantity may entail the risk of spoilage. The decision, therefore, requires a good deal of judgment and must be reviewed periodically.

During periods of threatened shortage, constant exercise of judgment and ingenuity on the part of purchasing personnel is required. A combina-

[2] "Risk Management—A Powerful Tool," *Purchasing World* (October 1989), p. 44.

TABLE 21-1. Representative Industries, Commodities and Hedge Vehicles

Industry	Commodity	Futures/Options	Exchange
Distillers	Grains	Corn/wheat	CBOT
Pet foods	Protein	Soybean meal	CBOT
Cereals	Grains	Corn/oats/wheat	CBOT
Food processing	Vegetable oils	Soybean oil	CBOT
Confectionery	Sugar/cocoa	Sugar/cocoa	CSC-NY
Bakery	Flour	Wheat	CBOT/KC
Metal fabricators	Copper	Copper	COMEX
Pollution control	Catalysts	Platinum/palladium	NYMEX
Transportation	Diesel fuel	Heating oil	NYMEX
Airlines	Jet fuel	Heating oil	NYMEX
Petrochemical	Feed stocks	Crude oil	NYMEX
Appliance	Aluminum	Aluminum	LME
Electronics	Circuitry	Silver	COMEX
Jewelry	Settings	Gold/silver	COMEX

CBOT—Chicago Board of Trade; CSC-NY—New York Coffee, Sugar & Cocoa Exchange; CBOT/KC—Chicago and Kansas City Board of Trade; COMEX—Commodity Exchange of New York; NYMEX—New York Mercantile Exchange; LME—London Mercantile Exchange.
Source: ''Risk Management—A Powerful Tool,'' *Purchasing World* (October 1989), p. 44.

tion of experience and true executive talent is necessary for managerial analysis and projection of future market conditions.

SPECULATIVE BUYING

The distinction between forward buying and speculative buying lies in their respective rationale. Forward buying is a response to operational considerations or supply–demand conditions. Speculative buying is conducted with the hope of profiting from price changes. Forward buying is a regular procurement practice; speculative buying is not.

When materials are to be bought for speculation, policy approval should be obtained from the highest executive authority in the organization. While pricing physical purchases based on futures prices meets wide acceptance, in many cases senior management resist the selling of futures and options contracts independently as a hedging mechanism.[3] To reduce risk, specific decisions about when and how much to buy may be made by a committee composed of representatives of purchasing, market research, and finance.

[3] ''Risk Management Reduces Price, Cost Savings,'' *Purchasing World* (May 1990), pp. 46–48.

Speculative Buying Compared to Gambling

Speculation and gambling are similar in some respects. Both practices make a prediction of future events, and both involve a substantial element of risk. However, there are two vital distinctions that justify speculative buying. Speculation is taking a financial interest in a risk that is already in existence, whereas gambling creates a financial risk that did not exist before. In buying ahead for speculative reasons, the buyer takes the risk of price changes from some other person who would otherwise be required to carry it. Thus there is merely the substitution of one risk taker for another. In gambling, the participants use some uncertain future event to create a financial risk. The event that determines the outcome for the gamblers has no necessary financial implications. A horse race or a ball game has uncertain outcomes but could occur with no money loss to anyone. Thus the gambler creates new financial hazards, whereas the speculator deals with existing hazards. A *Wall Street Journal* writer makes the following point:[4]

> Speculation should reduce the price consumers pay for goods produced with commodities that were hedged during the production process. They also help set a single price for commodities that are bought and sold at scores of locations around the country, and often around the world.

Gamblers perform no social or economic function. Speculators, on the other hand, assume a price fluctuation risk that is already present and in the process allow others to shift this risk to them. In the commodity exchanges, users of commodities are able to shift the risk of price fluctuations to speculators by the process of hedging, which is discussed in the following section.

HEDGING

One of the major risks of business is that of loss through adverse price fluctuations of raw material, in-process, and finished-goods inventories. Such risks can be substantially reduced for commodities for which organized futures markets exist through the practice of hedging. This section describes some aspects of the operations of commodity exchanges and discusses some of the ways purchasing can make use of hedging.

---

[4] "Don't Call Us Gamblers," *The Wall Street Journal* (October 19, 1990), p. R9.

Definition

Hedging is a procedure designed to minimize risks resulting from adverse price fluctuations in a cash commodity.* In simplest terms, hedging amounts to entering simultaneously into two transactions of a like amount—one a purchase, the other a sale—in two markets whose prices are known to move up and down together by approximately the same amounts. Any two commodity price series that move together can be used to accomplish the object of hedging—the cancellation of gains and losses from price changes—by buying one commodity and selling a like amount of the other for purchase and delivery at a later date. If prices go up, an inventory profit on the commodity bought will be realized; but, since prices move together and in like amount, a loss of an equivalent amount will be incurred in selling the second commodity. If prices go down, the buyer will lose on the purchase but gain a like amount on the sale for future delivery.

Hedging is, therefore, defined as the process of entering simultaneously into two contracts of an opposite nature—one in the cash market, the other in the future market—whose primary purpose is to protect operating profit margins. Essentially, it involves the transfer of price risk to a specialist in risk taking—the speculator.

In practice, it is virtually impossible to find two different commodity price series that move together so closely that they can be used for price protection. For this reason, among others, traders in a number of commodity fields have organized futures markets to serve this purpose.

Historical Development

Trading in futures contracts on an organized basis originated with the Chicago Board of Trade, which has been in operation since 1848. Today, there are over 50 commodities traded on a dozen different U.S. commodity exchanges. The major stock exchanges adopted futures trading in 1984.

The earliest markets and exchanges were developed around agricultural

---

* A complete 42-page report of hedging procedure and research on purchasing's role in it is G. J. Zenz, *Futures Trading and the Purchasing Executive* (New York: National Association of Purchasing Management and Merrill Lynch, Pierce, Fenner & Smith, Inc., 1971), available from Dr. Gary J. Zenz, Department of Marketing and Management, College of Business, Florida State University, Tallahassee, Florida 32306.

commodities such as wheat and corn. A special edition of *The Wall Street Journal* furnishes further historical facts.

> At harvest time, Midwestern farmers and grain shippers delivered their crops within days of each other, flooding the markets and driving down grain prices. . . . By spring, with most of the stored grain used up, grain prices shot up again. There they remained, only to plunge again in the fall.[5]

Today commodity trading has been broadened significantly to include such nonagricultural products as silver, lumber, copper, international currencies, ore, diamonds, and interest rates. This expanded development has sparked the interest of industrial firms as they attempt to protect fluctuating raw material cost and to stabilize international transactions conducted in an atmosphere of volatile prices and currencies.

In an attempt to reduce price risks, early American entrepreneurs developed what was known as the to-arrive contract. Under the terms of this agreement, the seller assured the delivery of goods at a future date at a price fixed at the time of the initial contract. Hence, the buyer had protection, and the seller bore the brunt of any risks associated with downward changes in price during the interval between the contracting and delivery dates.

These risks increased greatly as American markets expanded, resulting in greater in-transit time, the necessity of carrying larger inventories, extending credit, and so forth. In short, mechanization, industrialization, and large-scale production increased the risk of price fluctuations to the point that the seller often no longer could give the to-arrive price protection.

It was because of this risk dilemma that futures trading and commodity exchanges developed. Essentially, the exchange provided a physical meeting place for buyers and sellers and organized and regulated the trading of futures contracts. The exchange itself does not engage in buying or selling contracts; it merely acts as a clearing house for recording transactions. Exchanges gradually expanded their functions to include the supervision of some specifics of trading, including such considerations as trading hours, collateral transfer fees, margin requirements, and contract provisions. By formulating and enforcing trading rules, the exchanges help assure speculators and hedgers that their contracts will be honored.

A futures market is essentially a second market for a commodity, with its transactions limited to purchases and sales for delivery in future months. However, since the commodity concerned is the same in the futures market and in the regular market—usually called the spot or cash market—the prices will move up and down more or less in accord because both markets

---

[5] "Futures' Past," *The Wall Street Journal* (October 19, 1990), p. R7.

are affected by the same price-making forces. The hedger then takes one position (purchase or sale) in the cash market and the opposite (sale or purchase) in the futures market. Thus there is reasonable assurance that the gain or loss in one market will be offset for the most part by a loss or gain in the other.

Carrying Charges

Usually the price of a futures contract is higher than the cash commodity. The difference is represented by all or part of the charge of carrying (i.e., the cost of storage, insurance, and interest charges) the cash commodity to the futures month. For example, if cash wheat in April is selling for $5 a bushel and carrying costs are 5 cents a bushel per month, July wheat futures would theoretically sell for $5.15 per bushel.

However, if enough traders feel that there will be a greatly increased supply of wheat between April and July, it is possible that the futures price could be less than the cash price. This would result in what is called an inverted market, a condition that occurs infrequently.

Reasons for Hedging

Hedging has the advantage of safeguarding profit margins when sales contracts with fixed prices are negotiated, but the purchase of raw materials is postponed. Hedging may also be of benefit in protecting inventory values in a declining market period. Trading in futures can also be utilized to guarantee delivery of a raw material without storing physical stock and incurring finance and carrying charges. It may also be used to establish a favorable material price, again without necessitating the purchase of actual inventory.

The latter practices are not regarded as hedging because they may involve taking a position in futures without having a corresponding physical inventory or an established selling price. Nevertheless, for the purchasing executive they represent important tactical possibilities that are now being used to a greater extent than in the past. A related benefit of hedging is that banks will usually lend a greater percentage of inventory value pledged for collateral when this inventory is protected by a hedge.

Several factors determine the optional hedge and measure hedging effectiveness:

1. The correlation between a futures and its underlying cash price changes.

2. The relative payoff of a futures to its underlying cash position per unit of risk, as in one-period models.

3. The correlation between a cash price and the interest rate changes.

4. The correlation between a futures price and interest rate changes.

5. The relative payoff of a default-free bond to the cash position of per unit risk.[6]

The Buying Hedge

The buying hedge is used to establish the costs of raw materials when a sales contract has been executed that calls for their subsequent purchase. As an example, assume that on April 1, XYZ Company sells generators for delivery on September 30. It is reasonable to assume that the April 1 sales price is predicated upon raw material prices existing on April 1, in this instance for copper.

The selling manufacturer has three choices in this situation. The copper can be bought in April and held until September or whenever processing will begin. A firm price is established, but there will be appropriate storage, interest, and insurance costs on the copper.

The second alternative is to execute the buying hedge. This action will establish the copper cost with limited risk of price change and without incurring the cost of carrying physical inventory. Simply stated, the buying hedge involves the purchase of a futures contract at the time of the sales transaction (April 1) and the later sale of a futures contract when the physical copper is purchased. Since futures and cash prices tend to fluctuate together, any profit or loss because of a change in the cash price of copper between April and September 1 will be largely offset by a profit or loss in the futures contract. Diagrammatically the transactions involved in the buy hedge are

---

CASH

April 1—sell 25,000 lb, based on $1.20/lb prevailing price (copper in form of generators)

FUTURES

April 1—buy 25,000 lb September futures @ $1.25/lb (difference in cash and future prices owing to carrying charges)

---

[6] "An Intertemporal Measure of Hedging Effectiveness," *Journal of Futures Markets* (June 1990), pp. 307–321.

At this point, the manufacturer has hedged by entering into two contracts of an opposite nature, selling in the cash market and buying in the futures market.

Because the futures and cash markets tend to move together, a change in one price will be largely offset by a change in the price of the other market. Let us assume that on September 1 the price of copper has increased to $1.25 per pound. If the manufacturer had not hedged, the profit margin would have been cut considerably as the generators' sales prices were predicted on copper at $1.20 per pound. However, because a futures contract had been bought (in technical terms it is called "long" futures), the rise in the cash price of copper will be reflected in a rise in the price of September futures. Therefore, the loss sustained because the cash price advanced from $1.20 to $1.25 will be offset by a gain in the futures transaction when the September futures contract is sold.

The diagrammatic representation is completed as follows.

CASH

April 1—sell 25M lb @ $1.20/lb

Sept.1—buy 25M lb @ 1.25/lb
Loss $0.05/lb.

FUTURES: SEPTEMBER COPPER

April 1—buy 25M lb @ $1.25/lb

Sept. 1—sell 25M lb @ 1.30/lb
Gain $0.05/lb.

The hedging transaction is now complete. By taking the profit from the futures transaction and applying it to the cash price paid in August, the XYZ Company has in effect purchased its copper at $1.20 per pound, the price on which its sale was originally predicated.

But what if the price of copper drops, for example, to $1.15 in the cash market? Would not the manufacturer lose in the futures market because the purchase was at one price ($1.25) while the sale will be at a lower price ($1.15)? The answer is yes. In this case, there is a loss in the futures market. However, there is a "gain" in the cash market because XYZ Company originally anticipated paying $1.20 for the copper and they sold it at this

$1.20 price in the form of generators. Now in September when they actually buy the copper they have an abnormal profit (selling at $1.20, buying at $1.15) that offsets the futures loss.

The Selling Hedge

The selling hedge is used when the purchasing executive has a physical inventory whose value is declining because the open market price is dropping. Let us assume that XYZ Company normally carries a 60-day inventory of 1 million pounds of copper. Assume further that sales decline because of a cutback in automotive production so that this 1 million pounds now represents four months' average inventory. We can make the example even more realistic by assuming that the firm has forward purchase commitments that will continue to inflate the inventory.

Chances are that the slowdown in XYZ's automotive sales will be reflected elsewhere in the business world, and these pressures may cause the price of copper to decline. What can the purchasing executive do when inventory is excessive and continuing to expand while its value is declining?

The traditional approach would probably concentrate on the supply side of this inventory problem. An attempt would be made to defer future shipments from suppliers and allow time to use up the inventory. This procedure will take at least two months (in our illustration), and during this time relatively expensive copper will be used. Sales of XYZ's finished product will probably be predicated on the price in effect at time of shipment. This means that the firm will be losing, in a sense, its normal profit margin by using expensive copper while being restricted in the sales price of generators, which are predicated on the prevailing lower copper prices.

Another alternative for the traditional purchasing executive would be to sell the excess inventory in the open market. This is a cumbersome procedure that requires the development of sales contracts, negotiation of sales prices, and related concerns that are usually not within the purchasing domain.

The third alternative is to hedge the physical inventory price by selling futures contracts. Because the futures price will reflect declines in the cash market, the futures profit can be used to offset the diminishing cash value. By selling futures contracts, the purchasing executive minimizes inventory value losses without moving any physical stock. In diagrammatic form the selling hedge looks as follows.

CASH

April 1—have 500,000 lb excess inventory at today's value of $1.20/lb. A reduction in price is anticipated.

FUTURES

April 1—sell 500,000 lb (20 contracts) of July futures at today's price of $1.25/lb.

At this point the firm has hedged its excess inventory. It has entered into simultaneous transactions of an opposite nature—holding physical stock while selling contracts in the futures market. The loss or gain in one market should offset the loss or gain in the other market.

Let us assume that copper prices do decline so that on June 1, when the excess inventory has been used, the cash price is $1.10 per pound. The firm has lost 10 cents per pound on its physical inventory. However, the futures market will also reflect the lower price. And because this alert executive is short futures, when the futures contract is liquidated, a lower price will be paid than the sale price. Consequently, the firm will have a futures profit to offset the cash loss.

Again, using a diagrammatic illustration, the transaction would be

---

CASH

April 1—holds 500,000 excess @ $1.20/lb
June 1—sells the excess inventory in the form of generators at the reduced market price of $1.10/lb

 Loss $0.10/lb

FUTURES

April 1—sells 500,000 lb of July copper @ $1.25/lb
June 1—buys 500,000 lb of July copper @ $1.11/lb

 Gain $0.14/lb

The sell hedge has allowed XYZ Company to consume its excess inventory in a declining market while tying its price to the lower, declining cash commodity levels. This has been accomplished without moving or selling physical inventory. The purpose of the selling hedge is to keep the actual value of an inventory close to the declining market price.

If the prices of copper has risen between April and June, there would be, leaving basis considerations aside, a corresponding loss on the futures transaction with a gain on the physical inventory value. The hedge will still perform its purpose of establishing the inventory price at a predetermined level and avoiding profits or losses from commodity value changes.

However, if the firm was certain that prices would rise, it is obvious that they would merely enjoy increased profits from the price rise. As indicated in the buy hedge example, such perfect knowledge is rarely available, and therein lies the rationale for hedging.

Simplifying Assumptions

The transactions just cited make certain assumptions that should be examined here. It was assumed in the buy hedge that the changes in price in the cash and futures market were equal. When the cash market changed by 10 cents, the futures market changed by the same amount. This would constitute an ideal hedge, but in reality the changes between the two markets may not be exactly the same.

In the first illustration, April cash and September futures were used. During the intervening months, between the time the hedge was placed (April in this case), the potential supply–demand picture for copper may change. For example, an election in Chile in May could reduce that country's potential production and influence prospects for future supply. This could cause the futures price to rise more than the cash price, which reflects today's supply and demand. Another influencing possibility is a change in the U.S. tariff policies; this could increase imports and, therefore, depress futures to an amount lower than the cash price. These are just two of the factors that could cause the cash and futures markets to deviate from the partial or full carrying charge spread.

When the two markets do not fluctuate proportionately, the hedge may be imperfect. One can generalize, however, and say that prices usually move together and, therefore, hedges provide protection against major price fluctuations. In reality, the benefit of futures hedging is that one avoids the major risk of fluctuations in the price of the commodity, in exchange for the much smaller risk of fluctuations between the cash price and that of futures. There is a risk, but it is only a fraction of the risk one faces without a hedge.

A second assumption made in the previous examples was that the contract grade of the futures contract was the same as the grade used by the manufacturer. The grades may not be exactly the same. The difference determines the imperfection of the hedge. However, we assume that the relation, even if imperfect, is still close enough to eliminate major price risks, the hedger's main worry.

OTHER USES OF FUTURES MARKETS

Hedging, in the true sense of the word, involves a cash position (either in plant inventory or in a sales contract calling for future material requirements) and an offsetting futures position. Under these conditions, a loss or gain in one market will offset (within the limits already discussed) the gain or loss in the other market. However, futures markets may be effectively used by the sophisticated purchasing executive, providing that executive and management fully recognize the risks inherent in these practices. The use of the futures market for anticipatory pricing and as a supply assurance aid are logical, legitimate tools that purchasing should be prepared to utilize. In this context, we can view the following uses of futures trading as a possible exercise of the purchasing executive's best business judgment.

Anticipatory Pricing

The traditional responsibilities of the purchasing executive include obtaining material at the right price, time, quantity, and quality. We shall be concerned with the first two aspects (price and time) in the following review of futures trading. Note that we have now changed terminology. The use of futures trading is being substituted for hedging because the requirements of a cash-and-futures position will not be met in these applications as they were in the previous examples.

Purchasing executives obviously are very knowledgeable about the raw material they buy. By reviewing the trade papers and daily contacts with suppliers, they maintain a constant awareness or existing and impending supply–demand changes. Suppose a purchasing executive is convinced that today's price for one of the materials (silver) is very low, perhaps even artificially low. The usual procedure would be to check inventory, review projected sales, evaluate carrying charges, and balance all these variables against the advantages of increasing existing inventory buying at the low price. The result may suggest forward buying. Certainly management expects purchasing to explore continually such possible cost savings.

Assuming that approval is received, the executive will contract for additional supplies at the favorable price and will negotiate delivery schedules accordingly. If prices rise as anticipated, management is both impressed and pleased. But if prices decline, the firm is faced with an inflated inventory, resulting in carrying charges, and is paying a price during the delivery contract that is higher than the market. In effect, the action has involved the firm in considerable expense.

Traditional alternatives are few. An attempt can be made to cancel the contracts—which probably will be unsuccessful—or the excess inventory can be sold. This alternative is also likely to be unpalatable because of the difficulty in locating buyers and moving stock. In effect, there is likely to be no workable alternative except to wait for time to consume the material and heal the wounds.

Does this mean that anticipatory pricing is not a sound purchasing procedure? Definitely not: a right price is very often a judgment price and therefore subject to error. With intimate knowledge of the market, the purchasing executive will make a minimum of such decision mistakes.

But the purpose of this rather lengthy discussion is not to justify buying ahead when the conditions are extremely favorable. The purpose is to illustrate the use of futures trading as an alternate means of establishing a favorable price without carrying the stock, without paying full price for it, and with the flexibility to reverse the decision with minimum cost if conditions change. That is what anticipatory pricing via the futures market is all about.

Anticipatory pricing in the futures market simply means taking a long position—that is, buying a futures contract when the cash price appears favorable (this assumes, of course, that a normal basis differential exists). This will establish the price. Before the futures month reaches maturity, the contract is sold and profits are applied to offset the actual commodity purchase, whose price and value would have risen in the interim.

For example, assume that on February 1 silver is priced at $3.65 per troy ounce, which is considered an attractive price. After a review of anticipated sales, existing inventory, and carrying costs, it is decided to purchase 60,000 troy ounces of July futures to establish the price.

Assume further that by May 1 the price has risen to $4.24 per ounce, and it is decided that this is a normal price level. The futures contract can now be sold and the profit ($4.24–$3.65) used to offset the higher price paid when buying physical silver for actual production requirements.

Diagrammatically, the procedure would look as follows.

	FUTURES
Feb 1—buy July (assuming normal carrying charges) @ $3.75/oz	
May 1—sell July	@ 4.29/oz
Gain	$0.54/oz

By taking the 54 cents gain and subtracting this amount from the cash price prevailing on May 1 ($4.29/oz), the cost of silver has been reduced almost to the price prevailing on February 1—the most favorable price.

As can be seen, this low February price was established without incurring physical inventory or carrying costs. Because the margin requirement on such purchases is only a small percentage of the contract value (usually about 10 percent) and treasury bills can often be used as original margin, allowing the buyer to continue to receive interest, the cost of carrying the futures position from February to May is minimal.

If the price decision pegged in February is incorrect, the executive can liquidate the futures position at any time and absorb the losses. This is in contrast to taking in physical stock in February and then experiencing the disturbing downward price and having no alternative but to go out into the open market and sell the inventory, a procedure that, as has already been explained, is undesirable and perhaps impossible.

In summary, anticipatory pricing is fixing a favorable price by taking a long position in the futures market. It involves less risk and cost than purchasing physical stock at the favorable price level. The futures market also provides a means to leave the market if the pricing judgment proves incorrect, with a minimum of cost and effort.

Guarantee Supply

By purchasing futures contracts and taking delivery when they come due, the purchasing executive can guarantee supply even during periods of strikes or other shortages.

When a long strike assaulted western paper mills, big department stores bought large amounts of quality paper, stocked it, and supplied it to their printers. While others suffered shortages and price disruptions in publishing large catalogs, they rode out the strike in relative tranquility.[7]

The exchanges place extremely heavy penalties on nonperformance. This guarantees the buying company, which has a long position, delivery if any of the commodity is available. However, force majeure—acts of God, civil disturbance, and similar extreme events—could necessitate cash settlements rather than physical delivery. These would be rare occurrences.

An important consideration, when contemplating actual delivery, is that the grade of the commodity used may not be the same as the contract grade. Furthermore, the delivery point specified in the contract probably will not coincide with the manufacturing location at which the material will be used. However, brokers can usually arrange the exchange of goods and locations necessary to present a usable commodity. Cost premiums to adjust grades and locations are relatively minimal. It should be noted, however, that because of the variables (grades, locations, force majeure, etc.), the use of futures as a partial source of supply should be undertaken only after the purchasing executive has gained considerable expertise in futures trading.

---

[7] "Sometimes Hedging Is the Best Inflation Weapon," *Purchasing* (March 8, 1990), p. 63.

Summary of the Characteristics of Hedging

In summary, the futures market provides strategic tools for the purchasing executive in addition to straight price protection of a cash position. By effectively using anticipatory pricing procedures, the executive can establish prices without incurring inventory and carrying costs. In addition, future trading provides the flexibility necessary to liquidate a position if the initial pricing decision is in error or if supply–demand conditions change. Moreover, supply can be at least partially protected during periods of shortage. Finally the review of supply–demand information can significantly aid the executive in routine price negotiations, as well as providing background for important decisions concerning economical inventory levels.

The essential element in all hedging or futures transactions is the futures contract. It has been indicated previously that these contracts are legally binding agreements to buy or sell a specific quantity and quality of a commodity during a specific month. Although this is true, over 97 percent of all futures contracts are satisfied not by delivery but by a procedure known as offset; that is, buying back a futures contract that was previously sold, or vice versa. In other words, the purchasing executive and other futures traders will usually offset their futures position without taking delivery (the exception being the futures contract entered into as a supply mechanism). The firm pays or receives, as the case may be, the difference in price between the purchase and sale contract.

Basis has been defined as the difference between the cash and futures contract price. Favorable profits from futures trades can be enhanced by observing the amount and direction of basis changes. As has already been stated, futures contracts usually sell at premiums to cash market price because of the amount of full or partial carrying charges.

In general, then, carrying charges set the theoretical maximum by which futures can exceed the cash price. If this maximum is exceeded, it becomes profitable to buy the cash commodity and simultaneously sell the futures and eventually deliver against the futures contract. The effect of this action is to drive up the price of cash (the result of many people buying), drive down the futures price (resulting from heavy sales), or both. The net effect is to restore a normal carrying charge differential.

On the other hand, there is no automatic mechanism to correct an imbalance if carrying charges are absent (i.e., if futures should be equal to or less than cash). The cash price can go higher than futures because of predicted changes in supply and demand—for example, a strike or political upheaval in a major foreign producing country. Then perfect sell hedges will not be found, and the price protection value will be reduced. Under these conditions it may be better not to use the sell hedge. Of course, the inversion creates attractive hedging opportunities for prospective buy hedgers.

Hedging can reduce uncertainty, smooth out cash flows, and raise the value of the firm. A basis book, a means of assessing risk and position balance, can help the hedging officer's operational aspects as well as measure the hedging plan's success. A basis book includes such factors as: (1) the overall position, (2) the position basis, (3) the current basis, and (4) the net basis before carry. The position basis indicates the relationship of cash to futures on the settlement day. The current basis updates that relationship. The net basis before carry indicates the basis change in 32nds and an assigned value.[8] Purchasing managers and other executives find hedging to be a highly technical transaction.

SOME DIFFICULTIES IN HEDGING

Hedging has been described as the cancellation of gains and losses from price changes. This is an accurate description in the ideal situation. However, the situation frequently is not ideal, and purchasing personnel should be aware of some of the departures from the ideal that may be experienced in practice.

Basis versus Acceptable Grades

The prices quoted on the futures market are for the basis grade of the commodity, the grade in which the largest volume of business is transacted. All other acceptable grades have their prices set by the exchange in relation to the basis grade. In other words, to find the price of a particular grade, we add the established premium or discount to the price of the basis grade. This works well if the trade differentials and the exchange differentials between the grades are approximately the same.

This ideal relationship may not exist. To illustrate, assume that in a particular year the highest-quality grade was in short supply, whereas the basis grade was in average supply. Suppose Company A agreed to sell a specified quantity of finished goods requiring the highest-quality grade, and to price its finished goods on the prevailing price of the basis grade of raw material plus the exchange differential for the highest-quality grade. Company A then bought futures for the amount needed, expecting to buy the actual raw material when it was required for processing. By the time Company A got around to buying its actual raw material, the shortage conditions

---

[8] "Evaluating Hedge Success by Using the Basis Book," *Futures: The Magazine of Commodities and Options* (May 1990), pp. 42–44.

would have driven the price up, and the cost might be well above that on which it priced its finished goods. According to the theory of hedging, this loss should be offset by the gain Company A would realize on the sale of its futures contracts. But in this case the supply–demand conditions for the basis grades were normal, and so its price would not advance correspondingly. Thus Company A would have lost money, even though it had hedged its short position.

Of course, the outcome would have been the same if Company A had hedged a long spot position of high-quality raw materials by selling futures and then found that either the high-quality materials were in surplus supply or that the high-quality, supply–demand conditions were normal but that the basis grade was in short supply. One can work out several such situations, all of which serve to illustrate that hedging is not perfect price protection because of variations between the basis grade and other grades. However, it should be realized that the function of hedging is to *minimize* losses rather than to eliminate them.

Open Interest

Another point that often causes difficulty for the unskilled hedger is that the price of futures sometimes tends to be erratic during the month when the futures contracts must be fulfilled by completing the round turn—that is, making the opposite contract—or by making or taking delivery. This erratic price behavior is likely to be the result of either of two factors. First, the *open interest* is too small to permit the purchase or sale of a substantial number of contracts without significantly affecting the price. The open interest refers to the number of unliquidated contracts or open commitments. If the open interest in a particular month is 2000 contracts, this means that there are outstanding 2000 contracts to buy (long contracts) and 2000 contracts to sell (short contracts). If a particular hedger has 200 short contracts that must be covered by purchasing 200 contracts, it is evident that this action will tend to raise the price.

Certifiable Inventory

Another factor is the amount of the commodity certified for delivery in the month. If this amount is small, those who are "long" in the particular month will be reluctant to sell until the price has been bid up substantially. Suppose, for instance, that in the example there are 1000 contract lots certified for delivery. It is apparent that only 1000 of the 2000 outstanding contracts can be satisfied by actual delivery of commodity. The remaining short traders will have to fulfill their contracts by buying from the longs. Sensing this situation, the long traders will not sell until the price has advanced as much as they dare force it up. To avoid such squeezes, the experienced and careful hedger will use a futures month far enough ahead so that the hedge can be lifted before such price jockeying begins. If this is overlooked, and the delivery month approaches before the hedger is ready to lift the hedge, the hedge can be transferred forward. This is accomplished by buying to close out the hedge in the at-hand month and selling in a forward month to reestablish the hedge.

A hedger will also watch the open-interest figures, which are published daily, because they are a clue to the explanation of price behavior on the futures market. For example, if the price is up and the open interest is increased, this indicates new demand in the market and suggests that the market is strong and the price sound. On the other hand, if the price is up and the open interest is decreased, it suggests that the demand has come from shorts who have entered the market to cover their short commitments. Such a demand suggests not a basically strong market but rather a technical imbalance in the futures market. If prices are declining and the open interest is decreased, it suggests that the long interests are liquidating their holdings. If prices decline while the open interest increases, it suggests that short selling is the cause. From these clues the purchasing executive can glean information that will aid in interpreting price changes.

Size of Market

The prospective hedger should also consider the size of the futures market and its composition in terms of number and types of traders. Many of the futures markets are so small that a fairly large company attempting to use the market for hedging will find its single influence so great that its buying or selling forces prices up or down. Thus, it will determine prices rather than having them determined for it. Moreover, a firm should be careful about hedging in a market that is dominated by a few large companies, even though the firm itself may be small, because one can never be sure what action the few large companies may take. They might upset normal price relationships at any time by their activity and render the market worse than useless for hedging by other traders.

Dissimilar Products

Another point that should be kept in mind about hedging is that the protection it affords is reasonably complete only when the product for which the price is being hedged is identical with or very similar to the product traded on the futures market. If the products are identical, it is reasonable to expect the price series to move together. As the products diverge in characteristics, the expectation that their price series will move together decreases, because unrelated costs intervene. For example, an automobile tire manufacturer using cotton for its fabric will not get much protection from hedging its cotton inventory on the cotton futures market, since the price of tires is quite unrelated to the price of cotton. Similarly, a manufacturer of men's cotton shirts would get only moderate protection from hedging because the costs of labor and processing determine the price of shirts more than the price of cotton does. A manufacturer of cotton sheets would secure more protection because the cost of cotton is an important ingredient of total cost. A manufacturer of cotton batting would obtain still greater price protection because the price of cotton practically determines the price of batting.

It should not be inferred from the preceding paragraph that hedging is inappropriate for the tire and shirt makers. They can protect their cotton prices through hedging. The significant fact is that the protection of the price of cotton is less important to the total operations of the tire and shirt makers than it is to the sheet and batting makers.

Finally, and obviously, hedging is of the greatest importance to manufacturers who use raw materials that are subject to wide and sudden price fluctuations.

THE ROLE OF THE SPECULATOR

The speculator has always been an object of suspicion and censure by moralists, politicians, and the uninformed. However, as was already discussed in this chapter, speculators assume an existing and necessary risk. They are also a vital factor to the success of hedging, because the volume of trading by hedgers alone is not sufficient to support an active, year-round market. This essential market activity is created by the speculator, who buys and sells futures contracts on the basis of personal judgment in the hope of making a profit from the trading without needing or expecting to take possession of the commodity.

In the hedging process the speculator serves the dual function of creating activity (so a hedger can always find someone to take the other side of the transaction) and of stabilizing prices. The second function is also an important one. The hedger's interest in buying or selling is determined by the long or short position taken in the spot commodity. If several hedgers need protection against long positions, their combined selling of futures will tend to depress the price and destroy the normal relationship of spot and futures prices. The speculator, however, is looking at the price level in the light of its consistency with supply and demand. If several hedgers by their selling activity depressed the price abnormally, the speculator would step in and buy because it would appear that the price has gone down without sound underlying reasons. These purchases would tend to restore price to its proper level. This stabilizing influence for the market is an important economic contribution.

PURCHASING AND THE FUTURES MARKET

It is customary for an officer of a company or a purchasing committee to determine what policy is to be followed in trading on the futures markets. Where a purchasing committee is used, its members generally will consist of representatives from purchasing as well as general management, finance, sales, and production. It is the responsibility of the purchasing manager to advise this committee with respect to market conditions and to have a knowledge of all other pertinent factors required by the committee. The committee then decides on the quantity of coverage, which futures month to trade in, and other details of the hedging process.

In other companies the trading on commodity exchanges is entrusted solely to an officer of the company, who may or may not also be in charge of purchasing. In these instances the person responsible is a specialist who often has had long and successful experience in futures trading. Complete confidence of the principals of the company must be obtained, since trading results can have an important effect on the company's financial structure.

Any individual or company contemplating the use of a futures market for hedging should make a careful study of the commodity and its trading practices. Many costly mistakes can be made by the novice. A good broker can be of real assistance to the beginner until he or she has built up technical knowledge of the operations of the futures market through experience.

FINANCIAL FUTURES

Traditional hedging operations have centered on physical commodities as previously discussed. However, the ''future of futures'' includes interesting possibilities for the buyer to hedge the financial aspects of purchase transactions via financial futures contracts.

Money itself is the most widely used commodity—obviously exceeding products such as copper, lumber, and palladium. Futures contracts now exist that trade interest rates and the relative value of international currencies. Furthermore, relatively recent contracts have been developed involving stock exchange contracts and commodity options. Specific contracts include Eurodollars, Government National Mortgage Administration (GNMA) mortgages, Treasury bills (T-bills) and bonds (T-bonds), domestic certificates of deposit (CDs), and stock indexes. Present exchanges such as the Chicago Board of Trade and the Chicago Mercantile Exchange are being joined by newer exchanges specializing in financial futures, such as the International Futures Exchange, which uses computer access to tie in trading-access centers in New York, Chicago, London, Hong Kong, and Bermuda.

The development of these futures markets allows buyers to hedge the financial aspects of the purchasing process. In buying domestic products, they can hedge the dollar value of large purchases (such as capital equipment) against possible changes in interest rates during the period between the purchase and delivery. For example, during the early 1980s when the prime interest rate soared to 22 percent, buyers of capital equipment encountered staggering interest (either real or imputed) expenses. Hedging in interest rate contracts would have taken advantage of subsequent reductions in interest costs.

International purchasing transactions can now be approached with much less risk, as buyers hedge the amount of money involved in the international currencies market. That is, buyers hedge both the commodity and the currency components of the price risk.[9] Previously, foreign buying had significant financial risks because the relative value of the dollars against other countries' currency could fluctuate and greatly increase the real cost to the buyer. Hedging in international currencies now minimizes such risks.

Risk management could well become as important as value analysis and JIT ordering in developing the supply strategies of the twenty-first century.[10]

CHAPTER SUMMARY

The purchasing and materials managers decide their intent to use speculation and hedging as part of their overall strategy. The firm's financial executive consults with them on the matter or may take on the speculation and hedging function entirely. The highly specialized futures markets may distract the purchasing manager from the responsibilities of supplying the needs for raw materials, components, and services. In any event, the firm's executive committee and chief executive officer make certain that whoever has the responsibility, nothing should detract from successful futures trading.

Purchase timing favors the firm's strategic plans for controlling inventory, conserving cash, containing costs, and maintaining customer service levels that gain competitive advantage for the firm.

[9] "Out of Sample Effectiveness of a Joint Commodity and Currency Hedge: The Case of Soybean Meal in Italy," *Journal of Futures Markets* (June 1990), pp. 229–245.
[10] "Risk Management: A Purchasing Tool for the 21st Century," *Purchasing* (May 21, 1992), p. 40.

Discussion Questions

1. What is forward buying, hand-to-mouth buying, buying to current needs, and speculation buying?
2. Under what circumstances is forward buying the proper policy and why?
3. What is the principle distinction between forward buying and speculative buying?

4. What are the distinctions between speculative buying and gambling?
5. Describe the concept of risk management.
6. How should the purchasing manager sell risk management to senior management?
7. How would you relate investment inventory to purchase timing?
8. How can hedging raise the value of the firm?

Suggested Case

MF-1

22

Purchasing with Ethics and Social Responsibility

Norton Bingham owned an electrical parts and supply store in Los Angeles. Modestly successful over the years, Bingham bought from 25 suppliers and sold his electrical products to customers in about a three-mile radius. He knew many of the neighborhood children.

Bingham's 1991 sales revenues totaled $480,000. His costs amounted to $400,000. What steps should he take to set up college scholarships for neighborhood children? What should he do about bringing suppliers into participating with him in sponsoring the scholarships?

CHAPTER CONTENTS

Niccolò Machiavelli (1469–1527) described how sixteenth-century rulers applied power. His 1513 book, *The Prince,* became a code of behavior for leaders who acquired authority positions. He observed princes' rivals executed, banished, or demoted. Machiavelli urged removing the old regime, rather than demoting them to places in the new plan. From within, they may upset the mass consent and cohesion that the new managers need for survival.[1]

Today, executive development directors admonish managers to read *The Prince*—more often cited than read—when they take over new power positions. "Off with their heads" seems drastic by today's behavior standards; still, purchasing managers must assert their authority. To do so, they follow modified behavior codes—codes of ethics—that comprise personal, employers', and society's standards.

An organization reflects the social and ethical attitudes of its employees. In turn, these employees reflect to greater or lesser degrees the underlying attitudes of society in general. Therefore, as society's attitudes change, so do those of employees and organizations.

Purchasing employees are particularly sensitive to social and ethical changes and related issues because their professional responsibilities involve numerous interactions that bring up social and ethical concerns. This chapter highlights the issues most relevant to societal and ethical conduct and presents the alternatives that confront purchasing professionals.

Not many years ago the concerns mentioned in the title of this chapter were considered tangential to business operations and optional for management. Social responsibility consisted of providing support for the United Way, symphony orchestras, and release time for employees to serve on civic committees. Ethics was the practice of the golden rule, to be commended and practiced whenever it did not interfere with efficiency and profit. Public relations was a craft similar to advertising; it was to be employed whenever the company's reputation had suffered and its image needed to be revamped. This view prevailed at a time when it was easy to assume that free enterprise and the marketplace economy were beyond question and safe from attack by all but extreme radicals.

CHANGING ATTITUDES

The situation has changed, particularly with regard to social responsibility. Many events have brought about an increased sensitivity to social responsibility on the part of organizations. Four decades ago, business ethics formed

---

[1] Claude S. George, Jr., *The History of Management Thought,* 2nd ed. (Englewood Cliffs, NJ: Prentice Hall, 1972), pp. 43–47.

around statements like: "Inevitably the values of power and prestige come to take precedence over all others."[2] Today, concern about pollution, the dwindling of the nation's once-plentiful natural resources, consumer movements, government scandals, and the political implications of multinational corporate activities have all served to focus the public's attention on the activities of the business sector in our society.

Purchasing and business managers must deal wisely with these issues, or the political processes will mandate its own solutions. Now is a new era, in which the old single-dimension yardstick of business performance–profits is no longer adequate, and new multidimensional evaluations are being developed. Operating in such an environment presents an interesting and difficult challenge.

Public relations has evolved from what might be called a fire-fighting operation into a fire prevention operation. Businesses must now convince the public that whenever it cannot meet the highest expectations with regard to such matters as pollution, use of resources, and ethical behavior, the end product is worth the cost. This is definitely a new role for business; companies are now required not only to sell their product but also to sell themselves in an attempt to create an acceptable public image.

Purchasing is in the forefront of this developing concern of business because it allocates revenues and interacts with various publics, and in the process its actions directly affect the overall posture of the organization.

Today's college students will lead society's institutions in the future. How do they perceive ethical issues? Two Florida State University students surveyed student opinions on 27 ethical issues that The Conference Board, the business information service, had surveyed. The Board surveyed 300 chief executive officers and senior executives in the United States, Canada, Europe, Japan, and Australia. Table 22-1 displays the results when the 30 CEOs, 52 FSU business students, and 31 FSU nonbusiness students answered "yes" to the question, "Is This an Ethical Issue for Business?"[3]

The students had a higher number of affirmative answers on ethical issues for business than the CEOs, 19 out of 27 times. The nonbusiness students had a higher number of affirmative answers than business students, 17 out of 27 times. Results perhaps reflect perceptions before taking on the reality of heading a vast business enterprise. Perhaps, too, the results reflect the more stringent values of younger respondents, not as accountable for other people's actions as CEOs.

---

[2] Marquis W. Childs and Douglass Cater, *Ethics in a Business Society* (New York: Harper & Brothers, 1954), p. 18.

[3] Author's students' report, November 29, 1988, and The Conference Board Research Report No. 900, *Corporate Ethics* (1987).

TABLE 22-1. A Comparison of Business Ethics Opinions of Selected College Students and Corporate Chief Executive Officers

Is this an Ethical Issue?	52 Business Students	31 Nonbusiness Students	300 CEOs
1. Employee conflicts of interest	85%	86%	91%
2. Inappropriate gifts to corporate personnel	84	83	91
3. Sexual harassment	90	100	91
4. Unauthorized payments	93	90	85
5. Affirmative action	74	83	84
6. Employee privacy	77	97	84
7. Environmental issues	88	90	82
8. Employee health screening	59	59	79
9. Conflicts between company's ethics and foreign business practices	62	83	77
10. Security of company records	84	86	76
11. Workplace safety	81	93	76
12. Advertising content	88	62	74
13. Product safety standards	91	90	74
14. Corporate contributions	65	79	68
15. Shareholder interests	67	69	68
16. Corporate due process	86	83	65
17. Whistle-blowing	74	72	63
18. Employment at will	58	66	62
19. Disinvestment	47	72	59
20. Government contract issues	72	86	59
21. Financial and cash management procedures	72	76	55
22. Plant/facility closure and downsizing	58	83	55
23. Political action committees	63	66	55
24. Social issues raised by religious organizations	37	62	47
25. Comparable worth	60	59	43
26. Product pricing	47	38	42
27. Executive salaries	58	52	37

Source: Author's students' report, November 29, 1988, and The Conference Board Research Report No. 900, *Corporate Ethics,* 1987.

PURCHASING AND SOCIAL RESPONSIBILITY

Not everyone agrees that business should assume a leadership role in the area of social responsibility. A case can be made for the position that our economy will achieve its greatest efficiency if managers strive solely for maximum profits and do not voluntarily assume social responsibilities that entail costs. There is little doubt that this would be true (1) if the nation's economy operated in an ethical vacuum and (2) if efficiency were the only criterion by which business was measured. Business, however, does not operate in a vacuum. The public has definite expectations, and the economy cannot be sealed off from the rest of life. The public expects and demands a certain kind of performance on the part of the business sector.

The nature of the public's expectations differs from one period to another. It is important that the business community be sensitive and respond to these expectations because through various avenues, particularly political, the public determines the extent that business can ignore this message only at considerable risk to its future operational freedom.

Ernst & Whinney, the giant accounting firm, conducted a 1987 survey in conjunction with NAPM's Center for Advanced Purchasing Studies (CAPS) and cosponsored by *Purchasing World* magazine. E&W had conducted an earlier ethical survey in 1975. The new survey revealed that management ethical direction has changed negatively since 1975: less oral and written direction and less input from purchasing personnel has been implemented regarding ethics policy. The common practice still abounds for sales representatives to approach purchasing personnel bearing bait. Holiday gifts, small appliances, and clothing offers have increased. Survey results disclose a further dilemma: ''Buyers outside the purchasing department become a serious problem since these individuals are usually not subject to stringent ethical policy.''[4]

Covering other parts of the same survey, a business journal reports that:

> the vast majority of purchasing personnel conduct their business affairs in an ethical manner; however, they cannot agree on how ethical standards can be enforced. . . . Many buyers are subject to ambiguous directives from management about how to conduct business with suppliers. . . . A greater percentage (97 vs. 79) of respondents accepted favors in 1987 than did in 1975.[5]

---

[4] ''Ethical Practices of Industrial Purchasers,'' *Purchasing World* (June 1988), pp. 28–31.
[5] ''Ethical Practices in Purchasing,'' *Journal of Purchasing and Materials Management* (Winter 1990), pp. 19–26.

Materials

One area in which purchasing can play a socially responsible role is in the use of natural resources. A growing population with rising economic expectations will someday exhaust the finite resources of the planet. Depletion projections for oil and mineral resources show serious potential difficulties or shortages within the twenty-first century.

By utilizing vendors who share this social consciousness and operate efficiently and effectively without waste of precious resources, the purchasing department is able to procure many materials at the lowest cost and save the organization money. In addition, it acts in society's best interests by supporting businesses that do not pollute and waste limited natural resources.

The purchasing profession can also play a socially responsible role in its decision making regarding poisonous and hazardous substances. For example, the health dangers associated with asbestos have forced business organizations to think of substitute products. Although a social consciousness, per se, might not be the motivating factor that determines whether or not a company will stop purchasing asbestos products, the cost factors (i.e., product liability suits and worker compensation rates) have forced purchasing personnel to look for other products that will not only substitute for asbestos but hold down production costs as well. Some firms are purchasing asbestos substitutes. Although such substitutes add short-term increased costs to the final manufactured product, the future cost savings from protecting worker and consumer health and from precluding legal suits will be substantial.

Social responsibility will be mandated for the purchasing profession by a variety of federal and state laws and regulations if actions to safeguard the public welfare are not accepted voluntarily. For example, the Environmental Protection Agency instituted so-called closed-loop disposal regulations, which require organizations to follow very strict procedures for the disposal of hazardous wastes. Penalties for noncompliance are both civil and criminal, and any purchasing official whose responsibilities include contracting or arranging for a company's hazardous-waste disposal can be held liable.

Employee Adjustments

American business has accepted the fact that the complexity and interrelatedness of society's various problems demand some activities to enhance the social environment. For example, American companies have now begun donating time and resources to help in the development of literacy programs for their employees. United Technologies is furnishing space for tutoring sessions as well as hiring teachers to give classes in reading, writing, spelling, grammar, and other skills. Other companies are attacking the problems of alcohol and drug abuse, which may interfere with an employee's ability to function on the job. By helping employees achieve literacy or face substance abuse problems, business organizations will be able to cut some of the high costs resulting from employee absenteeism, lowered product quality, and decreased productivity. In short, in ethical, societal, and legal areas, the purchasing professional is in a position to assess the needs of society at large and react accordingly. In meeting these public concerns, purchasing projects the organization into action and in the process plays an important public relations role.

Value analysis is a useful operational technique in purchasing. It can help to reduce the use of critical materials and to adjust as much as possible to the use of replaceable rather than nonreplaceable resources. Value analysis has been primarily cost-oriented in the past but now encompasses broader concerns, including the social necessity of conserving resources.

Recycling

By prompting the use of recycled materials, purchasing managers can also be of positive service to their organizations and to society in general. The use of substitutes to replace scarce metals and recycled materials to replace virgin metals and the use of forms of transportation that minimize the consumption of power are all instances in which purchasing can affect the organization and, on a larger scale, society in general.

THE PURCHASING MANAGER AND ETHICS

Today, more than in the past, individuals involved in the business world are more concerned about ethics, but have a poor understanding of them. This concern stems from our increasing affluence. As the needs of a society are more adequately met, there is a tendency for its members to aspire to higher standards in nonmaterial areas. Concern about ethics has also been fostered by revelations of many unethical practices on the part of businesspeople and government officials in their dealings with one another.

The low level of ethical understanding stems from the fact that our society has become so predominantly secular that the typical businessperson has few ethical standards of reference. The subject of ethics is exceedingly complex, involving many philosophical and subjective issues. It is the very essence of ethics that each person must formulate his or her own system.

Business ethics may be defined as a self-generating system of moral standards to which a substantial majority of business executives give voluntary assent. It is a force within business that leads to industry-wide acceptance of certain standards of practical conduct. Here the standard is a relative one. It is a composite, a type of average, of what the group accepts and practices.

Personal ethics should be distinguished from business ethics or any other group ethics. Personal ethics have their source in a person's religion and philosophy of life. Here the standard may be—and in many cases is—absolute. In fact, unless the personal standard is fixed and is higher than the prevailing group level, the force of competition will lead to its erosion. As the standards and practices of individuals decline, the level of their group's ethics declines as well. In time, then, the level of business ethics degenerates, and there is no apparent baseline or minimal level. There must be some countervailing force, such as altruism, to offset the eroding effect of selfishness that is inherent in competition. This force comes from personal ethics that are derived from clearly defined moral standards. Figure 22-1 shows the relation of these two kinds of ethics to each other and to the laws of the society in which they operate.

In the purchasing department, ethical considerations abound at the buyer level. Buyers have a high level of exposure to unethical influences in their selection of suppliers. Selfish interests coupled with competition for the buying company's business may influence suppliers to offer gifts and other amenities. This is not only unethical but socially irresponsible, for product costs are invariably increased as a result.

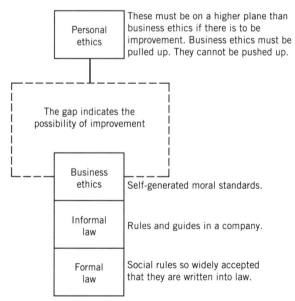

FIGURE 22-1. A model depicting the relationship to one another of personal ethics, business ethics, and the law.

It is difficult for buyers to maintain complete objectivity toward suppliers. Over time close relationships may develop. It is important that these relationships maintain a professional orientation and that transactions be conducted, to the greatest extent possible, without personal influence. For this reason it is both appropriate and desirable that an organization develop and maintain strict rules of conduct to guide its purchasing function.

The National Association of Purchasing Management urges its members to recognize the need for constant reinforcement:

> The most effective way for management to assure compliance with their ethical standards is to provide constant reinforcement of a formal written policy to both employees and suppliers. This can be accomplished by frequently bringing attention to their policies and by requiring employees to sign an annual statement attesting to the fact that they've read and agree to comply with the company's standards.[6]

Gifts from Suppliers

Gift giving, particularly at the holiday season, is a widespread business practice. Most gifts are meant as tokens of goodwill on the part of the giver. However, what the seller intends as a token of appreciation may take on a different significance in the mind of the recipient. After the purchasing person has a gratuity, the psychological balance may favor the seller in such a way that the buyer will find it difficult to remain absolutely unbiased in future transactions.

Gifts or favors become bribes when they are bestowed with the intent to influence unduly or corrupt. Although outright commercial bribery is illegal, there are many borderline cases in which neither the giver nor the receiver acknowledges that a bribe exists but in which the gratuity may subtly influence the purchasing decision.

Policies on Gifts. Many companies have established a definite policy limiting the gifts and entertainment offered to their personnel by vendors. Some companies permit the acceptance of gifts that are clearly promotional pieces. Others allow the recipient to decide whether the proffered gift is a bona fide goodwill gesture or an attempt at commercial bribery.

The problem of accepting gifts becomes especially acute during the holiday season. In some fields the volume of holiday gifts is so great that a morale problem is created among nonpurchasing employees of the receiving firm. In an effort to avoid this situation, some companies have adopted the practice of pooling all gifts and distributing them on some equitable or chance basis among all employees of the purchasing department or the

---

[6] *NAPM Program Aids Library 93*, "Ethics: A Solid Foundation," Leader's Guide, 1988, p. 6.

entire office force. This has the double advantage of both aiding morale and obscuring the identity of the giver so there is little danger of the gifts influencing the buyer.

Some suppliers have attempted to circumvent company-imposed restrictions on accepting gifts by sending gifts to the buyer's home, even addressing them to the buyer's spouse. In such cases it is extremely difficult to enforce company policy, and the integrity of the purchasing department personnel must be relied on to guide them in carrying out the official company policy. When such a practice is employed, it is unlikely that the gift is intended only as a goodwill gesture.

Gift and Entertainment Problems. Arguments can be advanced against the practice of giving gifts. Because gifts represent a cost to the donor firm, they will ultimately be reflected in the selling price of its goods. This means that the buyer firm pays for the gifts it receives. Another potential problem is the precedent such a practice may set. If one firm begins the practice of giving gifts, its competitors may feel compelled to follow, leading to competition among the firms in the value of the gifts given. Gifts of substantial value may be presented, and the purchasing person receiving such gifts may find it difficult to maintain a completely objective viewpoint in evaluating suppliers. The result may be diminution of competition in quality, service, and price—factors that should predominate in the purchasing decision.

Salespeople may also resort to excessive entertainment in an effort to influence an order. Exactly what constitutes excessive entertainment is a matter of interpretation. To accept excessive entertainment obviously compromises one's integrity and limits one's ability to be an objective agent of a company. Although proponents of gift giving and entertainment argue that they enhance morale and contribute to a better climate for business transactions, there is little rational justification for such practices. Purchasing executives cannot perform objectively or with maximum efficiency if their business sense is compromised.

All forms of extraordinary entertainment and gifts from suppliers should be prohibited as a matter of purchasing policy. Gifts received at times such as Christmas can be given to charity. Entertainment can be controlled by requiring a monthly report of all contacts after working hours between buyers and suppliers. This report may also include gifts received from vendors and an estimate of their value. Written reports put the buyer on record, and failure to report any such activities places the buyer in the position of concealing material facts. Company policy can be made and changed in the light of such reports.

The NAPM code on ethical behavior denounces all forms of commercial and government gratuities. Unbridled gift giving can eventually lead to commercial bribery and its attendant legal problems. The laws of agency, which apply to purchasing personnel, prohibit any action on the part of the agent that is detrimental to the interests of the principal. A number of states make commercial bribery a specific criminal offense.

THE PURCHASING MANAGER AND PUBLIC RELATIONS

A business firm has personal relationships running in many different directions. There are relationships between the firm and such groups as the government, the community, the industry, and the entire society. At any particular point in time one or another of these relationships may be of paramount importance, but ordinarily they are not of day-to-day concern to an organization. The three groups of greatest and most frequent concern to a firm are its customers, its employees, and its suppliers.

Since the purchasing department is responsible for supplier relations, it clearly has an important role in building and maintaining good public relations for the firm. In order to do this public relations job well, it is important first of all to have a clear understanding of the nature of the activity.

Some Definitions of Public Relations

Although there is no universally accepted definition of the term, the following definitions of public relations should serve to delineate its essential meaning. One very simple definition describes public relations as simply good morals and good manners. This definition clearly relates public relations to ethics. It suggests that before a firm can expect its good manners to be appreciated, they must be derived from good morals. Public relations, properly understood, is not a matter of putting a good face on bad practices. It consists of first practicing good morals and then conveying this to the public by exhibiting good manners.

Another definition of public relations calls it the production and distribution of a good reputation. This definition emphasizes the same point—that public relations involves doing the right thing as well as saying the right thing. Public relations specialists actually may not have a primary role in doing the things that create a favorable image. Public relations, when properly understood, is an attitude that must pervade an entire organization if the end result is to be favorable over the long run. In this sense, purchasing employees can be effective in both generating and maintaining a good reputation for their company.

A third definition describes public relations as the continuing process by which management endeavors to obtain the goodwill and understanding of its customers, its employees, and the public, inwardly through self-analysis and outwardly through all means of expression. This definition says less about the foundation of public relations, although the term self-analysis hints at its ethical origins. On the other hand, this definition is somewhat more explicit in describing the methods of practice of public relations. The three definitions are essentially consistent and, taken together, adequately convey the meaning of public relations in business.

It was stated earlier that the purchasing department practices public relations toward company suppliers. However, in the very broadest sense, it might be noted that this cannot be done effectively unless purchasing employees gain the willing cooperation of company employees—minor executives, major executives, and general management. This process may be thought of as internal public relations.

Internal Public Relations

A successful purchasing operation depends heavily on sound internal relations. Rapport with other functional areas within the company determines to a large extent whether purchasing's external relations will be satisfactory. Understanding the interrelationships between departments is essential to success. The realization that each function is dependent on the other makes for an effective operation.

The interdepartmental problems that inevitably arise can be overcome much more easily if a cooperative attitude exists. Problems of specification, quality levels, delivery times, and vendor qualification can be much more easily dealt with if purchasing personnel become aware of the fact that there may be more than one solution. If such an attitude exists in the purchasing department, others in the company will be favorably disposed toward the purchasing function and its efforts on behalf of the company.

A friendly atmosphere can be promoted by certain techniques available to all employees. These may range from formal reports to press releases, stories in company papers, bulletin board announcements, and informal visits with personnel in other departments. Every organization has its informal communications network, and employing it is an effective way to achieve good public relations. The informal communications system can also be used to gain useful information for the purchasing department from within the company.

Informal feedback channels can efficiently furnish information on acceptability of a product or shop problems with materials that are not important enough to get into official records. Frequently one product is more acceptable to the workers in the shop than another for reasons difficult to identify. Such knowledge is important to the purchasing personnel and can be used to avoid irritations that develop from such prejudices. Purchasing people can facilitate these informal communications if they recognize their possibilities.

Formal reports generally relay information to management. They deal with volume of expenditures, volume of materials, and effectiveness of supplier relations. Another kind of management report can also be quite effective: a regular report on markets, price trends, supply trends, substitute materials, improved materials, and new materials. If such reports are well written, they can be used by other departments as a guide to changing designs and manufacturing processes, enabling them to accommodate important shifts in the market.

External Public Relations

Sound external relations are built on a foundation of internal acceptance of the purchasing organization. A purchasing department cannot convey to the public an image of effectiveness, cooperativeness, and responsibility if its internal position is weak.

An important benefit of a favorable internal climate is the ease with which a vendor can be induced to assist in the solution of problems that require outside help or cooperative research. In many instances the vendor is well enough acquainted with problems that affect an entire industry to guide the company into avenues of research that will achieve the solution to the problem. Thus, good external relations are dependent on good internal relations, and the results of cooperation are expanded through the good relations between the purchasing department and its vendors.

Conversely, the purchasing department's help in the solution of a difficult problem through a vendor's resources is extremely helpful in improving internal relations. The company begins to look to purchasing for help.

Some Public Relations Tools and Techniques

A company's own public relations department is the best source of assistance in getting a better public relations job done in purchasing.

Next in importance to professional assistance is the use of certain public relations techniques. Perhaps, as mentioned before, doing an honest job in every interview is the best public relations opportunity for every purchasing employee. Here the purchasing personnel can indicate their appreciation for the information, advice, and services that are being offered by the vendor. Buyers should make themselves available to callers, so that visits do not have to be rescheduled to accommodate the purchasing department.

There is need for the exercise of good judgment in dealing with representatives of companies with whom there is no likelihood of doing immediate business. Explaining the situation as honestly and diplomatically as possible will save the time of both parties and keep open the possibility of later dealings.

Next in importance to the interview is the correspondence between the buyer and the seller. Here again, the proper attitude will show through in the correspondence. Letters are so important to public relations that many companies hire experts to help them improve their letter-writing practice. Where it is necessary to write complaints about quality or count deficiencies, price variations, or delivery failures, care must be taken to avoid negative attitudes.

Such devices as welcome folders identifying the persons who buy particular items, listing department heads and their responsibilities, and describing the company's product line help to initiate first-time callers. A welcome brochure can also be advantageously used to inform visitors of company policies regarding such matters as gratuities, payment for lunches, and acceptance of entertainment, so that embarrassment can be prevented.

It is the responsibility of the purchasing department to see to it that a salesperson's time is not wasted in needless waiting. Prompt admission to the interview area, or an acknowledgement of the salesperson's presence with advice about the amount of delay to be anticipated, is proper procedure. Another appointment may be arranged if the day is inconvenient for the buyer. Such consideration is appreciated and conveys the impression that the buyer is aware of the value of the salesperson's time.

An important public relations tool is vendor analysis, which, when combined with an informative report to vendors, is extremely helpful in advising them of their performance in the areas of service and delivery.

Another important practice is visiting vendors' plants. If the visit is made with proper preparation and by mutual agreement, good public relations will result. The purchasing representative should make a complete plant tour, noting such items as methods of manufacture, testing methods, shipping preparation, maintenance procedures, and new equipment. The representative should inquire about such factors as open orders, lead time to be anticipated, and trends in the price levels, all of which bear on present and future relationships with the vendor.

Professional Relations

The purchasing profession has a strong national organization. The National Association of Purchasing Management (NAPM), composed of local associations in all major industrial areas of the country, has in its memberships purchasing executives in all types of industrial and institutional purchasing. One of the active committees of NAPM focuses on public relations. This committee works to improve purchasing's image to its significant publics and to improve understanding of the professional quality and importance of the purchasing profession.

An advantage of membership in NAPM is the opportunity it gives its members for self-improvement and interactions with other purchasing people. Many chapters have well-developed speakers' bureaus and diversified professional development activities. NAPM chapters often have arrangements with educational institutions for the organization of purchasing conferences, institutes, seminars, and courses that influence public relations. Also, some chapters support scholarships in local universities. A former national chairperson of the public relations committee of NAPM has said, "Every member of the Purchasing profession lives in a goldfish bowl. . .both on and off the job. Everything he says or does is watched by the general public. It is just human nature for everyone to watch any person who is spending someone else's money."

In view of the public interest, ethics is a matter of great interest to the purchasing profession. Although ethics tend to be codified into neat little compilations of *do's* and *don'ts,* it is more than this. Rules and regulations will always be superficial because truly ethical conduct, coming from within, is the result of a conscious resolution of inner conflict between what people feel tempted to do and what they feel they ought to do.

Ethics deals with the person in society. Most people conform to the law, written and informal. This might be called the sphere of practical ethics. But many issues confronting a person transcend what society has reduced to rules. Furthermore, new situations arise when a person has to resolve a conflict between what society does and what individual ideals decree.

These considerations explain the endless discussions of how much of a gift is allowable, who pays for lunch, and whether the buyer should pay the cost of transportation on a plant visit. Attempts to reconcile the real with the ideal usually necessitate drawing up a set of rules for guidance. These rules as developed by a department, a company, or an association have the practical effect, at least, of raising the minimum standard of ethics for a profession, although they may leave many individual problems unresolved.

The following rules of conduct are found in NAPM's Principles and Standards of Purchasing Practice.*

1. To consider first the interest of the company in all transactions and to carry out and believe in its established policies.
2. To be receptive to competent counsel from colleagues and to be guided by such counsel without impairing the dignity and responsibility of the office.

---

*NAPM maintains a standing committee on ethics and morality in the profession to encourage high ethical practice.

3. To buy without prejudice, seeking to obtain the maximum ultimate value for each dollar of expenditure.
4. To strive consistently for knowledge of the materials and processes of manufacture, and to establish practical methods for the conduct of the office.
5. To subscribe to and work for honesty and truth in buying and selling, and to denounce all forms and manifestations of commercial bribery.
6. To accord a prompt and courteous reception, so far as conditions will permit, to all who call on a legitimate business mission.
7. To respect one's own obligations and to require that others' obligations be respected, consistent with good business practice.
8. To avoid sharp practice.
9. To counsel and assist fellow purchasing personnel in the performance of their duties, whenever the occasion permits.
10. To cooperate with all organizations and persons engaged in activities designed to enhance the development and standing of purchasing.

The Code of Ethics of the National Institute of Governmental Purchasing says that the purchasing agent:

1. Does not seek or accept a position as head or employee of a governmental purchasing agency unless fully in accord with the professional principles of governmental purchasing and unless [that agent] is confident of personal qualifications to serve under these principles to the advantage of the employing governmental jurisdiction.
2. Believes in the dignity and worth of the service rendered by government and is aware of a personal social responsibility as a trusted public servant.
3. Is governed by the highest ideals of honor and integrity in all public and personal relationships, in order to merit the respect and inspire the confidence of the agency and the public served.
4. Believes that personal aggrandizement or personal profit obtained through misuse of public or personal relationships is dishonest.
5. Keeps the employing governmental jurisdiction informed, through appropriate channels, on problems and progress of the agency served, but remains in the background by emphasizing the importance of the facts.
6. Resists encroachment on his or her control of personnel in order to preserve integrity as a professional administrator. Handles all per-

sonnel matters on a merit basis. Political, religious, and racial considerations carry no weight in personnel administration in the agency that he or she directs or serves.

7. Does not seek or dispense personal favors; handles each administrative problem objectively without discrimination, on the basis of principle and justice.

8. Subscribes to and supports the professional objectives of the National Institute of Governmental Purchasing.

SOCIAL RESPONSIBILITY AND BUSINESS GOALS

In discussing the rather subjective and sometimes emotional subject of social responsibility, one must begin by establishing whether it really is a legitimate concern of business and purchasing. Opponents of business involvement in social issues point out that maximizing profit is the paramount concern of business. They question the advisability of concentrating social power in the hands of business executives, and they often state that such action deprives stockholders of the right to allocate their dollars as they see fit.

Today, however, it is accepted that business is governed not only by explicit laws, but also by the sometimes shifting values of society. The values of society are recognized as potential legal constraints. Therefore, as stated earlier, business maintains sensitivity to public opinions and values in order to avoid being put in a rigid position bound by formal laws and regulations.

There is a good precedent for this view. Witness consumerism, the first quasi-organized approach in tapping society's views and opinions of the market. This movement had an impact on business almost equal to that of the labor movement of the 1940s, 1950s, and 1960s, when labor's rights were spelled out in legal terms. Although concern for social responsibility is a relatively new area of public interest, it has already been manifested in many legal restraints.

For example, the U.S. Senate faces ethics and campaign-finance reform. During 1989–1990, the Senate Select Committee on Ethics brought seven senators under investigation. Never before have so many senators come under investigation at once. The charges involved several ethical issues including intervening with federal regulators on a savings and loan association executive's behalf and accepting from him about $1.3 million in campaign funds.[7]

---

[7] *The Washington Post,* (January 24, 1990).

In this book, social responsibility will be considered in reference to such factors as concern about pollution (air and water), discrimination, hazardous waste products, and the depletion of our natural resources.

THE PURCHASING MANAGER AND SOCIAL RESPONSIBILITY

Purchasing managers are potentially one of the most important groups in American industry to play a role in instilling concern for action on social issues. Why? Simply because collectively they allocate the dollars of business. They have power, and power is what moves people and things.

For example, decisions to purchase capital equipment influences the level of both employment and prices. In the decision to increase or reduce inventories, the purchasing manager may be contributing to inflation or accelerating a recession. Buying from foreign producers entails a contribution either to international tensions or to international understanding. He or she fights reciprocity, because it treats suppliers and/or customers with special favor. The purchasing manager resists buying for employees because it robs local merchants of the selling opportunities by which they survive and grow. He or she opposes top-management pressure to solicit gifts for favorite charities in the corporation's name. When purchasing people discuss social issues, they instill ideas. When they encourage recycling in production processes, they influence waste control and the depletion rate of our natural resources. Some specific examples follow.

The purchasing manager can instill social awareness in suppliers (collectively this is almost all of American industry). This awareness can be instilled simply by discussing matters with the salespeople who call. The typical buyer sees between three and five salespeople a day; within a year this can represent over 1000 contacts. These are potentially powerful contacts.

For example, suppose the purchasing manager were to ask a salesperson, "How much money did you spend last year to change processes in order to reduce pollution?" or "How many minority employees did you add to your payroll last year?" or "How much did you spend on recycling research?" Chances are the salesperson will not know these things but will find out. He or she goes back and asks the vice president of sales, who asks the president. They will acquire the information, and it will be reported back. The result is that the supplying firm has had an inspiration of social thinking.

Purchasing has traditionally paid for intangibles such as service and quality—variables that have a great deal of subjectivity. A basic question is: Should (or can) a purchasing manager pay for the social responsibility of suppliers, as a subjective consideration in the buying decision? Some interesting and realistic situations can provide a basis for considering this matter.

Suppose competitive suppliers A and B are located across a state line from each other. The state in which B is located institutes pollution controls. The price from each vendor had been the same, but now B will have to increase price by 1 cent per unit. What does the purchasing manager do? Should he or she shift purchases to A and buy heavily from the polluter until the laws in A's state catch up with the environmental needs? Or should the purchasing manager, realizing the environmental benefits of B's actions, continue to buy from B?

To increase the complexity of the purchasing manager's environmental decision-making matrix, suppose company Z is a long-time supplier and desires to take voluntary steps to improve the environment. In addition, assume that Z company has been just equal with its competition, but now suggests a 10-cent increase if the proposed action is taken. Can the purchasing manager take the increase and directly pay for environmental action? In this situation, the purchasing manager probably cannot make the decision alone and must obtain an input of ideas.

The purchasing manager can be one of the practical instruments through which lofty concerns for social responsibility are put into action by business. What is necessary here is an increasing sensitivity to the issue of corporation citizenship and a close communication pipeline between the purchasing manager and top management on the matter of social issues. Perhaps statements about the socially responsible actions taken by suppliers should be added to the quarterly savings and inventory reports. These examples indicate that social responsibility is a significant part of the purchasing decision matrix.

Former *Harvard Business Review* editor Kenneth R. Andrews holds the familiar view that moral character is shaped by family, church, and education long before an individual joins a company to make a living.[8] However, a change in America's social contract has altered who or what shapes personal values, according to another observer:

> Corporations have become the focus of our concerns because today's individual spends most of his life in a corporate community—whether it is a university, a hospital or a factory. And it is that corporate community that has replaced the church, the extended family and even the community as the transmitter of values and ethics.[9]

---

[8] "Ethics in Practice," *Harvard Business Review* (September–October, 1989), pp. 99–103.
[9] "Mr. Diogenes, Call Your Office," *Financial World* (June 27, 1989), pp. 24–26.

DISADVANTAGED MINORITY BUYING

Purchasing from disadvantaged business enterprises is a specific and growing concern that was originally instigated by government actions. The National Minority Supplier Development Council was established in 1972 to accelerate acceptance of minority vendors through improved communications between majority and minority firms. The Small Business Investment Act of 1958 was a government move to aid small and disadvantaged companies by permitting subcontracting with these businesses on a negotiated rather than bidding basis.

The Public Works Act of 1977 requires that 10 percent of all federally funded construction contracts go to minority companies, and the Labor Department requires that 6.9 percent of a contractor's workforce be filled by women. All federal contracts of more than $50,000 must include a plan for subcontracting with small and disadvantaged firms. In 1978, Public Law 95-507 was passed; this law mandates that large contracts exceeding $500,000 and construction contracts exceeding $1 million include percentage goals for utilization of minority businesses. In addition, this law broadens the definition of minorities to include both socially and economically disadvantaged groups. Both these laws are being debated as possibly unnecessary and potentially costly to governmental projects.

American business has developed an increased sensitivity toward minority vendors. Corporations purchase from disadvantaged business enterprises because it makes economic sense as well as social sense. Purchases from minority-owned businesses by large corporations rose from $86 million in 1972 to more than $12 billion in 1988. The years from 1979–1988 showed a steady upward trend, as Figure 22-2 exhibits. Some of the specific reasons that have led to this increase include the following.

1. More minority businesses are offering the high-value goods and services that large corporations wish to buy.
2. More minority suppliers are available.
3. The number of minority businesses large enough to do business regionally and nationally has grown.
4. Public Law 95-507 has an incentive clause for government contracts that allows a corporation an additional profit or fee if it exceeds its minority purchasing goals.
5. More companies are establishing programs for complying with Public Law 95-507.

Business groups have also instigated their own programs to promote relations with minority firms. Such voluntary action is essential to long-term

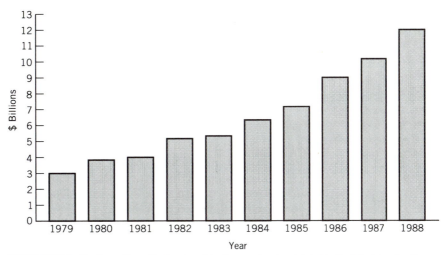

FIGURE 22-2. Purchases from disadvantaged business enterprises tripled in the latest decade. *Source:* Corporate members reports to Minority Supplier Development Council.

success for minority vendor programs. The dollar purchases have been showing considerable increases for individual concerns. A large percentage of this growth can be attributed to the fact that businesses are promoting minority business through the development of purchasing programs and the investment of corporate funds in minority firms.

The Business Consortium Fund makes corporate, state government, and foundation funds available as working capital loans for minority businesses. Loans range from $50,000 minimum to $250,000 maximum, with a maximum loan term of two years.[10]

When purchasing is evaluated only in terms of dollars saved, there may be little incentive to buy from minority firms. However, when the social impact of purchasing dollars is considered, a broader perspective is attained. Minority buying, scrap reclamation activities, and related social aspects of vendor choice are increasingly included in purchasing evaluation, in recognition of the influence on society of the purchasing manager's decision framework.

There is a significant and growing movement within business toward the acceptance of a social role. Although this change in goals may be somewhat difficult to reconcile with the classical theory of maximizing profit, our system of business organization has always shown a tendency to adapt to circumstances rather than to bear out pure theory. The present interest in social needs and demands may well be a response to a new level

[10] *The Business Consortium, Inc.* undated leaflet, 1412 Broadway, New York, New York.

of affluence and may alter to some extent the nature and operation of our economic institutions. In any case, purchasing managers should be keenly aware of developments in the area of social responsibility.

CHAPTER SUMMARY

Business has shown a growing movement toward accepting a social role and a stronger sense of social responsibility. The high level of prosperity that has prevailed in the United States has heightened the public's expectations of good business ethics standards. This prosperity has enabled business executives to concern themselves with matters such as corporate image and ethics rather than sheer survival.

The present adaptation to social needs and demands may well result as a response to a new level of affluence and government controls. Affluence and controls may alter to some extent the nature and operation of economic institutions. In any case, business managers should carefully observe the developments in public relations and ethics. Ethical businesspersons should lend their assistance to many of these changes that appear to offer the opportunity to practice both sound business and good ethics. A concerned public knows the high price that will be paid when business and civic leaders act on the basis of greed.

National professional associations publish ethical standards to guide those who purchase, sell, or manage materials. The current trend toward social accountability has prompted business and government to promote ethical standards. They urge their employees and vendors to follow good ethical behavior.

Social responsibility focuses on environmental matters. Natural resources show signs of running out, and the purchasing professional must face this reality. He or she should respond by taking decisive action; for example, by ordering shipments in reusable containers, substituting products that neither pollute nor waste resources, and recycling materials wherever possible.

Discussion Questions

1. What is the relation of a business to the social and ethical attitudes of society? How has this changed in the past few years?
2. Why is purchasing in the forefront of the developing business role in social and ethical attitudes and concerns?
3. Discuss the social responsibilities of purchasing.
4. What are the forces motivating business to accept social responsibility?
5. Discuss the role of the purchasing manager in business ethics.
6. Contrast personal and business ethics.

7. How does social responsibility affect business goals?

8. What is the role of the purchasing manager in these business goal decisions?

9. Discuss the concerns of purchasing in buying from minority vendors.

10. Why have purchases from minority-owned businesses increased?

Suggested Cases

ABC Corporation

Household Cleaners Corporation

Howell Chuck Company (A)

The Janmar Corporation

King County

McKeough Company

MF-1

Parktown 425

Thomas Ethics

Utopia School District

Warehouse Steel Company

Cases

ABC CORPORATION (A)

ABC Corporation, a manufacturer of electrical equipment, is in a highly competitive segment of its industry. For this reason, it has become necessary to search energetically for better and, frequently, radically different ways of performing standard operations in the manufacture of its product. Often it becomes necessary to develop special-purpose equipment, which bears little or no resemblance to any other machine or device, either in ABC's plant or in competitors' plants. This course of action has been dictated by the absolute need to eliminate every item of cost possible to ensure a profit.

Joe Hammel, the plant engineer, had an idea for such a radical device and was successful in selling his idea to management. Joe was authorized to discuss his idea with a number of firms engaged in the design and manufacture of special automated machinery. After a thorough search, one manufacturer was selected because it corroborated Joe's supposition that a machine built on Joe's principle would produce sizable savings.

A cost projection was made to establish rather firmly the cost of this equipment, and an involved method of payment was decided on. One of the unusual features was premium payments for early delivery of the equipment, and penalties for late delivery. The contract was undertaken in an aura of great optimism. However, despite the incentive of premium payments, the machine was not delivered on time. In fact, delivery was not made until several months after the penalty date. During this entire period, both ABC and the machine manufacturer encountered unexpected problems, and it became obvious that the design requirements exceeded the capabilities of the machinery manufacturer. To compound the problem, the person who had developed the original electrical circuitry and had done much of the basic research left the employ of the machinery manufacturer.

When it became obvious that no progress was being made, the impasse was resolved by taking delivery of the machine despite the fact that the original contract called for satisfactory performance under production conditions while still in the machine manufacturer's plant. The decision to take delivery was made in the hope that the technical resources of ABC could be successfully applied to the problem. After ABC invested much additional time and money, the machine finally began to operate as Joe originally had anticipated.

ABC was aware of its legal responsibilities in breaching the contract by taking delivery of equipment that failed to meet specifications. It did so because the machine manufacturer was near bankruptcy and could not invest further money in this piece of equipment. Had ABC forced the issue, it might have led to to the liquidation of the machine manufacturer. This would have exposed ABC to the hazard of losing many of its ideas which had been incorporated in the machine. The device was protected by a gentleman's agreement between ABC and the machine manufacturer, and the machine manufacturer had customers who were competitors of ABC.

This involved situation created many problems in public relations for ABC. Among them were the following:

1. How to deal with a supplier verging on bankruptcy on a matter involving costs in excess of contract.
2. How to supply know-how replacing that already contracted for.
3. How to protect design ideas that were mutually developed against becoming competitors' property.
4. How to deal with this supplier in the future so as to draw upon its knowledge about running undue risks; or, as an alternative, educating another supplier.

How would you handle each of the public relations problems listed?

ABC CORPORATION (B)

After two years of developmental work, the special machine referred to in ABC Corporation (A) began to function as originally anticipated. Labor costs had been minimized to a degree not previously realized in the industry.

There was one problem, however; raw material from one manufacturer seemed to work well in the machine, whereas material from another manufacturer (there were only two suppliers of any consequence of this material) seemed to perform erratically and at times could not be used at all.

Much time was devoted to finding the reasons for this variation in performance. After months of investigation and trial it appeared that some manufacturing procedure in the second vendor's plant made that product less acceptable.

Discussions were held with the supplier's representatives, but it was difficult to convince them that the processing of the product in their plant would have any bearing on the product's performance in the special machine. However, it was finally arranged for representatives of ABC's purchasing and quality control departments to view the manufacturing processes in both suppliers' plants.

The visiting team was given a step-by-step view of the material from the melt to the final slitting operations so that comparisons might be made. It was discovered that two steps in the manufacturing process accounted for the difficulties.

Although the offending manufacturer grudgingly agreed that its processes accounted for the problems on ABC's machine, the product was acceptable to other customers. It was, therefore, the uniqueness of ABC's machine that created the manufacturing differences. The unstated question was: Why change a manufacturing process that provides an acceptable product to all but ABC, and gives ABC difficulties only because it insists on using the material in a unique device?

It was obvious that changing the manufacturing process was going to be a rather costly undertaking. The supplier did admit, however, that some changes were being contemplated in its processing for reasons other than accommodating ABC. The company indicated that consideration would be given to ABC's problem when these changes were being planned if they would not greatly increase manufacturing costs.

A number of factors had to be considered at this point.

1. ABC is a sizable user of this expensive material. Its rate of use is increasing at more than industry-average rate. This makes ABC a better-than-average account and lends a degree of leverage to its bargaining.
2. At least two sources of supply for a material of this importance are highly desirable.
3. A third source is on the horizon but, although this source has spent millions of dollars in getting into this business, it has not yet succeeded in establishing itself as a dependable supplier.
4. The second source (the one with the product-producing problems for ABC) or the third (potential) source will need to make additional expenditures in mechanical processing equipment.
5. Should ABC's process be successful in producing a satisfactory product at lower costs, it is almost certain that ABC's competitors will discover a similar approach.
6. An alternative would be the development of another machine by ABC, designed to overcome the present limitations. This would not be easy, since many of the possibilities explored have proved to be unsatisfactory.

How should this problem be handled?

AJAX SEWING MACHINE COMPANY

The Ajax Sewing Machine Company has just received a large overseas order and has put production on a three-shift basis to meet it. But inventory has fallen to a minimum, and Ajax is considering reassigning its expediters to ensure that critical materials will come in on time.

Four key parts are purchased, respectively, from the Arkwright, Benton, Crowley, and Danielson companies. The four suppliers give rather poor service on deliveries, although they are more than satisfactory in other respects. Ajax, therefore, has made a practice of assigning one of its crack expediters to each of the four accounts.

On the basis of the past five years' experience, Ajax is able to tabulate the average days of delay experienced when each expediter is assigned to a particular supplier, as shown in Table 1.

Thus if Jones is assigned to the Danielson account, we may expect Danielson to be 11 days late in making its shipments. If Smith is given this assignment, the delay is reduced to 9 days.

An analysis by Ajax management shows that a delay at Arkwright will cost $125 per day; a delay at Benton, $50 per day; a delay at Crowley, $80 per day; and at Danielson, $100 per day.

Ajax has to assign four additional inspectors to handle the increased volume from the four suppliers. The cost of an inspector's mistake is $10 on an Arkwright part, $20 on a Benton part, $30 on a Crowley part, and $40 on a Danielson part.

The four inspectors—Herman, Abrams, Adams, and Johnson—vary considerably in their ability to catch errors. Herman has a 10 percent chance of letting an error go through in the course of a day, Abrams a 20 percent chance, Adams a 30 percent chance, and Johnson a 40 percent chance.

These estimates are based on the overall records of the four inspectors. However, when the records are analyzed by type of job, we see that Abrams has a bad record on the Benton parts, so that Abrams' chance of making an

TABLE 1. Days of Delay for Each Expediter

	Supplier			
Expediter	Arkwright	Benton	Crowley	Danielson
Jones	12	40	30.0	11
Smith	24	60	7.5	9
Peters	21	42	20.0	24
Hammond	16	36	12.5	8

TABLE 2. Chance of Error (%) on the Part of Various Inspectors

	Supplier			
Inspector	Arkwright	Benton	Crowley	Danielson
Herman	10	10	10	10
Abrams	20	25	10	20
Adams	30	30	30	10
Johnson	40	40	40	40

error on a Benton job is 25 percent. On a Crowley part, Abrams' record is very good, and the chance of error is only 10 percent. By the same token Adams has a particularly good record on Danielson-type jobs, with only one chance in ten of making an error.

For the others, the job analysis supports the original estimates. Table 2 shows the chances of a daily error.

1. How should the four expediters be assigned to minimize delay costs?
2. How should Ajax assign its inspectors to minimize the dollar value of its inspection errors?

AMERICAN ARBITRATION ASSOCIATION

The American Arbitration Association is a private, nonprofit organization established to aid businesses in finding solutions to legal disputes. Contracts between buyers and sellers sometimes contain what is called a future dispute clause. This clause establishes an agreement to settle disputes and claims in accordance with American Arbitration Association rules. Arbitration is invoked in lieu of a formal lawsuit. The following five recent disputes were submitted to arbitration.

1. The purchasing manager (PM) contracted to buy a large supply of corrugated boxes in a size for shipping a new line of merchandise her company had in production and would begin marketing in about four months. The delivery date was set at two months from the time of the agreement. Several days after she had submitted a purchase order, the PM received the order confirmation, and the deal was completely set.

Then the salesperson from the packaging company called about a week later with a special request, "Listen, we've got a warehousing problem here. We're about to rent some new space and it would make our inventory control a lot easier if you can take delivery on that order now.''

The buyer was willing, since she happened to have space to store the boxes till she needed them. However, she pointed out to the salesperson, ''I can take that shipment now, if I'm not required to make an inspection of the merchandise until I need it.'' Their agreement called for any defects to be reported within 14 days, and she didn't want to have to unpack all the boxes, then repack them for storage.

''That's no problem,'' the salesperson told her. ''Your 14-day inspection time won't begin until the original delivery date.''

They accepted shipment of the order and stored it on their premises. Two months later, when the shipment was opened, damage apparently caused by water was discovered.

The PM immediately called the supplier and learned that the salesman she had dealt with was no longer with the company, so she spoke to the sales manager. ''These boxes we ordered from you are water-damaged and can't be used.''

''There's nothing I can do about it now. You've had that order for two months.''

''Wait a minute,'' the buyer said. ''We agreed to take that order early for your convenience and your salesperson said that the inspection time didn't start until the original delivery date.''

''Well, the salesperson shouldn't have made a verbal agreement like that. Look at the order confirmation. It specifically says no changes can be made except in writing.''

''Well, he did make an agreement and since he was your salesperson, you're bound to it.''

''Nothing doing,'' was the supplier's reply. ''How do we know that you didn't damage those boxes yourselves? I'm afraid it's just too late to make a claim.'' Both parties repeated basically these same arguments before the arbitrator.

2. Martha Franklin, the purchasing manager for Graphics, Inc. one day felt the need for some advice on an order of paper and went to a wholesaler for help. She discussed her needs in full, explaining that the paper she wanted was to be printed and varnished and used as box wraps. The supplier was ready with quick advice. ''Got just what you need,'' he piped.

Following the agent's recommendation, Martha ordered 27,000 sheets of a certain 34 × 57-inch paper. The cost was $1500.

Soon after, the order was delivered and Martha's company put the paper through the various processes to prepare it for final gluing. When the company started gluing the paper to the boxes, the results were unsatisfactory. The paper blistered and could not be made to stick.

Pressed for time, Martha went to another supplier and got paper that proved satisfactory for the purpose, and her company was able to meet its obligation to the customer. Afterward, Martha totaled up expenses of $4000 in reprinting, finishing, and trucking the substituted paper. Then she let the first supplier know that her company had no intention of absorbing the cost. The tactic chosen by Martha's company was to deduct the expense from other invoices owed the supplier.

"You can just deduct $4000 from what we owe you," said Graphics officials, "and next time don't promise that a product can do a job unless you know what you're talking about."

"Who promised anything?" replied the supplier. "What I said amounted to no more than an opinion that the paper *might* be suitable."

"In fact," he went on, "the sales contract specifically states, *'Seller makes no warranties whatsoever, express or implied, as to suitability.'* That proves that you've got no gripe with me. If you couldn't make the paper perform satisfactorily, it wasn't due to any fault or defect in the paper. This is a case of bad judgment on your part and you can't hold me responsible for that!"

Martha's company decided to bring the matter to arbitration in accordance with the dispute settlement clause in the sales contract.

3. The sales manager of Eastville Specialty Cabinets was not in the habit of turning away business, but one day it looked as though he might have to.

The prospective customer, a life insurance company, had sent in a purchase order for a large supply of metal filing cabinets for a suburban branch under construction. To prevent duplication of moving costs, the insurance company had requested that the goods be shipped directly to the new office during the last week of May when construction was to be completed. But Eastville officials were not happy about this kind of arrangement. They did not like the possibility of having their already limited storage space taken up by the insurance company's goods, should the new quarters not be ready on schedule. When all was taken into consideration, Eastville's sales manager felt that the order wasn't worth the trouble if his company had to risk jeopardizing the movement of other orders.

He explained the situation to the insurance company's purchasing manager and after some discussion they worked out a solution. It appeared in the sales agreement as Section 14: If the buyer does not accept delivery on date requested, the goods will be stored at the buyer's expense.

The construction work progressed smoothly and to the relief of both the insurance company and the supplier, the building was ready on time. Eastville was notified and the goods were shipped. But upon their delivery the purchasing manager found them less than satisfactory. Apparently when they were crated the cabinets had been quite badly marred.

"Take them back," the purchasing manager told the driver. "We can't accept them in this condition."

The goods went back and the deficiencies were corrected. When Eastville asked the purchasing manager for shipping instructions, the firm was told that the local building department had closed the office down pending certain repairs by the contractor. Six weeks later, the manager called Eastville's sales office back. "We're in business again. Send the goods," he said.

Eastville did just that, but along with the cabinets came a bill for six weeks' storage.

"We won't pay," the purchasing manager's company replied. "That storage provision in the contract applied only if for some reason we were unable to receive goods on the date we requested. We did not intend to pay storage if the goods went back because of defects."

Eastville was adamant, however, and the case eventually found its way to the American Arbitration Association.

4. A buyer estimated that 3600 bundles of tile were needed to complete a land–sea trucking terminal. The supplier quoted a price of $14,000—$4 a bundle.

When the shipment arrived, the invoice was for 4800 bundles, not the 3600 ordered. He thought about it briefly and then decided to accept the shipment. "We might need the extra tiles," he reasoned. "Some of the men might be careless, there might be some pilferage—I'll keep the whole batch and see how many we use."

When the job was finished, the buyer discovered that his workers had used 500 extra bundles. He called the supplier to ask him to adjust the bill accordingly, charging the company for 4100 bundles. He was going to return the remaining 700 bundles.

The supplier was amenable to the return, mentioning in passing that as long as the tiles were still in factory-sealed cartons, he always allowed returns.

The buyer checked with his supervisor and learned that the cartons had all been opened at the beginning of the job. The workers had culled the damaged and broken tiles from the shipment, and these made up a great many of the remaining tiles. He went back to his supplier with this news, but still claimed that he had the right of return.

"After all," he said, "we only ordered 3600 bundles in the first place. The extra ones were your responsibility. Since we did use more than we anticipated, I'm perfectly willing to pay you for those. But it's ridiculous for me to have to pay for tiles that I didn't order and didn't use."

"If you had rejected the shipment on delivery, or told me that you might use some extra tiles at that time, I could have made it clear to you that I only accept returns if they are unopened," the supplier replied. "If you had found broken tiles in the shipment when you first received it, I would have given you credit for them; but now, since the cartons have been opened, there's every reason to believe that the tiles were damaged by the carelessness of your own workers. You have no way of proving to me that those tiles came to you in a damaged condition."

The buyer decided to invoke the arbitration clause on the purchase order his company used, and he and his supplier met a month later in front of an arbitrator to tell their stories.

5. The Whirlpool Corporation had purchased from a company in North Carolina an expensive piece of machinery. It was apparently loaded onto a truck of the McLean Trucking Company in good condition, but when it arrived at its Minneapolis destination the shipping case was broken. Whether the equipment was damaged could not be determined immediately, but the receiving clerk took the precaution of noting the defect on the receipt.

The original bill of lading contained a nine-month time limit for filing claims, and the Whirlpool executive apparently thought he had acted well within that limit when, a few weeks after the shipment arrived, he sent to McLean's depot a straight bill of lading on which he had written "Claim to be filed."

Believing he had preserved his rights to assert a claim, the Whirlpool executive took his time about expressing his claim in detail. He finally did so about a year after the shipment was received. The claim was for $488.86.

McLean's response must have come as a surprise to Whirlpool. The trucking company stated that, as no claim had been filed within nine months, it was too late to do so. Whirlpool replied that the notice expressed on the straight bill of lading did constitute a claim, but McLean refused to accept that interpretation.

1. How should the arbitration panel rule in each case?
2. Was there anything that could have been done to lessen the likelihood of each of these dispute's arising?

THE ANSON COMPANY

The Anson Company is one of the largest manufacturers of electrical generating equipment. Periodically over the last 20 years the company has booked more orders than its productive capacity can supply. At such times the company has resorted to subcontracting part of its work. This subcontracting has included not only the making of component parts but also some of the steps in the machining of parts that are to be finish-machined, tested, and assembled at the Anson plant.

Most of the subcontracting of machining operations involves heavy, cast-steel parts, some of which weigh more than 100,000 lbs. The Anson Company has three boring bars and milling machines with the capacity to handle pieces of this size. During periods of peak production, these machines operate on a three-shift basis but still are unable to keep up with the needs. The purchasing agent has arrangements with other metalworking firms using the same types of machine tools. Under these arrangements he has been able to place subcontracts with two firms located within 100 miles of the Anson plant.

Although Mr. Lightman, the purchasing agent, had never had occasion to make use of them, he knew of two other firms with machines of proper capacity for this type of work. These firms were located in Johnson City, 125 miles from the Anson plant and 80 miles from the city where the present subcontractors were located.

In the spring it became apparent that the work at the Anson plant was building up to the point that machining capacity for large pieces would be inadequate. Mr. Lightman, therefore, contacted the two subcontractors who had done this type of work before to inquire whether they could fit the jobs into their scheduled machining capacity. In the past there had been but minor differences in the prices quoted for this type of work. The prices were quoted in terms of the estimated number of hours of machining involved. The estimated hours were those determined by Anson engineers and used in its own cost calculations. A subcontractor who could machine a piece to specifications in fewer hours benefited from that efficiency. If it took longer, the subcontractor received no additional compensation.

The two subcontractors quoted identical prices for the machining of six castings, which were estimated to require 250 hours each. The castings were to be shipped directly from the foundry that cast them for the Anson Company. In this way the transportation costs, which were substantial because of the weight involved, would be minimized. Each casting was to be shipped by the foundry after it had passed an X-ray inspection. It was anticipated that the first casting would arrive at the subcontractor's plant on May 1 and that the other five would follow at 10-day intervals. It was necessary that all six castings be machined and delivered by July 15.

Bates Machinery Company, one of the subcontractors, had two boring bars large enough to handle the work. The Bates Company informed Mr. Lightman that it would schedule the Anson work on a three-shift basis on one of the machines and use the other for its own manufacturing purposes.

The Benson Machinery Company, the other subcontractor, had six machine tools in its plant capable of handling the work. The company believed that it would experience no problems in meeting the July 15 completion date.

In view of the fact that the subcontract would require the Bates Company to work at capacity and allow for no disruptions if the deadline was to be met, Mr. Lightman decided to subcontract with the Benson Company. Because of the tight schedule, a senior expediter was assigned to the contract and instructed to check once a week on the status of the work. On May 21, the first machined casting was delivered from the Benson Company; the second was delivered on June 4. The Benson Company regularly assured the expediter that the final deadline would be met. On June 12, Mr. Lightman and the expediter visited the Benson plant and discovered that only one machine had been scheduled to work on their castings. Several days of machining time had been lost through a breakdown of the machine. Mr. Lightman attempted to induce the Benson production manager to assign two machines to his job. However, Mr. Benson, the owner of the company, was on a two-week fishing trip in Canada and had set up production schedules for the plant before leaving. Neither the production manager nor the other executive wanted to countermand Mr. Benson's instructions. Mr. Lightman realized that if four of the six machines were put to work on his castings after Mr. Benson returned from his vacation, the deadline could still be met. However, he had no way of knowing whether Mr. Benson would take this action.

Mr. Lightman returned to the Anson plant and conferred with company executives. He pointed out that there were alternative courses of action available. They could leave the job with Benson and apply pressure to speed up the work. They could remove all or part of the work from the Benson plant and try to induce the Bates Company to machine some of the castings and have the others machined elsewhere. It appeared that there was no possibility of finding machine time at the Anson plant. Mr. Lightman was reasonably sure that he could place the work with one of the potential subcontractors in Johnson City. However, he noted that there would be substantial costs involved in moving the castings from the Benson plant to Johnson City.

Mr. Lightman's recommendation was that they permit the Benson Company to work on two of the castings and move the other two castings to the Bates Company plant for machining.

1. What action should Anson Company take to meet the July 15 deadline?

2. Was there anything that could have been done to prevent this siuation from arising?

BERG RAINGEAR, INC.

The Berg Raingear company manufactured a complete line of men's, women's, and children's raincoats as well as umbrellas and other types of raingear. Its annual sales were $12 million in 1993. The raingear was of two types, a rubberized fabric and chemically treated fabrics. Sales were evenly divided between the two types.

Annual purchases of Wein's rain repellent, a chemical used in treating the fabrics to produce the rain repellent, were approximately $200,000. This product was sold by its manufacturer both to clothing manufacturers and direct to the consumer in an aerosol spray can. Sales to consumers were backed by heavy consumer advertising, and broad consumer acceptance of the brand name had been achieved. Berg Raingear, Inc. was authorized by Wein to attach a special label to all its garments on which the solution was used.

Shortly before a new contract was to be negotiated with Wein, Ms. Frances Adams, chemicals buyer for Berg, was approached by a salesperson of the Madison Chemical Corporation. He stated that his company had developed a new waterproofing compound for textiles that was better than anything on the market. Madison Chemical was planning to introduce it to the industrial market first but hoped to begin to move the compound into the consumer market through an extensive advertising campaign within 12 months. The price of this new product was competitive with the Wein product.

A sample of the new product was delivered to the company research chemist for testing purposes. He reported back to Ms. Adams that this new product was the equal of that currently being purchased. However, he suggested that without much trouble he could develop a similar chemical compound that would be satisfactory and could be manufactured in the Berg plant at a savings of 15 percent over the price being paid to Wein. He estimated that were this course of action adopted, the necessary equipment could be purchased new for $115,000 or used for $50,000 or less.

Ms. Adams asked the chemist to give her a list of the chemical ingredients and their proportions in the product. She then called on two small local chemical plants and solicited bids for a waterproofing compound made to the Berg company specifications. One bid was received at a price of 5 percent below that then being paid to Wein.

1. Should Ms. Adams change suppliers?
2. Should Berg produce their own waterproofing compound?

BIELAW COMPANY

The Bielaw Company manufactures a varied line of industrial equipment and installations. Over the last 15 years the company had gradually been increasing the size and weight of many of its installations in order to meet customer requirements. A problem facing the company was the scarcity of special equipment to transport these large and heavy units. The company often had to sectionalize big units and reweld them on the job site. This was both time-consuming and costly. The cost added appreciably to the prices the company quoted its customers.

The railroad equipment used for such shipments were depressed-center cars, well cars, and heavy-duty flat cars. Because such equipment was in short supply, it was necessary to make arrangements with carriers at least six months in advance of requirements. The railroads distribute such special equipment through the Car Service Division of the Association of American Railroads, since many lines do not own cars of these kinds.

A shipper who required special equipment would place an order with the originating carrier. If this carrier was not able to furnish the car from its own equipment, it placed an order with the Car Service Division, which attempted to secure the equipment from another carrier. This procedure tended to make the shipping schedules of the Bielaw Company uncertain. There were occasions when the company had to make penalty payments under its contracts because of delays occasioned by the unavailability of rail equipment when needed. In addition, prompt loading and unloading of cars was necessary to avoid demurrage charges, and this was difficult to arrange when the cars had to be requisitioned six months in advance of use.

The traffic manager of the Bielaw Company prepared a special report for management on this problem. The report recommended the purchase of three specially designed railway well cars at an estimated cost of $250,000 each. As part of the reports she made a compilation of all charges paid during the previous 12 months for the rental of special equipment, which totaled $498,561. In addition, the report held that it was possible to design a car so as to permit larger dimensions of the pieces shipped, which would reduce cutting and welding cost. However, at the time the report was submitted, engineering feasibility studies on larger sectionalization had not been made.

Additional advantages stressed in the report included the competitive advantage of owning cars, which would permit guarantees to customers with respect to delivery dates. The two principal competitors of the Bielaw Company did not own special railway cars. The report pointed out that if Bielaw equipment could be redesigned to be shipped in larger sections, the savings could be used to quote lower prices than the two competing firms could offer.

The company made an additional saving through the reduction in blocking and tie-down costs. When the company used railway-owned cars, it frequently incurred costs in excess of $1000 per car for lumber and dunnage materials needed to secure the item against the hazards of travel. The report observed that such dunnage was completely lost, since the car moved on to another user after it was unloaded. With company-owned cars it would be possible to install permanent blocking and tie-down equipment that could be reused.

The report concluded that the payoff period on special rail equipment would be approximately 20 months, disregarding the sales advantages that might accrue to the company.

Mr. Lester, president of the company, discussed the report with his executive committee. He was of the opinion that the company should purchase the special cars as soon as possible. He planned to use this as a basis for underbidding competitors on a large government contract for which bids were due in 20 days. Mr. Lester thought that the savings would justify a substantially lower bid and that his competitors would be at a loss to understand the low bid until the special cars were placed in service. This could give the Bielaw Company a nine-month period during which it could underbid competition.

The executive committee discussed, without reaching a conclusion, whether this special equipment should be reserved for company use or made available through the Car Service Division to any user. The treasurer pointed out that the latter approach would increase the return to the company on its investment. He believed that conditions could be established that would permit all but the Bielaw Company's direct competitors to rent the equipment. The advertising manager thought that this was a good idea, since it was proposed to paint the cars the distinctive colors used on all Bielaw products and to emblazon the company name on the sides of the car.

The production manager and the purchasing agent felt that there should be further study before a decision was reached. They argued that engineering studies on sectionalization should be completed and firm bids should be secured from the manufacturers of the special cars before actions were taken that assumed the final profitability of this move. The traffic manager countered with the argument that the availablity of the cars when needed was sufficient reason for their purchase even if no larger sections could be carried and that they would pay for themselves even if the cars cost twice as much as she had estimated.

1. What decision would you make on the procurement of the special cars?

2. Is Mr. Lester correct in assuming that he will enjoy a nine-month price advantage over competitors?

3. Would you reserve the special cars for Bielaw Company use?

COURT DECISIONS ON PURCHASING ISSUES

The following cases from the courts of various states illustrate legal issues with which a purchasing agent should have some familiarity. Although the typical purchasing agent cannot have a lawyer's knowledge of the law, the agent should be aware of the legal implications of certain purchasing decisions.

1. A buyer entered into a contract with a seller for the purchase of scrap copper and agreed to secure the necessary government export licenses during the period preceding delivery. When the scrap was ready, the seller notified the buyer requesting shipping instructions and the necessary export licenses. But the buyer was unable to furnish the licenses then because of a federal government embargo on the scrap metal. The seller held the material at its plant and, when the period prescribed for delivery had elapsed, notified the buyer that it would not sell the material because of the buyer's failure to comply with the terms and conditions of the agreement.

The buyer sued the vendor for damages of $10,725 for breach of contract, claiming that the price of copper had gone up since the date they had entered into the contract. (*Bay State Smelting Co.* v. *Ferric Industries, Inc.*, 292 F 2d 96)

2. A seller sent a letter to a purchasing agent at his employer's address, offering to sell a hydraulic power cutter. The purchasing agent returned the letter to the seller with the notation. ''We wish to order the equipment as specified above.'' The purchasing agent signed his name below the notation.

The deal fell through, and the seller later sued the purchasing agent personally for the price of the cutter. The purchasing agent's defense was that he had signed as an agent for his company and was not personally liable. (*Sago* v. *Ashford,* 358 p2 599)

3. A buyer bought circuit breakers from a seller on COD terms. Before the breakers were unloaded at the buyer's plant, the buyer handed the seller's trucker a check in payment. While the unloading was in process, the trucker noticed that the check was not signed and returned it to the buyer. The buyer promised to get the check signed and delivered upon completion of the unloading. After the circuit breakers had been unloaded, the buyer

refused not only to sign the check, but also to return the circuit breakers. (*Gallagher* v. *Hockler,* 229 N.Y.S. 2d 623)

4. Randy Knitwear, a clothing manufacturer, purchased fabric from a textile manufacturer and finisher. This firm treated the fabric purchased by Randy with Cyana, a chemical resin made by American Cyanamid Company. Treatment with this trademarked resin was designed to prevent shrinkage, and textile manufacturers who used the product were authorized by American Cyanamid to sell them under the Cyana label and with the statement that they were Cyana finished.

After Randy Knitwear had made and sold garments with Cyana-treated fabric to customers, the company claimed that ordinary washing caused them to shrink and lose their shape. Randy Knitwear sued American Cyanamid for breach of warranty. Cyanamid maintained in court that the case should be dismissed because of lack of privity of contract between it and Randy. (*Randy Knitwear, Inc.* v. *American Cyanamid Co.,* New York Court of Appeals, 2-2262)

For each of these cases, analyze the facts, determine the point of law at issue, and make a decision.

DAVIS MILLS, INC.

Davis Mills, Inc. is one of the largest manufacturers of cotton fabrics and products made from cotton fabrics. The company has 16 plants scattered throughout the country. Headquarters are in Philadelphia, although the nearest plant is approximately 100 miles away. The company follows a policy of decentralized operations with a general manager at each plant responsible for the profit showing of that plant. The home-office staff departments formulate company policies that are to be followed by their counterpart departments at the various plants.

The director of purchases has found it desirable to hold an annual meeting with her several plant purchasing managers to discuss company policies and procedures. The major topic for consideration at the meeting held last year was purchasing reports. Up to that time there had been no requirement for the submission of reports by the various managers to the director of purchases or to their own general managers. Nor had there been any requirement for internal purchasing department reports at any of the works.

At the meeting all purchasing managers were asked to give their opinion on the value of a reporting system and what types of reports, if any, should be required on a company-wide basis. Those who had developed reporting systems were asked to describe them to the group.

The purchasing manager of the Chicago plant reported that he had developed a plan of reporting on the operations of his entire department to the general manager. He claimed several advantages for this type of reporting. In the first place, it provided an incentive for his assistants and employees to maintain a high level of performance, since they knew that their actions would be measured and reported upon annually. It had the virtue of requiring the purchasing manager to review the operations of his entire department in a thorough and quantitative manner, since this was the only way in which a useful and comprehensible report could be prepared. The process of preparing the report frequently brought to light procedures and methods that could be improved, and the purchasing manager felt that such matters were less likely to be observed in the ordinary course of business. Finally, he felt that the report served to call the contributions of the purchasing function to the attention of the general manager in an explicit way at least once each year. This, he believed, served to make the general manager more sympathetic to the needs of the purchasing department and gave the department a basis for requesting good treatment at budget time.

The purchasing manager of the St. Louis plant said that he had tried submitting an annual report to the general manager for a few years, but found that after the first year or two it received little attention. He attributed this to the fact that the report was essentially a series of statistical tables, which looked about the same from year to year unless they were studied more carefully than the general manager seemed willing to do. Consequently, he had come to the conclusion that the primary purpose of reporting was the internal discipline it required of departmental personnel. Therefore, he had shifted reporting to an intradepartmental basis. Each of the people reporting to the purchasing manager knew that his or her report would be completely reviewed and understood by the purchasing agent and, consequently, each person reported fully in order to make a good impression. The purchasing agent said that he then reported any unusual matters to the general manager informally when the occasion seemed right. The St. Louis purchasing manager argued that this method of reporting had the virtues of a departmental report without its stultifying effects.

The Denver purchasing manager argued in favor of formal, oral reports. He contended that written reports inevitably fell into a pattern of reporting on the routine affairs of the department that fit neatly into statistical form, whereas the significant things were usually those out-of-the-ordinary things that would not occur to a person in the process of preparing a written report. This purchasing manager therefore held monthly meetings of his employees at which they were asked to report informally on anything of consequence that had happened in their areas of work. In order to preserve the informal nature of the meeting, no minutes were kept or notes taken. However, after each meeting the purchasing manager made notes on the significant items. The general manager of the Denver plant, in turn, had quarterly meetings of the functional plant executives at which each executive was expected to report orally on the operations of his or her department. The purchasing manager reported to this meeting on the basis of the notes he had made on his own monthly meetings. He believed that this method of reporting brought to light the worthwhile things and saved his people the time and trouble of preparing written reports.

Some of the purchasing managers from the smaller plants argued against any form of reports. They thought that the important matters of purchasing performance were known to the general manager on the basis of daily contacts with the departments under his or her control. They argued that a purchasing department that could not justify itself without reports was not operating effectively and that their time could be spent more productively in improving performance than writing reports.

1. Evaluate the arguments in favor of each of the forms of reporting.
2. Design a reporting plan for Davis Mills, Inc. that would meet the needs of the company at the various levels of its purchasing operations.

EVANS CORPORATION

Evans Corporation is a relatively small company specializing in the design and manufacture of suspension seats for tractor and truck use. Traditionally the company has been engineering oriented, but a recent change in ownership resulted in an intensive analysis of all departments, attempting to integrate more efficiently the various functional areas.

The purchasing department, which spends approximately $60 million for purchased materials, supplies, and services annually, presently consists of the purchasing manager, Mr. Gray, nine buyers, and seven clerks. An analysis of the purchasing function revealed 25 percent of the total purchases to be steel, comprising over 200 separate items purchased from 10 different suppliers. Six steel suppliers represented direct mill purchasing, two were odd-lot, local steel warehouses, and two were national steel-warehousing firms. The majority of the suppliers had been supplying the Evans Corporation for many years.

When asked about the possibility of reducing the present number of suppliers, Mr. Gray admitted that the number could possibly be cut in half. However, he was quick to add one of his main justifications for not doing so was to have others to rely on should some suppliers fail to meet his requests during a period of high demand or supply shortage.

Historically, Evans Corporation had encountered quality problems with several of the smaller-volume steel items purchased. There had also been problems in delivery of several such items. Though Mr. Gray felt that Evans' suppliers were quite competitive on price, he thought that their quality and service standards left much to be desired. In the past no changes in suppliers had been made unless substantial cost savings could be proved.

1. Should Evans Corporation consolidate its steel purchases?
2. Should it develop a set of policy guidelines for use in selecting steel sources?
3. Should such a policy be applied to purchase of the other items needed by Evans?

EXPEDITING PROBLEMS

The subject of expediting was covered in the predinner professional development session of the Chicago Purchasing Managers' Association during its March meeting. Three members presented short case descriptions of recently expedited purchases with which they had been involved.

In introducing the subject, the panel moderator suggested that expediting of purchases could be accomplished by a wide variety of techniques. Among those listed were:

1. Purchase of delay-causing materials or components for supplier or, alternatively, furnishing such items from the buyer's own inventory.
2. Canceling contracts or threatening to do so.
3. Stationing of field expediters at supplier's plant.

Mr. Jones of the Medical Instruments Corporation reported that his expediting organization consisted of six expediters assigned individually to specific buyers to operate as a team. The expediters also are authorized to place routine repetitive orders and are required to perform special assignments. Mr. Jones reported as follows.

> The company entered into a procurement contract to purchase an electronic subsystem from a small, newly organized company. The subsystem was designed, developed, and sold to us for use. Samples were submitted and approved by engineering. Purchasing was made with a minimum of drawings in order not to delay delivery of the subsystem.

The first order for 1000 units was delivered at a reasonable rate, considering start-up by a new company. Quality problems were encountered but generally were resolved with a minimum of production interruption.

The second order was placed, also for accelerated delivery as experience with the first units did help sales of one of our investments. The shipment of units received against the second order was found to be 50 percent defective because of an electronic component. An examination of the units revealed substitute components had been inserted to save money. Many of these components were believed to be unacceptable for our product based on previous independent testing. Production was immediately halted.

The vendor flew in to resolve the problem. He said he could not obtain the components originally used for four weeks and besides, just starting up the line again once it was shut down would take four days. Our engineering division replied that to obtain data that might permit us to grant approval for the untested components would take 1000 hours (45 days) of environmental and reliability testing.

Management insisted on having the products for shipment before the end of the fiscal year but would not authorize use of substitute units. How would you proceed to get delivery of acceptable units in time to meet sales and profit objectives?

Mr. Roberts of the Steel Machinery Company reported that several months ago his company had been faced with the problem of locating quickly a new source for shell-molded steel castings. The company they were dealing with at that time had taken more government orders than it could handle, and the government had taken over almost its entire production by enforcing priority ratings. Even though most of the 3700 castings on order were considerably overdue, the company could not promise to produce any and further requested that the tooling be removed from its shop.

Mr. Robert's particular problem was that he needed castings in six weeks to meet production requirements of hand-strapping tools. Weekly usage of these castings was approximately 80. Mr. Roberts was not aware of any foundries within a reasonable distance that could produce similar castings.

Mr. Wier of the Electronic Testing Corporation reported that his expediting department consisted of seven people and that expediters were assigned according to products. They followed these basis expediting procedures:

1. Supplier order acknowledgment
2. Routine follow-up for delivery promise
3. Promise referral to shop
4. Acceptance or additional expediting

An order for an Electron Test Set (value $150,000) was placed in October, with a June delivery promise.

This was a new kind of testing machine that would reduce manufacturing cost significantly. Therefore, Mr. Wier's company was quite anxious to obtain early delivery.

In January the supplier said that it could not meet the June delivery date because of extended delivery from vendors on purchased components. The longest interval items were components from General Tool promised for September with a value of $340. A visit to General Tool showed that its production capacity was booked solid, with no overtime available. Electronic Testing's expediter was unable to improve the delivery date of the component even after discussions with General Tool's top management.

1. Can any of the moderator's suggested approaches to expediting be employed in these cases?
2. Are there any other approaches that might be tried to get delivery of required items on time?

FACTORY ENTERPRISES, INC.

Factory Enterprises, Inc., makes automobile air conditioners for car dealer installation. The firm owns the patents and makes the product at a sizable markup. As a result, the 20-year-old concern pays its private owners very well.

The enterprise shows growth in overseas sales at the very time that domestic market demand explodes. This exhausting situation calls for total effort by all company personnel: eight managers and supervisors, 30 factory workers, and six office employees.

Various people purchase materials and component parts, in addition to their regular duties. The production manager buys finned radiators and copper tubing. The shipping supervisor buys mounting assemblies, to which workers attach all of the component parts in the final process. The sales manager buys shipping cartons.

You have just joined the company as the purchasing manager.

1. Describe for the president the materials mangement concept. What would it do for the company and what would it do to the company?
2. What action steps would you follow to install the materials management concept if the president decides to adopt it?
3. Explain how sales and purchasing can help each other by establishing a good relationship.

4. European customers insist on ISO 9000 compliance. How should the company respond?

FERNER COMPANY

The Ferner Company produces electrical control equipment. Although a portion of its production is devoted to standard components, the bulk of its sales volume is derived from complex, custom-built installations. Annual sales were $60 million and had been rising at a 10 percent rate for the past five years.

The entire Ferner Company has for many years followed the policy of filling vacancies, whenever possible, by advancing personnel from within its organization. Shifts between functional areas are common.

When an opening for two expediters in the purchasing department developed in February, word spread quickly through the company. In addition, the employment manager was asked to secure applications from outside sources. He ran a classified advertisement in the local evening newspaper for a one-week period.

A number of applications were received, some of which were immediately discarded because there was no indication of the applicant's fitness for the position. After this screening, eight applicants were interviewed for the two expediter positions by the assistant director of purchases. He narrowed the list to four finalists.

1. Mr. Jones, employed as an expediter for two years by a company in the textile business. Mr. Jones was 22 years old and a high school graduate.

2. Ms. Spence, employed as a materials controller (storekeeper) by the Ferner Company, with four years of experience. One of her major responsibilities was the issuance of requisitions to the purchasing department for the purchase of materials when inventories dropped to predetermined order points. Prior to working for Ferner she had held employment as a retail clerk.

3. Mr. Wesley, a young man working for another company as a shipping clerk, with no experience in expediting or purchasing. He was in the process of completing a two-semester evening course in industrial purchasing at the local university.

4. Ms. Harvey, a sales correspondent in the Ferner Company service department who wanted to "get into purchasing." Ms. Harvey was a college graduate.

All these applicants were in the desired age bracket and all seemed alert and personable. After reviewing the application forms, studying the work records of each, and evaluating the personal interviews, the assistant director of purchases decided to promote Ms. Spence to one of the two positions. He was uncertain about the best prospect for the other vacancy.

In talking the matter over with his superior, the assistant director pointed out that he was being guided by four factors: (1) company policy on promotion from within; (2) character, knowledge of job procedures, and work habits; (3) the applicant's knowledge of company policy, products, and personnel; and (4) the prospect's potential for growth.

1. Do you agree with the promotion of Ms. Spence? Give reasons for and against.
2. Choose one of the three remaining applicants to fill the vacancy and present your reasons for selecting him/her and not the others.

GAMMA CORPORATION

Al Beta, purchasing vice president for the Gamma Corporation, was called into a top-management conference to hear about a new market being opened for the company's turbulators.

These were very high-priced items, manufactured to order, and it was anticipated that demand would be pretty much a one-shot affair. Sales office surveys indicated that the level of demand might range anywhere from 60 to 90 items.

Among the most important subassemblies for the turbulators were compressors. These were vendor-supplied on special order. Because of the job-lot nature of compressor production, reorder and setup cost were prohibitively high. Thus, Gamma would have to order all its compressors in one lot.

Since the demand might range from 60 to 90 turbulators, there was the danger of sales lost because of insufficient production if Gamma ordered only 60 compressors. But if more were ordered than were needed, unused compressors might have to be scrapped.

The sales office claimed that each lost sale represented $10,000 down the drain. Al estimated a loss of $5000 for each compressor scrapped. The question then was: How many compressors should be ordered?

So Al did some figuring. Since packaging, shipment, and other considerations made it necessary to order compressors in units 10, he reasoned that the question really was: Should 60, 70, 80, or 90 items be purchased? Now, if 60 compressors were bought and 60 turbulators manufactured, this

TABLE 1. Compressor Order Calculation

Number of Compressors Ordered	Actual Demand for Turbulators	Cost of Lost Sales ($1000)	Cost of Scrapping Compressors ($1000)	Overall Costs ($1000)
60	60	0	0	0
	70	100	0	100
	80	200	0	200
	90	300	0	300
70	60	0	50	50
	70	0	0	0
	80	100	0	100
	90	200	0	200
80	60	0	100	100
	70	0	50	50
	80	0	0	0
	90	100	0	100
90	60	0	150	150
	70	0	100	100
	80	0	50	50
	90	0	0	0

would turn out to be ideal—if sales amounted to 60 items. But if there was a demand for 70 items, a loss of $100,000 would be incurred. And if the market could actually absorb 90 units, the loss would be $300,000.

On the basis he constructed the chart shown in Table 1. Studying this chart, Al found the answer to his problem.

1. What was the solution, and how did Al find it?

THE GEER COMPANY

The Geer Company, a manufacturer of heavy-duty road-building equipment, was established in 1940 and grew slowly until 1972 when its sales volume was slightly in excess of $35 million. At that time the company went public and nonfamily management came into power. Aggressive management led to a tripling of volume by 1992.

During the period of slow growth the company's purchasing department consisted of a purchasing manager, who reported to the vice president, and three buyers. One buyer bought only steel. The other two buyers bought all other items. One expediting clerk, as well as the necessary clerks and typists to write purchase orders and check invoices, were also assigned to the department. Inventory control was not a part of purchasing but rather was reported to the production manager.

The Geer Company had operated a small foundry until 1976. When this facility was closed, the responsibility for buying ferrous castings was assigned to the production manager's office and was handled by a person who had been a supervisor in the foundry.

During the period of rapid expansion the company's manufacturing facilities were inadequate and it became necessary to subcontract a significant volume of machining operations. Two buyers who were responsible for subcontracts were assigned to the production manager. During the same period five new buyers and two expediters were added to the purchasing department.

The added work load in purchasing, the divided buying responsibilities, and the number of inexperienced buyers created many problems and brought complaints from the operating divisions of the company. Inexperienced employees in inventory control caused delays in placing orders. Late deliveries and incorrect ordering quantities frequently led to shortages and excesses in inventories, both of which were costly to the company.

Management finally decided to engage a consulting firm to aid in reorganizing the purchasing operation and to make recommendations about the responsibilities connected with the various buying functions.

1. As a consultant, how would you proceed to analyze this problem?
2. Prepare a recommended organization chart for the purchasing department.
3. Indicate how you would assign functions that, although not direct buying activities, are nonetheless closely related.

GOLDEN CITY

Early in 1995, the Golden City purchasing manager solicited bids for refractors. The specification provided that an aggregate award would be made to the low bidder. Bids were received from five firms interested in this contract. The bids were tabulated, along with the most recent price paid by Golden City, as shown in Table 1. The purchasing manager, in reviewing the bids, noted that there had been significant increases in items 1 and 4.

TABLE 1. Bids for Refractor Items

			Anderson Electric Corporation	Jones Supply Corporation	National Electric Company	Smith Electric Company	Stevens Supply Company	Previous Experience
(1) 200 each	Refractor, #4377E, complete with endural insides	each	9.18	9.19	9.33	12.30	9.19	8.07 (1994)
(2) 50 each	Refractor, #4334 CL, complete with endural insides	each	4.95	4.93	4.89	4.96	4.94	4.96 (1994)
(3) 100 each	Refractor, #4387 CL, *outside only*, for 4377 unit	each	4.09	4.07	4.04	4.39	4.08	3.97 (1994)
(4) 150 each	Refractor, #4189 VF, *outside only*, for 4179 unit	each	7.05	7.04	6.97	6.93	7.04	5.60 (1993)
(5) 25 each	Refractor, #4937, complete except *without* casting, for park unit	each	29.25	29.08	28.86	24.96	29.19	25.36 (1992)
(6) 25 each	Refractor, #4957 S.F., for #4937 Park Unit	each	1.93	1.93	1.91	1.84	1.91	2.04 (1992)
TOTAL NET AGGREGATE AMOUNT (after cash discount)			4286.20	4279.52	4285.96	4856.50	4283.23	
CASH DISCOUNT			1%	1%	1%	Net	1%	

She discussed this with all the bidders and was not completely satisfied with their explanation of the price changes.

The purchasing manager believed that it was in the city's best interest to request new bids on these two items and to make individual awards to each low bidder on the other items. All bidders were agreeable to this approach.

1. Should the purchasing manager carry out her plans?
2. Would your response be the same if this were an industrial buyer rather than a city buyer?

GORMAN PRODUCTS, INC.

The Gorman Products company was created by the merger of Gorman Cookware, a small Midwestern manufacturer of kitchen utensils, and the Electronics Products Company of Houston, Texas. The latter had annual sales of approximately $40 million, most of which consisted of subcontracts of missile components, for the company held the prime contract from the Defense Department. Gorman cookware sales were $20 million.

The executive board of the merged company had directed that unified corporate policies and procedures be established to the maximum extent possible. Mr. Ritchey, corporate purchasing manager, was uncertain how to proceed in establishing policies dealing with controlling the quantity of purchased materials and supplies. His problem can be illustrated by describing a major purchase of each of the two original companies.

One of Gorman's principal purchases is the chemical Teflon, used in coating its pots and pans. Fluctuations in Teflon usage had been as high as 70 percent from one period to the next, and future usage was predicted to increase greatly, thus accentuating the problem of purchasing the correct quantity. A further problem was presented by the fluctuating price of Teflon. In the past, Gorman had followed a policy of holding a 90-day supply of such items as a hedge against large price fluctuations. The generally accepted reordering period for all inputs was set at two weeks.

The purchasing department was in charge of inventory control. Storage space was a problem, and even though no critical shortages had resulted in the past, any sudden changes in the production rate could lead to such a problem. No physical inventory was taken, but the purchasing department felt that this was unnecessary as long as accurate records were kept.

Two of the most important purchases of Electronic Products were printed circuits, costing approximately 2 cents each, and transistors, some of which cost as much as $500 each. Approximately 80 transistors were needed monthly, and printed circuits were used at the rate of 600 per month.

Management policy had been to reorder these items every two months. The delivery cycle on both items had ranged from two to five weeks over the past four years. Quantities of printed circuits and transistors ordered were based on carrying one week's supply as a safety factor.

Mr. Ritchey was informed by the corporate controller that an inventory carrying charge of 24 percent was being assessed by management and that the average ordering cost was $6.

1. Should there be uniform policies relating to purchasing quantities?
2. What should be done about the difference in the reordering periods of two weeks and two months?
3. Should EOQ formulas be applied to printed circuits and transistor purchases?

HEARONS COMPANY

Angela Walker, purchasing manager for the Hearons Company, has engaged the services of a business consulting firm to advise her on a problem she suspects exists. She believes that she is paying a higher price than necessary for a major raw material because of the way in which she buys it. Her suspicions have developed because there have been no significant price variations over a period of several years for the commodity and because the several suppliers quote prices that are remarkably close.

The Hearons Company is a large paper manufacturing and converting firm with annual sales of $200 million. A major item of raw material bought in quantity by the firm is fiberglass yarn for use by one of its converting departments as a reinforcing medium in laminated combinations. The yarn is buried in the laminate between the two sheets of paper.

The company manufactures a number of grades of laminated combinations, some of which do not use any reinforcement, but all of which are processed on the same machinery. The company has six processing machines, and the yarn may be used on all, none, or combinations of them. There are periods when no fiberglass yarn is required and periods when it is consumed in large quantities. This causes swings in consumption of fiberglass yarn, depending on the product mix and machine schedules.

There is an additional complication in maintaining an adequate, but not excessive, inventory of fiberglass yarn. It is used in two different types that must be ordered and stored separately. In addition, the company can buy both types from only one of its three principal suppliers. Thus, the planning and scheduling of shipments of the two types from the three suppliers present some problems.

To address these problems, the company estimates at the beginning of each year the total amount of yarn of each type that will be required. The amount that will be purchased from each of the three suppliers is then determined. A blanket order is placed with each supplier in multiples of 30,000 lb, the quantity required for a single truckload.

As the year progresses, frequent inventories are taken to keep track of usage, and releases are issued in truckload quantities with as much advance notice as possible to the supplier. By keeping accurate usage records the company can spot trends in the usage and modify the original quantities covered by the blanket orders if necessary.

1. How can the consultant determine whether price competition exists for this commodity?
2. Is the method of purchasing a form of forward buying, since it does not involve protection against price fluctuations?
3. What steps can be taken to develop greater differences in the prices of the three suppliers?

HOUSEHOLD CLEANERS CORPORATION

Folding cartons for the soap pads and scouring cloths that Household Cleaners Corporation produces are manufactured in production runs of about 5 million units, valued at $50,000 to $120,000 per run. This is very attractive business for the carton industry, which is highly competitive. The volume of business available in these two types of cartons has increased over the last four years from $500,000 to about $2 million per year. Cartons represent 20 percent of product cost.

Rinkle Company has been the principal supplier. A careful check of the market indicated that the industry was protecting the Rinkle price list by submitting prices no lower than its schedule. In view of this situation, Cartoncorp was picked as a second source for soap pad cartons and Singer as a second source for scouring cloth cartons, both at the price levels established by Rinkle.

In the last few months a more aggressive interest has been shown by other sources of supply. Active Carton, through its sales vice president, requested that it be allowed to quote on a specific requirement for soap pad cartons, and North Industries made a similar request to quote on scouring cloths cartons through its president, Charles North.

Each of these companies quoted prices that were competitive with the prices paid Rinkle. They were told that they were competitive, but that this was not good enough to generate any business. Subsequently, they each indicated that they would quote a lower price if they were told what price was necessary. Such a situation, of course, would put Household Cleaners Corporation in the position of pricing their product. It puts Household in the position of protecting the Rinkle quote down to the price at which it would bring others in as an alternative source. Cartoncorp and Singer indicated a desire to have a share of the business at a lower price level, but each was unwilling to be labeled as a price cutter.

The major attaction was not merely the $5000 or $10,000 savings on specific orders, but the price competition it would provide over time to the carton program for the two kitchen cleaner products. Household would not have to use the lower prices as leverage to lower Rinkle's prices, but it would be available if Rinkle attempted to increase prices. The folding carton industry is competitive on prices, but all manufacturers think they are operating with depressed prices so that they are constantly alert to the opportunity to raise their prices. Price increases are usually effected by announcing in the trade journals that prices have been increased by 3 percent to 5 percent and then presenting the increase as though it were a fact. It is reasonable to assume that Singer and Cartoncorp would welcome any leadership taken by Rinkle in this regard. The lower-priced second suppliers could very well contribute to the avoidance of a $100,000-a-year cost increase.

Should Household Cleaner, however, set the price when it believes that its action would be publicized throughout the industry? If Household really wants these companies as alternate sources, which of the following should they be told?

1. Household Cleaners will not give them any further price information.
2. Household Cleaners does not intend to price their product for them.
3. They have enough information to quote a price that would interest Household Cleaners.
4. Any price they established must be based on how the business fits into their (suppliers') plant operations.
5. Any price they qoute will be held in confidence.

HOWELL CHUCK COMPANY (A)

The Howell Chuck Company is a manufacturer of chucks and similar accessories for original machine-tool equipment and replacement purposes. Approximately 500 employees work for the company. The purchasing department consists of the purchasing manager, who also functions as a treasurer, two buyers, and two clerical employees. Inventory records for raw materials and stores items are maintained in the purchasing department.

The purchasing manager and the two buyers make all final decisions about sources of supply, although heads of operating departments are permitted to recommend suppliers and the buyers often follow their recommendations. All salespersons are interviewed in the purchasing department. When the situation seems to warrant it, the buyers arrange for the head of a department to interview a salesperson.

Over the years the Howell Chuck Company has developed and followed a policy of loyalty to established suppliers. The experience of the company during periods of short supply convinced the purchasing agent of the wisdom of this policy. On many occasions the buyer was able to secure deliveries of items that competing firms had difficulty in securing because they had patronized many suppliers. The purchasing manager felt so strongly on this point that the buyers were instructed not to shift from an established supplier unless a price differential of more than 10 percent existed. If products were defective or unsatisfactory, the agent would notify a supplier that it was "on probation." If no additional problem shipments were received during the next six-month period, the supplier was retained. If a second unsatisfactory shipment was received, the supplier was called in for an interview before a drop decision was made.

During May a requisition was received from the head of the heat treatment department for a new welding outfit. The requisition recommended the make and model, which was priced at $36,000. The proposed supplier was a recognized firm in the field, although the company had not previously bought from it. The company bought similar equipment from Ace Welding Company, a local firm with whom it had dealt for more than 20 years. The proposed supplier did not sell the gas used by the welding equipment, but such gas was available from five local suppliers, including the Ace Welding Company.

The buyer who was processing the requisition called in the head of the heat treatment department and asked why the new supplier was recommended. The head said that inspection of the new equipment and discussions with the salesperson had convinced him that the equipment was clearly superior to that sold by Ace Welding Company. The new equipment sold for $3000 less than the equipment available from the old supplier. During the discussion it developed that the new salesperson had gone to the heat treatment department head without the consent of the purchasing department.

The purchasing manager had never made visits to supplier plants but had recently decided to change this policy. After discussions with his buyers, the purchasing manager had prepared a policy statement to govern plant visitations. Pertinent excerpts are quoted.

1. Visits shall only be made to suppliers who receive orders totaling more than $200,000 annually.
2. Usually each supplier shall be visited annually.
3. Supplier visits shall be made by purchasing department personnel only.
4. Potential suppliers shall only be visited if the proposed volume of purchases exceeds $200,000 annually.
5. Initial contact for a plant visit shall be made through the supplier's sales representative.
6. No undue entertainment or favors shall be accepted by purchasing personnel during a plant visit.

1. What should the buyer do about the requisition for the welding equipment.
2. Should steps be taken to prevent direct contact of salespersons and operating personnel within the company?
3. Is the Howell Chuck Company policy with respect to supplier loyalty sound?
4. Evaluate the proposed policies dealing with plant visitations.

HOWELL CHUCK COMPANY (B)

All purchases of major equipment made by the Howell Chuck Company were decided on by the executive committee of the company at the time that the annual capital budget was prepared. Members of this committee consisted of the president, executive vice president, secretary–treasurer, production manager, sales manager, and purchasing manager.

Requests for purchase of new equipment to meet new production requirements or to replace old equipment could be originated by the production manager, chief maintenance engineer, or the engineering and design section. It was expected that whoever initiated such a request would provide the executive committee with adequate information on which to act. A memorandum received by the executive committee prior to its capital budget session contained the following information.

When the executive committee met, each member was given a copy of the memorandum and after a brief discussion the decision was tabled and

---

November 19, 19___
To: Executive Committee
Subject: New Lathe

1. Recommend the purchase of a new 16-inch automatic lathe.

2. One of our lathes, purchased secondhand in 1986, breaks down frequently and is giving the production scheduling department considerable difficulty. I have checked this lathe over and believe that it will require a complete overhaul. My estimate of the costs of such an overhaul is $87,000 in direct labor and parts. Such an overhaul will prolong the life of this lathe by six years.

3. In checking through the catalogs of the various lathe manufacturers, I have come to the conclusion that we can buy a new 16-inch automatic lathe for $320,000.

4. The new machine will have a 15-year life before it would require a complete overhaul. It would provide us with an increased production potential of 25 percent for this one piece of equipment. I estimate that with the improvements this lathe contains we can save $37,000 in direct labor costs based on the same number of units of output, which is all that we require at this time. I believe that normal maintenance on this new lathe will be approximately $8000 less per year than on the present lathe.

5. The new lathe will require an additional $11,000 of special tooling and spare parts since it differs from any of our present lathes.

s/Fred Jones
Chief Maintenance Engineer

---

the memorandum sent back to Fred Jones with the request for additional information.

1. What additional information should Mr. Jones have furnished to the executive committee?

2. Is the procedure for major equipment purchases by the Howell Chuck Company sound? Can you suggest improvements?

INDUSTRY-WIDE PRICING

You are a purchaser of 3003-H12, 20-gauge aluminum coil. For six years you have bought from three firms, A, B, and C, paying "book" or industry quoted prices.

A potential new vendor, D, quotes you a price that is 15 percent below the quoted or published price for this commodity. Upon investigation you determine that the firms are equal in every respect, in quality, delivery, and service abilities and reputation.

In other words, the only difference in the potential new vendor is the 15 percent reduction in price, which represents a potential savings of $2500 annually.

In making the decision whether to add vendor D to your roster of suppliers, consider the following questions.

1. What are your obligations (if any) to firms A, B, and C?
2. What are your obligations (if any) to vendor D?
3. How likely is it that vendor D *knew* you were paying book price?
4. What is the easiest course for you to take?
5. What legal implications apply to this case?

ITALIANA, INC.

U.S. Industries of Chicago produces heavy equipment and is interested in obtaining a digital cutting press from a supplier in Italy, Italiana, Inc., at a delivered price of $21,500. Italiana is a well-established firm with a good international credit record and performance track.

U.S. Industries has never purchased internationally before. The buyer, Ted Sullivan, is concerned about the terms of the sale. Using a freight forwarder in New York, Sullivan receives the following data:

1. $21,500 CIF port of entry (New York).
2. Gross weight 3629 kilos.
3. Containerization $200.
4. Inland/freight handling $798.
5. Forwarding and documentation $90.
6. Ocean freight $2633.
7. Commercial risk insurance $105.
8. Marine insurance $167.15 (calculated at the rate of 1.1 times the total of items 1 through 7, $27,858.60, at 60 cents per $100).

Investigation revealed that Italiana included in the delivery price a 20 percent markup for sales expenses, along with a 10 percent markup for research and development and 10 percent for advertising.

1. What expenses should Sullivan attempt to negotiate out of the delivered price?
2. What is the CIF port-of-entry price according to Sullivan?

THE JANMAR CORPORATION

The Janmar Corporation was created in 1987 through the merger of Janson Company and the Mary W. Foods Corporation. Janson operated two large flour-milling plants, one in St. Paul and the other in Buffalo. In addition the company had 11 feed-mixing plants scattered throughout the Midwest and Plains states. Mary W. Foods produced various consumer food products in 12 plants and operated a frozen foods plant and a plant producing pet foods as well. These 14 plants were scattered throughout the United States. Janson, with sales of approximately $200 million, was headquartered in St. Paul, and Mary W. Foods, with approximately the same sales volume, was headquartered in Kansas City.

Prior to the merger, each plant of the Janson Company had responsibility for purchasing all required materials and supplies. Major equipment and a few common-use items were purchased centrally by a purchasing manager at the St. Paul headquarters.

Mary W. Foods operated with a centralized corporate purchasing department. The only buying permitted at the 14 plants was for orders of less than $2000. The company believed that such orders were important in developing local public relations in the plant communities. Responsibility for such purchases was assigned either to the plant office manager or to the plant production manager. All local purchases were made on bank-draft purchase orders. The individuals placing such orders were under instructions to attempt to secure an extra discount by reason of payment through the bank draft when the order was received by the vendor.

At the time of merger it was decided that the corporate headquarters would be located in St. Paul. It was planned that over a period of 18 months the Kansas City headquarters would be closed and a consolidation of staffs would take place. In some instances the Janson Company individual in charge of a department or staff function was named to the corresponding position in the new corporate organization, and in other instances this individual came from Mary W. Foods. This person's counterpart was frequently made an assistant.

The director of corporate purchasing had been the chief purchasing manager of the Mary W. Foods Corporation. The senior purchasing manager, who came from the Janson Company, was given the title of assistant director of corporate purchasing. Purchasing activities were to be moved to

St. Paul on July 1. The director believed that in the process of combining a centralized operation with a decentralized one, conflicts would arise, and also that it would be easier to gain cooperation from the purchasing personnel in both of the former firms if an outside specialist was hired to draft a purchasing department organization chart and policies manual.

Mr. Victor, who was engaged in this capacity, met with the director of corporate purchasing and the immediate superior. At this meeting, Mr. Victor discovered that traffic and transportation matters were to be assigned to a transportation manager who would have complete responsiblity for the purchasing of tractors, trailers, and all transportation equipment in addition to matters usually assigned to a traffic manager. He was also informed that grain buying for the milling operations would be under the direct control of the vice president for manufacturing. It also developed that various departments and divisions within the company would continue to make such purchases as advertising and promotional materials, service contracts, and printed forms.

In the discussions it developed that there was some doubt whether the senior Janson purchasing manager was capable of assuming the position of assistant director. It had, however, been decided that this agent would have responsibility for the buying of biological and pharmaceutical chemicals, important additives in the feed-manufacturing process. Mr. Victor also found that central receiving for the St. Paul milling complex had been a responsibility of this individual in the past.

The Janmar executive board had decided that the Buffalo milling plant was such a large operation that purchasing for the plant should remain decentralized except for basic grains. The board also decided that for the present it would continue the bank-draft purchasing system for each one of the Mary W. Foods plants and epxand it to the Janson plants.

On May 1, Mr. Victor submitted a proposed organization chart for the purchasing department along with a number of recommendations, some of which are summarized.

1. The company is too large for the position of assistant director to be eliminated. If there is doubt about the ability of the biological and pharmaceutical chemicals buyer, that individual should be assigned as acting assistant director and retain the chemical-buying responsibilities.

2. The amount of purchasing being done locally under the bank-draft system suggests that serious consideration should be given to consolidating such buying at the corporate level for all but emergency needs. Blanket purchase agreements and national contracts against which the individual plants can requisition direct from the vendor should be entered into as rapidly as possible.

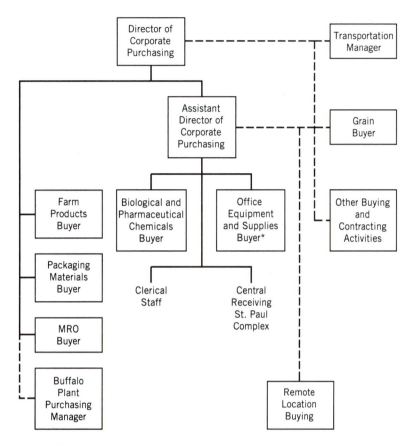

* The Office Equipment and Supplies Buyer handles also local small-order
  purchasing and materials release orders for St. Paul organization.

3. The director of corporate purchasing should have a greater degree of contact with and control over the buying activities not now assigned to purchasing.

1. Evaluate the proposed organization, shown in the illustration.
2. Will the reduction or elimination of local purchases at local plants affect community public relations? Should Mr. Victor's suggestions on local buying be adopted?
3. Is the policy of seeking an extra discount on purchases made by bank-draft purchase order sound? Should a similar procedure be adopted for larger corporation purchases?

JOHN ROBERTS MANUFACTURING COMPANY

The John Roberts Manufacturing Company is an air-conditioning equipment manufacturer in Houston, Texas, employing 800 people. It manufactures both window-type and large industrial air conditioners. It also has a line of automobile air conditioners.

The purchasing department is headed by Alice Harrison, the director of purchases. Reporting to Harrison are four purchasing managers and one full-time expediter. The purchasing director has a secretary who handles her filing, takes dictation, and types her correspondence. There are two typists who type approximately 2000 purchase orders and change orders each month. Approximately 65 percent of the items purchased are repetitive in nature; the balance are nonrepetitive and generally require considerable buyer attention. Practically all the maintenance, repair, and operating supplies (MRO) are purchased from local vendors.

The MRO stores and the receiving and shipping functions report to the director of purchasing. The company operates its own printing shop, which includes the stationery and office supply inventories. The supervisor of the printing and stationery department also reports to the director of purchasing. Responsibility for maintaining adequate inventories of stationery and office supplies as well as MRO supplies rests with the director of purchases.

An internal audit team has spotlighted the following problems, and management has asked the director of purchases to present a plan for correcting them.

1. A considerable number of items are delivered to the receiving department by local vendors before the receiving copy of the purchase order has reached the receiving department. This happens because deliveries are made within four to six hours on telephoned orders, whereas the typed copy of the purchase order is not received until the next day. This causes confusion, wasted effort, and delays in delivery to the requisitioner, who may have an urgent need for the specific item.

2. The typists are unable to handle the peak loads of purchase order typing. The adoption of traveling requisitions has reduced requisition writing but not the number of purchase orders. The use of blanket orders on large-usage items provided some relief for the typists when adopted one year ago. In order to avoid serious delays in the typing and mailing of purchase orders, considerable overtime expense is incurred.

3. Although the expediter appears to be competent, many items are received late, some of which cause serious production delays or hold up construction of needed facilities. Deliveries of capital equipment have been as much as four to five weeks late in some instances. This has seriously delayed the start-up of some production lines. Upon investigation by the

buyer, it was found that the vendor had not ben expediting all items from its own suppliers and subcontractors because it had been the vendor's practice to expedite only what is considered critical items based on past experience or pressure from its customers.

4. The company's value analysis program has bogged down because the buyers say that they are so busy placing orders and expediting that they do not have time for analyzing costs and devising ways to accomplish the desired functions at a lower cost while preserving or improving quality and reliability.

5. The auditors found several instances of vendor's products that did not meet specifications of physical qualities, and in some cases there were dimensional deviations. Although the suppliers replaced the material, they did not compensate the Roberts Company for labor expended up to the point of rejection, or for the loss of production time.

The vice president, to whom the director reports, has suggested that it might be possible to utilize the recently installed computer to overcome some of these problems. The controller supported the vice president's suggestion because of the accounting department's successful use of EDP.

1. What recommendations can you make to correct the problems facing the Roberts Company purchasing department?

JONES PRICE ANALYSIS

In reviewing new competitive quotes for an inlet fitting, Diana Jones noted the following:

Company A	$16.25
Company B	$18.70
Company C	$16.40
Company D	$16.35

Company B was the long-term supplier, was located nearby, and produced other items for Jones.

Because of the disparity in B's quotes, Jones requested a cost breakdown and was presented with the following cost–price breakdown:

Direct labor	$ 4.00
Direct material	5.00
Overhead (200% of direct labor)	8.00
Profit (10%)	1.70
	$18.70

Using B's figures, develop a potential negotiation strategy that Jones could use. Determine the following facts.

1. What is the very lowest price Company B should consider?
2. What are the relevant considerations Jones should address regarding the overhead and project calculations?
3. Should rebidding be allowed in this case?

KING COUNTY

Bids for ten 85-pound concrete-breaker pneumatic tools were requested by King County for delivery to the County Highway Department Service Center. Bids were to be opened at 2 P.M. in the county purchasing department.

The representative of the Speedy Contractors Supply Company arrived with their bid, which was time-stamped 2:01 P.M. He was infuriated about the parking conditions in the vicinity of the courthouse and told the purchasing manager so. He had been riding around for more than 15 minutes, trying to find a place to park. He also questioned the accuracy of the time stamp, for his watch showed that it was 1:59 when he submitted the bid. With this plausible explanation, the purchasing agent waived the one minute and accepted the bid for consideration.

When the bids were read, it was noted that the bid of the Speedy Contractors Supply Company was not signed. The representative said that he had intended to do this before submitting it; however, in the excitement caused by his difficulty he had neglected to do so. The purchasing manager felt that this was related to his trouble in not getting the bid in on time and allowed him to sign the bid.

When the bids were opened and read, that of Speedy Contractors was low. Later in the afternoon, the next lowest bidder protested to the purchasing manager about the acceptance of this bid and its late signature.

1. Should the Speedy Contractors bid have been accepted and entered into the competition by the purchasing manager?
2. Should Speedy Contractors receive the award?

LANDIS EVALUATION

Judy Landis, a recent purchasing major graduate from New Jersey, accepted employment as a metals buyer for Modine Mfg. Her responsibilities involve purchasing all metals and ferrous components (castings, extrusions, etc.) for eight manufacturing locations, accounting for approximately 250 items with an annual dollar volume of $25 million.

In the past, engineering dominated most purchasing source decisions, with the result that most suppliers were of long duration, and minimal sourcing changes. By relatively simple requests for bids, Landis opened potential business opportunities for alternative suppliers, with the result that substantial cost–price reductions were achieved with comparable quality, service and delivery, over a nine-month period.

Modine had no evaluation plan or system for purchasing, as such. Buyer annual reviews were mostly subjective, based on the overall impression of the buyer's efforts, coupled with a typical audit by the accounting staff relative to the overall departments adherence to corporate policy (e.g., at least two suppliers for each major component, minimal quality defects, inventory turnover ratios of a least 2:1, receipts correlated with amounts ordered, and "reasonable" lead time requirements). In addition, management held random annual inquiries with suppliers to determine their overall impression of their buyer counterparts.

Ms. Landis started her own running tally of her efforts which consisted of the following:

1. She performed a time/motion study of a typical days efforts to determine the amount of time spent on the following: follow-up of shipping dates for existing orders, interviews with salespersons of existing suppliers, interviews with potential suppliers, time spent with engineering issues, time spent checking on clerical type records such as verifying invoices relative to dollar accuracy and quantity compliance, time spent on administrative matters within the purchasing department, and nonproductive "idle" time.

She started a tally of all savings which were attributable to her individual efforts in the following format:

FIGURE 1. Savings Tally Sheet

Item	Previous Price	Present Price	Explanation of Change	Annual Usage	Estimated Annual Savings

Among the "explanation of change" were the following: renegotiation of prices with existing vendors, substitution of new suppliers with lower prices for comparable items, substitution of standard components for previous specially made items (all with proper interdepartmental approval), reduction of required inventory levels because of make–hold agreements.

The total dollar savings for the nine-month period now totals $800,000.

Consider the following:

1. Is it likely that substantial savings are available in such an engineering-oriented firm? Why?
2. What are the advantages/disadvantages of the "time/motion" procedure?
3. Why is a purchasing audit likely to be of value?
4. What are the limitations of the purchasing audit?
5. Is the running tally of savings as presented justified? What criteria could be added/deleted?
6. Assuming Modine had a profit margin of 5 percent, how would you present these efforts to the supervisor involved? What would be the equivalent amount of sales that would be necessary to equal Landis' efforts?
7. What are the morale ramifications if an organization does not specifically evaluate purchasing personnel performance?

McKEOUGH'S LEARNING CURVE

As a buyer of a specialty thermostat, you have selected the McKeough Company to produce your first order for 1000 pieces on the basis of the following competitive quotations:

McKeough	$8.10 each
Jones	9.25
Frost	9.20

The quality, delivery and service provided by McKeough were excellent for this initial order.

You now have a requisition to purchase 3000 more of the same thermostat. Your cost–price investigation of McKeough's price has produced the following information for the unit cost of the initial 1000 pieces.

Material	$ 1.90
Labor	0.25 hour at wage of $10.80 per hour
Overhead	100 percent of direct labor
Profit	11 percent of total cost

1. Determine the specific cost ingredients for McKeough's initial price.

2. Applying an 80 percent learning curve, what should the per-unit price be for the second order—assuming material costs remain constant?

3. What qualifications should you include in any learning curve application?

McKEOUGH'S NEGOTIATION CASE

The director of purchasing, Mr. Z, recently employed, was analyzing his new firm's purchasing procedures. He concluded that substantial savings could be realized by combining common items used by the 17 manufacturing locations.

Accordingly, he combined quantities for the common items and proceeded to obtain quotations, nationwide. One of the items was a small custommade brass connection, previously purchased from a medium-sized vendor located within 50 miles of the central corporate headquarters.

After a thorough nationwide search, the following relevant quotations were compared:

Previous Vendor F requoting on blanket quotation (5 million units annually)	$65.00/M
Vendor C	83.00/M
Vendor B	84.50/M
Vendor D	79.50/M

Mr. Z's natural reaction would have been to accept Vendor F's quotation. However, he decided to try a bit of psychology.

When Mr. McKeough, president of F Company called to ask how his price looked, he was given this response: "Well, it looks as if the competitive situation has really tightened; it looks like you will have to do better than this quote if you want the business." The following day, Mr. McKeough returned in person and offered a per-M quotation of $61.95. Mr. Z was surprised at the rapid response. He concluded that if a reduction could be offered so fast, perhaps additional leverage remained, so he informed Mr. McKeough, "Thanks Pat, that certainly looks better, but I am amazed at the extent of competitive pressures in this industry. Is it possible for you to requote?"

One week later Mr. McKeough again called on Mr. Z with a third quotation offering the part for $59.75 per M. Over lunch he asked Mr. Z whether F Company could now plan on receiving the blanket agreement. Mr. Z responded by saying, "You know Pat, our companies have had a long period of successful business relations, and I hope that our next year, when this item is again open for bids, you will be competitive." Mr. McKeough was startled. He asked, "Well, what do we have to do to get the business this year?" Mr. Z. responded, "Well, you wil have to quote below $56.00." Ten days later, Mr. McKeough again called on Mr. Z and presented a quote of $55.90. Mr. Z acknowledged the quote, and in response to Mr. McKeough's request for a reaction, indicated, "Well, Pat, this is a much better price, but the extent of competition on this part is very keen. However, price is not the only consideration, and I have decided to go along with you this year on the blanket agreement for $55.90."

Mr. McKeough beamed, indicated his keen appreciation, and expressed his desire to live up to the faith placed in his supplying organization. Subsequently, the blanket agreement was executed and parts were supplied throughout the year to the individual plant locations. Annual savings amounted to $45,500.

What about the ethics of Mr. Z's actions? Consider the following:

1. Is it ethical to mislead on a quotation?
2. Should buyers play hunches in negotiation?
3. Is it possible Mr. McKeough still enjoyed profits on this part?
4. Is it possible Mr. McKeough did not know his real cost of producing, or was he pricing on the basis of variable cost rather than total cost?

MEGALOPOLIS CITY

Claire F. Johnson, purchasing manager for the city of Megalopolis, recently presented a talk at a national meeting of government buyers on the subject of purchasing research. Excerpts of her talk are presented below.

We use value engineering in connection with our purchasing. This is an approach in which we analyze the component parts that enter into the makeup of an item in relation to its component costs in an attempt to learn its lowest cost denominator. We look at costs of labor, materials, amortization, overhead, and profit.

A recent example was our installation of street lighting. The value engineering study showed that it would be advantageous to buy the materials and contract for the labor. Our engineers estimated labor costs at $31 per unit. We were contracting for 50,000 units. Six bidders responded to our request for bids with quotations ranging from $59 to $63 per unit. This was $1.15 million more than our engineering analysis indicated. We rejected all bids and again advertised for bids. The new bids were approximately $500,000 lower. We decided to do the work ourselves. . . .

We introduced the concept of life-cycle costing on equipment purchases. Life-cycle costing is the determination of what an item would cost to perform its designated function through its total normal life. This covers the original cost of the equipment plus the total cost of maintenance of the equipment during its lifetime. We recently purchased garbage trucks on this basis. Suppliers requested to quote original cost of the trucks plus the total cost of maintenance for six years. Equipment cost would be paid immediately, plus maintenance on a monthly basis for six years. The low bidder did not have the lowest truck cost of the eight bidders who responded. . . .

We now apply value analysis cost engineering to the disposal of so-called junk. Formerly we sold used fire department hose to waste paper and bag dealers for less than $4 per ton. Our analysts applied value analysis techniques and we now receive more than $300 per ton for the hose, which is sold for end-use purposes such as boat bumpers, making drop pads for beer kegs, and to irrigation farms, which are not too concerned with a few leaks in the hose.

One additional illustration of purchasing research in the salvage field is the fact that we buy guinea pigs for $1.50 alive and sell them for $2.00 dead. We buy these animals for tuberculi research at the city sanitarium. Formerly, when the animal died it had to be incinerated and destroyed according to city health laws. Value analysts found a market at one of our local teaching hospitals, which buys the animals for purposes of student medical research. The only problem is that we have to freeze the animals as soon as they die. For an investment of $200 for a deep freeze we are able to secure a significant return on what was formerly of no economic value.

1. Do you consider each of these illustrations to be purchasing research?
2. Can value analysis have applicability to the purchases of a government agency, which must advertise for bids publicly and then accept the lowest responsible bid?
3. Should life-cycle costing be used by industrial purchasers?

MF-1

The steel buyer for the McKinegle Company, Herman Martinez, constantly educated himself in the technical aspects of the steel industry.

One of his major steel purchases was a commodity called aluminized steel, used to produce heat exchangers for industrial space heaters. Aluminized steel is simply regular cold-rolled steel with a protective coating applied to withstand high heat. The heat exchanger is a type of burner that receives and in effect captures the burning flame and acts as a means of storing the heat. Fans then blow the heat out of the exchanger into open areas.

The aluminized steel was purchased in 18-gauge (.0478) thickness, in sheets measuring 48 by 120 inches. These sheets were then stamped into the forms to produce the exchangers.

In a trade magazine, Mr. Martinez read that several major steel mills had developed a new type of steel to be sold to the automotive muffler industry to produce mufflers. The steel, called MF-1, was designed to withstand high heat. On closer review, Mr. Martinez determined that the chemical and physical properties of MF-1 were exactly the same as those of the product he was buying as aluminized steel, but at prices 40 percent below its price.

Mr. Martinez concluded that the steel companies were trying to compete with other commodities (such as ceramics, and nonferrous metals) for the muffler market, and in effect were establishing an entirely new commodity price. By calling it MF-1 the steel companies apparently were trying to keep this product separate and withhold it from competing with the established market for aluminized steel.

Mr. Martinez discussed the matter with his engineering and specification personnel, and with their concurrence placed an experimental order for MF-1. To his surprise the mill responded that this product was not available and was only to be sold to muffler producers. Two other steel mills responded to Mr. Martinez with the same reply.

If you were Mr. Martinez, what would you do in this situation? Potential savings if the MF-1 could be used were $500,000 per year.

In your analysis consider the following points.

1. Is it ethical for producers to label the same products with different names and charge different prices to different types of users?
2. Why do producers attempt commodity pricing?
3. What degree of technical knowledge must buyers possess and how do they obtain this knowledge?
4. How can buyers such as Mr. Martinez break the attempted stranglehold of commodity product pricing?
5. How would a value analysis program have helped in this example?

NELSON AUTO PARTS CORPORATION

The Nelson Auto Parts Corporation is one of the largest suppliers of automotive parts to original equipment manufacturers. Several years ago, the product engineering department with the company developed an automobile hubcap that would not rattle. The key feature of the new product was a shaped spring steel clip. Specifications for the clip were drawn up, and the Nelson Corporation's purchasing manager found two nearby suppliers willing to produce the clips. Samples were procured and tested and orders were placed.

After approximately 90 days both suppliers requested an increase in the contract price of 50 cents per 1000 units. Since the average daily use of the clips was 150,000 units, the increased cost per year would be between $30,000 and $40,000. Both suppliers argued that the increase was necessary because of the rigid standards the Nelson Corporation had imposed in the specifications for the part.

The purchasing manager for the Nelson Corporation also found that his inspection department was rejecting incoming shipments of the part at an unusually high rate. By talking to the head of the inspection department, he learned that the rejections were primarily because of the hardness test. Specifications allowed only a three-point spread in hardness. The inspection department superintendent said he could prove that a six-point spread would be satisfactory. He pointed out that, if the specifications were changed to allow the six-point spread, the rejection rate would drop to almost zero. In addition, the superintendent stated that the tests employed were far more extreme than the abuse that a typical consumer would give the product during the life of an automobile.

The purchasing manager also conferred with the head of the engineering department. He pointed out to the purchasing manager that during the 90-day period thousands of satisfactory clips had been supplied and, in view of this, he argued that the supplier could just as well make millions of satisfactory clips.

1. Should the supplier be granted the 50-cent increase?
2. What should the purchasing manager do about the apparent conflict in viewpoints within his company?
3. Could this situation have been avoided or alleviated sooner?
4. Is this a typical or an unusual type of problem?

PARKTOWN

A large supplier opening a branch in the city of Parktown invited the city purchasing agent to an open house, which included a display of the supplier's new products. Drinks and food were served and attendance prizes awarded. The city purchasing agent, believing he owed it to his agency to keep abreast of new products and sources of supply, accepted the invitation.

After the open house, he decided to purchase one of the new products for an application that had been troublesome for many years. The previous supplier whose firm was a local one, upon hearing of this and realizing that he would lose the business, called the city purchasing manager and said he thought that the purchasing manager was grossly unfair in securing these products from an out-of-town firm. He argued that the new supplier did not pay taxes in the city, but he did; besides, he had about the same products. He said that all the other cities he knew favored local merchants in their purchases.

1. Should the purchasing manager have accepted the invitation from the supplier? Why or why not?
2. How should the purchasing manager reply to the irate local supplier?

POWERS COMPANY

Ms. Abel, manager of purchases for the Powers Company, a rapidly expanding firm whose main line was manufacturing household and commercial appliances, was faced with the difficult problem or reorganizing her department. Because of the extremely rapid growth of the Powers Company during the past 10 years, she had noted that her buyers were becoming overloaded with the repetitious details of buying. Since her department had not grown in size during the past 10 years, the personnel were becoming so involved in their routine operations that they were not accomplishing her goals, which assumed that purchasing was a profit making function of the company

Because of public acceptance of the company's products, which were manufactured to high-quality standards and sold at competitive prices, as well as the improved economic conditions in the country, the sales of the company had expanded fivefold during the past 10 years. The dollars spent for purchased materials had expanded at the same rate. Despite this growth, the number of persons in the purchasing department had not expanded during these 10 years except for the addition of two clerks who maintained purchase records. In addition to Ms. Abel, the department consisted of 10 persons responsible for buying activities, eight secretaries, and the two clerks.

Although the personnel of the department were not sectioned formally, the buying personnel were in effect specialized. Their specifications were as follows:

1. Two buyers purchased raw materials. One, a 25-year veteran with the company and classified as a buyer, purchased all forms of aluminum and stainless steel. The other, an employee for 10 years, purchased all the carbon steel, copper, and brass, as well as tool steel for the machine shop. These two metal buyers shared a secretary.

2. Another buyer, who had been employed with the company for 18 years, 13 of which had been in the purchasing department, was now classified as an assistant purchasing agent and bought all the foundry products used, including die castings, permanent-mold castings, and sand castings. Aluminum, zinc, and stainless steel castings were also purchased by this buyer, who was also responsible for a modest quantity of forgings purchased for the larger appliances. A secretary was assigned to this buyer.

3. One buyer, who had been in the purchasing department 17 years, purchased all the switches, controls, and other electric and electronic components used in the company's products. He carried the title of assistant purchasing agent and had a full-time secretary.

4. Two people were responsible for purchasing capital equipment and MRO supplies. One, a 20-year employee, was classified as a buyer whose

major responsibility was the purchase of tools and equipment, including building additions, furniture, and similar items. A young buyer, with the company five years, purchased the MRO supplies used by the shop. Her purchases included small tools and dies, fixtures, and other materials required for maintenance and repair. She was classified as a buyer and shared a secretary with the capital equipment buyer.

5. A 12-year veteran of the company, originally hired for the advertising department, has spent the last eight years as a buyer of packing materials. He purchased all the containers, folding boxes, packaging supplies, and accessories used. He carried the title of buyer and had a full-time secretary.

6. Two members of the purchasing department were responsible for the purchase of all stampings and components required for production. One, a member of the department for 13 years and classified as an assistant purchasing manager, was responsible for the purchase of all molded plastic materials, as well as specialty stampings not fabricated by the company. The other, a member of the department for five years, was classified as a buyer and purchased all the fasteners, glass, ceramic, and rubber and wood components used for production requirements. Each had a secretary.

7. Although the company was equipped to do mechanical as well as organic finishing, it was not set up for chemical finishing. For this reason one person listed as a buyer was responsible for the processing and anodizing of aluminum, decorative plating of steel, and electropolishing of stainless steel components and subassemblies. She had been with the company for six years and had a full-time secretary.

Each buyer was completely responsible for the work in his or her area. The buyer processed all requisitions from the planning department, initiated inquiries, evaluated quotations, entered orders and expedited them, negotiated settlements regarding complaints on reject material, approved invoices, interviewed salespersons, and made inspection trips to new sources. All the buyer's letters and reports were dictated to the assigned secretary.

In addition to receiving and transcribing all dictation, the secretaries were responsible for maintaining the buyers' inquiry files, recording acknowledgments of purchase orders and receipts of materials, clearing invoices, and providing the buyer with daily follow-ups. The more experienced secretaries were competent to do some expediting for the buyer.

A records section was maintained in the department where all orders were recorded on a Kardex system showing order number, item, quantity, price, FOB point, and delivery schedule. In addition, after the invoices were received and recorded on the expediting copies of the purchase orders for use by the buyers, the invoices were recorded by date and quantity on the Kardex. The invoice date and quantity were checked against the receiving report date and quantity, and if they did not agree, were referred to the buyer, who was responsible for handling the discrepancy. After entry on the Kardex, the invoices were forwarded to the accounts payable department for payment. Two clerks handled the records section.

Ms. Abel's problem stemmed from the fact that, except for some minor variations, department personnel were doing exactly the same thing today that they had 10 years ago. With the greatly increased sales volume, the sheer quantity of paper processed by the purchasing department minimized the effectiveness of the buying personnel. The buyers complained that they were becoming paper pushers, and that because of the volume of work they were becoming less effective in creative purchasing.

For some time, Ms. Abel had been proud of the fact that despite the increasing volume of new products and the work load in the department her staff was able to handle the job, whereas engineering personnel had increased approximately three-fold and sales department personnel approximately four-fold over the decade.

Ms. Abel observed that with the heavy load on each of her buyers she was unable to obtain the profit potential possible through creative purchasing. Buyers were reluctant to explore new sources, either by plant visits or by giving a new company an opportunity to quote on new items. To accomplish their daily routine, buyers frequently shortened interviews with salespersons to the point that the salespersons were reluctant to discuss new materials or processes.

Following a purchasing research seminar at the state university, Ms. Abel realized that she was not using the personnel of her department as effectively as she could. Although she had always considered herself to be progressive in her thinking, she finally realized that she was not using tools available in her department to create profits for her company.

1. What purchasing research ideas would you introduce in Ms. Abel's department to restore morale and purchasing efficiency and to make the department again a profit-producing operation?

PRESSURE TANKS, INC. (A)

Pressure Tanks, Inc. manufactures compressed-gas cylinders, bulk-storage tanks for liquefied gases; chemical drums of stainless steel, nickel, or Monel; air receiver tanks; transport truck bodies for compressed liquefied gases; and seamless deep-drawn shells. Pressure Tanks, Inc. has three plants. The main plant, including corporate headquarters, is located in New England. The other two plants are located in Pennsylvania.

Management has asked Mr. Holmes, the corporate purchasing manager, to prepare an operating budget for his department. Prior to 1983, management had not expected departments to prepare or operate according to approved annual budgets. Concomitant with the preparation of the operating budget, Mr. Holmes decided to prepare a procedures manual for his department. He had been contemplating this step for several years and had accumulated much information but had never organized it.

When he came to the section dealing with reports, he realized that he had not required any written reports from his subordinates in the past. There were many verbal reports made to him, and in the past many business decisions had been made on the basis of informal written reports and oral discussion with buyers.

Recently Mr. Holmes had been submitting the following written reports to other executives in the company.

PERIODIC REPORTS

1. *Purchases, inventories, and disbursements of steel report.* This report, which was sent to the officers and all department heads, subdivided steel into flat-rolled sheets, billets, and products. This report gave a forecast of expected usage, inventories, and purchases three months into the future as well as current usage, inventories, and purchases. Mr. Holmes, who was also the steel buyer, issued this report.

2. *Monthly mill steel performance report.* This quality evaluation report was initiated by the product engineering department. The report was forwarded to Mr. Holmes, who analyzed it and wrote the cover letter for it. The purchasing department then sent copies of the report to the officers of Pressure Tanks, Inc. and copies of sections of the report to the steel-vending companies involved. This report was concerned with the grades of steel received, the quality of the steel, scrap resulting from defective material, and the nature of the defects.

   The sections sent to the steel companies were about the performance of that company's steel; that is, what percentage of their steel was defective, the nature of the defects, such as tears, voids, and so on.

3. *Yearly mill steel performance report.* This report was the annual composite of the monthly reports. Prepared by the purchasing department and the product engineering department, it also contained a vendor evaluation in the form of comments on the vendor's performance for the year. The vendors were not sent a copy of this report, but it was sent to the president, vice-president of manufacturing, and

secretary-treasurer, and copies were kept by the purchasing department and the product engineering department.

4. *Monthly supplies report.* The monthly supply report was prepared by the purchasing department to report on the inventories, usage, and purchases of coal, gas, and butane. This report was not sent to the officers, but only to interested department heads and plant managers.

SPECIAL REPORTS

1. *Casting requirements report.* This report was prepared by the purchasing department on all castings needed for cyclical orders in which the procurement time was three months or longer.

2. *Reciprocity report.* A reciprocity report was prepared by Mr. Holmes before any reciprocity contracts were negotiated. Mr. Holmes prepared a report of the proposal and sent it to the vice president of sales. A review of the reciprocity report was made by Mr. Holmes, the vice president of sales, and the market analyst before the vice president of sales negotiated the contract.

Reciprocity agreements were made on a one-year basis. No review was made of the cost of reciprocity, nor was a study made when the contract expired and was renegotiated for the next year. Investigations and reports were made only for initial proposals. If a competing vendor came in with a lower price during the contract year, a mental note was made of this and it would be mentioned to the vice president of sales when the existing reciprocity contract came up for renegotiation.

1. How should Mr. Holmes proceed in preparing an operating budget for the department?
2. Should he require written reports from his subordinates? If so, what subjects should they cover?
3. Do the reports now being made by Mr. Holmes provide a basis for the evaluation of his department?

PRESSURE TANKS, INC. (B)

Pressure Tanks, Inc. used a standard employee evaluation for all salaried employees. Employees were evaluated annually, the evaluation being scheduled one year from the date of hiring for or promotion to a new work assignment. The supervisor was supposed to prepare her rating on the basis of a personal interview. She used the following interview form.

PROGRESS REVIEW

Columns indicate merit or change in qualities listed, based on rater's own knowledge of specific acts that justify rating.

S—Absence of normal growth; must improve to hold own job
N—Normal growth and progress on job through experience
G—Good progress; better than average through special efforts

PERFORMANCE REVIEW

See performance review (pp. 656–659). Columns indicate where employee stands in relation to job standard or expected performance. Be sure to rate each quality independently of others to avoid the "halo effect."

O   Outstanding; falls in top 8 percent in any large representative group
A+   Adequate plus; above average
A   Adequate; average performance
A−   Adequate minus
I   Inadequate; must improve to hold job; failing in this category

PERSONAL CRITERIA

When a supervisor is interviewing an employee, we suggest that he or she look for certain qualities in each person. You will find a short description of what to look for in the nine categories common to all employees listed below. So that you have a better idea of the meaning of each of the five categories "For Supervisors Only," we list the *Webster's Dictionary* definition for each, together with a brief description and application.

Quality of Work: Consider neatness, accuracy, and general efficiency of work; does employee maintain high standards in this respect?
Quantity of Work: Consider the quantity of work turned out and promptness with which employee completes it.

EMPLOYEE PROGRESS AND PERFORMANCE REVIEW

Name _____ Date _____

Dept. _____ Job Title _____

Date Prior Report _____ Tentative
Date Next Review _____

Prepare rating carefully and accurately. Its value lies in the impartiality and sound judgment used by the rater. Judge each characteristic or trait separately or independently; that is, you should not let your evaluation of one trait unduly influence you on another. Place an "X" in the appropriate space.

PROGRESS				PERFORMANCE
S N G				O A+ A A− I

Quantity

O	Produces exceptional amount
A+	Usually does more than expected, works steadily
A	Normal output
A−	Below standard, slow producer, needs prodding
I	Unacceptable, wastes motions, no ambition

Initiative

O	Always alert, advances ideas, hunts work
A+	Plans work well, acts voluntarily on job
A	Needs average guidance, acts voluntarily in routine matters
A−	Shows occasional flashes, not consistent
I	Needs continual pushing

Cooperation

O	Goes out of way to work with others
A+	Always congenial, helpful, group conscious
A	Fulfills obligation to meet others halfway
A−	Reluctant to cooperate, difficult
I	Irritates, causes friction, quarrelsome

Personality

O	Very pleasing, inspires confidence, leader
A+	Outgoing, friendly, good habits, respected

PROGRESS			PERFORMANCE
S N G			O A+ A A− I

	A	Well adjusted, average friendly
	A −	Does not make friends easily, poor habits
	I	Negative, lacking, antagonizes, arouses resentment

Job Knowledge

	O	Expert in job, excellent understanding of related jobs
	A +	Thoroughly understands own and related jobs
	A	Adequately understands own and related jobs
	A −	Narrow concepts of own job only
	I	Limited know-how, inadequate training

Learning Ability

	O	Learns rapidly, excellent memory
	A +	Requires little instruction, grasps well
	A	Normal help only is needed to learn
	A −	Needs careful repetitive instruction
	I	Very slow, poor memory, cannot grasp ideas

Dependability

	O	Extremely reliable, minimum supervision
	A +	Dependable, seldom needs follow-up
	A	Average guidance, usually dependable
	A −	Requires more than normal supervision
	I	Unreliable, needs constant supervision

Judgment

	O	Shows excellent judgment, sound decisions
	A +	Uses common sense, most decisions accepted
	A	Judgment dependable in routine matters with little trouble resulting
	A −	Jumps at conclusions, frequently in error
	I	Poor sense of value, constantly in trouble because of poor judgment

FIVE NEEDS AT SUPERVISORY LEVEL

PROGRESS				PERFORMANCE
S N G				O A+ A A− I

Coordination, Planning

O	Exceptional planner, long- and short-range company concepts
A+	Lays out work to match own and other groups
A	Able to lay out and coordinate work in own department
A−	Takes short-range view, gets flustered easily
I	Inadequate planner, no sense of organizational relationship

Control

O	Exercises exceptional control with own responsibilities
A+	Rarely lets matters get out of hand, seldom needs to impress with authority
A	Requires normal follow-up to accomplish results within area of responsiblity
A−	Plans not always carried out, needs substantial supervision
I	Control inadequate, matters usually out of hand

Delegation

O	Exceptional skill in knowing what and how to delegate, and doing it
A+	Usually delegates properly and effectively
A	Occasionally does work that should be delegated
A−	Frequently does work that should be delegated
I	Incapable of delegating authority and responsibility

Development of Others

O	Excellent teacher, fully understands needs for improving subordinates
A+	Does good job training subordinates

PROGRESS		PERFORMANCE
S N G		O A+ A A− I

	A	Does adequate job training, scope may be limited
	A −	Occasionally lacks patience, limited concept of value of development
	I	Makes little effort to improve subordinates, lacks training techniques

Communication

	O	Exceptionally capable and effective in communication
	A +	Usually does good job in communication, good listener
	A	Communicates adequately (much of the time), usually listens patiently
	A −	Frequently fails to communicate, tends to listen impatiently
	I	Unwilling or unable to communicate

Initiative: Consider ability to act on own responsibility in the absence of instructions. Can this person start needed work and go ahead, or is he or she the type that has to be told what to do?

Cooperation: Consider willingness to work with and help others. Is employee willing to assume full share of work and responsibility? Does the cooperation exist in manner as well as act?

Personality: Consider appearance, tactfulness, self-confidence, integrity, loyalty, and the impression made on others.

Knowledge of Job: Consider how much employee knows about present job, other work closely related to it, and work in other departments.

Aptitude & Ability to Learn: Consider how quickly new work is learned, how well what is learned is retained, and the ease with which instructions are followed.

Dependability: Consider the amount of supervision required. Can you depend on this person's work? Is he or she punctual? Is the attendance record without fault?

Judgment: Consider the intelligence and thought used in arriving at decisions. Does this employee have the ability to think and act calmly, logically, and rapidly under stress?

Coordination (Definition: to arrange in due and relative order; to harmonize): Consider effectiveness in planning and carrying out of work and that of subordinates in light of interdepartmental relationships and of company goals.

Control: (Definition: to hold in restraint; to regulate; to govern; to subject to authority): Consider ability to ensure that plans and work assignments given to subordinates by this employee are completed effectively, in a timely manner, and economically.

Delegation (Definition: to entrust, commit, or deliver to another's care and management; to send with power to act as a representative): Consider employee's effectiveness in delegating authority and responsibility in order to afford self time to plan, control, and otherwise effectively supervise department or group.

Development of Others (Definition: gradual growth or advancement through progressive changes): Consider employee's interest in improving the performance of subordinates through training, as well as his or her effectiveness as a teacher. Is this person aiming to have one or more subordinates who could fill his or her shoes?

Communication: (Definition: information or intelligence imparted by word or writing): Consider whether the employee recognizes the value of conveying information, discussing ideas, and being a good listener. Do people clearly understand what employee is trying to convey?

Conclusion: It is intended that this report be prepared once each year. Certain persons may need to be reviewed more often. Reports are to be prepared by employee's supervisor and reviewed by the immediate supervisor.

Forms must be prepared in duplicate, the original for the office manager, the copy for future reference of person preparing report.

1. Should a standard form be used for all salaried employees?
2. What are the advantages and disadvantages of reviewing the completed form with each employee?
3. Is the annual scheduling of these evaluations appropriate?
4. Evaluate the form as to its suitability for purchasing personnel.

RADMER COUNTY

Radmer County is located in northern Wisconsin. The population in 1987 was estimated to be 24,000. The county seat, Hayson, had a population of 5000. Mr. Pippert was county purchasing manager. He had two clerks who took care of files, records, and typing for the department. There was also an assistant purchasing agent who handled purchasing matters of lesser importance and those of little interest to the purchasing manager.

The purchasing department was part of the county treasurer's office and did the purchasing for all county departments, including the consolidated school district, which was slightly larger than Radmer County itself. All purchases above a value of $200 had to bought through open, competitive bidding.

Gasoline, oil, and tires for the county road maintenance equipment, the county conservation department vehicles and boat motors, and county patrol cars accounted for one-fourth of all expenditures. For items of this type, an announcement was made in the local weekly newspaper and, upon inquiry, a potential supplier was given a specification sheet. Specification sheets were not unduly detailed. For example, a recent specification sheet for gasoline had octane rating, market grade, and two additives to establish the desired quality. Also included on the specification sheet were delivery date, point of delivery, and the quantity to be bought.

A major problem was the fact that Radmer County, being sparsely populated, had few potential suppliers for many items. Price was the most important factor in all purchase decisions.

The emphasis on price resulted from the fact that the department operated under a materials budget. An idea being considered to bring down prices further was cooperative purchasing. Meetings were being held to determine how many northern counties would sacrifice enough of the independence (legal obstacles, preferences among brand names and local dealers) to agree on a common standard for such items as gasoline and tires. According to Mr. Pippert's estimates, this would reduce the price of premium gasoline from $1.29 to $1.28 per gallon.

One other problem created by emphasis on the low-bid awards was that of "orphan equipment." Because the supplier may, and often does, change from year to year, the inventory of equipment consists of a mixture of brand names. The conservation department's outboard motors, for example, consisted of Evinrude, Johnson and Mercury, and a few other brands. This naturally poses a maintenance and spare parts problem. Other county departments purchasing in the area avoided this problem by long-term contracts, but, according to Mr. Pippert, this was impossible in Radmer County because of political "wrangling higher up."

1. What differences, if any, might one expect between a small government purchasing operation and that of a small industrial concern?
2. How can an isolated buyer, government or private, develop sufficient suppliers to ensure competition?
3. How might one establish cooperative buying by several counties in the light of such factors as political influences and demands by local suppliers in each county?

ROAD EQUIPMENT MANUFACTURING COMPANY

Road Equipment Manufacturing Company is one of the largest firms in its field. It manufactures a complete line of equipment used in road construction and maintenance. Since it sells to units of government that must buy on a low-bid basis or to contractors who in turn bid on construction jobs in the same manner, there is constant pressure from management on the purchasing and engineering departments to keep costs of materials and parts at a minimum.

Management repeatedly asks both the purchasing and engineering departments whether they have weighed the alternatives of making and buying the components that become a part of the equipment.

The purchasing policy manual contains the following statement concerning make or buy.

POLICY ON MAKE OR BUY

In arriving at the make-or-buy decision, purchasing will generally be best equipped to counsel in regard to the buy side of the decision-making process. Since purchasing is the contact with outside suppliers, its efforts should be directed toward obtaining all necessary information in this regard and should concern itself not with the details of costs of make but only that the appropriate departments have given adequate attention to them.

Specific assignments of responsibilities to the purchasing division that relate directly or indirectly to make or buy are as follows:

1. One buyer serves as a member of the make–buy committee, which controls parts in the fabrication inventory.
2. The director of the purchasing division acts as a member of the senior committee on pricing.
3. A purchasing division subcommittee on pricing is composed of the purchasing agent, supervisor of the purchasing cost estimating department, and the administrative buyer in charge of the subcontracting department.
4. The director of the purchasing division and the purchasing manager serve as members of the committee, which controls the outside procurement of end items that are destined for replacement parts sales activity.
5. The supervisor of the subcontract buying section serves as a member of the make—buy committee for control of manufactured assemblies.

The chief aims of purchasing in this area of activity are as follows.

1. Ensure that all facts needed to evaluate each situation from the standpoint of overall economy to the company are available.
2. Provide information on availability in industry of any specialized services or products that would be of value in the operations of the company.
3. Encourage company activity in need areas inadequately supplied by industry and ensure that due consideration is given before entering areas of activity that are already well supplied on a competitive basis.
4. Attention shall be given guarding against any decision, either make or buy, that will cause unnecessary or unjustifiable duplication of tooling or facilities.

When making make-or-buy decisions, purchasing department personnel will at all times give consideration to the fact that decisions of this type must never cause the end product to suffer in regard to specified quality, reliability, or delivery.

The two make-or-buy committees referred to in the policy statement each have a permanent representative from engineering and from general management. The committee's decision is final. The works manager, production manager, and controller receive a copy of each manufacturing or purchase analysis sheet prepared. Any comments they have are written in the remarks section of the form for the guidance of the three-person committee.

Three recent make-or-buy analyses are presented as Exhibits A, B, and C.

1. Evaluate the make-or-buy policy statement of the company.
2. Evaluate the committee structure used for make-or-buy decisions.
3. What decision should be made on the Locking Nut Wear Ring?
4. Do you agree with the decision regarding the other two items?

ROBERTS FIBRE PRODUCTS COMPANY

The Roberts Fibre Products Company operates 20 plants throughout the Midwest. The company manufactures fiberboard and, in some plant locations, also manufactures corrugated paper containers. Management is decentralized, each plant being under the control of a vice president in charge of manufacturing. Ms. Ward, purchasing manager for the plant in Capitol City, reports directly to the vice president in charge of manufacturing.

Ms. Ward's most important responsibility is the purchase of straw and wastepaper, the two principal raw materials used by the plant. In purchasing

ROUTE TO: INITIAL AND FORWARD 3. PRODUCT DIVN._____
1. WORKS MANAGER _____   4. CONTROLLER
2. PURCHASING _____   5. RETURN TO ORIGINATOR

MANUFACTURING OR PURCHASE ANALYSIS

PRODUCT	DESCRIPTION	DRAWING NO.	USAGE / YEAR		PART NO.	4210-3011	
MOWER	LOCKING NUT WEAR RING	B-5095	NEW	1993	EFFECTIVE DATE	9-15-93	EFFECTIVE WITH WORKS ORDER NO.
				*	Make	Buy	Review	**NEW ORDER**

IF PURCHASED

HISTORY		MADE AT	MATERIAL	DIRECT COST
DATE	ORDER NO.	QUAN		
9/15/93		1 to 3	VENDOR (ABC CO.)		42.70
9/15/93		1 to 3	OUR FOUNDRY		

IF MANUFACTURED

	MATERIAL	DIRECT LABOR	DIRECT COST	MFG. COST	ACTUAL DIRECT COST OF FIRST ORDER AFTER ABOVE DECISION
	4.00	27.33	31.33		

OTHER COST INVOLVED

| TOTAL DIRECT COST PER EACH | 42.70 | | 31.33 | | |
| AVERAGE YEARLY USAGE: NOT KNOWN | MIN. QUANTITY FOR REORDERS: | | | SAVINGS PER: YEAR EACH 11.67 | |

REMARKS: THIS IS A NEW PART RELEASE
SAVINGS EACH OF $11.67 IS BASED ON QUANTITY 1 TO 3
AVERAGE YEARLY USAGE IS NOT KNOWN AT THIS TIME.
THIS IS ROUGH CASTING ONLY.

ORIGINATOR	DATE	APPROVED	DATE	METHODS DEPT. APPROVAL OF HOURS	DECISION NOTED ON LEDGER	DATE	AFTER NOTATION RETURN ORIGINAL COPY TO COST DEPARTMENT	REVISION	DATE

EXHIBIT A. Mower

ROUTE TO: INITIAL AND FORWARD 3. PRODUCT DIVN. _____
1. WORKS MANAGER _____   4. CONTROLLER
2. PURCHASING _____   5. RETURN TO ORIGINATOR

MANUFACTURING OR PURCHASE ANALYSIS

PART NO. 1234-5678

PRODUCT	DESCRIPTION	DRAWING NO.	USAGE / YEAR	EFFECTIVE DATE 8-3-86			EFFECTIVE WITH WORKS ORDER NO.
				Make	Buy	Review	
DITCH DIGGER	ROPE-WIRE	I 1234-5678	1991 20 / 79 1992		*		AFTER X-1020

HISTORY

DATE	ORDER NO.	QUAN	MADE AT	IF PURCHASED		IF MANUFACTURED				ACTUAL DIRECT COST OF FIRST ORDER AFTER ABOVE DECISION
				MATERIAL	DIRECT COST	MATERIAL	DIRECT LABOR	DIRECT COST	MFG. COST	
7/92	2612-1131	20	OUR PLANT			11.00	1.60	13.24		
8/2/92	Quote	25	*Vendor (Specific)		10.73					

OTHER COST INVOLVED

	IF PURCHASED DIRECT COST	IF MANUFACTURED DIRECT COST
TOTAL DIRECT COST PER EACH	10.73	13.24

AVERAGE YEARLY USAGE: 50

MIN. QUANTITY FOR REORDERS: 25

SAVINGS PER YEAR EACH: 2.51   125.50

REMARKS: IT IS THE CONSENSUS THAT WE HENCEFORTH PURCHASE THE SUBJECT ROPE CUT TO THE LENGTH AND WITH THE ENDS WELDED AS PER OUR DRAWING. THIS ROPE WAS FORMERLY PURCHASED IN REEL LENGTH OF 1,000 FEET AND PIECES WERE CUT AND THE ENDS TAPED TEMPORARILY, STORED AND THE ENDS WERE FINALLY WELDED. THESE OPERATIONS WERE FOUND TO BE VERY AWKWARD.

*VENDOR - JOHN JONES CO.
1080 BLANK STREET
CHICAGO, ILLINOIS

ORIGINATOR	DATE	APPROVED	DATE	METHODS DEPT. APPROVAL OF HOURS	DECISION NOTED ON LEDGER	DATE	AFTER NOTATION RETURN ORIGINAL COPY TO COST DEPARTMENT	REVISION	DATE

EXHIBIT B. Ditch Digger.

ROUTE TO: INITIAL AND FORWARD 3. PRODUCT DIVN. _____
1. WORKS MANAGER _____ 4. CONTROLLER
2. PURCHASING 5. RETURN TO ORIGINATOR

MANUFACTURING OR PURCHASE ANALYSIS

PART NO.   5061-7801

PRODUCT	DESCRIPTION	DRAWING NO.	USAGE / YEAR		EFFECTIVE DATE			EFFECTIVE WITH WORKS ORDER NO.
EXCAVATOR	FABRICATED SWIVEL	D-1066	74 1990		8-24-65			NEXT ORDER
			36 1991		Make	Buy	Review	
			73 1992		*			

HISTORY

DATE	ORDER NO.	QUAN
1/31/93	1645-2030	8
8/24/93	NEW QUOTE	12

IF PURCHASED

MADE AT	MATERIAL	DIRECT COST
OUR PLANT		
VENDOR (FAB. ONLY)		*375.00

IF MANUFACTURED

	MATERIAL	DIRECT LABOR	DIRECT COST	MFG. COST	ACTUAL DIRECT COST OF FIRST ORDER AFTER ABOVE DECISION
	118.50	69.18	248.49		

OTHER COST INVOLVED

	IF PURCHASED DIRECT COST	IF MANUFACTURED DIRECT COST
OUR MACHINING	25.12	
OUR MISC.	7.94	
TOTAL DIRECT COST PER EACH	408.06	248.49

AVERAGE YEARLY USAGE: 60   MIN. QUANTITY FOR REORDERS: 12   SAVINGS PER YEAR   159.57 EACH   9574.20 PER YEAR

REMARKS: * TO DATE QUOTATION $375.00)
    415.00)
    470.00) MATERIAL & FABRICATION ONLY
    510.00)

IN VIEW OF THE ABOVE EVALUATION, CHANGE LEDGER TO "DEFINITELY MAKE"

ORIGINATOR	DATE	APPROVED	DATE	METHODS DEPT. APPROVAL OF HOURS	DECISION NOTED ON LEDGER	DATE	AFTER NOTATION RETURN ORIGINAL COPY TO COST DEPARTMENT	REVISION	DATE

EXHIBIT C. Excavator

these commodities she is guided largely by market prices as published in trade papers in the two fields. She also processes all purchase requisitions involving expenditures in excess of $250.

Reporting to Ms. Ward are Mr. Bond, inventory control clerk, and four clerical employees. Mr. Bond is authorized to purchase items not exceeding the $250 limitation. It is also his responsibility to requisition materials and parts on which he maintains inventory control cards whenever he notes that the supply of an item is too low. It is left to his discretion to determine the reorder point.

As insurance against plant shutdowns and slowdowns, the company maintains an inventory of replacement parts and fittings for its machinery and equipment. Each replacement part is tagged as it is received with such information as the part number and the supplier's identification. When a part is issued from stock, Mr. Bond is expected to make an entry on the tag, which is removed, noting the date and the equipment for which it is being used. He is then required to forward the tag, along with a requisition for replacement, to the purchasing agent.

Stock items may be requisitioned by any employee, and the requisition is then sent to the purchasing manager for processing. Requisitions involving purchases in excess of $10,000 are treated as capital expenditures. Requisitions for capital expenditures can be initiated only by the purchasing manager, the plant manager, or the plant superintendent and must be approved by the vice president. All such requisitions must be accompanied by a form showing the estimated costs, the reasons for the expenditures, the annual savings anticipated, and the proposed disposition of any old machinery or equipment.

A recent purchase of forklift trucks illustrates the procedure of the purchasing agent, Ms. Ward, with respect to the selection of a supplier for such items. The plant superintendent initiated the approved requistion. Ms. Ward then visited several fiberboard plants to determine the type of trucks they were using. She next arranged for three suppliers to send in demonstrator models so that her workers could try them. Her choice of supplier was based largely on the preference expressed by the workers who used the trucks.

Ms. Ward says that she likes to keep paperwork to a minimum because of the small size of the purchasing department. The two most frequently used forms are the purchase order requisition and the purchase order form. The requisition form has space for identification of the item, quantity desired, the department initiating the requisition, the purpose for which the item will be used, and the date by which it is required. The individual initiating the requisition fills in all this information. There is also space on the requisition for the purchasing agent to fill in the name of the supplier, the purchase order number, the price, terms of sale, and shipping information.

The purchase order is typed in triplicate by one of the clerical employees from the requisition form. One copy is sent to the supplier, one to the receiving department, and one is kept for the purchasing department files.

A postcard is used when follow-up of an order is indicated. The printed card contains a simple request for information as to the expected shipment date of an order, which is identified by purchase order number.

A special form is used when a fixed asset is being requested. This form is called the fixed-asset expenditure recommendation. In addition to identifying the asset and its proposed plant location, the form provides space for a description of the item, the reasons for making the acquisition, the estimated costs, detailed information about any assets that will be retired because of the purchase, and the recommended supplier.

1. Evaluate the purchasing procedures used by the company. Would you suggest any changes in procedures?
2. Evaluate the procedure followed by Ms. Ward in selecting the supplier of forklift trucks.
3. Can the follow-up procedure of this company be improved?
4. Should the company make use of the fixed-asset expenditure recommendation form for all purchases of fixed assets?

SELMA INSTRUMENTS COMPANY

The Selma Instruments Company was the successful bidder on a contract, offered by the prime contractor, for a component of an intercontinental missile. Two important items for this component had to be purchased from outside suppliers. These were 5000 instrument housings and 100,000 transitors. In bidding on this contract the company had cut its quotation approximately to cost. As a result, after the award, instructions were sent to all departments to increase their efficiency in every respect in order to meet the price commitment.

The purchasing manager discovered that the contract provided large progress payments during its two-year term. Therefore, the financing of inventories, one of the usual considerations in setting inventory levels, could be disregarded. Under these circumstances the company could place orders for immediate delivery of its entire requirements rather than spacing shipments over the two-year period.

Competition to supply the transistor and the instrument housings was keen, and the Selma Company was able to negotiate considerably lower prices than those originally estimated. The transistor order was given to a single supplier, and the housing order was split between two suppliers with whom the company had had a long and satisfactory relationship.

The transistors were purchased subject to the manufacturer's standard warranty. The packages stated plainly that replacement would be made for any transistor found to be defective within one year of the date of delivery. The Selma Company inspection department followed a different inspection practice depending on the product. When transportation costs were high, inspection was conducted at the supplier's plant. Statistical sampling techniques were used for high-volume technical items with close tolerance levels. When an item was procured that carried a guarantee (mostly shelf-stock items), a visual identity inspection by the receiving department was deemed sufficient.

After a period of 16 months, it was discovered that there had been an undue proportion of defective transistors. By this time about 30 percent of the transistors had gone into production.

Because the Selma Company had realized that all its departments would be working at or beyond their capacity, its contract with one of the housing suppliers had specified that inspection would be done at the supplier's plant by a Selma Company inspector. In this way the pressure on the Selma Company's inspection facilities would be reduced. Each housing required 45 minutes for inspection because of the close tolerances specified. The purchase from the second supplier of housings was governed by the standard clause of the Selma Company's purchase order, which stated, ''Material is subject to inspection for a period of 75 days after delivery.''

As source-inspected material was received from the supplier, it was moved directly to the production line. Housings from the other supplier were stored for later use. This procedure was followed by the inspection department because of the many activities it had to perform during the initial stages of the contract. Delivery by both housing suppliers was completed within four months. It was not until after seven months that housings from the second supplier moved onto the production line. The first 10 housings inspected were immediately rejected because holes had been drilled in the wrong places.

The supplier was called in at once but refused to take responsibility for replacement. It was pointed out that the Selma Company had had adequate time to inspect the housings and that if they had inspected them within the prescribed period, the error could have been corrected before the order was completed. Since the supplier had already been paid, it was assumed that the shipments had been satisfactory. The supplier agreed that the holes were slightly misplaced but pointed out that the Selma Company had dealt with the supplier company for years and had frequently specified closer tolerances than necessary and had not previously rejected goods that had exceeded tolerances. The supplier felt that he should have been warned if this contract was to be subject to different standards of acceptance.

1. What courses of action are open to the purchasing manager of the Selma Company in these two cases?
2. Could this situation have been avoided?
3. Should shelf-stock items be inspected as received if they are procured in such quantities that they will not be used before the guarantee period has passed?

SHARPE MACHINE CORPORATION

The Sharpe Machine Corporation was located in Michigan, with branch plants in Canton and Cincinnati, Ohio. Annual sales were in excess of $200 million. The company's major product line consisted of milling machines and lathes.

Fred L. Consel, vice president in charge of purchasing, had established a basic policy calling for annual review of all suppliers of major items. It was company policy to have for such items an approved list of four companies who would share in the business available. At the time of the annual review, the buyers were expected to evaluate potential new suppliers who might replace one or more of the current suppliers. A special evaluation form had been developed for this purpose (see Exhibit A).

Financial status was determined from the study of Dun & Bradstreet ratings and the most recent annual report of the prospective supplier. A supplier located within 200 miles was considered to be in an excellent location. Inventory breadth was determined by studying the supplier's catalogs. Depth of inventory, physical layout, administrative talent, and engineering talent could not be fully evluated without making a plant visitation. Delivery service ratings were based on the highway system between the supplier's plant and the Sharpe plants and on the availability of good common-carrier service between the two points.

The annual review of chuck suppliers had indicated an unsatisfactory condition with two of the current suppliers, and John Ozanne, tooling buyer, decided that he should replace both suppliers. He was uncertain which two new suppliers should be added (see Exhibit A). In talking this problem over with Mr. Consel, he pointed out that he thought the Adams Company was best and should be added to the approved list. However, he thought there might be problems with each of the others.

EXHIBIT A. Sharpe Machine Corporation New Supplier Evaluation Form

Product	Supplier	Financial Status	Location	Inventory		Physical Layout	Administrative Talent	Engineering Talent	Delivery Service
				Breadth	Depth				
16-inch 3-jaw chuck	Adams Co.	E[a]	E	E	E	G	G	G	E
	Ernst Bros.	E	P	E	E	C	F	E	G
	Ennis Corp.	E	E	G	G	N	E	E	E
	Tooling, Inc.	F	E	E	P	G	G	E	E
	General Tool Co.	F	E	E	E	E	E	E	P
	Murray Co.	E	E	E	E	G	P	P	E

[a]E = excellent, F = fair, C = correctable, G = good, P = poor, N = noncorrectable.

1. Which two suppliers should be added to the approved list?
2. What is the relative importance of the various evaluation factors?
3. Should any other factors be used in the evaluation?
4. Can this form be used or adapted for the evaluation of existing suppliers?

SMITH ELECTRONIC CORPORATION

The Smith Electronic Corporation is a large manufacturer of component parts for radio and television sets. The company purchases total about $300 million annually and are composed of more than 10,000 different items purchased from approximately 3000 suppliers. To improve the buying process, the purchasing agent developed a system for rating suppliers. She stated that the purpose of the system was to introduce an element of objectivity into an area of purchasing that is basically subjective.

The rating system was based on analysis of the inspection reports and the supplier's service and adherence to delivery commitments. Data for rating a supplier were recorded on a rating form developed by the purchasing agent (Exhibit A).

The volume of purchases for the current month was secured by tabulating invoices. The three-month average was derived from the vendor cards that the company maintains. No attempt is made to rate suppliers by individual types of products purchased. All purchases from one vendor are recorded on one line of the rating form.

Inspection reports provide the dollar volume of rejections and the percentage of rejections figures on the rating form. The percentage of rejections is based not on units, but rather on the value of the materials rejected divided by the value of the materials shipped by the supplier.

The expediting section rates the supplier in terms of adequacy of delivery. Four ratings were established for the evaluation of this factor.

1. *Excellent:* A supplier receives this rating only if there has been no need for expediting and if acceptance copies of the purchase order have been returned within seven days.
2. *Good:* A supplier receives this rating if the need for expediting or follow-up to secure order acknowledgments has been occasional rather than regular.
3. *Fair:* A supplier receives this rating if frequent expediting is required.

EXHIBIT A. Supplier Rating Form

| | Dollar Volume of | | | | | |
| | Purchases | | Rejections | | | |
Supplier	This Month	Three-Month Average	This Month	Three-Month Average	Monthly Rejection[a] (%)	Delivery	Comments
Adams Company	3722	2500	1210	505	20	Excellent	Very adaptable—accepts small orders
Baker Manufacturing	202	1420		160	11	Fair	Decrease percentage of business
J. I. Smith	9200	8500	980	2000	24	Good	Rejection rate still too high
Selma Instruments	6480	5500	2020	930	17	Good	Watch rejection rate closely

[a]Includes passed-on exception.

4. *Unsatisfactory:* A supplier who receives this rating seldom acknowledges orders, frequently misses delivery dates, or ships incomplete orders.

The buyer who placed orders with the supplier fills in the last column on the rating form. Comments are based on the services provided by the supplier's representative, the willingness of the supplier to handle rush or emergency orders, its ability and willingness to assist in the design and development of products to meet new requirements and its productive capacity.

Each month the purchasing manager sends a letter to each supplier indicating where each firm stands in relation to competitive suppliers. This letter is addressed to the sales manager of the company rather than the local salesperson. The purchasing manager feels that the salesperson should know the situation without being informed. In addition, if improvement is needed, the purchasing manager believes it will more likely be forthcoming if the customer informs the supplier of deficiencies rather than relying on the salesperson to do this.

1. Can vendors be rated objectively?
2. Should any other elements be included on this rating form?
3. Is the practice of rating the supplier in total, rather than by individual items purchased, sound?
4. Should suppliers be informed of their ratings?

SPACE SYSTEMS, INC.

Space Systems, Inc. is a major supplier of missile guidance systems for the United States Air Force. It received an initial contract for 50 guidance systems for a new missile on a cost-plus-fixed-fee contract. Many of the system components were purchased for subcontractors. One such subcontract was for a specially designed electronic component at a firm price of $100,000 each for 50 units.

The guidance system proved to be effective, and the Air Force began new negotiations for 300 additional guidance systems. The new contract was to be on an incentive contract. Under this contract, cost savings are shared on an agreed on basis between the government and the prime contractor, and costs above a target figure are not fully paid by the government. These terms provide an incentive to maintain or reduce costs.

Through auditing the production costs of its subcontractor for the electronic component, Space Systems became convinced that its manufacture was subject to an 80 percent learning curve. Because of the need for the 300 new units and additional ones for replacement purposes, it was decided to buy 350 of these electronic components. Using a log-log paper, Space Systems arrived at an average price that it would pay the subcontractor. The subcontractor, not understanding the learning curve concept, argued against this price.

1. Applying learning curve assumed by the buyer, what price should be paid for the 350 electronic components?
2. How should the supplier's objections be met?

STEPHEN MOTOR COMPANY, INC.

The Stephen Motor Company manufactures a diversified line of motor-driven vehicles. It has three operating divisions: outboard motors, road construction equipment, and garden equipment. The vice president in charge of each division has responsibility for both manufacture and sale of the products in his or her division. Certain departments in the company that serve all three divisions are grouped under a vice president in charge of staff activities. Included in this group is the purchasing department.

All purchases of major equipment and installations must have the prior approval of the board of directors. Each of the three divisions follows a slightly different approach in determining what equipment shall be purchased for replacement of existing equipment. In each of the divisions responsibility for equipment maintenance is assigned to a superintendent of maintenance. In the outboard motor division the superintendent reviews the condition of each piece of equipment during November and prepares a list of the equipment needing replacement for the board of directors the following January. When approval is given, he initiates the purchases through the purchasing department.

In reviewing the condition of equipment, the superintendent prepares an analysis of each item under his control on forms that he has adapted from the standard form developed by the Machinery and Allied Products Institute (MAPI). In his adaptation of the form he has included only 5 factors of comparison instead of the 12 or more factors suggested by MAPI. His 5 factors are direct labor, power, floor space, taxes and insurance, and normal maintenance. He justifies his exclusion of indirect labor by pointing out that indirect labor is generally computed as a percentage of direct labor. Thus its inclusion for both the old and the new equipment would not change the outcome. Defects and downtime are excluded because he says that all equipment in his division is kept in perfect order and, therefore, there can be no difference in these two factors between new and old equipment. Tooling is excluded as are supplies in the belief that these items will be used in approximately the same amounts for new and old equipment.

The equipment analysis forms are reviewed with the vice president in charge of the division, and any analysis that shows a cost advantage for new equipment is submitted to the board of directors. The board then determines which of the requests are to be approved for the ensuing 12-month period.

The superintendent of maintenance of the road construction equipment division does not believe that the MAPI formula provides a sound approach to the purchase of equipment. She argues that it is impossible to measure accurately the various factors of comparison. Furthermore, she believes that reliance on a formula approach to business decisions tends to inhibit the exercise of executive judgment. Therefore, she reviews her equipment annually and at the January meeting submits requests for board approval that are supported by data relating to age, downtime, rejection rates, and so on, for the equipment involved.

Requisitions for the purchase of equipment for the production lines in the garden equipment division are initiated at any time during the year when the superintendent of maintenance believes such action is indicated. At times he uses the equipment replacement formula and at other times he does not. He refuses to make an annual review to determine equipment needs for a 12-month forward period. He believes that this procedure is wasteful in that, once the board has approved a request, orders are placed immediately even though there may still be some months of useful life in the old equipment. Furthermore, he contends that competitive developments in garden equipment are such that changes in design may occur at any time during the year and require equipment changeover. If a division has used up its allocation of funds for equipment, it may experience difficulty with the board when it submits a supplementary request.

Mr. Ronald, purchasing manager for the Stephen Motor Company, has board of directors' approval for a policy of not leasing any production equipment. In securing approval, he cited as justification for his position the fact that in the long run costs of equipment are higher under a leasing plan. Furthermore, he contended that only companies with limited resources use the leasing method of procurement. If the Stephen Motor Company were to lease, he thought it might reflect adversely on the company's credit standing in the money markets.

Mr. Ronald does not approve of the purchase of used equipment for the company. He believes that if the company invests in equipment, it should be based on long-range plans and requirements. Used equipment is of value for a short-run producer who does not intend to remain in business for very long.

Furthermore, it is almost impossible to evaluate a piece of equipment that has been in use for some time, according to Mr. Ronald.

1. Compare the positions of the superintendent of maintenance for each of the divisions. Which position appears soundest?
2. Is Mr. Ronald correct in his policies on leasing and the purchase of used equipment?
3. Can variations in policies between divisions of a company be justified?

STITH FOREIGN STEEL

Mel Stith has been buying steel from domestic suppliers for the past eight years. While the opportunity to purchase from foreign suppliers has been a possiblity, Mr. Stith has refrained from such purchases because of the following:

1. He has held the view that it is unpatriotic to buy from foreign suppliers.
2. He is concerned that specific shipments may be of inferior or damaged quality.
3. His broker contacts cannot assure him that the value of the dollar versus the foreign currency will not vary between negotiation and receipt times.
4. He is concerned relative to unfavorable reactions from plant union personnel who would notice foreign purchases.
5. He dislikes the long in-transit time involved in foreign shipments.

In the last month, however, Stith has been made aware that his competitors have been purchasing a portion of their type 430 stainless from foreign (Japanese) suppliers and have enjoyed a 20 percent cost savings with equal or superior quality.

Stith has a requirement requisition in his hands covering 6 million pounds of type 430 stainless with 1 million pounds required each month during the next six-month period.

The foreign broker assures Stith that he can deliver steel within two months of an order, and will gurantee quality, price, and currency ratios for a six-month period.

1. Should Stith buy from foreign sources? If so, how much? If not, why?
2. Are his concerns legitimate, or do they have solutions?

3. Assuming he does buy foreign—how much should he commit of the present 6 million pound requisition.
4. What safeguards are available regarding such foreign purchases relative to contract terms and possible currency fluctuations?
5. How could currency hedging be used in this transaction?

TESTING AND PSYCHOLOGICAL ASSESSMENT

Personnel officers often use testing as a means of differentiating among candidates. Some firms use mechanical and psychological assessment to aid them in the evaluation process. The following case involves the use of tests and psychological assessment in an extensive search to fill the position of vice president of materials for a concern with annual sales of $150 million, comprising 17 plants scattered around the United States. The individual must have the ability to assume the important management function of commodity purchasing (copper, brass, etc.), including negotiations with top people in some of the largest producing plants in the United States. In addition the candidate chosen will have staff responsibility for all corporate procurement at central and plant locations.

Initial ads were placed in *The Wall Street Journal, Chicago Tribune, Milwaukee Journal,* and *Minneapolis Tribune.* Of approximately 150 candidates, six were called in for personal interviews, and two were singled out for further interviewing and testing. One of the two finalists was tested. The results, presented in Exhibit A, cover values, personality, aptitudes, and vocational interest. In addition, psychological assessment of this candidate was made by an independent organizational psychologist, and results are presented in Exhibit B. Would you give further consideration to this candidate? Why or why not? Specifically, evaluate the types of tests used, their relevance, and the psychological assessment.

OBJECTIVE OF REPORT

Mr. X is a candidate for a position as procurement, inventory, and materials manager. The job is described as the top job in the area. Mr. X is apparently a pro in this area. He has done very well for himself, for he has, apparently, a job just like this at the vice presidential level in another company.

The psychometric record is not particularly strong. His abilities are fair and good at best for a high-level job. He does not appear to be a strong decision maker. It may be that his experience and his contacts in particular will be useful to you at this point in time. One might wonder whether he got

EXHIBIT A. Psychometric data for Mr. X
Percentile Scores of Selected Variables

	1	4	11	23	40	60	77	89	96	99
	LOWEST		LOW		AVERAGE		HIGH			HIGHEST
STUDY OF VALUES										
Economic			*							
Political			***************							
Theoretical			***********							
Artistic			*********************************							
Altruistic			**************************************							
Religious			*******************************							
PERSONALITY										
Dominance			**********************							
Confidence			**************************							
Independence			*****							
Initiative			*********							
Persistence			********							
Flexibility			**							
Opportunism			****							
Introversion			*********							
Emotionally			*********							
Satisfaction			************************************							
Salesmanship			********************							

Vocational Interests

SIMILARITY	B	B+	A
POSSIBLE INTEREST			
SCIENTIFIC			
Biologist			
Mathematician			
Physicist			
Chemist			
Engineer			
PROCESS TECHNICAL			
Production Manager	BB		
Carpenter			
Teacher, Math and Science			
Printer			
Police Officer			
SOCIAL			
Personnel Manager	AA	AA	
Public Administrator	AA	AA	AA
Teacher, Social Science	AA	AA	
ARTISTIC			
Artist			
Musician Performer			

EXHIBIT A. Continued

DATA-CONTROL				
CPA Owner	BB			
CPA Senior	B+	B+		
Accountant	B+	B+		
Office Worker	B+	B+		
Purchasing Agent				
Banker				
Credit Manager	AA	AA	AA	
Computer Programmer	AA	AA	AA	
MANAGEMENT—SALES				
Association Executive				
President, Manufacturing				
Sales Manager				
Realtor	BB			
Insurance Salesperson	BB			
VERBAL				
Advertising				
Lawyer				
Writer				
NONVOCATIONAL SCALES				
Occupational Introversion	AA	AA		
Degree of Specialization	AA	AA		
Occupation Level	AA	AA		

Creativity	************************
ABILITIES AND APTITUDES	
Intelligence, Power	
—Timed	**********
—Untimed	*********************
Arithmetic Reasoning	********
Mechanical Comprehen.	***********************
Spatial Thinking	***************
MISCELLANEOUS	
Leadership Style	
Participative	******************
Directive	************

To: Zorro Manufacturing

Requested by: John Doe

MR. X REPORT

PERSONAL	WORK EXPERIENCE
Age: 53 Married Five children EDUCATION	● Payroll sorter, clerk ● Hearing-aid salesperson ● Self-employed salesperson ● Vice-president, purchasing
High school graduate Junior college graduate	

EXHIBIT B. Psychologist's report on Mr. X

to where he is right now because he was a very polite, affable man who simply didn't make any waves. Apart from trading on contacts and friendships from the past, we cannot see him pushing and angling to get results in a seller's market.

INTERESTS AND VALUES

As far as the function is concerned, the job that you are talking about is reasonably appropriate for him. His desire to work constructively with people is considerable. There is quite a bit of focus on social and public service jobs. He spends a fair amount of time in church and community activities.

Apart from that, he is like people in a number of the business control jobs and a bit like people in some of the sales jobs.

He is really very much people-oriented, and that is evident from his scores on the scale of values. He stresses the altruistic and religious values ahead of any others. We noted his involvement in church and community affairs. His wife, too, is so involved.

Next to his focus on altruistic and religious factors, he emphasizes the artistic value. He says at some point that he spends his leisure time in some sports activities and also visiting art galleries and museums.

Finally, at an average level, he makes a score for the political factor. His score on the economic value is at the bottom. He is not a materialistic person, and he may not be a very practical one. He does say that he would like to make a sizble income 10 years from now. However, we think that this man has a great deal of feeling for the good life. He has probably worked hard all his life, but he is not a dedicated businessperson in the sense of being totally committed to a business entrprise.

ABILITIES

His abilities are not very extraordinary. He placed at the 77th percentile on a measure of general intelligence. Compared with the general population, his score is not as good as the average college graduate at this point. In addition, on a timed intelligence measure, he scored at the 30th percentile. It is possible that this man is fairly superficial when it comes to problem solving. We would look to his low score on the theoretical factor and his low score on introversion, both of which suggest that he may be an impulsive thinker or an intuitive thinker. He may be fairly quick on the uptake, but if he doesn't catch on to something, he is not going to spend much time thinking it through.

His poor score on arithmetic reasoning doesn't look particularly desirable for the demands of the job. He is not strong when it comes to figure analysis or arithmetic reasoning.

His one strongest ability score is for mechanical comprehension. He apparently has some capacity to understand technology or technical processes and that could have helped him in a purchasing job in the manufacturing business.

We have commented about his possible style of approach to problem solving by suggesting that he may be reasonably alert but impulsive and not very patient in staying with a problem if he doesn't understand it immediately. His score on creativity is a bit above the average mark, and so he is capable of some imagination and openness to new ideas.

As far as personal salesmanship is concerned, he makes an average score. His kind of score would probably be appropriate for an inside sales job or an area such as purchasing, where he interviews people but doesn't particularly have to sell them. He could be moderately influential and probably a good representative of the company. In the latter, we are influenced by a number of the personality findings.

Personality

Mr. X probably owes a great deal of his success to the fact that he is a very pleasant and agreeable man. He probably gets along well and smoothly with most of the people he meets and is not a threat to anybody. An even-tempered and fair kind of person, he would give anybody the benefit of the doubt. His regard for people extends to a genuine concern about their development and doing what is right for others.

In addition, he is a reasonably forceful and quite confident person. He can establish himself fairly with other people, enjoys being with people, enjoys social stimulation.

His extreme sociability is evident from his low score on independence. Also evident is the fact that he is not much of a decision maker; he is not a man who can be very direct or tough in handling other people. His eagerness to please people would make it difficult for him to do or say anything that might disappoint people. He is the kind of man who can make everybody feel good but probably has to be prodded and pushed to move from here to there. He would find it very difficult to establish directions or set objectives on his own.

Overview and Recommendations

Mr. X is probably a tremendously easy person to work with. And is probably eminently likable. We also think that may be the secret of his success in life. It may be that people owe him a great many favors and that could be a basis for your giving him the job. However, on his own merits and in the long run we feel that you could find a much stronger candidate.

1. Evaluate Mr. X. Would you hire him? Why or why not?
2. What role should psychological assessment have in your decision?

THOMAS ETHICS

Tom Thomas has been buying steel from distributors and mill sources for a period of five years. The majority of his budget has been purchased from three mill sources, with the small varied quantities purchased from two local distributors. The distributors have been chosen on the basis of delivery facilities and price depending on specific purchase needs, with the majority concentrated with Lewis Steel. Annual purchases range from $1 million to $3 million per year.

Lewis Steel has invited 25 buyers to attend a weekend fishing expedition at a luxury resort located several hundred miles from Thomas' home. Lewis will provide transportation, plus all facilities including guides for the two-night, three-day excursion, with no expenses to the guests. In addition to all Lewis executives, there will be opportunities to socialize with the other buyers in attendance. Thomas is particularly interested in approaching the president of Lewis to propose an extensive make-and-hold arrangement, which could result in considerable (approximately 10 percent) overall savings.

Thomas feels that the relaxed social setting would provide an unusual opportunity to make his presentation, and feels the probable chance for success will be correspondingly enhanced. On the other hand he is concerned with the ethics of the situation, being concerned that his organization does not interpret the trip as representing undue influence on his buying choices.

1. What do you recommend Thomas do in this situation?
2. What should he tell/ask his superiors?
3. What type of statements should he make to Lewis in either accepting or rejecting the invitation.

UTOPIA SCHOOL DISTRICT

The purchasing manager of the Utopia School District solicited bids on new furniture for the high school. The sealed bids were opened and read publicly at the designated time, and the Riverview Office Equipment Company seemed to have submitted the low bid. Later when it did not receive the award, Riverview Office Equipment, which was located in one of the villages of the district, complained to a member of the board of trustees, "What goes on here? I am the low bidder and I should get the order." The trustee relayed the inquiry to the purchasing manager.

The purchasing manager explained to the trustee that the specification required delivery to the Utopia High School, and the low bidder had specified that his bid was "FOB shipping point with transportation charges prepaid and allowed." The trustee argued, "They are delivering the equipment to you at this price stated on the bid—what more do you want?"

The purchasing manager next explained that the Riverview bid also contained the statement: "Price in effect at the time of delivery." The trustee explained that most of this firm's bids are made in this manner, since the manufacturer will not give them a firm commitment, and he pointed out that as long as delivery is made immediately this is an unimportant question.

1. May the purchasing manager award the contract to the second low bidder?
2. What would you tell the low bidder and the village trustee?

THE WAGNER CORPORATION (A)

The Wagner Corporation is rated among the top five television set producers. Approximately 30 percent of its volume is obtained from government purchases of electronic components. With the appointment of a new director of purchases, a purchasing policy manual was prepared for the first time. A university professor with experience in purchasing was employed as a consultant to prepare this manual. Before writing the manual she interviewed key personnel in purchasing and other departments of the company and visited plant buyers at each of the branch plants.

In connection with the formulation of a policy on local purchasing, she realized that the new director of purchases was of the opinion that development and maintenance of community spirit were a responsibility of the industrial relations division and not purchasing. The director stated that price was the most important consideration in selecting sources. "Local sources offer convenience, but one should not pay a premium unless such convenience is crucial" seemed to represent the director's position. Professor Frank was uncertain whether she should include a policy statement on local purchases.

Because of the relatively large number of government orders received by the company and the frequent audits of such contracts, the director was insistent that three quotations be obtained on all purchases. Professor Frank therefore prepared the following policy statement.

THE WAGNER CORPORATION PURCHASING POLICY ON CHOICE OF VENDOR

General Policy

It is the policy of the purchasing division to buy materials and services from the lowest of at least three qualified bidders or to have an acceptable reason for doing otherwise.

Application of Policy

Because of the highly specialized nature of our business, the general purchasing policy must be modified to fit many special situations. These special situations are considered acceptable reasons for deviating from the general policy on the placement of orders.

A. Engineering Approval of Sources

In order to meet contract requirements and also Wagner specification, it is necessary that all parts of a critical nature be purchased from vendors who are approved by the engineering department. Only vendors who are on the approved list (referred to as WAL) can be considered eligible bidders for an individual part.

A one- or two-quote requisition may be satisfactorily explained by the comments "only approved source/sources" or "WAL."

The buyer may develop sources additional to those originally approved by engineering if warranted by considerations of *cost and time*.

No parts can be accepted from such a source until engineering approval is granted.

B. Special Tooling Requirements

Parts of a mechanical nature that require the purchase of special tooling are handled as follows.

1. Original order for parts and tools is placed on the basis of three competitive quotes. For some specialized operations such as impact extruding, it may not be possible to find three capable vendors.
2. Repetitive orders for the part will be placed with the tooled vendor as long as the quoted price remains compatible with that established on the competitive basis. The price may also be checked by obtaining an estimate for Wagner fabrication.

A requisition with fewer than the desired three quotes may be explained by the comments "only tooled source" or "tooled competitively."

C. Short Lead-Time Requirements

If a part is required in less than normal lead time, the purchase order for same may be based on fewer than three quotations, or it may possibly be placed with other than the low bidder.

If the lead time is too short to allow for normal quotation processes, the buyer may place the order on the basis of previous price experience with the qualified vendors, with consideration given to the vendor's delivery cycle and past record of performance. In certain emergencies small quantities of parts may be purchased from distributors at wholesale prices rather than direct from a vendor.

Consideration must be given to the cost of a line stoppage versus the added cost of the individual part.

D. Vendor Quality Level

In some instances, certain price differentials may be outweighed by a difference in the quality levels of the bidders. This would be true when the costs of additional inspection and of handling rejected parts would be of greater than the original savings.

E. Vendor Financial Stability

In certain instances a lower bid may be disregarded if the vendor is financially insecure. Membership in two credit organizations provides up-to-date information on such matters.

F. Purchase of Standard Catalog Items

Quotations are not listed on items that are of such a standard nature as to be covered by price lists published by the vendor. Buyers will purchase from the vendor with the lowest price listing compatible with the considerations of delivery, quality, and so forth.

G. Industry Standard Price

No quotations will be listed on requisitions for items for which there exists a single industry-wide price. Such requisitions are to carry a notation to this effect.

H. Sampling Plan for Receiving Inspection

In certain instances a low bid might be disqualified because the vendor would not accept our sampling plan for receiving inspection.

I. Vendor Loading

In certain instances an order may be directed to other than the low bidder if that vendor is overloaded. This is especially true when there are only two or three qualified bidders for a variety of part numbers. In situations of this nature, the buyer allocates the various parts in a manner to minimize the added costs.

J. Double-Source Protection

When production rates are high or parts of a highly critical nature, requirements, may be divided between two bidders. Here again the buyer must allocate the parts in a manner that achieves the desired protection at the least additional cost.

K. Transportation Costs

In some instances differences in transportation cost may direct an order to other than the low bidder.

L. Proprietary Items

Proprietary item is used here to identify parts that, because of patent rights or other reasons, are available from only one source. Only one price is available for such items.

Documentation Vendor Selection

Bids shall be posted on the reverse side of the requisition to which they apply. When the lowest bid is not selected or fewer than three bids were obtained, one or more of the previously stated reasons for such action shall be indicated on the reverse side of the requisition to which it applies.

Regulation and Control of Policy

All requisitions shall be checked by the administrative buyers to determine that vendor selections were made on a competitive-bid basis or that an acceptable reason for doing otherwise has been indicated. Only after this approval may requisitions be forwarded for the preparation and issuance of purchase orders.

1. Evaluate the director's position on local purchases.
2. Should Professor Frank draft a policy statement on local purchases? Prepare such a draft.
3. Evaluate the policy statement on vendor choice.

THE WAGNER CORPORATION (B)

In preparing the proposed purchasing policy manual, Professor Frank secured copies of correspondence with suppliers relative to holiday season gifts that had been mailed in December.

The first letter went to all purchasing department employees, the second to all suppliers.

In discussing this subject with Mr. Smith, Professor Frank was told of a unique suggestion made by a major supplier. After receiving the letter on gratuities, he had called on Mr. Smith and asked for permission to stage a holiday party at a local hotel to which all of the Wagner purchasing department personnel would be invited. He said that his company wanted to show appreciation for the many courtesies extended to his sales representatives. He stated further that he wanted all purchasing people to attend, not just those buyers and expediters with whom his company dealt. There would be no gifts given at the party.

1. Evaluate the letter to employees and the letter to suppliers.
2. How should Mr. Smith have handled the party request?

WAREHOUSE STEEL COMPANY

Dan Baldwin, a new buyer for the McKeough Company, advanced rapidly through the purchasing ranks by virtue of diligent purchasing practices. Starting with responsibility for MRO items, he had progressed to positions buying fabricated parts and was now responsible for steel and castings purchasing—major commodities for McKeough.

One of his major requisitioned items consisted of very thin steel of 0.008-, 0.010-, and 0.015-inch thicknesses, which were used in great volume to produce oil cooler tubes and fins. Baldwin purchased this steel to commercial strip steel specifications spelled out by the firm's specifications, which called for thickness tolerances of plus or minus 0.0005 inch.

Baldwin was surprised to discover that all previous purchases for this product had been made from the Warehouse Steel Company, a small steel distributor, at a price of 15 cents. This price represented a considerable savings over the quoted mill price of 18 cents. Annual usage was 5 million pounds, representing about $900,000 annually.

To determine how Warehouse Steel Company could afford to sell below mill prices, Baldwin called Warehouse's president, W. T. Hatch, and inquired how Warehouse could sell at below mill price. Mr. Hatch simply said, "We have ways," implying that Warehouse was getting a price break from

SUBJECT: Gratuities

I find it timely to direct a word to you on the subject of gratuities and to restate the policy under which all employees of the Wagner Corporation are to be governed in this regard.

1. It shall be the policy of the Wagner Corporation employees to be fair and impartial toward all with whom we do business and to select our sources of supply solely on the basis of merit. Vendors are to be selected strictly on the basis of price, quality, and delivery. Their appreciation for past and expected future business can best be shown by their continued efforts to excel in supplying the best quality material at the lowest prices and to meet required delivery schedules.

2. No employee of the company shall accept gifts of any form or value from anyone with whom he or she does business on behalf of the company, because such acceptance may place him or her in a difficult, prejudicial, or embarrassing position, or interfere in some ways with the discharge of his or her duties with impartial consideration for the interest of the company. This policy merely requires the application of common sense, simple honesty, and intelligence and does not, for example, require the refusal of advertising novelties.

The approach of the Holiday Season will no doubt bring thought to many business firms that they must do something to show their appreciation for business received. Any thoughts in the direction of the Wagner Corporation employees in this regard should be discouraged, and you, as our first line contact with the vendors, are to discourage any such thoughts. You are to carry out the principles of our company policy on the matter of gratuities by word of mouth to back up the letter (copy attached) that will be sent to all vendors again this year.

L. M. Smith

December 4, 19—

To Wagner Suppliers:

The approach of the Holiday Season prompts us to reiterate the policy of the Wagner Corporation with regard to the ethical code expected of our employees in their relations with our suppliers. This policy forbids the acceptance of gifts or favors of any form or value by our employees from anyone with whom they do business on behalf of the company.

We view with pride the cooperation and valuable services our many suppliers have extended in the past to help us meet our objectives. In order to carry out these objectives on an impartial basis, we ask that you continue your cooperation by respecting our policy on gratuities. This will save embarrassment to our employees as well as to your company. We shall appreciate your careful consideration and adherence to this policy in all transactions with our company.

We extend our very best wishes for the holiday season and a happy and prosperous New Year.

Very truly yours,
THE WAGNER CORPORATION
L. M. Smith, Director of Purchases

the mills but leaving the actual facts unclear. Subsequent probing by Baldwin produced no clearer responses.

Baldwin next called U.S. Steel and other mill representatives and pointedly asked (1) whether they were giving Warehouse lower prices and (2) whether they would give McKeough lower than 18 cents for direct sales. The mill reps checked with their headquarters and informed Baldwin that (1) they were not giving Warehouse Steel a lower price, and (2) they could not sell below the 18-cent price to any buyer of the strip steel product.

Frustrated, Baldwin continued to place his requirements for the 0.008-, 0.010-, and 0.015-inch materials with Warehouse.

One day six months later, Baldwin came across a technical article which referred to a steel product heretofore unknown to him. The product is called black plate, the steel used to make tin cans, to which a tin plating is later applied. In its raw form black plate is rolled to the very thin thickness of 0.008, 0.010, and 0.015 inch, the same as Baldwin's, but priced at only 11 cents. However, the commercial thickness tolerances of black plate are ±0.001—in contrast to the strip steel's tolerance of ±0.0005. All other specifications are the same; that is, all chemical and physical properties of the two products are exactly the same except for the commercial thickness tolerances.

Further investigation indicated that the black plate tolerances were written 15 years ago, when the three U.S. mills producing black plate were only 5 years old. Now Baldwin felt he had determined how Warehouse was able to sell "strip steel below mill prices. Warehouse was buying a black plate from the mills—knowing from experience that the newer mills with their newer equipment were actually producing black plate well under the ±0.001-inch commercial tolerances—selling the product to Baldwin's strip steel specifications, and pocketing the difference of 5 cents cwt. The facts of the case are shown in Table 1.

To prove his suspicions, Baldwin ordered a quantity of black plate, had it run through his plant operations, and found it performed perfectly. Armed with this information and experience, Baldwin approached Jack Murry, head of the specification department to explain his newfound savings. He asked Mr. Murry to change the specs for the 0.008, 0.010, and 0.015 steel to conform to commercial black plate specifications, which would allow him to (1) buy direct from the mill and eliminate the intermediary, Warehouse Steel, (2) save 5 cents cwt or $250,000 a year, and (3) still use the same product.

Baldwin was amazed to see Mr. Murry's reaction, which was summed up in the statement, "I don't want to fool around with our specifications—we know what we need, we know what we have, and we will not change for any buyer's whim."

Astonished, Baldwin was left with a dilemma. What should he do? How could he bring about a vital change in the specifications and effect the savings

TABLE 1. Comparison of Steel Sources

	Strip Steel	Black Plate
Vendors	Warehouse Steel	Mill, direct
Thickness	0.008, 0.010, 0.015 inch	0.008, 0.010, 0.015 inch
Tolerances	±0.0005 inch	±0.001 inch
Other mill specifications	Same as for black plate	Same as for strip steel
Price	18 cents CWT mill 15 cents CWT warehouse	11 cents CWT mill
Volume	5,000,000 pounds annually	

of $250,000, assuming that all findings about the products involved are correct?

1. Did Baldwin exceed his authority by ordering the black plate for trial?
2. Why was the head of specifications so obstinate?
3. How do mills use certain product categories to protect high profit margins?
4. How much technical knowledge do buyers need?
5. How may the McKeough Company provide an organizational alternative to take account of future product changes, changing needs, and changing production processes?
6. How would a value analysis program help in this case?

WELDON COFFEE ROASTERS, INC.

Ms. Williams is purchasing manager for Weldon Coffee Roasters, Inc., one of the five largest coffee roasters in the United States. One of her most important responsibilities is to keep informed on the daily fluctuations in the price of green coffee beans. To do this, she is in frequent communication with several commodity brokers.

When she believes that a significant price change is about to occur, she notifies Mr. Alberts, the company president. Mr. Alberts immediately calls a meeting of the executive committee. This committee consists of the executive vice president and the treasurer as well as Mr. Alberts and Ms. Williams.

The committee evaluates market trends in terms of the company's inventory position, official crop forecasts, past trends, "feel of the market," and political trends in coffee-producing nations. A decision is then reached whether to take a position in the futures market and how much to buy or sell. If the decision is affirmative, the purchasing manager is responsible for initiating the futures transaction. If inventories are high and the committee expects a price decline, she sells futures, If, for example, there has been a killing frost in Brazil, she would buy futures.

Weldon seldom uses the futures market for procuring green coffee beans. This is true even if there has been a sharp price increase in the spot coffee market so that spot prices are higher than might have to be paid for near-term futures contracts.

An example of one transaction follows. In early January the company bought 5000 bags of Colombia (high-quality) coffee at 45 cents per pound, to be delivered during the January–March period. This purchase was made to ensure an adequate supply of that particular type of bean and because the seller offered a discount of a half cent per pound from the current spot price.

In early February Ms. Williams feared a price decline, and the committee gave approval to sell a March futures contract for 3000 bags, the amount not yet used of the earlier purchase. Late in February the price declined about 2 cents on both the spot and futures markets. Weldon then got out of its futures contract by buying a 3000-bag March futures contract.

1. Is Weldon using the futures market for price protection or is it speculating?
2. Compute the profit or loss on the illustrated transactions.

Simulation Applications

Inventory control managers and buyers may estimate stock level sufficiency to meet expected future demand by simulating stock activity. The Monte Carlo simulation previously discussed in Chapter 2 uses probability of events occurring at random, based on past experience, to render a future activity likeness.

A typical simulation application would determine what stockout will occur in the following case. Demand or usage for a certain material varies. Records for a typical 10-week run show that the shop used zero on one of the weeks, used one on two of the weeks, used two on three of the weeks, and used three on four of the weeks. Future usage looks the same. Usage will vary but probably will vary like the past.

Lead time, or order-cycle time, for replenishing the material also varies. Two of the last 10 orders took two weeks to order, process the paperwork, and deliver. Six of the last 10 orders to a vendor took three weeks and two of the last 10 orders took four weeks.

Starting inventory amounts to 14 units, safety stock six as computed below, reorder point 12 as computed below, and ordering quantity 10.

REORDER POINT AND SAFETY STOCK

Reorder Point = maximum usage during longest lead time.
maximum usage: 3 units times longest lead time: 4 weeks
Maximum usage during longest lead time: $3 \times 4 = 12$ units.

Reorder Point = 12 Units

Safety Stock = maximum usage during longest lead time minus average usage during average lead time. Average usage: $(0.1)0 + (0.2)1 + (0.3)2 + (0.4)3 = 2.0$ units. Average lead time: $(0.2)2 + (0.6)3 + (0.2)4 = 3$ weeks. Average usage during average lead time: $2.0 \times 3 = 6$

Safety Stock = $12 - 6 = 6$ units
Keep in reserve but include in the inventory activity simulated here.

693

STOCKOUT

The Monte Carlo Simulation provides a means for checking for the likelihood of stockout. Computer software can run the simulation, but so can the back of an envelope as displayed here.

Run a 20-week simulation. Draw 9 columns. Label column 1 "Weeks." Number the rows Week 1, 2, 3,. . .to 20. Label column 2 "Received." Label column 3 "Beginning Inventory" and enter 14, the starting inventory stated above. Label column 4 "Demand Random Numbers." By computer or from a table select 20 random numbers and list them in column 4. Say the selected random numbers looks like this:

49 68 2 50 71 87 5 95 46 57 66 8 42 47 6 81 21 20 15 96.

On a separate sheet of paper, set up two probability distribution tables as follows:

Random Numbers	Probable Demand
00 to 09	0 units
10 to 29	1
30 to 59	2
60 to 99	3

Random Numbers	Probable Lead Time
00 to 19	2 weeks
20 to 79	3
80 to 99	4

Label column 5 "Demand." For Week 1 enter the Probable Demand 2 because Random Number 49 shows Probable Demand 2. Subtract 2 from Starting Inventory 14 and enter 12 in column 6 labeled "Ending Inventory."

Reorder Points

Since 12 falls at or below the reorder point 12, the time has come to reorder. Enter 10 the reorder quantity in column 7 labeled "Quantity on Order." To simulate lead times, select another shorter list of random numbers; say, 25 54 46 92 31. Enter Random Number 25 in column 8 labeled "Lead Time Random Numbers." In Column 9 labeled "Lead Times" enter 3, corresponding to Lead Time Random Number 25. Three rows down enter 10 in column 2 "Receipts" showing an increase of available stock for that week and add it to the "Beginning Inventory" in column 3. Assume that you reorder by close of week when reorder point appears and that delivery arrives at beginning of the week in time to increase "Beginning Inventory" for use that week.

Continue the Activity

Continue in like fashion for all the weeks. Compute the average ending inventory, average demand, average stockouts when demand exceeds inventory, average number of orders placed, and average lead times. Identify the maximums for each. Identify the number of times stockouts occur and when they occur. Be sure to include quantities delivered at the beginning of that week.

Adjustments

Set new reorder point and order quantity to prevent stockout, if your policy calls for zero stockout. For example, a hospital had better keep supplies of blood with zero stockouts. Sandwich bread, on the other hand, could tolerate perhaps a 5 percent stockout without incident. The Monte Carlo Simulation portrays stock activity to help the inventory control manager and buyer check the system's sufficiency and help answer the query, "What should I do?"

In summary, simulation provides a means for checking the outcome of decisions that bear on buying the right quantity as needed to sustain operations.

EXERCISE

Perform a simulation for 20 working days, starting with 100 units of XBE-3 in stock. Delivered price $100. Typical usage records show:

Daily Demand	Percent of the Time
7	10
8	20
9	30
10	40

Lead time records show two days 80 percent of the time and three days 20 percent of the time. Acquisition cost $30 per order; inventory carrying charge 0.2. Compute the number of stockouts, the average ending inventory highs and lows, average demand, and average lead time. What adjustment would you make for better inventory control of Item XBE-3?

The NAPM Report on Business

The NAPM Business Survey has forecast major turns in the business cycle since the early 1930s, except for four years during World War II. Since 1947, the results of the monthly survey reported in the NAPM "Report on Business" has provided a history of economic data. Extensive users include purchasers, economists, and forecasters in government, institutions, and the private sector. In recent years, the financial community and other countries began using the NAPM "Report on Business" as an analytical tool to forecast economic activity and to take appropriate actions in the market-place.[1]

Comparisons using an equation of the annual average of the Purchasing Managers' Index (PMI) with the percent change in real Gross National Product (GNP) indicates that the PMI can predict real GNP within 0.6 percent.

Indexes included in the NAPM "Report on Business" graphically depict the differences between indicators in signaling the end of a recession and the subsequent swings during the economic recovery which followed.[2] March 1991 through mid-1993 was one such period.[3]

Over 300 purchasing executives from manufacturing companies diversified both geographically and by industry compose the NAPM "Report on Business." They individually indicate what occurs with respect to their organizations' economic activity. Collectively, their survey predicts the seasonally adjusted Federal Reserve Board index of industrial activity. The monthly composite report carries the following details to the White House and to the American public, usually within three days.

1. *The Purchasing Managers' Index,* a predictive barometer, measures overall the indexes listed here.[4] Because an increase in industrial activity usually precedes (and also causes) an increase in overall macroeconomic activity, the composite index serves as a lead indi-

---

[1] "Forecasting with the Report on Business," *NAPM Insights* (August 1990), p. 22.
[2] Ibid., p. 25.
[3] Ibid. (June 1993), p. 23.
[4] A predictive or lead indicator reflects future changes in the economy. In contrast, a lagging indicator trails behind aggregate economic activity. Coincidental means that this measure reflects what currently occurs in the economy.

cator and represents the most widely used of the NAPM survey components.

For example, the Purchasing Managers' Index began to decline in the Spring of 1989. A reading below 50 indicates that the manufacturing economy is in a general decline; above 50, it is in a general expansion. For the entire economy to decline, the PMI would have to fall below 44 percent. It fell to 38.5 percent in February 1991, the tenth month below 50 percent, and began to improve in March.[5] Its climb brought it to 58.0 percent in January 1993, from where it declined to 51.1 in May 1993.

2. *The Production Index* reflects current levels of company production, a coincidental barometer. It faithfully mirrors the overall performance of the economy, usually leading government barometers by a month or two.[6]

3. *The New Orders Index,* a leading indicator, declined since mid-1990 to the lowest level (39.4 percent) since May 1982 (38.1 percent), which occurred in the tenth month of the previous recession. Economic decline does not bottom out until the New Order Index stops falling. Ultimately, an increase in New Orders will show (a) increases in production, (b) slower supplier deliveries, and (c) higher prices.[7]

A purchasing researcher reports from his studies that new orders and a new index based on new orders and vendor deliveries consistently lead the Purchasing Managers' Index by one month.[8]

4. *The Supplier Deliveries Index,* a leading barometer, sometimes leads general business by many months. Thus, it constitutes a highly reliable economic barometer. Persistent trends toward improved delivery performance means good news for purchasing managers in doing their jobs but potentially bad news for the overall economy, since relative ease in obtaining most items on schedule reflects decreased customer orders and production cutbacks.

5. *The Inventories Index* reflects levels of purchased materials held in company storerooms. This lagging indicator declined for the period 1989 to mid-1993. Purchasers seemed bent on lowering their inventory-to-sales ratio as manufacturers rode out the decline in sales.[9] A

---

[5] *"Report on Business," NAPM Insights* (June 1993), p. 23.

[6] Ibid. (December 1990), p. 16.

[7] Ibid.

[8] "Forecasting the NAPM Purchasing Managers' Index," *Journal of Purchasing and Materials Management* (Fall 1990), pp. 34–39.

[9] *NAPM Insights* (June 1993), p. 25.

railroad or trucker strike can devastate a JIT setup, reversing a lean-inventory policy back toward fatter just-in-case safety stocking.

6. *The Employment Index,* a lagging indicator, declined since early 1989 by layoffs, plant closings, reductions through attrition and hiring freezes, and voluntary early retirement programs.[10]

7. *The Price Index,* a lagging indicator, reflects world conditions. Purchasers fiercely resist price increases. At the peak of business cycles, sellers may prefer to cut prices slightly (or at least stop increasing them) rather than to cut production.

8. *The New Export Orders Index* increased sharply in March 1991. The index remained positive since it started in January 1988. History will develop a clearer picture of how this index will help purchasing managers to read the economy.[11]

9. *The Imports Index* began in October 1989. Trade agreements under international negotiations will impact this index.

10. *Buying policy* (hand-to-mouth versus forward buying) reports average leadtimes for three categories: capital expenditures, a predictive measure; production materials, a coincidental measure; and maintenance, repair, and operating supplies (MRO), a coincidental measure.

In summary, each index's graph as reported in *NAPM Insights* shows a 50 percent line. Any index reading above the line indicates that the economy generally expands. Below 50 percent, the economy generally declines. The distance from 50 percent indicates the strength of the expansion or the decline.[12]

[10] Ibid. (July 1992), p. 17.
[11] Ibid., p. 18.
[12] "Forecasting with the Report on Business," *NAPM Insights* (August 1990), pp. 22–23.

Useful Books and Periodicals for the Well-Stocked Purchasing Library

The well-stocked purchasing library should include the following:

Advanced Management Journal (New York: Society for Advancement of Management, quarterly): Short, readable articles on current management theory and practice.

Janet L. Ahrensfeld, Elin B. Christianson and David E. King, *Special Libraries: A Guide for Management* (New York: Special Libraries Association): A pamphlet for management on establishing or evaluating special libraries and information sources.

Business and Industry (Des Moines, IA: Business Magazines Inc.): The management purchasing magazine. Formerly *Iowa Business and Industry.*

Business Horizons (Bloomington: Graduate School of Business, Indiana University, bimonthly): Useful and well-written articles on all aspects of management and business planning.

Business Week: "Figures of the Week."

Buying Strategy Forecast (Newton, MA: Cahners Publishing Company): Biweekly short-term buying forecasts and strategies.

C P I Purchasing (Newton, MA: Cahners Publishing Company): The magazine about buying for the chemical and process industries. Provides database information on leadtimes, supply, pricing and forecasts, as well as articles on improving buying skills, successful purchasing and management strategies.

Chilton's Distribution, "Intermodal Guide." (July issue): Directory of air freight carriers/forwarders and commuters, computer systems and software, key trucklines, North American and international ports, ocean carriers, piggyback routes, transportation and distribution equipment, and public warehouses.

Congressional Staff Directory (annual): For frequent communication with Congressional staff.

Economic Indicators (U.S. Council of Economic Advisors, Washington, D.C.: U.S. Government Printing Office): Tables and charts of basic economic indicators for computing indexes and escalator-clause contracts.

Encyclopedia of Business Information Sources (Detroit, MI: Gale Research Company).

Europa Year Book (London: Europa Publications, Ltd. 2 volumes, annual): Comprehensive statistical abstract coverage on all countries.

Forbes: "The Forbes Index Components."

Fortune: "Economic Outlook."

Glossary of Key Purchasing Terms (Tempe, AZ: National Association of Purchasing Management, 1992).

Glossary of Packaging Terms (New York: Packaging Institute, USA).

Harvard Business Review

Industry Week: "Economic Trends" and business barometers.

701

Interfaces (Providence, RI: published jointly by The Institute of Management Sciences and the Operations Research Society of America, bimonthly): Usually nonmathematical articles on the use or application of MS/OR in business, industry, or government; order lot sizing, inventory control.

International Journal of Purchasing and Materials Management

H. Webster Johnson, Anthony J. Faria and Ernest L. Maier, *How to Use the Business Library, with Sources of Business Information* (Cincinnati, Ohio: South-Western).

Journal of Business Forecasting Methods & Systems (Flushing, NY: Graceway Publishing Company, quarterly): Methods and systems used in business and technological forecasting.

Journal of Business Strategy (Boston: Warren, Gorham & Lamont, quarterly): Aimed at the practical interests of managers in the area of strategic business planning.

Harold Kerzner, *Project Management: A Systems Approach to Planning, Scheduling, and Controlling*, 2nd ed. (New York: Van Nostrand Reinhold, 1984), 937 pages.

Management Contents: Tables of contents reproduced from a selection of better business management magazines.

Monthly Labor Review (U.S. Bureau of Labor Statistics, Washington, D.C.: U.S. Government Printing Office): Schedule of pending strikes and labor contracts up for renewal.

NAPM Insights

Predicasts Forecasts (Cleveland, OH: Predicasts Inc., quarterly with annual cumulations): Online counterpart is PTS U.S. Forecasts—first-place-to-check when looking for short- and long-range forecasts for leading economic indicators as well as for specific U.S. industries and products (arranged by a modified 7-digit SIC number). Date and page reference of the current journal from which the forecast statistics come.

Production and Inventory Management (Falls Church, VA: American Production and Inventory Control Society, quarterly): Reports on research and development, evaluating P&IC techniques, and detailing the applications of those techniques.

Project Management Quarterly (Drexel Hill, PA: Project Management Institute, 6 times a year).

Purchasing and Supply Management (Stamford, Lincolnshire, England: Institute of Purchasing & Supply): For American firms operating in England.

Purchasing Executives Bulletin (Waterford, CT: Bureau of Business Practice).

Purchasing Management (Minneapolis, MN: Purchasing Management Association Twin City, Bolger Publications Inc.).

Purchasing Management (Oakville, Ontario, Canada: Clifford Elliot & Associates Ltd.): Formerly *Purchasing Management Digest.*

Purchasing

Quality Progress (Milwaukee WI: American Society for Quality Control, monthly).

Sloan Management Review

Statistical Abstract of the United States (U.S. Bureau of the Census, Washington, D.C.: U.S. Government Printing Office, annual).

Survey of Current Business (U.S. Bureau of Economic Analysis, Department of Commerce, Washington, D.C.: U.S. Government Printing Office, monthly).

Thomas Register of American Manufacturers and *Thomas Register Catalog File* (17 volumes, annual) available on computer compact-disks.

Traffic Management (Boston: Cahners Publishing Company, monthly): A trade magazine for both transportation and distribution.

Traffic World (Washington, D.C.: Traffic Service Corporation, weekly): Industry news, current ICC decisions and orders, federal maritime news, legislative news, varying statistics, facilities and services of major U.S. and Canadian ports and of U.S. and foreign container lines, directory of air carriers and air forwarders.

Transportation Journal (Louisville, KY: American Society of Traffic and Transportation, quarterly): Practices and techniques in a wide range of transportation and physical distribution management topics.

U.S. Industrial Outlook (U.S. Bureau of Industrial Economics, Department of Commerce, Washington, D.C.: U.S. Government Printing Office, annual).

U.S. News & World Report

United States Government Manual (Washington, D.C.: Office of the Federal Register, General Services Administration, annual): Directory of government organizations.

The Wall Street Journal Source: Lorna M. Daniells, *Business Information Sources,* Revised Edition (Berkeley: University of California Press, 1985 and Ulrich's *International Periodicals Directory 1991–1992*).

Selected Bibliography

Benchmarking

H. J. Harrington, *Business Process Improvement: The Breakthrough Strategy for Total Quality, Productivity, and Competitiveness* (New York: McGraw-Hill, 1991), 274 pages. Chapter 9. Benchmarking process consisting of 14 potential internal activities and 16 possible external activities.

Allen Janger, *Measuring Managerial Layers and Spans* (New York: The Conference Board, Research Bulletin No. 237, 1989), 9 pages. Creating and using layer and span benchmarks to manage structure, using manager-friendly tools for organizing strategically, assuring cost-effective structure, and validating the benchmarking process.

Kathleen H. J. Leibfried and C. J. McNair, *Benchmarking: A Tool for Continuous Improvement* (New York: HarperCollins Publishers, 1992), 343 pages. Contrasts traditional operations improvement programs with benchmarking—a continuous process of measuring parts, services, prices, and practices against competitors or those companies known as the best in the business. Specific company examples of benchmarking and the firms' competitive progress through benchmarking.

Decision Support Systems

Michael W. Davis, *Applied Decision Support* (Englewood Cliffs, NJ: Prentice Hall, 1988), 256 pages. Concepts and applications of decision support systems.

Robert J. Thierauf, *User-Oriented Decision Support Systems: Accent on Problem Finding* (Englewood Cliffs, NJ: Prentice Hall, 1988), 381 pages. Design and use of computerized information systems.

Louis A. Wallis, *Decision-Support Systems in Marketing* (New York: The Conference Board, 1989), 13 pages. Report on major advances in information technology enhancing marketing decision making.

Distribution

James F. Robeson, editor-in-chief, *The Distribution Handbook* (New York: The Free Press, 1985), 970 pages. Reference guide on physical distribution planning, management, and analysis.

Hazardous Materials

Theodore H. Allegri, Sr., *Handling and Management of Hazardous Materials and Waste* (New York: Chapman and Hall, 1986), 458 pages. The regulation of hazardous materials, shipping and marking, recognizing and identifying, responding to incidents, hospital handling, Super fund, and Congressional acts.

International

The Ernst & Young Resource Guide to Global Markets 1991 (New York: John Wiley & Sons, 1991).

Robert M. Monczka and Larry C. Giunipero, *Purchasing Internationally: Concepts and Principles* (Chelsea, MI: Bookcrafters, 1990), 178 pages. Guide to international purchasing.

Lester Thurow, *Head to Head* (New York: William Morrow and Co., 1992). The coming economic battle among Japan, Europe, and America.

Inventory

Elwood S. Buffa and Jeffrey G. Miller, *Production-Inventory Systems,* 3rd ed. (Homewood, IL.: Richard D. Irwin, 1979), 744 pages. A definitive text on planning and controlling production systems.

Donald W. Fogarty, John H. Blackstone, Jr., and Thomas R. Hoffmann, *Production and Inventory Management,* 2nd ed. (South-Western Publishing, 1991), 870 pages. College textbook published in conjunction with the American Production and Inventory Control Society (APICS) whose practitioner-members use the book to prepare for certification examinations.

Just-in-Time

Joseph D. Blackburn, (ed.), *Time-Based Competition: The Next Battleground in American Manufacturing* (Homewood, IL: Business One Irwin, 1991), 341 pages. Quick response to customers and throughput-time reduction strengthen manufacturers' ability to compete. The process of time compression leads to just-in-time management. The stronger the perception of the plant's purchasing function, the better the productivity gain.

Carol J. McNair, William Mosconi, and Thomas Norris, *Beyond the Bottom Line: Measuring World Class Performance* (Homewood, IL: Dow Jones-Irwin, 1989), 212 pages. JIT and the management accounting system—now and in the future. The discipline and common sense that form the core of JIT's philosophy identify the "cost drivers." Events that use time cause cost. New manufacturing technologies make far-reaching changes on accounting systems.

Management Theory and Practice

Samuel C. Certo, *Modern Management: Quality, Ethics, and the Global Environment,* 5th ed. (Boston: Allyn & Bacon, 1992), 722 pages. Popular college text on principles and procedures.

John K. Clemens and Douglas F. Mayer, *The Classic Touch: Lessons in Leadership from Homer to Hemingway* (Homewood, IL: Dow Jones-Irwin, 1987), 213 pages. Getting others to commit themselves to their highest levels of achievement as the classics describe it.

Abraham L. Gitlow, *Being the Boss: The Importance of Leadership and Power* (Homewood, IL: Business One Irwin, 1992), 216 pages. A compilation of business policies, administrative practices, organizational behavior, and management techniques. Explores leadership and the exercise of power. The interaction of "stake-holders" (nonowner groups having a stake in the firm's activities) applies to vendors. Executive power and government regulations.

Ricky W. Griffin, *Management,* 3rd ed. (Boston: Houghton Mifflin Company, 1990), 884 pages. College textbook on management principles.

Justin G. Longenecker and Carlos W. Moore, *Small Business Management, An Entrepreneurial Emphasis,* 8th ed. (Cincinnati: South-Western Publishing, 1991), 866 pages. The process of startup and management of small firms.

Curtis E. Tate, Jr., Frank Hoy, W. Woodrow Stewart, James F. Cox, and Vida Scarpello, *Small Business Management & Entrepreneurship* (Boston: PWS-Kent Publishing Company, 1992), 859 pages. Planning, implementing, and operating a small business.

Daniel A. Wren, *The Evolution of Management Thought* 3rd ed. (New York: John Wiley, 1987), 451 pages. The backgrounds, ideas, and influences of management theory's major contributors since earliest times until the present.

Methods of Analysis

Harry F. Evarts, *Introduction to PERT* (Boston: Allyn & Bacon, 1964), 111 pages. An early work that describes what purchasing personnel need to know about network analysis, project planning and control, cost tradeoff to crash through delays, and probability of meeting scheduled dates.

Lyman Ott and David K. Hildebrand, *Statistical Thinking for Managers* (Boston: Duxbury Press, 1983), 849 pages. Making inferences and forecasts from data, making sense of it all.

Ralph M. Stair, Jr. and Barry Render, *Production and Operations Management: A Self-Correcting Approach* (Boston: Allyn & Bacon, 1980), 424 pages. An easy-to-use workbook on cost-analysis, decision theory, quality control, forecasting, inventory analysis, linear programming, distribution and transportation planning, work measurement, learning curves, waiting lines, maintenance and reliability, Monte Carlo simulation, and program evaluation and review technique (PERT).

Robert J. Thierauf, edited by Richard A. Grosse, *Decision Making through Operations Research* (New York: John Wiley, 1970), 570 pages. Comprehensive accurate explanation of the theory applied to problems that confront purchasing managers. Old but not stale.

Paradigms

Joel Parker, *Future Edge* (New York: William Morrow and Co., 1992). How business paradigms (boundary-setting rules) can fundamentally reorder an organization's universe.

Purchasing and Materials Management

Barrie Dale and John Oakland, *Quality Improvement through Standards* (Cheltenham, England: Stanley Thornes Publishers, 1991), 268 pages. Specifically for managers and specialists who must design a system for the management of quality and reliability, develop it, set up the system, and maintain it. Illustrates ISO 9000 series' impact on quality.

Donald W. Dobler, David N. Burt, and Lamar Lee, Jr., *Purchasing and Materials Management: Text and Cases,* 5th ed. (New York: McGraw-Hill Publishing, 1990), 843 pages. College textbook on private and public purchasing, with cases.

Economic Report of the President: Transmitted each year in February to the Congress, together with "The Annual Report of the Council of Economic Advisors," policies, strategies, and expectations for the future.

Peter L. Grieco, Jr., Michael W. Gozzo, and Jerry W. Claunch, *Just-in-Time Purchasing: In Pursuit of Excellence* (Plantsville, CT.: PT Publications, 1988), 199 pages. Guide to installing the just-in-time concept into the purchasing function.

Michiel R. Leenders and Harold E. Fearon, *Purchasing and Materials Management,* 10th ed. (Homewood, IL: Richard D. Irwin, 1993), 672 pages. Modern version of an early text on industrial purchasing.

Robert M. Monczka, Phillip L. Carter, and John H. Hoagland, *Purchasing Performance: Measurement and Control*. East Lansing: Michigan State University Business Studies, 1979), 331 pages. Research results on purchasing department performance.

William L. Scheyer, (ed.), *Handbook of Health Care Material Management* (Rockville, MD: Aspen Systems Corporation, 1985), 403 pages. A guide to establishing and managing functional hospital departments.

Quality

Barrie G. Dale and John S. Oakland, *Quality Improvement through Standards* (Cheltenham, England: Stanley Thornes Publishers, 1991), 268 pages. Explains how nonengineering manufacturing, commerce, and service industries can improve the quality of production, management, and service. Based on British Standards that relate to quality management.

H. J. Harrington, *The Improvement Process: How America's Leading Companies Improve Quality* (New York: McGraw-Hill, 1987), 239 pages. Describes excellence indicators for functional areas. For purchasing: premium freight cost, down-time because of parts shortages, number of parts off-spec'd to keep line going, cycle time from start of purchase request until items in house, and excess inventory.

Sud Ingle, *In Search of Perfection: How to Create/Maintain/Improve Quality* (Englewood Cliffs, NJ: Prentice Hall, 1985), 344 pages. How to implement the organizational improvement process using systematic statistical problem-solving methods, basic industrial statistics for nonstatisticians (statistical process control), and vendor quality control.

Ross H. Johnson and Richard T. Weber, *Buying Quality: How Purchasing, Quality Control, and Suppliers Work Together* (New York: Franklin Watts, 1985), 221 pages. The purchasing function, supplier evaluation and selection, strategy and motivation for supplier quality, and legal aspects.

Francis J. Walsh, Jr., *Current Practices in Measuring Quality* (New York: The Conference Board, Research Bulletin No. 234, 1989), 14 pages. How major U.S. firms organize their quality efforts, assess the profitability of quality programs, and link ratings to compensation.

Total Quality Management

Frank Caropreso, ed., *Managing Globally: Key Perspectives* (New York: The Conference Board, Report No. 972, 1991), 31 pages. Global companies share philosophies, strategies, plans, and concerns. Obstacles encountered and successes gained to meet and exceed customer expectations through total quality management.

Dana M. Cound, *A Leader's Journey to Quality* (Milwaukee: ASQC Quality Press, 1992), 184 pages. "Quality Is a Journey, Not a Destination." The evolving authority that attracts followers to perform. Approaches and methods that create a motivational atmosphere that improves quality and reliability.

Kenneth E. Ebel, *Achieving Excellence in Business: A Practical Guide to the Total Quality Transformation Process* (Milwaukee: ASQC Quality Press, 1991), 196 pages. A guide to understanding total quality management: principles and processes including procurement.

Lawrance Schein and Melissa A. Berman, eds., *Total Quality Performance: Highlights of a Conference* (New York: The Conference Board, Research Report No. 909, 1988), 94 pages. Results of a two-day conference in 1988 to examine the decade's experiences in corporate restructuring to make business more competitive and achieve economic survival. A panel of corporate leaders describe achieving error-free performance, meeting customer needs the first time every time, instilling a quality service ethic, and raising productivity, cutting costs, and expanding market share.

A. Donald Stratton, *An Approach to Quality Improvement that Works,* 2nd ed. (Milwaukee: ASQC Quality Press, 1991), 336 pages. Force field analysis for quality improvement. Lewin, Deming, and Ishikawa theories applied to continuous improvement.

Kathryn Troy, (ed.), *Baldrige Winners on World-Class Quality* (New York: The Conference Board, Report Number 990, 1992), 42 pages. Recent award winners discuss leading the way from quality vision to empowerment and building benchmarking capability.

Value Analysis

John H. Fasal, *Practical Value Analysis Methods* (New York: Hayden, 1972), 263 pages. Contributions from notable users of value analysis.

Glossary

ABC A method for classifying inventory into categories of high-value, less costly, and low-cost items. Based on Pareto's 80–20 rule.

Acceptance clause A statement on a purchase order that commits the seller to the buyer's terms and conditions.

Administered price A price that a manufacturer sets after calculating costs and desired profits from a fairly accurate knowledge of the total quantity of goods that the market will offer, and from an estimate of the probable sales volume at the predetermined price.

Agency The authority for person A to represent person B to a third person C. A purchasing agent has agency to represent his or her employer in buying–selling transactions with a vendor.

Bar coding A method of marking an item for fast and accurate readability. Vertical lines wide or narrow, light or dark, with spaces in between, represent letters and numbers.

Beginning inventory An inventory count at the last period's end.

Benchmarking A search for industry best practices that lead to superior performance.

Bill of materials A listing of all subassemblies, parts, or raw materials that go into an assembled product, showing the quantities of each and their source, like a requisition-to-buy number or from stock.

Blanket order Seller's agreement to provide one or more items over a period of time in exact specifications and price in quantities no fewer nor more than a designated amount.

Boilerplate An exhaustive list of terms and conditions, normally appearing on the back of a purchase order.

Breakeven analysis Comparing revenues with total costs to determine whether a process or a plant generates profit or loss.

Business cycle A recurring change in general business conditions. Useful in forecasting demand and price changes.

Buying to current needs Buying to cover requirements for the next 30, 60, or 90 days.

C.P.M. Certified Purchasing Manager, a recognition earned by examination and experience.

Capacity Reasonable output rate. Based on what products a firm produces and on which equipment.

Capital equipment Equipment so costly that the buyer depreciates the cost over a number of years. Typically involves large amounts of money and high-level decision makers.

Carrier A truckline or railway that transports a shipment from seller to buyer.

Carrying cost The cost to carry inventory for one year; computed by adding interest rate, insurance, storage space expense including taxes, stock deterioration or obsolescence loss, security expense, and labor expense after first placing into storage. Used in EOQ calculations.

CIF Cost, insurance, and freight to transport goods overseas.

Coincidal indicator A business economic index that changes when some other factor changes.

Commodity futures and hedging A method for reducing the risk of price declines between harvest time and delivery time.

Component A raw material, ingredient, part, or subassembly that goes into the assembly or manufacture of a finished product.

Conglomerate An enterprise that combines several enterprises into one.

Control chart A statistical device that plots randomness or non-randomness of deviations from a desired value.

Countertrade The international version of reciprocity whereby a company exchanges goods for goods. It may involve simple bartering between two parties, or it may engage a third party supplying goods to one party to enjoy trade with the other party.

Critical path method (CPM) The schedule and sequence of events that complete a project. Shows how to use resources.

Cross-functional buying A technique that involves the marketing, finance, engineering, production, traffic, and/or other business functions in the purchasing decision; it may bypass the purchasing department occasionally, but typically works with the purchasing department.

Data Information organized for analysis or used as a basis for a decision.

Data base A systematic collection of information organized for analysis.

Data processing Storing or processing raw data by a computer.

Delivered price What buyer pays seller for an item, plus incoming freight. Used in EOQ calculations.

Demand The need for a particular product or component. Comes from sales department forecasts and customer orders, production department, maintenance department, or some other requisitioner in the firm. Demand may not result in sales if the firm has no stock. Used in computing economic order quantity (EOQ), materials requirements planning (MRP), and lot sizing.

Dependent demand   Demand directly related to a production schedule for other items or end products.

Deterioration   Spoilage. Comes from storing an item too long unprotected. Considered in carrying cost calculations.

Direct labor   The labor to make a product or to perform a service.

Direct material   Material that makes a finished product.

Direct overhead   Expenses other than direct labor to convert direct material into finished products. Example: utilities consumed in manufacturing.

Discount   A deduction allowed by seller to buyer when buyer meets certain stated conditions, like buying large quantities or paying an invoice within a set time period.

Dock-to-stock   The process of moving incoming materials from the receiving dock directly to use or shelf without inspection, because the buyer previously certified the supplier as a quality shipper.

Earliest start date   The earliest date an activity can start. Used in critical path method (CPM) of scheduling a project or program evaluation and review (PERT).

Economic order quantity (EOQ)   The amount of product to order that causes the least cost to acquire and to carry in stock. Computed by formula, tabular display, or graphical method.

EDI   The *electronic data interchange* between buyer and seller who transact their business through computers connected by telephones.

Empowerment   The management practice of delegating authority as well as responsibility for decision making to an employee; for example, JIT works when management delegates to operators the power to shut down a production line when the operator detects defective quality.

Ending inventory   An inventory count at the end of a period.

Ethics   Personal values that guide behavior.

Expedite   To speed up a delivery.

Exponential smoothing   A mathematical technique that forecasts the next period's outcome based on the current period's forecast and actual outcome.

F.O.B.   Loaded *free on board* a carrier at a geographic point, like the seller's shipping dock or the buyer's receiving dock, where title to goods and risk of loss normally pass.

Fax   Facsimile of a form, quotation, or order sent through telephone wires.

Feedback   The information flowing back into a system.

FIFO   First in, first out method of inventory valuation.

Fixed cost   Cost that does not vary with production volume, like administrative salaries and property taxes.

Forecast   An estimated future demand. Useful in EOQ calculations.

Foreign Corrupt Practices Act (FCPA) of 1977   Empowers the U.S. government to deter corrupt practices by U.S. multinational companies, such as bribery and fraud.

Forward buying   Buying to cover requirements for 3 to 12 months.

Futures market   A second market for a commodity like grains, copper, and jet fuel, with its transactions limited to purchases and sales for delivery in future months.

GATT   The *General Agreement on Tariffs and Trade* arising from a 1947 Geneva conference where representatives from 23 countries reduced differential duties, import quotas, and other trade restrictions.

Hand-to-mouth buying   Buying to cover requirements for the next 30 days.

Hedging   Minimizing risk resulting from adverse price fluctuations in a cash commodity like grains, copper, and jet fuel.

Inbound traffic   A vendor's shipment transported to the buyer.

Independent demand   Demand unrelated to demand for other items. Examples include MRO items and finished goods.

Indirect cost   Cost not resulting directly from producing a product. Examples: air conditioning and lighting the plant.

Information   Knowledge derived from study, experience, or instruction.

Internal audit   A check on the processes, transactions, policies, and actual workings of a department to verify compliance with desired standards, conducted by persons within one's own firm.

Inventory   Raw materials, work in process, or finished goods. Expressed as quantity or money.

Inventory turnover   The number of times per year that the firm completely uses its inventory of a product or component part.

Inventory valuation   The dollar value of an inventory, either at cost or at market value, computed on a FIFO or LIFO basis.

ISO 9000   A registration process whereby a firm certifies a product, a production line, a plant containing several such lines, or an entire firm of one or several plants. Rigid rules apply to certification which may take years to complete. Purchasing managers promptly recognize certified companies.

JIT   Just-in-time.

Just-in-time purchasing   Buying for delivery to the user just as needed, without delay or storage. An output–input system.

Lagging indicator   A business economic index that changes after some other factor changes.

Latest start date   The latest date for starting an activity so as not to delay a project's completion; used in CPM and PERT.

Lead time   The time between determining the need for an item and delivering it to the production line, to storage, or to the user who requisitioned it.

Leading indicator   A business economic index that indicates future trends.

Learning curve   A graph showing steady reduction in direct labor to produce an item repeatedly. Experience shows workers and inspectors how to perform repetitive tasks in reduced time. Also *experience curve.*

Leasing   Acquiring the services but not the title of a fixed asset by means of a contractual arrangement whereby the owner of the property (lessor) allows another party (lessee) to use the services of the property for a specified period of time.

Life-cycle costing   The total cost of buying, installing, operating, maintaining, and disposing of equipment. Computed to compare alternative equipment choices.

LIFO   Last in, first out method of inventory valuation.

Liquidity banking   Adding money to strengthen banks.

Lot sizing   A planning method for ordering material to meet demand.

Make-or-buy   A choice whether to make a product or component part in-house or to buy it from a vendor.

Materials management   A business concept combining two or more functions into one group or department under a single head; such functions as purchasing, inventory planning and control, traffic, receiving and inspecting, and storage.

Min–max system   A plan for replenishing stock. Min—the order point, max—the maximum inventory. The difference fixes the order quantity.

Model Procurement Code   A guideline for public purchasing.

Models   Small representations of a proposed or existing transaction, used for testing outcomes under varying conditions.

MRO The *maintenance, repair, and operating* supplies consumed in support of producing the firm's finished goods.

MRP *Materials requirements planning* for acquiring and controlling the materials that flow into a production process.

Multiple sourcing Placing orders with two or more suppliers to avoid dominance by a single supplier or to avoid depending on just one supplier to keep the buyer supplied.

Negotiation The discussion process of buyer and seller with a view of reaching agreement.

Networking The process of developing and engaging in mutually beneficial relationships with peers or their personal computers.

Objectives Desired outcomes; for example, buyers may set cost reduction objectives for inbound transport costs and costs of rejects for the next quarter.

Obsolescence The process of an item becoming useless because a newer design replaces it.

Occupational Safety and Health Administration (OSHA) A watchdog within the Department of Labor set up in 1970 to monitor the quality of safety in producing and distributing goods and services.

Opportunity cost The earnings forgone from the next best way to use money. The firm could use the money tied up in inventory to invest at some rate of interest, thus avoiding opportunity cost. Some firms use opportunity cost in computing carrying cost.

Order point The inventory level that signals a buyer to replenish the stock; computed as forecasted usage during the replenishment lead time plus safety stock.

Ordering cost The cost to acquire a vendor's product. Includes cost to requisition; to conduct the purchase transaction; to expedite the product's delivery; to receive, inspect, and first put into storage; and the cost to audit the supplier's invoice and make payment. Used in EOQ calculations. Also *acquisition cost per order*.

Outsourcing The result of supplier partnering whereby a preferred supplier fills orders formerly spread out among several suppliers.

Paperless purchasing Buying without requisitions or hardcopy purchase orders.

Pareto's 80–20 rule Twenty percent of a firm's items in inventory may comprise 80 percent of the dollars tied up in inventory. Thus, the remaining 80 percent of the items comprise only 20 percent of inventory investment. The Italian economist's backward-J curves depicting these situations help to make inventory decisions based on the vital few, rather than on the trivial many. Basis for ABC analysis.

Partnering   A buyer and a single supplier working closely together for a long time period.

Procurement   The transaction that results in a business firm obtaining a product or a service. Consists in a chain of events, including determining a need, specifying the quality and design of a product or service to meet the need, finding a source, arranging shipment at an agreed-upon price and date, and delivering to the user, to the manufacturing line, or to storage.

Program evaluation and review technique (PERT)   A complex method of scheduling activities to construct a project or to conduct a process operation.

Public purchasing   Buying goods and services for not-for-profit organizations, such as schools, hospitals, the military, and contractors who perform work for the public—building bridges and highways, running buses and trains, and fighting fires.

Purchase order (P.O.)   A buyer's document formalizing a purchase transaction with a vendor.

Purchase requisition   A form conveying authority to the purchasing department to purchase specified materials in specified quantities within a specified time.

Purchasing   Buying products or services for commercial use, rather than for personal consumption.

Racketeer Influenced and Corrupt Organizations Act (RICO) of 1970   An act established to guard against corruption in business transactions.

Reciprocity   A mutual interchange of favors or privileges between buyer and seller, in a goodwill sense. In an illegal sense, coercion that one business person A exerts on another person B to compel B to buy from A or to sell to A.

Regression analysis   A mathematical technique for finding the degree of influence that an independent variable has on a dependent variable; for example, whether copper wire prices influence computer chip demand and to what extent.

Requisition   A form that conveys a users needs to the purchasing department. Results in a purchase order.

Reverse marketing   The buyer induces the supplier to sell.

Safety stock   Inventory that protects against fluctuations in demand or delays in replenishing working inventory.

Salvage   A transaction that recovers or restores usable materials, components, or equipment.

Semiconductor   A germanium or silicon wafer that conducts electricity better than an insulator but less than a good conductor. Used in controlling computers.

Simplification   Reducing the number of sizes and shapes for a product; a commercial term.

Simulation   An effort to try out the effects of a decision.

Single sourcing   Placing all or most orders with one supplier.

Social responsibility   Action that shows what the firm owes to society.

Socioeconomic   Pertains to people as well as their money.

Sourcing   Finding suppliers.

Speculative buying   Buying to cover requirements beyond 12 months.

Standardization   Agreement on design, size, and shape. An engineering term.

Statistical quality control (SQC)   A method of continuous monitoring during manufacture; to stop and reset the machines when quality drifts out of control.

Stockless purchasing   Buying for direct transport to user without placing the item in stock; for example, a distributor takes over the buyer's central distribution function for supplying stationery and office supplies, repetitive items, and MRO supplies, intent on reducing inventory thus reducing cost and simplifying the materials flow process.

Stockout   A lack of materials or component parts to meet demand.

Strategic goals   Long-term tasks for upper management to pursue that typically involve large sums of money and a long time period to achieve; for example, "shift inventory responsibilities to suppliers."

Strategic materials   The raw materials or other commodities that a nation needs for national defense, of which the nation's actual or potential supply falls below anticipated needs during a national emergency. The nation accumulates or stockpiles strategic materials before an emergency develops.

Strategic planning   A process that sets goals, assesses the business environment, and establishes plans to reach those goals utilizing available resources.

Strategic sourcing   Selecting those suppliers and materials with which to use long-term comprehensive purchasing contracts.

Subcontracting   The supplier (prime contractor) engages another firm to perform some essential service in order that the supplier may meet commitments made to the buyer.

Supplier certification Qualifying a vendor by rigid plant inspection and close monitoring of delivery and quality, leading to accepting deliveries without incoming inspection.

Surplus An oversupply of materials, components, equipment or similar items made unnecessary by the cancellation of a project.

Systems Groups of interacting, interrelated, or independent components, regarded as forming a harmonious, orderly function.

Systems contracting A long-term arrangement whereby the vendor stocks and delivers repeated-use materials.

Tactical goals Short-term action steps to achieve strategic goals; for example, ''Poll suppliers to find those willing to stock our inventory.''

Telecommunications Voice sounds or data sent through telephone wires.

Total costs Total fixed costs plus total variable costs. Used in breakeven analysis.

Total quality control (TQC) Managing entire operations from design to delivery that produce no defective products. Basic elements include process control, easy-to-see quality, insistence on compliance, line stop, correcting one's own errors, 100-percent check, and project-by-project improvement. See total quality management (TQM).

Total quality management (TQM) A system that focuses on customers' needs and continually reviews results in anticipation of improving performance.

Total quality service A system whereby the entire workforce seeks to satisfy customers' needs for service.

Tracing Following the paper trail of a shipment in order to locate the material.

Value-added concept Expresses the difference between the cost of component materials and the finished product's selling price. An operator who transforms the shape, size, composition, or place of a product adds value if the selling price exceeds the product's cost.

Value analysis Studying the function and purpose of a purchased item in order to determine its value.

Value engineering Studying the design and manufacture of a product to determine its value.

Value management An approach to value analysis by organizing the steps of identifying and eliminating unnecessary costs to provide the required function at the lowest cost.

Variable costs Costs that vary directly with quantity produced. Used in breakeven analysis.

Venture capital Funds for investing in new enterprise or projects.

Working inventory Active stock used in normal operations. The difference between maximum inventory and safety stock.

World-class Excellent to the degree that it obtains acceptance anywhere in the world.

INDEX